CONNECTING SOCIOLOGY TO OUR LIVES

CONNECTING SOCIOLOGY TO OUR LIVES

AN INTRODUCTION TO SOCIOLOGY

Tim Delaney

Paradigm Publishers
Boulder • London

Published in the United States by Paradigm Publishers, 2845 Wilderness Place, Boulder, CO 80301 USA.

Paradigm Publishers is the trade name of Birkenkamp & Company, LLC,
Dean Birkenkamp, President and Publisher.

Library of Congress Cataloging-in-Publication Data

Delaney, Tim.
Connecting sociology to our lives : an introduction to sociology / Tim Delaney.
p. cm.
Includes bibliographical references and index.
ISBN 978-1-61205-105-5 (pbk. : alk. paper)
1. Sociology. I. Title.
HM585.D45 2012
301--dc23

2011031844

Printed and bound in the United States of America on acid-free paper that meets the standards of the American National Standard for Permanence of Paper for Printed Library Materials.

Book design and composition in 11 point Bulmer by Jason Potter.

16 15 14 13 12 / 1 2 3 4 5

BRIEF CONTENTS

CONTENTS

LIST OF BOXES AND TABLES

LIST OF "A CLOSER LOOK" BOXES

LIST OF "CONNECTING SOCIOLOGY AND POPULAR CULTURE" BOXES

LIST OF TABLES

PREFACE AND ACKNOWLEDGMENTS

The beauty of teaching sociology is showing students its relevance to their lives. As I explain to my students, we *live* sociology on a daily basis. We socialize with other individuals and groups, and we are influenced by organizations, social institutions, and society's culture. While taking an introductory sociology class, students generally enjoy learning about their roles in society and how sociology is designed to help explain human behavior and the social forces and institutions that impact us all. In short, we live in a sociological world. Ideally, an introductory sociology course and a well-written text will convey this reality clearly to students.

Connecting Sociology to Our Lives is a concise, comprehensive, and brief introduction to the essential aspects of sociology. The text offers a straightforward presentation of key sociological concepts and issues covered in many introductory sociology texts, but in a manner that students will find both informative and relatively easy to comprehend.

HOW THE CHAPTERS WORK

Each chapter opens with an **Introductory Story** that brings the student experience together with the subject at hand.

Students are further engaged by three different kinds of **boxed material**:

- **"What Do You Think?"** boxed inserts pose questions that value student perspectives on sociological content—like the role of social science in day-to-day living.
- **"A Closer Look"** boxes zoom in on topics that have popular appeal and yet warrant deeper exploration—like the use of steroids in sports.
- **"Connecting Sociology and Popular Culture"** boxes show how contemporary music, art, and other cultural forms are linked to underlying social forces—like rap music and class "warfare."

Key Terms are highlighted throughout each chapter and clearly defined at the ends of chapters.

Each chapter concludes with a succinct **Summary** that recaps the chapter content in brief.

Discussion Questions and annotated **Web Links** at the end of each chapter lead students to explore further.

IN ADDITION

Entertaining **photos** are sprinkled throughout the text, adding to the lively content.

Tables of data arm students with information about subjects critical to sociological understanding like theory, poverty, gender, crime, education, and employment.

Global content connects students' lives to the economic and cultural scene at home and abroad.

A spotlight on **diversity** and **inequality** helps students walk in others' shoes—next door or around the world.

A **unique concluding chapter** focuses on **jobs** appropriate for students of sociology, showing the practical side of a theory-based discipline.

CLASSROOM SUPPORT

PowerPoint slides of tables and boxes in the text facilitate classroom discussion.

An author-written **Instructor's Manual** and **Test Bank** helps professors use the text readily.

Online access to the Test Bank through Respondus makes grading and course management easy.

Bundle this text with any Paradigm book of your choice for a single discounted price.

Write to *examcopies@paradigmpublishers.com* to create classroom textbook packages specially for your students.

ACKNOWLEDGMENTS

I would like to acknowledge all the work done by the good folks at Paradigm Publishers who helped with the final production of this book. Special thanks to Dean Birkenkamp and Jason Barry of Paradigm. I would like to express my gratitude to those who helped in the copy editing and production of this text too, especially Jennifer Kelland Fagan and Laura Esterman. As always, many thanks to Christina, my inspiration.

ABOUT THE AUTHOR

Tim Delaney is Associate Professor of Sociology and the Department Chair of Sociology at the State University of New York at Oswego, where he teaches a variety of courses including introductory sociology. He earned his B.S. in sociology from SUNY Brockport, a M.A. degree in sociology from California State University Dominquez Hills, and a Ph.D. in sociology from the University of Nevada–Las Vegas.

Delaney is the author of numerous books including *Classical and Contemporary Social Theory: Investigation and Application* (forthcoming 2012), *Sports: Why People Love Them!* (2009), *The Sociology of Sport* (2009), *Shameful Behaviors* (2008), *Simpsonology: There's A Little Bit of Springfield in All of Us!* (2008), *Seinology: The Sociology of Seinfeld* (2006), *American Street Gangs* (2006), *Contemporary Social Theory* (2005), and *Classical Social Theory* (2004). He has published more than 100 book reviews as well as numerous book chapters and journal and encyclopedia articles, and he has been published in five continents. Delaney is an outstanding teacher and has taught a wide variety of sociology and criminology courses.

Professor Delaney is listed as a "Media Expert" and regularly grants interviews with newspapers and radio show programs across the United States and Canada. He has also appeared on a number of local television entertainment and news programs.

Tim Delaney regularly presents papers at regional, national, and international conferences (including St. Petersburg and Moscow, Russia; Buenos Aires;

Dublin; London; Amsterdam; and Hamilton, New Zealand). Delaney maintains membership in ten professional associations.

Delaney has served as President of the New York State Sociological Association (NYSSA) in 2001 and 2004, Vice-President in 2000, and as Session Chair for more than a decade. Delaney is currently serving as co-Treasurer of the NYSSA.

SOCIOLOGY An Introduction

1

In 2010, University of South Carolina professor Mathieu Deflem proposed a sociology course called "Lady Gaga and the Sociology of Fame." During a 2011 60 Minutes *interview with Anderson Cooper, Lady Gaga (Stefani Joanne Angelina Germanotta) labeled herself "a student of the sociology of fame."*

Chapter 1

- Introductory Story
- The Sociological Perspective
- The Limitations of "Common Sense"
- The Sociological Imagination
- The Origins and Development of Sociology
- Applying the Sociological Perspective
- Summary, Glossary, Discussion Questions, and Web Links

INTRODUCTORY STORY

"What to wear, what to wear?" Nearly all of us have struggled from time to time when deciding what to wear on a date, to a social gathering that suggests casual dress, to class, or simply to a ball game. Most of us attempt to dress appropriately for the given social situation. Social customs often dictate such decisions. For example, formal dress wear is appropriate at most weddings and professional job interviews, whereas casual clothing is fine for a ball game or attending class in college. There are people, however, who challenge given social conventions. Lady Gaga comes to mind. When attending a New York Mets baseball game in the summer of 2010, Lady Gaga decided that simply wearing underwear was appropriate. At the 2010 Video Music Awards, Lady Gaga wore an even more controversial outfit: a dress made of meat. She had a meat purse as well. (The meat dress is currently on display at the Rock and Roll Hall of Fame in Cleveland.) A student of mine referred to it as a "death dress." If Lady Gaga's meat dress inspired some to refer to it as a "death dress," her 2011 Grammy Awards entrance, wherein she placed herself in an oversized egg to demonstrate "a rebirth of positivity," was meant to solicit the exact opposite reaction.

Lady Gaga, a current pop sensation, has challenged many of society's expectations, especially when it comes to clothing decisions. Lady Gaga and her often risqué clothing decisions adorn popular magazine covers and tabloid newspapers. But she is not the first entertainer to publicly challenge social decorum. In the past decade alone, Britney Spears, Paris Hilton, and Miley Cyrus, among others, have stimulated conversations about proper attire. And these entertainers were preceded by a host of others who flaunted social conventions such as proper choices in dress. Most popular culture analysts view Lady Gaga as the new Madonna. Although Madonna remains popular today, her perceived outrageous behavior in the 1980s and 1990s set the tone for public discourse and analysis.

Yet, the phenomenon of performers violating social conventions did not begin with Madonna either. In fact, every generation seems to have its Lady Gaga or Madonna. The 1960s, in particular, played witness to a number of social revolutions, including a sexual revolution. When the cast members of the Broadway musical *Hair* appeared nude on stage, they generated a great deal of social comment and controversy. At the same time, American cellist Charlotte Moorman was scandalizing classical music audiences by performing topless; in 1967, she was arrested for indecent exposure at a concert featuring a piece called "Opera Sextronique" by avant-garde composer Nam June Paik.

from the cast of 'Hair' in the 1960s to Lady GaGa or Madonna, Celebrities Maintain a Societal position that allows them to comment on Controversial issues. i.e, Moorman's topless performances & Gaga's 'born-this-way' egg

Sociology attempts to explain that while each of us is a unique individual, we are all influenced by society's conventions, norms, and values—concepts discussed in greater detail throughout this text. When high-profile people rock societal expectations, they open themselves to public discourse that may be supportive of or outraged by their expressions of individuality. Our reactions to the behaviors of others reflect our own perspectives about what constitutes proper or improper behavior. Examining the actions of others is the cornerstone of sociology.

whether you love or hate someone's actions reflects your own perception of normal

The beauty of sociology is its relevance to our lives. We all—every one of us—*live* sociology as we go about our daily activities in the contexts of family, school, workplace, and other social environments. Furthermore, all of us are, without realizing it, amateur sociologists as we go through each day observing and analyzing the human interactions that take place in our own relationships, in the society in which we live, and in the world around us. This analysis helps us to feel that our lives are meaningful and allows each of us to find his or her place in society.

Many popular comedians are very adept at using their sociological imaginations to observe and analyze the society we live in. For example, *Seinfeld* cocreators Jerry Seinfeld and Larry David managed to build a highly successful comedy series on the everyday encounters of young adults living in New York City. Much of the show's popularity stemmed from Seinfeld's and David's uncanny ability to satirize human behaviors and social interactions that most of us take for granted. Larry David has continued that tradition with the popular HBO series *Curb Your Enthusiasm*.

Late-night TV hosts like Jay Leno, Jon Stewart, and Stephen Colbert also rely on observational humor, providing an amateur sociological look at the day's headlines. The fact that such television programming serves as a primary source of news for

what are the dangers of this trend?

Late-night TV hosts Stephen Colbert and Jon Stewart provide their own unique amateur sociological look at the social world and human behavior. Shown here, Colbert and Stewart start the "Rally to Restore Sanity" on the Washington Mall. (© Tony Kurdzuk/Star Ledger/Corbis)

many viewers is, in itself, a phenomenon of interest to sociologists. As a specific example, survey data provided by the Pew Research Center revealed that in 2004, Americans under thirty cited late-night entertainment shows nearly as frequently as newspapers and broadcast news as their presidential-election news outlets of choice (McFarland 2004). A 2007 report by the Joan Shorenstein Center on the Press, Politics, and Public Policy confirmed the Pew Research results that young Americans (defined as those eighteen to thirty years old) are estranged from daily newspaper reading as a source of news and that television and the Internet are more likely to be their source of news. In addition, the Shorenstein research found that many young people find a bit of news here and there and do not make it a routine part of their day. This helps to explain how late-night entertainers become a source of news for younger people. Sociologists use information like this as an example of how societal norms and values change over time.

Performers like Lady Gaga, Madonna, and Adam Lambert understand that human behavior is generally dictated by ideals of proper behavior, and they choose to push the boundaries of conventional norms in an attempt to gain greater attention for themselves. In turn, they have profited tremendously because of their amateur sociological knowledge. And it does not take a sociology degree to realize that in contemporary society, an increasing number of people are seeking attention simply for the sake of seeing their names in the news, however briefly—a fulfillment of the prediction made by artist Andy Warhol: "In the future everyone will be world-famous for fifteen minutes" (Warhol 1968). With the proliferation of "reality" TV shows, the burgeoning of membership in social-networking sites such as Facebook, Twitter, MySpace, and LinkedIn, which encourage sharing bits

Shown on the set of Seinfeld, *cast members Jerry Seinfeld, Jason Alexander, and Michael Richards allowed the sociological imaginations of cocreators Larry David and Jerry Seinfeld to come to life on this highly popular TV series. (© Alan Levenson/Corbis)*

privacy is sacrificed for the "fame" of social media & 'reality' TV

of personal information, and the incessant use of digital cameras to photograph and video-record every mundane event, far more people in society are able to aspire to public fame than ever before. In the process, they seem willing to sacrifice a considerable amount of personal privacy, something that might have been difficult to imagine for an earlier generation. Thus, the amateur sociologist can easily observe that what is considered normal and acceptable in today's society is in some ways quite different from what it was in the past.

Whether or not one considers Andy Warhol's "Campbell's Soup Cans" as art is a matter of perspective. Sociologists examine the different social perspectives held by people. (iStockphoto)

Amateur sociologists, however, are not necessarily focused on the scientific aspects of their observations. Instead, they rely more on their creative imaginations. Though this can make for great entertainment, it does not always lead to valid or reliable conclusions about society or social behavior. And that is why it is important to understand the sociological perspective, which we will discuss next.

THE SOCIOLOGICAL PERSPECTIVE

To illustrate the importance of perspective, consider the old joke that goes, "Whether you enjoy the circus or not depends on whether you are in front of the elephants leading them into the circus tent or behind the elephants cleaning up after them." The joke is not so funny, but the lesson is important: enjoying the circus is a matter of perspective. A perspective represents one's view of something. Sociologists do not speculate on matters of culture and society; instead, they rely on a sociological perspective that encourages the scientific study of human behavior, groups, organizations, and society. Guided by theory and supported by research, sociologists attempt to uncover truths about the social world and present their findings in a coherent manner. By no means do sociologists claim to discover absolute truths; rather, they present findings that have an empirical basis of truth. In addition, while they are committed to the use of scientific methods, they also bring with them what famous twentieth-century sociologist C. Wright Mills called a sociological imagination—a perspective on how our private lives are influenced by the social environment and existing social forces.

"an empirical basis of truth"

At this point, you may be asking, Just what is the sociological perspective? and the more fundamental question, What exactly is sociology? Let us find out.

The sociological perspective is a broad conception that includes theoretical orientations used to analyze human behavior, groups, organizations, and entire societies; the use of a "sociological imagination"; and general tenets of human behavior. The various theoretical perspectives are discussed in Chapter 2, and the sociological imagination is described later in this chapter. For now, let us look first at the general tenets of human behavior.

Sociological Perspective:
- theoretical orientations
- "sociological imagination"
- general tenets of human behavior

Although sociologists come in many different flavors and orientations, most agree on a few basic tenets that constitute the **sociological perspective** (Eitzen and Sage 1989):

Survival necessitates social interactions

1. *Individuals are, by their nature, social beings.* There are two primary explanations for this. First, newborn babies are completely helpless and dependent on others for their survival. Second, in order to survive as a species, humans have formed groups as a defense mechanism against other animals and the environment. Furthermore, all humans typically live out their lives in a social environment and interact with others. For the most part, this is done out of necessity.

"Socially determined"

2. *Individuals are, for the most part, socially determined.* Because humans are social beings, they are products of their social environments. Humans learn primarily through trial and error, reinforcement, and modeling.

the masters of our own destinies, so to speak

3. *Individuals are capable of creating, sustaining, and changing the social forms within which they conduct their lives.* Humans are "puppets of their society," but "they are also puppeteers" (Eitzen and Sage 1989, p. 5). Thus, human life is not biologically predetermined, and individuals are capable (within certain social limitations) of making decisions to alter their life courses.

The sociological perspective places great emphasis on the ways in which social forces, such as the social institutions of family, education, politics, and economics, influence human behavior. These social forces are created by collective action over time, which makes them potentially amenable to change. Because of the significance of social forces, sociology tends to be a *macro-oriented* (large-scale) discipline. An examination of health-care availability for citizens of a particular nation is an example of a macro study. Sociologists, however, also acknowledge that even though individuals are products of the social world, they are still the captains of their own paths in life. That is, small-group participation and individual decision making play important roles in shaping who we are. Because of this, sociology also employs a *micro-orientation* in the study of human behavior. An analysis of the quality of health care provided to one individual family would be an example of a micro study.

What Do You Think?

The sociological perspective argues that humans are primarily social beings. What do you think this means? In what ways are humans both puppets and puppeteers in society?

As we will see throughout this book, some people face more obstacles due to social forces than others, and some people make better captains than others. These imbalances among people lead to a number of social inequalities and problems. A sociological analysis of society and culture helps to explain how social inequalities come to exist.

This book is organized as a guide through the fundamentals of how sociology is "done," followed by explorations of various facets of sociological inquiry. Chapter 2 presents the major theoretical perspectives used in sociology. Chapter

3 explains the methods of research typically used in sociology. Chapters 4 and 5 present two basic concepts in sociology: culture and socialization. Chapters 6 and 7 discuss deviance, crime, social control, and social stratification. In Chapters 8 through 13, we examine race and ethnicity, gender and sexuality, marriage and family, education, religion, economics and politics, health care, and the environment. Finally, Chapter 14 concludes the book by reinforcing the connections between sociology and our everyday lives.

Defining Sociology

Up to this point we have described the sociological perspective, but we have not yet provided a definition for this book's central topic: sociology. As you have probably already realized, sociology is a very broad field. In fact, sociology claims nearly everything related to human life as part of its domain. Sociology has traditionally been described as a social science that engages in rigorous research guided by theory.

In simplest terms, **sociology** can be defined as the systematic study of groups, organizations, societies, cultures, and the interactions between people. The word "sociology" is a hybrid of Latin and Greek: *socio* for "society" and *ology,* meaning "the study of." Thus, "sociology" literally means the study of society. The term "systematic" refers to the scientific approach used by most sociologists.

Although there is some debate as to whether sociology—or, indeed, any of the other social sciences—can be considered scientific, sociology is by definition a **science**, meaning that it deals with knowledge attained and tested through the scientific method. The **scientific method**, in turn, is defined as the pursuit of knowledge involving the stating of a problem, the collection of facts through observation and experiment, and the testing of ideas to determine whether they appear to be valid. As we see in Chapter 3, sociologists have a strong commitment to testing their theories through scientific methods such as statistical analysis.

What Do You Think?

Most sociologists argue that sociology is a science, but people in the natural sciences often view their disciplines as "real" science and have a hard time accepting the social sciences as legitimate science. What do you think? Which viewpoint do you agree with and why? At the conclusion of taking an introductory sociology course and reading this text, students should revisit this question.

The Social Sciences

We mentioned earlier that sociology is one of the **social sciences**. The social sciences, which also include such fields as anthropology, economics, history, political science, psychology, and philosophy, focus their study on the various components of human society. In contrast, the **natural sciences**, such as astronomy, biology, chemistry, geology, and physics, examine the physical features of

Social Sciences v. Natural Sciences
human society
physical features of nature

nature. Compared with social scientists, natural scientists often have an easier time conducting their studies because they can create controlled environments and manipulate the physical environment. The social scientist, in contrast, must study people in a dynamic environment where undetected or uncontrollable variables may influence events and behavior. Nevertheless, both social and natural scientists share a concern with furthering knowledge for its own sake. Thus, while a NASA scientist hopes to discover better ways to safeguard manned space exploration, a sociologist hopes to discover plausible explanations and solutions for social issues such as poverty, social inequality, social deviance, and crime.

The social science disciplines share a focus on human behavior but are uniquely divided by their respective specialized interests. Anthropologists generally study past cultures and preindustrial societies that continue today, as well as the origins of the human species. Physical anthropologists use archaeological techniques to discover evidence of human behavior from the past. Economists examine the ways in which goods and services are produced, distributed, and exchanged, as well as the market systems (e.g., money) that allow for trade. Historians trace the origins of particular events, people, and civilizations while pointing out the importance of such information for our contemporary society. Political scientists analyze and evaluate governments, international diplomacy, political parties, the rights of citizens, and matters in which power and political authority are exercised. Psychologists, like sociologists, are interested in a very wide range of human characteristics, including individual personalities, normal and abnormal behavior, and thoughts. Philosophers examine abstract theoretical notions such as the meaning of life, human existence, reason, and the moral and ethical implications of behavior.

Some of these disciplines, like economics and political science, are highly quantitative and rely on statistical data about such matters as market prices or voter preferences; others, like anthropology and history, tend to be more qualitative, relying on data addressing such questions as What was it like? or How does it feel?

To illustrate the different concentrations of each of the major social sciences, let us discuss a contemporary topic of some interest to most students: the use of anabolic steroids and other illegal performance-enhancing drugs among athletes. Athletes' use of steroids and performance-enhancing drugs extends to the young and old, men and women, and amateurs and professionals. During the early twenty-first century, a great deal of public attention was focused on this issue. How might each of the social sciences approach this topic?

The field of anthropology would likely examine the use of performance-enhancing aids by people of ancient cultures. Anthropologists will inform us that in a great many past cultures, athletes (and warriors) used some sort of erogenic (performance-enhancement) aid in hopes of reaching peak performance levels. In

natural scientists can better prevent against uncontrollable variables in their studies

Social Sciences

anthropologists	economists
past cultures; preindustrial societies, human origins	market systems, production, distribution, exchange
Historians	Political scientists
origins of ppl, events, civilizations; importance of each	analyze gov't, diplomacy, pol. parties, citizen rights, authority
psychologists	philosophers
personalities, behavior, thoughts	abstract notions; meaning of life, morals, etc.

fact, the very survival of the human species has been dependent upon its ability to develop technologies and methods to gain an advantage over an opponent.

Economists would be interested in the financial aspect of athletes taking performance-enhancing drugs, in terms of the athletes themselves, the professional sports industry, and the makers of such drugs. They would also examine the cost-benefit calculations that athletes make in their decision to take illegal performance-enhancing drugs. That is, the athlete compares the expected monetary gain (via the financial compensation that usually accompanies increased performance levels) versus the immediate costs of being caught (and risk of suspension or expulsion) and the long-term costs of rapidly deteriorating health in later life.

the varying Social Sciences approach the same problem in a multitude of ways

Historians, like anthropologists, might explain that people throughout time have used any means necessary to gain a competitive advantage over others and that current steroid use is an extension of the past.

Political scientists might concentrate on the congressional hearings investigating steroid use among professional athletes as well as the subsequent indictments and jail time for some of the participants. They might also assess voter attitudes about such drugs and the laws that proscribe their use.

Psychologists might investigate the decision-making processes and motivations of athletes willing to take dangerous and illegal substances. For example, do these athletes experience an enhanced self-image (via positive feedback from others or a personal belief that they look better) as a result of their steroid use? They may also examine behavioral changes such as "'roid rage"—violent behavioral outbursts that have been reported as a side effect of steroid use.

Philosophers would examine the moral and ethical notions of whether taking steroids is wrong. For example, is it wrong to use performance-enhancing drugs because doing so is a type of cheating? Or because it is against the law?

Students may ask, How do sociologists examine the use of performance-enhancing drugs by athletes? The answer to this question coincides with the previous description of sociology as a broad field with multiple focuses on human behavior. For example, sociologists acknowledge that taking performance-enhancing drugs is nothing new and is well documented in many cultures throughout history. Taking performance-enhancing drugs also reflects a greater drug-abuse problem found in contemporary American society, wherein people accept it as normal to take drugs as a means toward a desired end. Sociologists might also research the socioeconomic backgrounds of steroid users to determine whether social forces shaped their decisions to take illegal performance-enhancing drugs. They might examine the business of sports and the economic enticement that illicit drugs present to certain athletes. In short, the sociologist would examine nearly every facet related to steroid use, including the individual decision-making processes that lead some athletes to take illegal performance-enhancing drugs, while exploring why others do not take such drugs. Finally, regardless of which aspects of steroid use a sociologist might choose to study, he or she would rely on scientific research and data analysis to support or disprove the theories in question because using the scientific method is what makes a discipline a social science. (Note: A subfield of sociology known as sport sociology would be especially interested in topics like illegal steroid use. For a more in-depth analysis of this topic from a sport sociology perspective, see "A Closer Look" Box 1.1.)

THE LIMITATIONS OF "COMMON SENSE"

Science is one way of examining the world. Taking a commonsense approach to life is another. Faith and tradition, which we discuss briefly later in this chapter, are two more primary ways in which people look at the world. As a science, sociology teaches us to look beyond the many limitations of approaches to life based on common sense, faith, and tradition.

Sociologists recognize that what we generally refer to as common sense can be helpful to many people in many situations. Imagine how complicated life would be if we each had to stop and conduct a scientific study of our alternatives every time we were faced with a simple decision, such as whether to drive through an intersection on a yellow light! In everyday life, we use common sense to make many choices and solve many problems. However, sociologists also point out that what is labeled as common sense may not necessarily be accurate. For example, long ago, before people understood the law of gravity and its application, the world was assumed to be flat. This belief was based on a type of reasoning that dictated people, animals, and buildings would fall off if the world were not flat. This type of flawed logic led to a commonsense understanding of the natural environment.

Shown here at the New Zealand Cycling Tour of Southland, Floyd Landis was a winner of the prestigious Tour de France. However, he was disgraced after he had his title taken from him for testing positive for taking illegal substances. (AP Images)

The definition of **common sense** is also misleading, as having it is usually described as "the ability to see and act upon that which is obvious." But how many aspects of life are truly and inherently obvious? Most of us assume that when we take a step forward, the ground will remain stable. We take that for granted. However, during an earthquake, one of the very things we take for granted the most (the stability of the ground we stand on) may be taken from us. As another example, people once thought it obvious that you would catch a cold if you stayed out in freezing weather without wearing a coat, especially if your hair was wet. In reality, though, medical science later found that colds come from viruses. Further, where does commonsense knowledge come from? Are we born with it? How can common sense be obvious if it has to be learned?

> **What Do You Think?**
>
> Everyone has heard of the term "common sense," but what exactly is it? What do you think?

Most students can provide numerous examples of common sense, such as never putting a fork into an electrical outlet, not sticking your tongue on a pole covered with ice or placing your hands in boiling water, avoiding looking directly into the sun, never joking about hijacking a plane while going through airport security, and not attempting to attend a state dinner at the White House without an invitation (see "Connecting Sociology and Popular Culture" Box 1.2 for a discussion of White House party crashers Tareq and Michaele Salahi). And yet, none of these examples of common sense represents knowledge that we were born with; instead, we have learned all these things. The sociological perspective emphasizes that knowledge is gained through trial and error, experience, and the influences of others in the social environment. Experience teaches us to act routinely in most social situations. Before long, such expectations come to be viewed as common sense. However, because each of us has unique social experiences, we come to view common sense differently—we see it from our unique perspective. Thus, if one has not been exposed to a particular behavior—labeled by some as commonsense knowledge—one is not capable of acting in an obvious, or routine, manner.

Due to unique perspectives, "common sense" itself can vary person to person.

To this point, we have learned that what we call common sense is actually a result of learned behavior and that one person's perspective on what constitutes common sense may differ from another's. Another limitation of common sense is the fact that many people violate common sense. For example, it should be a matter of common sense not to try to outrun a train after the crossing gate has gone down; yet, we hear about people who violate this notion of common sense on a fairly regular basis.

This would-be skater is contemplating whether or not to heed the warning of "Thin Ice." Generally, common sense should prevail in such circumstances. What do you think happens next? (iStockphoto)

As another example, it should be common sense not to drive an automobile while distracted; yet, many people do so anyway. According to the Virginia Tech Transportation Institute (VTTI), driver inattention is the leading factor in most crashes and near crashes. Nearly 80 percent of crashes and 65 percent of near crashes involve some form of driver inattention within three seconds before the event (crash). The primary causes of driver inattention are drowsiness and distracting activities such as cell phone use. The latter is the most common distraction for drivers (*Virginia Tech News* 2006). Research conducted by VTTI has shown that driving while using a cell phone is more dangerous than drunk driving—leading to 2,300 fatalities and 330,000 serious accidents in 2003 (*The*

A Closer Look

Box 1.1 A Sociology-of-Sport Perspective on Anabolic Steroid Use

The use of anabolic steroids (and other performance-enhancing drugs) is a subject of great interest among many sport sociologists. Anabolic steroids are synthetic drugs that resemble natural androgenic (male) hormones such as testosterone. The effects of such hormones are both androgenic (controlling the secondary sexual characteristics in males) and anabolic (controlling the growth and development of many body tissues, especially muscle).

Although much of the discussion about steroid use centers on professional athletes, the use of anabolic steroids is not limited to athletes, bodybuilders, or males: many prepubescent athletes are experimenting with performance-enhancing drugs. "Studies show that nearly 5% of 12- to 18-year-old boys and up to 2% of girls have tried steroids. And in a 2004 survey, 19% of eighth-graders, 29% of 10th-graders and 42% of 12th-graders said that steroids were 'fairly easy' or 'very easy' to obtain" (O'Shea 2005, p. 8). Symptoms of children using steroids include mood swings (which are common among teens regardless of whether drugs are involved), obsession with body image, excessive acne that appears suddenly (generally on the face and back), and rapid gains in muscle size and strength (O'Shea 2005).

Why take anabolic steroids? Athletes consume steroids in hopes of gaining weight, strength, power, endurance, and aggressiveness. The anabolic effects help to accelerate the growth of muscle, bone, and red blood cells. When combined with a strenuous conditioning program, steroids do in fact aid the athlete in reaching the goal of added strength, speed, and muscle bulk. In essence, they give the athlete an edge over the competition. Clearly, competition is an integral aspect of sport. Competition is also an essential aspect of society in general as most cultures, including American culture, encourage individuals to strive and be "the best." In sport, success is clearly measured in terms of winning. And the higher the level of competition, the greater the emphasis placed on winning: society rewards winners with celebrity, status, admiration, and, of course, wealth. Because success is highly valued, gaining an edge over the competition becomes important. In sports, anabolic steroids have an aura of success.

What is the problem with people taking steroids? There are four primary areas of concern with regard to athletes taking steroids. The first deals with ethics and the spirit of sportsmanship. An excessive amount of unnatural testosterone provides an athlete with an advantage over the competition. When testosterone is introduced to the body in an unnatural manner, it becomes a form of cheating as it gives the athlete who takes a performance-enhancing drug, such as anabolic steroids, an unfair advantage over those who remain "clean." Cheating violates ethical codes of proper behavior, does not measure true athletic ability, and encourages further types of deviant behavior by showing that people who cheat can still become successful (Delaney and Madigan 2009a).

Citizen, 8/13/09). VTTI (2009) research indicates that the risk of accident increases 2.8 times when drivers are dialing a cell phone in a light vehicle or car and 1.3 times when they are talking or listening on a cell phone. Heavy vehicle or truck drivers are far more likely to be involved in an auto crash: 5.9 times while dialing a cell phone and 1.0 times when talking or listening on a cell phone.

Second, steroid use can cause an athlete to be disgraced if the use is discovered. For example, Floyd Landis, winner of the 2006 Tour de France, was stripped of his championship when an international sports court upheld doping charges against the cyclist. It was determined that Landis had taken an illicit dose of testosterone to win the bicycle race, which has been routinely subject to doping scandals. Landis, however, was the first tour winner to be stripped of his title for a doping violation. After repeatedly denying that he took performance-enhancing drugs, Landis admitted to cheating in May 2010. In professional baseball, a number of athletes have come forward and admitted to taking performance-enhancing drugs. Generally, they have escaped the "disgraced" stigma as Americans tend to forgive people who admit to a mistake, say they are sorry, and then move on. The general public is less forgiving when athletes (e.g., Sammy Sosa, Mark McGwire, Rafael Pamerio, and Barry Bonds) remain defiant in light of presumably overwhelming evidence of their guilt, even if they later come clean about their drug use. Athletes such as these risk stigmatization. In 2010, Roger Clemens faced indictment for lying to the U.S. Congress about his alleged drug use. His defiant behavior and the baseball world's general belief that he did take steroids have tarnished his reputation.

What Do You Think?

Some sport sociologists have argued that illegal steroid use reflects a moral crisis in society. Others believe it has more to do with a win-at-any-cost mentality. Many athletic achievements in major-league baseball (e.g., home run records and World Series championships) have been linked to athletes who have been found guilty of taking performance-enhancing drugs such as steroids. Are these records and achievements tainted? What do you think?

Third, any discussion of steroid use must include the issue of legality. Unless they are prescribed by a medical doctor, it is illegal to take anabolic steroids. Sociologists study crime and deviance; thus, the realization that people will take illegal drugs holds interest for them. Professional sports have banned a number of drugs; as a result, consuming them violates codes of conduct within respective sports.

The fourth concern with regard to taking anabolic steroids is health. Evidence has shown that excessive steroid use can lead to an enlarged heart, which may cause heart attacks (Swartz 2004). A number of professional wrestlers, for example, have died prematurely due, at least in part, to prolonged anabolic steroid use (Swartz 2004). Prolonged use of anabolic steroids has been implicated in breast, prostate, and testicular cancer, heart disease, sexual and reproductive disorders, immunodeficiencies, liver damage, and abnormal growth and premature sexual development in young girls (Delaney and Madigan 2009a).

Despite the many potential harmful effects of steroids, many people, especially athletes, continue to use and abuse anabolic steroids. They do so because they wish to achieve and have embraced the "winning is everything" doctrine.

A bigger concern now involves people who text while driving (TWD), which is far more difficult than holding a phone to one's ear and talking while driving. VTTI (2009) research indicates that a heavy vehicle operator texting while driving is a whopping twenty-three times more likely to crash than someone who is not texting. Avoiding TWD and driving while using a cell phone should

Connecting Sociology and Popular Culture

Box 1.2 Crashing a State Dinner Party at the White House

Undoubtedly, many of us have crashed a party. It is especially common for college students to crash fraternity or house parties; after all, the worst that can happen is that the crasher will be asked to leave. Outside the college environment, however, people are far less likely to crash random parties, let alone government-sponsored galas. Consider that there are birthday parties, graduation parties, holiday parties, wedding and anniversary parties, and many other kinds of parties within our general vicinity at any given time. Generally speaking, we do not crash them. And yes, the film Wedding Crashers starring Owen Wilson and Vince Vaughn made crashing wedding parties appear fun and relatively harmless, but common sense tells us, or should tell us, that crashing formal parties is taboo.

It takes a certain type of person—at the very least, one who is willing to challenge the conventional norms of society—to attend a party uninvited, as even hosts of college frat and house parties are likely to employ bouncers. In certain neighborhoods, attempting to crash a family party may lead to violent confrontations. With this in mind, most of us would consider it common sense not to attempt to crash a formal dinner hosted by the president of the United States at the White House. It does not take much thought to realize that the White House employs professional bouncers in the form of Secret Service agents and that, because the president is a person always at risk of assassination, security at a White House dinner is the ultimate in state-of-the-art protection.

What Do You Think?

The Salahis risked possible criminal charges in the pursuit of fifteen minutes of fame. What do you think? Does this behavior violate common sense? Do you believe crashing a party is a violation of common sense? Explain the sociological significance of crashing parties.

However, if we recall the earlier discussion in this chapter of the allure of "fifteen minutes of fame" for an increasing number of people in society, we will not be surprised to learn that one couple, so desperate for fame, did indeed crash a state dinner at the White House. In November 2009, Virginia socialites Tareq and Michaele Salahi infamously crashed the first state dinner given by the Obama White House, whose guest of honor was the prime minister of India. Although the couple went through magnetometers and other levels of screening, they were never asked to show their invitation (Argetsinger and Roberts 2009). The Salahis were photographed in a receiving line shaking hands with President Barack Obama and later in a chummy pose with Vice President Joe Biden. Imagine, two uninvited guests were able to gain a face-to-face audience with the most powerful person in the world!

If they had been trained assassins, the consequences would have been deadly. But the Salahis were merely publicity-seeking reality show wannabes: they were vying for a spot on Bravo's Real Housewives of D.C. In light of this security breach, and as common sense may dictate, the policies and procedures of the Secret Service were called for review. The Salahis did not face criminal charges; their lawyer defended them by insisting that they had done nothing wrong and suggested that their "fifteen minutes aren't over" (Meekand and Martinez 2009). And, indeed, Michaele Salahi's fifteen minutes of fame were not over, as it was announced later in 2010 that she would be added to the cast of The Real Housewives of D.C.

also, when other ppl violate common sense, they are at fault. But when we violate common sense, there's always mitigating circumstances

be common sense—but it is not. It is another example of knowledge that must be learned.

In short, what is often described as common sense should be thought of as learned knowledge that predicates behavior in a taken-for-granted directive. Although the sociological perspective prefers empirical over commonsense knowledge, sociologists would agree that acting in a commonsense manner is preferred to ignoring aspects of common sense. The White House party crashers Tareq and Michaele Salahi were lucky enough to get away with their breach of common sense, but generally speaking, those who choose to ignore "Danger: Thin Ice" signs are at risk of harm (see "Connecting Sociology and Popular Culture" Box 1.3 for a further explanation).

Michaele and Tareq Salahi violated protocol and common sense when they crashed a White House party in 2009. Michaele Salahi's fifteen minutes of fame continued, following her stint on Real Housewives of DC *(2010), when she made headlines for running off with Journey guitarist Neal Schon in 2011. (© Samantha Appleton/White House/Handout/CNP/Corbis)*

THE SOCIOLOGICAL IMAGINATION

Earlier in this chapter, we mentioned the concept of the sociological imagination. The **sociological imagination** is an aspect of the sociological perspective that highlights the importance of the social environment's influence on human behavior. The term was coined by eminent sociologist C. Wright Mills, who articulated how the social environment and the existing social forces (what he called "public issues") influence our private lives ("personal troubles"). Sociologists gain valuable insights into human behavior by employing the sociological imagination. As Mills (1959) states,

how "public issues" influence "personal troubles"

> The sociological imagination enables its possessor to understand the larger historical scene in terms of its meanings for the inner life and the external career of a variety of individuals. It enables him to take into account how individuals, in the welter of their daily experience, often become falsely conscious of their social positions. Within that welter, the framework of modern society is sought, and within that framework the psychologies of a variety of men and women are formulated. By such means the personal uneasiness of individuals is focused upon explicit troubles and the indifference of publics is transformed into involvement with public issues. (p. 5)

What Do You Think?

Because of the dangers posed by motorists using cell phones, it could be suggested that observing a driver with a cell phone in hand is similar to observing someone drinking from a bottle of booze while driving. What do you think?

By emphasizing the importance of the historical social context in which an individual is found, the sociological imagination combines the personal biography

Connecting Sociology and Popular Culture

Box 1.3 Demonstrating the Lack of Common Sense in Popular Television

If a GPS system instructs a driver to take a right-hand turn, but there is a lake on the right and not a street, common sense will dictate that it is best not to take that right-hand turn. But the Michael Scott character violated the commonsense principle in an episode of *The Office* after his GPS instructed him, "Turn right here." Michael's traveling companion, Dwight, suggested that the GPS most likely meant to turn right at the intersection just ahead. Michael countered that the GPS had said to turn right *here,* so that is what he did. They ended up in the lake.

When you think of a television or movie character lacking in common sense, who comes to mind? Is it Al Bundy from *Married with Children,* Bill and Ted from their excellent adventures, Michael Scott from *The Office,* or Will Ferrell from, well, let's face it, almost anything he has done? Popular culture certainly provides us with a vast assortment of people who seem to defy common sense, and yet they survive. Perhaps one of the more intriguing characters who defies common sense, and one who is well known to many college students, is Peter Griffin from *Family Guy.*

The animated comedy series *Family Guy* centers on the Griffin family, headed by Peter and his wife, Lois, who live in a suburban house with their three children: Meg (sixteen), Chris (thirteen), and Stewie (one), and their politically left-leaning, anthropomorphized, talking dog, Brian. Like Homer Simpson, Peter Griffin is a paunchy, opinionated couch potato who enjoys watching television and drinking beer. Peter is like Homer Simpson in another way as well: he lacks common sense and good judgment. Throughout the *Family Guy* series, Peter manages to find himself in numerous situations wherein he demonstrates his lack of common sense.

For example, in the "Road to Europe" (2002) episode, Peter and Lois both demonstrate a lack of common sense when they abandon their children to follow the rock band KISS on its five-city "KISS Stock" concert tour. As Peter and Lois pile into their car to embark on their adventure, thirteen-year-old Chris asks, "Hey, Dad, can me and Meg stay up late every night when you're at KISS Stock?" Instead of displaying proper parental guidance, Peter responds,

a more complete picture of the individual is found by combining their life history w/ their current behavior

(life history) of an individual along with his or her current behavior. In this manner, the sociologist has a more complete understanding of the individual. In other words, Mills is encouraging sociologists to take life histories into account when analyzing behavior and not simply to employ a snapshot view of human action.

Employing the sociological imagination helps individuals to realize that many of their problems are not due to personal shortcomings but rather are the result of social forces outside their control. To underscore this point, Mills (1959) made the distinction between "the personal troubles of milieu" and "the public issues of social structure":

1. *Troubles* occur within the character of the individual and within the range of her or his immediate relations with others. They have to do with the self

"You can do whatever you want, Chris." Common sense dictates that parents should not abandon their underaged kids, especially an infant, to go on tour to watch a rock band!

In the "Peter's Daughter" (2007) episode, the Griffin household is besieged by a flash flood that is wreaking havoc in their Quahog, Rhode Island, home. Thinking rationally, Lois instructs the family to seek higher ground as water inundates their living room. Ignoring his wife's commonsense approach to the crisis, Peter commands Meg to swim to the kitchen and retrieve his beer. He also tells her to make a sandwich for him while she is in the kitchen. Common sense would dictate that escaping with your life in a flood is more important than retrieving mundane items such as beer and a sandwich. Furthermore, as a parent, Peter should not place the life of his teenage daughter at risk. As it turns out, Meg almost drowns.

As the "Peter's Daughter" episode continues, sixteen-year-old Meg believes that she is pregnant. Peter grabs his shotgun and insists that Meg's boyfriend marry her. (This scene is meant to illustrate the concept of a "shotgun wedding.") As is customary, Meg's girlfriends throw a bachelorette party for her. However, as the party is held at the Griffin family home, the teenage girls feel awkward and are not sure what to do. Peter makes this worse by leaving the house only to return a little while later dressed as a police officer. When Meg answers the doorbell, Peter enters, claiming that the neighbors have complained about the noise coming from the party. He then makes reference to the complaint being false and starts a striptease that ends with a very uncomfortable lap dance for the bride to be—his daughter! Imagine the reactions that would ensue if a dad in real life did what Peter did for his daughter's bachelorette party. Most of us would agree that this behavior would violate common sense.

What Do You Think?

Have you ever witnessed someone violating common sense? Why do you think that person acted in such a manner? Have you ever violated common sense? If so, in what way? And why do you think you acted in that manner? Could a real-life Peter Griffin or Homer Simpson survive in American society? What do you think?

and with those limited areas of social life of which the person is directly and personally aware.

2. *Issues* transcend these local environments of the individual and the range of her or his inner life. They have to do with the organization of many milieus into the institutions of a historical society as a whole and form the larger structure of social and historical life. (p. 8)

• "troubles" are personal, sometimes internal
• "issues" are widespread & multi-affecting

Within this framework, the sociologist acknowledges that social forces, often out of the control of the individual, affect an individual's personal life—for both good and bad. The sociological imagination allows individuals to shift their focus from their own personal experiences and observations to a macro awareness of the role of public issues on their behaviors. Thus, it enables individuals to better understand their place in society and what they need to do in order to minimize the effects of negative social forces on their lives.

Mills (1959) argues that the distinction between *personal troubles* and *public issues* is an essential tool of the sociological imagination. As an example, students today may worry that even with a four-year-college degree, they may not find the type of gainful employment they desire. The sociological imagination reveals that such concerns do not necessarily reflect personal shortcomings but may instead be symptomatic of the changing socioeconomic realities of corporate restructuring, downsizing, and globalization. Many contemporary American workers have had to come to grips with this reality as plant closings and corporate layoffs have led to massive unemployment and caused personal troubles for scores of people. These former employees need not view themselves negatively because they could not control the causes of their dismissal, but they find themselves in deep personal trouble nonetheless.

Changing socioeconomic structures, a critical aspect of the sociological imagination, are linked to the origins and development of sociology, which is the topic we explore next.

THE ORIGINS AND DEVELOPMENT OF SOCIOLOGY

Sociology is one of the classic academic disciplines, having existed for nearly two centuries. This section of the chapter traces sociology's origins in empirical science and the ideas of social thinkers who challenged the dogmatism of faith and tradition that dominated European cultures in the centuries before the Enlightenment. We explore how political revolutions and the Industrial Revolution influenced social thinking, and how sociology developed as a discipline.

Empirical Science

In medieval Europe, most people abided by the principle of the divine right of kings, a socioreligious philosophy claiming that a select few people are born to be kings or nobles (i.e., rulers), while the majority (i.e., common people) are born to toil and to follow the rules dictated by rulers. Scholars trace this principle to passages in the *Holy Bible: Authorized King James Version* (1989), such as "there is no power but of God: the powers that be are ordained of God" (Romans 13:1). In this regard, the Catholic Church and the nobility worked cooperatively so that each entity could maintain power and control over the common people. For a commoner to dispute this socioreligious order was tantamount to challenging the word of God. Further, explanations regarding social life were to be accepted without question. Thus, the biblical passage "Render unto Caesar the things that are Caesar's, and to God the things that are God's" (Mark 12:17) was interpreted to mean that commoners were obligated to pay taxes to the powers that be and contribute to the church, regardless of the hardships this might impose on them. Similarly, if the church taught that the sun revolved around the Earth, using as evidence Psalm 104:5—"You fixed the earth upon its foundation, not to be moved forever" (*New American Bible* 1971)—the people were to accept such claims as the truth.

In addition, the functioning of medieval society depended heavily on adhering to tradition. For example, medieval society had a number of professions dictated by a system of guilds wherein apprentices learned trades from masters. It was common for a number of families to work within traditional trades established by their predecessors. Beyond economic considerations, tradition played an important role in power and politics. Rule by monarchs not only supported the divine right concept but also established the tradition of a system of power being handed down from one generation to another (usually via father to eldest son). It was assumed that where a king ruled, his eldest living son would follow suit. There was no empirical or rational reason for this; rather, it was a matter of tradition. Thus, it did not matter who was most qualified to rule; it was a matter of family heritage. The ceremonial role of British royalty today is based on such tradition.

Tradition also played a role in the matters of law via the notion of English common law. Common law refers to the system of laws originating and developed in England and based on court decisions, on the doctrines implicit in those decisions, and on customs and usages rather than on codified written laws. The tradition of common law established in the Middle Ages remains as ordinary today throughout most of the British Commonwealth as well as in the United States.

Considering these belief systems rooted in common sense, faith, and tradition, it is easy to understand how the concept of **empirical science**, which relies on observation and measurement as a way of acquiring knowledge, was a revolutionary idea in medieval Europe. Empirical science involves theory supported by research to ascertain scientific fact, and the presentation of scientific fact often unnerves people of power, as they may see science as a challenge to their authority. For example, in the early 1600s, Italian mathematician Galileo Galilei (1564–1642) provided evidence through the use of his refractive telescope that the Earth revolved around the sun—and not the opposite, as the church had maintained. Galileo's planetary theories were seen as a direct affront to the religious dogma that dominated society at that time, even though they were built on the theories of earlier scientists, notably Nicolaus Copernicus. Accused by the pope of heresy, Galileo was forced to retract his proposals and, despite his retraction, was held under house arrest for the last eight years of his life. Not until 1993 did the Roman Catholic Church officially acknowledge the accuracy of Galileo's science.

Liberal Idealism: The Age of Enlightenment

Scientists were not the only people challenging the existing social order at the end of the Middle Ages. Social thinkers such as Thomas Hobbes, John Locke, and Jean-Jacques Rousseau also made contributions to the study of society and human behavior. Like these Enlightenment thinkers, today's sociologists are concerned with the role of religion in society. Sociology is also concerned with the relationship between humans and their physical and social environments.

The Age of Enlightenment is a collective term used to describe a period during which the ideas of democracy and individualism, now widely accepted in Europe and the United States, were coming to the forefront. The traditional social orders of the Middle Ages were being challenged in such a way that governments were, for the first time, expected to answer to the needs of the people. Faced by such sweeping changes in society, many individual citizens were left confused as to their role. Should they listen to their religious leaders (faith), maintain a commitment to the way things had always been (tradition), or embrace the liberal ideas of democracy ushered in by reason and rationality (science)?

Similar to the role sociologists would play centuries later, the Enlightenment thinkers kept a watchful eye on the social arrangement of society. "Their central interest was the attainment of human and social perfectibility in the here and now rather than in some heavenly future. They considered rational education and scientific understanding of self and society the routes to all human and social progress" (Adams and Sydie 2001, p. 11). The Enlightenment thinkers stressed that human progress was contingent on embracing reason and rationality and that reason should not be constrained by faith, tradition, or sovereign power.

Thomas Hobbes (1588–1679) argued for the liberal idea that government should derive from human beings, not from divine right. Thus, the government should serve the people and be represented by the people, and rulers should not claim to be chosen by God to rule.

Some of the fundamental ideas articulated in the U.S. Constitution are rooted in the proposals presented by John Locke (1632–1694). Locke believed in God and in the idea that individuals are born with certain natural rights, which are given not by government or society but by God. This divine right gives all people equality, and it is echoed in the U.S. Declaration of Independence ("that

reason is above
faith, tradition,
& sovereign power

all men are created equal, that they are endowed by their Creator with certain unalienable Rights"). In his *Letter Concerning Toleration,* Locke ([1689] 1991) argued for the separation of church and state, another founding principle of the United States. Locke claims that whatsoever is lawful in the state cannot be prohibited by the magistrate in the church. On the other hand, Locke proclaimed that the state should prohibit the preaching or professing of any speculative opinions in any church because they have no jurisdiction over the civil rights of subjects.

Locke also believed in what he called the "social contract"—the idea that people give up a measure of their freedom in exchange for the benefits of social order, such as the protection of personal property. Yet, he argued, the government (the state) should be accountable to the people, and if the government fails to meet the needs of the people, the people have the right to overthrow the government.

Locke worked in the field of epistemology, the branch of philosophy that studies the nature of knowledge, its presuppositions and foundations, and its extent and validity. Locke came to believe that all knowledge is the result of experience. This contradicted the prevailing belief at the time that certain knowledge is inborn, or innate—a fallacy bearing similarities to the idea that we are born with common sense. To support his theory, Locke presented the concept of the "tabula rasa," or blank slate, to describe his idea that newborns start life with a mind that lacks predetermined thoughts or notions. In short, Locke suggested that humans are a product of their environment. Interestingly, the name John Locke was used as a character name in the popular TV show *LOST,* and he often reflected the philosophy of the real-life philosopher John Locke (see "Connecting Sociology and Popular Culture" Box 1.4).

Locke: Knowledge Come from Experience

Agreeing with Locke's basic principle, contemporary sociologists argue that knowledge is the result of experience, trial and error, and the socialization process. A leading early sociologist, George Herbert Mead (see Chapter 2) borrowed heavily from Locke's idea of the tabula rasa for his theory of the development of self.

Jean-Jacques Rousseau (1712–1778) was another Enlightenment philosopher who promoted the ideas of liberty, equality, and brotherhood, which contributed to the American and French revolutions, discussed in the next section.

The work of social thinkers like Hobbes, Locke, and Rousseau emphasized the grand, general, and very abstract systems of ideas that made rational sense. Their work, along with that of many other thinkers, such as Voltaire, Montesquieu, and René Descartes would spearhead a new movement of social reasoning known as the Age of Enlightenment (Delaney 2004, p. 10).

Connecting Sociology and Popular Culture

Box 1.4 John Locke and *LOST*

Like the Enlightenment philosopher with the same name, the character John Locke in the television series *LOST* believes in God and the rights of his fellow castaways. *LOST* is a fictional account of the survivors of a plane crash on a mysterious island—and island that seems to have properties that defy the laws of known physics. Both John Lockes are concerned with the relationship between nature and civilization. And, in essence, this relationship equates to basic survival.

Demonstrating one of many parallels with Enlightenment philosophy, the third episode of the show was titled "Tabula Rasa." In this episode, the island (with its mysterious powers provided by nature, God, or some other, unknown source) presents John Locke with a blank slate, or new beginning in life. Before crashing on the island, Locke was wheelchair bound. Now, inexplicably, in this environment, he can walk. He has also developed near-miraculous abilities to rejuvenate his body after he is injured on multiple occasions. With a willingness to shed preconceived ideas about himself, John Locke of *LOST* has a new lease on life. And for that reason, Locke has no desire to be rescued; he has developed "a spiritual bond with the mysterious island" (Keveney 2007, p. 1).

Since the crash, a passenger named Jack Shepard, a medical doctor, has served as the leader of the group. Most of the other survivors share Jack's desire to leave the island and return to their homes; as a result, they follow Jack's leadership. But other survivors—many of whom also have names echoing those of famous philosophers—have also been granted a clean slate and feel, as John Locke does, that they would rather stay on the island. Conflict inevitably emerges between the two factions. Echoing the argument of the philosopher John Locke that the people have the right to overthrow their government, the character John Locke challenges Jack's authority and eventually leads some of his followers away from the main group. The battle between the two would-be leaders, John and Jack, reflects some of the basic concepts of conflict theory (see Chapter 2), a leading sociological perspective on human behavior.

What Do You Think?

John Locke and George Herbert Mead argue that a baby is born as a blank slate, that is, lacking an innate sense of self or how to behave. The argument is not that the baby is literally blank, as a healthy baby will possess nerve endings and so forth, but rather that an infant's sense of self develops through interaction with others. What do you think?

Political Revolutions

The late eighteenth century witnessed radical changes in socioeconomic structures throughout the Western world because of the growing demand among citizens that their governments meet their needs and embrace the rationality of science as a guiding force of progress.

Predictably, many governments and sovereign rulers were determined to hold onto their absolute power. Rulers who held power via tradition and religious leaders who claimed to represent God responded in a conservative and reactionary manner and hoped to turn society back to a way of life that existed in the Middle Ages.

The Age of Enlightenment, however, had sparked the people's questioning of the traditional order of society. Thus, even though average men and women could not understand the scientific and philosophical ideas being developed in intellectual circles, they did comprehend that a government should meet the needs of the people. The seeds of democracy, or government by the people, had taken hold across Europe and its colonies. The people wanted a change. Revolutions became the course of action.

Two of the most significant revolutions in human history occurred in the late eighteenth century: the American Revolution and the French Revolution. In 1776, the United States declared its independence from England. The people had now crossed the line from talking about democracy to going about attaining it. At the end of a war that lasted eight years, the United States became the first democratically governed sovereign nation in the modern Western world.

The ramifications of the new American nation inspired the French Revolution of 1789, an event that ushered in more than a decade of violent social upheaval known as the Reign of Terror. During this period, along with many leaders of various revolutionary factions, many of France's nobles were killed, the centuries-old monarchy was overthrown, and King Louis XVI and his queen Marie Antoinette were both famously executed by guillotine. The nobility's dominant role in French society was ended forever. A new social structure would eventually emerge, but before this could happen, chaos ensued in France.

Among the many lessons of the French Revolution was the reality that a society cannot enjoy stability without a strong social structure. One cannot help but think of the twenty-first-century wars in Iraq and Afghanistan as examples of the relevance of this sociological lesson, as the lack of social structure in those countries has contributed to societal instability.

The Industrial Revolution

Political revolutions, however, would not be the greatest cause of social upheaval in modern history. Instead, it was the Industrial Revolution that radically changed a large number of societies around the world beginning in the late eighteenth century. The social change that occurred, especially during the early stages of the Industrial Revolution, would become the single most significant event to spark the development of sociology.

The Industrial Revolution began in the mid-1700s in England; over the ensuing decades, it spread throughout Western Europe, as well as to the United States and Canada. The Industrial Revolution was not a single event but rather a number of interrelated developments sparked by invention and scientific discovery. The once largely agricultural and rural world was about to be transformed to an industrial, urban one. Many farmworkers and rural inhabitants migrated to the cities in the hope of finding gainful employment in any of the growing number of factories. The use of machinery dramatically increased the productivity of material goods. In turn, this increased productivity sparked the demand for more raw materials, improved means of transportation, better communication, better-educated workers, and a more specialized division of labor.

Cities became overcrowded as more and more rural peasants arrived looking for employment. A population explosion, along with a decreasing child-mortality rate, further fueled overcrowding in densely populated neighborhoods. Poor city planning, or the complete lack thereof, transformed many small medieval towns into sprawling, chaotic, slum-filled cities characterized by poor sanitation and a great number of new and unique social problems. A number of concerned citizens and social thinkers alike began to take note of the terrible living conditions that many of the poor people had to endure. Eventually, reform movements were formed in an attempt to help the less fortunate. This development was in itself noteworthy as human history, until the Industrial Revolution, was dominated by a "survival of the fittest" principle. That is, the weak and old died off, and little attention was given to them. Families, not the government, took care of each other. But now, a number of moral reformers sought to make society better for all and wanted the government to help those most in need.

Political and social revolutions that challenged long-held traditions, an expanding urban world due to industrialization with all its growing social problems, and an emerging moral reform mentality would foreshadow the coming of sociology. Early sociologists such as Auguste Comte and Harriet Martineau (discussed further in Chapter 2) analyzed the transition of Western European societies that were once dominated by faith and tradition but now consisted of a growing number of people who encouraged "enlightened" thinking.

Auguste Comte (1798–1857) argued that societies, like organisms, evolve over time. Using a theory known as the law of three stages, he claimed that early societies were dominated by theological powers (stage 1) because religion provided simple answers to life's complicated questions. The average person was not capable of evolved thinking because of a lack of education. Eventually, societies evolved to a "metaphysical" stage that allowed for philosophical reasoning (stage 2). However, this evolved stage was simply a transition to the "positive" stage. It served as a bridge from ignorance to scientific thinking. Comte believed that the metaphysical stage was necessary because the jump to the final stage, positivism, was too drastic. The positive stage (stage 3) was a nod to his term, positivism. Positivism, for Comte, was similar to empiricism; it meant embracing a reliance on science for answering life's complicated questions. Comte recognized the rapidly changing nature of society and encouraged the scientific study of this development.

Harriet Martineau (1802–1876) was raised in an English family that valued education; she and her sisters were homeschooled and consequently enjoyed an advanced level of education not extended to most women of their day. Her upbringing was also unusual for the time in that her parents did not believe in worshipping a God but instead encouraged a commitment to meeting social needs. Like Comte in France, Martineau witnessed the early stages of industrialization in England. The social problems associated with any dense city sparked a desire in Martineau to help the less fortunate.

Comte and Martineau represent the earliest sociologists. Their combined commitment to empiricism and moral reform remain the cornerstones of sociology today. This is true whether sociologists embrace a quantitative or qualitative approach in research methodology (see Chapter 3) or immerse themselves with the lives of the less fortunate while they conduct work in such areas as public housing, public health care, gang-intervention programs, homelessness, and so on. The notion of moral reform extends to the present-day promotion of **social diversity**—the acceptance of people who are different from ourselves.

Social Diversity

Sociology promotes understanding and tolerance of others and instructs us to look beyond intuition, so-called common sense, and limited individual past experiences. The sociological perspective, while acknowledging that we are all unique individuals, holds that we are shaped by our social environment and our various group memberships. The sociological perspective also advances the notion that we can best understand ourselves, and our place in society, if we understand diverse groups. It is important to note, however, that if we only focus on the differences between people, we will fail to take note of the similarities between them. By acknowledging such similarities, it may become possible to achieve greater harmony among the diverse people of the world.

Many social constructs lead to the formation of diverse groups, including religion, gender, race and ethnicity, sexual orientation, age, social class, and so on. All these topics are of utmost concern for sociology and will, of course, be discussed in later chapters of this book. For now, it is important to note that the examination of diverse groups provides insights into how society is socially arranged and whether some group members or individuals are being treated fairly. People who are not treated equally experience social marginality. **Social marginality** refers to members who are not fully entrenched in society. Such people are excluded from full participation in mainstream society (see "Connecting Sociology and Popular Culture" Box 1.5 for a discussion of how one pop star has spoken out about social marginalization of the Roma).

As we have seen in this discussion, sociology originated in the ideas of the Enlightenment and empirical science, which challenged the traditions and faith that had previously dominated European thinking. In the eighteenth century, political revolutions and the Industrial Revolution brought about social changes that inspired the commitment to moral reform that would become the cornerstone of sociology. The commitment among sociologists to ensure that the rights of all people are protected has led to sociology's appreciation of social diversity and equality for all.

Connecting Sociology and Popular Culture

Box 1.5 Madonna and the Roma

The Roma, formerly known as "Gypsies," live mostly in Romania and other Eastern European nations. Their traditionally mobile culture makes it difficult to estimate their numbers. "Officially, there are approximately 500,000 Roma in Romania, but the real number could be closer to 2 million" (CNSNews.com 2009). They have been victims of prejudice and discrimination, treated as a marginalized people, throughout history. During World War II, for example, an estimated half million Roma were killed in Nazi concentration camps, and in the 1990s, Roma were among the groups targeted for ethnic cleansing in areas of the former Yugoslavia (Liegeois and Gheorghe 1995). The pattern continues to the present day: in the summer of 2010, French president Nicolas Sarkozy initiated a program to deport hundreds of Roma families who were allegedly living illegally in France. Critics charged that this was a ploy to gain approval from anti-immigration voters on the political Right in French politics (Carvajal 2010).

Attempting to draw attention to the plight of the Roma, pop star Madonna spoke out against discrimination against "Gypsies" during an August 2009 concert in Bucharest, Romania. During a break between songs, when Madonna told the crowd that it saddened her that the Roma were victims of discrimination, thousands in the crowd of 60,000 booed her. Yet, "Roma musicians and a Roma dancer were featured in her show, held just yards from the giant palace of ex-communist dictator Nicolae Ceausescu. Their performances were applauded by the crowd" (CNSNews.com 2009).

Interestingly enough, Madonna's statement of concern for the plight of the Roma was an example of utilizing the sociological imagination by realizing that many people are marginalized due to public issues beyond their control.

What Do You Think?

What other examples of marginalized people can you identify? What circumstances led to their marginalized status in society? What do you think?

APPLYING THE SOCIOLOGICAL PERSPECTIVE

In this chapter we have learned that the sociological perspective includes the use of a sociological imagination and that sociology proposes a number of general tenets about human behavior. They include the idea that individuals are social beings, are socially determined, and are capable of making decisions that may alter their life courses. Applying the sociological perspective to our daily lives provides benefits in a variety of ways. Listed below are a few more aspects of the sociological perspective worth noting:

1. *General enlightenment:* Just as the social thinkers of the Age of Enlightenment assessed the social structures of societies in their era, so today's sociologists continue to examine the social arrangements of societies around the world. Where they see injustices, sociologists will present critical evaluations.
2. *Informing the public:* Again, as social thinkers did centuries ago, today's sociologists often present evidence that is contrary to popular dogmatic belief. It is up to the ethical sociologist to inform the public of discovered injustices and to identify social problems.
3. *The pursuit of new knowledge through the use of science:* The roots of sociology are firmly entrenched in empirical science. The scientific method provides greater validity to the field of sociology in the eyes of an ever-expanding technological world. Supporting theory with research in an attempt to further increase the knowledge level of science remains an important aspect of sociology. Further, the pursuit of knowledge helps sociologists to transcend commonsense notions and provide viable solutions to the social problems previously identified. After all, merely criticizing an aspect of the social structure does nothing to solve the problem. Solutions require action.
4. *Global analysis:* Sociology's macro approach and commitment to promoting diversity places it in the forefront of global matters. The entire world is linked in one fashion or another (e.g., globalization, electronic communication), resulting in a global community. Sociology, then, assists individuals in their quest to find their place not only in their local communities but in the global one as well.

The relevance of sociology to the student's life is multifaceted as nearly every endeavor engaged in by individuals is of social consequence. Because sociology describes all elements of the social world, it is perhaps the most relevant to students of all academic disciplines. The sociological perspective has benefited humanity for nearly two centuries now. Many of the ideas of the early sociologists (e.g., moral reform, a commitment to science) continue to influence sociology today. In Chapter 2, we will learn about the ideas of many key early sociologists as well as about the major theoretical perspectives of sociology. The discussion of the major sociological theories completes the discussion of the sociological perspective.

SUMMARY

Sociology is an academic discipline that has existed for nearly two centuries. Sociology can be defined as the systematic study of groups, organizations, societies, cultures, and the interactions between people. The term "systematic" refers to the scientific approach used by most sociologists. Sociology is one of the social sciences.

Sociology proposes a perspective that includes such general notions as individuals are social beings (we crave being with others in the form of groups, including the family); we are socially determined (influenced by our past behaviors and other people and social institutions, not genetically predisposed to act a certain way); and we are capable of making decisions that may alter our life courses (we have free will).

An important element of the sociological perspective is the concept of the sociological imagination. The sociological imagination highlights the influence of existing social forces ("public issues") on our private lives ("personal troubles"). Thus, there exist instances beyond our control that influence our behavior.

Although sociology recognizes the value of utilizing a commonsense approach to life, sociologists point out that what one person may consider common sense is not necessarily universal. Furthermore, commonsense beliefs may, in fact, turn out to be fallacies under the test of empirical research. As a result, sociologists warn us not to rely on common sense for all social endeavors.

The origins of sociology are firmly entrenched in empirical science and the ideas of social thinkers who dared to challenge the dogmatism of faith and tradition predominant in European cultures before the Industrial Revolution. Empirical science relies on observation and measurement as a way of acquiring knowledge. The Enlightenment thinkers stressed that human progress was contingent on embracing reason and that reason should not be constrained by faith, tradition, or sovereign power. These "enlightened" ideals would go on to be embraced by the early sociologists.

Applying the sociological perspective to our daily lives provides benefits in a variety of ways, including enhancing general enlightenment, providing information to the public (information that may defy traditional or commonsense beliefs), advancing the scientific pursuit of knowledge, and furthering an analysis of social matters that extends globally.

Glossary

Common sense—Often viewed as prudent judgment based on the ability to see and act upon that which is obvious or believed to be innate knowledge. In actuality, common sense represents learned behavior that we take for granted.

Empirical science—The reliance on observation and measurement as a way of acquiring knowledge. This approach is in direct contrast to a reliance on common sense, faith, and tradition.

Natural sciences—Disciplines that include astronomy, biology, chemistry, geology, and physics, which examine the physical features of nature.

Science—Knowledge attained and tested through the scientific method.

Scientific method—The pursuit of knowledge involving the stating of a problem, the collection of facts through observation and experiment, and the testing of ideas to determine whether they appear to be valid or invalid.

Social diversity—A term encompassing the variety of people found in human society as a result of the many different social constructs (e.g., gender, race and ethnicity, sexual orientation, age, social class) used to categorize people.

Social marginality—A term referring to the unequal treatment of group members or individuals who are thus not fully entrenched in society. Such people are excluded from full participation in mainstream society.

Social sciences—Disciplines that include anthropology, economics, history, political science, psychology, and sociology, which focus their study on the various components of human society.

Sociological imagination—An aspect of the sociological perspective that demonstrates how our private lives are influenced by the social environment and existing social forces.

Sociological perspective—A framework utilized by sociologists to examine human behavior that involves such basic assumptions as that humans are products of their social environment and learning takes place primarily through trial and error, reinforcement, and modeling.

Sociology—The systematic study of groups, organizations, societies, and culture and the interactions between people.

Discussion Questions

1. The sociological imagination states that public issues may cause personal troubles. Describe how this has already happened in your lifetime. How is it likely to influence your life in the future?

2. The divine right of kings was the predominant principle during the Middle Ages in Europe. Are you aware of any sociopolitical states in the world today that apply a similar approach to ruling their citizens?

3. The Industrial Revolution dramatically changed the lives of Europeans and Americans. Today, we live in a postindustrial society characterized by jobs in the service industry. What does the future hold for the American worker? That is, what types of jobs skills do people need today in order to survive and succeed in society? In what ways are you preparing yourself to succeed in the society of the future?

4. There is a great deal of social diversity in American society. What would you do in an attempt to ensure that no group becomes marginalized from the greater society?

5. Have you ever displayed a behavior that violates common sense? Explain. Have you witnessed others who have violated common sense? Provide five examples. Why is it that people violate the principles of common sense?

Web Links

1. Learn all about sociology in the United States via the American Sociological Association's website at www.asanet.org. The numerous links provide information on a variety of subjects.

2. An important aspect of sociology is its application to real-life issues and social problems. Learn about applied sociology on the Society for Applied Sociology's website at www.appliedsoc.org.

3. Auguste Comte, often recognized as the founder of sociology, was a very brilliant but troubled individual. Learn more about this fascinating person on the History Guide website at www.historyguide.org/intellect/comte.html.

2

SOCIAL THEORY
Explaining How We View the World

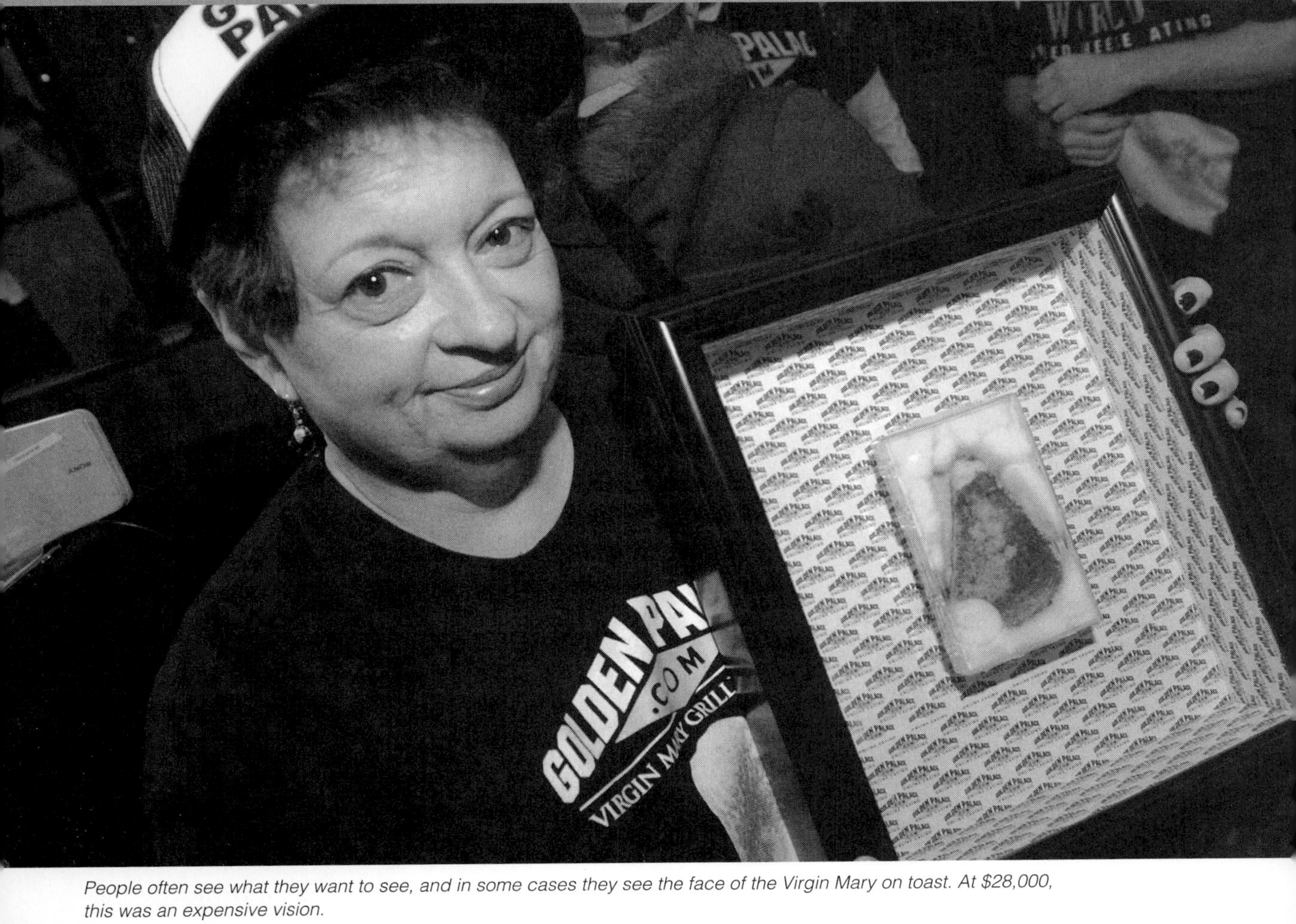

People often see what they want to see, and in some cases they see the face of the Virgin Mary on toast. At $28,000, this was an expensive vision.

Chapter 2

- Introductory Story
- Social Theory
- Early Sociologists: European Origins
- Early Sociologists in the United States
- The Major Theoretical Perspectives of Sociology
- Summary, Glossary, Discussion Questions, and Web Links

INTRODUCTORY STORY

The old cliché "beauty is in the eye of the beholder" embodies the idea that perception is selective. That is, we view the world from a personal perspective that is influenced by cultural elements and past experiences. Some people, for example, seem to find religious symbols embedded on the oddest items, including freezer doors and food products. In 2004, a grilled cheese sandwich sold for $28,000 on eBay (to Internet casino GoldenPalace.com) because some people believed it bore the face of the Virgin Mary (MSNBC 2004). Another person believed that his Funyuns onion-flavored snack resembled the Virgin Mary and the baby Jesus. He attempted to sell his mundane product on eBay but was only offered $609 by an anonymous bidder (*Post-Standard*, 12/7/05).

Another example of selective perception is the accusation that President George W. Bush and his daughter Jenna were agents of Satan because of a gesture they made at Bush's 2005 inauguration. During the ceremony, the president and his daughter flashed a "hook 'em horns!" symbol (the thumb is extended to cover the two middle fingers while the index and pinky fingers point upward) when the University of Texas band marched by their viewing area. This symbol is commonly used in an affectionate manner by University of Texas (UT) sports fans. However, the symbol has a variety of other meanings: it represents the "cuckold's horns," indicating that a man's wife is unfaithful; it is the International Sign Language symbol for "bullsh*t"; it is also the "sign of the devil" for heavy metal rockers and some Scandinavian nations. As a result, enough citizens in Norway interpreted Bush's "hook 'em horns!" gesture as a salute to Satan that Norwegian newspapers had to explain to their readers the intended meaning of the sign—as a tribute to the University of Texas. Furthermore, people with political agendas chose to interpret Bush's application of the UT symbol to their advantage (furthering the idea that Bush was the devil), even though he merely used a pop-culture symbol. To say that perception is selective in the way we view the world is an understatement, as demonstrated by the "hook 'em horns!" gesture and the meanings that people associate with its usage.

In this chapter, we discuss the concept of social theory, which guides sociologists in their quest to explain the social world. We step back in time to examine the ideas of the early sociologists and conclude by exploring some of the major contemporary schools of sociological thought.

SOCIAL THEORY

As individuals, we cannot help but contemplate the meanings of the social events that happen in our vicinity. Sociologists attempt to explain the meanings of social events and behaviors of those close to us, as well as of those from cultures around the world. Sociologists are guided by theoretical constructs that help them in their attempt to explain human behavior. Because of this, social theory is one of the most important aspects of sociology. In fact, sociology majors and minors are always required to take at least one social theory course in sociology in order to complete their degree requirements.

What is social theory? People often let the concept of social theory overwhelm them, but the truth is that most of us propose theories about social events and the behaviors of others on a fairly regular basis. Williams and McShane (1994) explain that people seem to "think of theory as something abstract and not really applicable to the 'real world'" (p. 1). They use rain as an example of theory in everyday life. When you see dark clouds forming in the sky and state, "It is going to rain," you have just expressed a simple theory. A more complex theory of rain would be that under certain circumstances, surface water evaporates and rises into the atmosphere. Certain atmospheric conditions cause water to condense, first into clouds and ultimately into drops of rain. This second theory is more complex as it specifies the conditions and processes involved (evaporation and condensation) and reflects a commitment to the scientific method discussed in Chapter 1.

Difference in stating it is going to rain & explaining why it is going to rain (application of Scientific Method)

Recall that the scientific method is described as a process wherein the pursuit of knowledge involves stating a problem and then collecting data through observation and experimentation. A number of theories about how rain occurs may be presented, but the ones that allow for empirical verification reflect the scientific method generally embraced by sociologists.

A **theory**, then, is a statement that proposes to explain or relate observed phenomena or a set of concepts. Social theory involves linking a set of interrelated concepts and/or observed phenomena in an attempt to establish a cause-effect relationship. A good theory is one that allows itself to be tested and supported or disproved by empirical research. Presenting ideas (theories) in the form of statements allows for empirical testing. Generally speaking, sociological theory is grounded in the scientific tradition of belief that social patterns exist; therefore, general abstract laws can be created through empirical study. As Jonathan Turner (2003) states, "Scientific theories begin with the assumption that the universe, including the social universe created by acting human beings, reveals certain basic and fundamental properties and processes that explain the ebb and flow of events in specific contexts. Because of this concern with discovering fundamental properties and processes, scientific theories are always stated abstractly, reign above specific events and highlight the underlying forces that drive these events" (p. 1).

Contemplation of the social world that surrounds us is an activity shared by humans throughout history. In Chapter 1, we learned that the development of sociology as a scientific discipline is traced to early industrialization in Europe. For centuries, Europeans were dominated by philosophies that embraced religious dogmatic thinking and the concept of the divine rights of kings. During the Enlightenment era, a number of social thinkers would challenge these long-held beliefs. The early European sociologists would be influenced by the Enlightenment mentality of challenging the status quo. They would also promote empirical research when seeking to validate their theories.

Sociology has been in existence for less than two centuries, but it has already amassed a great number of theoretical perspectives designed to explain the social world. As one of the social sciences, sociology is guided by these theoretical perspectives in an attempt to explain micro and macro aspects of human behavior. Sociologists maintain legitimacy in the academic world by demonstrating a commitment to the discovery and explanation of social reality. The wide variety of theoretical approaches used by sociologists reflects the reality that social thinkers are influenced by their own selective perceptions. Furthermore, it is beneficial for the field of sociology to embrace a variety of schools of thought because of the great cultural diversity that exists in the global community.

In this chapter we trace some of the major theorists who contributed to the development of sociology as a scientific discipline and examine the different theoretical perspectives that are active in sociology today.

EARLY SOCIOLOGISTS: EUROPEAN ORIGINS

A number of specific early European and American social thinkers helped shape the course and direction of sociology. Just as they were influenced by the social thinkers who preceded them, these thinkers went on to influence many of today's contemporary sociologists. Our discussion begins with Auguste Comte, the founder of sociology.

Auguste Comte (1798–1857)

The French social philosopher Auguste Comte first proposed the word "sociology" in 1838 in the fourth volume of *The Course of Positive Philosophy*. As mentioned in Chapter 1, the word "sociology" is a hybrid term composed of Latin and Greek parts—*socio* for "society" and *ology*, meaning "the study of." Thus, "sociology" literally means the study of society.

For Comte, his new positivist science, or **positivism**, was a coherent system of ideas guided by an intellectual and moral basis that allowed for science to intervene for the betterment of society (Hadden 1997). Further, Comte's idea of positivism is based on the idea that everything in society is observable and subject to patterns or laws. Discovering these laws would help sociologists explain human behavior. To prove the existence of laws, sociologists were expected to conduct and compile empirical research guided by theory. Comte believed strongly that the purpose of sociology as a discipline is to discover, define, and identify social patterns (K. Thompson 1975). Having gained knowledge of these laws, according to Comte, the sociologist would be equipped to aid in the progressive improvement of society.

Positivism -> Science intervenes for betterment of Society

Comte: Soc.'s purpose is to discover, define, & identify Social patterns
[Comte -> Social patterns]
[" -> improvement of Society]

Comte had first proposed the term "social physics" to describe his new science but discovered that Belgian social statistician Adolphe Quetelet had "stolen" the term from him (Coser 1977). His considering the term "social physics" made it clear that Comte wanted to model sociology after the natural sciences (Ritzer 2000b). Comte valued the field of physics because he believed it was the first discipline to free itself from the traditions of faith and metaphysics. Pointing to Galileo's struggle with the Catholic Church as the decisive moment marking science's attempt to break from theology, Comte conceived of sociology as a scientific discipline.

Social Statics
(Social structure)
- maintain social order
- justice system/etiquette

Social Dynamics
(Social change)
- stimulate, improve
- technology

Another important contribution to sociology from Comte was his use of the terms "social statics" and "social dynamics." Comte believed that in order for society to function, social forces had to be in place to guarantee the harmonious operation of all society's parts. Some of these forces are intended to maintain stability while others stimulate, or allow for, change. **Social statics** refer to the social forces that are designed to maintain the existing social order and bring harmony to all parts of society. Examples of social forces designed for stability are the justice system, law enforcement, and rules of etiquette. **Social dynamics**, in contrast, refer to the social forces that lead to social change. Comte believed these dynamic forces were important for the evolutionary (progressive) improvement of society. Advancement in technology, for example, constantly stimulates change, whether it involves the use of satellite technology or changes in the work setting (e.g., replacing assembly-line workers with automated machinery). Sociologists still study these social forces, but today they use the terms "social structure" in place of social statics and "social change" in place of social dynamics (Ritzer 2000b).

What Do You Think?

Do you agree with Comte's idea that a number of social forces in society are designed both to maintain stability and stimulate social change? Discuss examples of both. Are the social forces designed for stability more or less important than, or equally important as, the forces designed for change? What do you think?

Harriet Martineau (1802–1876) – not as important for class

Born in Norwich, England, Harriet Martineau is best known as Auguste Comte's translator. However, in addition to translating Comte's French publications into English, making them accessible to a much larger audience, she was also a prolific writer in her own right. Although much of her early writing was nonacademic, Martineau penned many sociological articles describing the social issues of her time. She traveled to different countries as well, which provided her with an opportunity to engage in cross-cultural analysis on a diverse set of subjects. These achievements are all the more remarkable in light of Martineau's physical disabilities: she was deaf and lacked the senses of smell and taste.

Martineau shared with her educated contemporaries a general belief in progress—the concept that human society is constantly moving forward and improving. However, she also noted that progress is sometimes interrupted by various crises. Martineau wanted sociology to concern itself with answering the fundamental question, What constitutes a better life for people? To address this question, Martineau believed that sociology should be committed to systematic, empirical observation. Further, any analysis of society must also include an examination of its *morals* (cultural values and beliefs) and *manners* (social interactions). Martineau studied prison settings and inmates because she believed that to truly

Martineau:
• What constitutes better life for ppl?
• morals + manners

understand the morals and manners of people, one must investigate the bad things that people do as well as the good and proper things.

good & bad in ppl Must be studied

Martineau also believed that sociology should be a critical and ethical field—that sociologists should work toward improving society and pointing out its ills. One of these ills was the unequal status of women. In her analysis of America's democratic ideal of social equality, for example, Martineau (1836–1837) pointed out that the U.S. Constitution (as it existed at that time) guaranteed equality and democracy, but not for women. This observation would help her formulate her feminist thinking, and Martineau went on to maintain a lifetime commitment to bettering women's place in society.

worked to better lives of women

Comte: Father of Soc.
Martineau: Mother of Soc.

Because of her influence on the field, Martineau is often referred to as the mother of sociology—a counterpart to Comte, whom some describe as the father of sociology (Lengermann and Niebrugge-Brantley 2000).

Herbert Spencer (1820–1903)

Throughout most of his life, the British scholar Herbert Spencer enjoyed critical acclaim for his works and theories. In fact, during the early years of American sociology, his ideas were much more influential than those of Comte, Karl Marx, Emile Durkheim, or Max Weber. By the mid-twentieth century, however, Spencer's works had been mostly forgotten. Even so, a discussion of his contributions to early sociology remains a constant in all introductory sociology textbooks.

Spencer: Social evolution occurs Culturally

As a firm believer in social evolution, Spencer argued that humans adapt to their environments culturally rather than biologically, like other organisms. Spencer believed that this occurred at both the micro (individual) and macro (societal) levels. Societies that meet the needs of cultural changes in the social environment are the fittest and therefore the most likely to survive. Spencer warned that societies must also protect themselves from other nations that pose a threat to their survival. Unsuccessful adaptation to these concerns leads to dissolution of the society, whereas successful adaptation leads to its survival. Successful adaptations handed down to the next generation will result in what Spencer described as "the survival of the fittest."

Cultural change propagates Society, unable to change leads to dissolution of Society

Curiously, Spencer's greatest contribution to social thought—the concept of the survival of the fittest—is mistakenly credited to Charles Darwin. Spencer first used the phrase "survival of the fittest" in 1864 in his *Principles of Biology*, many years before Darwin used the term "natural selection." Darwin's theory of natural selection was applied to the natural world, whereas Spencer's survival of the fittest was applied to the social world.

The concept of the survival of the fittest is also very relevant at the individual level as each of us is in competition with others for scarce resources. Students are in competition with one another for scholarships; athletes compete against one another to make the team, and once they do, they compete together against their opponents; graduates compete for scarce high-paying jobs; single people compete for the romantic affections of desirable partners; and so on. In short, there is no end to competition in life. A Spencerian perspective argues that the person who is fittest will achieve a positive outcome.

The **survival of the fittest** concept, according to Spencer, is an evolutionary process that entails individuals and societies meeting the needs of the changing social environment (Peel 1971). Those who are fittest will move on. Those who are unfit will die off.

What Do You Think?

Spencer's proponents would argue that the doctrine of the survival of the fittest is still relevant today. What do you think?

Karl Marx (1818–1883)

Nearly all students have heard the name Karl Marx. But what do you really know about him? The amount of literature available on Marx could fill a library. However, for our purposes, the most important elements of his theories, in terms of the early development of sociology, rest on class conflict, class struggle, and communism (see "Connecting Sociology and Popular Culture" Box 2.1 for a contemporary example of class struggle).

It should be noted that Marx never claimed to be a sociologist (among other things, he was an economist, historian, journalist, poet, philosopher, and humanist); rather, his theories were akin to sociological thought, and many sociologists have found them to be relevant to the field of sociology. His firsthand examination of the dreadful working conditions that most industrial workers of his day were forced to endure led Marx to conclude that the owners of the means of production were exploiting the workers. Furthermore, Marx believed that all history was an example of *class conflict* and *class struggle* between the haves and the have-nots. During the industrial age, the haves were the owners of the means of production, or **bourgeoisie**, while the have-nots were the workers, or the **proletariat**. In an attempt to maintain their power advantage, the bourgeoisie exploited the workers and prevented them from reaching their full human potential by means of demeaning, monotonous physical labor.

Marx:
class conflict
class struggle
communism

Marx's ideas on class struggle are still relevant today as many businesses, including major corporations, pursue a bottom-line strategy wherein profits for stockholders are more important than job security for workers. In his 1962 book *Capitalism and Freedom*, the Nobel Prize–winning economist Milton Friedman, an outspoken opponent of Marxism, famously wrote that the first responsibility of corporate officials should be "to make as much money for their stockholders as possible" (p. 133).

In carrying out this so-called responsibility over recent decades, the owners of the means of production in the United States have used their power position to relocate production facilities to developing nations where the labor force is paid significantly less than the U.S. minimum wage. As a result, many Americans have lost their jobs and are left feeling alienated and exploited. Marx defined *alienation* as a condition in which humans become dominated by forces of their own creation, which confront them as alien powers (Coser 1977; Cooper 1991). Marx argued that the capitalist system, by virtue of its structure, was responsible for four general types of alienation of the worker, all of which can be found in the domain of work: workers alienated (1) from the object(s) they produce, (2) from the process of production, (3) from their sense of self, and (4) from fellow workers.

For Marx, all matters of social theory, class struggle, social stratification, alienation, and so on, center on economic considerations. Marx believed that economics was the sole primary motivation for people to act. As a result, his critics would describe him as an "economic determinist," meaning that he believed social behavior to be determined by economics. Other early sociologists, such as Max Weber (whose work we discuss later in this chapter), would argue that social stratification and other matters of social concern could be determined by a number of factors, including not only economics but also politics, personal prestige, charisma, and so forth.

What Do You Think?

Should major corporations worry more about maximizing profits for shareholders than about maintaining jobs for their workers? How would you feel if you were a shareholder?

Marx believed that because the workers were exploited by the bourgeoisie, they would never reach their full human potential. In this regard, he came to view capitalism as an oppressive environment. He believed that **communism** would alleviate the suffering of the proletariat and thereby help workers to reach their full potential. Although later in his life Marx reluctantly admitted that capitalism increased economic production, he saw it merely as a necessary evil and a stepping-stone to communism. It was Marx's dream that the workers (the proletariat) would revolt against the bourgeoisie and a form a classless society based on communist ideology. It should be noted that Marx did not invent or create communism—he learned about it from Friedrich Engels, who learned about it from Germany's first communist, Moses Hess—but he was instrumental in popularizing it.

Marx's primary ideas on communism were articulated in *The Communist Manifesto*, a book he coauthored with Engels. Marx and Engels predicted that class inequality would end as the size and power of the working class increased, leading to collective control of property and the means of production. Under Marxist communism, governments would be unnecessary; as a result, governmental abuse

Even in death, Karl Marx attempts to unite the proletariat. Shown here, the tombstone of Marx reads "Workers of All Lands Unite."

of workers would end (Pampel 2000). The *Manifesto* was so powerful that it influenced all subsequent communist literature and proletariat revolutionary thought in general. Marx's theories were so significant that they would influence sociology's conflict theory, discussed later in this chapter.

Emile Durkheim (1858–1917)

The French sociologist Emile Durkheim enjoys many credits: he is known as the founder of modern sociology and the founder of functionalism"; he was also the first full professor of sociology (at the University of Bordeaux in 1895). Clearly Durkheim's contributions to sociology are immense. Most relevant to our discussion of early sociologists is the fact that he is acknowledged as the first sociologist actually to use the scientific method. His famous studies on suicide were based on statistical data and analysis that allowed him to categorize various types of suicide.

Durkheim ([1895] 1951) chose to study suicide because it is a relatively concrete and specific phenomenon that lends itself to statistical analysis. The importance of his study rests with the fact that Durkheim was able to show that this act, which is generally highly individualistic, could be understood sociologically (see "A Closer Look" Box 2.2 for a more in-depth analysis of the social aspects of suicide). As a sociologist, Durkheim was not concerned with any specific individual who had committed suicide (such an examination usually falls within the domain of psychology); instead he was interested in categorizing different types of suicide, thus demonstrating its social component.

Durkheim created a model that defined four categories of suicide—egoistic, altruistic, anomic, and fatalistic—and linked each with its degree of integration into, or regulation by, society. *Integration* refers to the degree to which collective sentiments are shared: Durkheim argued that when society is strongly integrated, it holds individuals under its control. *Regulation* refers to the degree of external constraint and pressure on people. Accordingly, altruistic suicide is associated with a high degree of integration and egoistic suicide with a low degree of integration, while fatalistic suicide is associated with high regulation and anomic suicide with low regulation.

for class → focus only on integration factor

The ultimate goal of science is prediction. Thus, sociologists would like to predict which individuals are candidates for suicide. Durkheim's types of suicide provide us with some insights:

Egoistic → low integration, social isolation

1. *Egoistic suicide:* High rates are likely to be found in societies, collectivities, or groups in which the individual is not well integrated into the larger social unit, such as someone who is suffering from deep depression or social isolation. A person who is dumped by a spouse or significant other, for example, may feel so depressed by this social disconnection from a loved one that she or he is compelled to commit suicide.
2. *Altruistic suicide:* This occurs when social integration is too strong. The individual is compelled by social forces into committing suicide, as happened in 1997 when thirty-nine members of the Heaven's Gate religious cult killed themselves by ingesting poison (ReligiousTolerance.org 1997). Altruistic suicide is also committed when social prestige is attached to the act; examples include the suicides of Japanese kamikaze pilots in World War II and Iraqi and Afghani Muslim suicide bombers seeking martyrdom.

Altruistic → too integrated, cult suicides + Kamikaze

People contemplate and often follow through on committing suicide. What could possibly be going on in the mind of this person standing on a building ledge? And how would Durkheim explain it?

3. *Anomic suicide:* Durkheim used the term "anomie" to describe a sense of normlessness among people. (Although the terms are not interchangeable, Durkheim's notion of anomie is similar to Marx's idea of alienation because such a condition negatively affects individuals as a result of social conditions.) Anomie generally occurs during periods of rapid social change for groups or individuals, when the usual norms break down. Workers who suddenly lose their jobs and people who suddenly lose large sums of money on the stock market would be candidates for anomic suicide. Interestingly, some large lottery winners report suffering from anomie. Some of these big winners have filed for bankruptcy within a few years, been attacked by family members, and been besieged by requests from strangers (Dorell 2006). ABC's *Good Morning America* (2009) provides a number of examples of lottery winners who have had bad luck, including a man who was kidnapped and murdered by his sister-in-law after winning $20 million, a two-time New Jersey winner who spent over $5.4 million in lottery winnings in just two years and now lives in a trailer, and a Pennsylvania winner of $16.2 million who now lives on food stamps and Social Security.

Anomic → Social changes i.e. winning lottery, losing job or money

4. *Fatalistic suicide:* Durkheim spent little time describing this category of suicide, but it is likely to occur when regulation is too excessive, leaving the individual with little or no sense of control over his or her own life. Candidates for this type of suicide would include people facing a life prison sentence or forced into slavery or prostitution.

Fatalistic → loss of control over own life

Connecting Sociology and Popular Culture

Box 2.1 Rap Music as an Expression of Class Struggle

Karl Marx argued that all history is an example of class struggle and class conflict between those who control the means of production and possess power (the haves) and those who do not (the have-nots). In most societies around the world today, there still exists a class struggle between such categories of people. In the United States, African Americans have historically found themselves disproportionately in the category of the have-nots.

Although the civil rights movement of the 1960s hoped and strove to establish equality, such a social condition failed to materialize fully. By the end of the 1960s, a number of African Americans, frustrated by the lack of equality in society, began to express a new racial consciousness that promoted Afrocentrism in all spheres of social life, including the arts. African American writing workshops began to spring up around the nation. Poetry and rhymes were performed live, generally accompanied by African music or drumming (Delaney 2006a). Performers like the Last Poets of Harlem gained national prominence. By the early 1970s, soul and funk artists Barry White and Isaac Hayes had begun to incorporate raps into their songs (Keyes 2002).

In the mid-1970s, another, now-common aspect of hip-hop began to emerge: the disc jockey (DJ). The DJ spun records at clubs and private parties. Over time, DJs developed such techniques as "phasing," "back spinning," and "scratching" (Keyes 2002). By the mid-1980s, rap had become popular in urban neighborhoods throughout the country as a way for younger African Americans to express frustration over the class struggle and conflict that many experienced. The relatively tame lyrics and themes of the 1980s gave way in the 1990s to angry messages laced with profanity. The new lyrics glorified violence and often referred to women in a derogatory fashion.

During the 1990s, gangsta rap gained popularity. Many rappers, such as the late Easy-E and Tupac Shakur, along with current rappers Dr. Dre and Snoop Dogg, used their actual gang and street credentials to give their lyrics legitimacy—"keeping it real." Having legit street cred is important to many of the have-nots; conversely, it is of little importance to those who

What Do You Think?

There are people, such as Kurt Cobain, former lead singer for Nirvana, who seem to "have it all" and yet commit suicide. Why do you think they do this? Did Cobain commit egoistic, altruistic, anomic, or fatalistic suicide? What do you think?

The application of the sociological imagination, discussed in Chapter 1, is very relevant to Durkheim's analysis of suicide: as he demonstrated, many individuals feel compelled to commit suicide (personal troubles) because of outside social forces (public issues).

Emile Durkheim's sociology was grounded in a macro (large-scale), functionalist perspective based on his belief that society is a system and that its parts (institutions) contribute to its stability and continual existence. As a result, Durkheim considered the study of society to be much more important than the study of individuals or groups of people found in society. As Durkheim ([1914] 1973) explains, "A great number of our mental states, including some of the most important ones, are of social origin. In this case then, it is the whole that, in a large measure, produces the part; consequently, it is impossible to attempt to explain the whole without

possess power in society. After all, people who control the means of production need not get into the trenches and prove themselves. Instead, they attempt to prove themselves in boardrooms and on Wall Street. In other words, the only street that people with power care to dominate is Wall Street, metaphorically speaking. Thus, it could be argued that those with power seek "Wall Street cred" because their power comes from financial credibility. And in reality, people with power control the streets in a different manner, with political and economic influence.

Gangsta rap today is still all about street credibility. Rapper 50 Cent claims to have been shot nine times, which gives him great street cred—but raises the bar for younger rappers. The violence that sometimes surrounds gangsta rap still has deadly consequences. In August 2009, for example, rapper C-Murder (real name Corey Miller) was sentenced to life in prison for killing a sixteen-year-old boy at a nightclub in Harvey, Louisiana (UPI.com 2009).

Rap music is just one example of popular culture that demonstrates the current state of class conflict and class struggle in society. Interestingly, many white kids also identify with the class struggle of African Americans and have embraced gangsta rap. Rapper Eminem, however, is one of the few white performers who has credibility in this genre. Rap music is also popular with many Hispanic youth who can identify with the class struggle that exists in the United States. Rapper Pitbull, for example, is a bilingual Cuban American Miami native with a number of chart-climbing songs. Pitbull, whose real name is Armando Christian Pérez, chose his stage name because of the symbolism inherent in the fact that pit bulls are outlawed in Dade County, where his hometown of Miami is located. He identifies with the class struggle of minorities in southern Florida and views pit bulls as animals too "stupid" to give up. Combining the outlaw spirit and never surrendering, Pérez views himself as also being too "stupid" to give up. Pitbull would appear to be winning his class struggle, as he has accumulated not only wealth through his rapping but also prestige: in August 2009 he was awarded a key to the city of Miami (*Post-Standard,* 8/21/09).

What Do You Think?

Is rap music an effective venue for performers and fans to express their frustration with the class struggle that exists in society? If Karl Marx were alive today, how would he react to rap music as a vehicle to express class struggle and conflict? What do you think?

explaining the part—without explaining, at least, the part as a result of the whole" (p. 149).

Max Weber (1864–1920)

German sociologist Max Weber conducted an extraordinary amount of empirical research and presented significant theoretical scholarship; among his more notable contributions are his ideas on rationalization, bureaucracy, and types of authority. Weber believed that sociologists actually had an advantage over natural scientists in conducting research because they possessed the ability to understand the phenomena under study. He used the German word *verstehen* (understanding) as a guiding principle in his interpretative approach to the study of human behavior. Weber contended that sociologists must examine the meanings behind

A Closer Look

Box 2.2 The Sociological Aspects of Suicide

The topic of suicide remains as relevant today as it did when Durkheim first studied it. According to the Centers for Disease Control and Prevention (CDC), suicide was the eleventh leading cause of death in 2007. More than 34,000 suicides occurred in the United States, the equivalent of 94 suicides per day, or one suicide every fifteen minutes (CDC 2010c). As alarming as these numbers are, it is even more common for people to contemplate suicide. According to the CDC (2010c), among young adults ages fifteen to twenty-four, there are approximately one to two hundred attempts for every completed suicide. In 2009, 13.8 percent of U.S. high school students reported that they had seriously considered attempting suicide during the twelve months preceding the survey (CDC 2010c).

Suicide statistics reveal a number of interesting patterns, one of which is gender differences. Women are more likely than men to attempt suicide, but men are almost four times as likely to succeed (CDC 2010c). Most experts attribute this gender difference to women attempting suicide as a "cry for help," whereas men are more determined to end their lives (Winik 2002). The method one uses to attempt suicide also has a significant correlation to the end results; women tend to use a more passive approach to suicide attempts (e.g., pills), while men use a more aggressive approach (e.g., a firearm). The CDC (2010c) reports that firearms are the most commonly used method of suicide among males (55.7 percent).

There are racial and ethnic disparities when it comes to suicide as well. Among American Indians/Alaska Natives ages fifteen to thirty-four, suicide is the second leading cause of death, and suicide rates among American Indians/Alaska Natives ages fifteen to thirty-four are 1.8 times the national average for that age group (CDC 2010c). Hispanic and black students in grades nine to twelve have higher percentages of suicide attempts (11.1 and 10.4 percent, respectively) than their white, non-Hispanic counterparts (6.5 percent).

Another interesting pattern involves geographic locations where people prefer to commit suicide. The most common location involves bridges and waterfalls. The most popular place in the United States for people to commit suicide is the Golden Gate Bridge, and the second most popular place is Niagara Falls. (Note: Students may want to watch the documentary *The Bridge* to learn more about this phenomenon.) In Niagara Falls, suicide statistics dating back to 1856 reveal that the most common month for people to

the actions of individuals. For Weber, *verstehen* was a rational procedure of study, not a subjective one. In fact, Weber argued that sociologists should be "value free" while conducting research.

Like Karl Marx, Weber examined the consequences of the Industrial Revolution for society. Unlike Marx, however, Weber focused on the potential benefits of industrialization, such as the reality that increased productivity results in a higher standard of living for a greater number of people. In Weber's view, industrialization was good for society because it was guided by constructs of rationalization. **Rationalization** can be defined as the product of scientific specialization and technical differentiation. Weber approved of industrialization's replacing favoritism and tradition with rationalization because the latter is based on scientific

commit suicide there is September (17 percent of total suicides) and the least common month is October (1 percent). The most common day is Monday and the most common time is 4:00 p.m. (Michelmore 2000).

Another aspect of suicide that reveals a social component is the phenomenon of suicide pacts, or predetermined plans, sometimes made between couples (e.g., dating or married partners) or among groups of people (e.g., cult members), for how and why to end their lives.

A large number of suicide victims tell someone of their plan to commit suicide, but that information is generally not acted upon (Winik 2002). The CDC reports that anywhere from 33 to 66 percent of suicide victims leave a note behind to explain their actions—revealing the social aspect of their suicide (Emeigh 2010; CDC 1988). Because so many people attempt to reach out to others about their suicidal aspirations, it is best to err on the side of caution. That is, if a friend or loved one expresses to you an inclination toward committing suicide, take some sort of action: contact a counselor, call another mutual friend or family member, or call a suicide hotline and ask for help.

Do individuals have a right to commit suicide? The answer to this question, at least in the United States, has been no; legally, people have not had the right to kill themselves—that is until 1994, when the state of Oregon passed the Oregon Death with Dignity Act by a slim (51 to 49 percent) vote. An attempt at appeal was handily defeated in 1997. This law allows a terminally ill patient to take an overdose of drugs under two conditions: two doctors agree the patient is terminally ill, and they believe the patient is of sound mind. In addition, the law protects counselors, physicians, and family members who provide aid and comfort, but do not administer the drugs, from being prosecuted or sued. On March 27, 1998, a woman in her eighties who was near death from breast cancer became the first person to legally end her life with barbiturates prescribed by an Oregon doctor. Advocates for the Oregon law saw it as a victory for personal autonomy and control over medical care when death is near. In 2006, in a 6–3 decision, the U.S. Supreme Court upheld the law—the only law of its kind in the nation (to date). However, a number of other states have passed laws that support do-not-resuscitate (DNR) and withdrawal-of-treatment decisions. People who support such laws claim that they would rather die with dignity than be kept alive by machines.

What Do You Think?

If a loved one informed you that he or she was thinking about committing suicide, what would you do? There is a great debate as to whether a person has the right to take his or her own life. What do you think?

principles. In one of his most powerful books, *The Protestant Ethic and the Spirit of Capitalism*, Weber ([1904–1905] 1958) explained that the spirit of capitalism involves the rational and calculating pursuit of maximum profit. He used rationalization as his primary reason to explain why capitalism and industrialization took hold in Western European nations and North America while other parts of the world failed to embrace it. Weber believed that only in modern capitalism does the desire for unlimited profit combine with the efficient use of reason (Pampel 2000). Weber also noted that rational systems need an efficient mechanism to operate them. This mechanism is called bureaucracy. According to Weber, **bureaucracies** are goal-oriented entities designed according to rational principles in order to efficiently attain the predetermined goals of the organization.

Weber introduced to sociology his concept of the ideal type as a means of studying the features of a bureaucracy. At its most basic level, an **ideal type** is a concept constructed by a sociologist to capture the principle features of some social phenomenon (e.g., a bureaucracy). An ideal type is essentially a measuring rod whose function is to compare empirical reality with preconceived notions of a phenomenon. Weber noted that as the complexity of society increases, bureaucracies continue to grow. The potential dysfunctional aspects of bureaucracy were not lost on Weber. Indeed, he warned that rationalization and bureaucracy were an inescapable fate of humanity. (Note: This idea is similar to Marx's notion of alienation, where individuals feel isolated and estranged.) In short, Weber viewed future society as an "iron cage" (unable to escape from bureaucracy and rationalization) rather than a semblance of Eden.

What Do You Think?

A bureaucracy, such as a college admissions or registrar's office, is designed to be efficient. At times, however, bureaucrats pay so much attention to the details of rules and regulations that they lose a sense of personal touch and consideration of individuals. Based on your own experiences with bureaucracies, what do you think?

EARLY SOCIOLOGISTS IN THE UNITED STATES

The discussion of Comte, Martineau, Spencer, Marx, Durkheim, and Weber covers the most significant influences on early sociology. All these people, however, lived and worked in Europe or Great Britain. Several Americans are worthy of special recognition as contributors to early sociological thought as well. It should be noted that a number of other European and American sociologists could also be mentioned, but space and time constraints do not allow for further review; this reality helps to explain why sociology majors are required to take a social theory course. In this text, four significant Americans have been chosen for discussion owing to their contributions to sociological thought: Jane Addams, Ida Wells-Barnett, George Herbert Mead, and W. E. B. Du Bois.

Jane Addams (1860–1935)

Addams was born in Cedarville, Illinois, and attended Rockford Female Seminary, a women's college that did not grant diplomas but instead provided graduates with a "testimonial"—a certificate used in place of a degree. Viewing this as an obvious example of sexual inequality, Addams embarked on a life of feminist thought and a desire to help disadvantaged youth.

In 1883, Addams traveled to Ireland and England. While in London, she became alarmed by the urban decay that included street prostitutes, drunken men, crippled children begging for food, and streets polluted with garbage and animal blood from slaughterhouses. Addams also visited the London Toynbee Hall, a settlement house designed to provide relief for the less fortunate. She became inspired to establish such a place in the United States. Ultimately, this would lead to her greatest contribution to society, and ultimately sociology: the creation of the Hull House settlement. Hull House was hugely successful, expanding in the first two decades after its founding in 1889 "from a single floor to a city-block complex of buildings including an art gallery, coffee shop, gymnasium, library, theater, museum of labor, dining rooms, music rooms, and housing facilities" (Lengermann and Niebrugge-Brantley 1998, p. 68).

Jane Addams → Hull House

The communal atmosphere of Hull House led Addams to develop a sociological theory based on the idea that people must begin to work collectively and cooperatively. Ideas of cooperation and progressive growth serve as the foundation for her major publications. Addams combined modified versions of progressiveness, social Darwinism, philosophic pragmatism, and social gospel Christianity into her general social theory. She proposed *reform social Darwinism*, a theoretical perspective that highlighted the need for morality to evolve along with scientific advancements. As for research, Addams believed that sociologists should employ ethnographic research, a type of observational study in which the researcher immerses him- or herself in the group under study (see Chapter 3 for a discussion of research methodologies). She incorporated a micro approach in order to better understand the needs of specific people. Both her theories and her research reflect a feminist framework and demonstrate a commitment to improving the social status of women. In short, Addams was an activist and a person who believed in moral social reform. She remains an instrumental figure in early sociological feminist thought.

Ida Wells-Barnett (1862–1931)

Perhaps the most unique social theorist of all those discussed in this chapter is Ida Wells-Barnett, a fearless civil rights crusader, suffragist, women's rights advocate, journalist, and public speaker. Ida Wells was born in Holly Springs, Mississippi, to enslaved parents who gained their freedom when the Civil War ended in 1865. In her autobiography, *Crusade for Justice*, Wells-Barnett credited her parents with instilling in her an interest in politics and a sense of morality that encouraged fighting for justice. Ida Wells attended Rust College in Mississippi. After college, she found concurrent jobs as a schoolteacher and journalist in Memphis.

In Memphis she first began to fight for racial and gender equality. In the truest sense of the concept of moral reform that early sociologists believed in so strongly (see Chapter 1), Ida Wells was very much a moral reformist. Her first major attempt at reform was a one-woman campaign against lynching, which she launched in 1883 by writing a series of articles in the *Free Speech* newspaper detailing, with empirical data, the horrors and racial terrorism that lynching represented (Lengermann and Niebrugge-Brantley 2000). In her first antilynching pamphlet, "Southern Horrors," Ida Wells described a case involving one of her close friends, Thomas Moss. Moss and two of his friends owned a successful grocery store in Memphis that was cutting into the profits of white-owned grocers. A group of angry white men eventually dragged Moss and his friends away from town and brutally murdered them. Wells's descriptions of the events deeply touched the black population of Memphis. Sensing her growing power as an activist in the community, a white-owned newspaper in Memphis called for the lynching of Ida Wells.

In 1884, long before Rosa Parks became famous for refusing to give her bus seat up to a white man, Ida Wells refused to give up her seat on a railroad car. Despite the 1875 Civil Rights Act banning discrimination on the basis of race in theaters, hotels, and other public places, Jim Crow–era tactics led railroad companies to ignore the law. (Note: "Jim Crow" refers to a period following the Civil War and before the civil rights movement of the 1960s when blacks were denied equal access to goods and services available to whites even though they were legally entitled to rights as American citizens.) Blacks were supposed to sit in the "smoker" cars, which were generally very dirty (smoker cars were immediately behind the engines). When a white man wanted Wells's seat in a nonsmoker car, she refused to give it up and was forcibly dragged out of it by the conductor and two other passengers. Wells sued the Chesapeake, Ohio and Southwestern Railroad Company and initially won, but when the railroad appealed, she lost and was ordered to pay court costs. Identified as a dissident by the southern white establishment, Ida Wells moved to Chicago where she worked with Jane Addams at Hull House and continued her career as a journalist. In 1895, she married F. L. Barnett, a Chicago lawyer and editor of a black newspaper. That same year she published her second book on lynching, *A Red Record*.

The relevance of Wells-Barnett to sociology cannot be overstated. She was a moral reformer who battled for the rights of women and blacks while fighting discrimination—mainstay topics in contemporary sociology. Her theoretical perspective was heavily influenced by the works of Karl Marx. Wells-Barnett argued that discrimination and oppression led to a two-class society of the "dominant" and the "dominated." These two groups (in the Marxist tradition) would engage in a class struggle. Domination by the power group is patterned by five factors:

1. *History:* sets of events that lead to power discrimination
2. *Ideology:* distortions and exaggerations of select events
3. *Material resources:* possession of resources, which equates to power
4. *Manners:* routinization of everyday interactions between dominants and subordinates

5. *Passion:* emotion and desire to control, which are the keys to domination (Lengermann and Niebrugge-Brantley 1998).

Ida Wells-Barnett is an underrated sociologist who believed in moral reform and shared all early sociologists' commitment to sociology as a science driven by theory and supported by empirical data.

George Herbert Mead (1863–1931)

Born in South Hadley, Massachusetts, George Herbert Mead is known for his pragmatic approach to the study of human behavior. Pragmatists believe that human beings reflect on the meaning of a stimulus before reacting to it. In this manner, according to Mead, humans are not like animals that simply respond to stimuli based on instinct; they are capable of reason and rational thought. The idea that humans have the capacity to reflect and decide on a course of action in any given situation implies that humans react on the basis of their perceptions and definitions of the situations in which they find themselves.

> **What Do You Think?**
>
> Rosa Parks is well known for refusing to give up her seat on a bus. Ida Wells-Barnett made a related gesture in an era when blacks were treated even more harshly, yet her campaign for justice is not nearly as famous. Why is this? What do you think?

Interestingly, Mead is considered one of the key figures in the development of American pragmatism even though he learned about pragmatism from John Dewey, a philosopher at the University of Chicago. Mead's pragmatism entailed the idea that truth and reality are not simply "out there" to be discovered; rather, they are created as humans act in—and toward—the world.

The human capacity for reflection is an instrumental component in the development of one's sense of self. Mead believed that the self is essentially a social structure that arises from social experience, or interaction with others. Like John Locke (see Chapter 1), who used the term "tabula rasa" to describe his idea that newborns start life without predetermined thoughts or notions, Mead believed that a baby is born a blank slate, without predispositions to develop any particular type of personality. (Of course, a baby is not literally blank, as a healthy baby will possess eyes, ears, nerve endings, and other biological faculties that will allow learning to occur.) The personality—the sense of self—that develops in each of us, according to Mead, is a product of each person's interactions with others.

The micro orientation of Mead's works is similar to that of another notable early American sociologist, Charles Horton Cooley (1864–1929). Cooley claimed that a sense of self requires *reflexivity*. For example, all students reading this book have a sense of self—that is, an idea of how they look to themselves and how they look to others. We have a sense of self because we reflect upon ourselves as objects. Cooley (1902) demonstrated the reflective nature of the self by comparing it to a looking glass (an old-fashioned term for mirror): "Each to each a looking glass, reflected the other that doth pass" (p. 183); we explore this concept in more detail later in the chapter. Mead argued that the development of self is critical for the creation of consciousness and the ability of the child to take on the role of the other. Mead believed that the development of self involved four stages:

1. *Imitation stage:* In this stage, the infant learns to imitate, through observation, the behaviors of others. He or she learns to communicate through gestures until the development of language. Imitation implies that behavior is learned.
2. *Play stage:* At this stage, the young child has learned to use language. The child now acts out, or plays, the roles of others. For example, a young girl may dress up like her mother. Children at this stage are learning the roles of others by role-playing. Role-playing also allows the child to become both the subject and the object, an important step in the development of self (Ritzer 2000b).
3. *Game stage:* At this stage, the child can now take the role of several others at the same time and is capable of understanding the relationships among these roles. Mead used the game of baseball to illustrate this stage. With baseball, as with all team sports, players must know not only their own roles but those of all their teammates as well. Knowing the rules of the game is another important aspect of the game stage as learning to abide by the rules implies that the child has learned self-control—an important aspect of group participation.
4. *Generalized other stage:* The generalized other develops from the successive and simultaneous use of many roles. The individual who reaches this stage can now take on the attitude of the entire community and acts on behalf of others instead of the self. The statement "I will not profit from this, but it will be good for the community" reflects a generalized other attitude.

Both George Herbert Mead and Charles Horton Cooley made significant contributions to symbolic interactionism, a micro sociological theoretical perspective discussed later in this chapter.

W. E. B. Du Bois (1868–1963)

Born in Great Barrington, Massachusetts, W. E. B. Du Bois graduated from Fisk University and went on to receive both a bachelor's degree and a doctorate from Harvard. In 1909 he helped to found the National Association for the Advancement of Colored People and became its first president. As Jane Addams was bringing to light the inequalities between men and women and promoting the idea of ethnographic research ("going native"), Du Bois (1903) was attacking racial inequality in the United States and promoting radical changes, including the use of force, to eradicate it. His investigative fieldwork on the African American community of Philadelphia (*The Philadelphia Negro* 1899) still stands today as a classic work of sociological research.

Du Bois envisioned sociology as a community-based profession whose top concern would be a commitment to social justice for all. Sharing the passion for moral reform of most early sociologists, Du Bois wanted sociologists to be activists. Having attended several lectures by Max Weber in Germany, Du Bois was influenced by the Weberian notion that sociologists must maintain a commitment to rigorous scientific sociological research.

Du Bois started the nation's second department of sociology at Atlanta University. (The first department of sociology was at the University of Chicago.) He led the annual Atlanta University Conference for the Study of Negro Problems, which became known for reliable sociological research on the South and founded two scholarly journals, *The Crisis* and *Phylon*. Du Bois recognized that his attempts to empower African Americans would be difficult because of the history of racism in the United States. Du Bois ([1903] 2007) stated, "The facing of so vast a prejudice could not but bring the inevitable self-questioning, self-disparagement, and lowering of ideals which ever accompany repression and breed in an atmosphere of contempt and hate" (p. 57). Frustrated by the lack of significant social change in race relations in the United States, Du Bois moved to the African nation of Ghana in 1961. He would die there two years later.

Although Du Bois made many significant contributions to sociology, perhaps his idea of double consciousness is most relevant to an introductory sociology course. In an 1897 *Atlantic Monthly* article titled "Strivings of the Negro People," but most often cited under the title "Of Our Spiritual Strivings" in *The Souls of Black Folk* (1903), Du Bois argued that one gains a sense of self through the eyes of others. This idea is similar to Cooley's "looking glass self." Du Bois distinguishes his concept from Cooley's by emphasizing the role of race in the perception of others. The introductory story in this chapter, regarding the "hook 'em horns!" gesture, highlights the selective role of perception. Whereas any given person may see herself as beautiful, another person may see ugliness. Du Bois (1903) theorized that nonblacks perceive black people on the basis of race rather than individual traits. As a result, Du Bois concluded, racism develops as a result of white stereotypes of black life; this, in turn, results in the exclusion of blacks from mainstream society. Ultimately, Du Bois's concept of double consciousness is similar to Cooley's looking glass self theory in that individuals are aware both of their own sense of self and of how they are perceived by others.

Du Bois & Cooley — Self-perception

THE MAJOR THEORETICAL PERSPECTIVES OF SOCIOLOGY

As sociology was a relatively new discipline, a limited number of sociologists proposed theoretical frameworks during the 1800s. These frameworks would dramatically change in the twentieth century and have continued to do so in the twenty-first century. Today, an abundance of sociologists is offering their theoretical ideas. Few of these people take the "grand" approach to social thinking, as such an endeavor involves establishing universal truths or laws about human behavior—a challenge beyond the capabilities of nearly all. Instead, most sociological theorists are specialized social thinkers who concentrate on a limited scope of sociological concerns. Thus, in sociology as it is practiced today, it is common to describe schools of thought rather than individual theorists who attempt to cover the broad spectrum of human behavior. These schools of thought, or theoretical perspectives, represent frameworks of similar thought among the many diverse social thinkers in sociology. The remainder of this chapter explores the three primary theories used in sociology: functionalism, conflict theory, and symbolic interactionism. It also presents a brief discussion of some of the other leading schools of thought (i.e., feminism, social-exchange theory, critical theory, and postmodernism).

Functionalism

Influenced by the earlier works of Auguste Comte, Herbert Spencer, and Emile Durkheim, functionalism reigned as sociology's dominant theoretical perspective during the 1950s and 1960s. For many sociologists, functionalism's primary tenets remain among the cornerstones of sociological theory. Functionalism is often referred to as structural functionalism because of its dual focus on the structural forces that shape human behavior and the attention given to systems needs. Proponents of functionalism are often called structural functionalists. Functionalism, originally designed by Talcott Parsons and expanded upon by Robert Merton, lives on through the ideas of neo- and poststructuralists such as Niklas Luhmann, Anthony Giddens, Neil Smelser, and Jeffrey C. Alexander. **Functionalism** is a macrosociological theory that examines the characteristics of social patterns, structures, systems, and institutions. Functionalists view society as having interrelated parts, which contribute to the functioning of the whole system. Whatever the characteristics of a society, they were developed to fit the specific needs of a given situation. Functionalism makes two basic assumptions:

1. All society's institutions (e.g., religion, politics, economics, education, sports, and the military) are linked together by a number of smaller interlinking systems that attempt to operate in harmony in order to secure the overall functional stability of the greater system.
2. There exists a general consensus on values and issues of right and wrong that allows the system to function properly.

The war on terrorism provides us with a nice example of how the two basic assumptions of functionalism come together. Immediately after the collapse of the World Trade Center's Twin Towers in New York City and reports of the attack on the Pentagon (along with a fourth hijacked plane that crashed in a field in Pennsylvania) on September 11, 2001, President George W. Bush mobilized many of society's institutions to take action. There existed, at that time, a general consensus among Americans that we had been attacked by terrorists and that something had to be done. With the support of the public that going to war was the right thing to do and that the attack upon the United States was wrong, the political institution mobilized the military institution. The remaining social institutions followed suit in near-blind obedience to this call-to-arms mentality sweeping across the United States. Without such a general consensus that military action was the right response, it would have been much more difficult for the president to justify the war on terrorism.

The events of September 11, 2001, have forever changed a number of aspects of culture. Americans are unlikely to ever forget these tragic events.

Talcott Parsons (1902–1979), the leading architect of functionalism, attempted to generate a grand theory of society that explained all social behavior with one theoretical framework. By design, his theory is abstract and elaborate. Parsons (1954) argued that sociological theory must use a limited number of important concepts to adequately grasp aspects of the objective external world. He also made clear his commitment to empirical research as the guiding force of his theory: "True scientific theory is not the product of idle 'speculation,' or spinning out the logical implications of assumptions, but of observation, reasoning and verification, starting with the facts and continually returning to the facts" (Parsons [1937] 1949, p. v).

Although functionalists generally study large social systems and how they strive to maintain stability and equilibrium, functionalism also addresses the fundamental sociological concern of explaining human behavior. Parsons's

([1937] 1949) *social-action theory*, an integral aspect of functionalism designed to explain human action (behavior), contains four steps:

1. *Motivation:* Social actors (individuals) are motivated to action, especially toward a desired goal. College students, for example, have the goal of attaining a college degree.
2. *Means:* Social actors must find the means to reach their goal. For some college students, finding the finances necessary to attend college presents a formidable challenge.
3. *Conditions:* Social actors must deal with conditions that hinder reaching the goal. College students seeking a degree must possess the necessary intellect, set aside the time to study and take examinations, overcome personal tragedies that occur while they are attending college, and so on.
4. *Work within the social system:* Social actors must learn to work within the social system in order to survive it. College students will have to fill out numerous forms, pass a large number of tests, fulfill the general education requirements, and meet other criteria in order to graduate.

Robert Merton (1910–2003), a middle-range theorist (someone who attempts to bridge macro and micro aspects), argues that just setting up a system and putting it in place does not guarantee that all aspects of the system operate at peak performance. Instead, certain aspects of a social system may have negative, or *dysfunctional*, components. Further, aspects of the system may be functional for some members of society but dysfunctional for others (Merton [1949] 1968). "Dysfunctional aspects of a society imply strain or stress or tension. A society tries to constrain dysfunctional elements somewhat as an organism might constrain a bacterial or viral infection. If the dysfunctional forces are too great, the social order is overwhelmed, disorganized, and possibly destroyed" (Cuzzort and King 1995, p. 252).

Merton also introduced the terms "manifest function" and "latent function" to sociological discourse. **Manifest functions** are the instances that occur that were planned on, intended, and consciously pursued. **Latent functions** are the unplanned, unintended functions of behavior. Merton's ([1949] 1968) research on the Hopi Indian Rain Dance illustrates the differences between these two concepts. The manifest function of a rain dance is, of course, to make it rain. The latent function of the rain dance, as Merton discovered, is the social solidarity provided by group participation toward a common goal. As college students can attest, the manifest function of education involves the imparting of knowledge from professors to students, whereas for many students the latent functions include social opportunities for dating and partying.

Conflict Theory

Students attend college for the manifest reason to learn and expand their level of knowledge, but also for the latent function of socializing. What do you suppose these students are doing—studying or updating their social network profiles?

Functionalism is driven by the idea that there is a general consensus in values and norms in society and that social institutions are integrated into a functioning whole. Conflict theory arose as a complete rejection of functionalism. Conflict theorists emphasize the role of power and claim that society's values and norms are those of the dominant power group, which are imposed on the masses. Conflict theory is a macro theory that attempts to explain the general structure of societies and demonstrate how those with power exploit those without it. Based primarily on the ideas of Karl Marx, the conflict perspective views society as a system of social structures and relationships shaped mainly by economic forces. However, it is important to note that Marx himself never used the term "conflict theory."

Those who control the means of production are the wealthy members of society, while those who do not are the poorer classes. Conflict theorists argue that because the economically wealthy control the means of production, they are able to dominate society. The economically wealthy, seeking to maintain their advantageous position, use their power to coerce and manipulate others. Economic disparity, conflict theorists argue, creates resentment and hostility within society. Thus, the potential for conflict always exists in any given society. Additionally, the conflict perspective pays close attention to the power of *special-interest groups* (groups that seek to fulfill their own best interests rather than the needs of the greater society), their role in society, and their battle to dominate scarce resources.

At its core, conflict theory argues that power is the root of all social relationships and the most precious scarce social resource. Thus, **conflict theory** can be defined as a theoretical perspective that views society as composed of competing elements (e.g., interest groups) that fight over scarce resources (e.g., wealth, power, and prestige) while acknowledging that power differentials ultimately determine the allocation and distribution of these scarce resources.

Of particular interest to many conflict theorists is the role of the power elite in society. C. Wright Mills, in particular, was convinced that major decisions regarding the course of history were made by the political, military, and economic institutions that constitute the power elite. Mills believed that the United States' military, industry, and politics were integrated to best meet their own needs. In *The Power Elite*, Mills (1956) wrote,

> The power elite is composed of men whose positions enable them to transcend the ordinary environments of ordinary men and women; they are in positions to make

> decisions having major consequences. . . . For they are in command of the major hierarchies and organizations of modern society. They rule the big corporations. They run the machinery of the state and claim its prerogatives. They direct the military establishment. They occupy the strategic command posts of the social structure, in which are now centered the effective means of the power and the wealth and the celebrity that they enjoy. (pp. 3–4)

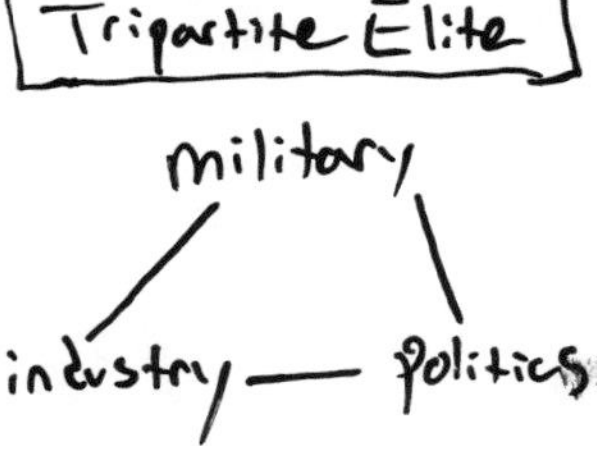

Mills labeled the connection between the military, industry, and politics the "triangle of power" or the "tripartite elite" and warned that these power elites were becoming a growing threat to American democracy. President Dwight D. Eisenhower echoed Mills's concerns when he used the phrase "military-industrial complex" in his 1961 farewell address to the nation (Encyclopedia.com 2011). Eisenhower believed that the Cold War was little more than a public relations scam to keep the military busy and the defense fully funded with taxpayers' money.

What Do You Think?

Many social commentators believe that this "tripartite elite" worked together to start and maintain the U.S. involvement in the wars in Iraq and Afghanistan. What do you think?

Conflict theory remains in vogue in contemporary sociology (especially compared to functionalism) as its general principles of power differentials, class struggle, and the inevitability of conflict are prevalent in societies across the globe. Today, conflict theorists do not limit themselves to issues of economics as the sole source of social inequality but have instead acknowledged such variables as race and ethnicity, gender, sexual orientation, and religious beliefs as possible causes of hostility between disparate groups.

What Do You Think?

Functionalists argue that members of society share an agreement about the general values and beliefs of society (a consensus), whereas conflict theorists argue that the values and beliefs of the ruling majority are forced onto the masses. What do you think?

Symbolic Interactionism

The term "symbolic interactionism," coined by Herbert Blumer (1937), is a theoretical perspective most generally associated with George Herbert Mead. It incorporates a social-psychological perspective and pays close attention to one's sense of self, self-esteem, and small-group interactions. Consequently, it is a micro theory. **Symbolic interactionism** is based on the idea that social reality is constructed in each human interaction through the use of symbols; that is, we communicate with one another through the use of symbols. *Symbols* include such things as words (language) and gestures (e.g., various hand signals). The importance of language is that it allows interacting individuals to discuss and understand ideas and events that transcend the immediate environment.

Symbolic interactionists believe that studying social interaction (as opposed to social systems) is the key to understanding human behavior. The interactionist perspective maintains a belief in the ability of actors to modify their behaviors to meet the needs of the present and the immediate environment. During interactions, social acts and events come to be defined in some manner by participating interactants based on personal perception.

The perception of events influences the manner in which people interact with one another. Perception is frequently selective, as people often see what they want to see. This is especially true if one's self-esteem is at stake. As noted in this chapter's introductory story, selective perception also leads to subjective definitions that individuals bring with them as they interact with others and view the world.

In this regard, it is interesting to note that I have studied street gang behavior quite extensively. I have found that many students wear tattoos without knowing that they also possess gang significance. When I warn them against wearing the tattoos visibly in certain neighborhoods or in front of specific people, they seem surprised. The sociological lesson here is the need to realize the importance of symbols and their sometimes multiple potential meanings (see "Connecting Sociology and Popular Culture" Box 2.3 to learn more about the multiple meanings of symbols).

Symbolic interactionism places great importance on issues related to self and self-esteem (see "A Closer Look" Box 2.4 for a further discussion of self-esteem and an example of a self-esteem test). Earlier in this chapter, we talked about Mead's theory of the development of self and about the looking glass self theory of another symbolic interactionist, Charles Horton Cooley. Cooley proposed that people develop a sense of self through the eyes of others; that is, we see ourselves through the eyes of others. We are concerned about our appearance to others because it is *our* appearance. The looking glass self theory has three key principles:

Self & Self-esteem [handwritten margin note]

1. Our imagining of our appearance to others
2. Our imagining of their judgment of our appearance
3. Our resulting self-feeling, such as pride or mortification

Therefore, an individual's self-image consists of imagined reactions of others to his or her appearance, demeanor, and behavior. In this regard, everyone we interact with serves as a mirror because we see ourselves through that person's reactions to our appearance. Generally, we are more concerned about the reactions of loved ones and the people whose opinions we most value. Their opinions and reactions to our appearance are important to us and play a great role in shaping our sense of self. The people closest to us are what Cooley called a *primary group*. "By primary groups, I mean those characterized by intimate face-to-face association and

Connecting Sociology and Popular Culture

Box 2.3 The Multiple Meanings of Symbols

Symbolic interactionism presents a theoretical perspective that individuals, groups, and cultures come to view the world through the use of symbols and their meanings. This explanation of how we view the world is limited by the realization that many symbols have multiple meanings—a fact that sometimes hampers effective communication between diverse people. The "hook 'em horns!" symbol described in the chapter's introductory story is only one example. The popular and controversial film *The Da Vinci Code* (2006) (adapted from Dan Brown's 2003 bestselling novel of the same name) describes a number of other examples of symbols with multiple meanings.

In this film, the main character, Robert Langdon (played by Tom Hanks), is a noted symbologist (a person who studies symbols). Early in the film, Langdon presents a slide show to an audience of learned scholars. He has asked audience members to shout out answers to his questions about the meaning of the displayed symbols. Viewing a swastika, the audience immediately gasps and proclaims it a sign of evil. This is understandable as most people equate the swastika with Nazi Germany (and some current hate groups).

However, as Langdon indicates throughout his presentation, symbols have multiple meanings—even the swastika. The symbol dates back to Neolithic times (more than 3,000 years ago). Derived from the Sanskrit *svasti,* meaning "well-being," the symbol has sacred meaning in the Hindu, Buddhist, and Jain religions. Early Christian traditions had another name for the swastika, the *crux gammata.* Displaying the swastika is prohibited within the European Union because of its Nazi association, but recently Hindu groups have attempted to display the symbol because of its spiritual meaning to them. Although most people are aware that the swastika has multiple meanings, nonetheless, the overwhelming feeling in most nations—especially in the West—is that the symbol now represents evil and hate because of its association with Nazi Germany.

The Da Vinci Code became the subject of protests by many groups, but especially Catholic and other Christian organizations who organized attempts to ban the showing of the movie in their nations. Among these nations were France, Canada, China, Greece, Hong Kong, the Philippines, South Korea, Venezuela, and many Latin American countries (ReligiousTolerance.org 2006). The attempted ban, which failed in nearly all cases, grew out of reasons beyond Langdon's discussion of the multiple meanings of popular symbols. The Roman Catholic Church and, even more so, the Catholic lay organization Opus Dei objected to the way they were portrayed in a negative light.

For the unacquainted, the main plot of the film centers on the hidden meaning of Leonardo da Vinci's famous painting *The Last Supper.* From the film's perspective, the painting reveals clues about the true meaning of the Holy Grail. The term "Holy Grail" derives from the Old French *sang réal,* meaning "royal blood" and referring to someone descended from royalty. A close look at *The Last Supper* reveals a feminine-looking figure to Jesus's immediate right (the viewer's left); this is traditionally believed to be the apostle John, but according to Dan Brown's plot, it is actually a woman, Mary Magdalene, whom some believe to have been Jesus's wife. The film further claims that Mary Magdalene was pregnant with Jesus's baby at the time of his crucifixion. Thus, the Holy Grail really refers to this child and his or her progeny as the lineage of Jesus.

The other symbols described in this film are too many to discuss here. But it is easy to imagine why some people were uncomfortable with this film and its interpretation of the meaning of symbols.

What Do You Think?

The swastika has a very negative connotation. In light of its multiple historic meanings, will the image of the swastika ever become positive again? What do you think? The novel *The Da Vinci Code* and the film based on it have been labeled, by some, as blasphemous. But perhaps the accusers do not understand the multiple meanings of symbols. What do you think?

cooperation. . . . The result of intimate association, psychologically, is a certain fusion of individualism in a common whole, so that one's very self, for many purposes at least, is the common life and purpose of the group" (Cooley 1909, p. 23). The primary group is relatively small in number, informal, and relatively permanent; it involves close personal relationships, face-to-face association, and relative intimacy between group members.

Symbolic interactionists note that many people alter their behavior in the public sphere in an attempt to present a positive appearance to others. Erving Goffman (1959) referred to this as the presentation of self. The presentation of self involves the attempt of actors to manipulate the environment while engaging in purposive behavior. Goffman reasoned that each of us has a sense of identity, a sense of self. We want others to see us in the same manner as we see ourselves. In other words, we have developed reality identity constructs for ourselves, and we want others to see us in the same fashion. Goffman's classic work on dramaturgy illustrates how actors perform depending on their environment. Goffman's work on dramaturgy was inspired by Shakespeare's *As You Like It*:

> All the world's a stage,
> And all the men and women merely players;
> They have their exits and their entrances;
> And one man in his time plays many parts.

Goffman claims that actors have "backstage" and "front-stage" personalities. *Front-stage* behaviors are designed as intentional performances using specific props to convey the role one is playing. The *backstage* persona represents the actor's "true self." In the backstage environment, the actor steps out of character and resumes his or her true self. Goffman used the role of the waitress to demonstrate the dramaturgical approach. While the waitress is serving customers, she is in her front-stage environment. Because she works for tips, she is likely to put on a persona that will make customers happy with their dining experience. While the waitress is in the kitchen, she lets her guard down and may complain or make jokes about the customers with other staff people.

Symbolic interactionism provides the most comprehensive analysis of micro and small-group behavior in sociology. The importance of self-esteem and self-concept has been debated by educators for decades and will likely remain an important topic of concern in the future. Gestures and emotions are other areas of study for symbolic interactionists. The symbolic-interactionist approach will remain a vital sociological theoretical perspective indefinitely (see Table 2.1 for a summary of the "big three" sociological theories).

A Closer Look

Box 2.4 A Measure of Self-Esteem

As described in this chapter, symbolic interactionism places a great deal of emphasis on the self and self-esteem. The process of how a sense of self develops has been provided from the perspective of a number of symbolic interactionists. But what is self-esteem, and how can we measure such a concept? Self-esteem is the manner in which an individual views him- or herself. That is, does the individual have a positive sense of self, a moderate sense of self, or a low sense of self? A number of scales have been designed to measure self-esteem. One of the most valid, reliable, and often cited was created by Morris Rosenberg (1965) (see Chapter 3 for a discussion of validity and reliability). The Rosenberg Self-Esteem Scale (RSE) represents an attempt to achieve a unidimensional measure of global self-esteem by asking respondents statements dealing with general feelings about themselves. The design of the RSE involves ten simple questions with four response choices, ranging from "strongly agree" to "strongly disagree."

If you would like to know your self-esteem measurement, take the test below. It should be noted that your measurement of self-esteem will likely change if you take the test again later (e.g., a month, a few months, or a year from now), as a number of personal and social factors affect the way one feels about oneself.

Instructions: Below is a list of statements dealing with general feelings you have about yourself. If you strongly agree with the statement, circle "SA"; if you agree, circle "A"; if you disagree, circle "D"; and if you strongly disagree, circle "SD."

1. On the whole, I am satisfied with myself. SA A D SD
2. * At times, I think I am no good at all. SA A D SD
3. I feel that I have a number of good qualities. SA A D SD
4. I am able to do things as well as most other people. SA A D SD
5. * I feel I do not have much to be proud of. SA A D SD
6. * I certainly feel useless at times. SA A D SD
7. I feel that I'm a person of worth, at least on an equal plane with others. SA A D SD
8. * I wish I could have more respect for myself. SA A D SD
9. * All in all, I am inclined to feel that I am a failure. SA A D SD
10. I take a positive attitude toward myself. SA A D SD

What Do You Think?

What personal and social factors in your life are currently affecting your self-esteem measurement?

Scoring: SA = 3 points, A = 2 points, D = 1 point, SD = 0 points. Questions with an asterisk (*) are reverse scored: SA = 0, A = 1, D = 2, SD = 3. Add the scores for all ten questions. The lowest possible score is zero, and the highest possible score is thirty. The higher the score, the higher your self-esteem. (Although researchers sometimes disagree with cutoffs for the levels of self-esteem, we will consider scores of twenty-four and above as constituting high self-esteem; twenty to twenty-three as constituting moderate self-esteem; and below twenty as constituting low self-esteem.)

For symbolic interactionists, we see our sense of self through the eyes of others during interaction. As a result, everyone we encounter is like a mirror that reflects our sense of self.

TABLE 2.1 Summary of the "Big Three" Sociological Theories

	FUNCTIONALISM	CONFLICT	SYMBOLIC INTERACTIONISM
Levels of analysis	Macro	Macro	Micro
Early proponents	Auguste Comte Herbert Spencer Emile Durkheim	Karl Marx	George Mead Charles Horton Cooley Herbert Blumer
Basic tenets	Society is a system of interrelated parts (social institutions). A consensus on values allows the system to function.	Power and inequality are found throughout society. Class struggle is inevitable.	Communication and interaction take place via the use of symbols.
Key points	Structures are designed to maintain societal stability. Social institutions and human behavior are evaluated based on their functionality. Dysfunctional activities threaten stability.	Resources are unequally distributed in society. Those in power will attempt to maintain their advantage; those without power will seek power. Conflict is inevitable.	Perception is selective. Self-esteem is the result of interactions with others.
Key terms	Structure Functions Social patterns Social institutions	Power Conflict Oppression Class struggle	Symbols Interactions Meanings Self-esteem

Other Theoretical Perspectives

Functionalism, conflict, and symbolic interactionism are often referred to as the "big three" sociological theoretical perspectives, and they represent the three theories examined in all introductory sociology textbooks. It is important to note that there are other vital theoretical perspectives in sociology beyond these.

One popular theoretical perspective in sociology is feminism. Feminist theory is an outgrowth of the general movement to empower women worldwide. Feminism highlights the importance of women, reveals the historical reality of how women have been subordinated to men, and attempts to bring about gender equity. Feminism is a women-centered approach to the study of human behavior and advocates for oppressed women. More than just a theory, feminism represents a social movement designed to empower women and bring about gender equality—especially with regard to the equal sharing of scarce social resources. Similar to conflict theorists, feminists argue that a two-class society exists in which men control the means of production and women are exploited. Equality in the workplace and the home is among feminists' chief concerns. It is worth noting that radical feminists hope to empower women to the point where they achieve gender dominance rather than gender equality.

Another important theoretical perspective is social-exchange theory. Originally articulated by George Homans (1910–1989), exchange theory emphasizes the ability of people to act rationally in their social interactions. For this reason, it is sometimes referred to as rational choice theory. Exchange theory started as a micro theory with Homans, grew into a middle-range theory with Peter Blau, and has expanded its focus to the macro level as network analysis theory during the contemporary era. At its basic roots, social-exchange theory combines the principles of behaviorism and elementary economics (along with other influences) and applies them to the concerns of sociology. Social-exchange theory is based on the idea that in every social interaction, there is an exchange between interactants. In other words, people always exchange something with others, whether it has economic or personal value (e.g., approval from others, love, affection, or self-esteem). Exchange theorists argue that actors will continue to interact with one another for as long as such exchanges are rewarding, and they will cease to interact when the costs are too high. In short, social-exchange theory can be defined as a theory that envisions social behavior as an exchange or activity, tangible or intangible, and more or less rewarding or costly, between at least two persons (Homans 1961).

Some contemporary sociologists offer alternatives to the more traditional sociological theories; these theories include postmodernist and critical theories. To think as a postmodernist, one must break away from the traditional, taken-for-granted perspectives and theoretical constructs. The concept often promoted in contemporary society of thinking "outside the box" would apply to postmodern theorists. Critical theory generally takes into account the role of power in social relations and concerns itself with social action. To separate itself from conflict theory, critical theory examines factors beyond economics in determining power relationships. (Note: Students who wish to learn more about these fascinating sociological theories are encouraged to take a social theory course where the discussion will be far more extensive than that provided in an introductory textbook.)

As we have learned in this chapter, sociologists attempt to present a coherent explanation of the world we live in. Social theorists spend a great amount of time contemplating the social world. In Chapter 3 we see how sociologists use research to test and support their views of the world.

Like social theorists, most people try to explain the meaning of social events in their own lives. Most individuals, however, take a less academic approach in their attempt to explain the world they live in. In "Connecting Sociology and Popular Culture" Box 2.5, we take one last look at an amateur's (nonacademic) perspective of the world. While reading this box, think about which of the major sociological theoretical perspectives the thoughts of Carlos Mencia most resemble.

SUMMARY

Social theory guides sociologists in their quest to explain the social world. A theory is a statement that proposes to explain or relate observed phenomena or a set of concepts. A properly designed theory allows itself to be tested empirically via research.

Auguste Comte coined the term "sociology," but more importantly, he set the tone for sociology as an empirical science grounded in the scientific tradition. Comte's works were translated into English by Harriet Martineau, who also wrote many sociological articles in her own right describing the social issues of her time. Herbert Spencer, a firm believer in social evolution, argued that humans adapt to their environments culturally, rather than biologically as the other organisms do. Spencer argued that those who are fittest will evolve and survive, while those who are not will perish. Although Karl Marx was not technically a sociologist, his theories and publications set the tone for a great deal of sociological thought, including influencing the popular conflict theory. French sociologist Emile Durkheim became the first full professor of sociology and gave scientific credibility to the field with his research on suicide. Max Weber's theoretical orientation led him to discuss the impact of rationalization and bureaucracy on the emerging industrial social world.

Among the significant early American sociologists are Jane Addams, who worked with underprivileged and underrepresented persons; Ida Wells-Barnett, a child of freed slaves who grew to write about the social injustices confronting African Americans; George Herbert Mead, who set the tone for modern symbolic-interactionist theory; and W. E. B. Du Bois, who wrote about problems confronting African Americans.

Contemporary sociology is dominated by schools of thought rather than individual social thinkers. The so-called "big three" theories of sociology are functionalism, conflict theory, and symbolic interactionism. Functionalism is a macrosociological theory that examines the characteristics of social patterns, structures, systems, and institutions. Conflict theory, also a macro theory, takes the perspective that society is composed of competing elements that fight over

Connecting Sociology and Popular Culture

Box 2.5 An Explanation of the World We Live in from the "Bad Boy of Comedy"

Academic folks are not the only "professionals" who earn a salary attempting to explain social life. News reporters, journalists, and a variety of social commentators (e.g., talk show hosts) are among the professionals who examine social life and offer their own spin on the social environment. Comedians also scrutinize the social world. The material of most comedians is contingent upon local, national, and world events. Comedians such as Jerry Seinfeld, Bill Maher, and the late George Carlin rely on observational humor—making fun of the everyday, mundane aspects of social life. Some comedians, like Chris Rock, infuse a cultural perspective into their brand of humor. And then there is Carlos "Bad Boy of Comedy" Mencia, a Latino comedian who hosted his own very popular show, *Mind of Mencia,* on Comedy Central from 2005 to 2008. (He remains an active and controversial comedian.)

Mencia downplays his bad boy image by stating that when he goes to East Los Angeles (a Latino barrio), the homeboys do not say, "Hey, watch out, p*ta, that dude tells jokes." (Note: According to the Urban Slang Dictionary, *p*ta* means "mother f*cker." The standard Spanish translation of *p*ta* is "whore" or "prostitute.") In other words, people with street cred are not worried about a bad boy comedian who tells edgy jokes.

Mencia is often controversial, certainly not politically correct (as contemporary academia generally requires of its social thinkers), often confrontational, and viciously honest. Born in Honduras and raised in East Los Angeles, Mencia has life experiences that differ radically from those of most traditional academic social thinkers. His first stand-up comedy album, *Take a Joke America,* made it clear that he is unapologetic about sharing his views of the social world. Most of his comedy would be considered too risqué for a mainstream textbook (he mocks illegal aliens, people with multiple personalities, women, white men, and so on), so students who are unaware of Mencia's brand of comedy are advised to visit (with caution) the Comedy Central website and view free clips of his show.

The conflict perspective is evident in Mencia's comedy. Born into a poor family, he has experienced life as a have-not. His jokes often take aim at power structures that dominate society. Functionalists could argue that Mencia's brand of comedy serves as a means to an end; specifically, his humor has provided him with an opportunity to earn wealth and fame. In this regard, Mencia's comedy is functional—for him. Mencia certainly relies on subcultural language and symbolism that has significant meaning to specific groups of people (e.g., Latinos/Hispanics); therefore, elements of his comedy reflect the symbolic-interactionist perspective. Because Mencia's comedy often offends women, one might be tempted automatically to discount the feminist perspective. However, feminist theorists would highlight the sexist tone of his comedy to demonstrate the heavily patriarchal nature of his upbringing. Mencia's willingness to think outside the box would, or should, appeal to postmodern theorists.

In short, this box demonstrates that nearly any element of social life can be examined from a sociological theoretical perspective.

What Do You Think?

Of the sociological theoretical perspectives that you have learned about in this chapter, which theory seems most appropriate in explaining the comedy of Carlos Mencia? What do you think?

scarce resources while acknowledging that power differentials ultimately determine the allocation and distribution of these scarce resources. Symbolic interactionism, a micro theory, is based on the idea that social reality is constructed in each human interaction through the use of symbols.

Among the other major sociological theories are feminism, which highlights the importance of women, reveals the historical reality of how women have been subordinated to men, and attempts to bring about gender equity; critical theory, which takes into account the role of power in social relations and concerns itself with social action; and postmodern theory, which proposes that social thinkers must break from traditional, taken-for-granted perspectives and theoretical constructs.

Glossary

Bourgeoisie—The owners of the means of production.

Bureaucracies—Goal-oriented entities designed according to rational principles in order to attain the predetermined goals of the organization efficiently.

Communism—A sociopolitical and economic system ideal made famous by Karl Marx involving the common ownership of the means of production and the elimination of the need for government. (Note: A true Marxist communist nation has never existed as all nations labeled as communistic have had governments, and the means of production were not owned by the people.)

Conflict theory—A theoretical perspective that views society as composed of competing elements (e.g., interest groups) that fight over scarce resources (e.g., wealth, power, and prestige) while acknowledging that power differentials ultimately determine the allocation and distribution of these scarce resources.

Functionalism—A macrosociological theory that examines the characteristics of social patterns, structures, systems, and institutions. Functionalists view society as having interrelated parts that contribute to the functioning of the whole system.

Ideal type—Essentially a measuring rod used by sociologists to compare empirical reality with preconceived notions of a phenomenon.

Latent functions—The unplanned, unintended aspects of behavior.

Manifest functions—Things that occur that were planned on, intended, and consciously pursued.

Positivism (as used by Auguste Comte)—A coherent system of ideas guided by an intellectual and moral basis that allows for science to intervene for the betterment of society.

Proletariat—The workers, or those without ownership of the means of production.
Rationalization—The product of scientific specialization and technical differentiation.
Social dynamics—The social forces that lead to social change.
Social statics—The social forces designed to maintain the existing social order and bring harmony to all the parts of society.
Survival of the fittest—A term coined by Herbert Spencer (used in conjunction with his idea of social evolution) to describe the cultural evolutionary process that entails individuals meeting the needs of the changing social environment, resulting in those who are fittest moving on, while those who are unfit die off.
Symbolic interactionism—A theoretical perspective based on the idea that social reality is constructed in each human interaction through the use of symbols. In other words, we communicate with one another through the use of symbols.
Theory—A statement that proposes to explain or relate observed phenomena or a set of concepts.
Verstehen—German for "understanding"; a guiding principle in Weber's interpretative approach to the study of human behavior.

Discussion Questions

1. What does Auguste Comte mean by the term "positivism"? Explain the relevance of positivism to the field of sociology.

2. Harriet Martineau wanted sociology to concern itself with answering the fundamental question, What constitutes a better life for people? What elements of society do you believe are important in order for all people of society to have a better life? What elements are necessary for you personally to have a better life?

3. Karl Marx dreamed of a world in which all people are treated equally and share equally in society's scarce resources. Many critics condemn Marx's ideas as utopian. In today's postmodern, materialistic world, do you think it is possible for a classless society to exist in which all the members of society share equally in social and natural resources? Explain.

4. Demonstrate the aspects of "backstage" and "front-stage" behaviors in your own life.

5. Discuss some of the advantages and disadvantages of functionalism. Discuss some of the advantages and disadvantages of social-conflict theory. Which of the two theories do you believe provides a more accurate view of the social world? Do you believe another sociological theory is better equipped to explain the social world? Explain.

Web Links

To learn more about the meanings and varieties of symbols, visit www.symbols.net.

To learn more about Auguste Comte and his application of positivism, visit http://changingminds.org/explanations/research/philosophies/positivism.htm.

To learn more about Harriet Martineau, visit www.webster.edu/~woolflm/martineau.html.

To learn more about Karl Marx and his theories, visitwww.bolender.com/Sociological%20Theory/Marx,%20Karl/marx,_karl.htm.

To learn more about or reach the National Suicide Prevention Lifeline, visit www.suicidepreventionlifeline.org.

3 RESEARCH METHODS
Testing Our View of the World

Despite the overwhelming research that clearly demonstrates the health risks of smoking, many people do it anyway.

Chapter 3

INTRODUCTORY STORY

A group of high school students has met at Smokers' Corner, a location on their school campus that is out of the view of teachers and administrators. They meet there every morning and during their lunch break. Although they have heard the warnings about the health risks of cigarette smoking, they choose to smoke anyway. They rationalize their behavior in an attempt to ignore the admonitions not to smoke. One of the students, Monty, states, "I do not believe that smoking is that bad for you." Chip responds, "I am more likely to die from a car crash than I am from smoking." Carole adds, "I like the way I look when I hold a cigarette." Agreeing with Carole, Susan proclaims, "And we look so cool when we smoke!"

Two other students, walking by Smokers' Corner, have overheard these four students, and one of them taunts the smokers by stating, "No one looks cool with a cancer stick in their mouth." The other passing student shouts, "Hundreds of thousands of people die every year from smoking, you know?"

Why is that some of these students have a theory that smoking is cool, while others have a theory that smoking leads to cancer and possible death? Which of these beliefs is accurate? The answers to these questions can be found by conducting social research. Scientific research has revealed the numerous harmful effects of smoking. It is such an objective truth that packages of cigarettes come with a warning proclaiming their dangers. In fact, over 400,000 Americans die each year as a result of smoking. Despite the empirical truths regarding the harmful effects, however, millions of people ignore the statistics and continue to smoke.

In this chapter, we learn about the importance of, and the need for, supporting sociological ideas and theories with social research. After all, ignoring the value of social research is akin to dogmatic thinking and mere speculation.

USING THE SCIENTIFIC METHOD

As stated in Chapter 1, sociology is an academic discipline guided by theory and supported by social research. In Chapter 2, we defined a theory as a statement that proposes to explain or relate observed phenomena or a set of concepts. Through the use of the scientific method, sociologists are able to explore facts that test their theories. The testing of theory with facts is what separates sociology from dogmatic thinking, philosophical speculation, and a reliance on tradition and so-called common sense. Social research may support or disprove a theory; at the very least, it may lead sociologists to modify their original theoretical approach. Ideally, social research attempts to uncover evidence about social realities. Objective evidence is the ultimate goal of any science. Sociologists and those committed to objectivity embrace the scientific method.

The validity of any science, sociology included, rests with its ability to test its theoretical beliefs with facts and data. Consequently, research methodologies serve as the backbone of sociology. Further, advancements in technology have allowed for even greater achievements in the field of research. Online databases, multimedia access, the Internet, and digital libraries all assist professionals and students in their quest for knowledge.

The Logic of the Scientific Method

As defined in Chapter 1, the scientific method involves the pursuit of knowledge by first stating a specific problem, followed by the collection of facts through observation and experiment, and the testing of ideas to determine whether they appear to be valid or invalid. As Hoover (1976) states, "Science has to do with the way questions are formulated and answered; science is a set of rules and forms for inquiry created by people who want reliable answers" (p. 5). Further, as Bernard Cohen (1989) explains, "science is not merely knowledge based on a collection of facts—after all, a telephone directory is a collection of facts, but that does not make phone company publications scientific treatises—it also provides knowledge to support, modify, or reject a theoretical construct or perspective" (p. 13).

The scientific method involves more than the mere aggregate of statistics; it possesses elements of logical reasoning and objectivity. **Logical reasoning** involves the discovery of causes for human behavior and social events. For example, if someone throws a rock through a window, the rock will cause the window to break. There is a direct link between the person who threw the rock and the window breaking. **Causal explanations** reveal a direct connection between events. This connection is often expressed by an "if-then" statement: if x occurs, then y will result. Determining the cause(s) of social action is the primary goal of science. *Objectivity* involves the researcher being self-conscious about his or her values and opinions. Although it is impossible for anyone to be completely objective and value free, the goal of sociological research is consistent with that of the natural sciences—to remain as detached as possible in order to best assure unbiased results. Objective research assists sociologists who test theoretical constructs regarding human behavior and social events (see "A Closer Look" Box 3.1 to learn more about objectivity and bias in social research).

The term "objectivity" is relatively straightforward in meaning: it refers to the reporting of observable phenomena, presented factually, and without bias. Whereas politicians and many talk show hosts regularly and purposely reveal a bias about matters of social interest, scientists conducting social research attempt to be unbiased. Nonetheless, accusations of bias are fairly common in the sciences. Often, reviewers of publications claim that an author has a bias when in reality the reviewer is actually revealing his or her own bias about how certain works should be presented to an audience. Thus, the people most likely to cast the bias stone are those who possess a biased opinion.

Interestingly enough, the term "bias" itself lacks a straightforward meaning. As sociologists Hammersley and Gomm (1997) explain, the concept of bias is itself ambiguous: "Sometimes, it is used to refer to the adoption of a particular perspective from which some things become salient and others merge into the background" (1). Although I have no hidden agenda and am not attempting to sway students toward any particular theory or socioeconomic or political outlook on life, this book is clearly intended to instill in students the value of the sociological perspective. Thus, it has a sociological bias.

There is a greater concern with regard to bias in social research, however, involving a conscious or unconscious tendency on the part of researchers to produce or interpret data in a way that inclines toward erroneous conclusions in line with their own goals (Hammersley and Gomm 1997). When a researcher has a biased goal, the collection, interpretation, and presentation of data may be falsified, even if unintentionally. "It has often been pointed out, for example, that once a particular interpretation, explanation or theory has been developed by a researcher, he or she may tend to interpret data in terms of it, be on the look out for data that would confirm it, or even shape data production process in ways that lead to error" (Hammersley and Gomm 1997, p. 3).

> **What Do You Think?**
>
> It could be argued that everyone who conducts research brings a personal perspective based on life experiences and that complete objectivity is therefore never possible. If this is true, is all research subject to bias? And if so, are all research results questionable? What do you think?

Objectivity is especially subject to bias when the researcher is hired by a private firm or a government entity that has a clear agenda. In an attempt to safeguard objectivity, many research agencies have developed conflict-of-interest codes. The National Institutes of Health (NIH), for example, citing an obligation to protect the public investment in science, has established the "Code of Federal Regulation"—a policy designed to, among other things, ensure objectivity in research (Kirschstein 2000). The NIH code states that objectivity must not be compromised by financial considerations or the pursuit of fame. Many colleges and universities require professors to complete conflict-of-interest forms when they serve as researchers (or consultants) for private or public entities.

At the heart of objectivity is a concern for ethics. That is, researchers must do everything in their power to attempt to remain loyal to the goal of objectivity in research. We discuss ethics in social research in greater detail later in this chapter.

Operationalization

Operationalization refers to specifying the various steps and procedures that a researcher will go through while conducting research. These steps and procedures generally involve identifying key concepts or variables to be examined and the specific hypotheses to be tested. Because each research project is unique, the operationalization plan is subject to a variety of social constructs. A social construct may be viewed as an idea or theory containing conceptual elements, generally considered to be subjective and not based on empirical evidence. As we learn in future chapters, concepts such as social class (Chapter 7), race and ethnicity (Chapter 8), and gender and sex (Chapter 9) are said to be socially constructed. In general, researchers identify a number of concepts and variables that will be tested. **Concepts** can be thought of as mental images used to categorize experiences. Forming concepts allows researchers to group similar things together and

A Closer Look

Box 3.1 Objectivity and Bias in Social Research

Objectivity in research is indeed important, as social policy and individual behavior may be shaped by the results presented in research findings. Consider, for example, the implications for the behavior of students (and most other human beings) if prolonged cell phone use, as many speculate, causes, or increases the possibility of, brain cancer. Authors of a ten-year study of 13,000 cell phone users announced in May 2010 that most participants were not at increased risk of developing meningioma (a common and frequently benign tumor) or glioma (a rarer but deadlier form of cancer) due to the radiation associated with cell phones. The research results did suggest, however, that using a cell phone for more than thirty minutes each day could increase the risk of glioma.

The authors of the paper citing this research (which appears in the *International Journal of Epidemiology*) worry that bias may have influenced the final results of the study because nearly a quarter of the $24 million study was funded by the cell phone industry (Kang 2010; *Post-Standard,* 5/17/10). The authors worry that cell phone use may have a stronger link to cancer risk than the data reveals. Scientists are continuing to investigate this question, studying whether cell phone use increases the risk of tumors on the ear's acoustic nerve and in the parotid gland, where saliva is produced. A separate study is also examining the effects of cell phone use on children, who are believed to be more susceptible than adults to the effects of radiation.

What Do You Think?

The tobacco industry hid the dangers of prolonged smoking for decades. Do you believe that the cell phone industry would hide evidence, if it exists, linking prolonged cell phone use with cancer? What do you think?

to separate dissimilar ones. **Variables** are measurable factors or characteristics that are subject to change in different situations. They are similar to concepts in that they categorize experiences, but they differ in that they must be concrete and measurable.

Typically, variables are divided into two categories: independent and dependent variables. An **independent variable** is one hypothesized to cause or influence another variable. A **dependent variable** is one that is influenced by an independent variable. For example, most students have heard their teachers proclaim, "The more hours you study, the higher your grade will be." This statement represents an attempt to link two specific variables: the number of hours a student studies (the independent variable) and the grade the student will receive for the class (the dependent variable). A student's grade is dependent upon the number of hours studied, while the number of hours studied is up to the individual student. Of course, variables other than the number of hours of studying will affect the grade a student receives, including the degree of difficulty of each course, the student's interest level, the competency of the professor, and so on.

Because variables other than those being directly investigated may influence an outcome, researchers are careful to distinguish between causes and effects and correlations. A *correlation* exists when a change in one variable (the hours one studies) is associated with a change in the other variable (the grade a student receives). Any number of variables, however, may be associated with the grade one receives in a class other than the total number of hours studied. For this reason, we are hesitant to say that one variable causes another to occur.

The principle that correlation does not equal causation can be illustrated in many ways. For example, research with college undergraduates has indicated that those who are very happy with their lives also tend to have many friends (Diener and Seligman 2002). Does happiness cause us to make friends? Or is it the other way around—does having a lot of friends make us happy? Or could it be that both variables (happiness and friendships) influence each other? If so, this would be an example of bidirectionality, or two-way causality. As another example, in certain years after World War II, researchers in the Netherlands observed an increase in both the number of storks nesting in chimneys and the number of human babies being born (Sapsford and Jupp 2006; Urdan 2001). Did the storks cause the babies to be born? Anyone who knows the basics of human biology knows they did not. However, an unusually cold winter might increase the number of storks building nests in chimneys (because chimneys emit warm air), and it might also increase the number of couples snuggling together in bed, leading to a higher rate of pregnancies. This is an example of a spurious correlation (also known as an illusory correlation or a lurking variable).

What Do You Think?

A number of variables influence the grades you receive in specific courses. How many such variables can you think of, and which have cause-and-effect relationships with other variables? What do you think?

Validity and Reliability

Another very important aspect of the scientific method is assuring validity and reliability. **Validity** refers to the degree that a finding, or measurement of a concept, accurately reflects the phenomenon under study. To assure validity, researchers generally use more than one method to measure a variable. If all the methods used to measure a concept provide similar results, the measurement is said to be valid. For example, we might measure a person's height using three different types of apparatus: a dressmaker's tape measure, a laser tape measure, and a yardstick. If the height measurement from all three is consistent, we have validity. **Reliability** refers to consistent results when the variable is tested repeatedly. The measurement of a particular concept is considered reliable if the same result occurs repeatedly. Using the example of measuring height, if we measure a person's height every Wednesday for three weeks and the results are the same, we have reliability.

To illustrate the issues of validity and reliability more fully, let us revisit the self-esteem test you took in Chapter 2. Your self-esteem test results would be considered valid if, in addition to that test, you took two different self-esteem tests, and all three tests indicated the same level of self-esteem (high, moderate, or low). Taking one test repeatedly and receiving the same score will make the results reliable. However, it is important to note that a measurement may be reliable but also invalid. Thus, if you received the same self-esteem score over and over, it may be reliable, but if the wrong key was used to measure your self-esteem score, the results would be invalid.

THE RESEARCH MODEL

As we see later in this chapter, sociologists utilize a wide variety of methodological approaches. Because of this variety, social researchers generally find it helpful to employ some sort of guideline or structure to keep their work as orderly as possible. This guideline is articulated as the research model. The **research model** is a step-by-step protocol that typically guides sociological research. It generally involves a seven- or eight-step process. (Note: Ultimately, researchers work with the research model variation that they are most comfortable with.) In the eight-step process, selecting a topic and defining the problem are treated as two separate steps. The outline below exemplifies the seven-step approach by combining the selection and definition processes.

1. *Selecting a specific topic and defining the problem:* As many professors and students alike can attest, simply getting started with a research project presents challenges. It is necessary not only to choose a topic worthy of academic study but also to specify the parameters of the study. For example, if the topic is juvenile delinquency, will the study focus on all forms of juvenile delinquency or just violent forms? Furthermore, what is meant by "delinquency"? Are we attempting to discover if the rate of delinquency is increasing or decreasing, or do we want to describe delinquency in a particular city or neighborhood? Do we want to look for a relationship between delinquency and decreasing school-attendance rates? These are just a few of the questions that must be considered when specifying a topic and defining a problem. For the purposes of illustration, let us narrow our research topic example to female gang participation—a very specific subtopic in the area of delinquency.

(handwritten margin notes:)
1. topic
2. literature
3. hypotheses
4. research method
5. Data collection
6. Analyze data
7. Conclude & Share

2. *Reviewing the literature:* It is important for researchers to acquaint themselves with as much information on their research topic as possible. (Note: Some sociologists combine steps 1 and 2 because they find it beneficial to conduct a review of the literature to stimulate their thoughts on the specific topic(s) to be studied.) A review of the literature helps researchers to structure the design of their own research, avoid the problems encountered by past researchers, and specify the variables to be measured in their own research. A review of the literature not only familiarizes the researcher with the existing theory and research on the subject but also affects the methods of research chosen by the researcher. Thus, for our study on female gangs, we will conduct a search of all available literature (such as books, journal articles, and crime reports) that discusses female gang activity.

3. *Formulating hypotheses:* After a review of the literature, the researcher is better equipped to address specific aspects of the research project. A **hypothesis** is a specific, testable statement concerning the research subject. "Hypotheses outline the propositions to be investigated and state the expected relationships between the variables of interest in the investigation. In other words, they are the researcher's best estimation of the expected results" (Kerr, Hall, and Kozub 2002, pp. 5–6). For example, the statement "Girls raised in a family with gang members already in it are more likely to join a gang than girls who come from nongang families" is a hypothesis. This statement allows itself to be tested via research.

4. *Selecting one or more research methods:* A number of researchers find that they prefer one method over another. This may reflect one's own bias or the fact that one's research skills are limited. It is crucial that researchers choose the most appropriate method for the investigation at hand. In other words, one method may be appropriate for one type of study but not for another. Sociologists use six basic methodological approaches, which are outlined in the following section of this chapter.

5. *Collecting data:* Once the research methods are chosen, it is time for the researcher to collect and record data accurately. Strict attention to accuracy and detail during the data-collection process is mandatory if the results are to be considered valid. The importance of data collection rests with the fact that it serves as the foundation upon which scientific inquiry is built (Kerr, Hall, and Kozub 2002). Issues of validity and reliability, discussed in the previous section, come into play during this step in the research process. Research data on gangs, for example, generally reveals that approximately 10 percent of all gang members are females (A. Campbell 1984; Office of Juvenile Justice and Delinquency Prevention 2000; Shelden, Tracy, and Brown 2001; Moore and Hagedorn 2001; and Delaney 2006a). Research data results on female gang-participation rates that vary significantly from this 10 percent

figure are generally questioned. However, if the research data on female gang participation in a particular city can be replicated, it will be considered valid.

6. *Analyzing the data:* Collecting the data is the starting point in determining whether the researcher's hypotheses are accurate. Establishing meaningful links between the facts (as determined by the collection of data) and stated hypotheses involves using whatever measurement techniques are appropriate. These measurement techniques may involve simple description or sophisticated statistical analysis. It should be noted that certain research methodologies, such as participant observation, generally do not involve hypotheses and therefore do not lend themselves to analysis. Nonetheless, all research methodologies generate some form of data, be they quantitative or qualitative (a distinction discussed in the following section).
7. *Stating conclusions and sharing the results:* The last step of the research model involves putting together a final report so that the results of the tested hypotheses can be shared with others in the field. Researchers hope to have their work published, but this is often easier said than done; a great deal of worthwhile research is never published. However, researchers can always find a conference at which to present their findings to their peers and colleagues. Researchers not only share their results but also indicate the implications of their study and suggest future research that could be fruitful in the continuing quest for the growth of knowledge.

Now that we have established a model to guide our research project, a number of very important decisions remain. Among the most important decisions confronting researchers is the choice of research methodologies and whether they hope to reveal the subjective (qualitative) or objective (quantitative) nature of a social phenomenon.

RESEARCH METHODS

As stated earlier, sociologists employ a variety of methods, or ways of getting information, to collect data in their effort to support or disprove a theory. The six primary methods used in sociology are

- survey research;
- observational studies;
- unobtrusive methods;
- content analysis;
- archival studies;
- experimentation.

Let us discuss each of these in detail.

Survey Research

Survey research is the most common, widely used approach in sociology. Moreover, it is not only popular in sociology but widely used in a variety of social science disciplines. If you are like most people, you have taken part in some sort of survey, whether you were approached by an interviewer at the mall and asked to answer questions about a specific product, were called by a telephone interviewer, or received a questionnaire in the mail. Mail (including Internet) questionnaires and face-to-face and telephone interviews represent the three types of survey research conducted by sociologists.

Survey research is not a new phenomenon; in fact, it has been utilized for centuries. For example, many ancient civilizations (e.g., Athens and Rome) took a census of their populations. A census is a type of survey that involves questioning an entire population. The U.S. Constitution mandates that a census be taken on a regular basis in order to assure equal representation of all citizens. This mandate once simply required a head count. With the rise of modern bureaucratic states and popular elections, precise measurement of people's opinions, attitudes, and behaviors became necessary. "The addition to the census of topics other than simple head counts was a matter of developing consciousness that the running of the state required more and more information about the status of the population and about organized entities such as farms, factories, and business enterprises" (Rossi, Wright, and Anderson 1983, p. 2).

The use of preelection surveys in the early 1900s revealed the value of forecasting, or predicting, future events. Early product testing designed to ascertain the buying habits of consumers foreshadowed the massive marketing campaigns utilized by companies today. Modern surveys have their roots in these humble beginnings.

Today, **survey research** involves taking a *sample* (a subset) of a population and administering a questionnaire or interview. A *population* can be defined as a totality of elements, such as all Democrats or Republicans, all retail chain store customers, or all left-handers. Because it is impossible to interview all elements of a larger population, survey researchers focus on a representative, random sample. As Martin Frankel (1983) explains, *survey sampling* "is a branch of statistics that concerns itself with the methods and techniques of selecting samples whose results may be projected to larger populations" (p. 21). Thus, a survey researcher need not interview all Democrats to find out whom they plan on voting for in a forthcoming election; rather, the researcher will interview a sample of Democrats. There are times when a researcher may employ a stratified random sample in order to gain a more precise measurement that reflects the total population. For example, if a researcher wants to conduct a survey that represents the total

U.S. population, he or she will make sure that 12 percent of the sample is African American and 13 percent is Latino—totals that reflect the proportional representation of these groups in the current U.S. population.

Survey research represents an effective method for measuring people's values, beliefs, attitudes, perceptions, motivations, and feelings on topic areas not directly accessible via observation. Further, certain topics, such as those related to sexual activity, drug use, and other private matters, are best addressed by survey research—just imagine if a researcher were to look through the windows of people's private homes to observe these behaviors!

Survey research is accomplished via interviews and questionnaires. As implied, researchers must formalize the questions they will ask respondents. This formal operationalization of the survey design represents an advantage of the survey research approach as it allows for easy replication by other researchers. The formalization aspect of survey design extends to the sampling plan (identifying the sample group), the questions to be asked, the coding of the responses, and data analysis.

The survey interview involves the researcher(s) obtaining information through face-to-face or telephone questioning. The face-to-face interview has the advantage of garnering the highest response rate of the three survey techniques, as it is generally more difficult to turn down a personal request for information than it is to discard a mailed questionnaire without answering it. Unfortunately, though, face-to-face interviews are the most costly and therefore represent a major disadvantage to researchers. A variation of the face-to-face interview is the focus group study. In the focus group setting, an interviewer poses questions to a small group of people in a more informal manner and encourages the free-flow sharing of ideas among those being interviewed and the interviewer. Telephone interviews are typically conducted as follows: a number of interviewers in a central location, under the supervision of a representative of the research project team, make calls to a predetermined number of respondents (provided by the researcher as part of the survey design) and read from scripted material (to assure consistency). Telephone interviewers generally start by asking the respondents if they are willing to answer a few questions on a specific topic. (Note: I have worked on numerous phone surveys and, depending on the type of research, experienced numerous respondents who refuse to participate or just hang up!) Although most surveys involving interviews consist of structured questions, unstructured interviews give the interviewer greater leeway in asking questions. Unstructured interviews are more commonly conducted by nonresearchers, such as talk show hosts and journalists in various fields (e.g., sports, fashion, and entertainment).

The questionnaire, a printed or written form used to gather information, is mailed to respondents who can answer the questions at their own pace. The major advantage of the questionnaire method is that it is the cheapest form of survey research and can therefore be used with large samples. As LaPiere (1994) explains, "The questionnaire is cheap, easy, and mechanical" (p. 56). Furthermore, it is generally believed that questionnaires produce the most honest responses because of the anonymity they convey to the respondents—often in an explicit statement (e.g., "Your answers will be used for statistical purposes only"), but in other cases through the simple fact that respondents do not have to provide their names or other identifying information. However, because it lacks a sense of personal involvement, the questionnaire survey has the lowest response rate of the three survey techniques. Typically, many respondents simply throw away the document. Students (and professors alike) can think back to times when they received a mail questionnaire and what they did with it.

Poorly worded questions or illogical question order may also affect the response rate of questionnaires (although these problems exist in interviews too). For example, imagine being asked to fill out a questionnaire that asks a number of questions about friendship but does not define the term "friendship" or "friend." Some respondents may consider coworkers, family members, members of the opposite sex, and so on to be friends; other respondents might think that a friend cannot be any of these other things. Thus, any data collected by researchers examining friendship will potentially be flawed so long as the critical term "friendship" itself is not defined.

In short, surveys provide much of the data used by sociologists, market researchers, political campaign workers, and a wide variety of social entities (e.g., law enforcement and health agencies). Survey data is also responsible for a great deal of our current knowledge about our society and the global community. It is important to note that survey research data is the result of *self-reporting*, that is, the researcher is relying on the validity of answers provided by respondents. Chances are, your professor has conducted her or his own survey in the past or is currently working on a survey now. Ask your professor to share her or his personal examples with you.

What Do You Think?

Survey research is the method most commonly used by sociologists. However, it is not the best option for all studies. Do you think survey research is a viable option for studying female gang participation and activity? Why or why not? How could survey research be used in the study of gangs? What do you think?

Observational Studies (or Field Studies)

Although survey research is the most popular method in sociology, sociologists are quick to point out that the type of research strategy used in collecting data must be appropriate to the study under consideration. In some cases, this appropriateness hinges on whether the data-collection method is indirect or direct. With survey research, the sociologist relies on the observations of others (the respondents). In this regard, surveys involve indirect research. In contrast, observational studies involve direct research because the researcher is observing, firsthand, the actions and behaviors of others in their social setting(s).

Everyone observes his or her social environment. Students sitting in the classroom are aware of other students (especially those nearest to them), the professor in the front of the room, and any other types of stimuli found in the social setting (e.g., the clock on the wall, people walking in the hallway outside the classroom door). In fact, all day long, we observe others. Simple observation of others, however, is not the same thing as the scientific pursuit of social research. Observation becomes a scientific endeavor only when observations

- become systematic;
- present a clear objective or purpose;
- involve careful record keeping;
- are tied to theory or broader sociological knowledge;
- are presented in some coherent manner that allows the results to be examined by others.

Observational research involves focusing on a social situation and meticulously recording key characteristics and events found in a specific setting. Stangor (2004) explains, "Observational research involves making observations of behavior and recording those observations in an objective manner. The observational approach is the oldest method of conducting research and is used routinely in psychology, anthropology, sociology, and many other fields" (p. 126). Ethnography, a popular variation of observational research, involves the study of an entire social setting in which the researcher asks the subjects for their perspectives on social reality.

Observational research is often a good option when survey methodology does not seem appropriate. Such is the case with studying female gang members. It does not make a great deal of sense to mail surveys or make random phone calls to a sample of a population asking people if they are gang members and, if so, to specify what types of criminal and delinquent acts they have committed. Randomly stopping people on the streets and asking to interview them about possible gang activity is not advisable either. Thus, when studying female gang members, observational research is a good option. There is one major drawback, however. How does one gain entry into such a deviant and often violent world? The answer involves having a connection, or an in, with a gang.

Sociologist John Quicker, the author of the first book written exclusively on female gang members (*Homegirls: Characterizing Chicana Gangs* 1983), gained access to female gangs in East Los Angeles through an introduction by one of his college students. Although now, in the twenty-first century, terms such as "homegirl," "homeboy," "homes," and "homie" are a part of popular urban slang, in 1983 the book title *Homegirls* was not only clever but new and insightful. Quicker (1983) states, "Chicana gang members use the affectionate terms 'homegirl' and 'homeboy' (sometimes shortened in speech to simply 'homes') to refer to other gang members. These terms take on the same affect as 'brother' and 'sister,' reflecting the family-like structure of the group" (p. 6). Observational research often provides sociologists like Quicker subjective insights that survey research cannot.

Members of the La Palanca gang flash signs to show their affiliation. Sociologists conduct research on gangs to learn more about their structure and behavior.

When conducting observational studies, the sociologist has three primary roles to choose from: participant as an announced observer; participant as an unannounced observer; and nonparticipant observer. **Announced participant observation** involves the researcher interacting with the group under study, informing the group of his or her purpose, and witnessing firsthand, or participating in, group activities. For example, the researcher might actually join a female street gang, with the consent of the gang members, to gain insights into the communal role of the group. In this case, the researcher would actively participate in group activities and talk with fellow participants about the value of group membership.

Participant observation has a major potential drawback: the observer may lose his or her objectivity, or detachment from the group. American Bill Buford, author of *Among the Thugs,* provides an example of a researcher losing detachment. Buford (1991) describes his becoming part of a gang of English hooligans who were actively involved in soccer violence. The adrenaline-induced euphoria experienced by the hooligans had an addictive quality that led Buford to full participation in acts of hooliganism. In fact, Buford became so attached to this group of hooligans that he was among a number of fans beaten by Italian police during the first round of the 1990 World Cup. Another potential problem with acknowledged (announced) participation in a group is the issue of reactivity. *Reactivity* occurs when the people being studied alter their behavior because they know they are being observed (Stangor 2004).

An announced participant observer researcher would not necessarily have to participate in group activities; thus, such a researcher might travel (move from setting to setting) with a street gang to observe its members' behaviors without engaging in actual gang activity. Quicker took this role when he studied Chicana gangs in East Los Angeles. I too have studied street gangs as an announced participant observer (Delaney 2006a). I announced my intentions to the gang, traveled with it, and recorded notes; but I never participated in gang activity.

The **unannounced participant observation** entails the researcher's interacting with a specific group under study without informing its members that they are being observed. Using our example of studying female gangs, the unannounced observer researcher would join the gang and act as a group member, all the while collecting data without the informed knowledge of the gang. The advantage of unannounced participant observation over the announced observer role is that it reduces the possibility of reactivity. Group members are unlikely to be guarded or to hold back information, just as they are unlikely to behave differently in the unannounced observer's presence.

Researchers opt for the unannounced observer role for a number of reasons. For example, in the late 1950s, a sociologist using the pseudonym "James Patrick" obtained entry into a Glasgow gang for four months, generally hanging out with members on weekends. The information Patrick obtained about the gang's violent activities was so insightful and overwhelming that he eventually feared for his life. Afraid of possible gang retaliation, he waited a number of years to publish his book *A Glasgow Gang Observed* (1973). In another scenario, a law enforcement officer may join a gang in an attempt to gain information leading to arrests and convictions of its members. As an unannounced observer, the undercover officer is able to obtain information that would be impossible to get if his identity and true intentions were announced. However, in order to avoid blowing his or her cover, the undercover agent may actually have to participate in illegal activity.

The third type of direct observation, **nonparticipant observation**, involves a researcher observing the group under study from such a distance that the group is unaware of his or her presence. For example, a gang researcher may investigate the behaviors of gang members by observing them through binoculars from the safety of a distant office building. While this may be a safer way of observing deviant or criminal behavior or eliminate the hassle of gaining permission to study a particular group (because the researcher does not have the contacts to gain entry), it has a major drawback in that the researcher is not afforded an opportunity to ask members questions in an attempt to elaborate on his or her observations.

Observational studies remain an excellent way of gathering data on a variety of topics, especially deviant, taboo, and illicit activities. The primary advantage of this method is the depth and intimacy of understanding that it brings to research. Observational research is much more flexible than survey research as the researcher is not tied to a prescripted set of questions. A major disadvantage is that sometimes the researcher becomes too close to the group under study and loses detachment or objectivity, as happened with Bill Buford and the soccer hooligans. Furthermore, unlike scientists who conduct controlled experiments, the observational researcher risks any number of intrusions that may interfere with effective data collection.

Unobtrusive Measures

Whereas observational studies involve the direct observation of behavior and social events by the researcher, unobtrusive measures entail indirect observation. **Unobtrusive research**, then, is a type of field observation in which the researcher does not interfere with, or become a part of, the behavior being studied. Unobtrusive measures allow the researcher to keep away from ongoing interaction. As True (1989) explains, "The word *unobtrusive* means that a person is not a part of the interaction and has no influence on it. When you're collecting data, the interaction is over" (p. 119). The researcher who utilizes unobtrusive measures is like a detective who attempts to uncover evidence about past behavior through the examination of clues left at the scene. This method examines physical traces left behind by participants. From this evidence, the researcher attempts to piece together past behavior. Thus, such measures do not require the cooperation of those under study. There are two primary categories of unobtrusive measures: erosion and accretion.

Measures of *erosion* reveal past behavior as a result of the wearing away of an item or area, such as worn-out carpet or pathways through backyards. Focusing on wear indicates, among other things, high traffic areas. Students can conduct their own unobtrusive research by moving a piece of furniture (that has not been previously moved for an extended period) in a carpeted room. The carpet under the couch will be fuller and cleaner than the worn-out area where people generally walk (and thus wear out the carpet). Most college campuses have areas of grass that have been worn away because people take shortcuts through grassy areas rather than following the path of the sidewalk. In such a scenario, the researcher need not be present to observe people walking across the previously grassy areas because evidence of erosion has been left behind (by those people who did not use the sidewalk). A grass outfield in baseball will reveal where the outfielders most commonly position themselves because, over the course of a season, the grass will be worn out in that area. It is easy to ascertain someone's favorite pair of jeans because they will be the most worn out. Examples of measures of erosion are nearly endless.

Measures of *accretion,* or accumulation, reveal evidence of past behavior based on deposited materials left behind by participants. For example, gang graffiti spray-painted on park benches indicates that gang members have been in the park. The researcher need not have witnessed the spray-painting directly to realize that gang members committed the criminal activity of destroying property because the gang members left evidence of their criminal behavior. An empty spray-paint can would be another example of a deposited material.

Gang graffiti provides a great deal of information to rival gangs, law enforcement, and gang researchers.

Unobtrusive research has an advantage over direct observation in that the problem of reactivity is nonexistent. On the other hand, it lacks the depth of participant observation studies. Researchers are not the only people who can utilize unobtrusive research, as measures of erosion and accretion are potentially helpful in a variety of decision-making processes. For example, let us say you are thinking about moving to a new city and you are not sure what neighborhoods are safest. Generally speaking, you can guess that a neighborhood where a majority of houses have bars on the windows (a physical trace and evidence of past behavior) is not a safe one.

Content Analysis

Sociologists need not rely on conducting their own research in an attempt to support or disprove a theory. Instead, they may choose to use existing sources of data. For example, as mentioned earlier, the U.S. government conducts a census based on survey research. Once this data has been collected, it exists as a form of written communication that can be analyzed by others for their own purposes; the U.S. Census Bureau (2010a) releases statistical reports of aggregated data shortly after census data is collected, and individual census records are available to the public for seventy-two years after a given census is completed. Newspapers, magazines, diaries, e-mails, letters, television programs, music, and art are all examples of written or oral forms of communication available for analysis by social researchers. These various contents are actually cultural artifacts that provide useful insights into human behavior. The **content analysis** methodology can be applied to any form of written or oral communication through the systematic recording of instances (under study) on tally sheets.

In conducting content analysis, sociologists search documents that may otherwise be ignored by other research methodologies. The examination of diaries and private letters, for example, often sheds light on an individual's most private feelings and experiences. Consider the private papers of Mother Teresa, who is often portrayed as a person with unshakeable faith who will undoubtedly be canonized as a saint by the Catholic Church (www.census.gov/po/pia/pia_guide.html). Her letters and diaries present a different impression of the nun and Nobel Peace Prize winner than is commonly presented to the public. In actuality, Mother Teresa's writings reveal that she sometimes felt helpless and that she was tempted to abandon her work for the poor and dying (Keys 2001). Such revelations may serve as an inspiration to others who question their own role in society and motivate them to continue. In one 1958 diary entry, Mother Teresa writes, "My smile is a great cloak that hides a multitude of pains." And because of her constant positive persona that included a "forever smile," many people felt, according to her, that "my faith, my hope and my love are overflowing and that my intimacy with God and union with His will fill my heart. If only they knew" (Catholic Church Religion News Blog 2002). In another passage, Mother Teresa writes, "I feel that God does not want me, that God is not God and that he does not really exist" (Catholic Church Religion News Blog 2002). The other methodologies we have discussed previously would ignore diaries and letters as sources of information and therefore fall short in providing a comprehensive look at a particular social event or human behavior.

The two major advantages of content analysis are that it is safe and it is economical. For example, it is both safer and more economical to conduct content analysis research on street gangs than it is to study them firsthand (observational research). Content analysis presents a potential disadvantage when researchers cannot find the information they are looking for and conclude that no evidence exists. As researchers are fond of saying, "Absence of evidence should not be confused with evidence of absence"; just because one cannot find information on a particular topic does not mean the information does not exist. In addition, because content analysis represents an indirect form of research, the researcher usually has no way to verify the accuracy of the contents. Most people realize that the availability of some sort of information on the Internet (or from any other source, for that matter) does not necessarily mean that it is accurate. Furthermore, news items available from wire services such as the Associated Press and Reuters, although they are generally "true" (factual), often do not present the full story. As a result, newspapers and news programs will provide us with news stories and information, but they quickly move on to the next story and seldom follow through to the conclusion of most of the stories they present.

Archival Research

As with content analysis, archival research involves the use of existing data. An archive is a place where old documents are kept (or stored). The government, businesses, and museums and libraries are all likely to have archives where they store old documents and oversized or oddly shaped files that do not neatly fit into other existing shelving. For many private people, the attic or basement may serve as an archive where tax documents, baby photo albums, yearbooks, and so on are stored. **Archival research** involves the analysis of documents and other materials found in an archive. In his study on suicide, Emile Durkheim ([1895] 1951) examined archival data from between 1841 and 1872 for seven European countries. Archival records contain a huge amount of information and must therefore be systematically coded. An often overlooked advantage of archival research rests with the realization that data collected decades ago for purposes that have nothing to do with present-day research are devoid of biases. Psychologist Jean Twenge, for example, used archival data in her 2006 book *Generation Me* when she compared contemporary attitudes toward social approval to the attitudes of young people in past decades.

Experiments

Although experimentation may seem to belong in the domain of the natural sciences, researchers in the social sciences may also conduct experiments. In an **experiment**, the researcher manipulates the independent variable and measures the dependent variable to discover the relationship between the two. One advantage of the experimental method is that it generally allows the researcher to control the environment so that outside variables do not influence the study.

A wide variety of experiments are available to researchers. The "classic," or basic, experimental design involves researchers working with two groups. It is important that these two groups are as identical as possible in all aspects relevant to the study. An initial measurement of the two groups is taken before the introduction of a treatment, or independent variable. Researchers then introduce a variable, or treatment, of some sort to one group, identified as the *experimental group,* but will not introduce this variable, or treatment, to the other group, known as the *control group.* The treatment introduced to the experimental group is the independent variable. Because experiments allow social researchers to test the effects of an independent variable on a dependent variable in an attempt to provide a causal inference, experimenters must be very specific in their descriptions of the independent variable (or treatment) used in their experimental design.

A classic, though regrettable, example of an experiment conducted on humans is the "Tuskegee Study of Untreated Syphilis in the Negro Male," commonly referred to as the "Tuskegee syphilis study" or simply the "Tuskegee experiment." In 1932, the U.S. Public Health Service initiated the Tuskegee syphilis study to document the natural history of syphilis. The subjects of the investigation were 399 poor black sharecroppers from Macon County, Alabama, with latent syphilis, and 201 men without the disease who served as controls. The physicians conducting the study deceived the men, telling them that they were being treated for "bad blood." In reality, the government officials went to extreme lengths to ensure that the men with syphilis received no therapy from any source (Jones 1993; CDC 2009c). Even when penicillin became the drug of choice to treat syphilis in 1947, researchers did not offer it to the subjects (CDC 2009c). The Tuskegee syphilis study lasted an incredible forty years and is considered one of the longest non-therapeutic experiments on human beings in medical history. The study is cited as a significant factor in the low participation of African Americans today in clinical trials, organ-donation programs, and routine preventive medical care (Thomas and Quinn 1991). On May 16, 1997, President Bill Clinton offered an apology, on behalf of the American government, to the surviving study participants, their families, and the Tuskegee community.

Although the nature of social research often makes it difficult for sociologists to use the types of laboratory experiments traditionally used in the natural sciences, it is fairly common among social psychologists and sociologists who embrace ethnomethodology to conduct breaching experiments.

Ethnomethodology is a branch of sociology that proposes social interaction is based on negotiated reality; it is an examination of the methods people commonly use to sustain some kind of consensus about the world and to solve problems characterized by highly irrational features. Sociologists who embrace ethnomethodology employ breaching experiments as their primary method of conducting research. Because they do not incorporate all the standard elements of a traditional experiment, breaching experiments are deemed quasi-experimental. Nonetheless, breaching experiments provide sociologists with a unique form of research.

Breaching experiments involve researchers deliberately interrupting the normal course of social interaction (Turner 2003). Ritzer (2000b) explains, "In breaching experiments, social reality is violated in order to shed light on the methods by which people construct social reality. The assumption behind this research is not only that the methodical production of social life occurs all the time but also that the participants are unaware that they are engaging in such actions. The objective of the breaching experiment is to disrupt normal procedures so that the process by which the everyday world is constructed or reconstructed can be observed and studied" (p. 386).

Harold Garfinkel, the leading proponent of ethnomethodology, believes that most people attempt to give order to their lives, and when their behavioral routines have been breached, they will attempt to normalize the resultant incongruities in their social lives. In one experiment, Garfinkel had his students act as if they were boarders in their own homes; as such, the students treated their parents as if they were landlords and acted in nonintimate ways while interacting with them. Family members generally demanded to know why the student was behaving in such an odd way. Many students also reported having difficulty with the assignment because of the drastic way it altered their own taken-for-granted world.

In another example of a breaching experiment, one of my former students informed me that he had held a party for his friends and did not tell them that the keg of beer was nonalcoholic. Inevitably, most of his friends acted as if they were drunk after drinking the beer. They were quite angry when they learned the next day that the beer had been nonalcoholic. The point is that their taken-for-granted reality was altered by a breaching experiment.

> **What Do You Think?**
>
> If you were old enough to drink alcohol legally and attended a party where people were drinking nonalcoholic beer from a keg they believed contained alcoholic beer, how would you expect people to react? How would you react? What do you think?

I have often had my introductory students conduct their own breaching experiments, and they find them to be very informative and entertaining. My students have placed "Wet Paint" signs on walls that were clearly not recently painted; placed "Out of Order" signs on a dorm elevator and then boarded it; placed a mattress and end table in an elevator to make it look like they lived in it; taken food items out of, or placed food items into, the shopping carts of total strangers at grocery stores; and so on. Students then report the reactions of those who witness these breaches of social reality, write about their own reactions to conducting such experiments, and discuss the social norms violated by these breaches. It is a fun exercise that provides a great learning experience about the social world we take for granted. Nonacademic people have also found the (monetary and entertaining) value of conducting social breaching experiments via such popular TV shows as *Candid Camera* and *Punk'd* (See "Connecting Sociology and Popular Culture" Box 3.2).

The advantage of experimental research is that it symbolizes "true" science—science used by those in the natural sciences. Experimental research provides cause-and-effect relationships between variables. Long-term experiments in a lab allow researchers the time to collect enough data to test theories at the level of the individual (Birnbaum 2000). Among the disadvantages of experiments is that they are costly and time-consuming. Further, they are difficult to execute in the social sciences because it is often impossible to control the social environment to the point where researchers are reasonably sure that outside variables have not contaminated the results of their experiment. Potential ethical problems exist with such experiments as well, as is evident in our earlier discussion of the Tuskegee syphilis study (ethical issues are discussed in greater detail later in this chapter).

Connecting Sociology and Popular Culture

Box 3.2 Punk'd by Ashton Kutcher: Celebrities Caught in Breaching Experiments

As described in this section, a breaching experiment involves the deliberate interruption of normal courses of social interaction. Most of us would not like to be victimized by a breaching experiment, especially one witnessed by an audience. However, we do seem to find enjoyment in watching others being "punk'd" by a breaching experiment. The popular television show *Candid Camera* and its many variations serve as evidence of this. The idea behind *Candid Camera* was to catch everyday people being confronted with unusual situations, sometimes involving the use of trick props designed to surprise the unsuspecting target of the show's hidden cameras. *Candid Camera,* created and produced by Allen Funt, originally as a radio show (*Candid Microphone*), first aired on television in 1948. When the victims were eventually told of the nature of their folly, the person who had set them up would say, "Smile, you're on *Candid Camera*!" Once they were in on the joke, victims would smile graciously.

Although most of *Candid Camera's* victims were everyday folks, the show sometimes targeted celebrities and entertainers. Audiences really seem to find delight in famous people being made the target of a joke, or as the popular vernacular would describe it, "punk'd!" A show known for specifically targeting celebrities, however, is Ashton Kutcher's *Punk'd,* which aired from 2003 to 2007 on MTV. Kutcher would begin each show with a description of the celebrity about to be punk'd and why he felt it necessary. The show usually took place in Los Angeles at common locations such as parking lots, restaurants, and hotel lobbies. Kutcher punk'd such celebrities as Halle Berry (Berry was told that she was barred from the premiere of her film *Gothika* because the number of people in the theater already exceeded the fire code), tennis star Andy Roddick (he was told that his automobile had been trapped by a Los Angeles mudslide), and Kanye West (who was told he could not film on Sundays without a special permit). At the conclusion of his pranks, Kutcher would usually say, "You just got punk'd!"

Ashton Kutcher's *Punk'd* was not the only contemporary version of prank shows that involved confronting people with unusual situations; others include *Just for Laugh Gags, The Jamie Kennedy Experiment, Howie Do It,* and *Girls Behaving Badly.* Clearly, there is a popular demand for breaching experiments. Pointing out the sociological relevance of popularized breaching experiments can provide great insights into the taken-for-granted and negotiated world that we live in.

What Do You Think?

If you were a TV producer who utilized breaching experiments as a theme, how would you demonstrate your sociological imagination? What do you think?

To review briefly the methods available to sociologists, let us return to our research example of studying female street gangs. Survey research seems an unlikely approach, as sending out a mass mailing or randomly phoning girls and women and asking them whether they belong to a street gang would be rather fruitless. If a researcher has access to a gang via a connection of some sort, observational research would be quite insightful. "Traveling" with a gang would pro-

Halle Berry reacts to being Punk'd by Ashton Kutcher. The show Punk'd *is a variation of a social breaching experiment.*

vide the researcher with information unknown to most citizens. Content analysis, via news reports on gang activity and police arrest and incident reports, would also be very beneficial. Studying gang graffiti is also a shrewd method. Archival data might be useful during the literature review stage but is not likely to be used as a method of data collection for this particular study, as we are interested in gang membership overall, not that specifically limited to crime records. Conducting experiments would be nearly impossible; after all, we could not tell females in one section of a neighborhood to join a gang so that we could study them and then tell females in another section of the neighborhood not to join a gang so that they could serve as our control group. A number of unobtrusive measures, however, may be beneficial to social researchers, as they could look for evidence of gang activity (e.g., bloodstains, destroyed property, discarded weapons) throughout a particular neighborhood. In short, many methods available to sociologists could be used to examine female gang activity, and yet the most popular method used by sociologists—survey research—is not the most viable.

It is important to note that social researchers are not limited to using just one methodology in testing a hypothesis. On the contrary, researchers should use as many methods as possible during the course of their study. Using multiple approaches is known as **triangulation**. Triangulation is used to overcome the shortcomings of one particular methodological approach while highlighting the value of using multiple approaches in the search for empirical verification. "This diversity of methods implies rich opportunities for cross-validating and cross-fertilizing research procedures, findings, and theories" (Brewer and Hunter 1989, p. 13). The use of multiple methods during sociological research provides a more comprehensive overview of the subject.

QUANTITATIVE AND QUALITATIVE APPROACHES

The introductory story at the beginning of this chapter described a variety of hypotheses about smoking that lend themselves to testing by social research. The harmful effects of smoking can be researched and quantified in terms of the numbers of people who die each year as a result of tobacco use, the medical costs to all citizens who pay for increased health insurance because of smokers, and so on. However, the theory that smoking is cool refers to a qualitative assessment, an idea that can also be researched. The following pages present the primary distinctions between quantitative and qualitative approaches to social research.

Quantitative Research

Quantitative research methods are the objective, logical tools of science that provide facts and figures describing patterns and events in social life. Social researchers who attempt to support their theories with statistical evidence use quantitative research. American sociology is especially quantitative primarily because of the use of computers for statistical analysis. The quantitative approach allows for the measurement of variables. As a result, quantitative studies employ an accepted definition of a theory, based on the interrelationship of the variables, and incorporate authoritative terms (descriptions of variables) in their study. These terms are explicitly written in an operational language (Creswell 1994).

The quantification—assignment of numbers to observations—of social research has many benefits for sociologists. First, it increases intersubjective agreement on the nature of observed behaviors and, consequently, provides objectivity. Second, quantification increases the amount of information about observed behavior that can be provided in a concise, logical manner. Third, statistical analysis allows for comparative research studies (B. Cohen 1989).

Quantitative methods are generally used in survey research. Typically, questions are predetermined with fixed answers that allow for codification of responses. "Structuring questions, developing categories and variables, and counting responses and observations" are critical aspects of the quantitative approach (Nardi 2003, p. 16). An example would be the U.S. census. The census involves respondents answering a number of questions with fixed, categorical possible responses. Ultimately, the census will provide easy-access statistical information on a number of variables, including the total U.S. population, number of men and women, number of persons by age, racial or ethnic categories, number of people living below the poverty level, and so on. The quantification of the U.S. census allows for an objective (intersubjective) review of data on U.S. citizens presented in a concise manner that lends itself to comparison with past and future census data.

The use of statistics is the trademark of quantitative methods. Statistics are used in social research as a means of influencing others with regard to various social issues. The modern meaning of statistics—numeric evidence—dates back to the 1830s (Best 2001). Statistics provide researchers with specific bits of information. This information is used in a variety of fashions, including shaping and supporting people's attitudes, opinions, and knowledge level. For example, many people may believe that during times of recession and high unemployment the crime rate will increase. However, data collected by the Federal Bureau of Investigation (FBI) for the first half of 2009 indicates that the overall crime rate fell 4.4 percent across the United States despite high unemployment, home foreclosures, and layoffs (FBI 2009). This included a 10 percent drop in murders and manslaughters and a 6.1 percent drop in property crimes. Sociologist Richard Rosenfeld, who studies crime trends, states, "That's a remarkable decline, given the economic conditions" (*Post-Standard,* 12/22/09). Rosenfeld believes there are several possible explanations, including that extended unemployment benefits, food stamps, and other government-driven economic stimuli have cushioned and delayed for many people the big blows that come from a recession; with more people home from work, it is harder for burglars to break into a house or apartment unnoticed by neighbors; and people are engaging in technology-driven "smart-policing" efforts. Whereas Rosenfeld is astonished by the FBI's statistics, James Alan Fox, a criminal justice professor, is not surprised by the lowering crime rates and, instead, cites the FBI's recent data as support for his belief that citizens without work do not typically go on crime sprees (*Post-Standard,* 12/22/09). Notice how Rosenfeld and Fox both cite the same statistics even though they possess different attitudes toward and beliefs about crime in times of recession. Such is the nature of statistics. As the cliché goes, "Statistics never lie, but you can make them say whatever you want."

Statistics come into play in a variety of social settings and have practical purposes. The weather, for example, is filled with statistics, including the temperature, humidity level, heat index, wind direction, wind chill, normal highs and lows for a specific date, probability for rain or snow, and so on. Many people rely on this statistical data to help them plan their daily activities, both for work and for leisure.

Statistics also possess a qualitative component. In sports, for example, statistics allow not only for an easy comparison between athletes (e.g., batting averages) but for a quality assessment that leads sports fans to claim one player is better than another based on statistics. Sports are filled with statistics. And with the advent of technology, many men and women now participate in fantasy football leagues that rely on real-life statistics. Fantasy sports leagues are especially popular with college-aged persons, but many students might be surprised to learn about their sociological roots (see "Connecting Sociology and Popular Culture" Box 3.3 to learn more).

Also of note is the reality that many students seem to have a fear of statistics and suffer from what Kerr, Hall, and Kozub (2002) call "numerophobia"—the fear of numbers. Often times, as soon as a professor starts describing a number of statistics in class, many students become uneasy, and eventually one will ask, "Will this stuff be on the test?" Or a student may comment after taking an objective exam (multiple choice), "There were too many questions about statistics," even if just five to seven of fifty questions consisted of statistics. Students and non-students alike tend to fear statistics (as if they were our enemy) and become easily overwhelmed when too many stats are described in class (see "A Closer Look" Box 3.4 for a further analysis of the problem adults have with numbers). For these students, let us make an explicit point of stating that statistics are not the enemy. Statistics provide social researchers with a great deal of useful information. Furthermore, despite the many wisecracks about how one can manipulate and lie with statistics, it is important to recognize that statistics themselves are generally neutral. For example, the speedometer reading on your car is not a value judgment; it is simply a reading of how fast your car is going.

In short, a quantitative research methodology relies on the use of numbers, or statistics, that allow social researchers to gather information and test theory. Statistical analysis generated by the sociologist allows not only for an objective explanation of an event or behavior but, ideally, for the prediction of future events or behaviors.

Qualitative Research

Qualitative research is a generic term used to describe a range of different research approaches that support different theoretical assumptions such as

Connecting Sociology and Popular Culture

Box 3.3 Fantasy Sports Leagues: With Roots in Sociology

Enjoyed by men and women alike, fantasy sports leagues are a growing pop-culture phenomenon. Participants act as "owners" of sports franchises and "draft" players for their teams. The fantasy teams then compete against one another via the real-life statistics of the players. Although many students may believe fantasy sports leagues are a recent invention, the idea of picking players and running a contest based on real statistics has been around for a long time. "Conventional wisdom holds that fantasy sports were officially born in 1980 when a group of baseball fans including magazine writer and editor Dan Okrent founded Rotisserie League Baseball over lunch at a Manhattan restaurant called La Rotisserie Franchise" (Frost 2006, p. 1). However, as Sam Walker, author of *Fantasyland: A Season on Baseball's Lunatic Fringe* (2006) explains, Rotisserie-style baseball was "only the live birth" of fantasy sports. Walker adds that the conception of fantasy sports leagues dates back to 1960 when then Harvard sociologist William Gamson started the "Baseball Seminar" where he and his colleagues would form rosters that earned points based on players' final statistics, such as their batting average, runs batted in, earned run average, and wins. Participants anted up $10 each in those early days to play in the fantasy baseball league. Gamson (currently teaching at Boston College) still participates in what is now called the "National Baseball Seminar." League fees are a modest $24 per participant (Frost 2006).

Fantasy sports leagues have grown and developed a great deal since their early sociological roots. Participants now use their computers to join and follow the leagues they belong to. Statistics are updated daily—in some cases, instantly—as they occur on the field, so winning and losing fantasy teams can be determined very quickly based on the actual performances of real-life players. Winners of fantasy sports league competitions may be rewarded with real-life monetary prizes (generated from participation fees).

At present, fantasy sports leagues around the world encompass nearly every form of organized team sport, and individual sports such as golf and tennis also have fantasy sports appeal. According to Fantasy Sports Ventures (FSV) (2009), an estimated 15 million Americans play fantasy sports, each spending an average of $154 per year on fantasy games and related products. FSV, in an attempt to capitalize on this lucrative and rapidly growing $2 billion industry, established itself in 2006 as a sports consulting/advisory service. FSV consists of a team of entrepreneurs and sports media executives. FSV has formed the Fantasy Players Network, an aggregation of more than four hundred leading fantasy sports websites and related properties. FSV owns a number of sites specializing in professional football, baseball, basketball, and hockey, as well as college football and basketball, and has affiliate sites as well. FSV does much more than simply provide a service to sports enthusiasts; it also sells ad space, which, of course, allows the organization to generate revenue.

If only Professor William Gamson had fantasized about how big his sports league would grow! If he had applied for a trademark for his fantasy sports concept, one can only imagine how much money he would have generated. We might all be playing "Gamson Sports Leagues" instead of fantasy sports leagues. At the very least, we can thank a sociologist for stimulating the creation of the fantasy sports league craze.

What Do You Think?

As you continue to learn more about sociology, apply your sociological imagination to finding a way to connect statistics (or any research methodology, for that matter) to an area of interest that you possess. Is it possible that you could help to stimulate something as popular as fantasy sports leagues? What do you think?

A Closer Look

Box 3.4 Quantitative Illiteracy

Based on data compiled by U.S. Department of Education's National Assessment of Adult Literacy (NAAL), Americans are lousy with numbers. NAAL periodically measures three forms of literacy—prose, document, and quantitative—among adults, including college students. Quantitative literacy refers to the knowledge and skills required to perform quantitative tasks (i.e., to identify and perform computations, either alone or sequentially, using numbers embedded in printed materials). Examples include figuring out a tip, completing an order form, or determining the amount of interest on a loan from an advertisement (Greenberg, Dunleavy, and Kutner 2008; NAAL 2009).

Quantitative illiteracy (also known as innumeracy or numerophobia) has led to a number of startling problems, including the realization that most college students cannot perform common tasks ranging from understanding credit card offers to comparing the cost per ounce of food (MSNBC 2010). In its most recent study, NAAL (2009) found that more than half of the students surveyed at four-year schools and more than 75 percent at two-year colleges could not interpret a table about exercise and blood pressure, compare credit card offers with different interest rates and annual fees, or summarize the results of a survey about parental involvement in school (MSNBC 2010). In addition, results from the NAAL survey reveal that only 42 percent of Americans were able to pick out two items on a menu, add them, and calculate a tip; only one in five could reliably calculate mortgage interest; 22 percent could not figure out a weekly salary after learning the hourly pay rate; just 13 percent of Americans were deemed "proficient" in quantitative skills (only one in ten women, one in twenty-five Hispanics, and one in fifty African Americans); and a staggering 20 million Americans pay someone to complete their IRS-1040-EZ tax return, a form with approximately ten blanks to fill out (MSNBC 2010).

Although it could be argued that most adults armed with a calculator could manage to accomplish many of the rudimentary skills described above, people who do not have fundamental math skills enter the job and economic markets unprepared to handle a vast array of simple problems. Possessing quantitative literacy comes as a result of developing reading and comprehension skills and, of course, memorizing the basic mathematical tables taught in elementary school. The social problem of grave quantitative illiteracy means that the vast majority of Americans are lacking in logic and reasoning skills.

What Do You Think?

In an advanced rational society such as the United States, how is it possible that Americans are so inept in quantitative skills? Is it possible to develop logic and reason without possessing quantitative skills? What do you think?

symbolic interactionism, phenomenology (the examination of the conscious experience of individuals), and ethnomethodology (a theoretical perspective that seeks to understand human behavior by examining the methods that people employ to make sense of the world) (Flick, von Kardorff, and Steinke 2004). Qualitative methods attempt to uncover the subjective nature of human behavior and social events. Thus, while the U.S. census may provide valuable objective data to sociologists, it does not provide subjective information on qualitative areas of interest, such as the number of Americans who are happy with their lives. In addition, whereas quantitative questions are highly structured and force respondents to choose from answer choices provided, qualitative research questions are generally less structured and more flexible because they tend to be open-ended. Open-ended questions are those that cannot be answered with a simple yes or no and that allow respondents to answer using their own words rather than choosing from a menu of predetermined responses.

The flexible nature of qualitative questions leads them to be a little more ambiguous than quantitative ones. As Creswell (1994) explains, "In qualitative designs, terms are defined tentatively because the meanings of words will emerge from the informants" (p. 112). For example, if we reexamine the introductory chapter story that suggests some people think it is cool to smoke, we realize that the meaning of "cool" was never spelled out. To dwell on the coolness aspect of smoking, a quantitative question might restrict respondents to a scale of one to ten, with ten being the most cool, in answering the question "How cool do you consider smoking to be?" A qualitative research question, in contrast, could ask respondents, "Do you think smoking is cool, and why do you think it is, or is not, cool?"

Sociologists who conduct observational studies most commonly use qualitative methods. As Silverman (2001) explains, quantitative researchers often ignore observation because they view it as a nonreliable from of data collection. Further, quantitative methodologists argue that qualitative research is less objective than the quantitative variety, as qualitative research findings are more open to interpretation. "Quantitative measurements are quantitatively accurate; qualitative evaluations are always subject to errors of human judgment" (LaPiere 1994, p. 56). Despite these criticisms of qualitative research, it is important to note that both quantitative and qualitative approaches to social research are beneficial to sociologists, as both provide information, or data.

Qualitative research provides the answer to why certain behaviors occur rather than simply providing statistics regarding specific behaviors. Silverman (2001) states, "'Authenticity' rather than reliability is often the issue in qualitative research. The aim is usually to gather an authentic understanding of people's experiences and it is believed that open-ended questions are the most effective route towards this end" (p. 13). The advantage of qualitative research, then, rests with its ability to explain human behavior from the point of view of the participants themselves. "Qualitative research claims to describe life-worlds 'from the inside out,' from the point of view of the people who participate. By so doing it seeks to contribute to a better understanding of social realities and to draw attention to processes, meaning patterns and structural features" (Flick, von Kardorff, and Steinke 2004, p. 3).

A study on amateur stripping ("The Case of Amateur Stripping: Sex Codes and Egalitarianism in a Heterosocial Setting") by Thomas Calhoun, Rhonda Fisher, and Julie Ann Harms Cannon (1998) provides us with an example of qualitative research. The authors argue that, while a number of studies have examined professional stripping in strip clubs, the growing phenomenon of amateur stripping (defined as stripping by individuals who engage in the activity primarily during contests but do not see it as a full- or part-time occupation) has been mostly ignored. Calhoun and his colleagues interviewed audience members, announcers, disc jockeys, and security staff who participated in amateur stripping contests at a popular college bar in a Midwestern city. The contest was open to both men and women and occurred once a week on Thursdays. The authors attended amateur strip contests and took notes of their observations as the contests took place. They learned that most of the amateur strippers were college students who stripped for money and fun and that those meeting sexual stereotypes about the most attractive men and women (men with big muscles, small waists, and tight butts; "Playboy-type" women) consistently won the contests, received the loudest applause, and earned the largest tips. The amateur strippers generally found the experience to be positive both from a financial standpoint and in terms of positive self-esteem enhancement.

As with quantitative research, qualitative research will always have a place in sociology. The two approaches actually complement one another, as one (quantitative) provides objective, hard data, and the other (qualitative) provides valuable insights into human social behavior.

What Do You Think?

Suppose you were given the sociological task of measuring the degree of happiness among students at your campus. How would you go about such a research project? Would you use a quantitative or qualitative approach? What do you think?

ETHICS AND IDEAL RESEARCH

Earlier in this chapter we discussed the Tuskegee syphilis study and commented on the ethical violations associated with deceiving the study's subjects and preventing them from receiving medical treatment. While deception is not the only way in which research can be unethical, it is an issue that often arises in social research, as sociologists are often concerned with obtaining data on people's behavior when they are not being influenced by knowledge of what the researcher is looking for.

Social research is important; after all, it provides knowledge and leads to scientific advancements. However, it should not come at the cost of human dignity or life. As we have seen, social research has not always been ideal in this aspect, as many human subjects over the years have had their dignity, safety, and lives compromised under the guise of research. For this reason, this chapter concludes with an important discussion of ethics and of the factors that contribute to ideal research.

Ethics in Social Research

Today's notions of research ethics date back to ancient professional codes such as the medical Hippocratic oath from the fifth century bce (Alderson 2004), in which the physician promises to do no harm, to treat sick people with the appropriate remedies and with compassion, and to keep patients' confidential information private. In the twentieth century, as universities and other institutions became increasingly conscious of the need to monitor the research being conducted under their auspices, they began to set up committees to evaluate the ethical dimensions of proposed studies. In the United States today, these committees, known as institutional review boards, have the authority to approve, modify, or disapprove research to ensure that the rights of human subjects are not violated.

The American Sociological Association (ASA), the major professional organization for American sociology, has developed a code of ethics that sociologists are expected to abide by. The principles and standards of this code are to be used as guidelines when sociologists engage in professional activities. These ethical standards are written broadly in order to apply to sociologists in varied roles. The ASA (2006) provides five general ethical principles for the discipline (see Table 3.1).

Sociological research implies that the focus is on people and human societies. It is essential that the safety of human subjects is always the top priority of social researchers. Typically, when humans are involved in sociological research, sociologists are required to inform the subjects (something that, as we noted earlier, was not done in the infamous Tuskegee syphilis study). This is known as informed consent. Informed consent refers to the process by which researchers provide research subjects with important information about the study, including any possible harmful effects that might result from their participation. Research subjects should never be coerced into participation, and they should volunteer to participate in research of their own free will. Any possible physical or mental harm resulting from research should be put in writing so that participants are fully aware of the potential dangers they face. Likewise, it is important for social researchers to have subjects sign a waiver, or an informed-consent form, to protect themselves from possible lawsuits if participation in the research project does cause harm to the subject(s).

TABLE 3.1 The American Sociological Association's Code of Ethics (in Abbreviated Form)

Principle A. *Professional competence*: Sociologists strive to maintain the highest levels of competence in their work, and they will undertake only those tasks for which they are qualified by education, training, or experience.

Principle B. *Integrity:* Sociologists are to be honest, fair, and respectful of others in their professional activities–in research, teaching, practice, and service. They do not knowingly make statements that are false, misleading, or deceptive.

Principle C. *Professional and scientific responsibility:* Sociologists adhere to the highest scientific and professional standards and accept responsibility for their work. Sociologists value the public trust in sociology and are concerned about their ethical behavior and that of other sociologists that might compromise that trust.

Principle D. *Respect for people's rights, dignity, and diversity:* Sociologists respect the rights, dignity, and worth of all people. They strive to eliminate bias in their professional activities, and they do not tolerate any form of discrimination based on age, gender, race, ethnicity, national origin, religion, sexual orientation, disability, health conditions, or marital, domestic, or parental status.

Principle E. *Social responsibility:* Sociologists are aware of their professional and scientific responsibility to the communities and societies in which they live and work. They apply and make public their knowledge in order to contribute to the public good. When undertaking research they strive to advance the science of sociology and to serve the public good.

(Note: The most recent ASA code of ethics was approved by the ASA membership in June 1997.)

These issues and others are addressed in the ASA's (2006) specific code of ethics for social research:

1. Maintain objectivity and integrity in research.
2. Respect the subject's right to privacy and dignity.
3. Protect subjects from personal harm.
4. Preserve confidentiality.
5. Seek informed consent when data are collected from research participants or when behavior occurs in a private context.
6. Acknowledge research collaboration and assistance.
7. Disclose all sources of financial support

Despite a code of ethics that accompanies every academic discipline and the generally proper ethical behavior of most researchers, there are a number of well-documented examples of ethical problems associated with social research. One of the most widely cited cases of ethical breaches in social research is Laud Humphreys's Tearoom Sex Study research.

What Do You Think?

As described earlier in this chapter, sociological research includes observational studies where the subjects are not aware of the fact that research is being conducted. Is this unethical behavior on the part of sociologists? What do you think?

Humphreys (1930–1988), an ordained Episcopalian priest, husband, and father, is best known for his 1970 published PhD dissertation (Washington University), *Tearoom Trade: Impersonal Sex in Public Places.* The term "tearoom" is slang for a public place where men meet for anonymous sexual encounters. Humphreys studied male-male fellatio in public restrooms. He concluded that men like to meet in restrooms because they provide privacy in public places. The 1998 comedy hit film *There's Something About Mary* involves a humorous scene in which Ben Stiller's character, Ted, inadvertently stumbles upon a large number of men engaging in fellatio in a field adjacent to a public highway rest stop. The police show up and arrest the participants, including Ted. It is worth noting that, in real life, "tearoom sex" accounts for the majority of homosexual arrests in the United States.

Humphreys studied the tearoom trade in an attempt to understand this phenomenon and to determine the kind of men who participate in this type of sexual activity. (As a closeted gay man, Humphreys was also attempting to gain some insight into his own personal life. Humphreys left his wife in 1980 to live with his protégé Brian Miller.) In order to conduct his ethnographic, observational study, Humphreys offered to serve as a "watchqueen"—a person who keeps an eye out for police and other individuals about to enter the restroom. While playing this role, Humphreys observed hundreds of acts of fellatio. In his notes, he carefully recorded specific details of the tearoom trade, including "signaling" (e.g., foot tapping, hand waving, and body positioning), maneuvering, contracting, foreplay, and payoff.

Sociologists have criticized Humphreys's tearoom study on ethical grounds because he ignored the rules of informed consent, he masqueraded as a voyeur, and he wrote down the license plate numbers of subjects and later tracked them down (via Motor Vehicle Department records) at their homes to ask follow-up questions. Humphreys discovered that nearly half of his subjects were outwardly heterosexual men who hid their behaviors from their wives and family. Instead of considering the private lives of these men, Humphreys would ask the wives a number of embarrassing questions about their husband's secret lives. In many cases, the women had been oblivious of their husbands' double lives before Humphreys arrived on the scene. There is also reason to wonder whether Humphreys was telling the truth when he said he was a "watchqueen," or whether in fact he was an active participant because it is questionable whether "watchqueens" actually exist; the tearoom participants probably would have been suspicious if he did not participate in sexual acts (see "Connecting Sociology and Popular Culture" Box 3.5 for a further analysis of the tea trade).

> **What Do You Think?**
>
> Was Laud Humphreys out of line when he followed his subjects home to ask them questions about their tearoom sexual behavior? Why or why not? If you were a married male hiding your secret homosexual life, how would you react to a researcher "outing" you to your wife? If you were a woman married to a man living a secret gay life, how would you react to a researcher "outing" your husband? What do you think?

Ideal Research

Choosing the most appropriate research methodology is an important ingredient in ideal research (Frey 1989). Designing a research project so that others can replicate it is another important factor in conducting ideal research. Replication allows for reliability and validity. In this regard, other researchers may either support or challenge an original claim. The replication of studies is a feature that distinguishes science from speculation, personal judgment, and dogmatism. Clearly stated social research brings sociological inquiry out of the mind and into public view for others to support or challenge. In this regard, social research is "ideal."

Scientific research involves a code of honor. As True (1989) states, "The scientific method is a way to conduct research according to rules that specify objec-

> **Connecting Sociology and Popular Culture**
>
> ### Box 3.5 Laud Humphreys and Senator Larry Craig
>
> Although Laud Humphreys published his classic study in 1970, it remains relevant today as many of the same specific tearoom details he outlined are standard signals police watch for when investigating lewd-conduct complaints in men's public restrooms. Consider, for example, the highly publicized arrest by a plainclothes police officer of Senator Larry Craig (R-ID) in June 2007 at a Minnesota airport. As detailed by Laura MacDonald in her *New York Times* article, "America's Toe-Tapping Menace," the police report of Senator Craig's behavior followed the steps detailed by Humphreys. "First is the approach: Mr. Craig allegedly peeks into the stall. Then comes positioning: he takes the stall next to the (undercover) policeman. Signaling: Senator Craig allegedly taps his foot and touches it to the officer's shoe, which was positioned close to the divider, then slides his hand along the bottom of the stall. There are more phases in Mr. Humphreys' full lexicon—maneuvering, contracting, foreplay, and payoff—but Mr. Craig was arrested after the officer presumed he had 'signaled'" (MacDonald 2007).
>
> Senator Craig, who is married and leads an outwardly heterosexual lifestyle, pleaded guilty to misdemeanor disorderly conduct, received one year of probation, and paid more than $500 in fines and fees. He has adamantly denied being gay. Although he initially stated that he would step down from his public office, Craig changed his mind and remained in office. This incident became a pop-culture reference point for stand-up comedians such as Jay Leno, Jimmy Kimmel, Jimmy Fallon, and David Letterman.
>
> > **What Do You Think?**
> >
> > Should police officers hide out in public restrooms looking for tearoom-type sexual behaviors? Critics have argued this is a type of entrapment. How likely is it that Senator Craig was, or was not, signaling for sex? What do you think?

tivity, honesty, thoroughness, and service to the scientific world" (p. 33). Ideally, social research is conducted in an objective manner and supported by empirical verification in an attempt to increase the overall level of knowledge. The cardinal principles behind ideal research are integrity, empirical verification, contributions to knowledge, and publication (True 1989).

Ideal sociological research involves the advancement of knowledge and the betterment of society. It should be conducted ethically, and at the very least, human subjects should be made aware of their participation and free from deceptive, harmful studies. Above all else, the safety and dignity of human participants should be the top priority of all social research. When research is conducted in accord with these principles, it has the potential to contribute to the improvement of people's lives and society as a whole.

SUMMARY

Sociologists use a variety of research methods to test their theoretical perspectives and ideas regarding social behavior, issues, and events. The attempt to support or disprove theory with data and facts separates sociology from dogmatic thinking, philosophic speculation, and reliance on so-called common sense. The scientific method involves operationalizing the research question and designing a study whose results will be both valid and reliable.

A seven-step research model guides sociologists. This model serves as the design of the research project at hand. Six primary research methodologies are available to sociologists: survey research, observational research, unobtrusive research, content analysis, archival research, and experimentation (especially breaching experiments). Survey research is the most popular method used by sociologists. However, survey research may have to be abandoned in favor of some other alternative if it is not appropriate to the study under consideration. The use of multiple research methods is recommended whenever possible as a diverse approach yields greater insight.

Maintaining a commitment to the scientific method, sociology is geared to explain both the quantitative and qualitative dimensions of social reality. Quantitative research methods (that use numbers) provide objective analysis via facts and figures that describe patterns and events in social life. Qualitative research strategies attempt to uncover the subjective nature of human behavior and social events via words and descriptions provided by the subjects themselves. Whereas quantitative research is quite structured and forces respondents to choose from predetermined answer choices, qualitative research questions are generally less structured and more flexible because they tend to be open-ended.

Although the vast majority of research conducted by social scientists is ethical, there are instances in which researchers have violated codes of ethical behavior as established within the discipline. The American Sociological Association's code of ethics is the basis for ethical decisions in sociological research.

Glossary

Announced participant observation—A research method that involves the **researcher** interacting with the group under study, informing the group of his or her purpose, and witnessing firsthand or participating in group activities.

Archival research—The analysis of existing data (usually old documents or oversized files) and other materials found in an archive.

Causal explanations—Direct connections between events that explain cause and effect.

Concepts—Mental images humans use to categorize experiences.

Content analysis—A type of methodology that can be applied to any form of written or oral communication through the systematic recording of instances (under study) on tally sheets.

Dependent variable—A measurable trait hypothesized to be influenced by the independent variable.

Experiment—A research methodology that involves the researcher manipulating the independent variable and measuring the dependent variable to discover the relationship between the two.

Hypothesis—An untested statement that attempts to predict the relationship between variables and renders itself testable for validity.

Independent variable—A measurable trait hypothesized to cause or influence another variable.

Logical reasoning—The search for causes of human behavior and social events.

Nonparticipant observation—A research method that involves the researcher observing the group under study from such a distance that the group is unaware of his or her presence.

Observational research—Research that entails researchers focusing on a social situation and carefully and objectively recording key characteristics and events found in a specific setting.

Operationalization—The specification of the various steps and procedures that the researcher will go through while conducting research.

Qualitative research—Research involving the use of methods that provide a subjective descriptive analysis of human behavior and social events.

Quantitative research—Research involving the use of methods that provide facts and figures describing patterns and events in social life.

Reliability—The achievement of consistent results when a variable is tested repeatedly.

Research model—A step-by-step protocol that typically guides sociological research.

Survey research—Research that involves taking a sample (a subset) of a population and administering a questionnaire or interview as a means of collecting data.

Triangulation—The practice of using more than one research method during the course of a study.

Unannounced participant observation—A research method that involves the researcher interacting with a specific group without informing its members that they are being studied.

Unobtrusive research—An indirect form of observation that examines physical traces left behind by participants. There are two primary categories of unobtrusive measures: erosion and accretion.

Validity—The degree that a finding, or measurement, of a concept accurately reflects the phenomenon under study.

Variables—Measurable traits or characteristics that are subject to change under different situations; similar to concepts.

Discussion Questions

1. If you were going to study gang behavior, what type of research methodology(s) would you use? Explain.
2. Explain the respective advantages and disadvantages of quantitative and qualitative research.
3. Are there limits to an investigator's responsibility for participants? What should these limits be?
4. Should confidentiality always be kept while conducting social research? What if the researcher witnesses criminal or unethical behavior conducted by group members under study. Should the researcher report it to the police?
5. How would you define the term "ethics"? What does ethical behavior mean to you? What is an example of unethical behavior?

Web Links

To learn more about fantasy sports, visit www.fantasysp.com and www.fantasysportsventures.com.

To view the full code of ethics, visit the ASA website at www.asanet.org/about/ethics.cfm.

To learn more about the Hippocratic oath, visit www.medword.com/hippocrates.html.

To view episodes of Ashton Kutcher's *Punk'd,* visit www.mtv.com/shows/punkd/series.jhtml.

4 CULTURE AND SOCIAL STRUCTURE

Although torn jeans have historically been associated with being poor, or with someone who performs hard labor, many young people pay a high price for such jeans as a fashion statement.

Chapter Four

- Introductory Story
- Defining Culture
- Material Culture
- The Allure of Popular Culture
- The Diversity of Culture
- Social Structure: Groups, Organizations, and Social Institutions
- Summary, Glossary, Discussion Questions, and Web Links

INTRODUCTORY STORY

Imagine that you are working as a clerk in a donut shop. One day, a would-be robber jumps over the counter and starts to take the cash out of your register. How would you react? Would you worry that the robber might have a gun or some other type of weapon? Would you freeze? Or panic and start yelling and running around?

Maybe you would react as one Dunkin' Donuts employee did: by fighting back and clobbering the man with a novelty mug. As first reported in the *Record* of Bergen County, New Jersey, the clerk (who happens to be named Dustin Hoffmann) was less concerned about his personal safety than he was about how he would look on the video-sharing site YouTube if the store's security tape was broadcast and subsequently appeared on this popular website. Hoffmann explained, "What was going through my mind at that point was that the security tape is either going to show me run away and hide in the office or whack this guy in the head, so I just grabbed the cup and clocked the guy pretty hard" (*Post-Standard,* 12/15/07).

That Hoffmann cared more about his image on YouTube than about his own personal safety says a great deal about contemporary culture. Advancements in technology, such as video-sharing websites, e-commerce (e.g., online shopping), e-banking, and the constant and public use of cell phones and text messaging, have altered many aspects of society. Technology represents just one important aspect of culture. It also happens to be a valued characteristic of society.

This chapter explains the meaning of culture and the elements of which it is composed, explores the differences between material and **nonmaterial culture** and between popular and high culture, and discusses the diversity of culture, including subcultures and countercultures. We also learn about the kinds of groups, organizations, and social institutions that make up society's structure.

DEFINING CULTURE

All societies comprise both culture and social structure. Analyzing culture and society's social structure is a cornerstone of sociology. After all, as we have seen in the preceding chapters, sociology is literally the "study of society." We examine society's social structure later in this chapter, so let us take a closer look at culture now.

Culture may be defined as the shared knowledge, values, norms, and behavioral patterns of a given society that are passed on from one generation to the next, forming a way of life for its members. Because culture is viewed as the set of ideas shared within society, it becomes the social determinant of behavior. That is, culture serves as a script for acceptable behavior—it gives order to life. Culture exists before we are born; consequently, we are born into a system filled with expectations. And because culture generally changes only in gradual increments, it provides social stability and social control. This last point is emphasized by the realization that culture does not change every time a child is born—that would be absurd. Abiding by the rules of culture generally garners rewards, while violating the cultural expectations may lead to punishments or sanctions.

This is not to say that culture cannot be changed but rather that in stable societies, change generally occurs slowly. For example, consider the role of technology in culture. Students, perhaps more than most members of society, use the latest technologies in communication. Cellular phones, in particular, help us keep in constant contact with significant others. The ubiquity of cell phones has seemingly revolutionized communication in the twenty-first century. There is a common perception, especially among younger people, that life without a cell phone and the ability to text friends and family members would be akin to going back to the Stone Age. However, communication studies professor Gary Krug argues that the greatest changes in communications took place in the nineteenth century, not the twentieth or twenty-first. As Krug (2005) explains: "In that earlier century and for the first time in human history, the message was commonly separate from the messenger, becoming electronic. The speed of the rider on horseback was superseded. The manufacture of books and papers became inexpensive enough to finally permeate the great masses of people in the industrializing world. Most of the basic forms of narrative, the semiotic conventions of images, and the large social relations formed between mass society and mass media appeared over 100 years ago" (p. 1).

As Krug indicates, technological change in communication has been a constant feature of society; it is not a radically new concept unique to today's culture. In other words, while technology changes society, advancements in technology are a constant feature of culture. Although some changes are more dramatic than others, many forms of change persist over generations and centuries. In every case, it is up to the members of society to either adapt to the cultural changes or risk lagging behind those who do.

You may have noticed the repeated use of the word "society" in relation to the description of culture thus far in this chapter. It is important to note that the terms "culture" and "society" are related but have different meanings. Whereas culture refers to a shared way of life, **society** pertains to a group of persons who interact with one another as members of a collectivity within a defined territory and a highly structured system of human organization. This system helps to shape the social structure of society.

What Do You Think?

The mass production of digital technology has provided people with access to wide ranging forms of information. Does digital technology simply create more quantity rather than quality of information? What do you think?

A society is the largest collection of people in group form. People within a society share a common heritage and culture. A society is viewed as a totality of social systems. Social systems include local communities, schools, business firms, kinship units, and so on. All societies are dependent upon the interchanges among and continuation of subsystems that serve as their foundations.

Symbols and Language

All members of a culture use a system of symbols and language to communicate with others in the same culture. Although today's society uses technologically advanced forms of communication, the use of symbols and language remains as the foundation.

Symbols: Successful communication is dependent upon a common understanding of gestures, symbols, and language. **Symbols** are items that possess meaning and represent something else to people in a society. (Note: Recall that in Chapter 2 we learned that symbols can have multiple and confusing meanings for people.) Realizing that the letters of an alphabet are merely symbols (that have meaning to people), we can say that symbols are the building blocks of language.

Symbols are so common in our culture that we take many of them for granted. Traffic signals are among the most obvious symbols that we take for granted. We do, however, become keenly aware of the importance of symbols when someone misinterprets them. For example, in baseball, it is common for a catcher to flash signals to the pitcher. Elementary signals include the index finger to indicate a fastball, two fingers for a curveball, and three fingers for change-up pitch. If a catcher flashes a sign for a fastball "down the middle" (directly over home plate) but the pitcher reads the sign as a pitch out (a ball thrown outside and away from the batter), the ball is going to sail out of the catcher's reach.

Gestures represent the most basic form of communication. A gesture occurs when a person uses limbs, body parts, or facial expressions to convey a thought. The upturned palm is one of the oldest and most widely understood signals in the world. It can symbolize a general request for help. A homeless person may hold out an upturned palm in hopes of receiving a donation from a passerby. A student using a computer only to have it mysteriously shut down may hold an upturned palm toward the computer as if to say, "What do you want from me?"

What Do You Think?

Most of us can identify any number of gestures with common meaning. For example, what gesture do you use for "Be silent"? Do you know a gesture to signal "Advance"? Can you think of other gestures common in your culture? What do you think?

Language: **Language** is an abstract set of symbols that can be strung together in an infinite number of ways to express ideas and thoughts. Some languages, such as English, are spoken nearly everywhere in the world, while others, such as many Native American languages, are far more localized and specific to their own cultures.

Within a given society, different dialects of the same language may be spoken. Anyone who has traveled around the United States has heard a variety of regional variations of American English. Regionalism—linguistic dialect specific to certain geographical areas—is just one aspect of variations in the same language found within one society. For example, if you greet your friends by saying, "Hi, guys," and wear "sneakers" to walk to the store to buy some "soda," chances are you live in the northeastern United States; if you greet your friends by saying, "Hello, y'all," and wear "tennis shoes" to walk to the store for some "coke," chances are you live in the southeastern United States.

Language tells us a good deal about what is important and relevant to a culture. For example, as technology alters the world in which people live, it also changes their perceptions, thoughts, and symbolic interpretations of the world (Krug 2005). Changes in technology, as well as changing cultural values, often lead to the creation of new words. This helps explain why hundreds of new words are added to dictionaries with every new edition (Pyle 2000).

If the total number of words spoken by a culture of people is an indication of changing cultural values and norms and technologies, then English-speaking people are quite dynamic. According to the Global Language Monitor (GLM), the English language, as of June 2009, contained over 1 million words. GLM estimates the millionth English word, "Web 2.0," was added to the language on June 10, 2009. Web 2.0 refers to the second, more social generation of the Internet (Shaer 2009). As with many new words, Web 2.0 is a product of the popular culture. For more examples of recent pop-culture words added to the English dictionary, see "Connecting Sociology and Popular Culture" Box 4.1.

The idea that language reflects the perceptions and observations of people was famously articulated by Edward Sapir and Benjamin Whorf, who both studied Native American languages and culture. Their linguistic relativity theory, known as the Sapir-Whorf hypothesis, suggests that language not only reflects but also helps to shape people's perceptions of reality. While working for the Hartford Fire Insurance Company, Whorf investigated insurance claims resulting from fire damage. He came to believe that the English language contributed (figuratively speaking) to some fires. Whorf learned that some of the fires he investigated were unintentionally started by people who lit matches near empty gasoline cans. The English word "empty" conjures the perception that the gasoline cans are safe because they contain no gasoline; in actuality, empty drums contain fumes, making them far more dangerous than full tanks of gasoline. In this regard, language leads people to interpret certain events from a cultural perspective. As we see later in this chapter, the use of language helps to shape subcultural interpretations of events as well.

Although Sapir and Whorf never tested their hypothesis empirically, most subsequent research in this area has supported the basic premise that language reflects the perceptions and observations of people (Deutscher 2010).

Beliefs, Norms, and Values

Beyond symbols and language, a culture is characterized by the way its members think, feel, and make judgments about the world around them. These patterns of thinking, feeling, and judging can be described as beliefs, norms, and values.

Beliefs and ideologies: **Beliefs** are mental acts that involve placing trust or confidence in another, a cause, or a condition. When we believe in something, we are

Connecting Sociology and Popular Culture

Box 4.1 The Ever-Changing Lexicon: Slang, Pop-Culture Words, and Buzzwords

Slang, or the language of popular culture, has existed for generations. Using the slang of a certain social group can help someone identify with that group, while using slang of another group, such as that of an older generation, can signal that the speaker is an outsider. Today most people chuckle at outdated slang expressions like "hep cat" and "the bee's knees." Slang words can also change their meaning: in the 1950s, a "flame" was the object of someone's romantic desire ("He brought his new flame to the party"); by the 1990s "flame" was a verb meaning to criticize someone harshly via e-mail or an online forum.

As various slang expressions die out, new ones are added; these contemporary terms are what we usually think of as pop-culture words. Numerous pop-culture words are added to the English lexicon annually. The following are recent additions:

IED: abbreviation for "improvised explosive device" of the kind that has become common in the wars in Iraq and Afghanistan
Bellig: belligerent and drunk
Bromance: a close "buddy" relationship between two or more heterosexual, often action-sports-participating males
Crunk: a style of southern rap music
Dudevorce: the end of a friendship between two males over a lame disagreement, usually concerning a girl
Epic fail: big mistake
FOMO: acronym for "fear of missing out"
Papi chulo: male friend; an attractive male who dresses well
Pleather: a plastic fabric made to look like leather
Telenovela: a Latin American soap opera

The terms "retweeting," "sexting" and "cyberbullying" were added to the *Concise Oxford English Dictionary* in 2011. Retweeting occurs when someone reposts or forwards a message posted by another user on a social-networking site such as Twitter. Sexting refers to sending sexually explicit text or photos to another person via a mobile phone. Cyberbullying involves, as the name implies, bullying, not face-to-face but instead by sending intimidating or threatening electronic communication via the Internet (C. Smith 2011).

Buzzwords may be considered a subset of pop-culture words, as they reflect changes in technology and are more akin to computer jargon. John Walston, author of *The Buzzword Dictionary* (2006), provides a large number of buzzwords used in society. He also established a buzzword website in 2000. The entries include the following:

404: a derogatory term used to describe someone who is completely clueless, derived from the computer error message "404 Not Found"
Connectile dysfunction: the inability to get a connection, especially a cell phone connection
Cyberslackers: employees who use the Internet during work hours to surf the Web
Jitterati: what the digital generation becomes after one too many cups of coffee

In 2011, the jargon expressions of LOL ("laugh out loud"), FYI ("for your information"), and OMG ("oh my God") were added to the *Oxford English Dictionary* (CNN.com 2011).

People who are interested in language often keep their eyes and ears open for new words and expressions; they may also keep lists of them and even try to invent new ones. From a sociological perspective, it is important to realize how the creation of new words reflects changes in cultural norms and values. Such is the power of language in a society.

What Do You Think?

What words do you and your friends use that are not found in a dictionary but should be? In what ways do these words reflect a change in values or norms in the culture you belong to? What do you think?

convinced of its truth, actuality, or validity. As a matter of illustration, imagine that the car you are driving breaks down at 3:00 a.m. and you phone your best friend for help. Sensing fear in your voice, your friend promises to pick you up in fifteen minutes. If you trust your friend to be there in fifteen minutes, you have a belief in the validity of your friend's promise. You also have a very good friend if he or she actually arrives in fifteen minutes at that hour of the morning.

When a number of similar beliefs, or tenets, are linked together at the cultural level, they may be transformed into a society's ideology. An **ideology** may be thought of as a body of ideas, or a doctrine, that reflects the social needs and aspirations of a society. This doctrine forms the basis of the socioeconomic and political social system of a society. As a result, a society's ideology justifies its social structure (e.g., the allocation of the fiscal budget). American culture is dominated by an ideology centered on representative democracy.

Norms: Although the creation of norms is based on abstract cultural ideals and beliefs, they constitute specific requirements of proper behavior. **Norms** are socially defined rules and expectations regarding human behavior. They are generally enforced by sanctions (punishments). Sociologists divide norms into three categories: folkways, mores, and laws.

Folkways are the conventional rules of everyday life that people follow almost automatically as they go about their ordinary activities. They constitute the most basic level of norms; they are enforced with informal sanctions, such as mild joking or ridicule, when they are violated. Folkways may be looked at as the basic mannerisms of a culture. For example, it is common courtesy (a norm expectation) to hold the door open for the person behind you. The sanction for violating this folkway may include the second person letting out a frustrated sigh or a dirty glance aimed toward the person who failed to hold the door open. Some sociologists argue that a rising "culture of shamelessness"—an increasing number of people engaging in behaviors that in the past would have brought the perpetrator embarrassment, shame, and a lower sense of self—is leading to the deterioration, or at the least an alteration, of basic etiquette in the everyday world (See "A Closer Look" Box 4.2). If this is true, we are likely to witness a great number of changes in folkway expectations.

Mores are more serious norms than folkways. They constitute the basic moral judgments of a society—so much so that they are viewed as essential to society's well-being and existence. Violating mores will result in much stronger sanctions. Such violations include committing murder, rape, incest, pedophilia, and cannibalism. The most serious of mores are transformed into laws.

Laws are norms that have been written down by a political authority; their breach entails designated punishments (sanctions) that officials (e.g., the police,

A Closer Look

Box 4.2 The "Culture of Shamelessness"

Is there a rising culture of shamelessness in the United States? That is, are people shamelessly engaging in behaviors today that in the past would have brought embarrassment, shame, and a lower sense of self? The culture of shamelessness is especially highlighted by the willingness of individuals to shame themselves.

People who shame themselves are, in effect, challenging the cultural norms of society. Self-shamers are telling the world that they are willing to engage in behaviors that society finds inappropriate, and they do not care about the possible negative consequences. Self-shaming generally creates a sense of excitement for the participants, and their need for thrills outweighs the value of attaining full acceptability within the greater community. As a result of this exhilaration, some self-shamers may actually enjoy a heightened sense of self (Delaney 2008a).

Many celebrities, including Miley Cyrus shown here, dress provocatively and are accused by some parents of setting a bad example for the kids who idolize them.

The MTV show *Jackass,* originally shown from 2000 to 2002, features Johnny Knoxville, Bam Margera, and others performing a variety of dangerous, asinine, sadomasochistic, and self-harming stunts and pranks in an effort to entertain an audience. Since 2002, two *Jackass* films have been released. Despite the fact that the majority of the population views the *Jackass* behavior of Knoxville and crew as shameful, if not ludicrous, these actors apparently do not experience shame. Knoxville and Margera are ambassadors for the growing culture of shamelessness as, while their behavior should not be emulated by others, they are laughing all the way to the bank.

In the growing culture of shamelessness, individuals are flashing skin more freely. Visitors to New York City's Times Square have no doubt come across the Naked Cowboy, a legendary figure who stands in the middle of Times Square wearing only underpants and cowboy boots while holding a guitar in an attempt to draw people's attention to himself. Celebrities such

judges, district attorneys, probation officers) have been empowered to enforce. Laws, then, are formal rules and principles governing the affairs of community members. The purpose of laws is to maintain social order and the common morality of society. "The law" may be viewed as a system of judicial administration consumed with legal action or proceedings. Further, because laws exist formally, they are easier to change than informal norms (folkways).

Values: Of these three aspects of culture, perhaps the most deeply rooted are **values:** the things we cherish and place importance on, that have worth. Examples

as Britney Spears, Lindsey Lohan, and Paris Hilton are photographed flashing body parts in an effort to gain publicity.

A growing number of college women and men are taking their clothes off in a less public arena at nude parties. Naked parties are a rage at many northeastern colleges, including such Ivy League colleges as Yale and Brown. Students at Brown University claim naked parties began there back in the 1980s. Since then, the idea has caught on and spread to Wesleyan, Wellesley, Columbia, the Massachusetts Institute of Technology, and Yale (Aviv 2007).

A great deal of shameless behavior occurs in cyberspace, especially via such social networks as Facebook, MySpace, Twitter, and YouTube. People who maintain sites on these social-mixer meeting places often display personal photos of themselves in "compromising" positions (e.g., sexually explicit or drunk photos). Sexting has also become quite popular in recent years, especially with younger people. Sexting involves sending naked, or near naked, photos of oneself to others via a text message. Based on research data compiled by Teenage Research Unlimited, 22 percent of teenage girls and 18 percent of teenage boys have taken nude or seminude photos of themselves and sent them to someone (O'Brien 2008). In addition, a third of young adults age twenty to twenty-six have sexted. Participants in sexting describe the behavior as a form of digital flirting.

Although sexting is meant as harmless fun, a number of potential legal problems arise when such behavior involves minors, including charging teens who send and receive such images with child pornography and possible felony obscenity charges. Prosecutors may also charge someone who receives a sext photo as a sex offender (*The Citizen*, 2/5/09).

Self-shaming fuels the culture of shamelessness. When people are willing to engage in behaviors previously labeled as shameful, there is seemingly little hope for those who cling to past notions of morality. And yet, maybe the growing culture of shamelessness merely reflects cultural social change in expected behavior.

What Do You Think?

I have utilized a wide variety of research methods to test the theory that there is a growing culture of shamelessness in society. Although these are described in the book *Shameful Behaviors* (2008), I purposely omitted that information from this "A Closer Look" box so that this question may be asked: of the six types of research methodologies available to sociologists (discussed in Chapter 3), which would you use to support or dispute the theory that there is a growing culture of shamelessness in society? What do you think?

of values in U.S. society would include success, equality, loyalty, and family. Some values, like keeping one's word or respecting human life, are relatively universal; others, like individualism or chastity, differ widely from one culture to another.

Public figures, such as entertainers and politicians, have always valued attention. But today an increasing number of people want the spotlight turned on them, if only for a brief period. In Chapter 1 we referred to artist Andy Warhol's idea that everyone will have fifteen minutes of fame. The increasing popularity of reality television shows—which place the focus on everyday people—stems in part from a culture that values fame and attention. There are people willing to embarrass themselves publicly on shows such as *The Jerry Springer Show* and *Maury,* even if it means exposing embarrassing moments in their private lives.

Nielson Media Research ratings indicate that the most-watched TV show in the United States in the years 2004 through 2011 was *American Idol.* From a sociological standpoint, *American Idol*'s popularity reveals a great deal about American values. On the one hand, we value people with talent who perform well under pressure and go on to become successful through hard work. On the other hand, we seem to find value in comparing ourselves to others with less talent than ourselves (see "Connecting Sociology and Popular Culture" Box 4.3).

MATERIAL CULTURE

Up to this point we have discussed aspects of culture that refer to abstract, intangible things a society creates. But what about a society's physical, tangible creations—its clothing, buildings, automobiles, electronic devices, and other merchandise? These cultural manifestations are known as **material culture**.

Throughout history, people of all cultures have possessed material items. Before the rise of consumerism, however, most people had relatively few material possessions, including such basic items as cooking and eating utensils, farming and gardening tools, weapons, clothing, simple furniture, and other household items. The era of consumerism, which developed as a consequence of the Industrial Revolution, vastly increased the average person's ability to acquire material possessions. The popular adage "Whoever dies with the most toys wins" is evidence of contemporary society's assumption that most people are driven to own as many material goods as possible.

According to this assumption, a young person joining the workforce and earning a modest salary will wish to possess a number of specific items (e.g., nice clothing, an automobile, home furnishings) that contribute to the comfort and convenience of everyday life. Once these basics are secured, he or she will move on to a desire for more and more "toys" (e.g., video games; big-screen, high-definition televisions; tickets to prized sporting events; exotic vacations). Thus, people's striving for success has created a culture predicated on materialism.

From a sociological perspective, it may be said that we desire material items because they have practical and cultural value and meaning. Unfortunately, many of us lack the money to purchase the material items we need or desire. As a result, we work. Some people go to college in hopes of finding a high-paying job, which in turn will allow them to purchase more material goods.

Counter to this theory, American sociologist Thorstein Veblen (1857–1929) argued that humans have an "instinct of workmanship"—a natural desire and

Materialism v. Workmanship

willingness to work. In his essay "The Instinct of Workmanship and the Irksomeness of Labor," Veblen described human physical weakness in comparison to the other animals of earth: "Man's great advantage over other species in the struggle for survival has been his superior facility in turning the forces of the environment to account" (1964, p. 80). Thus, in Veblen's view, the very survival of the human species has been contingent on workmanship; he believed that workmanship provides us with a sense of purpose in life and allows us to feel we have contributed to society in a positive manner.

Cubicle work settings are common for many people.

The importance of Veblen's instinct of workmanship is as relevant today as a century ago. Despite all the trappings afforded by a culture centered on conspicuous consumption and leisure, it would seem that the majority of people still have a sense of pride in workmanship. Workmanship itself is something to be emulated. And this is true among people of all social classes as all workers, regardless of their type of work, can take pride in a job well done.

A corollary of Veblen's argument is the idea that we all compare ourselves to others: we tend to show disdain toward those who do not engage in productive activity and to admire productive members of society. In Veblen's words, "Under the canon of conduct imposed by the instinct of workmanship, efficiency, serviceability, commends itself, and inefficiency or futility is odious. Man contemplates his own conduct and that of his neighbors, and passes a judgment of complacency or of dispraise.... Under the guidance of this taste for good work, men are compared with one another and with the accepted ideals of efficiency, and are rated and graded by the commonsense of their fellows according to a conventional scheme of merit and demerit" (1964, pp. 89–90).

If the premise is true that we like to compare levels of workmanship, it might be interesting to compare the number of hours worked on the job in a number of industrialized nations. Data provided in Table 4.1 reveal that in 1997, U.S. workers put in the largest annual number of hours per worker of the fourteen industrialized nations cited. In 2008, U.S. workers were no longer number one in this category, but they still ranked near the top. In 2008, the Netherlands had the lowest figure for average annual hours worked per worker. (It should be noted that figures among developing nations are not available.)

Although many sociologists downplay the validity of human instincts as a major influence on behavior, Veblen's theory of workmanship is applicable in explaining

Connecting Sociology and Popular Culture

Box 4.3 The Popularity of *American Idol*

First airing on June 11, 2002, *American Idol* has provided FOX Television with Top 5 ratings since its second season. It has been the number one show on television since its fifth season (2006). Using the simple format of a singing competition, the show attempts to discover the best young singer in the United States through a series of nationwide auditions. Because *American Idol* hopes to discover new talent, contestants are not allowed to have any current record deals or to be signed with any talent agency. So that its parent corporation (19 Entertainment) can profit from the would-be *Idol* winners, all contestants are required to sign over to19 Entertainment the exclusive right of refusal for the management and merchandising of their talent; they are also obligated to sign with 19 Entertainment's record company, Sony/BMG.

American Idol *is consistently one of the most popular shows on TV, and many other shows are spinoffs of the pop-culture phenomenon. Shown here are the original* Idol *judges, Randy Jackson, Paula Abdul, and Simon Cowell.*

During the early audition rounds, tens of thousands of *Idol* hopefuls will try out, first in front of preliminary judges and ultimately—if they are lucky—in front of the show's three primary judges. Hosted by DJ Ryan Seacrest, *Idol* has had a panel of three star judges for most of its run: Randy Jackson (record producer and bass player), Paula Abdul (popular recording artist), and Simon Cowell (producer and manager). In 2009 (Season 8), the show added a fourth judge, Kara DioGuardi (singer-songwriter). In 2010, Paula Abdul was replaced by comedian Ellen DeGeneres. In 2011, Cowell, DioGuardi, and DeGeneres left the show, leaving Randy Jackson as the sole original judge. Jackson was joined by singing legend Steven Tyler of Aerosmith and recording artist and actress Jennifer Lopez. The trio of Tyler, Lopez, and Jackson worked very well and contributed to the success of the show. Contestants that make it through the first round are invited to Hollywood for the semifinal round, where they go through a more rigorous screening. Eventually, the top twelve are determined. From that point on, singers are eliminated on a weekly basis until, eventually, a winner is

why people of all social classes value material goods. He realized that although many people dislike work and seek to avoid it in favor of leisure pursuits, engaging in conspicuous leisure and consuming products conspicuously becomes reputable because they are evidence of pecuniary strength (the ability to purchase material goods). Thus, pecuniary strength is both reputable and honorable because it presents itself as evi-

chosen. Although the judges determine who reaches the final round, the television viewing audience determines the next American Idol.

American Idol has proven to be as profitable as it is entertaining. 19 Entertainment has earned profits exceeding $100 million, FOX Television is winning the key demographic audience (eighteen to forty-nine), and the American public has been treated to great singing performances. Because we value being entertained by talented performers, many *Idol* contestants, such as Kelly Clarkson, Carrie Underwood, Clay Aiken, Chris Daughtry, and Taylor Hicks, have sold millions of units (CDs).

However, *American Idol* has also discovered that viewing audiences enjoy watching people with less talent make fools of themselves during the early round of tryouts. Many contestants clearly lack singing ability but audition for *Idol* anyway. They may actually think they have talent, may have been told by significant others that they do, or may merely be seeking their fifteen minutes of fame via a public shaming by the *American Idol* judges (Simon Cowell is known for his brutal assessments of contestants who lack singing talent).

Another aspect of American culture is revealed in the popular *Idol* show. Although we may find joy in the public humiliation of others, there comes a point at which we begin to feel sorry for a contestant who seems completely oblivious of his or her lack of talent and surprised by the resulting shaming. William Hung, for example, became an American cultural icon after his terrible rendition of Ricky Martin's "She Bangs." The judges ripped Hung, and Cowell stated, "You can't sing, you can't dance, so what do you want me to say?" Hung was the butt of comedians' jokes for weeks. *Saturday Night Live* lampooned him. Hung achieved his fifteen minutes of fame, though probably not in quite the way he had envisioned.

It would have been reasonable to assume that Hung would simply disappear from the American pop-culture consciousness after his failed audition. However, the public felt sorry for Hung. He started receiving e-mails from supportive fans. His video audition hit the Internet and turned him into a Web cult hero. The mainstream media became aware of his growing popularity, and before long he was appearing on talk shows, characterized as a "lovable loser." In September 2004, Hung threw out the first pitch at a Los Angeles Dodgers baseball game. And most shocking of all, Hung was offered a record deal from Koch Entertainment. His first album, "Inspiration," includes Ricky Martin's "She Bangs" and "Shake Your Bon Bon" and reached as high as number thirty-four in the charts. And although his next two albums—yes, two!—never reached the charts, he has sold nearly 300,000 units. Today, Hung enjoys his own website, and his merchandise can be found on eBay.

Since 2004, there seems to be an annual William Hung–type story in which some other untalented person achieves fame on *American Idol* because he or she cannot sing.

What Do You Think?

Do you agree that *American Idol* reflects some of the values of American society? Beyond the values described in this box, what other American values are displayed by this popular television show? Do you enjoy the opening round of *American Idol*? Why or why not? Or do you prefer the actual talent aspect of *American Idol*? What do you think?

dence of success and superiority. Industrial workers may find honor and demonstrate pecuniary strength through means of conspicuous consumption, but those able to engage in a life of leisure, free from working obligations, possess even greater pecuniary strength. Industrial workers engage in conspicuous consumption to demonstrate pecuniary strength even though they will never reach the elite level of the business

TABLE 4.1 Average Annual Hours Worked per Worker

COUNTRY	1997	2008
Australia	1,866	1,721
Canada	1,734	1,734
Denmark	1,688*	1,610
France	1,656	1,542
Germany	1,559	1,432
Ireland	1,656	1,601
Japan	1,889	1,772
Netherlands	1,679*	1,389
New Zealand	1,838	1,753
Norway	1,399	1,422
Sweden	1,552	1,625
Switzerland	1,643	1,643
United Kingdom	1,731	1,653
United States	1,966	1,792

*1997 data for Denmark and the Netherlands were only available for males. In 2008, Greece had the highest average annual hours worked per worker; however, 1997 data for Greece were not available, therefore Greece was not included in this table.

Source: 1997 data provided by the International Labour Office; see ILO News 1999. For 2008 data, see Organization for Economic Co-Operation and Development 2009.

owners. Furthermore, the continued consumption of physical comfort goods on the part of workers serves to increase further the profits of the business owners, resulting in an ever-increasing economic gap between the two groups.

The conspicuous consumption and conspicuous leisure that emerged in Veblen's era have been transformed into a consumer culture in the contemporary era. The "consumer revolution" represents a fundamental shift in the culture of modern society, as one can see from browsing through the photographs in Peter Menzel's 1995 book *Material World: A Global Family Portrait* (see p. xx). As anthropologist Grant McCracken (1990) explains, "The consumer goods on which the consumer lavishes time, attention, and income are charged with cultural meaning. Consumers use this meaning for entirely cultural purposes. They use the meaning of the consumer goods to express cultural categories and principles, cultivate ideals, create and sustain lifestyles, construct notions of the self, and create (and survive) social change. Consumption is thoroughly cultural in character" (p. xi). We tend to view our possessions as extensions of ourselves, of who we are (Belk 1988). As a result, the material objects found in any given society are "social communicators" of cultural values.

What Do You Think?

Industrial work—repetitive physical labor in factories—was much more common in the United States during Veblen's era than it is today. Has the instinct of workmanship been altered now that industrial jobs are less common? What do you think?

THE ALLURE OF POPULAR CULTURE

Beyond a description of the elements of culture and the material/nonmaterial distinction, culture can be divided into the categories of popular, folk, and high culture. Although manifestations of these three forms of culture can sometimes cross boundaries, they are also often at odds with one another.

Popular Culture

Popular culture is generally recognized as the vernacular or people's culture that predominates in society at a given time. Thus, it involves the aspects of social life in which the public is most actively involved. As the culture of the people, popular culture is determined by the interactions among people in their everyday activities: current clothing and hairstyling fashions and fads, the use of slang, greeting rituals, and the foods people eat are all examples of popular culture. Popular culture also involves aspects of the mass media—including television, film, music, cyberspace, sports, fads, advertising, news programming, and print publications—and the content presented by these media. With these descriptions in mind, **popular culture** may be defined as the items (products) and forms of expression and identity that are frequently encountered or widely accepted, commonly liked or approved, and characteristic of a particular society at a given time.

Pop. Culture – 'at a given time"

Popular culture allows large heterogeneous masses of people to identify collectively. It plays an inclusionary role in society as it unites people in terms of acceptable forms of behavior. Along with forging a sense of identity that binds individuals to the greater society, consuming pop-culture items often enhances individuals' prestige in their peer group. Further, popular culture, unlike folk or high culture, provides individuals with a chance to change the prevailing sentiments and norms of behavior. Thus, popular culture appeals to people because it provides opportunities for both individual happiness and communal bonding (Delaney 2007).

Sociologists examine the aspects of social life found in society, including the everyday activities of people. The relevance of popular culture to sociology helps to explain, in large part, the focus of this text in connecting sociology and popular culture.

High Culture

When people hear the word "culture," they often think of museums, libraries, theaters, concert halls and opera houses, and the works of the visual, literary, and performing arts that are offered in such venues. This association is not incorrect, but it refers to one form of culture: high culture. **High culture** is not mass-produced or meant for mass consumption. It belongs to the social elite; the fine arts, opera, theater, and high intellectualism are associated with members of the upper socioeconomic classes, who are presumed to have the extensive experience, training, or reflection required to appreciate items of high culture. Such items seldom cross into the pop-culture domain. Consequently, popular culture is often looked down upon as superficial compared to the sophistication of high culture. This does not mean, however, that social elites do not participate in popular culture or that members of the masses do not participate in high culture. For example, millions of people enjoy visiting art museums. See Table 4.2 for a listing of the most-visited art museums in the world.

What Do You Think?

Museums are generally considered within the domain of high culture, but if millions of people visit them, would that not qualify museums as "popular"? What do you think?

Folk Culture

The third type of culture, folk culture, is similar to pop culture because of the mass participation it embodies; it is also similar to high culture because it is often manifested in timeless, classic art forms. **Folk culture** represents the traditional way of doing things. Consequently, it is not as amenable to change and is much more static than popular culture.

Folk culture represents a simpler lifestyle that is generally conservative, largely self-sufficient, and often characteristic of rural life. It generally discourages radical innovation and expects group members to conform to traditional modes of behavior adopted by the community. Folk culture is local in orientation and noncommercial. In brief, folk culture promises stability, whereas popular culture is generally looking for something new or fresh.

Because of this, popular culture often represents an intrusion and a challenge to folk culture. At times, certain elements of folk culture (e.g., Turkish rugs, Mexican blankets, Irish fairy tales) find their way into the world of popular culture. Generally, when this happens, the folk items gradually lose their original form. For example, zoris are a traditional style of Japanese footwear consisting of a flat sole made of woven straw and a thong-shaped pair of straps running from between the big toe and second toe to the sides of the foot. You may recognize this description as applying to flip-flops or go-aheads, which became fashionable in the mid-2000s when manufacturers began to offer them in countless colors, materials, heel heights, and other variations, some of which are barely recognizable as deriving from the original zoris.

TABLE 4.2 World's Most-Visited Art Museums in 2008

MUSEUM	NUMBER OF VISITORS (MILLIONS)
Louvre (Paris)	8.5
British Museum (London)	5.9
National Gallery of Art (Washington, DC)	4.96
Tate Modern (London)	4.95
Metropolitan Museum of Art (New York City)	4.82

Source: USA Today 2009.

The Formation of Popular Culture

As described in Chapter 1, throughout most of human history before the political and industrial revolutions of the eighteenth century, the masses were influenced by dogmatic forms of rule and traditions dictated by leaders and local folk cultures. People were spread throughout small cities and rural areas—conditions that were not conducive to the quick spreading of fashions and fads inherent in popular culture. With the beginning of the industrial era, the rural masses began to migrate to cities, leading to the urbanization of most Western societies.

Urbanization is a key ingredient in the formation of popular culture. People who once lived in homogeneous small villages or farms found themselves in crowded cities marked by great cultural diversity. As historian J. M. Roberts (1996) observed, the city in the early days of industrialization was "a crucible of new social reforms and ideas," a place where people were free for the first time from the strong norms that restricted them when they lived in rural communities (p. 333). As they shared the urban environment, these diverse people would come to see themselves as a collectivity as a result of common, or popular, forms of expression. Thus, many scholars trace the beginning of the popular-culture phenomenon to the rise of the middle class brought on by the Industrial Revolution.

Industrialization also brought with it mass production; developments in transportation, such as the locomotive and the steamship; advancements in building technology; increased literacy; improvements in education and public health; and the emergence of efficient forms of commercial printing, representing the first step in the formation of a mass media (e.g., the penny press, magazines, and pamphlets). All these factors contributed to the blossoming of popular culture. By the mid-nineteenth century, mass-produced illustrated newspapers and weekly and monthly magazines were the best source of information for a public with a growing interest in social and economic affairs. The ideas expressed in print provided a starting point for popular discourse on all sorts of topics. Fueled by further technological growth, popular culture was greatly influenced by the emerging forms of mass media throughout the twentieth century. Films, broadcast radio, and television all had a profound influence on culture. By the late twentieth and early twenty-first centuries, the advancement of computer technology had led to many new forms of popular culture, especially those related to the Internet.

So, urbanization, industrialization, the mass media, and the continuous growth in technology since the late 1970s have all been significant factors in the formation of popular culture. These factors continue to shape it today.

The Role of Individualism

A seemingly contradictory source of popular culture is individualism. *Individualism* is a belief in the primary importance of the individual and in the virtues of self-reliance and personal independence. It is a doctrine that advocates for the individual's freedom from government regulation in the pursuit of economic goals. At the opposite end of the spectrum is collectivism, in which the goals and welfare of the group are valued more highly than those of individual group members.

Individualism encourages the development and expression of each person's unique character and personality. When a culture places a high value on the pursuit of personal happiness and independence, collective goals and interests may be compromised. Few nations in the world place such a high value on individualism as the United States (Hofstede 2001). Americans tend to believe that society exists for the benefit of individual people; this sentiment is popularly expressed by the statement, "You can't tell me what to do. I have rights. I'm an American."

Americans do indeed have individual rights in their homeland. However, such a belief system has a number of potential negative aspects. For example, in an article published in the *University of Chicago Chronicle,* William Harms (2007) claims that Americans are particularly challenged in their ability to understand someone else's point of view because they are part of a culture that encourages individualism. In contrast, Harms suggests, Chinese people, who live in a society that encourages a collectivist attitude among its members, are much more adept at determining another person's perspective.

Psychologists Boaz Keysar and Shali Wu (Harms 2007) conducted an experiment wherein they established two groups of students from the University of Chicago: one consisting of twenty people from China and another consisting of twenty non-Asian Americans. The researchers hypothesized that interdependence would aid people in focusing on others and away from themselves. To test their hypothesis, they conducted games that involved taking the perspective of one's partner. The Chinese subjects proved so adept at perspective taking that they completed their tasks twice as fast as the American group. Keysar and Wu found that the American group was significantly slower at the task because many of them failed to consider their partner's perspective at least once during the experiment. The researchers also concluded that the interdependence that pervades Chinese culture has such an effect on individual members that they more easily take into account the perspectives of others (Harms 2007).

Collective participation is a major ingredient in popular culture. However, the role of individualism is also important as the very premise of individual rights encourages creativity and new ways of thinking. Individuals are encouraged to express themselves and to think outside the box. Theoretically, there are no limitations to what an individual may think, express, and accomplish. Furthermore, individuals may choose to participate in all that is popular for popularity's sake, or they may choose a course of action off the beaten track. Freethinking people, or "pathfinders," can affect popular culture by their creative thinking, action, and embrace of the concept of individuality. Inevitably, of course, once a unique style becomes adopted by others, it ceases to be unique: it becomes popular.

Opinion Leaders

> **What Do You Think?**
>
> As an individual, you can choose to go with the flow, or you can choose to set your own course in life. Do you suppose that you will be a pathfinder and influence popular culture during your lifetime, or will you follow others? What do you think?

The role of individualism as an influence on popular culture is exemplified by another form as well, namely, opinion leaders. The concept of opinion leaders was first formulated by sociologists Elihu Katz and Paul Lazarsfeld (1955) in their analysis of the flow of mass communications. Katz and Lazarsfeld (1955) defined opinion leaders as "individuals who were likely to influence other persons in their immediate environment" (p. 3). The contemporary definition of **opinion leaders**—as individuals who serve as a type of role model for, and exert a great deal of influence over, others—has only been slightly modified from the original. Opinion leaders are not leaders in the usual sense because they do not head formal organizations; nor are they public figures such as newspaper columnists, critics, or media personalities, whose influence is exerted indirectly via organized media or authority structures. Instead, their influence is direct and derives from their informal status as highly informed, respected, or connected individuals (Watts and Dodds 2007).

Katz and Lazarsfeld argued that opinion leaders, who are few in total number, act as intermediaries between the mass media and the majority of society. Opinion leaders—such as town residents who frequently write letters to the editor of the local newspaper—have a way of influencing the beliefs and attitudes of others in such a manner that they stimulate behavioral change among their cohorts. Marketing companies and politicians often seek the endorsement of opinion leaders as a means of communicating their product or message to the public. For example, an apparel manufacturer may look to female celebrities as opinion leaders and offer them free samples of garments in exchange for their wearing them in a photo shoot. A testimonial from an opinion leader can have great influence over others. A testimonial from an opinion leader in the field of medicine, for example, can hold great sway in the field of pharmaceuticals as this person's endorsement of a product can represent huge sales increases.

THE DIVERSITY OF CULTURE

Cultures vary a great deal, and each is unique in several ways. The diversity of culture results from each society's adaptation to its specific natural environment (e.g., climate and geography) and the traditional customs, habits, values, and norms that develop over time in that culture, forming a way of life for its people. Some nations, such as Japan, Saudi Arabia, and Sweden, are referred to as homogeneous societies because they consist mainly of people who share a common culture and generally come from similar social, religious, political, and economic backgrounds. On the other hand, some nations, such as the United States and Canada, are heterogeneous societies because they consist of people who are dissimilar in regard to social characteristics such as religion, race and ethnicity, political orientation, and economic background.

Many people embrace cultural diversity because they enjoy certain aspects of cultures different from that to which they are most accustomed. For example, a person raised in an Italian American household may enjoy Chinese cuisine, European clothing, and Latin music. Sociologists use the term "cultural borrowing" to describe the phenomenon of the spread of material and nonmaterial culture from one society to the next. Cultural change takes place in a society through the discovery and invention of new objects and ideas and through the normalization of aspects of different cultures. However, all people of a given society do not accept social change at the same pace. Sociologists use the term "cultural lag" to describe this failure to keep up with significant changes in society. People who visit or move to a foreign country may experience anxiety or feelings of surprise, disorientation, and uncertainty because the norms and values of that culture are so different from those they are accustomed to; sociologists refer to this phenomenon as culture shock.

In this photo, cultural diversity is demonstrated from a technological standpoint, as these two people rely on a horse-drawn carriage for transportation and yet they recognize the value of computers.

At times diversity in cultural viewpoints may also lead to tension and conflict, as behaviors deemed acceptable in one culture may not be perceived as such in another. For example, American actor Richard Gere caused a scandal in India when he kissed Indian film star Shilpa Shetty on the cheek at a 2007 press conference for an HIV/AIDS prevention program. Not only did angry citizens burn Gere in effigy, but the Indian government issued an arrest warrant for both him and Shetty on obscenity charges (BBC News 2007).

Such tension and conflict may be a result of ethnocentric thinking. **Ethnocentrism** is the tendency for members of a society to use their culture's norms and values as standards for judging other cultures or to believe that their culture is "right" and others are "wrong." Ethnocentrism is not inherently a bad thing: it allows people to feel proud of their heritage and who they are; it also reinforces social stability and promotes group loyalty and solidarity. For example, Irish Americans who celebrate St. Patrick's Day and Mexican Americans who celebrate Cinco de Mayo are expressing positive aspects of ethnocentrism. However, ethnocentrism may also block cooperation among groups and societies and sometimes stimulates people to feel superior to others because they believe theirs is the "best" culture.

Disparity in cultural ideals rooted in ethnocentrism may lead to conflict and, in extreme cases, war (see "A Closer Look" Box 4.4 for a specific example of cultural ideals that clash). Violent ethnic conflicts are all too common all over the world; consider events in Bosnia and other parts of the former Yugoslavia, in Rwanda, in Sudan's western Darfur region and the country's southern provinces, and between Catholics and Protestants in Northern Ireland. Ethnocentrism has also been a contributing factor to incidents of vandalism and other violence against Islamic mosques and individual Muslim citizens in the United States.

A Closer Look

Box 4.4 Cruel and Unusual Cultural Customs?

Differences in cultural traditions contributed to conflict among a group of hunters in Wisconsin after a Hmong immigrant hunter was accused of trespassing on private land. During the November 2004 hunting season, a group of deer hunters in Birchwood, Wisconsin, were surprised to find a trespasser, Chai Vang, in their tree stand. After being asked to leave, Vang opened fire on the hunters with his semiautomatic assault rifle, killing six and wounding three others. Vang claimed that he felt threatened by the group of white hunters. Clashes between white hunters and Hmong refugees from Laos have occurred before in the Birchwood area, but never with such deadly consequences. Cultural differences—the Hmong do not understand the concept of private property, which is customary in the United States, and therefore hunt wherever they see fit—were deemed the primary reason for the dispute (*Post-Standard*, 11/23/04). Vang was later convicted of six counts of first-degree, intentional homicide and three counts of attempted homicide.

Most immigrants bring with them customs from their old country. (Note: My immigrant ancestors certainly brought with them the customs of their homeland.) As was the case with Chai Vang, these old customs can come into conflict with the culture of the new country. In another example, a Mexican couple living in California disciplined their son via an ancient method passed down from their sixteenth-century Aztec ancestors. They held a hot chili under their son's nose until the pungent smoke scorched his sinuses. This form of corporal punishment, like most others, is generally frowned on in American culture and, in this instance, led to a social worker (who discovered the incident) to declare such discipline "cruel and unusual" punishment (Gurza 2000). Corporal punishment (physical punishment, such as flogging, whipping, and spanking, inflicted on an offender's body) was once common in the United States for adults as well as children, but changes in cultural ideals have led to a major decline in this type of discipline.

What Do You Think?

Do you think the Mexican couple described above was justified in the form of discipline used? Were you spanked for misbehaving when you were young? How did that make you feel? If you have children, do you think you will spank them when they misbehave? Why or why not? How should children who misbehave be punished? What do you think?

Taking into account the fact that cultural norms, values, and beliefs may vary within any given society, it should not come as a surprise that radically different ideals of cultural expectations exist throughout the world.

Consider the differences between Amsterdam, the largest city in the Netherlands, and Riyadh, the capital of Saudi Arabia. In Amsterdam, "coffee shops" sell marijuana and hashish and provide a place for patrons to smoke these products openly. Prostitutes, whose trade is legal, lounge in storefront windows under soft neon lights displaying their "goods" for would-be buyers in the famous Red Light District. Under Dutch law, same-sex marriages are recognized and carry the same legal rights as intersex marriages; euthanasia, under strict guidelines, is also allowed.

Window shopping takes on an entirely different meaning in Amsterdam's "Red Light District," where prostitution is open and legal.

In Saudi Arabia, on the other hand, the law forbids the use of not only drugs but also alcohol. In contrast to the freedom of religion that has existed in the Netherlands for centuries, only one religion is practiced in Riyadh: Islam. The Saudi religious police—the Committee for the Propagation of Virtue and Prevention of Vice—enforce a strict code of morality. This code not only forbids prostitution but also restricts what many would consider the rights of women to enjoy pursuits such as sitting next to a man who is not a relative at a movie theater or chatting with a man over a cup of coffee (Shahzad 2003). It also forbids the sale of Barbie dolls because they are considered a threat to morality. The revealing clothes of the "Jewish" toy (the Barbie doll) are deemed offensive to Islam (*USA Today,* 9/10/03). (Note: A spokesperson for the Committee for the Propagation of Virtue and Prevention of Vice claims that Barbie was modeled after a real-life Jewish woman.)

In light of the great diversity of culture that exists throughout the world, we might wonder if the notion of a global civil society can ever be realized. Cultural globalization may exist in forms of transportation, commerce, and communications, but is it possible for a true global community to exist? On the positive side, Lipschutz (2005) suggests that globalized activism is more prevalent today than ever before in human history. And yet, intolerance, discrimination, and prejudice continue to plague humanity. (Note: Intolerance, discrimination, and prejudice are discussed in Chapter 8.)

What Do You Think?

Would you have an easier time adapting to the cultural norms found in Amsterdam or Riyadh? Should the United States adopt any of above described cultural norms found in Riyadh or Amsterdam? What do you think?

Subcultures and Countercultures

Differences in cultural values, norms, and beliefs contribute to the formation of subcultures and countercultures. Subcultural participation allows people who share certain cultural values and norms that contrast with those of the prevailing culture to feel as though they are part of group. Countercultures are formed when people feel that the prevailing norms and values of society need to be dramatically altered.

Subcultures: A **subculture** is a culture within a culture consisting of a category of people who share a distinctive set of cultural beliefs and behaviors that distinguish them from the larger society. Members of a subculture generally agree with most of the cultural aspects of the greater society but share a key characteristic that provides them with a sense of identity. Among the many examples of subcultures are students, bodybuilders, rodeo clowns, runway models, gang members, Goths, and surfers.

Sharing a love for riding waves and sustaining the ocean helps these surfers form a very distinctive subculture.

Members of a subculture identify one another in a number of ways, such as by style of clothing, mannerisms, accessories, and language. It is as easy to point out a Goth as a surfer dude because of all these characteristics. Goths wear layers of dark clothes; surfers wear colorful shorts and tank tops. Goths like to wear emblems that convey the "dark side"; surfers like to wear shells and shark teeth. As described earlier in this chapter, language is an important aspect of culture. Language is especially important for subcultures as group members like to create their own unique form of communication. An interesting point about subcultural language is that it often catches on with the larger society. For example, everyone knows what the surfer terms "stoked" (excited) and "wipeout" (crash) mean; they have become part of the mainstream.

Countercultures: A **counterculture** has norms, values, and beliefs that consciously oppose the dominant culture. Counterculture groups seek societal change. Depending on one's perspective, countercultures may be viewed as positive (e.g., civil rights movements) or negative (e.g., extremist hate groups). When a large segment of a population embraces a counterculture, it may be transformed into a social

What Do You Think?

There are literally thousands of subcultures in Western societies such as the United States and Canada. How many subcultures do you belong to? What do you think?

movement. In this regard, a plurality of individuals, groups, or organizations possess a shared collective identity in pursuing a cause and seeking to reach goals. These goals differ from those of the prevailing, existing culture.

Ken Goffman (2004) summarizes the primary characteristics of a counterculture:

1. Countercultures assign primacy to individuality at the expense of social conventions and governmental constraints.
2. Countercultures challenge authoritarianism in both obvious and subtle forms.
3. Countercultures embrace individual and social change. (p. 29)

Countercultures were especially prevalent during the 1960s in the United States when people reacted against the social norms of the 1950s (i.e., respect for authority, racial segregation, and discrimination against women). Beginning in 1964, students across the United States began to stage demonstrations opposing the Vietnam War; over the next several years, these demonstrations continued to gain such momentum that people began to be identified with either support for the war (dominant culture) or opposition to it (counterculture). Around the same time, court decisions mandating desegregation in schools and other public places led to boycotts and other demonstrations by African Americans against Jim Crow laws; as with the antiwar movement, the civil rights movement became a means of identification for many people, white as well as black. Women also began to stage demonstrations for equal rights, or "women's liberation," as it was known at the time. Being a feminist was another way of belonging to a counterculture. Finally, individuals who rejected the entire idea of a consumer-oriented society became known as hippies and experimented with drugs as a means of challenging the traditional ethos of authority.

Successful countercultures manage to transform society in a lasting manner by eventually becoming mainstreamed into the prevailing social system. A cursory glance at U.S. history in the 1970s shows that the United States pulled out of Vietnam, Jim Crow laws were almost universally repealed, and equal opportunities for women and minorities in the workplace were mandated. Had the above countercultures not existed, these social changes might not have taken place when they did.

The prevalence of countercultures during the 1960s was reflected in many forms of popular culture, including the film industry. And although the 1950s witnessed a few classic counterculture films that remain popular today (e.g., *The Wild One* [1953]; *Rebel Without a Cause* [1955]), movies like *The Misfits* (1961), *Scorpion Rising* (1963), *Magical Mystery Tour* (1967), *Barbarella* (1968), *Alice's*

Restaurant (1969), and *Easy Rider* (1969) brought the counterculture film industry the greatest notoriety. The popularity of this genre would continue throughout the 1970s with such classics as *Woodstock* (1970), *A Clockwork Orange* (1971), *Billy Jack* (1971), *Serpico* (1973), *Dog Day Afternoon* (1975), *Up in Smoke* (1978), and *Apocalypse Now* (1979). The 1980s brought us such counterculture films as *Altered States* (1980), *Platoon* (1976), and *Drugstore Cowboy* (1989). Though fewer counterculture films were produced in the 1990s and 2000s, the trend continued with *The Doors* (1991), *Smoke* (1995), *Fight Club* (1999), *Boondock Saints* (1999), *Requiem for a Dream,* (2000), *V for Vendetta* (2006), and *Grindhouse* (2007). Each of these films contains, of course, subject matter that challenges the prevailing norms and values of society, which is why they are characterized as counterculture films (see "Connecting Sociology and Popular Culture" Box 4.5 for a closer look at the sociological significance of counterculture films like *Fight Club,* starring Brad Pitt, Edward Norton, and Helena Bonham Carter).

Why are we discussing movies at such length? It has been pretty well established at this point in the text that sociologists study human behavior. In an overly simplistic summation, macrosociologists look at the big picture and examine how social systems and institutions operate, while microsociologists look at the everyday behaviors of individuals and groups. Although no sociologist examines every aspect of social life (every sociologist has his or her own bias as to what constitutes a worthy study), there is always at least one sociologist examining every aspect of culture. With this in mind, the study of movies is inherently sociologically significant. Macrosociologists will examine, among other things, trends in movie viewing and analyze the industry with regard to the way gays, women, and minorities are portrayed in film. Microsociologists will find individual viewing habits of greater interest because they provide insights into the personalities of individuals.

If you ask someone you recently met the simple question, What type of movies do you like? you can gain a great deal of information about that person's general beliefs and outlook on life. For example, some people like action films, others like comedy, and still others enjoy romance. A sociologist would want to know why certain people enjoy specific genres. Of equal interest, perhaps, are the people who do not enjoy watching movies of any kind. Why would someone not like to watch a movie, any movie, when there exists a nearly endless supply of films? The answer may be sociologically significant.

The study of movies has sociological merit for other reasons as well. For instance, movies represent an integral aspect of popular culture. Movies also often reflect the prevailing sentiments of society. During wartime, for example, it is common for Hollywood to produce hero-based war movies where the good guys always win, albeit after great struggle and sacrifice. On the other hand, a number

Connecting Sociology and Popular Culture

Box 4.5 *Fight Club* and the Sociological Significance of Counterculture Movies

Fight Club, based on the novel of the same title by Chuck Palahniuk (1995), opened to mostly bad reviews and a lackluster box office in 1999, but since then it has become one of the biggest DVD hits of all time. As with all films based on a novel, there are a number of differences between the two. But the basic plot remains fairly consistent.

In the film, the narrator, a "recall cocoordinator" for a major car company, suffers from a bout of insomnia and starts to attend support group meetings as a means of releasing emotional stress. While returning from a business trip, he meets Tyler Durden (Brad Pitt), a fellow frequent business traveler who happens to be a salesperson. (Note: The true meaning of the narrator's "meeting" Tyler is revealed later in the film.) The two exchange pleasantries and head to their separate homes. Much to his chagrin, the narrator discovers that his apartment has exploded, and he now has no place to go. Reaching into his pocket, he grabs a business card with Tyler's phone number on it in hopes of crashing with his new acquaintance.

Later, the narrator and Tyler bond over a discussion centered on disdain for materialism and the modern male (they believe males have become too feminized in contemporary society). Then, Tyler surprises the narrator by asking him to punch him, at which point the two realize that they enjoy the therapeutic physical release that fighting provides. (The enjoyment of random brawling is a counterculture behavioral attitude.) The narrator moves in with Tyler, and the two fight each other on the streets regularly. One night, as a number of people stand around watching them fight, one onlooker asks to be next. Before long, the growing interest in street brawling leads Tyler and the narrator to form a fight club, which grows so quickly that Tyler, a psychotic anarchist with bomb-making skills, decides to form an army of men who share his antimaterialistic views.

As is the case with growing counterculture movements, Tyler decides to establish a number of Fight Club rules:

> You do not talk about FIGHT CLUB.
> You DO NOT talk about FIGHT CLUB.

of movies are produced to appeal to an undercurrent in the population that seeks to challenge and change prevailing norms, values, and attitudes. Counterculture films reflect this social discontent.

SOCIAL STRUCTURE: GROUPS, ORGANIZATIONS, AND SOCIAL INSTITUTIONS

As pointed out at the beginning of this chapter, all societies have a culture and a social structure. We have learned that culture plays an important role in people's lives; this is also true of social structure. A society's **social structure** consists of its prevailing social organization—the groups to which people belong—and its prevailing social arrangements, or institutions.

If someone yells, "Stop," the fight is over.
Only two guys to a fight.
One fight at a time.
No shirts, no shoes.
Fights will go on as long as they have to.
If this is your first night at FIGHT CLUB, you HAVE to fight.

Many of these rules have become a part of popular culture. The rules in the film are symbolic of countercultures themselves, as the bigger any counterculture becomes, the greater its need for organization also becomes. The 1960s countercultures that stood against war and for equal rights for women and minorities shifted from radical fringe participation to mainstream acceptance.

The Fight Club quickly evolves into "Project Mayhem," with Tyler giving homework assignments to his followers. The first assignment mandates that each member pick a fight with a stranger and then let the stranger win. Tyler's followers obey his every command. He soon assigns his followers tasks that involve random acts of violence and destruction toward corporations. At the conclusion of the film, Tyler's army has planted bombs in eleven financial buildings. It is Tyler's goal to destroy the credit card financial industry. He reasons that if credit card debt is erased, then regular people win, and corporations lose. Such a scenario makes one wonder, How many counterculture groups are out there? Are they as dangerous as "Project Mayhem"? Or will counterculture groups yet to be formed stimulate positive change in society?

As for *Fight Club,* the rebel message behind the film has also become mainstream and materialistic as the 2000s witnessed numerous men's and women's fight clubs springing up across the country. In addition, a *Fight Club* video game was released in 2004, and a *Fight Club* musical has been in development for years.

What Do You Think?

In order for a counterculture ultimately to reach its goal of changing cultural norms and values, it must become popularized. Once it has become popularized and accepted by the mainstream, does it cease to be a counterculture? Can you identify current counterculture movements that seem likely to become accepted by mainstream society? What do you think?

As Juette and Berger (2008) explain, "Sociologists use the concept of social structure to refer to patterns of social interaction and relationships that endure over time and that enable and/or constrain people's choices and opportunities. Social structure is, in a sense, external to individuals insofar as it is not of their own making and exists prior to their engagement with the world" (p. 4). However, these authors go on to point out that "people are not mere dupes or passive recipients of social structures; they are thinking, self-reflexive beings who are capable of assessing their circumstances, choosing among alternative courses of action, and consequently shaping their own behavior" (p. 7).

As thinking humans, we possess free will and are capable of choosing from a wide variety of courses of action. However, our choices are influenced by our social group memberships and the institutions of the social structure in which we live.

Groups, Aggregates, and Categories

Most species gather in groups. Geese fly in flocks, fish swim in schools, wild dogs and hyenas run in packs, and chimpanzees live in societies made up of groups and affiliated cliques. Humans also form groups and have done so throughout history for safety and basic survival. In contemporary society, social interaction continues to play an important role in an individual's life. Everyone wants to feel part of a group or community (Maslow 1954). Individuals want to experience a sense of unity with their fellows. By joining together in groups, individuals become a part of a whole. The group provides them with an identity because of their membership. Individual personalities allow for the maintenance of self-identity.

Although it might be tempting to think of any gathering of people as a group, that would be a mistake, as certain parameters create a distinction between groups, aggregates, and categories. A **social group** is defined as two or more people who interact regularly and in a manner defined by some common purpose, a set of norms, and a structure of statuses and roles (social positions). Two general requirements must be met for a number of people to qualify as a group: (1) they must interact with one another in an organized fashion, and (2) they must identify themselves as group members because of shared views, goals, traits, or circumstances. Core members of a street gang would qualify as a social group, for example. Gang members identify one another based on such qualities as wearing certain colors and clothing, tattoos, hand signals, language, jewelry, and the use of graffiti. And when they congregate, they do so for one or more reasons.

An aggregate, on the other hand, consists of a number of people who happen to be clustered in one place at a given time—for example, at a bus stop, train station, airport, sporting event, or movie theater. Although aggregates are simply a collection of people who happen to be in a specific place at a specific time, these people do share a purpose. For example, people standing in line to buy a movie ticket comprise an aggregate; they have not met for a random purpose but have a common reason for being there.

A **category** includes a number of people who share a particular attribute but who may have never met. Examples of categories of people include all oldest daughters, all left-handers, Democrats, Republicans, football fans, and so on.

> **What Do You Think?**
>
> How would you describe the collection of people in your classroom? Do they form a group, aggregate, or category? What do you think?

Group dynamics: There are a number of dynamic influences on social groups beginning with the size of the group itself. The definition of a group places a minimum requirement of at least two persons. It may seem odd that two people would qualify as group, but that is the case because of the work of

German sociologist Georg Simmel, who coined the terms "dyad" and "triad." A **dyad** is a two-person group, and a **triad** is a three-person group. Simmel argued that the simple addition of one more person to a two-person group changes the dynamics radically. In a dyad, each member retains an equal level of individuality and decision-making power (at least theoretically). The dyad is characterized by direct and immediate reciprocity, and each member is dependent on the other for group decisions. Furthermore, if one member of a dyad withdraws or chooses to leave the group (as in the case of a romantic breakup), it will dissolve.

The addition of a third person to a dyad causes radical and fundamental changes to the group structure. In simplest terms, a third person can

- take the role of a nonpartisan arbitrator or mediator to settle or mediate disputes among the original two (such as a marriage counselor who is trying to help a married couple keep their marriage intact);
- deliberately seek to cause disputes between the other two in order to gain an advantage or superiority (divide and conquer);
- become the object of competition between the other two (an effect known as *tertius gaudens,* Latin for "third who enjoys").

Another group dynamic that interests sociologists is the distinction between primary and secondary groups. American sociologist Charles Horton Cooley described **primary groups** as characterized by intimate, face-to-face association and cooperation. Members of a primary group share a sense of "we-ness" involving the sort of sympathy and mutual identification for which saying "we" (as in, "We always get together for the holidays") is a natural expression. It is the "we" feeling that helps to create a bond characterized by group loyalty. Most people will belong to a number of small primary groups. We are born into a family, then form playgroups during childhood, and later form cliques of primary association. In adulthood, many people will form their own family groups; they will also belong to work groups and leisure groups. Through these associations, individuals develop a sense of self.

Secondary groups encompass the relatively impersonal relationships we have with others. In secondary groups there is little social intimacy or mutual understanding among the members. Secondary groups are larger and more anonymous than primary groups. Membership in secondary groups is based on some common interest or activity that brings people together to interact. Members of a college class, for example, would constitute a secondary group. Most work colleagues have a secondary-group relationship with each other. A cashier and regular shoppers have a secondary-group relationship.

A group is also influenced by its type of leader. In simplest terms, groups have two types of leader (Cartwright and Zander 1968): the instrumental (task-oriented) leader and the expressive (emotional) leader. The *instrumental leader* is consumed with achieving goals and attempts to keep group members focused and on target toward achieving the desired ends. The effective instrumental leader possesses critical-thinking and problem-solving skills and is a skilled communicator. Instrumental leaders generally adopt an authoritarian style of leadership because they feel the need to keep everyone in line. The *expressive leader* focuses on maintaining harmony among members. Such a leader shows concern for members' feelings and works to ensure that everyone stays satisfied and happy. In this regard, expressive leaders tend to adopt a laissez-faire style of leadership. An expressive leader is also more likely than an instrumental leader to adopt a democratic leadership style, which encourages input from group members. Because the instrumental leader possesses an authoritarian leadership style, he or she is less likely to incorporate input from others.

Group cohesion, another dynamic of social groups, refers to the sense of solidarity among group members. Both expressive and instrumental leaders value group cohesion, but for different reasons. The expressive leader values group cohesion because of his or her desire to have all group members get along and look forward to working on projects together. The instrumental leader, on the other hand, values group cohesion because he or she believes this is an effective component of keeping group members focused on the group's goals. To this end, the instrumental leader is much more concerned about group conformity. Because these group members understand the need for conformity and its value, they tend to overcomply to the point where they take on a groupthink mentality.

As described by sociologist Irving Janis (1972, 1982), *groupthink* refers to the phenomenon of group members keeping their own opinions and ideas to themselves rather than expressing them to the group. They will do this even when they know that their private ideas are better than those expressed. Groupthink occurs when group members feel pressure to overconform.

ascribed Status- born in to it

Social positions: Within groups, individuals may occupy any of several **social positions**, referred to by sociologists as statuses. There are two types of social status: ascribed status and achieved status. An **ascribed status** is any status a person receives through birth. Illustrations include one's race or ethnicity, ancestry, and gender. Because ascribed statuses are assigned to us at birth, we cannot generally alter them. An **achieved status** is any status that a person attains or earns through individual effort, choice, or competition. There are far more examples of achieved status than ascribed status. College graduate, professional athlete, teacher, bowling league champion, nurse, priest, and restaurant owner are just a few examples of achieved statuses.

Everyone possesses many social positions, or social statuses, and with specific social positions come corresponding expectations of behavior. Sociologists refer to such cultural expectations as **roles**. A social role may be defined as entailing culturally determined rights, duties, and expectations associated with specific social positions. The role of a college student involves attending class, reading assigned materials, participating in class discussions, completing assignments (e.g., tests, term papers), attending school events, and representing the college in a positive manner within the greater community. A college student, of course, holds many other social statuses simultaneously. These other positions may include being a son or daughter, a sibling, a parent, an employee, a friend, an athlete, and so on.

Holding many statuses at any given time may lead to role conflict, a stressful situation that occurs when opposing expectations are attached to different statuses held by the same person. For example, a college student-athlete may experience role conflict when she is expected to attend an extra practice session at the same time as a test is scheduled for one of her academic classes. This student-athlete will experience additional role conflict if she is suddenly called into work by her employer or asked by her mother to help out a family member in an emergency. How can such a conflict be resolved? Ultimately, this student-athlete will have to prioritize her life. The status deemed most important will take precedence. Sociologists refer to a prioritized status as a master status. A master status is the status that dominates one's identity. For most undergraduates, the status of student is likely to be their master status. However, college students who are raising a young child will likely view being a parent as a master status. A star basketball player on a Division I team may view being an athlete as a master status.

Another form of stress associated with social roles is role strain. Role strain occurs when conflicting expectations are placed on an individual within one role, such as that of student. Most students have undoubtedly heard that the college years may be "the best years of their lives." If this is the case, a college student must find a way to balance social life with academic expectations. Is it is more important to hang out with friends all night or to study for a test? Trying to do too much results in the cliché of "burning the candle at both ends," which eventually leads to strain within the role of college student.

What Do You Think?

As a college student taking an introductory sociology course, what is your master status? What master status do you believe your classmates claim? What do you think?

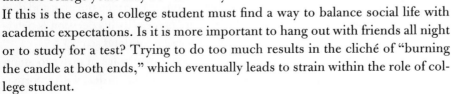

Organizations

Another important aspect of a society's social structure is social organizations. An organization is a social unit, consisting of a group of persons, deliberately constructed to seek predetermined ends or goals. Nearly all the activities we engage in are influenced by organizations. There are hospitals and clinics for our health needs, fitness centers and organized sports leagues for our recreational needs, professional clinics for our counseling needs, food stores to provide our food, oil companies to provide gas stations with our motor fuel, and so on. Nearly everything we encounter throughout the day has a relationship to an organization. Most people wake up to the sound of an alarm clock or computer, devices that were created by organizations. After getting out of their beds (made by another organization), most people go to the bathroom. The bathroom is filled with items made by organizations. The sewer lines that dispose of our waste are maintained by an organization. In a matter of a few waking minutes, we have already been exposed to a large number of organizations, directly or indirectly.

Despite their great diversity, all organizations share a number of characteristics. First, they all serve a specific purpose and are designed in such a way as to meet predetermined goals. All organizations are staffed by a number of people who (typically) have specialized job tasks to perform. This specialization leads to a division of labor. All organizations also have rules and regulations that their employees must abide by, and in many cases these rules extend to the customers who patronize the organization. As Chu (2006) summarizes, "[Formal] organizations have explicit goals, specified productive processes to achieve those goals, official roles, clear statuses, rights and duties" (p. 3).

What Do You Think?

Trace your typical day and try to count all the different organizations you come into contact with, whether directly or indirectly. Will that number exceed fifty, one hundred, two hundred, more? What do you think?

A key term associated with organizations is bureaucracy. A bureaucracy is the formal administrative structure used by an organization to meet its goal. (Recall that in Chapter 2 we discussed Max Weber's concept of bureaucracy.) Bureaucracy is the mechanism that drives an organization. The college you attend is a huge organization consisting of multiple offices. The registrar's office, for example, is responsible for registering students for classes. In an ideal situation, the system allows for a smooth registration period every semester. Administrators and students must follow certain rules during registration, including regulations concerning the time and date that specific student groups are allowed to register (generally this decision is determined based on rank, with seniors registering before juniors, and so on.)

Ideally, a bureaucracy is set up based on rational principles in order to attain stated goals efficiently. Offices are ranked in a hierarchical order, with information flowing up the chain of command and directives flowing down. The organization's operations are characterized by impersonal rules that explicitly outline duties, responsibilities, standardized procedures, and expectations for officeholders' conduct. Offices are highly specialized. Only through bureaucracies are large-scale planning and coordination, both for the modern state and the modern economy, possible.

> **What Do You Think?**
>
> How efficient is the bureaucratic system at your college? What do you think?

Social Institutions

Social institutions are forms of organizations that perform basic functions (e.g., organization, direction, and execution) in a society and are strongly supported by a society's culture. Social institutions include, among others, marriage, the family, the economic system, education, religion, sports, health care, and the military. Thus, social institutions are not buildings or places but rather structures of relationships, roles, obligations, and functions in society.

As an example, let us consider the social institution of politics. (Note: Politics is discussed in further detail in Chapter 12.) As an organizational structure, the political system includes political leaders who are responsible for creating, implementing, and overseeing the law. In the United States, the president is responsible for creating an economic budget, which must then be approved or modified by Congress. This economic budget must take into consideration all the major elements of the social structure, and a review of a president's budget reflects the priority given to specific social institutions within society.

SUMMARY

All societies are composed of a culture and a social structure, and both of these elements help to shape individuals' behavior and give order to our lives. Culture includes the shared symbols and language, knowledge, values, norms, and behavioral patterns of a given society. The use of symbols and language allows members of a society to communicate and fosters the transmission of culture from one generation to the next.

Culture is difficult to change, but changes do occur. In contemporary culture, technology has played an increasingly important role in shaping human lives. Culture consists of material and nonmaterial aspects. Whereas nonmaterial culture consists of the more abstract creations of society, material culture refers to the physical, tangible products it produces.

Contemporary culture is dominated by aspects of popular culture. Popular culture refers to the aspects of society (products and forms of expression and identity) that are frequently encountered or widely accepted, whereas high culture refers to the fine arts and literature intended to be appreciated by an elite audience.

Each society has a unique culture; as a result, there is a great deal of cultural diversity in the world. Many societies possess cultural diversity within their boundaries. Subcultures, for example, highlight cultural diversity. In some instances, a large segment of society may seek major changes in cultural ideals. When this is the case, a counterculture movement may sweep a society.

The social structure of society includes the social groups and individual social positions (statuses) held by individuals, organizations, and social institutions.

Glossary

Achieved status—Any status that a person attains or earns through individual effort, choice, or competition.

Aggregate—The total number of people who happen to be clustered in the same place at the same time.

Ascribed status—Any status a person receives through birth.

Beliefs—The mental acts that involve placing trust or confidence in another, a cause, or a condition.

Category—A number of people who share a particular attribute but who may have never met.

Counterculture—A social movement with norms, values, and beliefs that consciously oppose the dominant culture.

Culture—The shared knowledge, values, norms, and behavioral patterns of a given society that are passed on from one generation to the next and form a way of life for its members.

Dyad—A two-person group.

Ethnocentrism—The tendency for members of a society to use their culture's norms and values as standards for judging other cultures.

Folk culture—The local, noncommercial, traditional way of doing things.

Folkways—The conventional rules of everyday life that people follow almost automatically as they go about their ordinary activities.

Gestures—The most basic form of communication. Gestures occur when we move limbs or body parts or make facial expressions in an attempt to convey a thought.

High culture—Culture that is not mass-produced or meant for mass consumption and generally consists of the fine arts, opera, theater, and high intellectualism.

Ideology—A body of ideas, or doctrine, that reflects the social needs and aspirations of a society.

Language—A set of symbols that can be strung together in an infinite number of ways to express ideas and abstract thoughts and that enables people to think and to communicate with one another.

Laws—The formal norms of society that have been written down by a political authority that come with designated punishments (sanctions) for their violation that officials (e.g., the police, judges, district attorneys, probation officers) have been empowered to enforce.

Material culture—The physical, tangible creations of a society (e.g., clothing, merchandise, electronic devices, automobiles, art, and so on).

Mores—Norms that are more serious than folkways and constitute the basic moral judgments of a society.

Nonmaterial culture—The abstract creations of society, such as beliefs, ideologies, norms, and values.

Norms—Socially defined rules and expectations regarding human behavior.

Opinion leaders—Individuals who serve as a type of role model for, and exert a great deal of influence over, others.

Popular culture—The items (products) and forms of expression and identity that are frequently encountered or widely accepted, commonly liked or approved, and characteristic of a particular society at a given time.

Primary groups—Those groups characterized by intimate, face-to-face association and cooperation.

Roles—Culturally determined rights, duties, and expectations associated with specific social positions.

Secondary groups—Those groups characterized by relatively impersonal relationships, with little social intimacy or mutual understanding among members.

Social group—A set of two or more people who interact regularly and in a manner defined by some common purpose, a set of norms, and a structure of statuses and roles (social positions).

Social institutions—Forms of social organizations with a structure consisting of social positions, roles, norms, and values designed to organize relatively stable patterns of human activity.

Social positions—The statuses and roles that individuals hold within a group.

Social structure—The prevailing social organization and social arrangements of a society.

Society—A group of persons who interact with one another as members of a collectivity within a defined territory and a highly structured system of human organization.

Subculture—A culture within a culture consisting of a category of people who share a distinctive set of cultural beliefs and behaviors that distinguish them from the larger society.

Symbols—Items that possess meaning and represent something else to people in a society.

Triad—A three-person group.
Values—Things we cherish and place importance on, that have worth.

Discussion Questions

1. How do Americans balance their desire to possess material goods with a sense of the importance of the nonmaterial aspects of society?
2. Describe your ideal work situation. What would be your occupation, how many hours per week would you work, how much would you earn, and would you be in charge or working for someone else? Would you work harder than, as hard, or not as hard as your colleagues?
3. Discuss slang language or buzzwords that you and your friends use. Will your language patterns influence popular culture, reflect it, or both?
4. Describe the major elements of at least one subculture to which you belong.
5. If you were in charge of the nation's economic budget, how would you allocate revenue?

Web Links

To learn more about the average hours worked per week by workers around the world, visit www.billshrink.com/blog/working-around-the-world.
To learn more about sexting, visit www.cbsnews.com/stories/2009/01/15/national/main4723161.shtml.
To learn about Chinese folk culture, visit www.chinesefolkculture.com.
To learn more about regional differences in dialect in map form, visit www.hcs.harvard.edu/~golder/dialect/maps.php.
To learn more about buzzwords, visit www.buzzwhack.com.

SOCIALIZATION

5

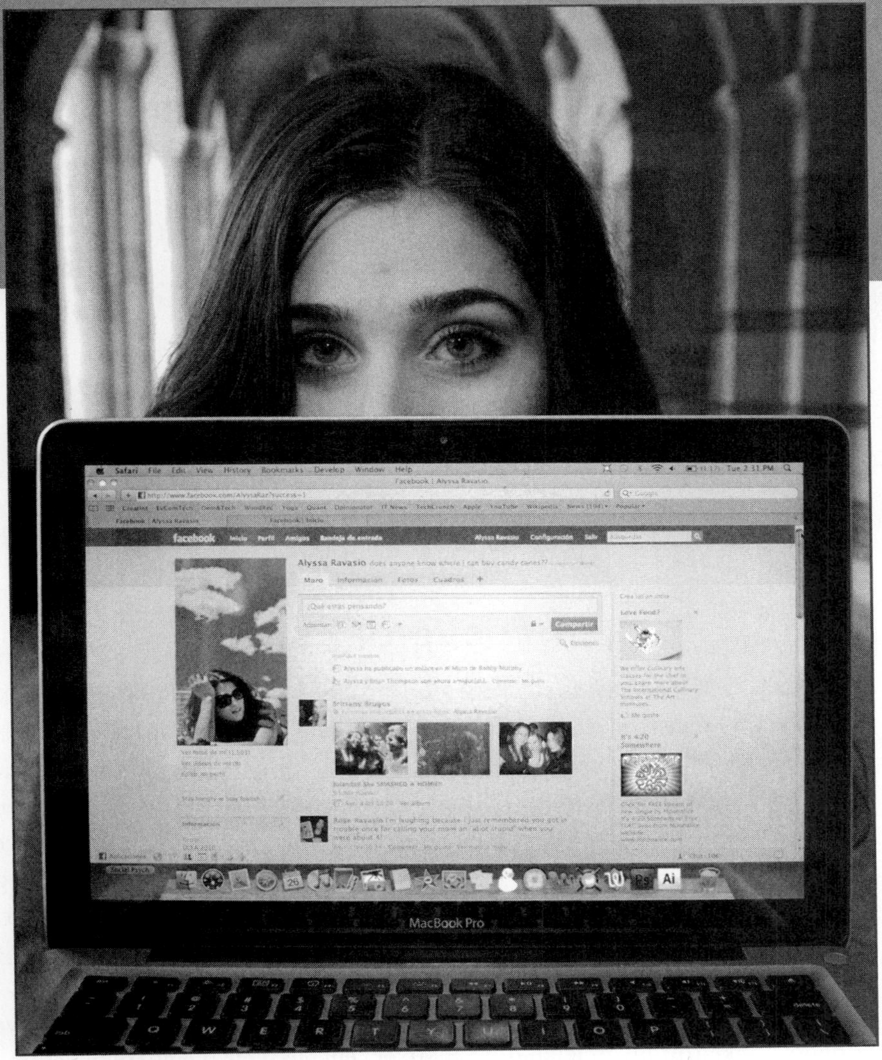

An increasing number of people are spending a great deal of time on social network sites such as Facebook.

Chapter 5

INTRODUCTORY STORY

Michelle, age nineteen, is a college student. She has several hundred friends and tries to find time to socialize with as many of them as she can on a daily basis. Her parents wonder how she can possibly find time to mingle with so many friends and keep up with her studies. Michelle's parents are from the phone book generation; Michelle belongs to the Facebook generation. For any readers who have not heard, Facebook, an online social-mixer site designed for young people, gives users the opportunity to maintain a large number of friendships. However, the name Facebook is a little misleading, as most of Michelle's several hundred friends are not face-to-face relationships but rather virtual ones.

Facebook, and other online social-networking sites such as MySpace, Twitter, Bebo, LinkedIn, inCircle, and RSS Mixer, enable their members to set up personal profiles; create links to photos, achievements, and buddy lists; and keep in touch with friends. The concept of the friend is important with Facebook. Members are able—and encouraged—to ask other members to be their "friends." If one is accepted as a friend (or "friended," in Facebook jargon), he or she can view personal pages and share information. Friends can sign each other's "walls."

Many Facebook members, like Michelle, attempt to secure as many friends as possible. For Michelle, the fact that she has hundreds of online friends is a sign of her popularity, an enhancement of her self-esteem. In her continual efforts to friend more and more people, Michelle also has an account on MySpace. Some days she is so busy checking her online pages that she has little time for actual friendships, much less to keep up with her college coursework. Despite this, Michelle is quite content with her social life. She has learned to accept this type of socializing as the norm.

If Michelle's self-esteem is based on the total number of friends she has on Facebook, she may be setting herself up for disappointment, as her hundreds of friends pale in comparison to the friend lists of most celebrities. In 2009, the race to become the first person with 1 million followers on Facebook was won by Ashton Kutcher. A year later, Lady Gaga became the first person to attain 10 million Facebook fans. Lady Gaga narrowly beat out President Barack Obama, who had more than 9.96 million followers when she broke the eight-figure barrier in July 2010 (D. Thomas 2010). Lady Gaga also had 5 million Twitter followers at the time she reached this milestone.

It is common for many of Michelle's peers to spend a great deal of time interacting by means of a variety of electronic gadgets—so much so that many phone-book-generation parents find themselves asking their Facebook-generation children to help them learn to use new electronic media, so that they too can join online networking sites, text message on cell phones, listen to music on MP3 players, play video games, and watch movies on smartphone screens. As this chapter shows, Michelle's behavior reflects the socialization process to which she has been exposed by her peers. Socialization is typically assumed to flow in one direction—from parent to child—but we can see from this example that it sometimes flows in the opposite direction as well. The socialization process shapes all of us; as a result, it is very important to sociologists.

THE SOCIALIZATION PROCESS

Socialization involves developmental changes brought about as a result of individuals interacting with other people (Schaffer 1984). Sociologists view socialization as a lifelong process of learning—one that spans from infancy to old age. Although early-childhood development is generally emphasized as the most critical time for learning, ideally each of us will continue to learn throughout our lifetimes. We learn by interacting with others.

An infant is nearly completely dependent on caregivers for survival. These caregivers (e.g., parents, other family members, legal guardians, friends, babysitters) teach the child necessary, basic rules of life designed to aid the infant's survival. At birth, all infants are very narcissistic, meaning that they think only of their own needs and want immediate gratification. If they are hungry or thirsty, they will usually cry and scream (as if dying!), regardless of the time of day or night or whether other family members are trying to sleep. Infants do not behave badly on purpose; since they have not been socialized, they do not know how to behave properly. They have biological needs (for food, warmth, removal of discomfort, etc.), and they respond to these needs biologically.

However, the child lives in a social world where biological urges must be controlled. The child must learn to conform to societal expectations. The "spoiled" child continues to scream and throw temper tantrums in an attempt to get what he or she wants, but this behavior is considered very annoying by most people and is seldom tolerated in society.

Parents (and guardians) are responsible for the early primary socialization of their children and, together, parents and children form an important primary group.

The socialization process is responsible for taming this narcissism. One of the goals of socialization is to teach children that they cannot have whatever they want whenever they want it. The real world seldom provides instant gratification for all individual needs, biological or social. It is hoped that, by the time they reach school age, all children will have learned this basic fact. Adults who act in such a childish and narcissistic manner are seldom taken seriously.

Clearly, learning is a critical aspect of the socialization process. As a result, sociologists define **socialization** as a process of social development and learning that occurs as individuals interact with one another and learn about society's expectations for acceptable behavior. Through socialization individuals acquire a social identity. Loy and Ingham (1981) describe socialization as "an interactional process whereby a person acquires a social identity, learns appropriate role behavior, and in general conforms to expectations held by members of the social systems to which he belongs or aspires to belong" (p. 189).

In order for the socialization process to be effective, individuals must learn to internalize the messages being sent to them. In this manner, the expectations of society are added to the "script" of response patterns of individuals; they have learned to respond to various stimuli in a routine fashion (everyday courtesy and manners, formal etiquette, knowing when to speak and when to remain quiet, etc.). The chapter's opening vignette about Michelle and her use of social-networking sites to keep in touch with friends reflects the concept of internalizing the cultural norms and expectations of her generation. Her desire to acquire as many virtual friends as possible is a particular aspect of the socialization process that she has chosen to embrace.

In a broader sense, people who are properly socialized and have internalized the cultural expectations of the greater society are able to function properly in a variety of social settings. Each of us performs a number of social roles in society; in some settings an individual may be in a position of power (e.g., a vice president in a major corporation), while in other settings this same person may have little or no power (e.g., as a customer in a grocery store, a spectator at a ball game, or an airline passenger checking in for a flight). Within this matrix of statuses and their contingent role demands, individuals must be capable of transforming identities. Thus, the socialization process prepares the social actor to perform appropriately in all social settings.

Furthermore, sociologists note that the socialization process is critical for the survival and stability of the greater society itself. After all, it is the support and maintenance of the existing social structure that allows society to continue. However, as we learned in Chapter 4, society can be altered when dramatic changes in culture occur, such as changing beliefs, norms, and values, and as the result of significant social events.

Our family is instrumental in our Socialization

Primary Groups

Socialization is most effective in **primary groups**. Charles Horton Cooley (1909) describes primary groups as "those characterized by intimate face-to-face association and cooperation.... The result of intimate association, psychologically, is a certain fusion of individualities in a common whole, so that one's very self, for many purposes at least, is the common life and purpose of the group" (p. 23). These associations are primary in several senses, but chiefly in that they are fundamental in forming the social nature and ideals of the individual. As described in Chapter 4, members of a primary group share a sense of "we-ness"—a sort of sympathy and mutual identification for which "we" is a natural expression. The primary group is relatively small and often informal, involves close personal relationships, and plays an important role in shaping an individual's sense of self. According to Cooley (1909), the fundamental properties of the primary group include

1. face-to-face association;
2. an unspecified nature of associations;
3. relative permanence;
4. a small number of persons involved;
5. relative intimacy among the participants.

Cooley argued that individuals are prone toward the whole (the group) in order to share a "we" feeling with others. Humans do this despite their instinctively and initially bound selfishness. Thus, Cooley believed that individuals are born with biological needs that must be fulfilled; yet, the fulfillment of these needs can only be met through group participation. Cooley (1909) stated that the most important primary groups are the family, peers, and the immediate community or neighborhood. Dependence on a group leads to mutual appreciation among group members. Group membership becomes a valued commodity, and the opinions of primary group members, understandably, are very important.

Neglected children do not receive the love and nurturing environment that is so critical in their human development.

The Neglected or Abandoned Child

In an ideal world, every child would be raised in a loving and nurturing environment. Unfortunately, this is not always the case. Far too often, children are neglected and abused. Although Chapter 10 discusses family abuse, it is also worth noting here in order to demonstrate the importance of human interaction for the developing child. Child abuse may take many forms; however, the most commonly reported form of abuse, and the most relevant category here, is child neglect. Child neglect may be defined as the failure of caregivers to provide adequate emotional and physical care for a child.

Horrific examples of neglect involve a child being deprived of contact with others. The neglected child may be tethered to a bedpost, underfed—leading to malnourishment—left to live with the stench of waste that has not been cleared away, and denied interaction with other humans. A famous example is the girl known as "Genie," who came to the attention of authorities at age thirteen when her mother, who was visually impaired and fleeing from an abusive husband, brought her to a welfare office seeking help. Genie had spent most of her life isolated in a closed room, tied to a potty chair. Her few social interactions had involved hostile treatment by her father (Curtiss 1977). Such a neglected child will not develop properly, will lack the ability to communicate with others, and is at risk for premature death.

In extreme cases of neglect, a child may be abandoned and left to survive, or die, on his or her own. Studies on such **feral children** (children raised in social isolation without human contact or who receive minimal human contact from a very young age) reveal just how important the socialization process is. Although documented cases of feral children are very rare, they are quite profound from a sociological (and psychological) perspective. When a feral child is raised by animals, he or she may exhibit (within certain physical and mental limits) behaviors similar to those of the care-animal (Benzaquen 2006; Newton 2002; Harlan and Pillard 1976). For example, Ivan Mishukov, an abandoned Russian child who was protected by a pack of stray dogs, came to howl and bite when humans attempted to separate him from the dogs (see "A Closer Look" Box 5.1).

Through his begging, Ivan was able to maintain some of the language skills he had acquired before being abandoned at age four. In some ways, Ivan is lucky, in that children with some human experience before isolation are more easily rehabilitated after being rescued.

An infant with a normally functioning brain has the capacity to learn to speak but will only speak if encouraged, through socialization with humans, to do so.

A Closer Look

Box 5.1 Ivan Mishukov: A Feral Child Living Among Dogs

Ivan Mishukov was a six-year-old boy who had spent two years living with a pack of stray dogs in Moscow when his story was told by a journalist, Galina Mashtakova (Newton 2002; Whitehouse 1998). Mashtakova describes how Ivan, just one of 2 million homeless children in Russia, made friends with the dogs, which in turn looked out for him. Surviving brutally cold Moscow winter nights takes a great deal of ingenuity for a feral child and a pack of dogs. The dogs would sniff out warm hiding places, such as sewers next to hot-water pipes, cellars, and unoccupied buildings. Ivan, relying on the limited language skills he had developed before his parents abandoned him, would approach adults, beg for food, and share it with the dogs. The dogs would protect Ivan from human and other animal threats.

On several occasions, police attempted to separate Ivan from his pack of dogs. But Ivan refused to come forward, and the dogs viciously guarded him. The police then set a meat-bait trap in the storage room of a restaurant where the dogs searched for leftovers. After the dogs were trapped, social workers rescued the lice- and sore-ridden boy, who howled and attempted to bite them. Ivan was quarantined in a children's home where he received medical and psychological treatment (Whitehouse 1998).

What Do You Think?

If you were confronted by a six-year-old child and a pack of stray dogs, what would you do? Would you give them food, run away, or find help? What sorts of conditions could have led to Ivan's parents abandoning their son at age four? What do you think?

Many child-development theorists believe it is critically important for certain aspects of human development to be nurtured in infancy (Resnick et al. 1997; Farran and Haskins 1980; Masten and Gewirtz 2006; Elkind 2001). As Turner (2006) explains, "Human potentials that are hard-wired into our neuroanatomy must be activated within a certain timeframe; if they are not activated, it will be difficult to acquire in full human measure those capacities that make us human and allow us to participate in society" (p. 119).

Genie, whom we mentioned earlier, provided researchers with an opportunity to test this theory. When first taken into protective custody, Genie was almost entirely mute. A team of therapists worked intensively to bring her vocabulary and social skills up to the norm for her age, and Genie initially showed rapid progress, learning to dress herself and to communicate with basic words and short phrases (e.g., "I want Curtiss play piano" to indicate that she would like to listen to her therapist playing the piano) (Rymer 1994). However, she never gained linguistic fluency, and after a few years—during which, unfortunately, she was transferred to a series of unhappy foster homes—she regressed into silence. Today she lives in an adult-care facility (James 2008).

As was clear in the case of Ivan, a dog cannot teach a young child how to speak any language. A parent can teach a child every language. Cases of feral children remind us of how important the socialization process is. The socialization process reveals how we become human. Without human interaction and socialization, infants will not develop properly; they will not become "human."

THEORIES OF SOCIALIZATION AND HUMAN DEVELOPMENT

The discussion of neglected and feral children highlights the nature-versus-nurture debate regarding how human development occurs. Biology (nature) certainly dictates a number of physical attributes (e.g., skin color, hair color, eye color, ancestry) and plays a role as to whether an individual is physiologically capable of learning, but does it dictate behavior? According to sociologists, socialization, past experiences, modeling, and motives—in short, the environment (nurture)—most significantly influence human behavior. It might help to think of social forces and natural innate traits, in terms of their significance for human behavior, as two ends of a "nature-nurture continuum." Both forces play a role in human development, but in sociology, the pendulum swings toward nurture.

A number of significant theories have been put forth in an attempt to explain how human development occurs. Some of these theories favor the nature approach while others rely more heavily on the nurture approach. Considering that sociology leans heavily on the importance of learning, most sociologists embrace human-development theories that emphasize the importance of nurturing factors. To illustrate both the nurture and nature approaches to human development, two classical psychological theories are discussed here. We begin with Sigmund Freud and his theory of psychoanalysis.

Sigmund Freud and Psychoanalysis

Sigmund Freud (1856–1939) was a medical doctor specializing in neurology during an era when most causes of human behavior were deemed biological in origin. Freud developed his theory of psychoanalysis through years of treating patients for mental or emotional problems. For years during and after Freud's lifetime, psychoanalysis was a dominant theory, but in recent decades it has largely been replaced by other approaches to treating mental disorders.

Freud was primarily concerned with how the individual personality develops. Freud's model of personality is based on the concept of a dynamic unconscious, which gives rise to drives, instincts, and urges that are nearly uncontrollable. Freud believed that one's personality is composed of three structures: the id, the ego, and the superego. The *id* (Latin for "it") is totally unconscious of, or unconnected to, reality and is consumed with satisfying basic human drives, or instincts. An **instinct** may be defined as an innate impulse, or tendency to act, that is common to a given species. Whether humans possess instincts is a matter of debate, but for Freud, among the chief basic instincts are sexual gratification and aggressive tendencies.

It is the id that makes the young child so self-centered and preoccupied with immediate gratification, even at the expense of the needs of others (e.g., parents and siblings). A hungry child will scream out for attention, even if it is 3:00 a.m. and other family members are asleep. In adulthood, the instincts that humans possess are often suppressed by societal expectations of proper behavior, a fact reflected by Freud's concept of the *superego* (Latin for "above or beyond the ego"), as it is the superego that enables us to control our behavior and meet the needs of the greater society. The superego must determine what is proper behavior or, in a cultural sense, moral behavior. When an individual has a fully developed superego, he or she has developed a conscience.

Freud uses the concept of the *ego* (Latin for "I") to explain how individuals manage to fulfill the needs of the id in a culturally acceptable manner. For example, in an attempt to fulfill one's need for sexual gratification, one should find a willing partner and not force him- or herself upon an unwilling other. The id will induce individuals to take advantage of opportunities presented (e.g., a person whose judgment is impaired by alcohol or drugs) while the superego instructs the individual to abide by society's laws and values (it is immoral and illegal to take advantage of incapacitated individuals). Thus, the properly socialized person will not take advantage of another person who is incapable of giving informed consent. The ego is necessary, according to Freud, because id and superego are in a constant battle.

Although sociologists downplay the impact of any possible human instinct(s) on behavior, they do find validity in the idea that each of us must learn to take care of our personal needs within the cultural framework of a society's given norms and values.

What Do You Think?

Recall from Chapter 4 that sociologist Thorstein Veblen proposed that humans have an "instinct of workmanship." Observation of humans will reveal that many people possess a strong motivation to work hard. But does this motivation reflect an instinct or a learned behavior dictated by necessity? Further, does it appear that all humans have an instinct to work hard? What do you think?

Jean Piaget and Cognitive Development

In contrast to Freud's psychoanalytic theory, which emphasizes the importance of unconscious thoughts, cognitive theories highlight conscious thoughts (Santrock 2007). Cognitive-development theories are aptly named, considering that **cognition** itself may be defined as the mental process of knowing and includes such aspects as perception, awareness, reasoning, judgment, and learning.

The leading proponent of cognitive-development theories was Swiss psychologist Jean Piaget (1896–1980), who studied human cognition by observing his own three children as they grew from infancy to adulthood. He was especially interested in what children know and how they come to know. Based on his observations, Piaget ([1936] 1952, 1954) proposed that every child goes through four stages of development, each associated with increasingly complex cognitive abilities to learn and reason.

1. *Sensorimotor stage* (from birth to age two): In this stage of development, the child is still in the sensory phase. His or her understanding of the world is limited to direct contact, such as sucking, touching, listening, or looking. At this stage, babies do not know that their bodies are separate from the environment. Infants are also unable to recognize cause and effect (Flavel, Miller, and Miller 2002). By age two, the child has developed simple problem-solving skills, such as how to find a toy that is not immediately available (Gunter, Oates, and Blades 2005).
2. *Preoperational stage* (ages two to seven): In this stage of development, the child learns to understand and articulate speech and symbols, progressing from basic words and phrases to lengthy sentences, as well as gaining the abilities to read and write. Symbolic representation, however, is quite limited and results in an unyielding and inflexible manner of thinking; for example, a preoperational child has difficulty imagining what a scene looks like from the viewpoint of another person in a different location. Thus, according to Piaget, the child lacks the ability to perform specific operations that entail relatively abstract ideas.
3. *Concrete operational stage* (ages seven to eleven): At this stage, the child is capable of performing specific (concrete) tasks that involve basic formulas,

such as mathematical calculations. In this regard, logic and reasoning are replacing intuitive thought, so long as they are applied to concrete examples. Children at this age are also capable of playing team games.

4. *Formal operational stage* (ages twelve through adolescence): During this final stage of Piaget's cognitive-development theory, children have learned to think abstractly and to use logical deductive skills and reasoning. The adolescent is capable of looking at a problem, thinking of courses of action, and deciding which course might be best. She is also capable of thinking of ideal situations, expressed as "What if . . . ?" Parents of adolescents can attest to their children's tendency to criticize the way things are in the world, now that they are capable of imagining more ideal solutions to society's problems.

Cognitive-development theories such as Piaget's reflect the definition parameter of socialization as a learning *process.* As the word "process" implies, development occurs as a result of a systematic series of actions that take place in a definite manner. In this regard, human development follows a scripted course. In the decades since Piaget proposed his theory, critics have pointed out that not all children follow this script. For one thing, some children may lack the physiological or mental capacity to develop at a "normal" pace. For another, today's neuroimaging techniques have allowed researchers to assess infants' brain activity, which has revealed more sophisticated mental processes at younger ages than Piaget thought possible (Baillargeon 2004; Luo and Baillargeon 2005). Finally, it is not difficult to argue that many adults, let alone teenagers, lack—or at least do not make use of—the ability to think abstractly (stage 4).

Social-Learning Theory

Sociologists believe that we are all free beings capable of deciding our own courses of action. That is, behavior is not fixed, or predetermined, as the nature end of the nature-nurture continuum would suggest. (It should be noted, however, that sociologists do not ignore the fact that social structures and achieved and ascribed statuses may limit the choices available to each of us.)

Proponents of this perspective elaborate on the process of learning itself. They propose that learning is a three-step procedure that entails three critical aspects: acquisition, instigation, and maintenance. *Acquisition* refers to the initial introduction of a behavior; *instigation* occurs when the individual actually participates in some form of behavior; and *maintenance* refers to the repetitive and consistent participation in a behavior over a period. An individual initially learns a behavior either through direct interaction with others, wherein such behavior is reinforced, or indirectly through observation. Thus, human development is the result of environmental experiences.

Social learning generally takes place through two primary methods: conditioning and modeling. **Conditioning** is a learning process whereby individuals associate certain behaviors with rewards and others with punishments. Children's behavior is generally subject to evaluation by parents and other caregivers. When a child behaves appropriately (as deemed by significant others) and is rewarded by praise or other means, the usual consequence is continued suitable behavior on the part of that child. In this manner, proper behavior has been reinforced. Reinforcement is used in an attempt to secure a conditioned response to a given stimulus. Reinforcement is a powerful tool in human development, as it attempts to influence individuals to conform to specific norms and values. Reinforcement is the result of contact between great numbers of people in society, and although parents and the immediate family are the most important agents of socialization, when the child reaches a certain age (around the third grade), the reinforcement of peers becomes very important. Conversely, inappropriate behavior may lead to a punishment. Punishments are undesirable consequences used to discourage the offender from further engaging in objectionable behavior.

Along with conditioning, the child learns behavior through observation and **modeling**. Simply observing how others behave represents a learning opportunity, and, indeed, daily activities generally present children with countless opportunities to observe the behaviors of others. On the first day of school, many children manage to ride a bus, proceed from the playground to the classroom, and negotiate many other behaviors by watching what the other students do and imitating their behavior.

Modeling teaches children countless positive behaviors, but a child may also learn less desirable behaviors, such as how to smoke, by observing older children or by watching adults on television or in movies. Thus, one may serve as a model without wanting to, or even without knowing it. Children exposed to delinquent gang members may find a fascination with their lifestyle and become wannabes—meaning that they want to be gang members when they grow older. Children living in economically disadvantaged neighborhoods who observe gang members with new clothes, shiny bling, and cash, in essence, may see them as role models. In this case, parental intervention is critical as such children are at risk of "turning" (becoming gang members).

Symbolic Interactionism

Of the four human-development theories discussed in this chapter, the symbolic-interactionist approach is the most sociological. As described in Chapter 2, symbolic interactionism is a theory based on the idea that social reality is constructed in each human interaction through the use of symbols. The most critical aspect of human development from the symbolic-interactionist perspective is the development of self, which occurs through reflexive behavior. *Reflexive behavior* involves individuals observing, interpreting, and evaluating their own behaviors from the perspective of others. Learning to take the perspective of another is a fundamental aspect of the socialization process because this ability reflects the development of self. Cooley believed that early childhood is a critical time in the development of self. For Cooley, however, primary group participation is very important for children, for it is within the primary group that children develop a sense of self. "The self develops in a group context, and the group that Cooley called the primary group is the real seat of self-development" (Reynolds 1993, p. 36).

George Herbert Mead's development-of-self concept provides the most fundamental symbolic-interactionist theory of human development. Mead believed that the self was composed of two parts, the "I" and the "me." The **"I"** represents the subjective (or egocentric) aspect of the self; it is impulsive, spontaneous, and creative. The **"me"** represents the objective (socialized) aspect of self and develops through interaction with others and the internalization of the norms and values of the greater community. The "me" reflects upon the self in relation to the expectations of society.

Mead (1934) believed that children learn to control their impulsive urges to respond to outside stimuli because of the expectations of others. Eventually, the "me" comes to dominate the "I," and when this happens, human development has succeeded. For example, when a mother disciplines a child, the child's "I" sense of self wishes to protest via a variety of means, such as throwing a temper tantrum; however, when the child reaches a point of realization that such a negative behavior will be frowned upon and therefore decides to keep his or her emotions in check, the "me" has developed.

The "me" develops through a set of stages (imitation, play, game, and generalized other), which were explained in our discussion of Mead's theories in Chapter 2. For our purposes here, the point is that when the actor shares the perspective of a reference group, she has, in Mead's terms, taken on the attitudes of the generalized other (the community). The generalized other stage represents the fully developed self. At this stage of development, the individual not only identifies with significant others (specific people) but also with the attitudes of the group or community as a whole. The generalized other is not a person; instead, it is a person's conscious awareness of the society that he or she is a part of (Cockerham 1995).

Although one might be tempted to compare Mead's concept of the "I" with Freud's concept of the id, this would be a mistake. Freud's id is tied to innate biological urges, whereas Mead's "I" is not. Mead's theory of self discounts biological notions and embraces instead the nurture aspects of human development.

AGENTS OF SOCIALIZATION

In Chapter 4, we discovered the importance of culture. In this chapter we have found that individuals learn about culture through the socialization process. We are socialized via a number of cultural outlets known collectively as the agents of socialization. **Agents of socialization** are sources of culture; they are people, groups, organizations, and institutions that teach us what we need to know in order to function properly in society. Agents of socialization include, among others, the family, schools, peer groups, the mass media, religion, employers, and the government. Although most of these agents of socialization will be discussed in later chapters, a brief examination of each is warranted here.

Parents and the Family

The most important agents of socialization for any individual are those that are most highly revered and trusted. They are primary groups. The first primary group encountered by a child is the family—especially his or her parent(s). The family includes a number of significant others, including parents, siblings, and other close relatives. The family is a primary agent of socialization because it plays a major role in shaping a person's self.

It is within the family structure that most of us first experience face-to-face associations. Face-to-face associations "involve a considerable variety of signals—visual, vocal, and bodily—that are integrated into coherent patterns of communicative significance to the other person and that additionally need to be synchronized with the response patterns of that other person if some meaningful interchange is to result" (Schaffer 1984, pp. 44–45). Schaffer (1984) argues that gazing is the most versatile of all interactive responses: "From their very first encounter with the newborn baby mothers attempt to bring about mutual gazing. They do so by aligning their face in the same vertical plane as the infant's, so that the two sets of eyes can meet—a position known as 'en face'" (p. 45). The infant locks onto the mother's face, identifies with it, and forms a bond based on this association.

When a baby meets a parent's gaze, the parent cannot help but imagine what the baby might be thinking. Parents attempt to communicate with their babies, but this is generally quite difficult because babies lack language skills. Babies also attempt to communicate with their caregivers about what they need and what they are feeling, but they are literally at a loss for words. In an attempt to overcome this communication breakdown, a number of professionals promote teaching sign language to hearing babies. Proponents of teaching "baby sign language" argue that infants are capable of communicating with signs long before they are capable of speaking words in a coherent fashion. "A Closer Look" Box 5.2 provides a brief overview of one very popular program that teaches parents how to communicate with hearing infants via sign language.

A Closer Look

Box 5.2 Teaching Sign Language to Hearing Infants

One of my relatives has an infant son who has been taught sign language. It is quite fascinating to watch an infant, who is still too young to talk, communicate with family members through the use of sign language. Any family member who has dinner with this infant quickly learns the signs (gestures) for "more," "please," and "thank you." This infant's parents used the Baby Signs approach to teaching sign language. The Baby Signs program is neatly packaged with such learning tools as instructional DVDs for parents; picture books that teach signs used at mealtime, bath time, and bedtime and with pets; and an instructional guide to explain why teaching sign language to infants is beneficial to childhood development and thus assists in the socialization process.

Before children learn verbal and written language, they are capable of using sign language to communicate their feelings, needs, and desires.

What Do You Think?

Proponents of teaching sign language to hearing infants claim that the parent-child bond is strengthened through the ability to communicate through the use of signs. How might this ability influence the socialization process? What do you think?

The founders of the Baby Signs program, Linda Acredola and Susan Goodwyn (2006), claim that many important benefits are associated with an infant's ability to communicate through sign language: signing reduces frustration for both parents and infants; it lets babies share their world with those they love; it strengthens the parent-infant bond; it helps parents realize how smart their babies are; and it helps to enhance infant self-esteem. The Baby Signs approach clearly has a heavy symbolic-interactionist perspective, especially with its focus on self-esteem enhancement. Furthermore, because symbolic interactionists argue that the use of gestures is an important precursor to the development of language, teaching infants how to use sign language will help stimulate human development. Teaching infants how to use sign language, together with the corresponding learning on the part of infants, represents active participation in the socialization process.

As the primary agents of socialization, parents have a tough job. Parents must, at minimum, provide food, clothing, and shelter for their children. Depending upon cultural norms, parents are also expected to provide a loving and nurturing environment wherein children feel safe, secure, and loved. It is reasoned that such an environment will assist children in their growth and development as individuals. Because the process of human development begins the moment a baby is born, parents face a number of immediate decisions, including where to bed the infant.

Prevailing sentiment in the United States for the past 150 years or so has encouraged the idea that a baby should have its own crib to sleep in. Parents were warned that sleeping with an infant could have dangerous consequences, including the potential for a baby to be crushed to death if the parent rolled on top of the infant during sleep. Materialistic societies of the West have also equated bed sharing with poverty, as people with money would be able to provide separate bedrooms for children. Since the 1970s, however, a number of parents have opted for the *family-bed method,* wherein the child sleeps in the same bed with the parents. Parents who promote this method argue that children sleep better in a family bed; as a result, the parents also sleep better because they do not have to wake up to a baby crying for attention (Thevenin 1987). The sleeping arrangement for a young family represents just the beginning of the numerous decisions parents must make in the course of raising and socializing a child.

Many parents, understandably, are unsure as to what constitutes the best way to socialize children. For example, some parents believe in the tough-love approach, while others believe in spoiling their children. *Tough love* refers to treating another person strictly or firmly with the intent of helping him or her in the long run. A parent who punishes a child for misbehaving by taking away a privilege (e.g., a sleepover at a friend's house or an opportunity to go to a ball game with the rest of the family) is said to be issuing tough love. Although the victim of tough love may not see it immediately, such treatment implies love and affection, as the parent is hoping to instill in the child proper values and a sense of responsibility for his or her actions.

Conversely, some parents would rather be friends with their kids than serve as adult authority figures. Many child-development experts criticize this approach, arguing that children need structure and boundaries and that it is up to parents to establish these parameters (Baumrind 1966, 1967). Another potentially unhealthy approach to parenting involves spoiling children. As Harvey Karp, MD, author of *The Happiest Toddler on the Block* (2004), explains, a spoiled child is demanding, self-centered, and unreasonable (Rauh 2009). Karp acknowledges that it may be easier to get along with children when they get their way, but giving in to their demands ultimately makes them feel isolated and confused. Furthermore, the spoiled child typically grows into a spoiled adult, and spoiled adults have trouble maintaining a job, a spouse, and friendships. Spoiling a child is not simply a matter of overindulgence in material goods, such as extravagant toys; instead, it is the manner in which a parent treats a child. According to psychologist Ruth A. Peters, author of *Laying Down the Law* (2003), among parental mistakes that may lead to spoiling a child are making the child the center of the world, ignoring positive behavior, accidentally rewarding negative behavior, failing to establish clear limits, not enforcing rules consistently, not holding a child accountable for his or her behavior, giving in to temper tantrums, and acting like spoiled children themselves.

A prime example of a spoiled child is the girl who is socialized into believing that she is a princess. A girl comes to think of herself this way because of "princess parenting" (see "Connecting Sociology and Popular Culture" Box 5.3).

The family provides the child with more than face-to-face association. It is the main channel for the transmission of language, names, land and housing, local social standing, and religion (Bertaux and Thompson 2005). The family indoctrinates the child with a system of social values and aspirations, fears, worldviews, domestic skills, taken-for-granted ways of behaving, attitudes about the body, models for parenting and marriage, and so on (Bertaux and Thompson 2005). In addition, the family provides children with a social position in terms of race, ethnicity, and ancestry. Thus, the role of family extends to the intergenerational transmission of cultural values. In this regard, who we are, socially and personally, is rooted in our families (P. Thompson 2005). Because of the importance of family, the period wherein a child interacts with parents, caregivers, and other significant family members is referred to as *primary socialization.* We discuss the family in greater detail in Chapter 10.

Day Care and School

Raised within the family structure, the young child receives mostly consistent messages about social expectations from an extended number of significant others. However, when children start going to school (or even earlier, if they are in day care during the infant and toddler years), they begin to interact with a number of other children and adults with potentially different outlooks on proper behavior, norms, values, and cultural beliefs. These different outlooks on life may confuse the child, but they may also enhance an appreciation for diversity of thought and action. Attending school represents the beginning of the *secondary socialization* process. This is because parental influence usually declines as the child progresses

Connecting Sociology and Popular Culture

Box 5.3 Princess Parenting and the Princess Syndrome

Princess parenting is a process that generally begins at birth with parents dressing baby girls in "princess" baby shirts and "her royal highness" bibs; they may also buy princess-themed photo albums and picture frames to showcase pictures of their new baby. As Martha Irvine (2009) explains, "By the time those girls are toddlers, many are drawn to the princess dresses, crowns and even makeup. And it goes on and on. Barbie has many princess-oriented items, including a top-selling 'Princess and the Pauper' DVD. . . . And then, of course, there's the undisputed leader in all things princess: The Walt Disney Co. In 2000, Disney began grouping several of its female movie characters together as the 'Disney Princesses'—from 'Sleeping Beauty' to the more recent 'Mulan'" (p. C2).

Many young girls love to dress and act as princesses. This behavior is often encouraged by their mothers.

The princess is generally outfitted in pink clothes with lots of frills and sparkles. Her bedroom may include a pink princess theme and a play area with a princess castle. As a result, the princess comes to see the world as a fairy tale, with herself as the star.

Because the princess has been pampered throughout her childhood and placed on a pedestal, she comes to think of herself as overly special and develops a delusional sense of entitlement. This phenomenon is known as the *princess syndrome*.

The delusions of grandeur generated by princess parenting also lead to the development of narcissistic traits. Based on their research findings, Jean Twenge and W. Keith Campbell, coauthors of *The Narcissism Epidemic: Living in the Age of Entitlement* (2009), found that college-age women today are developing narcissistic traits at a rate four times that of men. The authors attribute this high rate of narcissism to the princess syndrome, given that a generation of young women have been socialized by parents and the media (especially Disney) to embrace the princess fantasy. Among the characteristics of the princess in adulthood are extreme insecurity, the urge to be the center of attention (drama-queen behavior), wanting everyone to know she is a princess, failure to take responsibility for things, and a desire to be waited on.

through school. The role of the educational system on an individual's socialization is discussed in Chapter 11.

Peer Groups

As the young child grows older, the opinions, values, and norms of peers become increasingly important. A **peer group** consists of associates of a similar age and

The series finale of the TV show *Samantha Who?* ("With this Ring" 2009) provides us with a fictional account of the adult princess. Andrea Belladonna (Jennifer Esposito), the adult princess, is getting married to an NBA star, Tony Dane (McKinley Freeman). The marriage is actually a sham, as Dane is gay, but his agent fears he will lose endorsement deals if the truth about his sexual orientation is revealed. Andrea loves the idea of marrying a wealthy celebrity because she craves the attention, the paparazzi, and the idea of people talking about her. Andrea's princess dream is rooted as a classic case of social mobility—the idea that a woman can use marriage as a strategy to rise in the social strata. Although certainly not politically correct, this idea holds true within the princess fantasy. And in this particular example, by marrying Dane, Andrea will achieve a rise in socioeconomic status.

What Do You Think?

Were you, or was anyone you know, raised in the princess fantasy? Have you ever met someone with the princess syndrome? What are some reasons parents would raise a child this way? Is there a male equivalent—a prince syndrome? What are the pros and cons of being raised in such a fantasy world? What do you think?

At the start of this episode, Andrea and her bridesmaids, Samantha (Christina Applegate) and Dena (Melissa McCarthy), are being pampered by hunky men who serve them champagne and chocolate-covered strawberries in the aptly named "Princess Suite" of a luxurious hotel. As is customary with *Samantha Who?,* the Samantha character narrates each episode. Samantha states, "I guess a lot of girls have this princess fantasy. . . . Living in luxury, totally pampered . . . I'm trying to understand it. In fact, I'm trying really hard." Samantha has reservations about her best friend's marrying for reasons other than love. But she keeps quiet as Andrea happily proclaims, "After I'm married tomorrow, I will have to learn to be self-indulgent and demanding." Such is the life of a princess!

As it turns out, however, there is hope for Andrea. At the last minute she changes her mind about marrying Tony Dane when her average-looking would-be boyfriend, Seth, shows up outside the church and declares his love for her. Perhaps Seth will turn out to be her Prince Charming. We are left to wonder.

Whether feminists or others wish that princess parenting were a thing of the past, it still exists. A number of girls like the idea of being princesses: parents, especially fathers, often call their daughters "princess," and many moms like creating a fantasy world for their daughters. The royal wedding of Prince William and Kate Middleton in 2011 "fueled a bonanza of opportunities for niche entrepreneurs" in the princess fantasy world. For example, in London, girls eight to eleven years old attended a series of weeklong summer camps to learn about princesses. For US$4,000, the camps taught girls about modern and historic princesses, royal history, phone etiquette, how to take compliments, and what to do if you suddenly find food wedged between your teeth (Dodds 2011). Does this seem over the top? Feminists are not the only people worried about the phenomenon of "princess parenting."

usually from the same social status and background. Peers enjoy a certain amount of autonomy and egalitarianism as each friend possesses relatively equal status within the group. Peer group participation affords members an opportunity to explore the limits of adult rules and expectations. In this manner, the child is being socialized into accepting the idea that norms, values, and beliefs are not fixed entities. This freedom is exciting to most children and helps to explain why they value praise and acknowledgment from their peers. Furthermore, this newfound freedom underscores the concern that parents have for the friendships their children establish and maintain.

Children (as well as adults) may also be concerned with joining a new, more desirable peer group. They may rehearse their behavior in an attempt to achieve this desired position (or role). Sociologists refer to this process as *anticipatory socialization.*

The Mass Media

Providing news, information, and entertainment is the trademark of the contemporary mass media. According to Real (1996), "The term *media* refers to all communication relays and technologies" (p. 9). The word "mass" refers to the large size of the media's audience (Ryan and Wentworth 1999). Put together, the **mass media** collectively become the vehicle by which large numbers of people are informed about important happenings in society. "[The] most narrow view of the mass media refers precisely to the technological apparatus that literally carries or transmits information. That is the strictest sense of the word *medium*: a means of communicating information" (Ryan and Wentworth 1999, p. 10). Real (1996) concurs and states, "Any device that relays messages is a medium. Any technology that ritually structures culture is a medium in the broadest sense" (p. 9).

The mass media consist of television, radio, motion pictures, newspapers, books, magazines, and sound recordings. Typically, the media are divided into two major categories: *print media,* including newspapers, magazines, and books, and *electronic media,* including television, radio, motion pictures, and the Internet. Traditionally, the mass media have been viewed as forms of communication that permit a one-way flow of information from a source to an audience (Ryan and Wentworth 1999). However, as Delaney and Wilcox (2002) indicate, with the increased use of the Internet, the development of interactive television, and the ability to text-message such things as votes for the next American Idol, in conjunction with the older interactive medium of call-in radio programs, the idea of mass media as merely a one-way form of communication is no longer accurate. Bryant and Bryant (2003) concur by stating, "With the advent of newer forms of mediated communication, in which the end is both producer and consumer and assumes considerable agency over media content through interactivity and other means of selectivity and control, the potential for productive entertainment research is almost unlimited" (p. 213).

As an agent of socialization, the mass media involve many issues of sociological interest related to its impact on the viewing audience. These concerns are far too numerous to discuss in here, but the significant amount of time people spend interacting with the mass media is certainly worthy of articulation. Consider, for example, that "computer games (whether on a TV-linked games machine, a computer or a Gameboy) are played by two-thirds of children and young people aged 6–17" (Livingstone 2002, p. 62). Playing video games is not limited to children; young adults also have time on their hands to play games. People of all ages are not just playing video games online; they are also watching videos online. And why not? The videos are there, and they are generally free. Missed a televised TV show? Go online; the networks broadcast their shows on their websites. And a host of online sites, such as Hulu and YouTube, also have sites linking users to their favorite TV shows. Watching television shows online is just one small aspect of the market for viewing videos online. Millions of people enjoy going online to watch random videos, music videos, and blooper videos (see "Connecting Sociology and Popular Culture" Box 5.4 to learn more about viewing videos online).

The growing popularity of viewing videos online has not, apparently, made much of a dent in television viewing. "Despite all the hype about new media displacing old media, for most children television remains far and away the most popular medium in terms of time spent with it.... Television is watched by 99% of children and young people aged 6–17" (Livingstone 2002, p. 60). In 2006, Americans averaged 9.5 hours per day with the media, and television, at 4.5 hours per day, was by far the most popular medium (Ohlemacher 2006a). The popularity of television viewing has actually increased since 2006. According to Nielsen statistics, Americans watched, on average, nearly five hours of television per day in 2008 (Gandossy 2009). There are no indications that traditional television watching will decrease in the near future.

Due to the popularity of television viewing, parents and child-development experts alike are concerned about the images children are seeing. This includes television programming and advertising directed toward children. "Food advertising in particular has been singled out as potentially damaging in its relentless promotion of fatty and sugary products" (Gunter, Oates, and Blades 2005, p. 29). Research on young children and the effects of advertising reveals that the majority of children below the age of seven or eight do not have a well-developed understanding of advertising's persuasive intent (Gunter, Oates, and Blades 2005; John 1999). In fact, Smith and Atkin (2003) argue that children ages four to twelve are uniquely "susceptible to advertising content given their inability to differentiate programs from commercials as well as to comprehend selling intent" (p. 320). Research on adolescents and advertising indicates that they, like adults, are capable of seeing through advertisers' techniques. However, adolescents are more

Connecting Sociology and Popular Culture

Box 5.4 Viewing Videos Online

How many videos are people viewing online? According to comScore (2009), an industry expert, Internet users viewed 12.7 billion online videos during the month of November 2008. This figure represents an astounding 34 percent increase from one year prior. The most watched video site belongs to Google Sites, with YouTube accounting for more than 98 percent of all videos viewed at that property. Fox Interactive Media, which includes MySpace, ranks second with 439 million videos viewed, followed by Viacom Digital with 325 million; Yahoo! Sites, 304 million; Microsoft Sites, 296 million; Hulu, 226 million; Turner Network, 214 million; Disney Online, 137 million; AOL LLC, 115 million; and ESPN, 95 million (comScore 2009). People certainly are watching a lot of videos.

How many people are watching videos? According to comScore (2009), more than 146 million U.S. Internet users watched an average of eighty-seven videos per month in November 2008. Google Sites attracted 98 million online video viewers, or approximately two-thirds of all Internet users who watched video during that month. Fox Interactive ranked second with 58.1 million viewers, followed by 40 million viewers of videos on Yahoo! Sites. The typical online video viewer watched 273 minutes of video (in November 2008), and the average video lasted 3.1 minutes. By contrast, the average duration of online video viewing at Hulu was 11.9 minutes, higher than for any other video property in the top ten sites (comScore 2009). Jordan Hoffner, YouTube's director of content, offers this explanation for why the site is so popular: "YouTube is a clip culture" (Graham 2008, p. 12B). The term "clip culture" is especially applicable in contemporary society for younger viewers who are stereotyped as having short attention spans. With a short-attention-span audience in mind, YouTube had a ten-minute video limit.

However, YouTube has paid attention to the growing popularity of Hulu, an online video site introduced to the general public by NBC Universal and News Corp's 20th Century Fox. Hulu offers full-length episodes of such popular shows as *Saturday Night Live, Family Guy,* and *The Simpsons,* along with other NBC, ABC, and Fox shows. In response, YouTube nixed its ten-minute limit rule and now offers full-length videos of partner CBS programming. Hoffner states, "We saw that there was a demand for a longer form, and a market that's growing, so we decided to try it" (Graham 2008, p. 12B).

How much has Hulu grown? As previously stated,

susceptible to peer pressure and therefore vulnerable to advertising geared toward their generation (Gunter, Oates, and Blades 2005).

What Do You Think?

People of all ages are spending a great deal of time with one form or another of the mass media. Do you foresee any negative consequences to individuals, or society in general, when so much time is spent with the mass media? What do you think?

Debates over the prevalence of the mass media and its effects on consumers have led to attempts by special-interest groups to suppress particular media outlets. One example would include attempts by certain individuals or groups to ban specific books based on their content (see "A Closer Look" Box 5.5). However, only occasionally are they successful, as the First Amendment has consistently steered such protests of freedom of expression away from government-imposed controls on what the media may present

Hulu ranked sixth in videos watched in November 2008 at 226 million videos. According to data from Nielsen Online (2009), Hulu had climbed to second place in the video viewing market in total streams with 373 million in April 2009. In all, Hulu had jumped 490 percent from April 2008 to April 2009. The huge growth makes Hulu the fastest-growing property, or brand, among the top ten sites. Jon Gibs, vice president of media and analytics at Nielsen Online states, "Historically, short form, clip-length video ruled streaming on the web. . . . Hulu, along with pure-play providers like Veoh and the TV networks, has spent the past two years trying to convince consumers that the Internet can be a good place to watch full length programming as well. April's strong showings of Hulu, Fox, and ABC suggest that consumers are beginning to listen" (Nielsen Online 2009).

Nielsen Online (2009) data also reveal that middle-aged viewers (ages thirty-five to forty-nine) are leading the charge in full-length video viewing. Their analysis showed that time spent viewing per viewer in April 2009 had grown 29 percent over the past six months among people ages thirty-five to forty-nine, making this cohort the fastest-growing group in terms of time spent viewing per viewer. Gibs concludes, "Hulu's growth in time viewing illustrates that they are setting the pace in the video market. Although this growth has a lot to do with a good interface and excellent programming, Hulu's aggressive marketing campaign, starting with their first TV ad at the Super Bowl, seems to have given them a bounce that they haven't yet fallen from" (Nielsen Online 2009).

Will the trend of watching videos online continue? The simple answer would appear to be yes. In May 2010, the five-year anniversary of YouTube, it was revealed that YouTube streams more than 2 billion video views per day (Pham 2010). The average YouTube viewer sticks around for about fifteen minutes a day while TV commands the average person's viewing for over four hours per day. In an effort to continue its growth, YouTube's marketing strategy now includes an attempt to challenge traditional television viewing by offering a number of full-length movies, two-hour concerts, and live sporting events—some in high-definition and 3D (Pham 2010).

What Do You Think?

What does all this online video viewing say about us as a society? Does the time spent watching videos come at the expense of doing something productive, such as working or studying? What do you think?

(Bogart 2005). One thing is for certain: the mass media have a tremendous impact on children and adults. As Marie Winn (2002) aptly put it in her book *The Plug-in Drug,* we spend so much time with television, computers, and video games, we risk becoming a nation of mediated zombies.

Other Agents of Socialization

In addition to those described so far, a number of other agents of socialization have an impact on the socialization of individuals. This section discusses three of the principal ones: religion, employers, and the government.

The importance of religion varies a great deal from one individual to another. For some, the advice of religious leaders and religious readings serve as beacons of

A Closer Look

Box 5.5 Read a Banned Book

Perhaps we should read more. Librarians and college professors certainly encourage people to read. And if you really want to stimulate your brain, read a banned book. In 1982, the American Library Association launched its National Banned Books Week (it occurs during the last week of September each year) in an effort to guarantee our rights and our freedom to read, especially books deemed dangerous by government and special interests.

Books are banned for a variety of reasons. Government officials may consider certain publications a threat to national security because the contents contain potentially dangerous information (e.g., books that explain how to make bombs and carry out terrorist attacks). Government officials may also ban books that go against the prevailing ideology. Books used in public schools may be banned simply because parents find portions of them offensive. For example, West Marion High School in Foxworth, a rural Mississippi town, banned the book *Fahrenheit 451* because a parent complained to the superintendent about the use of the phrase "God damn" in the book. The book was removed from the required reading list shortly thereafter. Interestingly enough, *Fahrenheit 451* is a futuristic tale of a society in which all printed materials are banned. The title is a reference to the temperature at which paper catches fire and starts to burn (Banned Books and Authors 2011).

What Do You Think?

In an open society like the United States, should the public be forbidden to read certain literature? Read a banned book to stimulate your cognitive thought process and ask yourself, Why was this book banned? Who would be harmed by such a book? What do you think?

truth that must be followed. Other people, however, lead a more secular life, and religion has little significance for them (see Chapter 11 for a more in-depth review of religion).

Most people work because they have to make a living. As a result, employers play an important role in our lives. Employers provide a wage or salary that allows us to secure the resources necessary to survive. Ideally, employers also provide workers with benefits such as adequate health insurance and a retirement fund. When a breadwinner loses his or her job, the entire family may suffer. (Chapter 12 discusses the importance of economics.)

The type of sociopolitical structure (government) found in a society will have a great deal of influence on individuals and socialization. The government determines what is legal and illegal (see Chapter 6) and legislates our civil lives (see Chapter 12).

The family, schools, peer groups, the mass media, religion, employers, and the government are the primary examples of the agents of socialization. They affect individuals to varying degrees, but collectively, the agents of socialization are responsible for the transmission of culture from one generation to the next.

VIRTUAL SOCIALIZATION

Today, many people spend a great deal of time communicating with one another in the virtual world (cyberspace) rather than in face-to-face interactions. This process is called **virtual socialization**, and its influence on our lives is increasing. In 2008, 84 percent of Americans reported that they were more dependent on their home computer than just three years previously (Kelton Research and Support 2008). The amount of time spent in the cyberworld generally comes at the cost of less time spent with personal relationships in the real world; in a 2008 study, 65 percent of Americans were found to spend more time with their computers than with their significant others (Kelton Research and Support 2008). The average visit to a social-networking site lasts more than twenty-one minutes, up from almost fifteen minutes in 2007, and consumers make numerous visits each day (see "A Closer Look" Box 5.6 for a discussion of compulsive Internet use).

Our fascination with the virtual world has not developed overnight, even though for some it may seem that way. For nearly the past two generations, people have been raised in an increasingly electronic world. The use of computers is no longer a fascination; it has become a necessity and is treated as a given. As Herbert Spencer might say, those who embrace the virtual world are fitter and therefore more likely to survive and flourish. Today's children and young adults have used computers their entire lives. Socializing online is a norm for them, and social networking in cyberspace fulfills the purpose of staying connected. Perhaps the best attraction of the cyberworld is the instant access people have to each other's lives.

As illustrated in the chapter's introductory story, many young adults maintain social relationships in the virtual world with such social-networking sites as Facebook and MySpace. Open to anyone now, Facebook was originally created in 2004 by Mark Zuckerberg and a few of his classmates at Harvard University as a social-networking site for college students. Using a college e-mail account, a student could set up a home page through his or her college's network. Users created personal home pages, shared information about themselves and others, and searched for new (and old) friends to be accepted within a circle of comrades. Until 2008, MySpace, founded in 2003 by Web entrepreneurs Tom Anderson and

A Closer Look

Box 5.6 Compulsive Internet Use

Along with the increased use of this new medium comes a new phenomenon: a growing number of people risk becoming addicted to the Internet. Compulsive Internet use—characterized by such behavior in people as "an inability to stop themselves from using computers, rising levels of tolerance that drive them to seek ever longer sessions online, and withdrawal symptoms like anger and craving when prevented from logging on" (Fackler 2008, p. A9)—has been identified as a mental-health issue in many countries, including the United States.

Researchers in South Korea believe that Internet addiction is a big problem in their country. Ahn Dong-hyun, a child psychiatrist at Hanyang University in Seoul, led a government-financed survey on the problem and found that "up to 30 percent of South Koreans under 18, or about 2.4 million people, are at risk of Internet addiction" (Fackler 2008, p. A9). They spend at least two hours a day online, usually playing games or chatting, and in extreme cases users have started dropping dead from exhaustion after playing online games for days at a time. A growing number of South Korean children are skipping school to stay online (Fackler 2008). To address this social problem, the South Korean government has established a number of Internet-addiction counseling centers in addition to nearly one hundred treatment programs at local hospitals.

"In the United States, Dr. Jerald J. Block, a psychiatrist at Oregon Health and Science University, estimates that up to nine million Americans may be at risk for the disorder, which he calls pathological computer use. Only a handful of clinics in the United States specialize in treating it, he said" (Fackler 2008, p. A9).

What Do You Think?

Are you, or is anyone you know, addicted to the Internet? That is, do you find yourself compelled to go online to "see what's happening"? Are you at risk for Internet addiction? What do you think?

Chris DeWolfe and purchased by Rupert Murdoch in 2005 for $580 million, was far more popular than Facebook (Harold 2007). At the beginning of 2008, Hitwise US, a leading virtual-world Web-research company, reported that MySpace maintained about 72 percent of the social-networking market, while Facebook held 16 percent. Hitwise US (2008) also reported that MySpace was so popular that only two other websites enjoyed higher total cybermarket shares in January 2008: www.google.com (5.37 percent) and mail.yahoo.com (4.91 percent), with www.myspace.com at 4.49 percent.

However, once Facebook allowed nonstudents to use its social-networking site, the number of subscribers increased dramatically, and by mid-2008, Facebook had surpassed MySpace. By August 2010, Facebook's membership neared 600 million, and its popularity has so surpassed MySpace that many have begun to wonder whether MySpace will survive. To put the number of people on Facebook in perspective, if it were a nation, it would be the third most populous nation in the world. Data provided by Facebook (2010) reveal a number of interesting other statistics. For example, more than 50 percent of all Facebook users log on at least once a day; the average user has 130 friends; there are more than 30 billion photographs posted each month; people spend over 700 billion minutes per month on Facebook; there are over 900 million objects that people interact with (papers, groups, events, and community pages); and about 70 percent of Facebook users are outside the United States.

As a commercial enterprise, Facebook was valued at over $50 billion in 2011. Facebook has become such a social phenomenon that *Time* magazine named Mark Zuckerberg the 2010 Person of the Year because of his influence on culture. A film about Zuckerberg and Facebook, *The Social Network,* was released in 2010. It was a 2011 Academy Award nominee for Best Film (as well as for seven other categories; it won three). Facebook received kudos from the Gay & Lesbian Alliance Against Defamation (GLADD) in 2011 when it expanded its romantic-status options to include "domestic partnership." GLADD's president, Jarrett Barrios, said, "By acknowledging the relationships of countless loving and committed same-sex couples in the U.S. and abroad, Facebook has set a new standard of inclusion for social media" (CBS News 2011). With examples such as these, it is clear to see that Facebook is a *social* network.

In 2010, Twitter surpassed MySpace in online traffic for the first time. "Twitter's lead over MySpace was marginal—96 million versus 95 million—but the trend over time paints a prettier picture of the microblogging service. Between August 2009 and August 2010, Twitter grew 76 percent while MySpace dropped 17 percent" (CNN.com 2010b, p. 1). People still turn to Twitter to tweet messages, but the social-networking site has expanded its front page to allow easier access to photos, videos, and other information without using other websites or programs (CNN.com 2010b).

People tweet all sorts of messages on Twitter, most of which are mundane in nature. Most followers of Twitter use the site to read recent tweets from their favorite celebrities or athletes. Celebrities and athletes enjoy Twitter because they, and not the media, control the flow of information. In early 2011, Charlie Sheen, a famous television and movie star, was constantly in the news for a series of bizarre interviews and odd antics, including claims that he possessed "tiger blood" that allowed him to party for days at a time without sleep and repeated joking claims that he was an alien warlock from Mars. After his March 1, 2011, interview on ABC's *20/20* aired, Sheen posted his first tweet on Twitter, "Winning . . . ! Choose

Your Vice . . ." Twenty-four hours later, Sheen had over 1 million followers. By March 6, he had more than 2 million followers clamoring for his words (not necessarily of wisdom!).

Publicity-seeking celebrities are not the only people using Twitter as a means of virtually connecting with others. A number of businesses, including restaurants, pay attention to tweets from customers. In a story run by the Associated Press in 2010, for example, a man (Tony Bosco) posted a tweet about all the negative reviews he had read of a restaurant (Wow Bao in Chicago), asking if the food was "going to suck as much as [the] reviews suggest." Almost immediately afterwards, the restaurant sent Bosco a coupon to find out for himself, free of charge. Bosco went to the restaurant the next night and posted pictures of the food on Twitter. "Conversations about food that only happened between friends are now public thanks to the Internet. And the microblogging site Twitter has only sped up the conversation. Whether it's reviews before the meal or the service afterward, opinions are voiced freely—and restaurants have taken notice" (*The Citizen,* 9/26/10, p. C4).

The old adage "If you can't beat 'em, join 'em" applies to another unlikely partner of Twitter, the traditional news media. As discussed in Chapter 1, young people are not getting their daily dose of news from newspapers or network television news programs; as a result, a number of news outlets tweet "news as it happens." They then suggest Twitter followers turn to their respective news outlets for further and more in-depth news analysis. Tweeting about sporting events, in particular, has become popular among traditional news media folks.

Because of the growing allure of social-networking sites, the Ford Motor Company in 2010 introduced the concept of linking Facebook, Twitter, and LinkedIn to an application called Listen. Speak. Rate. Share. that provides users with information such as restaurant, fuel, and rest locations (Translogic 2010). Seemingly, there is no end in sight to the application of social networking. We are all being socialized into the virtual world, willingly or not. It is fascinating to speculate about social-networking sites in the near and distant future and to wonder about the implications of people spending so much time in the virtual world.

Despite the huge popularity of Facebook, MySpace presently remains most popular with its original audience: people in the music industry and those who follow bands and like to watch videos of band performances. However, for those who seek enjoyment via videos, YouTube has become an increasingly popular site. People of all ages enjoy watching YouTube (owned by Google, Inc.) videos. Loading short recordings of personal behavior or the behaviors of others has become a predominant feature of the electronic generation that has been raised on all manner of virtual experiences. And contemporary society is filled with people who are essentially voyeurs who love to watch the escapades of others, as evidenced by the popularity of such TV shows as *America's Funniest Home Videos* and *World's Wackiest Videos.* We observe people's follies and triumphs and watch the latest music videos, all on YouTube. Consider, for example, that on July 16, 2010, Justin Bieber's music video for "Baby" became the most-watched video ever on YouTube with more than 246 million hits. Bieber, the latest hit fad singer, thanked his fans—known as "Beliebers"—appropriately enough by tweeting to them. The most-watched nonmusic video (as of July 2010) on YouTube was "Charlie Bit My Finger," a viral video watched by more than 210 million viewers (*Sun Sentinel,* 7/16/10).

The ease of accessibility to the cyberworld provides users with numerous opportunities to socialize in a virtual setting and access a great deal of information (albeit inaccurate at times). However, the benefits of the virtual world have a price. There are only twenty-four hours in a day. Time spent socializing in the virtual world comes at the cost of less face time with friends or less time for work or school. Something has to give.

Another concern about the virtual world is unwanted persons gaining access to home pages thought to be restricted. "The provocative profiles and photos that some young children have created have led to a number of potential pedophile and child pornography issues. . . . MySpace is an attractive cyber tool for pedophiles because many youngsters post seemingly innocent photos online that tantalize sex perverts" (Delaney 2008a, p. 85).

In other cases, people may use social-networking sites to slam other people in a highly negative manner. And such hurtful words and misinformation may cause harm to an individual's emotional well-being and sense of self. The use of technologies such as the Internet, cell phones, or other devices to send or post text or images with the intent of intimidating, hurting, or embarrassing another person is known as **cyberbullying**. Cyberbullying can include not only such acts as simply continuing to send e-mails to someone who wants no contact with the sender but also more dangerous acts, such as sending threats, sexual remarks, and hate speech and posting false statements as fact in order to humiliate the victim. Thus, bullying, once confined to the schoolyard or the dorm, can now make its way around the world instantly via the Internet. Hurtful images and videos spread just as quickly. In some cases, the victims of cyberbullying are so traumatized they may commit suicide. The Associated Press has found at least twelve cases in the United States since 2003 in which children and young adults between the ages of eleven and eighteen have killed themselves after falling victim to some form of cyberbullying (*The Citizen,* 10/1/10). The shocking suicide of a college student whose sex life was broadcast over the Web in September 2010 illustrates the alarming negative potential of the Internet. The student, Tyler Clementi, an eighteen-year-old Rutgers University freshman, jumped to his death from the George Washington Bridge after his roommate and another classmate allegedly used a webcam to secretly broadcast his dorm-room sexual encounters with another man. His being "outed" via an online broadcast was too much for Clementi. A spokesperson for the New Jersey gay-rights group Garden State Equality indicated that the case may be pursued as a hate crime if it can be proved that the defendants acted because they believed Clementi was gay (Schwartz 2010; Hu 2010).

In some cases, people cross the line and commit criminal acts. In a 2008 Staten Island, New York, case, for example, a judge ruled that sending a MySpace friend request to anyone who has an order of protection against you is against the law. Criminal court judge Matthew A. Sciarrino Jr. ruled that even though MySpace users can ignore, deny, or block friend requests, a request was still contact, and no contact was allowed under the temporary order of protection (Feuer 2008).

A number of social conventions that lead to awkward face-to-face exchanges in communication also exist on social-networking sites. For example, let us say you unexpectedly come into contact with a friend you have not seen in a while and begin to exchange pleasantries, such as, "How are your parents doing?" or "How did your spouse's surgery turn out?" only to find out that your friend's mom or dad passed away two years ago and that the surgery was unsuccessful. You would feel bad that you did not know about the news and even worse that you had introduced a topic that left both parties uneasy. Well, Facebook is experiencing this same type of scenario. Facebook will periodically post messages on members' home pages reminding them that they have not contacted this or that friend for a while and urging them to do so. However, as Jenna Wortham (2010) reported in a *New York Times* article, Facebook has suggested that members get back in touch with people who are now deceased. Such an intrusion from an impersonal social-networking site may make members uneasy and remind them of past events better left alone. A Facebook spokesperson explains, "It's a very sensitive topic, and, of course, seeing deceased friends pop up can be painful.... And with people passing away every day, we're never going to be perfect at catching it" (Wortham 2010). With over 500 million Facebook members (in July 2010), there is roughly one Facebook employee for every 350,000 members (Wortham 2010). Clearly, mistakes will be made.

Undoubtedly, as the popularity of social networking and virtual socialization continues to increase, we will witness a number of other negative by-products of this advanced form of technology. In this regard, the virtual network is not always "social."

It would be a mistake to believe that virtual socialization is limited to social-networking sites. **Virtual reality**—technology that allows users to interact with a computer-simulated environment—has become a growing characteristic of contemporary society. Simulated environments, accessible as visual experiences displayed on a computer screen or as stereoscopic displays, are utilized by a variety of social institutions, organizations, groups, and individuals. The military, for example, uses virtual reality to train pilots, parachutists, and combat soldiers. The medical community uses virtual medicine to train surgeons for surgery and to experiment, virtually, with new, radical procedures. These simulations lower the cost of training doctors, provide assistance to doctors in performing difficult or complex procedures, reduce the need for animal experimentation, and afford accessible remote consultations. The field of psychology also utilizes virtual reality to treat people who suffer from phobias. In 2006, the U.S. government developed the concept of a virtual border fence (the SBI*net* program) along the U.S.-Mexican border equipped with radars and surveillance cameras to catch people—especially drug smugglers—entering the country illegally. However, in March 2010, beset by technical problems and cost overruns, this "virtual fence" form of border patrolling was abandoned (Gaynor 2010; Hsu 2010).

What Do You Think?

Is technology, bias, bullying, ignorance, or something else responsible for negative behaviors such as posting a roommate's private moments in the virtual world? What do you think?

Virtual reality gives individuals an opportunity to transcend the real world by creating a fantasy world. In this fantasy world, participants can create a whimsical version of themselves. In essence, participants in virtual realities have created a new sense self (through the use of an avatar). It could be argued that they have "self-socialized" an identity based on a make-believe reality (see "Connecting Sociology and Popular Culture" Box 5.7 for a description of self-socialization via the virtual self). Seemingly, there is no end in sight for the utilization of virtual reality; thus, virtual socialization will continue to expand in the future.

In the 2009 blockbuster film *Avatar* (the first film to crack the $2 billion figure), virtual characters come face-to-face with "real" characters. This epic science fiction film, written and directed by James Cameron, is set in the future (2154) on the planet Pandora, where humans are mining a precious mineral called unobtanium (meaning "unobtainable precious metal"). The expansion of the mining industry threatens the existence of a local tribe of Na'vi (a sentient humanoid species indigenous to the planet). A team of human researchers interacts with the natives of Pandora through the use of avatars. The use of 3D special effects provides movie viewers with a sense of escape not easily duplicated in traditional 2D film formats. *Avatar*'s popularity reflects our growing socialization and human embrace of the virtual world.

Connecting Sociology and Popular Culture

Box 5.7 The Virtual Self

Have you ever wanted to run away and start all over again? To find a new job and new friends and to create a new identity and a new sense of self? For a variety of practical reasons, this is not feasible for most of us. However, many people are finding comfort in the cyberworld and have created a "virtual self"—a sort of alter ego and an identity hidden from others. There are numerous virtual worlds to choose from. One of the most popular is Second Life (SL). According to its website's home page, "Second Life is an online, 3D virtual world imaged and created entirely by its residents."

Second Life is an Internet-based virtual world that was initiated in 2003. SL users, of whom there were more than 20 million in 2008, are known as "residents." These residents establish a virtual reality persona and interact with other participants as "avatars." (Note: The word "avatar" comes from Hindu mythology and refers to a Hindu deity in reincarnated form.) An avatar (usually abbreviated to "av," "avi," or "ava") appears in human form with a wide range of physical attributes. An avatar may be customized to a variety of forms. It may reflect the image of the user or may be made up. Users can take on several personas if they wish. Avatars interact with one another via text-based communication.

The SL world has its own economy and a currency, Linden dollars (L$)—named for game creator Linden Lab. Residents create goods and services, buy and sell items, and attempt to make a living. As SL, as well as other virtual worlds, continues to expand and improve, it becomes more lifelike. However, despite its attempt to resemble real life, it remains a virtual world, and its residents remain apart from those of us interacting in the real world.

Another popular virtual reality world wherein participants create a virtual self via an avatar is World of Warcraft (WoW), a massively multiplayer online role-playing game (MMORPG). (Note: Some gamers simply use the acronym "MMO," for massively multiplayer online.) According to its website, WoW has more than 11 million monthly subscribers, making it the world's most-subscribed-to MMORPG. Players control their character avatars while going on quests in a virtual world filled with monsters and numerous other avatars. As the characters become more experienced and successfully complete quests, they gain a variety of talents and skills. Players can also team up with other avatars and participate in group quests and challenges. This allows for further character development and achievement of different levels of skill.

What Do You Think?

How would one go about self-socializing in a new, virtual reality? Have you ever escaped to a virtual world or wanted to do so? If you have assumed a virtual identity, describe your experiences as a virtual self. How do virtual realities compare to the real world? What do you think?

ADULT SOCIALIZATION

As mentioned at the outset of this chapter, socialization does not end in childhood; it is a lifelong process that continues throughout adulthood. Children become young adults, young adults become middle-agers, and the middle-aged become elderly. The adult life cycle presents new situations that require the learning of new roles. High school graduates may go to college, find a job, or join the armed services. College graduates seek a career. Many young adults get married and start a family. Half of those married will get divorced and return to being single, perhaps with parental responsibilities. Some of these people will get married a second or third time. In the process, some people will move far from their birth homes and childhood friends, while others will stay put. Some parents may face an empty nest when their children grow up and move out of the house. Retirement and old age welcome those who have made it that far. In short, there is no end to the possibilities for life-learning situations and the corresponding changes in role expectations that confront us as we go through life. In each case, a socialization process accompanies the transition in the life cycle.

Among the social concerns related to the aging process are the risks of people becoming socially isolated from loved ones and being victimized by ageism (see "A Closer Look" Box 5.8 for further elaboration on social isolation). **Ageism** refers to prejudice, discrimination, and negative stereotyping directed against people because of their age. Societies with youth-centered cultures, such as that in the United States, contribute to negative attitudes toward middle-aged and elderly adults. Workers in their fifties and early sixties, for example, are especially vulnerable to the negative consequences of the recession and economic down-spiral that began in 2008. According to the U.S. Bureau of Labor Statistics, about 1.6 million U.S. adults aged fifty-five to sixty-four were unemployed in November 2010, nearly triple the number at beginning of the recession (Garber 2010).

When the economy is suffering, employers become increasingly reluctant to hire people older than fifty. They may worry that older adults have lost their peak productive capacity or are out of touch with contemporary trends in the workplace. Or they may believe they can hire a younger person with less experience at a lower rate of pay. At the very least, employers realize that older workers are much closer to retirement than younger workers; they may therefore view the training and development of older workers as not cost-efficient. A 2009 survey conducted by ExecuNet, a recruiting and consulting network for business leaders, found that 91 percent of 258 employers surveyed considered age to be a significant factor beyond fifty. Only 5 percent of the 258 employers surveyed reported that age was never a factor (Garber 2010).

Human resources professionals and hiring managers, however, realize that workers over fifty are more likely to stay at the job longer, be more dedicated, and be absent less often than the average thirty-year-old (Garber 2010). Furthermore, aging adults are protected from age discrimination by the federal government's Age Discrimination in Employment Act of 1967, which prohibits employment discrimination based on age with regard to employees and prospective employees

A Closer Look

Box 5.8 Social Isolation

The importance of primary group participation and interaction with other humans comes to the forefront with our look at the negative effects of social isolation. Social isolation may occur at any point during one's passage through the *life cycle*—a series of developmental stages that begins at birth and continues, ideally, through old age. **Social isolation** is a state, or process, wherein a person loses significant communication and interaction with others, leading to psychological, emotional, and/or developmental problems. According to research (2004 General Social Survey) conducted by sociologists McPherson, Smith-Lovin, and Brashears (2006), Americans are especially vulnerable to social isolation. Consider, for example, that Americans, on average, report having just two close friends, down from three close friends as reported in the same comprehensive poll in 1985. Further, the number of people indicating that they had no close person with whom to discuss important matters nearly tripled from 1985 to 2004. These weakening bonds of friendship have far-reaching effects that include having fewer people to turn to in a time of crisis, fewer visitors for elderly persons in nursing homes, fewer confidants to discuss important social issues (e.g., filling out important medical and insurance forms), fewer bonding opportunities, and so on. Friendships have declined for many reasons, including a longer average work week, longer commute times, increased television viewing and computer use, and more time spent by younger people in the virtual world.

In an attempt to alleviate social isolation, many older persons have learned to embrace technology as a means of communicating with loved ones. An increasing number of older adults, including parents and grandparents, have learned to text-message their children and grandchildren. They may not be "double-thumbers" (people capable of texting at high speed by using both thumbs), but they are capable of punching in letters on a tiny cell phone pad. In many cases, these older adults have been granted friend status on their children's and grandchildren's MySpace and Facebook pages. Thus, the same tools that have created social distance between older and younger family members may be used to stay connected. Virtual socialization to the rescue!

What Do You Think?

Some young adults may consider it creepy when an older person joins a social network as a friend. They may also find it necessary to create a watered-down version of their home page to avoid disapproval from people of their parents' generation. What do you think?

age forty or older. Despite this law, many older workers find it hard to find a job, especially when the economy is bad.

A number of seniors are embracing technology not only to keep in contact with younger family members but also as a way to socialize with friends their own age. For example, the popular Nintendo Wii game is not just for kids and young adults. An increasing number of elderly people enjoy this wireless game that allows them to "play" their favorite sports, especially bowling. Wii players sit or stand in front of big-screen TV and manipulate a wireless controller that translates their motions to the screen. Bowling, which has always been a favorite with the GI Generation, is extremely popular in senior centers today in its virtual incarnation. It is so popular that many senior centers have Wii bowling leagues (Moos 2008). Nintendo has capitalized on this popularity by setting up exhibits of Wii games at conferences of the American Association of Retired Persons and at senior-living industry conventions.

Video gaming, such as playing Wii, allows elderly persons a chance to enjoy and engage in sporting activities.

Seniors learning to play video games is a clear example that learning and socialization continue throughout one's lifetime. It seems that an old dog can learn new tricks—that is, if he or she is socialized properly.

SUMMARY

Through the socialization process, we learn about culture's expectations, norms, and values. Socialization involves developmental changes brought about as the result of individuals interacting with other people, especially significant others. Sociologists view socialization as a lifelong process of learning that starts in infancy and continues throughout adulthood. Socialization is most effective in primary groups. The socialization process is so important that without it, we would not quite be human.

The socialization process accompanies human development. A number of significant theories have been put forth in an attempt to explain how human development occurs. Some of these theories favor the nature approach, while others rely more heavily on the nurture approach. Because sociologists lean heavily toward the nurture end of the nature-nurture continuum, sociological human-development theories emphasize the importance of learning (via socialization), past experience, modeling, and motivation.

Significant others, known as agents of socialization, are responsible for teaching us cultural expectations. The most important agents of socialization are one's parents (or guardians) and immediate family members. Parents and family members provide us with our initial, or primary, training. Schools, peers, the media, religion, the government, and employers are among the important agents that provide us with secondary socialization.

In contemporary culture, a number of people spend a great deal of time interacting with one another virtually rather than face-to-face. This process is called virtual socialization, and its influence on our lives is increasing. Virtual socialization is accomplished through the use of computers and other electronic devices. Older adults have learned to embrace technology as a means of keeping in contact with significant others, especially younger family members. Finding a way to keep in contact with significant others is very important, as the average American reports having just two close friends with whom to share the intimate details of his or her life.

Glossary

Ageism—Prejudice, discrimination, and negative stereotyping directed against people because of their age.

Agents of socialization—Sources of culture, including people, groups, organizations, and institutions, that teach us what we need to know in order to function properly in society.

Cognition—The mental process of knowing, which includes such aspects as perception, awareness, reasoning, judgment, and knowledge.

Conditioning—A learning process whereby individuals associate certain behaviors with rewards and others with punishments.

Cyberbullying—The use of technologies such as the Internet, cell phones, and other devices used to send or post text or images with the intent of intimidating, hurting, or embarrassing another person.

Feral children—Children raised in social isolation without human contact or who receive minimal human contact from a very young age.

"I"—The subjective (or egocentric) aspect of the self. The "I" is impulsive, spontaneous, and creative.

Instinct—An innate impulse, or tendency to act, that is common to a given species.

Mass media—The various media by which large numbers of people are informed about important happenings in society.

"Me"—The objective (socialized) aspect of self that develops through interaction with others and the internalization of the norms and values of the greater community.

Modeling—The process of learning by observing and imitating significant others.

Peer group—Associates of a similar age and usually from the same social status and background.

Primary groups—Relatively small groups whose members share a sense of "weness," intimacy, and mutual identification.

Social isolation—A state or process wherein a person loses significant communication and interaction with others, leading to psychological, emotional, and/or developmental problems.

Socialization—A process of social development and learning that occurs as individuals interact with one another and learn about society's expectations for acceptable behavior.

Virtual reality—Technology that creates a computer-simulated environment and allows users to interact within its domain.

Virtual socialization—A process that involves people learning about cultural expectations through communication and interaction with significant others in the virtual world (cyberspace).

Discussion Questions

1. Compare and contrast nature and nurture theories of human development.
2. Whom do you consider to be your primary group now that you are in college?
3. Modeling theory suggests that a child's behavior is influenced through observation, including by watching television. Do you think children can pick up bad behaviors by watching violent television shows or films? Do you think children can pick up good behaviors by watching wholesome television shows or films?
4. Have you ever maintained a strictly virtual relationship?

Web Links

To learn more about feral children, visit www.world-mysteries.com/sci_feralc.htm.

To learn more about Second Life, visit www.secondlife.com.

To learn more about World of Warcraft, visit www.worldofwarcraft.com.

To learn more about neuroimaging techniques, visit www.psych.illinois.edu/infantlab.

To learn more about the U.S. government's "virtual fence" (the SBI*net* program), visit www.dhs.gov/xlibrary/assets/sbinetfactsheet.pdf.

To learn more about aging in a youth-centered culture, visit www.nevcoeducation.com/store/index.php?main_page=product_info&products_id=381.

6 DEVIANCE, CRIME, AND SOCIAL CONTROL

The established society often views the behaviors and fads of the younger society as deviant and a sign of cultural decay. In this photo, taken in Brooklyn, NY, Sen. Eric Adams led a campaign to "Stop the Sag!"

Chapter 6

- Introductory Story
- Social Deviance
- Sociological Explanations of Deviance
- Crime
- Social Control and the Criminal Justice System
- Summary, Glossary, Discussion Questions, and Web Links

INTRODUCTORY STORY

If you are like most students, you have attended at least one wedding ceremony in your life. Although marriage customs around the world vary a great deal (see Chapter 10), most wedding ceremonies are relatively traditional, or "normal." However, it is not unusual to hear of wedding ceremonies that fall outside the norm, such as underwater ceremonies, skydiving marriages, or couples who have married while riding a Ferris wheel or rollercoaster. Think of the weddings you have attended. Were any of these ceremonies what you might call "deviant"?

In all likelihood, few compare to the wedding of Patricia Montenez, of France, who married Claude Darcy in August 1996 (*Post-Standard,* 9/1/96). You see, Darcy had died two and a half years before the ceremony took place. Darcy, a police officer in Marseille, France, was killed by an assailant while on duty. Montenez and Darcy were engaged at the time and had a son. Darcy's parents challenged Montenez's desire to proceed with the unusual wedding, and their wishes were upheld by a French court of law. Darcy's parents had argued that two prenuptial agreements were the only evidence of their son's desire to marry Montenez, and they had expired before his death. Eventually that court decision was overturned when a little detective work by Montenez's lawyer led to a doctor who testified that he had written the wrong date on the documents, meaning they were still valid when Darcy was killed. French president Jacques Chirac issued a decree allowing the wedding. About one hundred guests, including dozens of uniformed police officers, attended the brief ceremony. At Montenez's side, where Darcy would have stood, there was just an empty chair.

Some people have theme weddings in which the bride and groom dress the part of their favorite characters, such as Ken and Barbie or Romeo and Juliet. In some instances, theme weddings may involve the entire wedding party and guests portraying characters from popular movies, such as *Star Wars, Shrek, Beauty and the Beast,* or *The Lion King.* At least one wedding in Scotland has been organized around a theme from the film *Braveheart* wherein the wedding party and guests converged in an open Scottish field to perform a reenactment of the battle-charge scene (Barker 2001).

These wedding scenarios reflect challenges to time-honored ideals of marriage ceremonies in which tradition dictates a certain level of decorum and protocol. In other words, they violated social norms. Generally speaking, behaviors or activities that violate social norms are labeled as deviant. Cultural norms and ideals of morality are underlying themes when discussing deviance. All groups, organizations, and societies have rules of acceptable behavior. Rules have existed throughout time, and individuals are expected to abide by them. Society not only teaches us to conform to cultural norms but provides a number of social-control agents that serve as reminders and enforcers of rules and laws.

However, understanding social deviance is not as simple as one might think. This chapter explores the various ways in which sociology explains and classifies deviance. It also examines crime and efforts at social control.

SOCIAL DEVIANCE

When you read and thought about the introductory story in this chapter, did you notice yourself judging the participants of these nontraditional wedding ceremonies—or, for that matter, people who get married in traditional ceremonies? Judging other people's behavior is typical. As Goode (2001) explains, "Humans are evaluative creatures. We continually make judgments about the behavior of others" (p. 3). We cannot help but evaluate others because we must all meet so many expectations. Many students have already evaluated their peers in the classroom. In most cases, these evaluations are based on limited contact. Is the student sleeping in the back row hungover from a rough night of drinking? Or is that sleeping student exhausted from working the late shift in order to pay for college? Most likely, the professor will evaluate the student's sleeping behavior as deviant and maybe even insulting.

Sooner or later, everyone will do something that someone else disapproves of. These violations may be mild, such as belching in public or "flipping the bird" (raising the middle finger) at someone, or they may be more serious acts, such as assault or murder. Either way, when people violate the norms of a group, organization, or society, they risk potential negative reactions from others.

Defining Deviance

The sociological study of deviant behavior reveals that a number of circumstances influence how some behaviors come to be defined as deviant, while others are defined as acceptable. After all, no behavior is inherently deviant; all behaviors must be defined, or labeled, as deviant in order to be deviant. But what is deviance? And what makes a particular behavior deviant? Is deviant behavior the same thing as criminal behavior? These are just a few of the questions associated with the study of deviance. For the purposes of this text, **deviance** refers to any behavior that is labeled by some members of society or specific subcultural groups as an unacceptable violation of their social norms and that elicits negative reactions from others. In short, deviance involves diverging from accepted group norms. Further, people who commit such acts are considered **deviants**.

A statistical component is sometimes incorporated into definitions of deviance: according to this view, deviance is that which is unusual, rare, or uncommon. For example, Frank Schmalleger (2004) defines deviance as "human activity that violates social norms or is statistically different from the average" (p. 9). Henry Vandenburgh combines a standard definition of deviance with a statistical aspect: "In one sense, *deviance* is behavior that goes against norms, that is, behavior patterns that we expect others (and ourselves) to engage in. In another sense, deviance has a statistical definition. It's unusual behavior—behavior we seldom see others engage in" (2004, p. 4). However, Vandenburgh and others recognize the inherent problem with equating deviance merely to the statistical rare occurrence. For example, if a college student takes just three years to earn a bachelor's degree, does that make him or her a deviant? It is statistically rare, but this student is not a deviant. People who wash their hands two hundred times a day or read five books a day are not deviants just because their behavior is uncommon. As Goode (2001) explains, "Deviance may overlap with rarity, but it is far more than rarity by itself. It is entirely possible, even likely, that something of a correlation exists between rarity and deviance—that extremely rare actions are more likely to be deviant than common ones—but we cannot base our definition of deviance on rarity" (p. 23).

Morality plays a role in determining whether certain behaviors are labeled deviant or not. However, identifying certain behaviors as moral or immoral inevitably involves subjective interpretations. For example, in the United States, a taboo prohibits people from going naked in public. Women are not even allowed to go topless at the beach, something that men are allowed to do. Many people have challenged this nudity restriction displayed by "moral" Americans. For example, in the 1990s in Rochester, New York, "Patricia Marks, a New York county judge, overturned the convictions of 10 women who had been arrested for publicly displaying their breasts. The women, known as the Topfree Ten, had been arrested after baring their chests during a picnic" (Schmalleger 2004, p. 9). These women believed that they should have the right to bare their chests in public since men are allowed to do so. Judge Marks agreed with the women, ruling that the New York statute was sexist and gender biased.

As another example of morality's role in determining deviant behavior, consider the subcultural fashion of a number of contemporary youth and young adults who wear saggy pants so low that the butt is exposed. Such a style is perceived negatively by members of mainstream society. New York State senator Eric Adams (D-Brooklyn), a former police captain, believes that such a style reflects a "high tolerance for antisocial behavior" (*New York Times,* 4/1/10). As a result, Senator Adams cosponsored the posting of six "Stop the Sag" billboards throughout Brooklyn targeting the saggy trend. The billboard messages also proclaimed, "We Are Better Than This! Raise Your Pants, Raise Your Image." Adams equated wearing jeans at the waist as a sign of respect for oneself and society (Pearson 2010). The "pull up your saggy pants" theme of the billboards reminded many of the 2010 *American Idol* audition of Larry "The General" Platt, whose song "Pants on the Ground" included such lyrics as "Looking like a fool, with your pants on the ground." The "Pants on the Ground" lyrics became a mainstay of popular culture throughout 2010, and the song itself reached the top rankings in iTunes downloads. (Note: The sixty-two-year-old Platt was ineligible for *American Idol* consideration because of his age, but the producers let him audition in front of the judges anyway.) Both Senator Adams and community activist Larry Platt argued that saggy pants are disrespectful and compromise community standards of morality.

There are, however, some instances of behavior that nearly all agree are immoral. Most likely, all of us consider cannibalism to be depraved. In December 2003, a German man went on trial for cannibalism. Armin Meiwes, forty-two, admitted to having fantasies since childhood about killing and eating another human being. Meiwes wanted some-

What Do You Think?

Many teens walk around with saggy pants exposing their butts and underwear while hanging out in public. Some cities have created ordinances to forbid this. Should there be laws that dictate how people dress in public? What do you think?

one to become "a part of him." He placed an advertisement on the Internet and received four hundred responses from people who wanted to join him in acting out his fantasy. Meiwes finally met with Bernd Juergen Brandes, who reportedly agreed to fulfill Meiwes's fantasy by saying, "Now that you can see my body, I hope you'll find me tasty" (*Post-Standard,* 12/4/03). Meiwes stabbed his victim, froze some of his dismembered body parts, and ate the flesh over a period of months. He videotaped himself killing Brandes. The tape was used as evidence to prosecute Meiwes.

Painting graffiti on walls is an example of criminal activity that is often embraced by members of a deviant subculture seeking a way to express themselves.

Further complicating any attempt to establish a universal definition of deviance is the realization that deviance varies from culture to culture. As we learned in Chapter 4, cultures vary a great deal, and since each culture creates its own folkways, norms, and laws, it stands to reason that behaviors labeled as deviant will vary from culture to culture. Thus, if we reconsider the United States and its conservative stand on what constitutes proper public attire, especially on the part of women, we learn that it is actually quite liberal when compared to societies of the Middle East. Some Islamic women, depending on class, education, and country, are expected to wear loose, flowing clothing that covers them from head to toe, even to the point where it is impossible to see their faces. As a result, it is very unlikely that there is any debate there as to whether these women should be allowed to go naked at public picnics—or at beaches and other swimming venues, as is widely accepted for men, women, and children in some parts of Europe. On the other hand, in the Red Light District of Amsterdam, women can be seen displaying their bodies in store windows. These nearly nude women are selling themselves like any other commodity prominently displayed. The customer who is willing to pay for sex with these women merely steps into the back room behind these display fronts. This type of transaction is viewed simply as an exchange of money for a service provided. In short, each society is responsible for establishing norms, and these norms ultimately determine deviance.

> **What Do You Think?**
>
> A number of Americans find it peculiar for Islamic women to dress modestly from head to toe; yet, they do not find it odd when Roman Catholic nuns wear clothing that is equally concealing. Why is this the case? What do you think?

At this point, you may be thinking, or assuming, that deviance possesses an inherently negative connotation. Sociologists, however, point out that there are instances in which deviance can be described in positive terms. **Positive deviance** refers to behavior in which a rule violation generates a positive reaction from others. Some acts of civil disobedience, such as Rosa Parks's refusal to give up her bus seat on December 1, 1955, in Montgomery, Alabama, which set the tone for the civil rights movement, and Harriet Tubman's attempts to free slaves through the Underground Railroad prior to and during the Civil War, are considered examples of positive deviance. People who violate the established norms, or laws, in an attempt to help others who are being victimized are generally acknowledged as "fighting the good fight" for necessary moral reform.

As this brief discussion of deviance illustrates, labeling something as "deviant" is clearly a matter of social construction. Cultural norms, ideals of morality, and individuals and institutions occupying positions of power play the major roles in determining what is, and what is not, considered social deviance. Sociologist Howard Becker (1963) perhaps best sums up this notion of deviance as a matter of social construction by claiming that it is not the act itself that makes an act deviant, but the reaction to, or the labeling of, the act.

What Do You Think?

If deviance is a matter of social construction, are any social acts inherently deviant? Have you or any of your friends engaged in behavior that you did not consider deviant but that others perceived as such? What do you think?

Despite the complexities of determining what is and is not deviant behavior, there is a consensus that deviance, in one form or another, exists in all societies. This leads us to a fundamental question: why do people commit deviant acts? As the following pages illustrate, there are a number of sociological explanations for deviance.

Even when surrounded by people, individuals may feel a sense of anomie, or social distance from the greater society.

SOCIOLOGICAL EXPLANATIONS OF DEVIANCE

Sociological theories incorporate a diverse, multicausal framework in their explanation of deviant behavior. Factors and theories including social disorganization, anomie and strain, cultures and subcultures, social bonds and control, social learning, labeling, and conflict are all recognized and studied as causes of, and explanations for, deviance.

Social-Disorganization Theory (Chicago School)

Social-disorganization theory, which emphasizes that certain neighborhoods (social environments) are more likely to produce crime and delinquency, is one of the most popular and lasting sociological approaches in explaining deviance. Social-disorganization theory developed from the early ecological research on urban development conducted by sociologists at the University of Chicago during the 1920s and 1930s. Researchers at Chicago discovered that high rates of crime and delinquency were found in areas with high rates of other social problems (e.g., high unemployment, high percentage of single-parent families, low levels of education). They theorized that people in such neighborhoods feel marginalized from the larger community because of limited financial resources being allocated to meet their needs.

Social disorganization itself is caused by rapid social change, which disrupts the normal operation of a local area. In neighborhoods where the family and friendship groups are solidly grounded in societal norms and where stability is present, social organization generally exists as well. But in a socially disorganized area, dominant values and norms compete with other, sometimes deviant values and norms. As different cultural ideas emerge and as the values and norms of the younger generation clash with those of the older generation, social cohesion breaks down, and a new set of norms emerges. The behaviors and attitudes of the new generation are likely to be labeled as deviant by the adherents of the previously established norms (and vice versa).

Anomie or Strain Theory

Anomie theory, or strain theory as it is sometimes called, was established by Robert Merton, who borrowed Emile Durkheim's term "anomie," which comes from the Greek *anomia,* meaning "without law." In his 1893 book *The Division of Labor in Society,* Durkheim used the word "anomie" to refer to a condition of deregulation occurring in society. This deregulation, or normlessness, left people confused about societal expectations, which in turn served to encourage deviant behavior. Borrowing from Durkheim, sociologists define **anomie** as the absence of norms, or normlessness.

Durkheim argued that people are confronted with anomie when they are not faced with sufficient moral constraints or do not have a clear concept of what is and is not acceptable behavior. Durkheim viewed anomie as a pathology, which implied that deviant behaviors and the problems of the world could be cured: with the proper level of regulation and a clear understanding of proper morality, people could form a cohesive, smoothly operating society.

Durkheim argued that deviance and crime serve a functional role in society. The fact that certain behaviors are labeled as inappropriate and unacceptable means that members of society have a script for acceptable behavior. When people break the rules, or laws, of society and are subsequently punished, it serves as a reminder to others of the consequences for violating norms and morality. Deviance, then, helps to establish and maintain boundaries of acceptable behavior. Deviance may also serve as a barometer (a measuring device) of social strain in society. When a society experiences a great deal of deviance, such a trend reflects a growing dissatisfaction with the rules of that society. Society must respond to deviance and crime in order to maintain its own cohesiveness. As a result of crime and deviance, each society creates a large number of occupational categories. Workers such as police officers, correctional officers, probation officers, and private security guards all owe their jobs to the violators of cultural norms and community standards of morality.

What Do You Think?

Durkheim argued that deviance and crime serve a function in society. Do you think the society you live in, or any society, would be better off if deviance did not exist? What do you think?

Merton's anomie theory (first published as "Social Structure and Anomie" in 1938) is based on the premise that society encourages all persons to attain culturally desirable goals, but the opportunities to reach these goals are not equal for all members of society. Certain people, especially members of minority groups and the lower social classes, often encounter barriers to success not encountered by the wealthy and privileged members of society. Faced with the strain of being unable to realize their aspirations, some people seek unconventional or illegal means in the pursuit of culturally defined goals. Merton ([1949] 1968) argued that when individuals are faced with the strain caused by anomic conditions, they have a choice among five modes of adaptation:

1. *Conformity:* This involves abiding by convention and accepting things as they are. Conformists have accepted the major goals of society and the approved ways of attaining them. This is the most common mode of behavior. The realization that most people follow the rules helps to explain why most citizens are not criminals, even those who reside in high-crime neighborhoods.
2. *Innovation:* This mode of behavior is often used by those who have accepted the prescribed goals of society but use atypical (illegitimate) means to attain them. Innovation is the most common deviant adaptation of behavior. For many members of society, deviant adaptation (e.g., bank robbery) may actually represent a more efficient means of reaching a goal than the approved means to do so (e.g., working hard at a menial job earning minimum wage). This helps to explain why a disproportionate number of street criminals are from the lower socioeconomic classes and why successful businesspersons are very unlikely to rob a convenience store for $50.
3. *Ritualism:* This adaptation is viewed as deviant by some researchers but not by others. Ritualists reject higher goals but work toward less lofty goals

by institutionally approved means. Low-level administrative assistants and clerks are an example of ritualists. Ritualists simply go through the motions day after day, are never really happy with life, but have found relative happiness through scaling down their ambitions. Students may want to ask themselves whether this is a deviant behavior.

4. *Retreatism:* Retreatists reject both society's goals and the means of attaining them. Rather than innovate or conform, these people choose to cut themselves off from the world (e.g., monks, social hermits, drug addicts, and street people). This mode of adaptation has become increasingly common in the postmodern world.
5. *Rebellion:* These people are so upset (strained) with the current social structure and/or value system that they seek to destroy it rather than accept or modify it through legitimate means. Anarchists, nihilists, and militant groups are among those who subscribe to rebellion.

Of these five behavioral adaptations, Merton considered three (innovation, retreatism, and rebellion) to be deviant; in his view, the other two (conformity and ritualism) were not. It should be noted that a number of sociologists consider ritualism to be a deviant adaptation.

Subculture/Cultural Deviance Theory

By the 1950s and early 1960s, sociologists were studying deviant behavior in the context of a new sociological concept, the subculture. As described in Chapter 4, a subculture refers to a category of people found within the greater society. Subculture members share many of the same ideas, values, and norms of the greater society, but they differ in specific other areas. Subculture theorists believe that deviants who violate certain rules adhere more closely to the norms of their subcultural group than to those of the larger society. "Cultural deviance theory proposes that delinquency is a result of a desire to conform to cultural values that are to some extent in conflict with those of conventional society. In part, this perspective is a direct offshoot of social disorganization theory because part of that theory ... suggests that criminal values and traditions emerge within communities most affected by social disorganization" (Shelden, Tracy, and Brown 2001, p. 172).

The concept of reference groups emerged along with that of subcultures. Reference groups may include family, friends, colleagues, and inspirational others. In many ways, reference groups are similar to subcultures; in fact, this "reference point" idea leads to the formation of a subculture. For example, if a juvenile is raised in a family that has gang members, he or she may seek a peer group of gang members to join. Subcultures are formed when reference group members share a number of common goals and traits. The reference group serves as the point of comparison or contrast in evaluating one's own status and forming judgments about oneself. The reference group concept is particularly useful in accounting for the choices made among possible alternative courses of action. "The concept of reference group can ... greatly facilitate research on the manner in which each actor's orientation toward his world is structured" (Shibutani 1955, p. 563). Within the framework of the reference group, members feel a great sense of loyalty to each other, they aspire to gain or maintain acceptance, and consequently, group norms take on a higher value than society's norms. When these events occur, a subculture has been formed. If the subculture sanctions various forms of deviant behavior, members of this subculture will freely participate in such activities because they have come to value the judgments of others found within the reference group.

Social-Bond and Control Theory

Social-bond and control theory is a unique perspective for explaining deviant and delinquent behavior. Instead of asking why deviants commit acts of deviance, this perspective asks, "Why doesn't everyone participate in deviance?" In other words, what prevents everyone from being deviant? The answer is socialization. Citizens are socialized to conform to rules. Social-bond and control theorists believe that deviance simply reflects poor socialization. Thus, in order to eliminate or minimize deviance, society must find a way to get individuals to form a bond with society. The key to forming bonds and attachments to society rests with proper socialization. "Proper socialization leads to conformity, while improper socialization leads to nonconformity. Delinquency is one consequence of improper socialization" (Shelden, Tracy, and Brown 2001, p. 175). Delinquency, then, is the result of the weakening, breakdown, or absence of effective social controls. Deviants are people who have not developed bonds with the society that spawned them.

Control theory has a number of variations, all of which assume one basic point: "Human beings, young or old, must be held in check, or somehow controlled, if criminal or delinquent tendencies are to be repressed" (Shoemaker 2000, p. 160). Sykes and Matza (1957) believe that deviance cannot be explained simply as an absence of social controls; instead, it must also involve a "will to delinquency." Thus, to become deviant one must be willing to participate in delinquent acts. Furthermore, once individuals have found a way to justify their willingness to commit deviant behavior, they become free to commit additional acts of deviancy.

The most popular version of control theory, put forth by Travis Hirschi, holds that all humans are basically antisocial, and all are capable of committing deviance and crime. Only when people have formed a bond with the greater society do they refrain from committing deviant acts. Socialization leads to this social bond. Significant others teach each new generation the rules and expectations of society. When individuals internalize these rules, they have formed a bond with society. According to Hirschi (1969), this bond includes four major elements: *attachment,* or ties of affection (e.g., family and friends); *commitment,* or dedication to long-term goals (e.g., children going to school and planning for college), a type of delayed gratification; *involvement,* eliminating unstructured time and getting involved with group activities (e.g., playing sports, joining civic organizations); and *belief* in the morality of the law (e.g., stealing is indeed wrong). Adults, especially parents, must make sure that their children have embraced these four elements of the social bond, or their children will be at increased risk for participating in deviance. In short, the best way to keep children away from delinquency is to keep them busy with socially productive activities. Adults must also reaffirm their social bond to society; otherwise, they too risk being lured by deviance.

Social-Learning Theory

As the name implies, **social-learning theory** is based on the idea that individuals learn how to become delinquent. "One of the first theorists to associate the origins of crime with a learning process was Gabriel Tarde. In his book *The Law of Imitation,* Tarde argued that crime results from one person's imitating the actions of another. Although he also took into account biological and psychological factors, he believed that crime is essentially a social product" (Kratcoski and Kratcoski 1996, p. 56). An individual learns behavior through interaction with others, whether directly (by being taught) or indirectly (through observation). Through interaction with others, individuals learn the norms, beliefs, attitudes, and values treasured by the interactants.

According to the social-learning theory perspective, youths learn to become delinquent through three related processes: acquisition, instigation, and maintenance. *Acquisition* refers to the initial introduction to a deviant form of behavior (e.g., one juvenile offers cigarettes or alcohol to another juvenile). *Instigation* occurs when the individual actually participates in some form of delinquent behavior (e.g., a juvenile accepts the offer of an opportunity to smoke or drink). *Maintenance* refers to participation in the delinquent behavior consistently over a period. Only in this way will deviant or criminal behavior persist.

Edwin Sutherland is considered to be among the most prominent of all social-learning theorists. According to Sutherland's theory of differential association, the more an individual associates with criminals and deviants, the more likely he or she will be to learn and accept their behaviors, values, attitudes, and beliefs (Sutherland and Cressey 1978). Continued association reinforces these behaviors and values, which Sutherland refers to as modeling influences. Over time, the individual comes to view attitudes and beliefs that are deviant (as defined by society and especially the criminal justice system) as acceptable; at that point, the individual will attempt to justify or rationalize deviant activities inspired by these attitudes and beliefs.

The key to social-learning theory is that criminal and deviant behavior is learned through socialization; it is not an inherited trait. If the greatest number of associations that youths have are the positive, conventional ones of society, then they will be more likely to embrace those values. Conversely, if youths' primary associations are with deviants, the likelihood increases that they will become deviant themselves.

The primary criticism of this theory relates to the vagueness of the term "association." Sutherland and Cressey (1978) admitted that their differential-association theory was not precise enough to make rigorous empirical tests possible; thus, the theory is difficult to evaluate scientifically. Despite this criticism, differential-association social-learning theory remains one of the most popular theories of delinquent and criminal behavior. This theory's core idea has become popularized with the following statement often expressed by parents: "We don't want you hanging out with that group of people because they are a bad influence on you."

Labeling Theory

One of the most prominent symbolic-interactionist approaches to the study and explanation of deviant and criminal behavior is offered by the labeling perspective. Labeling theorists do not examine how or why people become delinquents and criminals; instead, they concentrate on the effects of being labeled as deviant. Furthermore, labeling theorists attempt to uncover the processes that lead to who gets to decide what is deviant and criminal (the labelers) and how it is that certain behaviors come to be labeled criminal while others are legal. Labeling theorists investigate such factors as religion, social class, race, and sex, as well as the relationships between these factors and the formulation of criminal definitions and the major causes of crime itself.

What Do You Think?

Social class often intersects with the labeling process. That is, when wealthy people do something odd, it tends to be labeled as quaint or eccentric, but when poor people engage in similar behaviors, they are called deviant. Why is this? What do you think?

The effects of labeling are often revealed in early childhood. A child who is constantly told he or she is "no good" and "will never amount to anything" will develop a negative self-image. Negative labels tend to produce a negative self-image, which in turn results in negative behavior. In order to escape this negative label, the individual may seek the company of those who offer a more positive one.

Labeling is an important factor in the creation of a deviant identity. The allocation of labels is often determined by social-control agents, and it is not unusual for these unwanted labels to consume the identity of individuals; when this occurs, a self-fulfilling prophecy has been created. A **self-fulfilling prophecy** consists of people taking to heart the labels bestowed upon them, coming to view themselves in terms of those labels, and then acting in ways that correspond to those labels. When this happens, conventional society often shuns the deviant. At the same time, a deviant group may accept the person and teach him or her to reject the rejecters.

Individuals' rejection of negative labels bestowed upon them by their rejecters is similar to Sykes and Matza's (1957) neutralizing "condemnation of the condemners" technique, whereby the motives and behaviors of those who disapprove of a behavior are deemed suspect. This is one of five **techniques of neutralization** that Sykes and Matza articulated, allowing people to free themselves of negative labels bestowed upon them for committing delinquent acts. The other four techniques of neutralization are denial of responsibility (e.g., "I didn't mean it"), denial of injury ("No one was really hurt by my act"), denial of the victim ("They had it coming"), and appealing to higher loyalties ("I answer to a higher power than societal laws").

Furthermore, negative labels often leave people feeling stigmatized (disgraced). Erving Goffman (1963) used the term "**stigma**" to describe the labels used by society to devalue certain of its members and certain social groups. Stigmas fuel the negative self-fulfilling prophecy that specific members of society may possess.

Edwin Lemert (1951) developed the concepts of primary and secondary deviance. **Primary deviance** applies to individuals who are guilty of committing acts of deviance that remain undetected or unrecognized by others. With **secondary deviance**, the actor has been identified and labeled as a deviant. The process of moving from primary to secondary deviance is often complex, but the critical determination is societal reaction and identification. The individual has been labeled as a deviant when he or she reaches the secondary level of deviance.

Conflict Theory

Whereas functionalism views society from a consensus perspective that relies on shared values, norms, and beliefs regarding morality, conflict theory highlights the imbalance of power found in society, especially in light of the economic and social inequalities present in all societies. Inspired by the ideas of Karl Marx, conflict theorists argue that those who control the means of production are in a social position to dictate to others what is right and wrong behavior. Conflict theorists do not view the law as expressing a broad consensus among the masses to protect the members of society; rather, they see it as a means of forcing one group's beliefs and way of life onto others.

For conflict theorists, the most important variable to study is power. Those in power—the power elite—may exercise both legitimate and illegitimate means of maintaining their advantageous position, for they have a vested interest in doing so. These power elites are the very people who are in a position to impose both their will and their ideas of what constitutes deviance. This power position is especially important in the creation and enforcement of laws and the administration of sanctions against nonconformists.

Conversely, the conflict perspective also teaches that those without power will want some, and they will find some way of demonstrating what little power they have. This often entails participating in illegal and deviant activities (e.g., rebellion).

Quinney (1977) linked crime to the modern capitalist political and economic system, suggesting that the capitalist system itself produces a number of social problems. This is especially true for the economically marginalized, such as the oppressed lower working class, the poor, and racial and ethnic minorities. Those in power (the capitalists) will exert their control over those without power. From this perspective, the capitalistic system creates inequality in such forms as the development of an **underclass**, that is, the extremely poor populations that have been abandoned in inner cities due to *capital flight* (the exodus of businesses) and *white flight* (the exodus of middle- and upper-class persons—mostly whites). The designation of an underclass area is determined when a census tract zone reaches a poverty level of over 40 percent. Although the term "underclass" does not innately possess a racial or ethnic connotation, the majority of underclass neighborhoods are occupied by such minority groups as blacks and Hispanics/Latinos.

Conflict theorists also highlight the shifting labor market (which began during the 1970s) as another cause of economic disparity, thus deviance. In their view, the United States has reached the last stage of the Industrial Revolution, as manufacturing and factory jobs are disappearing and are being replaced by service-economy jobs that require highly skilled, educated workers. Data provided by the U.S. Bureau of Labor Statistics (2009a) reveal that in 2008, 116,451,700 (77.2 percent) of the 150,931,700 total jobs were in the service-providing sector of the economy. In contrast, in 1970 approximately 63 percent of all jobs were in the

TABLE 6.1 2009 Unemployment Rate by Level of Education

LEVEL OF EDUCATION	UNEMPLOYMENT RATE (%)
Doctoral degree	2.5
Professional degree	2.3
Master's degree	3.9
Bachelor's degree	5.2
Associate's degree	6.8
Some college, no degree	8.6
High school graduate	9.7
Less than a high school diploma	14.6

Source: U.S. Bureau of Labor Statistics 2009c.

service economy (Godbout 1993). For those lacking the job skills that the service sector demands, finding a job will become increasingly difficult. Those most likely to suffer from this continuing shift in the labor market are the poorly educated. As Table 6.1 reveals, as one's level of education decreases, the unemployment rate increases (except in the top two categories). (Note: Chapter 11 shows that median weekly earnings increase as one's level of education increases.)

It should be pointed out, however, that deviance and crime exist in all societies—industrialized or not—and that they existed long before the advent of industrialization. It would be simplistic and inaccurate solely to blame capitalism as the cause of all forms of deviance and crime.

CRIME

Crime is simply defined as any deviant behavior that violates a law. However, intent is often a critical aspect of criminal activity. Bartol (1995) states, "Intentional means that the behavior did not occur accidentally or under duress. To be held criminally responsible, a person must have known what he or she was doing during the criminal act and must have known that it was wrong" (p. 17). Thus, crime contains two aspects: an *act* (or, in some cases, the failure to act when the law requires it) and *criminal intent* (in legal terminology, *mens rea,* or a "guilty mind"). Intent varies by degree, ranging from willful conduct at one extreme to negligence (meaning that the criminal act was not deliberate) at the other. Prosecutors consider the degree of intent in determining

What Do You Think?

We have described a variety of theoretical perspectives that attempt to explain deviance. Of the theories presented here, which strikes you as the most valid? What are your reasons for choosing this theory? What do you think?

Connecting Sociology and Popular Culture

Box 6.1 *Mens Rea* and Other Aspects of the Law in *Legally Blonde*

Legally Blonde was released in 2001, and its opening gross proceeds of more than $20 million made it a "sleeper hit." It went on to gross over $96 million in North America alone. *Legally Blonde* propelled Reese Witherspoon as a leading actress—and one of the highest paid in the industry. The fashionable adventures of Witherspoon's character, Elle Woods, at Harvard also inspired a number of female law students (Elkins 2010).

Elle Woods is a bubbly, outgoing blonde sorority girl who struggles to be taken seriously, especially by her boyfriend Warner Huntington III (Matthew Davis). After she graduates from CULA (a fictitious California University in Los Angeles) with a degree in fashion merchandising, Warner breaks up with her to attend Harvard Law School. He also tells Elle that he needs to date and marry a woman with a better pedigree than she in order to advance his legal and political aspirations. Eager to win Warner back, Elle decides to take the Law School Admission Test (the graduate entrance exam into law school) and earns a very high score. She then produces a video personal statement, something quite rare for students to do in 2001. The personal statement is quite comical because it has little to do with law school. In fact, the most relevant legal aspect of the admissions video occurs when she shouts, "I object," after receiving some unwanted attention from a passerby (Elkins 2010). Elle is accepted into Harvard not so much because of her qualifications but because of the uniqueness of her personal statement.

Despite a number of early setbacks, Elle works hard toward her law degree. At one point in the film, she helps her new best friend, Paulette Bonafonte (Jennifer Coolidge), retrieve her beloved dog from an ex-boyfriend, Dewey Newcombe. Elle proclaims, "I'm Elle Woods. Miss Bonafante's attorney. And I'm here to discuss the legal situation at hand. Do you understand what subject matter jurisdiction is? Well, due to habeas corpus, you and Miss Bonafante had a common law marriage which heretofore entitles her to what is legally referred to as equitable division of the assets. Due to the fact that you've retained this residence, Miss Bonafante is entitled to full canine property ownership and will be enforcing said ownership right now." And with that, Elle and Paulette drive off with the dog, leaving a dumbfounded ex-boyfriend behind in the rearview mirror.

Elle eventually wins an internship with Professor Callahan (Victor Garber). Elle, Warner, and Warner's

whether, for example, to charge someone with first-degree murder, second-degree murder, negligent manslaughter, or justifiable homicide (e.g., self-defense).

Have you ever worried about being a crime victim? It seems as though crime exists everywhere and a cursory reading of the "police blotter" section of a typical newspaper or online news site reminds us that crime exists in a variety of forms. Typically, crimes are classified into one of five categories, each of which is examined in the following pages: street crime, white-collar crime, victimless crime, organized crime, and political crime. (Note: A discussion of hate crimes appears in Chapter 8.) We also discuss reporting crime and the compilation of crime statistics.

new girlfriend, Vivian Kensington (Selma Blair), are assigned to a case that involves defending Brooke Taylor-Wyndham (Ali Larter), a famous fitness instructor accused of murdering her billionaire husband. Brooke was once Elle's fitness instructor, and they also belong to the same sorority. As a result, they develop an instant admiration for each other. While Elle is visiting her in jail, Brooke discloses her alibi but makes Elle promise not to reveal it (Brooke admits that she had liposuction on the day of the murder, but public knowledge that a fitness guru relies on liposuction to stay in shape would ruin her reputation). When pressed by Professor Callahan, the lead lawyer for the defense, for Brooke's alibi, Elle refuses and is dropped from his legal team. Callahan also makes a sexual advance toward Elle. When Brooke learns about this, she fires Callahan and hires Elle to defend her.

Ill-prepared but undaunted by the challenge of her first court case, a murder trial at that, Elle is instructed by the judge to begin questioning. Elle states, "First of all, I would like to point out that not only is there no proof in this case, but there is a complete lack of *mens rea,* which, by definition tells us there can be no crime." The judge chastises her by asking why she is giving a vocabulary lesson when she should be questioning her witness. Elle begins her questioning of Chutney Windham, daughter of the deceased. Chutney claims that at the time of murder, she was in the shower washing her hair. Recalling Chutney's earlier admission that she had had a perm earlier in the day at the hair salon, Elle quickly points out that the first cardinal rule of perm maintenance forbids wetting one's hair due to the risk of deactivating the ammonium thioglycolate. And because Chutney has had many perms in the past, Elle suspects that Chutney not only was not in the shower but had time to kill Mr. Windham and hide the gun. Without realizing what she is saying, Chutney yells, "I didn't mean to shoot him. I thought it was you (pointing at Brooke) walking through the door." And with that, everyone in the court knows Chutney accidentally killed her own father. Brooke is a free woman, and Elle has won her first murder trial.

What Do You Think?

Elle Woods believes strongly in her abilities and refuses to let people tell her what she can and cannot do. How realistic is her success in *Legally Blonde*? That is, could a person with a degree in fashion merchandising gain entrance into Harvard Law School? What do you think?

Street Crime

Street crime is a loose term used by many sociologists, criminologists, and law enforcement agencies to describe criminal acts committed in public outdoor places, including streets, playgrounds, shopping areas, business districts, and even residential neighborhoods; it encompasses infractions like purse snatching, painting graffiti on public buildings, and acts of vandalism. Sociologists who study street crime use the distinction made by the Federal Bureau of Investigation (FBI) in classifying the wide variety of crimes that fit this parameter. The FBI divides street crime into two subcategories: violent offenses and property offenses. Violent offenses include homicide, assault, forcible rape, and robbery. Property offenses include burglary, larceny-theft, and motor vehicle theft.

The most serious of all violent offenses is homicide, or the killing of one human being by another. Homicide includes a variety of behaviors that may be either non-deviant or deviant. In many societies, killing to protect oneself or others (especially loved ones) is not considered deviant; such behavior does not generally violate social norms. There are two forms of homicide: noncriminal and criminal. Noncriminal homicide includes excusable and justifiable homicide. Excusable homicides are accidents or misfortunes involving neither negligence nor unlawful intent (i.e., hunting accidents). Justifiable homicides result from necessity or the lawful duty to protect oneself or others (e.g., a police officer who kills a suspect within line-of-duty guidelines or a home owner who, in self-defense, kills an attacking intruder). Criminal homicides (those causing the death of another person without legal justification or excuse) include murder and manslaughter. Murder is the act of taking a human life unlawfully. The FBI defines murder as "the willful killing of one human being by another." Variations of murder include premeditated murder, also known as first-degree murder ("murder one" in police jargon), in which the killing was planned ahead of time, and felony murder, which refers to killings that occur during the commission of a felony such as rape or robbery. Felony murders are often not premeditated, but the law treats them as if they were. Murder is punishable by life in prison and sometimes by execution. Manslaughter can be negligent or nonnegligent. Nonnegligent manslaughter is an intentional killing that lacks "malice of forethought of murder" (premeditation). Heat-of-passion crimes are examples of nonnegligent manslaughter. A heat-of-passion killing requires that the offender have been adequately provoked by the victim and that the killing occurred before the offender's blood had "cooled." For example, if someone returns home to find his or her spouse in bed with another person and, angrily and immediately, reacts to the situation by killing the spouse and/or the other person, such a killing is ruled a heat-of-passion crime because the killer was provoked and acted without malice aforethought—he or she had never intended to come home and kill someone. Negligent manslaughter is an unintentional killing that takes place during the commission of a misdemeanor violation, such as reckless driving, which might lead, say, to the death of a person crossing the street.

Assault is another major violent offense. "Assault is the intentional infliction of bodily injury on another person, or attempt to inflict such injury. It becomes aggravated assault when the intention is to inflict serious bodily injury. Aggravated assault is often accompanied by the use of a deadly or dangerous weapon" (Bartol and Bartol 2005, p. 286). Simple assault is applied to acts of violence against a person that inflict less than serious bodily injury without a deadly weapon (e.g., punching someone in the gut over a disagreement).

Another violent offense is robbery. Robbery is the unlawful taking of, or the attempt to take, property that belongs to another by use or threat of force. Rape, commonly viewed as unwanted sex forced by one person on another, actually takes a variety of forms. The FBI's Uniform Crime Reports (UCR) distinguish among three categories of rape: (1) forcible rape, (2) statutory rape, and (3) attempted forcible rape. "Some jurisdictions draw a distinction between forcible rape with the use of a weapon and forcible rape without the use of weapon. Although the UCR . . . does not make such a distinction, it does, however, record statistics on the use of weapons associated with the crime of rape. Other types of rapes include spousal rape, gang rape, and homosexual rape" (Schmalleger 2004, p. 54). As we learn later in this chapter, rape is a highly underreported crime, as victims often fear the stigma attached to it.

Citizens are far more likely to be victimized by property offenses than by street crime offenses. Property crime occurs when something of value is taken from its owner by a perpetrator. One type of property offense is burglary, or breaking and entering. Burglary involves taking someone else's property or goods by stealth (without the owner's knowledge). Because the potential threat to home occupants (even if not home at the time of the initial break-in) is so high, most jurisdictions punish burglary as a felony. It is also common for states to enact laws creating different degrees of burglary. For example, nighttime forced entry into a home is more heavily punished than a daytime entry into a nonresidential structure by an unarmed offender (Siegel 1995). Nearly two out of three burglaries are residential in nature, and the largest percentage involves forcible entry (e.g., breaking a window or picking a lock). **Larceny-theft** refers to the illegal carrying away of personal property belonging to another with the purpose of depriving the owner of its possession and with the intent to convert this property to the taker's own use. Larceny generally refers to such crimes as shoplifting (theft of merchandise offered for sale in a store or other business), passing bad checks, and other forms of theft (e.g., downloading music illegally from the Internet) that do not involve force, threats to the victim, or forced entry. (See "Connecting Sociology and Popular Culture" Box 6.2 for a discussion on downloading music.) Motor vehicle theft involves the theft, or attempted theft, of any motorized vehicle (e.g., an automobile, truck, bus, tractor, boat, riding lawn mower, or snowmobile).

White-Collar Crime

Coined by Edwin Sutherland in his 1939 presidential address to the American Sociological Association, the term "white-collar crime" has since become recognized throughout the world. Sutherland defined **white-collar crime** as "crime

Connecting Sociology and Popular Culture

Box 6.2 Downloading Music

For generations now, people have made copies of sound recordings without paying for them. In the 1960s, the state-of-the-art copying method involved using a tape recorder to tape music played on a phonograph or heard via a radio broadcast. With improvements in technology, the ability to record music without paying for it has advanced radically. Since the mid-1990s, it has been fairly common for young people, including college students, to download and share music on the Internet.

Many students may not know, however, that the Recording Industry Association of America (RIAA) considers this behavior to be criminal activity, as it involves the theft of intellectual property (copyrighted material). Since 2003, the RIAA—whose corporate membership makes 90 percent of the nation's recorded music—has been regularly suing people who steal recorded material via downloading and file-sharing programs such as LimeWire and Kazaa (Seely 2007).

College students are among those who have been on the receiving end of the RIAA's wrath. The RIAA estimates that college students downloaded 1.6 billion songs in 2007 without paying for them (Seely 2007). To combat this, the RIAA obtains Internet addresses of individuals who use file-sharing programs (from the file-sharing companies themselves), send the offenders warning letters and/or bills for the estimated dollar value of the material stolen, and then threaten to sue if the perpetrator refuses to pay. Most recipients of such letters decide to settle with the RIAA, but in a highly publicized case, one such music sharer, a Boston University graduate student, fought back—and lost. On July 31, 2009, a federal jury ordered the student to pay $675,000 to four record labels. The student admitted in court that he had downloaded and distributed thirty songs online. The only issue for the jury to decide was how much in damages to award the record labels. Under federal copyright law (Title 17

committed by a person of respectability and high status in the course of his occupation" ([1949] 1983, p. 7). Although the definition has been modified over the years to include almost any nonstreet crime—such as tax evasion, receiving illegal Social Security payments, identity theft, and buying on credit with no intention of paying for the merchandise—most white-collar crime is committed by professionals during the course of their occupation. White-collar crime includes such activities as the manufacture and distribution of unsafe products (e.g., automobiles, toys, and household appliances) that lead to consumer deaths, embezzlement (stealing from an organization via a position of trust, such as bookkeeper or cashier), price fixing (collaborating with other businesses to sell goods or services to the public at a certain price), and extortion (obtaining money or property through coercion or threats). Physicians who defraud insurance companies or government programs such as Medicare are also guilty of white-collar crime.

The FBI recognizes a specific category of white-collar crime called corporate fraud. In 2002, in the wake of corporate scandals such as those perpetrated by Enron and Worldcom, President George W. Bush created a corporate-fraud task

of the United States Code), the recording companies were entitled to between $759 and $30,000 per infringement. The law also allows as much as $150,000 per track if the jury finds the infringements were willful (*The Citizen,* 8/1/09).

Currently, the RIAA works with colleges and universities in an attempt to curtail this deviant behavior by cutting off college aid to students who illegally download music off the Internet. Many college students justify their behavior by claiming that they want to sample music before deciding whether to purchase an entire CD. A number of people believe that music should be shared with others freely. Most students, however, do admit that downloading music without paying for it is wrong.

College students, of course, are not the only people who illegally download music. In 2009, a federal jury ruled that Jammie Thomas-Rasset, a thirty-two-year-old mother of four from Brainerd, Minnesota, had violated music copyrights and ordered her to pay recording companies $1.92 million—$80,000 per song for the twenty-four songs she copied. In this case, Thomas-Rasset was unwilling to pay the fine for committing the crime. When asked about the jury's decision, she replied, "There's no way they're ever going to get that. I'm a mom, limited means, so I'm not going to worry about it now" (*Post-Standard,* 6/19/09, p. A15). In January 2010, the judge who oversaw the Thomas-Rasset case reduced the fine to just $2,250 per song (Masnick 2010). Both Thomas-Rasset and the recording industry plan to appeal the decision further.

What Do You Think?

Have you ever downloaded music from the Internet or file-sharing programs without paying for it? Do you consider this theft? Why or why not? Do you believe recording artists deserve to paid for their labor? Or do you believe that file sharing is a legitimate means of spreading the popularity of music? What do you think?

force to investigate and prosecute such crimes (Gongloff 2002). Corporate fraud involves accounting schemes and obstruction of justice committed by executives or corporate representatives in order to benefit their businesses. According to the FBI (2006), corporate fraud involves the following activities:

1. Falsification of financial information, including false accounting entries, bogus trades designed to inflate profit or hide losses, and false transactions designed to evade regulatory oversight.
2. Self-dealing by corporate insiders, including insider trading, kickbacks, backdating of executive stock options, misuse of corporate property for personal gain, and individual tax violations related to self-dealing.
3. Fraud in connection with an otherwise legitimately operated mutual or hedge fund: late trading, certain market-timing schemes, falsification of net asset values, and other fraudulent or abusive trading practices by, within, or involving a mutual or hedge fund (see Box 6.3 for an example of a hedge fund fraud scheme).
4. Obstruction of justice designed to conceal any of the above-noted types of criminal conduct, particularly when the obstruction impedes the inquiries

of the Securities and Exchange Commission (SEC), other regulatory agencies, or law enforcement agencies.

This brief glimpse into the scope of white-collar crime should help us to understand that white-collar crime costs society far more than street crimes; this is true both in terms of loss of life and total dollars. And yet, white-collar criminals often get away with their crimes. How is this? The answer rests with the realization that white-collar criminals typically hold positions of high status, and their crimes are difficult to detect because few people have the necessary access or knowledge to expose what they are up to. Furthermore, high-ranking officials are in a position to prevent effective investigation when wrongdoing is suspected. They are also in a position to cover their steps and may attempt to set up underlings as scapegoats. Even when a white-collar criminal has been arrested, prosecution is more difficult than for a street criminal, and it is hampered by the fact that underfunded agencies (e.g., the SEC and the Environmental Protection Agency) are responsible for detecting white-collar crimes. White-collar criminals are generally able to hire high-priced law firms to work on their defense. Judges and juries are sometimes biased in favor of the white-collar criminal if he or she is a pillar of the community. If found guilty of a crime, white-collar criminals generally receive far more lenient sentences than street criminals and are incarcerated in low-level security prisons (see "A Closer Look" Box 6.3 for a discussion of the white-collar crimes of Bernard Madoff).

Victimless Crimes

Victimless crimes can be defined as illegal acts in which all direct participants are willing and consenting adults. If a minor is involved or if all parties are not willing participants, it is not a victimless crime. However, the term "victimless crime" is somewhat misleading, as it implies not that there is never a victim but rather that such crimes do not require a victim. Examples of victimless crimes include recreational drug use, prostitution, and some forms of gambling.

Take prostitution, for example. In most cases the prostitute provides a service and the customer (or "john") pays for it. End of transaction, no victims. But is this really the case? Closer analysis reveals that in many scenarios involving prostitution, someone may be victimized. One potential victim is the customer, who may acquire a sexually transmitted disease (STD) through contact with the prostitute or who may be set up and robbed, even killed, by the prostitute (with or without assistance from accomplices). The prostitute is also a potential victim, as she or he—male prostitutes are not unusual—risks acquiring STDs from johns and may be subjected to bodily injury, theft, or even murder in the course of

A Closer Look

Box 6.3 The Extraordinary Evil Crimes of Bernard Madoff

The defendant sits passively throughout an hour-and-a-half-long hearing as his victims call him a "beast," an "animal," and a "lowlife." The judge declares that he has committed "extraordinarily evil" crimes (McCool and Graybow 2009). Who is this evil person? A mass murderer? A sadistic pedophile? No, it is seventy-one-year-old Bernard Madoff, the former NASDAQ chairman who was found guilty of operating a classic Ponzi scheme—paying off early investors with funds from subsequent clients and sending out fraudulent investment statements to keep the illusion of profit alive, while skimming lavish percentages for his own use (Zambito and Smith 2008). In March 2009, Madoff pleaded guilty to eleven federal crimes, including securities fraud, wire fraud, mail fraud, money laundering, making false statements, perjury, theft from an employee benefit plan, and making false filings with the SEC (U.S. Attorney Southern District of New York 2009). Prosecutors estimated that as much as $170 billion had flowed through the principal Madoff account over decades and claimed that Bernard L. Madoff Investment Securities showed $65 billion in customer accounts when the firm was only able to collect $1.2 billion to return to investors. Because Madoff pleaded guilty, however, he could not be forced to testify about how the crimes were committed and which of his associates may have been involved (Henriques and Healy 2009).

White collar criminals, such as Bernard Madoff (shown here), do far more damage to society than street criminals.

Among those duped by Madoff were New York Mets coowners Fred Wilpon and Saul Katz. Many of Madoff's victims lost their life savings, were forced to sell their homes, or had to apply for government assistance to buy food (McCool and Graybow 2009). In June 2009, U.S. District Judge Denny Chin sentenced Madoff to the maximum penalty of 150 years in prison and ordered him to pay $170 billion—symbolic of the amount of money that flowed through Madoff Investment Securities.

What Do You Think?

Can you imagine how an organization like Madoff Investment Securities could get caught up in running a Ponzi scheme? What would it take to get away with such a scheme over a period of many years? Do you think Madoff's 150-year sentence is fair? What do you think?

Although described as a "victimless" crime, prostitution in most societies is illegal, and people may in fact be victimized because of this behavior.

an encounter; nor are incidents in which prostitutes are cheated, robbed, beaten, or even killed by their pimps uncommon. Furthermore, the prostitute may have been coerced into performing her role by unscrupulous others. Human trafficking in adults and children for purposes of prostitution occurs all around the world, including in the United States (U.S. Department of State 2010). Finally, family members of the prostitute and the customer may also become victimized by all the aforementioned scenarios.

Organized Crime

Organized crime (sometimes called syndicate crime) involves criminal activity committed by members of formal organizations that exist to operate profitable illicit enterprises (e.g., insurance fraud, counterfeiting, tax evasion, and money laundering). As Stephen Schneider (2002) states, "Organized crime can be broadly defined as two or more persons conspiring together on a continuing and secretive basis, with the aim of committing one or more serious crimes to obtain, directly or indirectly, a financial or other material benefit" (p. 1112). Organized crime exists to meet the needs of a public that lacks access through legitimate means to certain goods and services. Wherever there is a demand for prohibited goods and services (e.g., prostitution, drugs, pornography, gambling, or smuggling), there is an opportunity for organized crime to become a major supplier (Best and Luckenbill 1994).

Some forms of organized crime, such as smuggling, necessitate crossing national borders. Despite the historical prevalence of organized smuggling, most organized crime groups prior to the 1980s were confined to and controlled specific local territories and seldom sought to expand their operations outside their spheres of influence. Schneider (2002) explains that since the 1980s, however, organized crime has increasingly become international in character: "The unprecedented frequency with which criminal groups and activities now cross national boundaries, combined with the global structure and reach of some crime groups, has led to the emerging spectre of what is now commonly referred to as transnational organized crime" (p. 1112).

From a structural standpoint, organized crime is generally characterized by violence, corruption, and criminal monopoly. The use or threat of violence serves two critical functions. First, systematic extortion (the collection of payments from people), accomplished through threats and intimidation, provides the organization with needed funds (Chambliss 1988; Cressey 1969). Extortionists may also demand that their victims conduct exclusive business relationships with other businesses already under the control of the crime syndicate. For example, organized criminals may demand that a restaurant subscribe to their linen service, garbage-removal, and liquor-sales companies, and the like. This reality underscores the second function of violence, which is gaining control of the market—establishing a monopoly.

Political Crime

Political crime refers to acts directed against a government or state. There are many types of political crime, ranging from criminal acts committed by individuals and groups (e.g., espionage, treason, illegal campaign finance, illegal influence by lobbyists, illegal wiretapping, unauthorized video-recording, and viewing private e-mails of and by politicians and/or government officials) to those committed by entire governments as they attempt to prevent or control dissent within their borders.

The Jack Abramoff scandal provides a good example of how individuals and groups of people can become interconnected via a variety of political crimes. One of Washington's most prominent Republican lobbyists, Abramoff helped the Louisiana Coushatta tribe secure legal rights to open a casino. In return, the tribe donated hundreds of thousands of dollars to Republican political groups (Schmidt 2005). Tribal money found its way into the campaign coffers of many members of Congress as well (Schmidt 2005). When another Louisiana tribe, the Jena Band of Choctaws, won the governor's support for a casino years later, Abramoff turned to his political friends in the U.S. Senate and House, among other prominent persons, for help to block the Choctaws' casino bid. They did this to guarantee that profits would continue to roll into the Coushatta tribe and eventually back into the hands of the politicians who supported them (Schmidt 2005). On March 29, 2006, U.S. District Judge Paul C. Huck sentenced Abramoff to five years and ten months in prison for his role in the fraudulent purchase of a fleet of casino cruise boats. Abramoff received the shortest possible prison term under sentencing guidelines because he promised to aid federal officials in the ongoing investigation (Whoriskey and Branigin 2006).

Governments may commit political crimes as well. In the United States, a number of people wonder if the passage in 2001 of the USA PATRIOT Act and the 2003 establishment of the Department of Homeland Security intrude upon and violate individual rights. The PATRIOT Act was established in response to the terrorist attacks of September 11, 2001. "The Act gives federal officials greater authority to track and intercept communications, both for law enforcement and foreign intelligence gathering purposes" (Doyle 2002, p. 1). Civil liberties groups worry that the nation's intelligence system, designed to protect innocent Americans from terrorism, has eroded long-held individual rights and privacy. Among such concerns are the lowering of the burden of proof for secret surveillance against citizens and noncitizens alike, the expansion of the secretary of the Treasury's authority to investigate suspected cases of money laundering, expanded powers to seize property, and expanded definitions of crime for activities such as harboring terrorists and engaging in biological warfare.

Criminal Statistics

One might imagine, with five major categories of crime (street, white-collar, victimless, organized, and political), there must be a great deal of criminal activity occurring in society. So how much crime is there? A simple answer would go something like this: there is a great deal of crime, but no one knows for sure how much. It is not that we have no idea how much crime exists in society; we do not know the precise number of crimes, criminals, or victims of crime. But we are not entirely clueless, as FBI's Uniform Crime Reports, compiled since 1930, serve as an official source of U.S. crime statistics. The UCR classifies crime according to a number of categories, such as geographical region of the country, age, sex, race, and degree of seriousness. Serious crimes are called index crimes (criminal homicide, forcible rape, robbery, aggravated assault, burglary, larceny-theft, motor vehicle theft, and arson), while nonserious crimes are called nonindex crimes (e.g., vandalism; carrying weapons; buying, receiving, and possessing stolen property) (Bartol 1995).

Based on data provided by the UCR (2008), we can come up with a more precise answer to the question, How much crime is there? A violent crime occurs every 22.8 seconds (e.g., one murder every 31.8 minutes, one forcible rape every 5.6 minutes, one robbery every 1.3 minutes, one aggravated assault every 36.8 seconds), and a property crime occurs every 3 seconds (e.g., one burglary every 14.6 seconds, one larceny-theft every 4.5 seconds, and one motor vehicle theft every 25 seconds) in the United States.

Relying on official criminal statistics can be a little misleading, however, because the UCR data represent only those crimes known to the police. And while certain crimes, such as homicide, are mostly reported, other crimes, such as assaults and rape, are underreported. The crime of rape, for example, often goes unreported because some victims feel shame as a result of the traumatic experience, and others worry about reprisals. Most colleges and universities attempt to educate students about the danger of acquaintance rape—sexual assault perpetrated by an offender known to the victim—and yet many victims still do not report the crime. According to the U.S. Department of Justice (2002), "Fewer than 5 percent of college women who are victims of rape or attempted rape report it to police.... In one report, over 40 percent of those raped who did not report the incident said they did not do so because they feared reprisal by the assailant or others. In addition, some rape victims may fear the emotional trauma of the legal process itself" (p. 4). Furthermore, FBI statistics do not include rapes against males, even though some researchers believe male rape victims suffer greater physical injury than female victims (U.S. Department of Justice 2002).

> **What Do You Think?**
>
> Thinking back over the past year, can you remember a time when you broke the law (e.g., took items that did not belong to you, used drugs, or drove recklessly)? What were your thoughts at the time? Did you know you were breaking the law, or did the fact that your behavior was illegal only occur to you later? What do you think?

Because of the underreporting of crime, researchers often conduct victimization surveys, wherein they ask a representative sample of people about their experiences with crime. In addition, the Bureau of Justice Statistics conducts its own annual National Crime Victimization Survey (NCVS) (Schmalleger 2004). The NCVS, initiated in 1972, provides data from a variety of victimization surveys. Its data consists of information elicited through interviews with members of randomly selected households throughout the nation. Like other self-report measures, the NCVS may reveal a number of crimes that were never reported to the police. Self-report studies of perpetrators reveal that minor criminal activity is extensive and widespread (e.g., illegal drug use, underage alcohol consumption), especially among youth. In short, a great deal of minor crime is occurring, and very little of it shows up in official crime reports.

SOCIAL CONTROL AND THE CRIMINAL JUSTICE SYSTEM

Any group, organization, or society that creates rules will also design means of enforcing them. These means of enforcement, including all efforts and means used to ensure conformity to cultural norms, are forms of social control. **Social control** encompasses all the processes used to prevent deviant behavior. In simplest terms, there are two primary types of social control: internal and external.

Internal Social Control

Internal social control, sometimes called indirect social control, regulates behavior through ideological or cultural manipulation. It is accomplished through the socialization process. Socialization, described in Chapter 5, is a learning process whereby individuals, from the time of birth, are influenced by the agents of socialization (e.g., the family, peers, schools, religion, and the mass media). When individuals accept the ideas and norms presented to them, they have internalized society's expectations. A great deal of conformity comes about as a result of internalizing norms, values, and beliefs; thus, through the process of socialization, most of us learn to follow most of the laws of society routinely without having to be told to do so. Violations of such norms are usually confronted with mild **sanctions** (punishments) such as a frown or heavy sigh. Proper displays of behavior are reinforced with a smile or nod of gratitude. Since most people seek the approval of others, internal social control can be very effective.

External Social Control

With external social control, sometimes called direct social control, regulation of behavior comes from exterior social-control agents, such as the police, the judicial system, and other authority figures—people in our lives who are watching our behavior. Those with legitimate authority are in a position to levy sanctions against norm violators. Formal sanctions (punishments) can be used for violations of specific rules and laws. The major reason for the use of formal sanctions is deterrence. Deterrence is the idea that the threat of punishment should be enough to stop individuals from breaking the law. Research has shown that the threat of punishment is an effective deterrent for some crimes (e.g., property crime) but not for violent offenses. Parents and guardians are the first direct social-control agents in the life of individuals. Soon, a number of other adults take on this role, including teachers and school administrators, sports coaches, store owners, and police officers. The primary formal social-control agents are law enforcement agencies, the judicial system, and the legislative system.

The Criminal Justice System

External, or direct, social control is accomplished via the criminal justice system. The **criminal justice system** consists of law enforcement efforts to curtail crime, the judicial system, and the legislative system.

Law Enforcement: The first line of defense against lawbreakers is law enforcement—the police. The police are responsible for the suppression of crime. Suppression efforts vary from one police agency to the next. The suppression process generally includes police getting to know the nature and scope of criminal activity within their jurisdictions, gathering information and intelligence, creating a comprehensive database, and developing strategies to eliminate, or at least reduce, criminal activity. Proactive strategies center on fact gathering so that the police can stop crime before it occurs. Reactive strategies involve the everyday interaction between the police and law violators. Most police work is reactive. The average patrol officer generally comes into contact with crimes that either are in progress or have recently occurred. As the foot soldiers in the battle against crime, the police are often blamed for social injustices that they did not create and are held accountable for labeling citizens as criminals. "Social critics view the police as oppressors that protect the privileged at the expense of the poor, disadvantaged, and politically disenfranchised. The police view themselves as practical crime fighters caught in a web of political intrigue" (Sanders 1994, p. 178). As described in "Connecting Sociology and Popular Culture" Box 6.4, the daily activities of police officers hold a certain fascination for people as many TV viewers turn to cop shows for entertainment purposes.

Police academy officers are shown here being sworn in to duty; soon, they will join the front line of defense between street criminals and citizens.

The Judicial System: Before an alleged criminal goes to court, he or she must, of course, be arrested for committing a crime. "To make a legal arrest, the police must have probable cause, which is a set of facts that would lead a reasonable person to believe a crime has been committed and the person arrested committed it" (Regoli and Hewitt 2003, p. 339). Immediately upon being arrested, all subjects must be read their rights, as per the 1966 *Miranda v. Arizona* Supreme Court ruling. (The *Miranda* ruling forever changed police action as it mandated that all suspects must thenceforward have their rights expressed to them by police before any interrogation can take place). In cop shows, police often use such phrases as "Read him his rights," "Mirandize him," and so on.

After an arrest has been made, the suspect must go through booking. A booking is the official recording of a person brought into detention after being arrested. Once suspects have been booked, they are fingerprinted and photographed (a mug shot is taken). An interrogation period follows. During an interrogation, the police ask the suspect a number of questions. In some cases, a suspect may be placed in a lineup. A lineup involves the suspect standing next to other uninvolved persons while a witness tries to identify him or her from behind a one-way mirror.

Connecting Sociology and Popular Culture

Box 6.4 Cop Shows, Films, and Videos

The role of law enforcement in society intrigues Americans. We are concerned about justice and equality and expect law enforcement officers to be among the most ethical and moralistic members of society. Most police officers perform their duties honorably; others do not. An indicator of the importance of law enforcement and how well, or how poorly, its members perform is demonstrated in popular culture in a variety of fashions including the numerous cop shows on television, as well as police-related films, YouTube videos, and video games.

In some TV shows, such as *COPS, Hawaii Five-0, The FBI, Hill Street Blues, NYPD Blue, Detroit 1-8-7, Southland, CSI,* and *Law & Order,* the police are shown in a mostly positive manner. *COPS,* for example, is filmed in a documentary style at rotating locales. Film crews follow beat cops as they perform their daily duties, often involving unusual and even idiotic behavior on the part of everyday citizens and perpetrators. On cable, TruTV broadcasts such cop shows as *Hot Pursuit* (police chases) and *Inside American Jails.* Viewers are especially attracted to the police-chase scenes as the onboard police car cameras allow viewers to gain the perspective of law enforcement officers. Much like hockey viewers who watch a hockey game waiting for a fight to occur, viewers of *Hot Pursuit* await the nearly inevitable car wreck at the conclusion of most aired police chases.

Other TV cop shows paint the men and women of law enforcement in a less than flattering manner. *Reno 911* (a spoof of *COPS*), for example, involves a film crew following Reno, Nevada, police officers as they perform their daily duties, but the officers generally come across looking incompetent, unethical, and immoral. Shows such as *The Sopranos* provide a criminal's perspective of police officers. Not surprisingly, the police come across in a negative manner on these shows.

Countless films involve law enforcement as well. Once again, cops are at times shown in a mostly positive manner, such as in the *Die Hard* and *Lethal Weapon* movies. Other films portray some police officers in a positive manner while others are shown to be corrupt; examples include *S.W.A.T., Training Day,* and the *Dirty Harry* movies. In other cases, law enforcement agencies or the police are shown to be mostly incompetent or corrupt. These movies include the *Smokey and the Bandit* films, *Gone in Sixty Seconds,* and the *Bourne Identity* films.

Popular culture also provides glimpses of the world of law enforcement through videos and video games. Yahoo.com alone lists over sixty examples of police video games. Once again, these games' portrayal of police varies from one extreme (proficiency) to the other (ineptness). The violent nature of video games, especially police video games, makes them the target of a wide variety of activist groups that claim playing violent video games contributes to acts of deviant violence. There is no conclusive evidence to support this contention, and yet it persists. Nearly 2.5 million police-related videos on YouTube provide film coverage of police chases, police brutality, and so on.

What Do You Think?

In various popular-culture outlets, law enforcement is shown in both positive and negative lights. Based on your personal experiences, which TV shows, films, or videos seem to portray the police most accurately? What do you think?

In some cases, a suspect may be freed before going to court (e.g., if new information surfaces to clear the suspect) or may reach a plea bargain (a deal with the district attorney's office) before going to trial.

Just as the police may use discretion (personal judgment) when making an arrest, prosecutors sometimes use their own discretion as to whether to proceed to trial in specific cases. They may feel that the evidence is too weak or will not hold up in court, the suspect's prior arrest record is clean, or the seriousness of the offense is too light; they may even fear not being able to get a conviction and therefore refuse to try the case in court. Under such circumstances, a prosecutor may order the case to be heard by a grand jury. A grand jury is a group of people selected and sworn in by a court, just like jurors chosen to serve on a trial jury. Unlike trial jurors, however, grand juries do not decide if someone is guilty of criminal charges that have been brought against them. Instead, they listen to evidence to decide if someone should be charged with a crime. Grand jurors may serve for up to thirty-six months, although, unlike trial jurors, they do not convene every day.

Prosecution is a critical element in suppression efforts. The prosecutor is supposed to act in the best interests of the state (or "the people"). After making an arrest and going through the booking process, a police officer can do little else except rely on prosecutors to get convictions against those who commit crimes. It is the prosecutor's job to find enough additional information to make a conviction. The prosecutor, then, is the second line of defense against crime, or "the regulator within the criminal justice system" (Shelden, Tracy, and Brown 2001, p. 253).

The courts are, ideally, the legitimate segment of the criminal justice system. The court is presumed to consist of an unbiased judge, preexisting legal norms and rules that do not change on a case-by-case basis, due process, and (typically) a jury of peers. The court is the setting for routine legal procedures where objectivity is supposed to reign. However, most judges in U.S. jurisdictions are elected and wish to be reelected. With that in mind, a judge's personal bias, subjectivity, and political ambition may at times interfere with the objectivity of judicial proceedings. Ideally, innocent people are found not guilty, and guilty people are incarcerated (see "A Closer Look" Box 6.5 for an examination of the incarceration rate in the United States). In reality, this is not always the case. Those found guilty can seek a second trial, via an appeal of their conviction, where they may or may not find a more favorable decision.

The Legislative System: The police can only enforce the laws; they cannot create new ones or ignore existing ones. Laws are formal norms. They are the most

A Closer Look

Box 6.5 Incarceration in the United States

The judicial system attempts to determine whether an accused person is actually guilty of a crime. When an individual is found guilty, he or she may face incarceration. This is especially true for Americans, as the United States imprisons more people than any other country in the world. According to the Pew Center on the States (2009), at the start of 2009, there were 2.3 million incarcerated American adults. To put this figure into perspective, the far more populous nation of China ranked second, with 1.5 million citizens behind bars, and Russia was a distant third with 890,000 inmates (Pew Center on the States 2008). Furthermore, if we add the number of people on probation or parole in the United States, there are more than 7.3 million Americans in the corrections system. This figure equates to one in every thirty-one U.S. adults. In 1985, the rate was one in seventy-seven adults.

As previously mentioned, the United States also has the highest rate of incarcerated citizens in the world, outpacing such nations as South Africa and Iran. Virginia senator Jim Webb (2009) has declared, "With 5% of the world's population, our country now houses nearly 25% of the world's reported prisoners. We currently incarcerate 756 inmates per 100,000 residents, a rate nearly five times the average worldwide of 158 for every 100,000" (p. 4). As a matter of comparison, Germany has a rate of 93 people in prison for every 100,000 persons (Pew Center on the States 2008). The costs associated with maintaining U.S. corrections facilities are equally staggering: Local, state, and federal spending on corrections adds up to about $68 billion annually (Webb 2009). Webb (2009) argues that most U.S. prisons are overcrowded, ill-managed places of violence, physical abuse, and hate, "making them breeding grounds that perpetuate and magnify the same types of behavior we purport to fear" (p. 4).

The American judicial system's tough sentencing laws and record number of imprisoned nonviolent drug offenders contribute to the high incarceration rate found in the United States. According to data provided by Congress's Joint Economic Committee, drug offenders constitute nearly 33 percent of the prison population. An estimated 60 percent of incarcerated drug offenders are nonviolent (passive users or minor dealers) (Webb 2009). "The continued incarceration of drug offenders has done nothing to break-up the power of the multibillion-dollar illegal drug trade" (Webb 2009, p. 5). In addition, "more than one in eight prisoners in the U.S. has serious mental illness. Advocates of a new system of 'mental-health courts' say that, with treatment, many of them could become lawful and productive, reducing overcrowding in our nation's prison system at the same time" (Foster, Orr, and Laing 2009, p. 6). Since 2002, Congress has allocated millions of dollars to establish mental-health courts, which operate in about two hundred jurisdictions across the United States.

What Do You Think?

What do these crime statistics say about us as a nation? Does it concern you that the United States incarcerates more people than any other nation in the world? Would you consider replacing incarceration with some other form of punishment for nonviolent offenders? Should nonviolent recreational drug users be incarcerated? What do you think?

important norms of society. Laws are a form of government social control created by the legislative system (Black 1995). Ideally, they are established to protect a society's citizens from each other and from outside threats. Sociologists view the creation of laws as part of an ongoing social process. Representing varying theoretical perspectives, sociologists also generally agree that the legal system reflects the values of those in positions of power with the ability to exercise authority. As a result, many laws are controversial and not necessarily agreed upon by a majority of citizens. Social-conflict theorists, for example, believe that those in power use the justice system to maintain their social high status while at the same time keeping others subservient. Conflict theorists argue that the very fact that a disproportionate number of the poor are arrested for criminal activities and minority poor claim to be victimized by the police stems from the imbalance of power found in society.

Consider, for example, drug use. Certain drugs, such as alcohol and tobacco (with nicotine as a natural ingredient and hundreds of added chemicals), are legal, and yet their use often has deadly consequences. Tobacco alone is responsible for 400,000 premature deaths per year in the United States; yet, it is legal. Why? Conflict theorists would point out that tobacco has traditionally been viewed as a "cash crop"—meaning that capitalists make money from the sale and distribution of tobacco products. The tobacco industry has very powerful lobbyists who influence politicians to keep the drug legal. Alcohol, which is not even considered a drug by some users, enjoys the same cash-crop advantage as tobacco. On the other hand, marijuana has traditionally been viewed as a drug of choice among persons of lower socioeconomic status and therefore has not benefited from a powerful pro-marijuana lobbying industry—that is, until recently. Throughout the 2000s, a relatively powerful pro-marijuana lobby has emerged because of the medical benefits the drug presents. Although it is deemed illegal by the federal government, a number of states have legalized medical marijuana, decriminalized the possession of small amounts of pot, and pushed legislation to legalize marijuana.

As described throughout this chapter, cultural norms are strongly influenced by ideals of morality. Social control of deviant behavior is deemed necessary in order to assure conformity to rules and the relatively smooth operation of society. Much of the discussion of social control here, however, centers on how societies curtail the deviant behaviors of individuals. It is important to note that dominant groups within a society will, at times, attempt to control the behavior of other large groups.

> **What Do You Think?**
>
> Some people who drink alcohol regularly do not view it as a drug. And yet, many of these same people look down upon those who smoke pot. Why is this the case? Should marijuana be federally legalized for medical purposes? What about legalizing marijuana for recreational purposes? What do you think?

In extreme cases, social control may come in the form of genocide. Genocide (combining *geno* from the Greek for "race" or "tribe" with the Latin *cide* for "killing"), a term coined by a Polish Jewish lawyer named Raphael Lemkin in 1944, refers to the mass murder of one group of people by another group. Recent research conducted by Bradley Campbell (2009) suggests that "genocide is normally a form of social control—a response to behavior defined as deviant. . . . The perpetrators express moral grievances against the targeted ethnic groups" (p. 155). Campbell (2009) provides examples of genocide in recent history and connects specific moral grievances levied against targeted groups. His examples include Nazi Germany's claim that Jews were clannish, aloof, and distant; Rwandan Hutus' grievances against Tutsis as clannish and possessing a disproportionate share of places in secondary and higher education; and the numerous grievances of the government and Arab militias in the Sudan against the African Muslims of Darfur.

SUMMARY

Social norms have existed throughout human history. All societies create norms and expect citizens to abide by them. Cultural norms are directly connected to issues of morality and ideals of proper behavior. Deviance is said to occur when people violate social norms. Like social norms, deviance is a matter of social definition and social construction. That is, all behaviors must be labeled and defined by society as deviant in order to be deviant. The most serious social norm is a law. When people violate a law, they have committed a crime. Those found guilty of committing a crime may face arrest, prosecution, conviction, and incarceration.

Sociologists have presented a number of theories, including social-disorganization theory, anomie or strain theory, social-bond and control theory, social-learning theory, labeling theory, and conflict theory, in an attempt to best explain why deviance and crime occur.

There are a number of different ways to categorize crime. This chapter discussed the following categories: street crime, white-collar crime, victimless crime, organized crime, and political crime. There are also a number of subcategories of crime within each broader classification scheme.

Genocide, the mass murder of people, represents an extreme form of political criminal behavior.

Criminal activity is quite common in the United States. Crime statistics are compiled via the FBI's Uniform Crime Reports. The data provided by the UCR represents official statistics. However, many researchers believe that a great deal of crime is not reflected in the UCR because of underreporting. As a result, the Bureau of Justice Statistics conducts victimization surveys whereby a number of people are randomly contacted and interviewed about their experiences with crime.

All groups, organizations, and societies establish social norms, expect group members to abide by them, and implement mechanisms to control behavior. This process is known as social control. In simplest terms, there are two primary types of social control: internal and external. Internal social control, sometimes called indirect social control, regulates behavior through ideological or cultural manipulation. It is accomplished through the socialization process. With external social control, sometimes called direct social control, regulation of behavior comes from the criminal justice system. The criminal justice system consists of law enforcement efforts to curtail crime, the judicial system, and the legislative system.

Glossary

Anomie—The absence of norms, or normlessness.

Crime—Any deviant behavior that violates a law.

Criminal justice system—The official system used by society to curtail criminality. The criminal justice system includes law enforcement, judicial courts, and legislative bodies.

Deviance—Any behavior that is likely to be defined, by some members of society or specific subcultural groups, as an unacceptable violation of a social norm and that elicits negative reactions from others.

Deviants—People who violate social norms by committing acts of deviancy.

Larceny-theft—Stealing property with the purpose of depriving the owner of its possession and with the intent to convert this property to the taker's own use.

Organized crime (sometimes called syndicate crime)—Criminal activity committed by members of formal organizations that exist to operate profitable illicit enterprises (e.g., insurance fraud, counterfeiting, tax evasion, prostitution, and money laundering).

Political crime—Crime committed by political officials during the course of their incumbency.

Positive deviance—An instance in which a rule violation generates a positive reaction from others.

Primary deviance—The deviance of individuals whose actions remain undetected or unrecognized by others.

Sanctions—Punishments for violating specific rules and laws.

Secondary deviance—The deviance of actors who have been identified and labeled as deviants.

Self-fulfilling prophecy—A process that involves people taking to heart the labels bestowed on them, coming to see themselves in terms of those labels, and then acting in correspondence with them.

Social control—The processes used for preventing deviant behavior.

Social-learning theory—A theoretical perspective based on the idea that individuals learn how to become delinquent through interaction with others, whether directly (by being taught) or indirectly (through observation).

Stigma—A mark of disgrace, or negative label, used by those in power to devalue certain members of society (or groups).

Street crime—A criminal act committed in an outdoor, public place, such as a street, playground, shopping area, business district, or residential neighborhood.

Techniques of neutralization—Ways that delinquents and norm violators attempt to rationalize, neutralize, and temporarily suspend their commitment to societal values, providing them with the freedom to commit delinquent acts.

Underclass—Denizens of a census tract wherein 40 percent of the residents live in poverty.

Victimless crimes—Illegal acts in which all direct participants are willing and consenting adults.

White-collar crime—Professional (nonstreet) crime committed by high-status people.

Discussion Questions

1. How would you define deviance? Are there any behaviors that at least some people in society would not label as deviant?
2. Have you committed any deviant acts? Apply a theoretical perspective to explain why you behaved as you did.
3. Why do some athletes cheat and take performance-enhancing drugs? Is it immoral for athletes to take performance-enhancing drugs?
4. Are victimless crimes labeled properly? If not, how would you define crimes such as prostitution and illegal drug use?
5. Do you believe the criminal justice system in the United States is fair to all people? Why or why not? What would you do to change the system for the better?

Web Links

To view a wide variety of unusual wedding photos, visit http://damncoolpics.blogspot.com/2009/06/worlds-most-unusual-weddings.html.

To learn more about doping scandals in sports, visit www.cbc.ca/sports/indepth/drugs/stories/top10.html.

To learn more about racial profiling, including "driving while black," visit www.aclu.org/racialjustice/racialprofiling/index.html.

To learn more about U.S. copyright law, visit www.copyright.gov.

The Creative Commons is an alternative to traditional views of copyright ownership. To learn more, visit http://creativecommons.org/about/what-is-cc.

To learn more about white-collar crime, visit www.federalcrimesblog.com.
To learn more about corporate crime, visit www.fbi.gov/publications/financial/fcs_report2006/financial_crime_2006.htm.
To learn more about official crime statistics, visit the Bureau of Justice website at http://bjs.ojp.usdoj.gov.

7 SOCIAL STRATIFICATION

Although medical doctors often incur a high debt by the time they graduate from medical school, they also enjoy a high salary.

Chapter 7

- Introductory Story
- Stratification and Social Class
- Theories of Social Stratification
- Social Stratification Systems and Social Mobility
- Social Stratification Systems
- Poverty and Homelessness
- Global Stratification and Inequality
- Summary, Glossary, Discussion Questions, and Web Links

INTRODUCTORY STORY

According to *Forbes* magazine, the leading tracker of the world's wealthiest persons, 2008 marked the first time that the number of billionaires in the world surpassed four figures (Kroll 2008). Chances are you are like me—not on that list! In 2008, there were 1,125 billionaires who had a total net worth exceeding $4.4 trillion, a figure nearly $1 trillion higher than in 2007. Although just four of the world's top twenty richest were from the United States in 2008 (compared to half of the top twenty in 2006), Americans still represent 42 percent of the total billionaires.

The collapse of the Soviet Union has spearheaded a booming economy for select Russians, as eighty-seven billionaires are found in Russia. This total far exceeds Germany's fifty-nine, although that nation ranked third in terms of having the most billionaires. An increasing number of young billionaires appeared on the 2008 list, with *Forbes* finding fifty under the age of forty. Of these under-age-forty billionaires, 68 percent had built their fortunes from scratch, including Google cofounders Sergey Brin and Larry Page and Facebook founder Mark Zuckerberg, who at age twenty-three is believed to be the youngest self-made billionaire in history (Kroll 2008).

The year 2008 also marked the first time in thirteen years that Bill Gates was not the world's richest person. But do not worry too much for him; according to Forbes.com (2009), Gates regained his number one ranking in 2009 despite losing more than $18 billion in one calendar year. As of 2009, Gates, a self-made billionaire, was worth $40 billion. It should be noted that he did not "lose" the entire $18 billion; he gave $3.8 billion in charitable donations. The rest of the losses reflected investments he made outside Microsoft (Forbes.com 2009). Gates's good friend and fellow philanthropist Warren Buffett was the second-richest person in the world in 2009, with a fortune listed at $37 billion. Like Gates, Buffett is a self-made billionaire, and he too lost billions of dollars—25 billion to be exact—between 2008 and 2009. Buffett, the world's richest person in 2008, lost his money in the stock market. Gates and Buffett are not the only billionaires who lost massive amounts of money in the 2008–2009 global economic collapse. The third-richest person, Carlos Slim Helu, a Mexican telecom tycoon whose self-made fortune was worth $35 billion in 2009, also lost $25 billion in one year.

The number of millionaires around the world is also increasing. There were more than 10 million people with assets of at least $1 million around the world in 2007.

> The combined wealth of the globe's millionaires grew to nearly $41 trillion [in 2007], an increase of 9 percent from a year before.... That means their average wealth was more than $4 million, the highest it's ever been. Home values were not included in asset totals.... The ranks of the wealthy are growing fastest in the developing economies of India, China and Brazil. The number of millionaires in India grew by about 23 percent. The United States still reigns supreme when it comes to fat wallets, though: One in every three millionaires in the world lives in America. (*Post-Standard,* 6/25/08, p. A1)

The number of millionaires and billionaires may be increasing, but, unfortunately, so too is the number of people living in poverty. Furthermore, the number of people living in poverty far exceeds the number of people living in luxury. The World Bank, for example, estimates that there are nearly 1 billion people living in poverty worldwide. The great disparity between the economically rich and poor represents one significant variable in social stratification. Economics, social prestige, and political power represent the most commonly cited variables in social stratification and thus are the focus of attention in this chapter. Chapters 8 (race and ethnicity) and 9 (gender inequality) discuss how social stratification occurs beyond the economic realm.

STRATIFICATION AND SOCIAL CLASS

Stratification refers to layers. While geologists may concern themselves with such things as the layers of the Earth's subsurface (crust, mantle, and core), sociologists are concerned about the layers found in the social world (e.g., an overly simplified division consisting of upper, middle, and lower social classes). Some form of stratification exists in all groups, organizations, and societies. Students, for example, are stratified based on their class standing (senior, junior, sophomore, and freshman). Athletes are divided by first string, second string, and third string. Specific sports themselves are more prestigious than others and therefore lend themselves to a ranking system. In most high schools across the United States, football is king, generally followed by other such traditional sports as basketball and baseball. (Note: The popularity of sports is subject to variation at any given high school, but as a generality, football is the most prestigious sport.) A ranking system is deeply entrenched in the social institution of the military, with members ranking from private to general. Generals are further stratified based on the number of stars they have earned: a four-star general has higher rank than a one-star general.

A critical aspect of social stratification is the built-in corresponding value component that characterizes the higher rank. Thus, a military general enjoys more prestige than a private, the starting quarterback enjoys more prestige than a third-string punter, and seniors in college enjoy more perks (e.g., earlier course registration) than freshmen. Because members of a higher rank enjoy privileges over their lower-ranked counterparts, social stratification may be viewed as institutionalized social inequality. Taking into account these key components, sociologists define **social stratification** as a system for ranking members of a social system into levels with different or unequal evaluations. In this regard, social stratification reveals patterns of social inequality found within a society.

> **What Do You Think?**
>
> Sociologists believe that some form of stratification exists in all groups and organizations. Think of the wide variety of groups and organizations that you belong to or encounter on a regular basis. What type of ranking system exists within each? Where do you rank within each structure? What do you think?

From the sociological perspective, social stratification may also be viewed as the hierarchal or horizontal division of society based on rank, strata, or social class. All societies are characterized by a stratification dimension that places people in some sort of social stratum or classification system. This classification system leads to the development of socioeconomic classes. Sociologists use the term "**social class**" to describe a broad group of people with common economic, cultural, or political status (e.g., the working class or the professional class).

Dimensions of Social Stratification

Most societies have three major dimensions of stratification: social prestige, political power, and economics. The **social prestige** dimension of stratification is tied to what people think about others. Generally, people who are thought highly of have high prestige or social status. In contrast, those who are thought of negatively have a low level of prestige. There are many ways to attain social prestige, including family name, geographic residence, level of education, occupation or career, public exposure, accomplishments, social titles, and celebrity status. We take a closer look at many of these social-prestige variables later in this chapter during our discussion of theories of social stratification.

The political dimension of stratification is usually expressed in terms of **power**. Although power may be expressed in a number of ways—including physical strength and the ability to make people do things even against their will—the political system is the means by which legitimate power is exercised. Thus, holding political office, voting, lobbying, contributing to campaigns, and participating in boycotts, strikes, and demonstrations are all means by which people exercise power. Since power is a relatively abstract concept, it is difficult to measure. However, power is clearly distributed unequally in society as a minority of people enjoy a great deal of power, while the majority do not.

Although most people want power and prestige, many believe that money will provide both. As a result, the economic dimension of stratification systems holds most people's attention and focus. The economic dimension involves two key variables: income and wealth.

Income: **Income** refers to the amount of money that a person or family receives over a period, generally a calendar year (e.g., reported income on a tax return). In 2009, the median household income in the United States was $50,112 (U.S. Census Bureau 2010b). Households in the western region of the United States earned the highest median income at $54,876, followed by those in the Northeast ($50,112), Midwest ($49,922), and South ($45,417).

There is great income disparity in the United States. Based on 2008 U.S. census data, the highest-earning 20 percent of families (with incomes of at least $113,000 a year and with a mean or average of $187,000) received 47.3 percent of all income (Macionis 2010). Conversely, the lowest-paid 20 percent (with incomes below $28,000 a year and averaging $16,000) received just 4.1 percent of all income (Macionis 2010). Furthermore, in 2003, the median cash bonus for an American CEO was $605,000. "Chief executives of big companies now average more than $10 million a year in total compensation—370 times more than the pay of the average hourly worker. The median weekly salary [in 2003] was $620 (half of all workers earned more, half, earned less). Adjusted for inflation, that's slightly lower than the 2002 median wage" (Brenner 2004, pp. 10, 12). In the New York City borough of Manhattan, the top fifth of earners makes fifty-two times what the lowest fifth makes—$365,826 compared with $7,047—which is roughly comparable to the income disparity in Namibia (*Post-Standard,* 9/5/05, p. A8). Like many other Western societies, the United States rewards entertainers and elite athletes with extremely high salaries (see "Connecting Sociology and Popular Culture" Box 7.1), while workers such as firefighters, police officers, and school teachers, who provide essential services enabling society to function in an orderly manner, receive annual salaries much closer to the median household income.

When I ask students, "Why are you in college?" most respond that they anticipate finding a good job upon graduation. Generally, a good job means a professional career wherein the graduate will earn a substantial income in a profession that allows the graduate an opportunity to showcase the skills learned in college. Is this a realistic goal? "A Closer Look" Box 7.2 examines the job market and a number of fields that are likely to provide a good income for college graduates. (Note: Chapter 14 discusses job opportunities for sociology majors.)

Wealth: The second element of economic stratification is wealth. **Wealth** refers to the total value of everything that a person or family owns, minus any debts owed. It is similar in meaning to the term "net worth." To be wealthy is to have a plentiful supply of material goods, property, and/or money. Wealth, then, refers to an accumulation of resources. Wealth could be (and often is) looked at as one's ability to do what one wants to do, when one wants to do it; being "independently wealthy" means having enough wealth that one can live comfortably without having to work at a job. Thus, wealth is a measure of one's breadth of immediately available choices of courses of action. For example, wealthy people can go on vacation when and where they want. In contrast, when people without wealth receive vacation days or furlough time from their jobs, they are likely to take a **staycation** (home-based period off work) instead of traveling to a pleasurable destination. The decision to "staycate" can be caused by high gas prices or just a lack of money to pay for restaurant meals, hotel stays, and other travel expenses.

Connecting Sociology and Popular Culture

Box 7.1 Select Salaries of Entertainers and Nonentertainers

Every year, *Parade* (a magazine found inside most Sunday newspapers) prints an annual "What People Earn" roundup of select salaries of entertainers, athletes, and regular folks. This well-researched annual feature allows readers to compare their salaries with those of others. In many cases the results can be quite enlightening.

Table 7.1 lists a few examples of the 2008 salaries of entertainers and athletes cited by *Parade*.

Beach homes, especially this one in Malibu, California, are prestigious not just because of their value, but also because of their geographic location.

As a matter of comparison, consider the salaries of a number of folks who perform regular jobs listed in Table 7.2.

The primary reason top U.S. entertainers and professional athletes are paid such high salaries compared to most workers (and most actors and athletes) is reflected in the value system of many Western societies, including the United States. That is, members of the public value being entertained and diverted from the everyday problems of life, and they are willing to pay for it. We also value people who perform at peak levels in social arenas that most of us cannot duplicate. Sports fans marvel at the achievements of top athletes because they do things the rest of us cannot. We go to movies as a form of escape from the mundane, and we support top actors by renting movies and purchasing movie tickets and snacks from the concession stands at the theater. Thus, the high salaries of top entertainers and athletes are made possible by the people who perform regular jobs.

Data collected and analyzed by leading sociologists and economists reveal that the disparity in wealth is much more extreme than the disparity in income in the United States. In 2007, the top 1 percent of households owned 34.6 percent of all privately held wealth (money earned, homes, automobiles, stocks, bonds, real estate, and businesses), and the next 19 percent had 50.5 percent, which means that just 20 percent of the people owned 85 percent, leaving just 15 percent of the wealth for the bottom 80 percent of Americans (Domhoff 2010; Wolff 2010; Macionis 2010).

Prestige: Economic success is often equated with prestige, as people with money generally garner more respect in Western societies than the poor. Furthermore,

TABLE 7.1 2008 Select Salaries of Entertainers and Athletes

OCCUPATION	NAME	AGE	SALARY
Doll	Barbie	50	$3.3 billion
Actor	Tyler Perry	39	$125 million
Pro golfer	Tiger Woods	33	$110 million
Rapper	Jay-Z	39	$82 million
Singer	Beyoncé	27	$80 million
Baseball player	Alex Rodriguez	33	$34 million
Actress	Jennifer Aniston	40	$27 million
Author	John Grisham	54	$25 million
TV host	Kelly Ripa	38	$8 million
Race car driver	Danica Patrick	27	$7 million
Actress/comedian	Tina Fey	38	$4.6 million
Supermodel	Carolyn Murphy	33	$4.5 million
Actor	Patrick Dempsey	43	$3.5 million
Singer	Britney Spears	27	$2.2 million

Source: *Parade,* 4/12/09.

TABLE 7.2 2008 Select Salaries of Regular Folks

OCCUPATION	NAME	AGE	SALARY
Trial attorney	Joshua Gropper	43	$400,000
Federal investigator	William Bailey	55	$111,100
Pet sitter/ dog walker	Tammy Roussin	37	$100,000
Math teacher	Ann Sin	34	$66,000
Public-housing analyst	Leroy Ferguson	44	$65,000
Probation officer	Michael Olson	44	$58,000
Letter carrier	Deborah Blakeney	47	$53,700
MRI technician	Laurie Metoyer	37	$48,000
Deputy sheriff	Dave Dougherty	42	$47,000
Social worker	Aubrey Carter	24	$45,800
Library director	Pradeep Das	58	$41,000
Realtor	Kathleen Mason	44	$38,000
Sports blogger	Josh Bacott	31	$10,000

Source: *Parade,* 4/12/09.

What Do You Think?

Examine the salaries and occupations in the two lists. Do you think the salaries reflect the value to society of the various individuals? What do they indicate about our value system and priorities? What do you think?

wealthy people tend to have more power than those who are poor. Thus, there is an overlapping relationship between social prestige, political power, and economics. As a means of combining the effects of these three dimensions of social stratification on individuals and groups, sociologists use the term "socioeconomic status." **Socioeconomic status** is a composite term that includes a person's income, wealth, occupational prestige, and educational attainment. Occupational prestige is determined by such factors as the level of pay, the desirability of the job, the amount of education required for the job, and the amount of physical labor involved. Professional (white-collar) jobs have more prestige than physically demanding (blue-collar) ones. Using this composite, someone with a high income and/or net worth, a professional job, and a high level of education enjoys a favorably high socioeconomic status. Conversely, someone who is economically poor, possesses a physically demanding job, and is poorly educated, has a low socioeconomic status.

A Closer Look

Box 7.2 The Recession's Impact on the Job Market

Like the general public at large, college students are very concerned about the job market. And for good reason, as the labor force has witnessed a number of significant changes over the past few years, especially in light of the recession that began in December 2007. Many people who once earned relatively large salaries have been forced to live on far less or have lost their jobs altogether. As economist George Anders explained in a 2009 *Parade* article, "The frantic race to keep up with the Joneses has been put on hold. And as layoff notices and foreclosures sweep the country, being able to count on a dependable paycheck suddenly has become goal No. 1" (p. 6).

During the period from December 2007 (when the U.S. economy slipped into recession) through April 2009, at least 4.4 million jobs were lost. In February 2009, the national unemployment rate reached 8.1 percent—its highest level in twenty-six years (Anders 2009). Based on data provided by the U.S. Bureau of Labor Statistics (BLS) (2009b), the national unemployment rate hit 9.4 percent five months later. Fifteen states and the District of Columbia reported jobless rates of at least 10 percent in July 2009. "Michigan continued to have the highest unemployment rate among the states, 15.0 percent. Rhode Island recorded the next highest rate, 12.7 percent; followed by Nevada, 12.5 percent; California and Oregon, 11.9 percent each; and South Carolina, 11.8 percent. The rates in California, Nevada, and Rhode Island set new series highs, along with the rate in Georgia (10.3 percent)" (U.S. Bureau of Labor Statistics 2009b). One's level of education is correlated with unemployment rates. According to the BLS, those with a college degree had a 4.1 percent unemployment rate in March 2009, those with a high school diploma had an 8.3 percent unemployment rate, and those with no high school diploma had a 12.6 percent unemployment rate (Anders 2009).

Citing statistics from the Bureau of Economic Analysis, Anders (2009) explains that there is some good news: "Despite devastating job losses, average salaries and personal savings rates have increased. The national average weekly income rose 2.5%, from $598 in 2007 to $613 in 2008. Inflation increased just .1% over the same period. The personal savings rate rose from .9% in January 2007 to 5% in January 2009" (p. 6). The increase in personal savings reflects a sense of cautiousness among Americans who fear that the shaky economy is a sign to those with a steady income to increase savings wherever they can. The flip side to those with savings is the average U.S. household credit card debt of $10,728 (in January 2009).

Among the bright spots in the job market are the following: police officers (even when budgets are tight, law enforcement is one of the last areas to be cut); speech therapist (school systems are hiring to comply with federal disability laws, and an aging population, coupled with a growing number of trauma victims, has increased demand in this area); search-engine gurus (businesses hire these tech whizzes to get listings to show up more prominently on Google and other search engines); registered nurses (there is a nationwide shortage of nurses); and internal auditors (the government, banks, and insurers need safeguards against fraud) (Anders 2009).

What Do You Think?

What expectations do you have regarding your job prospects when you graduate? How well prepared will you be for the job market and the career you plan to pursue? What do you think?

THEORIES OF SOCIAL STRATIFICATION

As we have discussed, societies are stratified based on three major dimensions: social prestige, political power, and economic standing. Two classical theorists—Karl Marx and Emile Durkheim—provide us with the basic foundation of theories of social stratification.

> **What Do You Think?**
>
> What is your current socioeconomic status? What is it likely to be twenty years from now? What factors do you anticipate will determine your future socioeconomic status? What do you think?

Karl Marx as an "Economic Determinist"

Marx argued that economic forces give rise to social classes and that a class struggle between the owners of the means of production and the workers was inevitable. Thus, for Marx, the most important aspect of social stratification was economics—especially in regard to the ownership of the means of production. Marx's solitary focus on economics as the root of social class formation has led observers to refer to him as an "economic determinist."

A closer examination of Marx's class theory reveals that he frequently used the term "class" in his writings, but he lacked a systematic treatment of its usage (So 1990). Nonetheless, it is quite clear that he viewed social classes as structures that are external to, and coercive of, people (Ritzer 2000a). Social classes come about as the result of the distribution of property. Marx noted that the possession of property is especially critical for industrial production. Those who control the means of production own property. They maintain control over others (workers) by manipulating the social system in a manner that allows property to be privately owned (rather than owned collectively by all). The political system allows private property to remain in the hands of a few, thus assuring an ongoing imbalance of power. The power brokers of the economic system, in turn, influence legislation in such a manner as to provide an advantage for the owners of the means of production. "Marx's thesis that political conditions are determined by industrial conditions seems to stem from the generalized assertion of an absolute and universal primacy of production over all other structures of economy and society" (Delaney 2004, p. 74).

Marx believed that capitalistic societies tend to create conditions favorable to class polarization. The distinct social classes, recognizing what courses of action best suit their needs, will become more and more homogeneous internally. These two factors contribute to Marx's idea that conflict is inevitable among the social classes. Class struggle also mandates the need for the ruling class to control the proletariat. In order to eliminate class struggle (and social class distinctions) Marx proposed the abolition of all social classes through the implementation of communism. Under Marx's conception of communism, the means of production would be commonly owned by the people, and the profits from production would be shared among the masses. Private property would be eliminated in favor of common ownership, meaning, again, that the people would own all property. When people controlled property and the means of production equally, social classes would be eliminated. Thus, communism was meant to be a classless society in which every person worked to produce for the totality based on his or her individual skills and then reaped the benefits from the collectivity. With a classless society, class conflict would also be eliminated. Furthermore, because the people controlled the means of production, power would be taken away from the few and given to the collectivity.

Marx was so sure of his communistic ideal that he attempted to educate people throughout Europe that it was in their best interest to overthrow existing social systems in favor of communism. He expected that once the masses became consciously aware of the fact that they were being exploited, they would join a massive workers' revolt. This idea that members of the working class would recognize the courses of action that would best suit their own specific needs was articulated in Marx's concept of class consciousness. **Class consciousness** refers to an awareness of belonging to a class in the social order with definite economic interests; it is the realization of where one stands within the socioeconomic strata. Once again, economics—one's position relative to the means of production and access to scarce resources—becomes the primary factor that shapes class consciousness. It was Marx's hope that members of the proletariat would become conscious of their low status within the social stratification system and revolt against the ruling class.

However, due to **false consciousness**—the inability to recognize clearly the instruments of one's oppression or exploitation as one's own creation, as when members of an oppressed class unwittingly adopt the views of the oppressor class—the proletariat failed to unite against the bourgeoisie and remained dominated by the social forces it helped to create. Marx overestimated the willingness of "workers of all lands [to] unite."

What Do You Think?

Although Marx used the related terms "class consciousness" and "false consciousness" in relation to entire social classes rather than individuals, it is possible for each of us, as individuals, to apply these terms to our own lives. In this manner, when did you become consciously aware of your social class? Have you ever engaged in behavior that Marx would label false consciousness? What do you think?

Max Weber: A Multicausal Approach to Social Stratification

Max Weber agreed with Marx that a social class is a category of persons with a common specific causal component of their life chances and that this causal component is manifested by economic interests (possession of goods and opportunities for income). Weber also agreed that members of a social class are aware of their social position in society. This acknowledgment can cause persons with a similar economic background to regard themselves as a "we" group and to categorize other economic classes as "they" groups (Coser 1977). (Note: Chapter 8 discusses the "we-they" categorization system in terms of racial and ethnic identity.)

According to Weber, economics is also tied to social prestige in that those with money, over time, will eventually ascend to the top status positions in society. Equally true is the realization that the economically poor will almost always find themselves in the bottom social-prestige strata. With this line of reasoning, social stratification will always consist of the haves and the have-nots. And although it is impossible for an entire social class of low economic standing to ascend to higher strata within society, Weber did note that some individuals are capable of bridging the gap between low economic status and high social prestige and/or political power. Thus, Weber believed that an individual can occupy a low social status in one sphere of life while possessing a high status in another sphere. For example, a religious leader may have little money (economic poverty) but be respected (social prestige) by his or her followers. Conversely, a wealthy person may not enjoy a great deal of social prestige if the money was attained through illegitimate means (e.g., drug dealing or prostitution). In another scenario, a local politician may exert a high level of political power but earn a small salary and enjoy little social prestige.

Within a Weberian scheme of social stratification, people may earn social prestige from a variety of sources beyond wealth and income. Consider the following variables as possible sources of social prestige:

- *Family name:* At every level—local, regional, and national—certain family names carry a sense of prestige.
- *Geographic residence:* Within every locality, certain neighborhoods are more prestigious than others. Furthermore, certain states or regions are more prestigious than others. In some cases, prestige is based on safety. Thus, because some cities are "safer" (defined in terms of crime rates) than others, they are more prestigious.
- *Level of education:* It is generally accepted that the higher one's level of education, the more prestige one has. A college graduate, for example, enjoys a higher level of social prestige than a high school dropout.
- *Celebrity status:* Movie stars and star athletes generally enjoy a high level of social prestige. Wherever they go, the paparazzi will follow. If they wish to host a press conference to get a message out, the media will show up—a

What Do You Think?

Members of certain families, such as the Kennedy, Rockefeller, Bush, and Clinton families, are accorded a great deal of prestige in U.S. society. What is this prestige based on? Within your own community, what reputation does your family name have and why? What do you think?

> **What Do You Think?**
>
> Cities such as Camden, New Jersey, Detroit, Michigan, and St. Louis, Missouri, are routinely ranked among the most dangerous cities in the country. Would it be prestigious to live there? Are there certain areas of your own community where you would prefer to live compared to other areas? Are certain geographic regions more desirable than others? If so, why? What do you think?

forum will be provided. And because they have a forum, many members of general society come to value their opinions.

- *Titles:* In nearly all professions, favorable job titles are sought after. There is a certain built-in prestige associated with being a CEO or president of a corporation. Political titles such as senator, governor, or mayor are also generally looked upon favorably.
- *Accomplishments:* Gaining some sort of public acknowledgment for an achievement (e.g., receiving a reward for saving someone's life, earning a military honor for service above and beyond the call of duty, or even becoming the title holder for one's state in the Miss America pageant) provides a forum for the recipient to express his or her views on a particular issue, political or otherwise. An opportunity such as this may be parlayed into a profitable future, not to mention positive social prestige.

> **What Do You Think?**
>
> What types of accomplishments do you hope to achieve in your lifetime? Will others consider them prestigious? How will your accomplishments affect your standing in the social strata? What do you think?

It should be noted that the variables discussed above do not always have universal acceptance. For example, not all people place a great deal of importance on the size of someone's salary, as listed in "Connecting Sociology and Popular Culture" Box 7.1. Similarly, not everyone is impressed by a job title, and a job title valued in one profession may not be looked upon similarly in another. In an episode of the TV sitcom *Seinfeld* titled "The Bookstore" (1998), the Elaine character (played by Julia Louis-Dreyfus) attempts to explain the importance of her job to the Jerry character (played by Jerry Seinfeld), based on her job title. She quickly finds out that her title does not have as much meaning as she thought when she realizes that others, who presumably have less prestige than she, have the same title. In an earlier scene, Elaine has humiliated herself by getting drunk at an office party and then making out with a coworker. She is now with her friends Jerry and George at the local coffee shop as she attempts to explain her mortification and its consequences.

Elaine: Do you know how embarrassing this is to someone in my position?

Jerry: What is your position?

Elaine (proudly proclaims): I am an associate.

George: Hey, me too!

Waitress (while filling their cups of coffee): Yeah, me too.

As this episode of *Seinfeld* illustrates, revered titles in one field do not always carry the same meaning and weight in another. Thus, a title may provide a sense of social prestige for people within a given profession, but that does not guarantee that a title brings automatic prestige to others outside the profession.

The Social Construction of Class

The discussion of Marx's and Weber's theories on social stratification reveals an underlying sociological theme: social class, like race (Chapter 8) and gender (Chapter 9), is a matter of social construction. Marx believed that social class was constructed almost entirely by economic parameters, whereas Weber believed that social class was based on a wide variety of variables. The concept of the social construction of class is of particular concern to sociology because sociologists examine the ways all forms of power are socially developed and maintained. For example, forms of cultural capital or class status are developed by joining the right social clubs, knowing the right people, reading the right books, attending the right events, and the like. If someone wants to be thought of as having high social class, cultural expectations dictate attending high-cultural events (see Chapter 4), such as the opera, Broadway plays, museum openings, and charity balls. If someone wants to be thought of as "one of the people," he or she will attend pop-culture events, such as rock concerts, ballgames, blockbuster films, and backyard barbecues. A person who craves street credibility (see "Connecting Sociology and Popular Culture" Box 2.1) will commit street or violent crime and get involved with gunfire. We learn these class roles through experience and social interactions. Through fulfilling these roles, we help to construct our own social class standing.

SOCIAL STRATIFICATION SYSTEMS AND SOCIAL MOBILITY

How much socioeconomic mobility exists in society? The answer to this question depends largely on a society's system of stratification. As a rule, individuals have the greatest opportunity for social mobility with an open system of stratification. An *open stratification system* allows for mobility up and down the social hierarchy for all members of society. In this type of system, achieved statuses have substantial influence. An **achieved status** is any trait assigned to a person through individual effort and merit. The status of college graduate is an example of an achieved status because a college degree is something an individual must earn.

Conversely, in a closed stratification system, there is very little mobility. Those born poor will almost certainly remain poor, and those born wealthy will nearly always remain wealthy. In this type of stratification system, ascribed statuses largely determine a person's social position throughout life. An **ascribed status** is any trait assigned to an individual at birth (e.g., one's race or ethnicity, national origin, and gender).

SOCIAL STRATIFICATION SYSTEMS

Sociologists generally acknowledge three distinct types of social stratification systems based on their degree of mobility: caste, estate or feudal, and class systems. The caste system affords little or no mobility, the estate or feudal system allows for modest mobility opportunities, and the class system provides the greatest opportunity for mobility.

Caste: The least mobility is found in caste systems (Marger 2006). A caste is a grouping of people. A caste system consists of legally or formally defined groupings that are determined at birth and not subject to change. In such a system, a person is born into a particular group, or caste, and must remain in that caste throughout life. Thus, ascribed characteristics entirely determine one's life chances of social mobility, and personal achievement (achieved statuses) has little or no influence. In a caste system, the privileged class is allowed access to desired goods and services, while the group discriminated against is denied equal access. Access to desired goods and services (e.g., a quality education, proper medical care, job opportunities) greatly increases a person's chances of upward social mobility. Examples include India's caste system, which was based on religion and existed for centuries. The caste system was officially abolished in 1949, but it continues to exert considerable influence on social behavior, especially in rural areas, today.

As another example, from 1948 to 1991, the nation of South Africa was governed under a policy of racial discrimination known as apartheid (literally meaning "apartness"). Apartheid was a system of laws and procedures intended to oppress the rights of blacks and mixed-race people (known as "coloreds") while maintaining white supremacy within the ranks of the government as well as society. Under this system of legal discrimination, more than 25 million nonwhite Africans had their rights rescinded while the fewer than 5 million whites held the power of government. Despite the efforts of a number of humanitarians and writers to highlight the injustices of apartheid, for decades most of the world turned a blind eye to this blatant and open form of discrimination. The resistance movement of the African National Congress eventually gained critical aid from Nelson Mandela's worldwide public plea for assistance after his release from a long prison sentence.

It should also be noted that Mandela's release from prison was the result of worldwide public pressure. For example, during the 1980s, there were many demonstrations on college campuses to pressure universities to divest themselves of their South African stock holdings (see "Connecting Sociology and Popular Culture" Box 7.3 for a racial struggle of a different type that takes place, in a fictional manner, in South Africa).

Living in a public housing project lacks prestige and safety.

Estate or feudal system: The estate or feudal stratification system offers only modestly greater mobility opportunities than found in the caste system. In the estate system, status is determined on the basis of land ownership, which is often accompanied by some type of formal title (e.g., lord or baron). Typically, the high-status groups are those who own land (means of production), and the rest of the population works for them. Some variation of the estate system has been found in most of the world at some point, including Europe during the Middle Ages and China and Russia in the nineteenth and early twentieth centuries. The Latin American hacienda system, some of which remains intact today, is another example of the estate system. Because land ownership is passed down from one generation to the next, ascribed status primarily determines one's social position and chances of social mobility.

Class system: The highest degree of mobility is found in a class system. The social class system allows people the opportunity to ascend and descend the socioeconomic ladder. The United States has a social class system. In the U.S. class system, all people (at least theoretically) have a chance for social mobility. In the class system, both ascribed and achieved statuses have significant effects on people's income, wealth, and social position. Ascribed status has influence in the sense that those born into wealthy families generally enjoy a higher status than those born into poorer families. In addition, wealthy persons will have opportunities that the poor will not (e.g., better nutrition and medical care; access to better schools, private tutoring, and job connections). However, achieved statuses also play a role in the class system because those people who attain high levels of

Connecting Sociology and Popular Culture

Box 7.3 Apartheid in *District 9*

The fictional account of aliens from outer space depicted in the 2009 blockbuster movie *District 9* presents us with many interesting parallels between the real-life struggle of blacks in apartheid South Africa and the alien refugees of Johannesburg's District 9 area. A documentary-style presentation at the beginning of *District 9* informs the viewing audience about the arrival of a spaceship that has mysteriously stopped operating and is somehow hovering over the city of Johannesburg. After a few weeks, the malnourished aliens are assisted to Earth by government forces. The aliens are given a place to reside on the outskirts of the city as guests and are initially taken care of by the government (a type of welfare). Over time, a number of residents of Johannesburg begin to complain that the money spent on the growing alien population (over 1 million) would be better spent on them. Echoing past and present-day complaints about immigration, the residents would prefer that the aliens went back home. But the aliens do not have the means to return home. Under pressure from South Africans, the government turns to the Multi-National United (MNU) for help. The MNU, by all appearances, is similar to the United Nations. The MNU, however, is the second-leading manufacturer of weapons and, as a result, has ulterior motives when dealing with the aliens.

The aliens have now been in Johannesburg for two decades. Government assistance is nearly nonexistent. Consequently, the refugee home of the aliens has been transformed into a ghetto. Like nonwhite South Africans under apartheid, the aliens find themselves living in squalid conditions. Isolated from those who control the means of production, District 9 becomes a lonely ghetto inhabited by a growing underclass. Under apartheid, nonwhite South Africans also became an underclass and found themselves isolated from the benefits of the ruling class. The aliens in District 9 are confronted by a number of social problems including discrimination, stereotypical and negative portrayal of their group as an underclass—the aliens in *District 9* are referred to as "prawns"(a derogatory term used by the residents)—squalid living conditions, hunger and malnourishment, and a growing criminal presence.

What Do You Think?

In the early 1980s social observers began to use the term "yuppie" (from the acronym for "young upwardly mobile professional") to refer to college graduates in their twenties who were pursuing careers in prestigious professions such as law and medicine. Instead of being admired for striving to improve their social status, yuppies were widely criticized for being materialistic and overly ambitious. Was this criticism justified? In today's society, is upward mobility generally admired or criticized? What do you think?

education or make successful personal and economic decisions can improve their opportunity for upward mobility.

Although most people think of social mobility in terms of an upward gain in social position, it is possible in the class system for wealthy people to lose their fortunes, therefore lowering their socioeconomic position in life.

Social Mobility

What exactly is meant by social mobility? **Social mobility** refers to the degree to which an individual, family, or group changes its status within the social stratification system—usually expressed in terms of income, wealth, level of edu-

Black South Africans under apartheid were confronted by many of these same problems.

Although the audience is clearly set up to recognize the similarities between apartheid in South Africa and the segregation of aliens from earthlings in *District 9,* the film takes an interesting sci-fi turn in presentation. It manages to be political without being preachy. Some people will be pleased by this; others will not. It also provides an interesting perspective on the term "race" (see Chapter 8 for a discussion of race).

Many audience members may be unaware of another similarity between the film *District 9* and a specific real-life occurrence in South Africa during the time of apartheid. *District 9* film director Neill Blomkamp (who is known for his documentary-style films), a native of South Africa, was stirred by the events of Cape Town's now defunct District Six—a site where different ethnic groups, including blacks, whites, Asians, Muslims, and Christians, lived together in relative harmony. "Because of its proximity to Cape Town's port, District Six was a frequent stop for American, British, and Italian sailors whose ships made frequent ports of call there—making it very cosmopolitan" (Johnson 2009, p. 1). As a model for urban diversity at its best, District Six was viewed as a threat to the apartheid government, which was intent on promoting a separate development for different ethnic groups. As a result, the government swooped in on District Six in 1965 and forcibly removed the inhabitants. Over 60,000 people were relocated to the bleak plains of the Cape Flats several kilometers away (District Six Museum 2003). Blomkamp, drawing inspiration from this event, designed the alien compound and alien relocation plan used in *District 9* along the lines of those used in District Six.

Students are encouraged to learn about District Six and apartheid and then watch the film *District 9.* It will be an informative and entertaining manner of learning. (Web links are provided at the end of this chapter.)

What Do You Think?

What social conditions made it possible for a system like apartheid to dominate a country in the late twentieth century? Do any comparable forms of segregation exist in the world today? If aliens from outer space actually arrived on Earth, how would we treat them? How would they treat us? What do you think?

cation, or occupation—over a period. There are two primary categories of social mobility: intragenerational mobility (within a generation) and intergenerational mobility (across generations). *Intragenerational mobility* is defined as changes in an individual's social status over a single lifetime—for example, when a child from a lower-socioeconomic-status family enjoys wealth in adulthood after earning a college degree that led to a high-paying professional occupation. *Intergenerational mobility* is defined as changes in social status from the parents' generation to their children's generation. For example, a working-class couple may struggle to make ends meet, never enjoying wealth but providing opportunities for their children to pursue a quality education and enjoy a higher socioeconomic status than themselves.

Open stratification systems provide the best opportunity for upward mobility. However, the type of stratification system becomes far less important if the economy is weak. Thus, while it is true that large numbers of people may enjoy upward mobility during times of economic prosperity, very few people will attain upward mobility if the economy is stagnant. Once again, we see the importance of the economic system for people's life chances. Furthermore, people who face discrimination based on an ascribed characteristic will face even greater structural barriers in times of economic turmoil in their quest for upward mobility.

In their study of intergenerational social mobility, Emily Beller and Michael Hout (2006) compared men's and women's rates of social mobility: "Among men, 32 percent were immobile (their occupation was in the same category as their father's), 37 percent were upwardly mobile, and 32 percent were downwardly mobile. Fifteen percent of the mobility was driven by structural change in the economy, or economic growth—more professional jobs and fewer farm jobs were available to sons than to their fathers" (p. 23). The news was much better for women as "27 percent were immobile, 46 percent were upwardly mobile, and 28 percent were downwardly mobile" (Beller and Hout 2006, p. 23). Beller and Hout believe that increased economic growth and greater opportunities (especially for women) are the primary factors influencing upward social mobility in the past few generations.

POVERTY AND HOMELESSNESS

> **What Do You Think?**
>
> A number of factors are tied to upward mobility. A strong economy would seem to benefit the greatest number of people in their pursuit of upward mobility. Based on today's economy, what are your chances for upward mobility over the next twenty to thirty years? What do you think?

The introductory story of this chapter reminded us of the great wealth enjoyed by a select few members of society. However, there are far more economically poor people than there are wealthy ones. This has been the case throughout human history. And until fairly recently, the poor were not recognized as a distinct status group. Sociologist Georg Simmel ([1908] 1971) believed that the poor only emerged as a status group when society recognized poverty as a special status and then assigned others to assist them. Historically, the poor were on their own to either survive or perish. Civilized societies feel compelled to assist the poor and hope to end poverty. Students may recall our discussion in Chapter 2 of Jane Addams's creation of Hull House in Chicago. Hull House started the settlement-house movement in the United States. Needless to say, ending poverty is a daunting challenge, even in times of economic prosperity.

Defining Poverty

Although most of us have a general understanding of what poverty is, it is important, especially for governments, to establish clear parameters in order to ascertain the degree and instance of poverty. **Poverty** can be defined as the lack of basic necessities, goods, or means of support. It prevents people from consuming, owning, or doing things that are an essential part of belonging to the society in which they live (Saunders 2005). "At its core, poverty restricts people's ability to live a decent life because it imposes restrictions on what they can buy or do, and hence be. Those who are poor must devote all of their resources to meeting their basic needs, with nothing left over with which to exercise the freedom to consume and participate" (Saunders 2005, p. 59). In extreme cases, people may face destitution—a state of having absolutely none of the necessities of life. Widespread destitution is likely to occur in countries at war or facing famine or drought.

The Demographics of Poverty

Poverty is not restricted to nations besieged by war on their soil or those that face famine or drought. The United States, one of the wealthiest nations in the world, has a relatively huge number of people living in poverty. The recession that began in 2007 contributed to a steady increase in the number of Americans living in poverty. According to the U.S. census, there were 36.5 million Americans living in poverty in 2006 and 37.3 million in 2007 (12.5 percent poverty rate) (U.S. Census Bureau 2008b). In 2008, the figure increased to 39.8 million, a poverty rate of 13.2 percent (Eckholm 2009). The *poverty rate* refers to the percentage of people living in poverty. The number of seniors sixty-five and older living in poverty increased from 3.4 million in 2006 to 3.6 million (9.7 percent) in 2007. The poverty rate for those age eighteen to sixty-four was 10.9 percent. The U.S. Census Bureau (2008b) data also revealed that 14.2 percent of people in the South lived in poverty in 2007 compared to 11.4 percent in the Northeast, 11.1 percent in the Midwest, and 12.0 percent in the West. In addition, 24.5 percent of blacks lived in poverty in 2007 compared to 21.5 percent of Hispanics, 10.2 percent of Asians, and 8.2 percent of non-Hispanic whites.

The Xhosa family of South Africa are shown in front of their impoverished home.

The perception of poverty often involves an image of the urban poor. However, it should be noted that the poor can be found in rural areas and in the suburbs. For example, according to 2010 data provided by the Brookings Institution, the number of poor grew by 25 percent in the suburbs from 2000 to 2008—a growth rate nearly five times higher than that for the nation's largest cities—making the suburbs home to the largest and fastest-growing poor population in the United States (Stith 2010).

Gender also plays a role in poverty rates, as women are far more likely than men to be poor. Women who are single parents and women of color are especially vulnerable to poverty. According to the National Poverty Center (2009), "Poverty rates are highest for families headed by single women, particularly if they are black or Hispanic. In 2007, 28.3 percent of households headed by single women were poor, while 13.6 percent of households headed by single men and 4.9 percent of married-couple households lived in poverty" (p. 2). That women are more likely to be poor than men has led sociologists to use the term "feminization of poverty." Dianna Pearce popularized this term in her 1978 article "The Feminization of Poverty: Women, Work, and Welfare," in which she cited data to support her claim that almost two-thirds of the poor over the age of sixteen were women entering the labor force between 1950 and the mid-1970s. She argued that the blame for this feminization of poverty belonged to the government because it did not find a way to support divorced and single women (Delaney 2006a).

Slightly more than one-third of the poor are children. In 2008, more than 13 million persons under the age of eighteen (19 percent of children) lived in poverty (Institute for Research on Poverty 2009). A disproportionate number of these poor children are black or Hispanic.

This Asian man is among the working poor, who barely make enough money to survive.

It is also interesting to note that not all the poor are jobless. A significant number of people work full-time and yet still live in poverty. These people are referred to as the "working poor." The **working poor** are those persons who spend twenty-seven weeks or more per year in the labor force, working or looking for work, but whose incomes still fall below the official poverty level (U.S. Department of Labor 2008). In 2006, there were 7.4 million working poor in the United States (U.S. Department of Labor 2008). In 2007, there were 7.5 million working poor in the United States, a figure that represents 5.1 percent of all people who were in the labor force (Nelson 2009). The working poor are more likely to be women than men and, proportionately, black or Hispanic. The working poor are also more likely to be poorly educated and concentrated in nonprofessional or service-oriented occupations such as sales clerks and restaurant workers (e.g., dishwashers and waitresses).

The History of "Official" Poverty Thresholds and Poverty Guidelines

In 1964, President Lyndon B. Johnson declared a "War on Poverty" during his first State of the Union address. Acknowledging poverty as a national concern (a social problem), Johnson set into motion a series of bills and acts creating programs such as Head Start, food stamps, work study, Medicare, and Medicaid, all of which still exist today (Siegel 2004). In an attempt to measure the progress of the "War on Poverty," poverty scales, or thresholds, were established by the federal government—specifically, the Office of Economic Opportunity. The key variable used in the 1960s to determine poverty thresholds was the cost of food, thus the required food budget calculated for families of various sizes and compositions by the U.S. Department of Agriculture (Weinberg 2006).

Based on research conducted by Mollie Orshansky (1963, 1965), a researcher for the Social Security Administration, the U.S. Department of Agriculture determined that food represented about one-third of after-tax income for the typical family. "This relationship yielded a 'multiplier' of three, that is, the minimally adequate food budgets were multiplied by a factor of three to obtain 124 poverty thresholds that differed by family size, number of children, age and sex of head, and farm or nonfarm residence (adjustments were made for families of size one and two)" (Weinberg 2006, p. 2). In 1969, the U.S. Bureau of Budget (now the Office of Management and Budget) adopted the Orshansky measure as the standard government poverty measure (Weinberg 2006). Each year the government computes a low-cost food budget and multiplies by three. Families whose incomes are less than this amount are considered poor; those earning above this figure are considered "not poor."

The U.S. government, then, in an effort to calculate "official" numbers of poor—as determined by U.S. Census Bureau data—uses an absolute measurement. *Absolute poverty* thresholds are calculated by the costs of minimal "necessary" consumption goods, such as food and shelter, which are fixed at a point in time and updated solely for price changes. The European Community uses relative thresholds to facilitate cross-national comparisons of poverty (Weinberg 2006). *Relative poverty* thresholds are developed by reference to the actual expenditures (or income) of the population (U.S. Census Bureau 2009). "Thus, under a relative poverty measure, only if the incomes for the families at the bottom of the income distribution improve *relative* to the rest of the distribution would poverty decline" (Weinberg 2006, p. 5).

Since the early formation of poverty guidelines, the Office of Economic Opportunity no longer uses poverty thresholds. Similar to poverty thresholds, poverty guidelines are used to determine eligibility for such government programs as

Head Start, food stamps, the National School Lunch Program, the Low-Income Home Energy Assistance Program, and the Children's Health Insurance Program (U.S. Department of Health and Human Services 2009a). However, while poverty thresholds make a distinction between age and nonage units, the poverty guidelines do not. In addition, whereas poverty thresholds were consistent for all fifty states and the District of Columbia, there are separate poverty guidelines for Alaska and Hawaii. (The calculated food costs for Alaska and Hawaii are deemed significantly different than those of the forty-eight contiguous states and the District of Columbia.) The poverty guidelines are not defined for Puerto Rico, the U.S. Virgin Islands, American Samoa, Guam, the Republic of the Marshall Islands, the Federated States of Micronesia, the Commonwealth of the Northern Mariana Islands, and Palau (Department of Health and Human Services 2009a).

The poverty guidelines differ by family size and, as stated above, by location. The 2009 official poverty guidelines for the forty-eight contiguous states were $22,050 for a family of four; $18,301 for three-person families; $14,570 for a two-person family; and $10,830 for a single person (U.S. Department of Health and Human Services 2009a). (For a closer examination of the 2009 poverty guidelines see Table 7.3.)

It is nearly impossible for households to survive at or below the poverty level. Costs for food, especially healthy foods (see Chapter 13), health care, child care,

TABLE 7.3 2009 Poverty Guidelines

NUMBER OF PERSONS IN FAMILY OR HOUSEHOLD	FORTY-EIGHT CONTIGUOUS STATES AND WASHINGTON, DC ($)	ALASKA ($)	HAWAII ($)
1	10,830	13,530	12,460
2	14,570	18,210	16,760
3	18,310	22,890	21,060
4	22,050	27,570	25,360
5	25,790	32,250	29,660
6	29,530	36,930	33,960
7	33,270	41,610	38,260
8	37,010	46,290	42,560

Source: U.S. Department of Health and Human Services 2009a.

Note: For families with more than eight persons in the forty-eight contiguous states and the District of Columbia, add $3,740 for each additional person, add $4,680 in Alaska for each additional person, and add $4,300 in Hawaii for each additional person.

and housing continue to rise at a faster pace than poverty thresholds. That the poverty levels are set so low leads to the perception that the government does not want to acknowledge the true number of people who find it hard to make ends meet.

What Do You Think?

Consider the official U.S. poverty rate for a household like yours. Would it be possible for your family to survive at the official poverty threshold? What changes in your lifestyle would you need to make to do so? What do you think?

Homelessness

Every city, large and small, has a homeless population. The homeless can be found in parks, under bridges, lying on city benches, underground in subway stations, above ground at bus stops, and waiting in line outside soup kitchens and homeless shelters. Yet, despite their visibility, they are often unnoticed by most citizens, who go about their business either oblivious to their presence or hopeful that they will not be bothered by a homeless person approaching them and asking for assistance.

How does someone become homeless? It may start with an illness or injury that causes the person to miss more days of work than the employer allows. Then a chain reaction may occur: the worker is laid off and thereby loses his or her health insurance. Now he or she cannot pay for medical care, so becomes sicker, unable to look for a new job. Over the next few months, savings are exhausted, and the person can no longer pay the mortgage or rent. Maybe this person turns to living in his or her car . . . then has to sell it or cannot afford to have it repaired. Now the person is destitute. Many destitute people end up homeless.

Joining the destitute are a number of drug addicts and alcoholics who become homeless because they spend all their money on drugs or alcohol and have alienated loved ones who can, or will, no longer help them. Their daily activities are consumed by finding ways to raise money for a fix. If they had help fighting their addictions, many homeless drug addicts and alcoholics could perhaps be rehabilitated.

The deinstitutionalization of the mentally ill contributed to the influx of members of this group becoming homeless. Deinstitutionalization refers to the release of people from mental hospitals into local communities, generally the streets. Deinstitutionalization began during the John F. Kennedy administration and continued during the Johnson administration via the Mental Retardation Facilities and Community Mental Health Centers Construction Act of 1963 (Public Law 88-164) when it was determined that a large number of the institutionalized were simply developmentally challenged and not mentally ill. The relatively recent introduction of antipsychotic drugs has enabled many patients to function better as long as they take their medication. Deinstitutionalization continued during the 1980s under the administration of Ronald Reagan; at that time it was conducted primarily to reduce federal human-service program costs (Kaiser Commission 2007).

The dilemma of deinstitutionalization continues today, as mental hospitals cannot legally retain a patient who wishes to leave and is not a danger to him- or herself or others. When taking antipsychotic medication, many individuals with severe mental illness are able to function reasonably well, but when released to live on their own, they often stop taking their medication and consequently slip into behavior and thought patterns that make them unable to hold a job or even take care of themselves properly. Consequently, many deinstitutionalized mentally ill individuals have found themselves living on the streets, homeless and fending for themselves. (In some cases, the homeless are subjected to cruelty. See "Connecting Sociology and Popular Culture" Box 7.4 for an example of a crude form of mistreating the homeless.) The lack of proper and regular medical treatment assures that these people will most likely never become fully functional members of society.

Although the U.S. government attempts to assist this group through such agencies as the Department of Housing and Urban Development, countless people remain homeless. The word "countless" is more than just an expression in this case, as it truly is difficult to count the total number of homeless persons. In 2007, estimates for the United States ranged from 744,000 to 3.5 million (National Coalition for the Homeless 2007). Who are the homeless? The demographics of homelessness in the U.S. reveal that single men constitute 51 percent of the homeless population, families with children 30 percent, single women 17 percent, and unaccompanied youth 2 percent. Forty-two percent of the homeless are African American, 39 percent white, 13 percent Hispanic, 4 percent Native American, and 2 percent Asian. Approximately 16 percent of the homeless are mentally ill, and 26 percent are substance abusers (National Coalition for the Homeless 2007).

The National Alliance to End Homelessness, in cooperation with Veterans Affairs and the U.S. Census Bureau, estimates that between 23 and 40 percent of the homeless in 2006 were veterans. This is an alarming figure, considering that just 11 percent of the general adult population are veterans (National Alliance to End Homelessness 2008). They are veterans from a variety of wars, including World War II, the Korean and Vietnam wars, Grenada, Panama, Lebanon, and the Iraq and Afghanistan wars. The Veterans Administration (VA) believes that the early presence of veterans from the Iraq and Afghanistan wars is particularly disconcerting, as it took roughly a decade for the lives of Vietnam veterans to unravel to the point that significant numbers showed up among the homeless (*The Citizen,* 11/8/07). Advocates to end homelessness worry that repeated deploy-

Connecting Sociology and Popular Culture

Box 7.4 "Bum Fights": The Degradation of People Down and Out?

It is often stated that there are three basic necessities for human survival: food, clothing, and shelter. Shelter refers to having a home, or at the very least, a safe harbor. Most of us take for granted that we have a home to return to at the end of the day and from which to start the next day. Our home represents a safe port in an often dangerous world. Finding oneself homeless and living on the street presents many challenges, such as finding adequate food and clothing and avoiding the many dangers associated with daily street life. The homeless, who are already living with the indignity of having fallen so far in the ranks of the social strata, must worry about the threat of humans' most dangerous enemy—other humans. On occasion, the homeless turn on one another; on other occasions, they fall victim to random attacks from the nonhomeless. Street thugs and drunken delinquents have been documented as attacking homeless people just because they wanted to have some fun. Such senseless brutality against those who can barely defend themselves is one of humanity's least desirable traits.

In recent years, a new level of senseless brutality against the homeless has reached the domain of popular culture—"bum fights." Bum fights are staged acts of violence wherein homeless people, usually men, are paid to fight one another for the entertainment of the viewers. In most cases, these fights are filmed; many of the videos appear on YouTube and other websites. There exists a specific film series called *Bumfights* created by Indecline Films. The videos feature homeless men in metropolitan areas (primarily San Diego and Las Vegas) fighting and attempting amateur stunts in exchange for money, alcohol, and other incentives. *Bumfights* are brutal video depictions of street life, portrayed with rapid-cut, handheld camera images. Most of the images are too brutal to describe here, but suffice it to say that the participants often endure violent attacks that may include being set on fire; some receive payment to defecate on a sidewalk or pull their own teeth out with pliers, and so on.

As one might imagine, the *Bumfights* videos are condemned by numerous organizations, such as the National Coalition for the Homeless. They have been banned in a number of countries, including England, Scotland, Northern Ireland, and Canada, and most mainstream retail video outlets refuse to rent or sell them.

Numerous other street fight videos are available online beyond the *Bumfights* series. The wide variety of violent street fight videos available online includes out-and-out brawls, gang fights, ghetto fights, girl fights, school fights, random street fights, and so on.

What Do You Think?

Do "bum fights" represent a new low in the degradation of humans? Why would people be willing to pay others to engage in such fights? What do you think?

ments leave newer veterans particularly vulnerable to homelessness. As the plight of war veterans illustrates, the challenge to end homelessness in the United States will be daunting.

> **What Do You Think?**
>
> What would it take to end homelessness in the United States? Can the root causes of homelessness be eradicated, or is it better to address the problem by providing shelter to those who are already homeless? What do you think?

GLOBAL STRATIFICATION AND INEQUALITY

As noted in the introductory story, over 1 billion people in the world live in constant poverty. If the challenge to end homelessness and poverty in the United States is daunting, what chance is there to end global stratification and inequality? After all, there exists a great disparity in income and wealth at the global level, not just in the United States. Worldwide, people living in poverty face a variety of social problems. "People living in poverty are generally malnourished; they are refugees, homeless, or have inadequate shelter; they have no health care; their homes and neighborhoods have little or no sanitation or clean water supplies, they are usually illiterate and have no access to education or educational opportunities; they have no energy supplies; they are often unemployed or underemployed; and because they are generally powerless, they have the least amount of human rights" (Delaney 2006a, pp. 105–106).

The populations of a number of nations in Africa, Latin America, and the Caribbean basin rank among the world's poorest. The distribution of income and wealth is far more unequal in these areas than in any other part of the globe. As Engerman and Sokoloff (2006) state, "For the most part, the least developed of these societies have small populations and are in Central America, the Caribbean basin, or the Andes. Among those [nations] with less than 60 percent of the world per capita income, for example, are Belize, Bolivia, Ecuador, Guatemala, Guyana, Haiti, Honduras, Jamaica, Nicaragua, and Suriname. Even the most populous nations, Brazil and Mexico, barely manage to match the world average, which means that significant proportions of their populations fall below international poverty lines or are unable to enjoy basic services such as access to sanitation" (p. 43).

The living conditions for people in many African nations is more dire than in Latin America and the Caribbean basin as most of the poorest nations in the world, based on gross domestic product (GDP), are found in Africa (see Table 7.4).

Arguably, the poorest of the poor in Africa are women. Most poor women in Africa do not have access to the education that would be their path out of poverty. Women in rural Africa farm small plots and sell fruits and vegetables and other items in their villages while men work in mines or perform other migrant labor far from home. Often the absent men take on second wives and create other families, never to return. Those men who return to their home villages and wives are often infected with HIV (Hunter-Gault 2006). The farming techniques utilized by the poor in Africa contribute to the negative economic spiral. For example, farmers often grow the same crops in the same fields year after year; they do not fertilize, and they do not terrace their fields. When the soil wears out, they clear a new plot of land. When erosion eventually occurs, the topsoil disappears, and farmers cannot produce food in those areas any longer (Beaubien 2006). The combination of poor education, poor farming skills, and a lack of proper medical care are among the contributing factors to continuing poverty in the developing world.

TABLE 7.4 Top 10 Poorest Nations in the World

COUNTRY	GDP PER CAPITA (US$)
Democratic Republic of Congo	300
Zimbabwe	500
Liberia	500
Guinea-Bissau	600
Somalia	600
Comoros	600
Solomon Islands*	600
Niger	700
Ethiopia	700
Central African Republic	700

Source: Maps of World 2008.
*Not located in Africa; located in Oceania.

As stated earlier, civil society feels compelled to assist the poor and hopes to end poverty. Governments have collaborated to establish a number of organizations, including the World Bank and the International Monetary Fund (IMF), to help fight global stratification and inequality. According to its website, the World Bank is a source of financial and technical assistance to developing countries around the world. It is not a bank in the traditional sense; instead, it is made up of two unique development institutions owned by 185 member countries—the International Bank for Reconstruction and Development and the International Development Association. The World Bank's primary goal is global poverty reduction and the improvement of living conditions. It oversees $55 billion in readily tradable assets (Weisman 2007b). With this money, it provides low-interest loans and interest-free credit to developing countries for education, health, and other purposes.

The modern World Bank office building in Washington, D.C.

The IMF is an international organization with 185 member countries (as of 2008). It was established to promote international monetary cooperation and exchange stability, to foster economic growth, and to provide temporary financial assistance to countries to help them ease balance payments (IMF 2008a). In the 1990s, the IMF helped to stabilize the world economy

A Closer Look

Box 7.5 The International Monetary Fund

The International Monetary Fund is an institution of global economic governance that emerged from the UN Monetary and Financial Conference, held at Bretton Woods, New Hampshire, in July 1944 (Scholte 2000a). The 1940s marked an era when the victors of World War II created vast cooperative superstructures for the world economy (Weisman 2006). The IMF hopes to achieve global stability by helping developing nations in transition to achieve stability while they continue to grow (Stiglitz 2002). "Until recently it debated whether it should be concerned with poverty—that was the responsibility of the World Bank—but today it has even taken that on board" (Stiglitz 2002, p. 195). According to its website, the IMF conducts three main types of work: surveillance, lending, and technical assistance (IMF 2008b). *Surveillance* involves monitoring economic and financial developments and the provision of policy advice aimed especially at crisis prevention. In its *lending* capacity, it extends financial aid to countries with balance-of-payments difficulties in order to provide temporary financing to support policies aimed at correcting the underlying problems that created financial difficulties. The IMF also provides *technical assistance* and training in its areas of expertise. The IMF further plays an important role in the fight against money laundering and terrorism (IMF 2008b). Officially, the IMF deals only with governments. However, over the years the institution has conducted dialogues with various associations from civil society (e.g., academic associations). In this context, civil society refers to a broad collectivity of nongovernmental, noncommercial, less formal organizations (Scholte 2000a). IMF officials explain that because the world economy is constantly changing, the IMF must change with it.

What Do You Think?

Considering the rates of poverty that continue to exist around the world, are the World Bank and IMF doing a good-enough job assisting poorer nations? What are some of the obstacles they face? How could their work be more effective? What do you think?

after markets collapsed in Latin America, Russia, and Asia. "Though critics often have rued its interventionism, the fund was widely hailed as a heroic guardian of the global financial system" (Weisman 2007a). (See "A Closer Look" Box 7.5 to learn more about the IMF.)

A number of organizations beyond the IMF are attempting to help the less fortunate around the world. Some are affiliated with governmental agencies like the United Nations; others rely on private donors to finance their efforts. The United Nations, for example, was affiliated with 14,000 nongovernmental organizations (NGOs) in over 120 countries in 2010 (NGO.org 2010). A random sampling of these organizations includes Earth Charter, the Education with Enterprise Trust, Good Neighbors International, the International Agency for Economic Development, the Nuclear Age Peace Foundation, and the World Information Transfer. Students have most likely heard of the Peace Corps, Doctors Without Borders, and Habitat for Humanity. The Peace Corps, created in 1961 under President Kennedy, promotes world peace and friendship and has as its primary mission providing people in interested countries job-skills training (Peace Corps 2008). Created in 1971, Doctors Without Borders is an agency that operates independently of any political, military, or religious agenda and is committed to bringing quality medical care to people caught in crisis (e.g., people threatened by violence, neglect, or catastrophe) primarily due to armed conflict, epidemic, malnutrition, exclusion from health care, or natural disaster (Doctors Without Borders 2010). Habitat for Humanity builds homes for low-income families around the world. Whenever possible, the organization builds sustainable, energy-efficient, and healthy housing (Habitat for Humanity 2010).

Global awareness has caused a heightened debate over the responsibility to aid the poor. Do the developed nations owe the poorer nations assistance, and if so, how much and how will the distribution work? Officials from the IMF and World Bank insist that they are making every effort to help the poor. However, these organizations are not without critics. Although pleased with their goals, advocates to end world poverty do not necessarily agree with their methods. Christine Koggel, for one, argues that the World Bank is politically and economically biased by the industrial nations that fund it: "Its powerful place in the global context, its acceptance and endorsement of a discourse and set of policies about the virtues of capitalism and global markets, and its funding that ties aid to the implementation of neoliberal policies undermine the idea that it can hear or interpret well what is said by 'poor people in poor countries'" (2007, p. 20). In support of Koggel's observation, the *New York Times* claimed in an October 15, 2007, article that the World Bank neglects agriculture in impoverished sub-Saharan Africa, where most people depend on a farming economy for their livelihoods (Dugger 2007). Because of the criticism sometimes directed toward the World Bank and the IMF, supporting NGOs has become increasingly popular.

Ironically, the IMF is suffering a financial crisis as it faces a shrunken loan portfolio and lost operating income and is running a deficit (Weisman 2007a). Critics also claim that the IMF has abandoned its "traditional insistence on neutrality and objectivity with explicitly moral arguments as they seek to elaborate and justify a particular vision of international economic governance" (Jacqueline Best 2006, pp. 307–308).

It bears repeating that ending global stratification and social inequality remains an overwhelming challenge. And a classless society, as once envisioned by Karl Marx, seems highly unlikely to materialize anytime soon.

SUMMARY

Social stratification is a classification system in which people are divided into layers or strata. A corresponding level of social status generally accompanies people based on their position in society. Some form of stratification exists in all groups, organizations, and societies.

Most societies have three major dimensions of stratification: social prestige, political power, and economics. Social prestige is tied to what people think about others. Generally, people who are thought highly of have high prestige or social status. There are a number of ways to attain high prestige, including family name, level of education, occupation or career, accomplishments, social titles, and celebrity status. When people are not highly thought of, they have low social prestige. The political dimension of stratification is usually expressed in terms of power. The economic dimension of stratification is connected to one's income and wealth. Karl Marx argued that economics is the most important aspect of social stratification, whereas Max Weber believed that all three elements—prestige, political power, and economics—affect status.

There is great disparity among people based on wealth and income. The wealthy generally enjoy political power and social prestige. However, it is possible for nonwealthy people to possess prestige or relative political power, especially at the local level. In most cases, the wealthy are able to maintain their advantageous social positions, while the poor fill subordinate roles in society. However, it is possible for people in an open stratification system (the class system) to gain upward mobility. It is also possible for people to fall from their lofty hierarchal positions. In the open stratification system, achieved statuses have substantial influence on one's life chances. Closed systems of stratification (the caste and feudal or estate systems) pretty much lock people into social positions based on ascribed characteristics.

Social inequality most clearly manifests itself via poverty and homelessness. Poverty and homelessness are problems in the United States and nearly all nations of the world. A number of organizations exist to combat social inequality. People living in poverty face a variety of social problems, including malnourishment, homelessness, living conditions that may involve little or no sanitation or clean water, illiteracy, and a sense of powerlessness. That 1 billion people worldwide live in poverty is evidence that organizational attempts by civil society to eliminate poverty have, for the most part, failed.

Glossary

Achieved status—Any trait assigned to a person through individual effort and merit.

Ascribed status—Any trait assigned to an individual at birth.

Class consciousness—One's realization of where he or she stands within the socioeconomic strata.

False consciousness—The inability to see clearly where one's own best interest lies.

Income—The amount of money that a person or family receives over a period, generally a calendar year.

Poverty—The lacking of basic necessities, goods, or means of support.

Social class—A broad group of people having common economic, cultural, or political status (e.g., the working class or the professional class).

Social mobility—The degree to which an individual, family, or group changes status within the social stratification system throughout the life course.

Social prestige—A dimension of stratification tied to what people think about others.

Social stratification—The ranking of members of a social system according to levels with different or unequal evaluations.

Socioeconomic status—A composite term that includes a person's income, wealth, occupational prestige, and educational attainment.

Staycation—A vacation spent at home instead of traveling to a pleasurable destination, due perhaps to high gas prices or a simple shortage of money.

Wealth—The total value of everything that a person or family owns, minus any debts owed.

Working poor—Those persons who spend twenty-seven weeks or more in the labor force, working or looking for work, but whose incomes still fall below the official poverty level.

Discussion Questions

1. Who is the wealthiest person you know? Would you consider this person to be prestigious? Does this person have political power?
2. Do you believe the combined wealth of the richest members of society should be shared with the poorest? Why or why not?
3. If every American were given $1 million, what would happen?
4. Describe how your life would be if you were a peasant during the medieval feudal era. How would it compare with life today?

5. Do you believe the younger generation will enjoy upward social mobility similar to that of the past few generations?

6. When you have seen homeless people, what thoughts have entered your mind? Have you ever helped a homeless person?

Web Links

To learn more about the job market, see the Bureau of Labor of Statistics' *Occupational Outlook Handbook* at www.bls.gov/oco.

To learn more about the World Bank, visit its website at www.worldbank.org.

To learn more about the International Monetary Fund, visit its website at www.imf.org.

To learn more about homelessness, visit the website of the National Coalition for the Homeless at www.nationalhomeless.org/publications/facts/Why.pdf.

To learn more about poverty in the United States, visit http://aspe.hhs.gov/POVERTY.

To learn more about South Africa and apartheid, visit www.overcomingapartheid.msu.edu.

To learn more about the film *District 9,* visit the official website at www.district9movie.com.

To learn more about Cape Town's District Six, visit www.southafrica.info/about/history/districtsix.htm.

To learn more about NGOs, visit www.ngo.org/links/list.htm.

8 RACE AND ETHNICITY

Shown here is a multicultural box of Crayola crayons that depict skin color ranging from black to white with six other shades in between.

Chapter 8

INTRODUCTORY STORY

Finally, it was Friday. A great buzz filled the halls of Ridgemont High School. The Ridgemont Panthers were hosting the visiting Alcorn High School Indians in the annual contest between these two bitter crosstown rivals. Players, coaches, students, faculty and staff, and most of the Ridgemont community were looking forward to the big game. As was customary at Ridgemont High, a huge pep rally was scheduled for the last period of the school day. Pep rallies are designed to inspire young players to play hard and to remind them that the community backs them. Pep rallies also ignite fans into a near frenzy of anticipation as the student body is encouraged to yell and scream in support of the team. Yes, everyone was stoked for the pep rally.

Well, not everyone. A couple of students, Naomi and Kevin, were feeling uneasy. Having attended many pep rallies in the past, they knew what to expect. The marching band and cheerleaders did not make them feel uneasy; nor did the players. It was the bonfire and burning effigy of an "Indian," as well as the posters around campus that sported such slogans as "Scalp the Indians" and "Redmen Are Deadmen," that bothered Naomi and Kevin. For you see, these two students were Native Americans. To them it was deeply offensive to reduce the Alcorn High Indians to caricatures and celebrate acts of violence against indigenous peoples.

The use of so-called Indian imagery in sports has come under criticism throughout the United States during the past few decades. Native American advocacy groups point out that Indian imagery (team nicknames, mascots, and logos) is based on negative stereotypes, prejudice, and discrimination. As this chapter shows, the use of such imagery exemplifies some of the issues that sociology addresses when examining the subject of race and ethnicity.

THE SOCIAL CONSTRUCTION OF RACE AND ETHNICITY

As people interact with one another, especially strangers, they tend to examine each other based initially on physical characteristics. They may wonder, for example, Does the person who is approaching me pose a bodily threat? Or is this person a potential friend or maybe a future dating partner? If I were in trouble, would this stranger help me or take advantage of me?

Why do people judge others based on their outward appearance? Well, quite simply, it is the first thing we see, and we generally do not learn what is "inside" the vast majority of people we see in a given day. How, then, do we ascertain whether a stranger is a threat, a potential friend and ally, or something else? Most people rely on past experiences, trial and error, and stereotypes that accompany certain characteristics of people. For example, a stranger to a "tough" neighborhood may fear that a group of young adolescent males hanging out in front of the convenience store is a threat because the youths look like gang members. But how does the stranger reach the conclusion that the young people are gang members? What if they happen to be members of a local volunteer group meeting to do charity work and are simply cooling off by having a soda or sports drink?

When people make judgments about others based on limited information, they are generally using mental shortcuts rooted in stereotypes—and stereotypes are sometimes dead wrong (i.e., all groups of juveniles hanging out are not delinquents or gang members). However, at times individuals make judgments about strangers based solely on their visible behavior and appearance, and they are correct (e.g., law enforcement officers are trained to identify behavioral characteristics common to drunk drivers).

Among the many physical characteristics by which people judge one another is skin color. Indeed, races have traditionally been classified solely on the basis of their most easily observable anatomical trait: skin color (Marger 2006). Many Americans are described as white or black. But most humans are neither very fair nor very dark but some shade of brown (M. Harris 2004). A simple test can illustrate this point. If a "white" person holds a sheet of white paper next to her skin, and a "black" person holds a sheet of black paper next to hers, they are both likely to find that their skin color is some shade in between white and black. It is worth noting that Crayola, the manufacturer of crayons and other markers, has a line of "multicultural" crayons described as an assortment of realistic skin tones that range from white to black with six other shades in between. These crayons will reveal that most "white" people's skin is closer in color to peach than to white.

Skin color itself—in most animals, not just humans—results from the presence of an amino acid derivative known as melanin. While melanin protects the upper levels of the skin from being damaged by the sun's ultraviolet rays (M. Harris 2004), it also decreases the body's ability to produce Vitamin D in response to sun exposure. In general, the closer to the equator ancestral groups are from, the darker their skin, and the farther from the equator, the lighter the skin. However, there are significant individual differences in skin color; moreover, a genetic variation known as albinism, in which the person has very little melanin, can and does occur in all racial groups.

Typically, a **race** is defined as a group of people who share some socially recognized physical characteristic (such as skin color or shared hereditary traits) that distinguishes them from other groups of people. This definition uses a biological aspect to determine racial categories but acknowledges that such a classification scheme is socially constructed. Increasingly, the social sciences, including sociology, have come to reject biological notions of race in favor of an approach that regards race as a social concept (Omi and Winant 2004).

What Do You Think?

Why is skin color used to determine races of people? Why not use some other physical characteristic, such as eye color, hair color, or height? What do you think?

Race

Although, as we have seen, race is largely a social construct, that is not to say it is not a scientifically valid way of distinguishing people. A number of academic disciplines utilize classification systems for race. In biology, race refers to a population of humans based on certain hereditary characteristics that differentiate them from other human groups (Marger 2006). Physical anthropologists distinguish racial groups either by *phenotype*—visible anatomical features such as skin color, hair texture, and body and facial shape—or by *genotype*—genetic specifications inherited from one's parents (Marger 2006).

The sociological origin of socially constructing the concept of race dates back (at least) to the nineteenth century, when Max Weber discounted biological explanations for racial conflict and pointed instead to the social and political factors that helped to foster it (Omi and Winant 2004; Ernst 1947). During his 1904 visit to the United States, Weber correctly observed that African Americans were not fully assimilated socially and politically, and he predicted a rise in racial tensions between white and black America (Delaney 2004; Weber [1926] 1975). Considering that African Americans had not been fully assimilated in the United States prior to Weber's visit, such a prediction was not an example of foresight out of the clear blue. After all, blacks were subjected to slavery in the South and generally unequal status in the rest of society, even during the post–Civil War decades, which consisted of the formation of the Ku Klux Klan, lynchings, and the Jim Crow era. The discussion of Weber's view of race in the United States is interesting from a sociological perspective because it reveals how sociologists from different nations became aware of race relations as a sociological area of interest. Weber's views on race relations were developed in Germany and reinforced during his only trip to the United States in 1904.

And just a few years after Weber's visit, on the night of July 4, 1910, the tensions between blacks and whites erupted in massive race riots around the country as a reaction to the heavyweight championship fight in which the African American boxer Jack Johnson defeated Jim Jeffries (popularly known as the "Great White Hope") (*New York Tribune,* 7/5/10).

Racial riots continued sporadically throughout the twentieth century. African Americans, however, were not the only racial group to experience discrimination by the white majority in the United States. As we see in the next section of this chapter, discrimination has also been practiced against European immigrants (especially those from non-English-speaking countries), Hispanic and Latino Americans, Asian Americans, and Native Americans.

As the twenty-first century progresses, sociologists have increasingly placed the concept of race in a sociohistorical context (Omi and Winant 2004). Furthermore, a number of sociologists, along with a growing number of citizens, have attempted to downplay classifying people by race altogether. Nonetheless, and despite the limitations of doing so, most social institutions (e.g., the media, politics, and economics) and people themselves acknowledge racial categories based on skin color.

Ethnicity

An **ethnicity** is a category of people recognized as distinct based on social or cultural factors. An ethnic group shares cultural characteristics: nationality, religion, language, geographic residence, values, and so on. Ethnic groups have a shared sense of history and fate that connects members together in a meaningful manner, and many ethnic groups take great pride in their cultural history. Ethnic groups have traditionally been described as subgroups of racial groups (Marger 2006). For example, the French, Irish, English, and Germans are ethnic groups under the Caucasian racial umbrella, while the Chinese, Japanese, and Filipinos are examples of ethnic groups found within the Asian race. The classification in recent U.S. censuses of Hispanics/Latinos as an ethnic rather than a racial group (consisting of such ancestral groups such as Mexicans, Cubans, and Puerto Ricans) has clouded this idea of an ethnic group as a subgroup of a larger racial group. Ethnic groupings further illustrate the socially constructed aspect of race—albeit on a smaller level.

Racism and Other Terms

When an individual is judged solely on the basis of his or her race, that individual may fall victim to racism. The most commonly described form of racism is *interracism,* which occurs between different categories of races. When describing interracism, most people simply use the term "racism." **Racism** involves any attitude, belief, behavior, or social arrangement that has the intent, or the ultimate effect, of favoring one racial category of people over another. Racism involves denying equal access to goods and services to all racial groups in society. A racist perspective denies the idea of equality among all people and promotes an ideology that one racial group is superior to another (Doob 1999). Marger (2006) concurs and states that racism is "the belief that humans are subdivided into distinct hereditary groups that are innately different in their social behavior and mental capacities and that can therefore be ranked as superior or inferior. The presumed superiority of some groups and inferiority of others is subsequently used to legitimate the unequal distribution of the society's resources, specifically, various forms of wealth, prestige, and power" (p. 25).

The sociological perspective dictates that racism, in any form, is the result of learned behavior; that is, no one is born a racist. People become racist because they are exposed to significant others who display racist attitudes, beliefs, and behaviors and thereby pass them on to others. The sociological perspective of racism as learned behavior is further exhibited by the realization that a less described from of racism, known as intraracism, also exists. *Intraracism* (sometimes referred to as colorism) occurs between members of the same race who condemn those with darker or lighter skin tones than their own. For example, very dark-skinned African Americans may be discriminated against by lighter-skinned blacks for being so dark; conversely, darker-skinned blacks may view lighter-skinned blacks as not "black-looking" enough. In its acknowledgment of the existence of intraracism, the National Association for the Advancement of Black People (2011), founded in 2003, proclaims on its home page that "Black/African Americans w/ Negroid features are welcome to join" but that "intraracism ... will not be tolerated, practiced, or allowed."

As shown below in this chapter's section titled "The We-They Character of Race and Ethnicity," racism can be further distinguished via analysis of racism at the institutional versus the individual level. For now, we turn to a discussion of prejudice.

The word "prejudice" literally means a judgment formed without knowledge. Prejudice involves a mind-set whereby an individual or group accepts negative social definitions of others (LeMay 2005). Thus, **prejudice** can be defined as negative beliefs and overgeneralizations concerning a group of people involving a judgment against an individual based on a rigid and fixed mental image applied to all individuals of that group. Ethnic and racial prejudices are characterized by several features, including categorical or generalized thoughts, negative assumptions about an individual based on group membership, and inflexible thinking. The ideas that all Polish people are stupid and all French people are arrogant are examples of prejudicial thinking.

A common type of prejudice is the stereotype. *Stereotypes* are oversimplified and exaggerated beliefs about a group of people. A stereotype presumes that any one person within a group possesses specific characteristics regarded as embodying that group. The beliefs that all black people make good athletes and all Japanese people make good scientists are examples of stereotypes. As Marger (2006) explains, "Once we learn the stereotypes attached to particular groups, we tend to subsequently perceive individual members according to those generalized images" (p. 63).

Bigots often employ stereotypes with their flawed reasoning. A bigot is a person who identifies strongly with his or her own group, religion, race, or political view and is intolerant of those who are different. *Bigotry* refers to a person's use of a set of interrelated attitudes and beliefs to define an entire group of people in an inferior way. Archie Bunker, the main character of the 1970s television show *All in the Family,* expertly portrayed a bigot. (Note: *All in the Family* is still on the air via television syndication and YouTube.)

Another key term related to the analysis of racism is discrimination. **Discrimination** refers to behavior that treats people unequally on the basis of an ascribed status, such as race or gender. Discrimination can be viewed as applied prejudice (LeMay 2005). That is, while prejudice refers to a negative *belief* about someone, discrimination refers to actual *behavior* that involves treating someone unequally. Thus, someone may be guilty of prejudice but not discrimination, whereas someone who discriminates is by definition also prejudicial.

Racial profiling is connected to discrimination. As defined by the American Civil Liberties Union (ACLU) (2005), *racial profiling* refers to "the discriminatory practice by law enforcement officials of targeting individuals for suspicion of crime based on the individual's race, ethnicity, religion or national origin." In this context, law enforcement officials include all those "acting in a policing capacity in public or private settings, such as security guards at department stores, airport security agents, police officers, and, more recently, airline pilots who have ordered passengers to disembark from flights because the passengers' ethnicity aroused the pilots' suspicions" (ACLU 2005). Racial profiling examples include using race to determine which drivers to stop for minor traffic violations (commonly referred to as "driving while black or brown") and the use of race to determine which pedestrians to search for illegal contraband. It is important to note, however, that "racial profiling does not refer to the act of a law enforcement agent pursuing a suspect in which the specific description of the suspect includes race or ethnicity in combination with other identifying factors" (ACLU 2005).

Proving instances of racial profiling by law enforcement is often problematic. Law enforcement agencies defend the inclusion of race as one of several factors in suspect profiling, arguing that criminal profiling based on any characteristic is a time-tested and universal police tool and that excluding race as a variable is illogical. Thus, if a call goes out to patrol cars that a suspected burglary is in progress, police officers will benefit if they are given information about the suspected burglars. Information would include the number of suspects, gender, race, height and weight, age, clothing worn, and so on. The responding officers certainly cannot interrogate all citizens in the area of the burglary in their attempt to protect and serve the community. On the other hand, critics of racial profiling argue that all too often, responding officers are more likely to view minorities as suspects for the crime in question (see "Connecting Sociology and Popular Culture" Box 8.1 for a highly publicized incident that involved an allegation of racial profiling).

Connecting Sociology and Popular Culture

Box 8.1 The Beer Summit: Deconstructing Racial Profiling

An allegation of racial profiling from July 2009 became such a huge part of popular and academic discourse that it gained a pop-culture reference as "The Beer Summit." The summit came about after an incident near Harvard Square in Cambridge, Massachusetts. Based on a Cambridge Police Department incident report (#9005127), an African American man named Henry Louis Gates was placed under arrest at a Ware Street residential location "after being observed exhibiting loud and tumultuous behavior, in a public place, directed at a uniformed police officer who was present investigating a report of a crime in progress. These actions on the behalf of Gates served no legitimate purpose and caused citizens by this location to stop and take notice while appearing surprised and alarmed." Sergeant James Crowley and Officer James Figueroa were responding to a report by Gates's neighbor Lucia Whalen that two men were forcing their way into the home. When the 911 dispatcher asked Whalen whether the two men were black, white, or Hispanic, she replied, "One looked kind of Hispanic, but I'm not really sure" (Goodnough 2009a).

As it turned out, the fifty-eight-year-old Gates—a highly renowned scholar and Harvard professor—was returning home from a trip to China and had simply been trying, with the help of his driver, to enter his own house, whose front door was stuck. Unaware that a neighbor suspected foul play, the two eventually succeeded in pushing their way into Gates's home. When Crowley arrived at the residence, he asked Gates to come outside and speak with him and show his identification. Gates yelled at Crowley, "Why, because I'm a black man in America?" Gates reportedly continued, "Ya, I'll speak with your mama outside!" Gates's agitated state, apparently caused by the belief that he was a victim of racial profiling, led Crowley to arrest, handcuff, and transport him to police headquarters, where he was held for hours (Goodnough 2009b).

A short time later, when asked about the incident, President Barack Obama replied that the police had acted "stupidly." This upset many folks in law enforcement, including Crowley. Crowley, a police academy expert on racial profiling, insisted that he had "acted appropriately." While conducting an interview with WBZTV, Crowley claimed, "Mr. Gates was given plenty of opportunities to stop what he was doing. He didn't. He acted very irrational, he controlled the outcome of that event.... There was a lot of yelling, there was references to my mother, something you wouldn't expect from anybody that should be grateful that you were there investigating a report of a crime in progress, let alone a Harvard professor" (WBZTV .com 2009). Gates accused Crowley of entering his home without permission. He also asked for the sergeant's name and badge number because he was unhappy about his treatment (WBZTV .com 2009).

Although the charges against Gates were subsequently dropped, news programs and outlets of all sorts, including blogs, offered emotionally charged opinions about the incident. In an attempt to defuse the situation, President Obama invited both Gates and Crowley to join him at the White House to sit down, have a beer, and discuss things. On July 30, 2009, Gates, Crowley, and Obama met and shared a beer. (Vice President Joe Biden joined the group but did not have a beer as he does not drink alcohol.) When Obama learned that both Gates and Crowley had already spent time talking to each other, he praised them for doing so. In the end, Gates and Crowley "agreed to disagree" about the confrontation that had led to Gates's arrest. Obama reported that the Beer Summit conversation centered on moving forward and not reliving the events of the previous two weeks.

What Do You Think?

Was Gates's arrest the result of racial profiling? Did Crowley act appropriately or inappropriately? How might events have been different if Gates had been white? Should race be taken out of the criminal profiling formula used by law enforcement? A 911 dispatcher's asking for a description that entailed race might be considered profiling on the part of the public, but it may also reveal that this is standard police procedure What do you think?

U.S. President Barack Obama and Vice President Joseph Biden meet with Sgt. James Crowley and Professor Henry Louis Gates to discuss racial profiling while drinking a beer in the Rose Garden outside of the Oval Office.

As "Connecting Sociology and Popular Culture" Box 8.1 concludes, Gates, Crowley, and Obama felt it best to move on and "agree to disagree" about past events. In essence, the Gates-Crowley incident may have been defused, but the greater issue of racial profiling remained unresolved. This prompts us to ask, What can be done to lessen the animosity that exists between many members of diverse racial and ethnic groups? After all, it would appear that many people in society are intent on focusing on the differences rather than the similarities among people. This is problematic, to say the least. Perhaps if people focused on similarities, we would all come to see each other as members of the same race: the human race.

After all, we are all much more closely related than we might think. For example, genealogists have documented links between otherwise dissimilar individuals. President Barack Obama is a distant cousin of former vice president Dick Cheney, British prime minister Winston Churchill, and Civil War general Robert E. Lee. Obama is also a distant cousin of actor Brad Pitt. Pitt's girlfriend, Angelina Jolie, is a distant cousin of Hillary Clinton (Lavoie 2008). As for First Lady Michelle Obama, genealogical research published in 2009 indicates that she had at least one great-great-great-grandfather who was white and another ancestor believed to be Native American (Swarns and Kantor 2009). Indeed, genetic studies indicate that many people who look like they may belong to one particular race might actually have a significant proportion of genes of another race. Furthermore, DNA evidence reveals a genetic link between Jews and Palestinians, two groups who have been locked in a bitter struggle for more than a century yet share a common ancestry dating back 4,000 years (Kraft 2000).

You may be asking yourself, Why do diverse people not concentrate more on their social and genetic similarities than on their cultural differences? Part of the answer lies with our discussion in Chapter 4 of the power of culture. It is also partly explained by the "we-they" mentality that most people possess. (Note: The "we-they" distinction is discussed later in this chapter.)

RACIAL AND ETHNIC STRATIFICATION IN THE UNITED STATES

Chapter 7 explored stratification primarily from a social class perspective. Stratification also exists among racial and ethnic groups. Nearly all multiethnic societies

Angelina Jolie and Hilary Clinton are distant cousins.

have a hierarchical arrangement of ethnic groups wherein one establishes itself as the dominant group with the power to shape the course of ethnic relations. Other, subordinate ethnic groups possess less power and take a correspondingly subordinate position in the hierarchy, with the least powerful groups finding themselves at the bottom of this ranking system (Marger 2006). In this fashion, a system of ethnic stratification takes hold in society. **Ethnic stratification**, then, is a system of ranking ethnic groups with the dominant group on top and the less powerful groups taking positions lower in the hierarchy. Using this system of ethnic stratification, sociologists are able to distinguish majority-minority and dominant-subordinate social systems.

In order to best understand the ethnic-stratification system in the United States, it is necessary to identify the major racial and ethnic groups that populate the nation. Typically, the following categories of people are recognized in the United States: white non-Hispanic, Hispanic, African American, Asian, American Indian, and "other" (e.g., Hawaiian or other Pacific Islander). The U.S. government modified these categories slightly on its Census 2010 form. Question 8 of the census asked respondents, "Is Person 1 of Hispanic, Latino, or Spanish origin?" Respondents indicating yes to this question were given four suboptions: Mexican,

Mexican American, Chicano; Puerto Rican; Cuban; and "Other," with directions to specify, for example Argentinean, Colombian, Dominican, Nicaraguan, Salvadoran, and so on. Census respondents were asked in Question 9, "What is Person 1's race?" Respondents could check one or more boxes. The first option was "white" with no elaboration; that is, no suboptions were made available for ancestry. The other options for Question 9 were black, African American, or Negro; American Indian or Alaska Native (identify tribe); Asian Indian; Chinese; Filipino; Japanese; Korean; Vietnamese; Other Asian (with multiple options); Native American; Guamanian or Chamorro; Samoan; and Other Pacific Islander (with multiple options provided).

Five hundred years ago, the geographical area that is now the United States was populated almost entirely by indigenous peoples. As more and more people emigrated from Europe, the population shifted toward a white majority, displacing the Native Americans. The Europeans also brought with them slaves from Africa, making blacks the largest minority group. Because of slavery, African Americans had consistently represented the largest minority group, until the early 2000s, when Hispanics became the largest minority group.

As the majority and dominant group throughout U.S. history, white non-Hispanics have represented the power group among Americans. Demographic data from the 2005 census reveals that whites represent 68 percent of the population; Hispanics (a term used for people with ethnic backgrounds in Spanish-speaking countries), 14.5 percent; African Americans, 12.8 percent; Asians and others, 4 percent; and Native Americans, 1 percent. The demographics of the United States are changing quickly, and according to projections, by 2050 minorities will make up 49 percent of the total U.S. population (compared to 25 percent in 1990). Hispanics are the fastest-growing minority group in the United States, and by 2050 there will be more Hispanics than all other minorities combined (Ginsberg 2003). The two primary causes of the rapid Hispanic population growth are massive immigration and a high birthrate. The Asian population is also growing quite quickly, and the U.S. census estimates Asians will represent 8 percent of the total U.S. population by 2050 (Ohlemacher 2006b).

The following pages give a brief synopsis of each major racial and ethnic category in the United States. Clearly, such a review is succinct by design, as it would be impossible to provide full coverage of the diversity of each of these categories of people. However, the coverage provides a glimpse of the sociological perspective of each category. (Note: Most sociology departments offer a wide range of courses on race and ethnicity. Students interested in learning more about the topic are encouraged to take such courses.)

White Non-Hispanic Americans

Based on 2005 census data, white non-Hispanic Americans (sometimes referred to as European Americans) represent the largest racial group in the United States. At 68 percent, whites make up more than two-thirds of the total population. During the seventeenth century, English immigrants colonized Massachusetts and Virginia. Along with the English, other immigrants from Western Europe, especially from Wales, Scotland, and Germany, settled in North America. Since the earliest days of the United States, white Anglo-Saxon Protestants, or WASPs, have dominated the socioeconomic and political landscape. They established their political power in 1790 with the passage of the Naturalization Act, legislation declaring that only white immigrants could apply for citizenship.

Between 1820 and 1992, nearly 60 million immigrants entered the United States legally. Most of them were white Europeans; however, despite being racially similar to the dominant race in the United States, they came from a variety of countries, spoke many different languages, belonged to many different religious, political, and ethnic categories, and were often victims of intraracism. As immigrants, they generally lacked the skills necessary to compete in the job market, struggled with learning English, and experienced prejudice and discrimination. Some changed their names and denied their ethnic heritages to gain social and economic mobility in their pursuit of the "American dream." These non-Anglo-Saxon immigrants resided in concentrated urban areas that became known as *ethnic ghettos*. Multiple-dwelling units became a source of profit for slum owners. Sanitation conditions were poor, and high-density living fueled crime. These early immigrants looked forward to moving out of the ghettos as quickly as possible; as a result, they embraced assimilation. As one ethnic immigrant group, such as Irish Catholics, moved out of the ghetto, other, new immigrant groups, such as Eastern European Jews, moved in and replaced them. Each time this happened, the immigrant neighborhoods in the ghettos fell into further decay.

Although all white people, as a racial group, certainly do not enjoy a high socioeconomic status, they fare much better financially today than most other groups in the United States. White Americans are very diverse and consist of a number of ethnic, or ancestral, groups (see Table 8.1 for a listing of the largest European ancestries in the United States in 2000).

Hispanic (Latino) Americans

There is debate among scholars—and, more importantly, among Hispanic or Latino people themselves—as to which term is more acceptable: "Hispanic" or

TABLE 8.1 Largest Reported European Ancestries in the United States in 2000

ANCESTRY	NUMBER (MILLIONS)	PERCENTAGE OF TOTAL U.S. POPULATION
German	42.8	15.2
Irish	30.5	10.8
English	24.5	8.7
Italian	15.6	5.6
Polish	9.0	3.2
French	8.3	3.0
Scottish	4.9	1.7
Dutch	4.5	1.6
Norwegian	4.5	1.6
Scotch-Irish	4.3	1.5
Swedish	4.0	1.4

Source: U.S. Census Bureau 2000.

"Latino." In some regions of the United States, especially Southern California, the term "Chicano" is preferred. Chicanos identify with their indigenous ancestors (Mayans or Aztecs) and are slightly militant in their insistence on usage of the term "Chicano." Those who prefer the term "Hispanic" generally do so because they trace their roots to Spanish and indigenous ancestors who resided in Mexico and the Southwest (before it became a part of the United States). People who prefer the term "Latino" generally identify with ancestors from Puerto Rico, Ecuador, the Dominican Republic, and other areas of Central America. (Note: This text uses both "Hispanic" and "Latino," and no disrespect is intended to those who prefer one term over the other.)

Until fairly recently, Hispanics were categorized as a racial group with many subcategories of ethnic groups. Today, because of their great diversity, Latinos are viewed as an ethnic group made up of distinct people of different geographic ancestry. As stated earlier in the text, Hispanics collectively constitute 14.5 percent of the total U.S. population and are the largest minority group. Marger (2006) puts the total number of Latinos in the United States in perspective by stating, "There are more people of Mexican origin in Los Angeles than in all but one city in Mexico; in New York City, there are more Puerto Ricans than in San Juan; and only in Havana are there more Cubans than in Miami" (p. 303). The three largest categories of Hispanics are Mexican Americans, Puerto Ricans, and Cuban Americans.

Hispanic people are very diverse; as a result, it is difficult to describe a stereotypical Hispanic. Still, most Hispanic ethnic groups have been influenced significantly by Spain and the Spanish language and culture. This heritage continues today. Most Mexican Americans are *mestizos* (meaning "mixed blood" and referring to their blended Spanish and indigenous ancestry), whereas many other Latinos (e.g., Cubans, Puerto Ricans, and Brazilians) have African heritage as well. "If a common theme runs through the unique histories and experiences of the several Hispanic groups in the United States, it is their intermediate ethnic status between Euro-American groups, on one hand, and African Americans, on the other. In several important respects, Hispanics are an ethnic minority 'in between'" (Marger 2006, p. 304). As an "in-between" group, Hispanics have not suffered from prejudice and discrimination to the same degree as African Americans; yet, nor have they historically enjoyed full participation in the American power structure.

African Americans

Based on our current knowledge of the origins of humanity, all our ancestors can be traced back to Africa. The migration patterns of our earliest ancestors led to the spread of the human race across the globe. Despite Africa's legacy as the "cradle of humanity," Africans have often faced prejudice and discrimination. No truer example of this reality can be found elsewhere than in the United States. The African American experience in the United States has been (and remains, for many) drastically different from that preached by American idealism.

Africans have had a unique experience in the Americas. They came with the earliest Europeans, usually as indentured servants; however, by the late 1600s, more and more Africans were transported to the colonies as slaves. The history of slavery in world civilization has often been told, but a quick recap is in order. Ancient cultures such as the Babylonians, Egyptians, and Romans held slaves, and the practice continued in Europe and Asia throughout the Middle Ages. Anyone, regardless of race or ethnicity, could be enslaved as a result of military conquest, piracy, or an inability to pay his or her debts. As Islamic culture flourished in the ninth and tenth centuries, Arabs began to invade the sub-Saharan regions of the continent and enslave black Africans. Portugal and eventually other European nations became involved in the African slave trade in the 1400s. When the Europeans started settling in the Americas and developed large plantations (e.g., tobacco, sugar, indigo, and cotton), they increasingly brought African slaves with them. The slave trade became highly lucrative for Europeans.

For more than two hundred years, Africans suffered as slaves. In an attempt to justify their behavior, slave owners developed a racist ideology that included viewing Africans as less than human. Even after slavery was abolished in 1865 (by virtue of the Thirteenth Amendment) and Africans were granted citizenship by the Civil Rights Act of 1866, they still suffered from extreme prejudice and discrimination. The Reconstruction period that immediately followed the end of the Civil War ushered in the Jim Crow era—typified by efforts to deny African Americans equal access to goods and services, the right to vote, and so forth. Segregation also characterized this period. The Supreme Court's 1896 *Plessy v. Ferguson* decision established a "separate-but-equal" philosophy designed to continue the unfair treatment of blacks. After World War II, the effects of Jim Crow were diminishing but had not disappeared. During the 1950s and 1960s, blacks stood up for their rights and challenged the dominant power structure of the United States. In 1954, for example, the ruling in *Brown v. Board of Education of Topeka* invalidated the *Plessy v. Ferguson* decision.

Because so many Africans were brought to the United States as slaves, they have historically been the largest minority group. However, as previously stated, Hispanics now occupy that status. Still, African Americans make up 12.8 percent of the total U.S. population. The largest percentage of blacks can trace their ancestral roots to the African slave trade, but a number of ethnically diverse U.S. blacks trace their heritage to the West Indies and such Caribbean nations as Haiti, Jamaica, Trinidad, and the Dominican Republic. Although a number of African Americans have gained great success in the United States, many still suffer from prejudice, discrimination, low education levels, and high rates of incarceration.

What Do You Think?

African Americans have long been the largest minority in the United States. Now that Hispanics outnumber them, what will the socioeconomic effect, if any, be on blacks as the second-largest minority group? What do you think?

Asian Americans

As with every other category of Americans, Asian Americans are also quite diverse. Generally looked upon as members of a single racial category, Asian Americans consist of many ethnic groups (e.g., Chinese, Japanese, Korean, Vietnamese, and Filipino American). Asian Americans share a number of characteristics with other immigrant groups; specifically, they were victims of prejudice and discrimination upon their earliest arrival in the United States.

The Asian experience in the United States can be divided into two distinct eras of immigration: the first wave and the second (and current) wave. The first wave occurred roughly from the middle of the nineteenth to the early twentieth century. The Chinese were the first to arrive, followed by the Japanese, and then smaller numbers of Koreans and Filipinos. These early Asian immigrants were employed mostly as unskilled laborers for construction and agricultural work (Marger 2006). Asian immigration was quite limited during this first wave because of strict U.S. laws limiting it. For example, the Page Act of 1875 (Sect. 141, 18 Stat. 477) was designed to limit the immigration of Chinese men who would serve as a cheap source of labor and "immoral" Chinese women (who would engage in prostitution) (Peffer 1986; Museum of Learning 2010). From 1882 to 1943, the U.S. government severely curtailed immigration from China to the United States via Chinese Exclusion Laws. In 1882 an act (22 Stat. 58) suspended immigration of Chinese laborers for ten years and prohibited the naturalization of Chinese already in the United States (U.S. National Archives and Records Administration 2010). In 1892, passage of the Act to Prohibit the Coming of Chinese Persons into the United States (27 Stat. 25), referred to as the Geary Act, also severely restricted Chinese immigration (U.S. National Archives and Records Administration 2010). When China and the United States became allies in World War II, President Franklin D. Roosevelt signed the Act to Repeal the Chinese Exclusion Acts, to Establish Quotas, and for Other Purposes (57 Stat. 600-1). Nonetheless, until the Immigration Act of October 1965 (79 Stat. 911), numerous laws continued to restrict Chinese immigration (U.S. National Archives and Records Administration 2010).

The second (and current) wave of Asian immigration began with the shift in U.S. immigration policy brought about by the Immigration and Nationality Act of 1965. The new Asian immigrants are far more diverse. Some are highly educated and trained for skilled jobs, while others come from such war-torn areas as Vietnam, Laos, and Cambodia. This second wave of Asian immigration has contributed to this group's comprising 4 percent of the total U.S. population. In many areas, Asian Americans equal or exceed white Americans in income, educational attainment, life expectancy, and so on. Conversely, poorer Asian Americans suffer the same plight as other people of lower socioeconomic status: they are victims of prejudice and discrimination.

Native Americans

When the European explorers first arrived in 1492, the Western Hemisphere was populated by many diverse cultures and tribes of indigenous people who became known collectively as "Indians" to Europeans. Christopher Columbus thought that he had arrived in India, when he actually landed in San Salvador, and he mistakenly labeled the native people he encountered "Indians." The misnaming of the indigenous people of the Americas by the Europeans foreshadowed the misunderstandings, distrust, and hostility that later developed between the two races of people.

The great diversity of native peoples is illustrated by the estimated 260 different nations (or tribes) that inhabited the Americas (Winik 1999). They were differentiated by, among other things, great differences in geography and climate in the United States. The Indian way of life in the forested Northeast was not the same as that in the muggy, near-tropical jungles of Florida and Louisiana or on the grassy plains of the Dakotas or in the arid Southwest. Thus, any collective generalization about Native Americans is difficult, to say the least.

However, at least one major characteristic is shared by all native people: the harsh treatment they were subjected to by the Europeans and, later, white Americans. The indigenous peoples of the North and South American continents were decimated by European explorers and settlers between the sixteenth and eighteenth centuries, then by North American westward expansion in the nineteenth century. The Europeans did not simply exterminate millions of people; they conducted a sustained population reduction over hundreds of years through mass eradication campaigns, starvation, and the introduction of diseases (Marsico 2010). Such policies are an example of **genocide**, the intentional attempt to exterminate a race of people by a more dominant population.

After facing near extinction, Native Americans, once described as the "vanishing Americans," have made modest gains in their population (see "Connecting Sociology and Popular Culture" Box 8.2 for a discussion of the use of Indian imagery in sports). Today, they represent over 1 percent of the total U.S. population. Unfortunately, Native Americans as a group suffer from many social problems, including the highest rate of poverty and the shortest life expectancy of any category of Americans. The extreme poverty Native Americans suffer from has led to many other problems, including high rates of alcoholism, poor health, and high rates of depression and suicide (Winik 1999). A 2009 Centers for Disease Control and Prevention report revealed that 11.7 percent of Native American deaths between 2001 and 2005 were due to alcohol; the national rate is 3.3 percent (*Post-Standard*, 8/22/09). In brief, despite the positive increase in population growth, Native Americans suffer disproportionately (when compared to all other racial and ethnic groups) when it comes to any number of social problems.

The feud between Native Americans and the U.S. government is not limited to the past. On occasion, the U.S. government has had direct conflicts with Native American organizations or tribes. For example, in 1973 followers of the American Indian Movement (AIM) staged a seventy-one-day occupation of Wounded Knee, South Dakota. In response, the U.S. Marshals Service was called in to assist in a resolution. The AIM surrendered on May 8, 1973. Two Indians were killed, and one marshal was seriously wounded (U.S. Marshals Service 2010). Among the biggest contemporary concerns of native peoples is the Indian Trust Fund lawsuit. Congress first established the Indian Trust in 1887 to hold proceeds from government-arranged leases of Indian lands (Belczyk 2010). The Indian Trust consists of about 56 million acres of land; 10 million of those belong to individual Indians, and the other 46 million acres are held in trust for various tribes (Streshinsky 2009). In 2009, the U.S. government announced that a settlement agreement worth more than $3.4 billion had been reached in a thirteen-year class-action lawsuit claiming mismanagement of trust funds against the U.S. Department of the Interior. For those who brought the suit, the settlement agreement was about more than money; it was about anger and frustration stemming from years of poverty and victimization, decades of unfunded mandates, and a piecemeal web of legacy laws (Streshinsky 2009).

This sign "No Sovereign Nation, No Reservation" depicts the ill will shown by many non-Native Americans toward Native people.

It is somewhat amazing that so many people have forgotten, or choose not to accept, that Native Americans (Indians) were settled in the Americas long before European settlers arrived. Perhaps one of the most ignorant things a racist can say to an Indian is, "Why don't you go back to your own country" (see "A Closer Look" Box 8.3 for a story of a Native American professor who was told by a student to do that).

Is the Term "Minority" Outdated?

The demographic changes in the United States increasingly mean that whites are no longer the majority (defined as comprising at least 51 percent of the population): as of 2006, this was the case in four states (California, Hawaii, New Mexico, and Texas). In other states (Maryland, Georgia, and Nevada), the share of white people fell below 60 percent in 2006. Most likely, by 2060 there will be no clear majority racial or ethnic group in the United States. Thus, from a statistical standpoint, it becomes increasingly pointless to speak in terms of a majority-minority relationship. However, as sociologists point out, the term "minority" extends beyond a numbers game; it also refers to a differential in power. In this manner, a **minority group** is a group of disadvantaged citizens—specifically, the underprivileged at the lower end of the stratification hierarchy.

Connecting Sociology and Popular Culture

Box 8.2 The Use of Indian Imagery in Sports

This chapter's introductory story briefly introduced the idea that many Native Americans consider the use of Indian imagery in sports offensive. Sports teams routinely use nicknames, logos, and mascots as a means of conveying an identity. There is a great deal of symbolism involved with sports nicknames, logos, and mascots. "A group's symbols serve two fundamental purposes—they bind together the individual members of a group, and they separate one group from another.... Using symbols to achieve solidarity and community is a common group practice" (Eitzen 1999, p. 29). Many sports teams use Native American imagery for their nicknames, logos, and mascots and insist that they are doing this to bring honor to Native Americans.

However, various Native American groups and academic scholars argue that the practice of using Indian imagery amounts to a form of racism. In their view, the use of Indian mascots places Native Americans on a parallel level with animals, relies on racist logos and practices, and constitutes an obscenity, considering the history of genocide perpetrated against native peoples by Europeans and Americans (Meyer 2002; Davis-Delano 2009). Is it any wonder that descendants of a people who were nearly obliterated by Europeans and Americans find it very difficult to accept "Indians" as sports mascots?

Many Native Americans and sociologists consider the "Redskin" nickname as the most racist of all U.S. sport franchises. Shown here are fans of the Washington Redskins dressed in Native American costume.

Sports teams that use Indian imagery often also engage in behavior known as "playing Indian." Playing Indian involves building a type of team spirit by displaying stereotypical Native American behaviors for entertainment purposes (King and Springwood 2001). For example, students at Simpson College in Indianola, Iowa, shout "a victory cheer known as the 'Scalp Song' and use idioms of Indianness in their annual rituals such as homecoming" (King and Springwood 2001, p. 3). Playing Indian may include wearing face paint, which had spiritual meaning for native peoples. Another example is the "tomahawk chop" and the chant that goes with it, practiced by Florida State University and Atlanta Braves fans. This practice is a sort of team

A growing number of people is perceiving the application of the word "minority" to specific racial and ethnic groups as offensive; as a result its usage has fallen out of vogue. However, it would seem that until all groups share equally in socioeconomic and political power, some will be designated as holding minority status. This is due in part, as sociologists point out, to the fact that minority status can be applied to groups based on characteristics beyond race and ethnicity, such as gender, age, and physical disability.

cheer, used especially when the team is doing particularly well, to express the idea that the "Indians" are about to attack, crying out with their well-known war whoops as they chop up their opponents with small axes. Most Native Americans find this conduct demeaning to them.

Of the many professional sports teams that utilize Indian imagery, perhaps none is as offensive as the National Football League's Washington Redskins. The Redskins organization argues that the word "redskin" is neutral and that its use of the name "Redskins" honors American Indians. Many Native Americans strongly disagree that the concept of redskin is an honor and have challenged the use of that term in various courts of law. For example, in 1992, seven Native Americans filed an action before the U.S. Patent and Trademark Office to cancel six Redskins trademarks because they were "scandalous" and "disparaging" to Native American peoples (MacDowall 2010). More recently, in 2009, Native Americans again unsuccessfully challenged the use of the word "Redskins" by the Washington, D.C., franchise in *Harjo v. Pro Football Inc.* (565 F.3d 880; D.C. Cir. 2009) (MacDowall 2010). It should be pointed out that nearly all dictionaries characterize "redskin" (the *R* word) in the same way as they do "nigger" (the *N* word)—that is, as an offensive term or offensive slang. Native American advocates point out that people should be as uncomfortable saying the *R* word as they are saying the *N* word. Furthermore, they find it more than ironic that the Redskins franchise is located in the U.S. national capital city, considering that Washington, D.C., has long been the symbol of broken promises to and treaties with Native Americans.

The issue of sports teams using Indian imagery in nicknames, logos, and mascots will not disappear until offensive usages of such imagery no longer exist in sports. Some believe Native Americans are being honored by teams who use Indian imagery (Davis-Delano 2009). In the U.S. military there is an expression: "No honor is given if no honor is received." In other words, one cannot claim to have honored another if the other does not view the act as such. Other people try to ignore the Native American nickname, logo, and mascot issue by saying, "It's just political correctness." That is not true. Native Americans are people. They are not mascots. Eliminating offensive Indian imagery is a matter of correctness.

What Do You Think?

Many Native Americans, academics, and others believe that sports teams should eliminate the usage of Indian imagery. Imagine the social reaction, they say, if the Washington team changed its nickname to "N***ers" and claimed that it did so to honor African Americans! That is what they say people should imagine every time they see the Redskins' logo. Do you find the use of Indian imagery offensive? What do you think?

THE WE-THEY CHARACTER OF RACE AND ETHNICITY

As discussed in Chapter 4, cultures around the world are quite unique and cherish their own sets of norms, values, and beliefs. There also exists a tendency among like-minded people to view their way of life as "right" or proper. This line of thinking is known as ethnocentrism. Recall that **ethnocentrism** refers to the tendency of people from one cultural group to judge other cultures by the

A Closer Look

Box 8.3 "Go Back to Your Own Country"

What does it mean to tell a Native American, "Go back to your own country"? Is this a sign of hate or perhaps of ignorance? Or it is a Halloween prank gone terribly wrong? A colleague of mine at the State University of New York, Oswego, Kevin White, a Native American (Akwesasne Mohawk), had to wrestle with these questions and more while teaching, ironically, his "Native Americans 100" class shortly before noon on October 31, 2003. During class a student wearing a headdress ran into Professor White's classroom, fired a suction cup arrow from a bow, and shouted, "Go back to your own country" (Mohr 2003a, p. B1). The student claimed he was simply involved with a Halloween prank. A number of students in White's class were outraged and considered the incident a hate crime. One student was quoted as saying, "I'm part Native American and this was the biggest form of racism I've ever seen" (Mohr 2003a, p. B1). The student who dressed and acted like a stereotypical "Indian" was charged not with a hate crime but with disorderly conduct. Still, the incident stirred the passions of many Native American academics across the nation and among White's friends and colleagues. The student offender maintained that the incident was simply a prank. The university did not charge the student with a hate crime because of the language of its policy on hate crimes. That language has since been changed so that such an incident today could be classified as a hate crime (White 2010).

As Professor White (2010) explained, the student appeared before a local judge in city court (Oswego, New York) on disorderly conduct charges and was ordered to apologize to the entire class. The student left school on his own accord, saying that he was suffering after having been identified as the culprit publicly and that the humiliation was more than he could endure. Professor White wonders whether the student thought about his being humiliated before or after the incident. As for his reaction to being told, "Go back to your own country," Professor White's reaction was, "I am already here!"

What Do You Think?

Why is "Why don't you go back to your own country" an odd question to ask of a Native American? What do you think?

standards of their own. An ethnocentric viewpoint generates a "we" feeling that is shared by members of a group. Ethnocentrism promotes group solidarity and group pride (a positive aspect), but it also generally involves viewing other groups as inferior (a negative aspect).

When one group deems itself superior, it usually displays acts of intolerance toward others. Stereotypes, racism, and prejudice are by-products of intolerance. This section examines the social effects of "we-they" thinking in group interactions and group identity. It also describes how racism can exist on both the individual and the institutional level. Finally, it scrutinizes the "color-blind," or race-neutral, perspective and explores why race continues to matter in a society that claims to hold equality as an ideal.

"We" Groups

As we learned in Chapter 5, social interaction plays a significant role in an individual's life, and it is important for us to feel as though we belong, or fit into a group. Individuals like to experience a sense of unity with their fellows. Group participation provides a sense of "we-ness," where saying "we" is natural. For example, members of a specific racial or ethnic group might say, "We have long been victims of prejudice and discrimination." The creation of the "we" category involves a sense of community. Ethnic communities are deeply rooted in common sentiments, common experience, and a common history. Sharing a common history not only gives an ethnic group a common ancestry and descent but also becomes a significant basis for organizing the present. Often, the historical past is selectively interpreted from the perspective, and from the needs, of the present. Ethnic groups often share special-purpose associations to further their political and/or economic needs (e.g., the American Jewish Committee, National Association for the Advancement of Colored People, the Anti-Defamation League, and the Urban League).

However, racial and ethnic groups are not completely autonomous and self-contained. "Instead, they are a part of a larger societal system that influences, shapes, and partially determines their life circumstances. Internally, groups often attempt to maintain their distinctive 'we-ness'" (Shibutani and Kwan 1965, p. 47). Once an in-group establishes itself as a "we" group, its members come to seen by external groups for their "they-ness" (Rose 1981). Thus, the creation of a "we" parameter implies that a "they" label has also been established to refer to out-groups. As Ringer and Lawless (1989) explain, "When an ethnic group defines itself as a distinctive group it must face the fact that the larger society also perceives it as a distinctive entity" (p. 19).

"They" Groups

Interestingly, although it is made up of other "we" groups, "they" is generally viewed or recognized as representing the larger society itself. Even more ironically, the outside society, or "they," comes to view the initial "we" group as a "they." Thus, the determination of "we" and "they" groups is a matter of perspective. "However, despite this apparent agreement on the designation of distinctiveness, major differences exist between the ethnic group and larger society over the specifics of this definition. For example, on the cognitive level, larger society's definition of the ethnic group is primarily a function of its own beliefs about the group, which may not basically correspond with the group's own beliefs about itself nor even with the 'real nature of the group'" (Ringer and Lawless 1989,

p. 19). The larger society comes to view specific ethnic groups in an oversimplified manner and may fail to grasp the social realities of such groups. Historically, misunderstandings between "we" and "they" groups result in discriminatory treatment by dominant groups over smaller, less powerful ones.

The "we-they" dichotomy was influenced by the work of famous French linguistic anthropologist Claude Levi-Strauss (1962) and his concept of binary opposition. Some of his binary opposites are fairly straightforward, such as raw versus cooked, while others are used as a means of creating a social hierarchy. Consider, for example, the Western cultural meanings of "white" and "black," wherein white is associated with purity and goodness, and black is considered a sign of darkness and evil. Such interpretations of white and black carried over to the realm of race, where Europeans, who are white, viewed Africans as inferior because of their skin color and the meanings associated with being black.

In should be noted that the "we-they" social relationship extends beyond racial and ethnic distinctions. Street gangs identify one another on the basis of affiliation. Athletes and sports fans have long drawn distinctions between "us" and "them." Budgetary concerns between different departments within the same organization often create adversarial rivalries expressed in such ways as, "If that other department (them) receives its requested funds, there will not be enough money left for us to make our budgetary requests." Charities also compete with one another when requesting funds from the government and public donations.

What Do You Think?

Think of the groups you belong to ("we" groups) and determine the corresponding "they" groups. Is there any way to avoid the "we-they" group parameter in life? What do you think?

Individual and Institutional Racism

Earlier in this chapter, the term "racism" was introduced. It is now important to point out that racism occurs at two levels: the micro level (individual or interpersonal racism) and the macro level (institutional or ideological racism). **Individual racism** refers to unequal treatment and behavior on the part of a member or group of one race against a person or group of another race. For example, a store manager may refuse to hire a qualified person just because of his or her race or ethnicity. Although individual racism is fairly common, most researchers indicate that the total number of incidents of prejudice and discrimination is declining (Tepperman and Blain 2006). However, as Doob (1999) indicates, "While individual racism is surely less common than in the past, the impact of particular incidents can be shocking" (p. 7). An informed person who watches the news can find daily examples of shocking acts of individual racism.

Institutional racism involves widespread, large-scale, structured discrimination on the basis of race or ethnicity. "Institutional racism involves impersonal forces that are likely to disproportionately impact on minority group members, restricting opportunities for success in mainstream society by providing inferior facilities and limiting access" (Doob 1999, p. 8).

> **What Do You Think?**
>
> Based on your observations and experiences, do you think acts of individual racism are commonplace or isolated incidents? Have you noticed any of your friends or family members acting in a racist manner? What do you think?

Many social institutions are arranged in such a manner as to disadvantage those without socioeconomic or political power. As Sage (1993) explains, "Racism is a salient aspect of the structure of American society. The most important aspect of this form of stratification is that it excludes people of color from equal access to socially valued rewards and resources. These people tend to have less wealth, power, and social prestige than do other Americans. Moreover, racism has built-in policies and practices that systematically discriminate against people in employment, housing, policies, education, health care, and many other areas. These conditions result in fewer human resources and diminished life chances for African-Americans" (p. 6).

One example of institutional racism is *redlining,* which involves marking out specific areas where some people (usually based on race or ethnicity) are refused goods or services. Mild forms of redlining may include denying taxicab service or delivery of takeout foods to certain neighborhoods. More extreme forms of redlining occur in real estate and the banking and mortgage industries (e.g., Federal Housing Administration policies from the 1930s to the 1960s). In these cases, minority members will not be shown homes in certain neighborhoods, and qualified minority members will have their loan requests denied. Although redlining in real estate and mortgage lending has been illegal since 1968, when the Fair Housing Act became law, critics charge that it still takes place today.

Institutional racist policies also extend to other social institutions. For example, in 2004, the restaurant chain Cracker Barrel was ordered to pay $8.7 million to settle allegations that it mistreated black customers and discriminated against black employees. More than forty plaintiffs in sixteen states claimed that blacks were denied service, assigned to segregated seating, subjected to racial slurs, and even served food taken from the garbage (*Post-Standard,* 9/10/04). Based on numerous news reports in 2006, Rose Rock, mother of African American comedian Chris Rock, claimed that she had been a victim of discrimination at a South Carolina Cracker Barrel restaurant (Tapper 2006). She reported being seated but then ignored for thirty minutes. (Note: At this writing, Cracker Barrel authorities were still investigating the accusation.)

In 1998, Nationwide Insurance was ordered to pay a record $100 million in a federal suit over racial redlining. Civil rights advocates hailed the judgment as a civil rights landmark, arguing that the decision underscored redlining practices in sectors beyond the banking and mortgage industries—which have long been held up as exemplars of institutions that employ discriminatory redlining practices (Fulwood 1998).

Why Race Matters

Some are uncomfortable with categorizing people by race and ethnicity. As we shall see, however, race does matter—and for a wide variety of reasons. It matters because society is not color-blind. Most people see others based on their skin color. If this were not true, racism in all its forms would not exist. But as we know, racism, prejudice, discrimination, and intolerance exist in the United States and throughout most parts of the world.

If race did not matter, society would be color-blind, and the playing field would be level for all people regardless of their race. "The color-blind or race neutral perspective holds that in an environment where institutional racism and discrimination have been replaced by equal opportunity, one's qualifications, not one's color or ethnicity, should be the mechanism by which upward mobility is achieved. Color as a cultural style may be expressed and consumed through music, dress, or vernacular but race as a system which confers privileges and shapes life chances is viewed as an atavistic and inaccurate accounting of U.S. race relations" (Gallagher 2009, p. 91). A majority of white Americans believe discrimination no longer exists against racial minorities; however, a majority of black Americans see a field that remains quite uneven (Gallagher 2009).

Believing that today's society is color-blind allows one to think of institutional racism as a thing of the past, but again, this is not reality. Higginbotham and Andersen (2009) would have us consider two more points: schools in the United States are now more segregated than thirty years ago, and some successful plans for desegregation are being dismantled (Frankenberg, Lee, and Orfield 2003). There is a 61 percent gap between black and white household incomes (DeNavas-Walt, Proctor, and Lee 2006). Based on interviews of nearly 77,000 Americans age sixteen or older, a 2005 Justice Department study found that black, Hispanic, and white motorists are equally likely to be pulled over by police, but blacks and Hispanics are much more likely to be searched, handcuffed, arrested, and subjected to force or the threat of it (Sniffen 2005).

Race complicates the legal system with regard to crime on Native American reservations. The system relies largely on race to determine jurisdiction and then charges law enforcement and prosecutors with the sometimes delicate task of determining a person's race (*Missoulian,* 9/6/10). In most states, federal and tribal authorities can arrest and prosecute Indians on Indian lands, but criminal offenses by non-Indians are handled by federal or state authorities (*Missoulian,* 9/6/10). According to B. J. Jones, director of the Tribal Judicial Institute at the University of North Dakota School of Law, there is no clear-cut definition of who is an Indian (*Missoulian,* 9/6/10). The Shane Maggi case illustrates many of these points. Maggi was accused of terrorizing a Native American couple at their home on the Blackfeet Indian Reservation in Montana for more than two hours on the night of May 16, 2007. Maggi was tried as a Native American for committing crimes against a Native American couple on a reservation and was sentenced to more than forty-two years in prison. However, the U.S. Court of Appeals for the Ninth Circuit overturned Maggi's March 2010 conviction because he did not meet the definition of Native American: he was not enrolled in the tribe. As a result, tribal police were not allowed to arrest or prosecute him (*Missoulian,* 9/6/10).

Race matters for reasons beyond the social; certain medical issues pertain to race as well. Thus, having knowledge about one's own race may be critical to disease prevention and treatment and long-term care for individuals. Consider, for example, the fact that although nearly all people of northern European descent can enjoy milk and milk products, many people of other races are lactose intolerant, meaning that they cannot drink milk or consume dairy products without an adverse digestive reaction. About 75 percent of African American, Jewish, Native American, and Mexican American adults cannot digest much milk; neither can about 90 percent of Asian Americans. Lactose intolerance can be managed by taking a chemical called lactase, which is available in pill form and in some dairy-based products such as specially formulated milk (vos Savant 2005). As another example, young blacks are twenty times as likely as whites to suffer heart failure. This illness strikes one in every one hundred blacks under the age of fifty (*Post-Standard,* 3/19/09). Interestingly enough, there is a specific treatment for heart disease that is most effective for blacks: BiDil. BiDil represents the first medication approved by the Food and Drug Administration for a specific racial group (Jewell 2005).

For years, medical research had shown that African American patients do better on kidney dialysis (a life-sustaining process for removing waste and excess water from the blood that acts as an artificial replacement for lost kidney function in people with renal failure) than their white counterparts (Johns Hopkins Medicine 2011). However, 2011 Johns Hopkins research has shown that younger blacks—those under the age of fifty—actually do much worse on dialysis than equally sick whites who undergo the same blood-filtering process (Johns Hopkins Medicine 2011). Dorry L. Segev, the lead medical doctor who headed this research at the Johns Hopkins University School of Medicine, claims that black patients between the ages of eighteen and thirty are twice as likely to die on dialysis than their white counterparts; those ages thirty-one to forty are one and a half times as likely to die (Johns Hopkins Medicine 2011). As a result, younger black patients are advised to opt for a kidney transfer instead of dialysis. As we can see, when it comes to kidney treatment options, race matters.

Another relatively new medical procedure that is giving new hope to patients with a number of cancers and immune-deficiency disorders is bone marrow transplantation. Bone marrow is a spongy tissue found inside the bones, and patients with leukemia, aplastic anemia, and some immunodeficiencies have their healthy stem cells destroyed along with unhealthy ones during chemotherapy and radiation therapies (Columbia Presbyterian Medical Center 2010). There is a 35 percent chance that a patient's sibling will be a perfect bone marrow match (Columbia Presbyterian Medical Center 2010). A patient without a close relative to serve as a match can turn to national registries to seek donors. However, the picture is significantly different depending on the patient's race, because the markers used in matching bone marrow are inherited, and patients are most likely to match someone of their own race or ethnicity. This becomes even more difficult when a person is multiracial. A white person has an 80 to 90 percent chance of finding a donor; blacks, Hispanics, and Asian-Americans have about a 40 percent chance; and multiracial persons have a much lower chance (Moses 2010). Native Americans have slightly more than a 1 percent chance of finding a donor because of the 7 million donors on the national registry, only about 80,000 are Native American (Moses 2010, p. A5). As the numbers would indicate, a multiracial person who is partly Native American will have less than a 1 percent chance of finding a donor.

The above discussion of why race matters is a mere sampling of the social and medical reasons why it is important for individuals to know their racial and ethnic background and to understand the possible consequences of their categorization.

Conducting genealogical research into one's own ancestral background might prove quite beneficial for medical purposes, but it may also reveal surprising or shocking information (see "A Closer Look" Box 8.4 for an example of one person's search for the truth about his past).

THE CAUSES AND EFFECTS OF PREJUDICE AND DISCRIMINATION

Individual and institutional racism, prejudice, and discrimination exist because of ignorance, hatred, and intolerance among diverse individuals and groups. We can do many things to fight hatred and intolerance (see "A Closer Look" Box 8.5), but how do we explain its occurrence? This section looks at three theoretical explanations for why prejudice and discrimination exist. It also examines the effects of prejudice and discrimination, both on the people who engage in these practices

A Closer Look

Box 8.4 Genealogical Research and Why Race Matters

In late February 2010, an intriguing news story spread across the wire services and Internet news outlets. A long-time neo-Nazi skinhead named Pawel (he asked that his last name not be revealed because of threats against his life) took a closer look at himself in the mirror and was alarmed by what he found: he was no longer the man he considered himself to be. Pawel, a thirty-three-year-old Pole living in Warsaw, had a long history of bigotry. He belonged to a group of skinheads who imitated Nazi salutes and enjoyed harassing the few Jewish residents of Warsaw. "Before 1939, Poland was home to more than three million Jews, more than 90 percent of whom were killed by the Nazis. Most who survived emigrated. Of the fewer than 50,000 who remained in Poland, many abandoned or hid their Judaism during decades of Communist oppression in which political pogroms against Jews persisted" (Bilefsky 2010). Consumed with fascist ideology, Pawel and his intolerant buddies, heads shaved and filled with racist hatred, once took a train ride to the remains of the Auschwitz concentration camp, where they cracked jokes about the Holocaust.

Pawel joined the army and married a fellow skinhead at age eighteen. At age twenty-two, his wife, Paulina, suspected that she had Jewish roots. The couple went to a genealogical institute and discovered that they both had registered Jewish maternal grandparents. When Pawel confronted his parents, they revealed that his maternal grandmother was Jewish and had survived the war hidden in a monastery by a group of nuns. His paternal grandfather, also a Jew, had seven brothers and sisters, most of whom perished in the Holocaust. Pawel stated that he could not look in the mirror for weeks (Bilefsky 2010). Confused by his newfound ancestral roots, he felt guilty for his past racist behavior. Imagine, the very people he discriminated against, the people he treated like the dirt beneath his shoes, were, in fact, his people. Eventually, he decided to embrace his newfound ethnic background, and at age twenty-four Pawel was circumcised. Two years later, he decided to become an ultra-Orthodox Jew. He and his wife are raising their two children in a Jewish home. He is now a victim of anti-Semitism, and many of his tormentors were once his friends.

What Do You Think?

Imagine the transformation in Pawel's life since he discovered his ancestral background. How would Pawel respond to the question, Why does race matter? Is it possible that if you researched your own genetic ancestry, you would find connections you did not expect? What do you think?

and on those who are subjected to them. We conclude with a discussion of the most extreme form of discriminatory behavior: hate crimes.

The Psychological Approach

Psychological theories of why prejudice and discrimination exist focus on how psychological needs are fulfilled. One of the earliest psychological theories explains prejudice as a means by which people express hostility as a result of frustration (Marger 2006). According to John Dollard et al. (1939), *scapegoating* is an essential feature of this approach. In brief, people who have difficulty achieving highly desired goals tend to respond with a pattern of aggression. Because certain social forces block attempts to reach these goals, some people direct their attention toward substitutes—scapegoats.

However, many people are frustrated by their life circumstances and yet do not resort to acts of discrimination or prejudicial feelings. As Thomas Adorno et al. (1950) explain, becoming aggressive and blaming others for their own inadequacies is most common among persons with the authoritarian personality type, which is characterized by, among other traits, intolerance, insecurity, excessive conformity, submissiveness to authority, and rigid stereotyping thought patterns. The concept of an authoritarian personality helps to explain why some people turn to prejudice and discrimination when frustrated while others do not.

Rosen and Crockett (1969) argue that some racial and ethnic groups differ in their orientation toward achievement, especially with regard to their drive for upward mobility. They use the concept of achievement syndrome to explain this drive. The implication of this theory is that some groups (and individuals), because of a drive to succeed, may use prejudice and discrimination to get ahead.

Theories that suggest certain personality types are prone to prejudice and discrimination are popular on the one hand because they offer simple explanations about a complicated issue—especially when compared to sociological theories that emphasize the role of power imbalances within society. On the other hand, sociologists tend to discredit psychological theories because they reduce the explanation of prejudice and discrimination to personality traits while mostly ignoring the social conditions that lead to them. Furthermore, a large number of people who are not extremists (authoritarian personalities) are prejudicial and discriminate against others.

Normative Theories

The normative approach centers on the idea that people feel compelled to abide by the norms of their group. That is, we follow the rules that dominate in-group associations. As we learned in Chapter 5, people are socialized to follow group norms. The socialization process is the key to learning and behavior. Thus, one's reference groups have a strong influence over behavior. In this regard, one's social environment shapes individual thoughts and actions. Prejudice and discrimination, then, are explained within the framework of social norms and people who feel obligated to follow them. From this viewpoint, tolerant people have been raised in an environment that instills respect for others, whereas bigots emerge out of social experiences where intolerance is the norm.

Power-Conflict Theories

Psychological and normative theories help to explain how discrimination and prejudice are transmitted and sustained, but they fail to explain how or why they arise in the first place. Sociologists focus on the imbalance of power between individuals and among diverse groups. Sociologists believe that an imbalance of power leads to different outlooks on life and that prejudice and discrimination are used as power resources that can be tapped as new conflict situations demand (Marger 2006). The power-conflict approach argues that those in power use discrimination and prejudice as weapons to maintain their power positions (e.g., via institutional racism).

Sociological power-conflict theories, however, are less effective in explaining why subordinate groups engage in prejudice and discrimination. Clearly, members from all racial and ethnic groups are capable of holding prejudicial thoughts and of behaving in a discriminatory manner. This leaves us with the realization that prejudice and discrimination are products of group interests that can be used by any group in an attempt to protect and enhance its own interests (Marger 2006).

What Do You Think?

Which theoretical approach best explains why prejudice and discrimination exist? How would you explain their occurrence in society? What do you think?

The Effects of Prejudice and Discrimination

Prejudice and discrimination exist in some form in every society. Consequently, from the functionalist perspective, they must serve a purpose. The effects of prejudice and discrimination vary based on whether one is a victim or perpetrator. From the perspective of those who discriminate and hold prejudicial beliefs (perpetrators), prejudice

1. provides scapegoats for certain social problems. A scapegoat is a readily available, often weaker (lacking in socioeconomic power), and (generally) innocent person or group blamed by others for specific societal problems. Scapegoats are the targets of prejudice and discrimination.
2. gives the majority, or power, group an opportunity, via institutional racism, to prevent subordinate groups from becoming a threat (to the power group) politically, economically, and socially.
3. serves to enhance the self-esteem of the majority or dominant group. One of the easiest ways for people to feel good about themselves (or superior) is to put others down. Prejudice and discrimination, then, serve as a self-esteem-enhancement mechanism.

From the perspective of the victimized group, the effects of prejudice may involve the following consequences:

1. Members of a victimized group often unite.
2. Because of this unification, victimized groups are better able to preserve their heritage.
3. Furthermore, this unification can lead to efforts for social change (i.e., finding or demanding courses of action designed to end prejudice and discrimination).

Throughout history, the dominant group of any particular society has typically victimized subordinate groups. Beyond the above-mentioned possibility of group members uniting with others in their "we" group, people can react in a number of ways to the effects of prejudice and discrimination. I refer to these reactions to subordination as the "seven *A*'s":

1. *Acceptance:* simply accepting things as they are. The Marxist/conflict perspective would refer to this as an example of false consciousness.
2. *Avoidance:* removing oneself from that neighborhood or society.
3. *Assimilation:* merging and blending in with the greater general society. (Note: Assimilation is discussed later in this chapter.)
4. *Aggression:* acting out with violence and hostility toward the power group.
5. *Action:* taking social action to correct the wrongs of society.
6. *Appeal to a higher loyalty:* turning to God or some other entity for guidance or relief.
7. *Anxiety:* failing to act at all. This is different from acceptance in that victims of prejudice or discrimination may not accept their plight but fear the consequences of acting out against it.

What Do You Think?

The Seven *A*'s represent a few examples of reactions to subordination. Can you think of others? They do not have to start with the letter *A*, but as a form of mental exercise, see if you can make them. What do you think?

Hate Crimes

One of the severest effects of prejudice involves hate crimes. The Federal Bureau of Investigation (FBI) defines a **hate crime**, also known as a bias crime, as "a criminal offense committed against a person, property, or society that is motivated, in whole or in part, by the offender's bias against a race, religion, disability, sexual orientation, or ethnicity/national origin" (FBI 2004). In response to the growing number of reported bias crimes in the late 1970s—from lynchings to cross burnings to vandalism of synagogues—the term "hate crime" entered the nation vocabulary in the early 1980s (FBI 2004; Gerstenfeld 2004). Racist skinheads and the National Socialist Party of America (NSPA) were among the leading hate groups that helped to trigger the need for special legislation to fight bias crimes via hate-crime legislation. Fans of popular culture may recall that the NSPA was satirized in the 1980 movie *The Blues Brothers.* In this film, the character brothers Elwood (Dan Aykroyd) and Jake (John Belushi) Blues run down a group of Illinois NSPA members attempting to cross a bridge on their way to a hate rally. Elwood, the driver of the car, calmly states, "Illinois Nazis." Jake responds, "I hate the Illinois Nazis."

In response to the growing national concern over crimes motivated by bias, Congress enacted the Hate Crime Statistics Act of 1990. Among other things, this law directed the attorney general to collect data "about crimes that manifest evidence of prejudice based on race, religion, sexual orientation, or ethnicity" (FBI 2004). In 1994, Congress passed the Violent Crime Control and Law Enforcement Act, which amended the Hate Crime Statistics Act to include both physical and mental disabilities. According to the FBI (2008a), in 2007, 2,025 law enforcement agencies reported 7,624 hate-crime incidents involving 9,006 offenses. There were 7,621 single-bias incidents that involved 8,999 offenses, 9,527 victims, and 6,962 offenders. Table 8.2 presents a breakdown of the 7,621 single-bias incidents reported in 2007 based on category.

Among the leading nongovernmental organizations attempting to track the number of hate crimes is the Southern Poverty Law Center (SPLC). The SPLC was founded in 1971 as a small civil rights firm located in Montgomery, Alabama, the birthplace of the civil rights movement. Its motto is "Fighting Hate, Teaching Tolerance, Seeking Justice." To learn more about the Southern Poverty Law Center, see "A Closer Look" Box 8.3.

TABLE 8.2 Single-Bias Hate-Crime Incidents, 2007

CATEGORY	PERCENTAGE
Race	50.8
Religion	18.4
Sexual orientation	16.6
Ethnicity or national origin	13.2
Disability	0.9

Source: FBI 2008a.

PATTERNS OF INTERRACIAL AND INTERETHNIC CONTACT

History has shown that when very diverse groups of people come in contact, the consequences are generally negative. Negative patterns include the following:

1. *Expulsion or population transfer:* the forced uprooting and ejection of a minority group from the society of the dominant majority. For example, the Roma (Gypsies) have been forced out of most European countries. There are believed to be approximately 12 million Roma scattered

A Closer Look

Box 8.5 Fighting Hatred and Intolerance

The Southern Poverty Law Center was founded in 1971 by Morris Dees and Joe Levin, two Montgomery, Alabama, lawyers who shared a commitment to racial equality (SPLC 2010). The SPLC investigates hate activity throughout the United States and provides this information to the public via a number of publications and its website. The organization also conducts training sessions for police, schools, and civil rights and community groups, and its associates often serve as experts at hearings and conferences (SPLC 2010).

The chief publication of the SPLC with regard to hate-group activity is its quarterly *SPLC Report,* which in spring 2009 documented 926 hate-group chapters in the United States. This figure represents a 54 percent increase since 2000 and a 4 percent gain over 2007. "The number of hate groups active in the United States continued to grow in 2008 as racist extremists were fueled by immigration tensions, a faltering economy and the election of the first black president, an SPLC investigation has found.... Obama may have smashed the ultimate political barrier to African Americans, but his presidency and the recession are creating a perfect storm for white supremacists intent on swelling their ranks" (SPLC 2009, p. 1).

Hate groups, of course, are not solely the domain of whites, as a large number of minority hate groups, especially black hate groups, also exist in the United States. The leading black hate group, the black separatists, is tied to the Nation of Islam. Furthermore, there is a black Ku Klux Klan organization, although the number of chapters is small compared to other major hate groups (Hale 2008).

As mentioned above, the number of hate groups in the United States has grown throughout the first decade of the 2000s. According to the SPLC (2011), there were 1,002 documented hate groups in the United States in 2010. California, the nation's most populous state, has the largest number at sixty-eight; even South Dakota, the last state to serve as home to a hate group, now has two. See Table 8.3 for a listing of the largest categories of hate groups operating in the United States in 2010. Not listed in Table 8.3 are 122 "general hate" categories that include antigay (seventeen), radical traditional Catholic (seventeen),

throughout the world. Many Roma mask their ethnic origin out of fear of discrimination.

2. *Annihilation or genocide:* the mass murder of a minority group by the dominant group in an attempt to eliminate the minority group. Bradley Campbell (2009) argues that genocide is a form of social control wherein the "perpetrators express moral grievances against the targeted" (p. 155). The examples are too numerous to document here, but they include the Nazis versus the Jews (and other groups), the Turks versus the Armenians, and the European settlers in the Americas versus the American Indians.
3. *Segregation:* the separation of races; the formal restriction of contact between racial or ethnic groups with denial of access to superior facilities

TABLE 8.3 Hate Groups Operating in the United States, 2010

TYPE OF GROUP	NUMBER IN OPERATION
Ku Klux Klan	221
Neo-Nazi	170
Black separatist	149
White nationalist	136
Racist skinhead	136
Neo-Confederate	42
Christian identity	26

Source: SPLC 2011.

racist music (fifteen), Holocaust denial (eight), anti-Muslim (five), and other (forty-seven).

In *Ten Ways to Fight Hate,* the SPLC (2000b) states that the ten best ways to fight hate are to

1. act (do something);
2. unite;
3. support the victims;
4. do your homework (learn about the group);
5. create an alternative (do not attend a hate rally);
6. speak up;
7. lobby leaders;
8. look long range (e.g., create a bias-response team);
9. teach tolerance (bias is taught at home, but so is tolerance);
10. dig deeper (look into the social issues that cause hate crimes).

The SPLC also provides the publication "101 Tools for Tolerance" (2000a), which, as the title implies, provides 101 ideas for tolerance, along with ideas about how to promote equity and diversity. (Note: Because of the document's length, these tools are not listed here, but they can be found online at the website provided at the end of this chapter.)

What Do You Think?

There were more than one thousand documented hate groups operating in the United States in 2010. The Southern Poverty Law Center provides us with ten ideas on how to fight hate groups. Is it possible to eliminate, or at the very least reduce, the number of hate groups in the United States? What do you think?

and opportunities to subordinate groups. Examples include the former South African policy of apartheid and the U.S. doctrine of "separate-but-equal" public facilities for blacks.

4. *Enslavement:* the literal ownership of a population of people, whereby owners have complete control over slaves. Slavery was legal in parts of the United States until 1865, when the Thirteenth Amendment to the U.S. Constitution abolished the practice of "involuntary servitude." The International Labour Organization (2010) estimates that 12.3 million people are enslaved around the world today.

Although all peoples have failed to exercise tolerance at some time in history, and despite the numerous examples of ethnic conflict and genocide across the globe, sociologists remain among those who refuse simply to accept racial intolerance as an inevitable reality. There are some possible solutions to the negative effects of intergroup contact. These include assimilation, pluralism or multiculturalism, and amalgamation. Let us examine each of these.

Assimilation (Melting Pot Theory)

The word "assimilate" derives from the Latin *assimulare,* which means "to make similar" (Feagin and Feagin 2004). The basic idea behind **assimilation** is that people who move from one nation to another should learn, as quickly as possible, to accept the culture of the new homeland. Assimilation, then, involves the cultural blending of two or more previously distinct groups. It involves conformity to and acceptance of the dominant culture. As sociologist Robert E. Park explains, European out-migration (during the nineteenth and twentieth centuries) was a major catalyst for social reorganization around the globe, especially in the United States (Feagin and Feagin 2004). Park (1950) argued that out-migration leads to recurring cycles in intergroup history (between in-groups and out-groups): contact, competition, accommodation, and assimilation. In theory, the faster immigrant groups assimilate to the greater society, the faster they will receive acceptance by the dominant group. The adage "If you can't beat 'em, join 'em" comes into play here. Thus, while many European immigrant groups (starting with the Irish and continuing with the Italians, Poles, and so on) faced a great deal of prejudice and discrimination when they first arrived in the United States, they came to enjoy relative equality due to cultural assimilation. Over time, these immigrant groups abandoned the cultural ways of their ancestors, and their heritages became compromised; in the process, however, the dominant society slowly accepted them. "Ideally, then, at the point of complete assimilation, there are no longer distinct ethnic groups. Rather, there is a homogenous society in which ethnicity is not a basis of social differentiation and plays no role in the distribution of wealth, power, and prestige" (Marger 2006, p. 101).

For generations, social policy makers promoted assimilation as the primary means of resolving ethnic differences in the United States. Functionalists argue that assimilation policies help to eliminate conflict among diverse groups because everyone belongs to the same group. In this regard, there are no "they" racial or ethnic groups, just one big "we" group of Americans.

Conflict theorists believe that assimilation does not work with racially different categories because the dominant group generally refuses to give up power to those deemed significantly different, or socioeconomically inferior. According to this view, assimilation worked quite well with European ethnic groups primarily because they were all white. They were also willing participants in the idea of assimilating to the greater society. Many nonwhites do not wish to assimilate and value their own cultural heritages. As a result, a new prevailing sentiment exists in the United States—one that promotes multiculturalism, or pluralism.

Multiculturalism or Pluralism (Salad Bowl Theory)

For the past generation or so, U.S. policy makers have endorsed the idea of multiculturalism, or pluralism, instead of assimilation. **Pluralism** is the idea that all groups have something positive to add to the greater society and that each racial and ethnic group ("we" group) should maintain its cultural heritage. However, while maintaining old customs, these groups would also have the right to participate fully in the greater society's political and economic institutions.

This approach works on the assumptions that the greater society can be taught to value the differences among people via diversity education and that the greater society will be willing to give up its dominant socioeconomic power. Public school education, for example, has fully embraced the multiculturalism ideal and teaches students to value all people as equals and to accept the cultural differences that may exist between them. Many businesses value workers with a background in diversity training and awareness because of the diverse nature of most workplaces. Thus, pluralism teaches that all groups should be treated equally and should share equally in society's scarce resources.

As the conflict perspective predicts, people in a power position are almost always reluctant to relinquish their power voluntarily. As a result, the pluralistic approach has, at best, mixed results (Dobbin, Kalev, and Kelly 2007). The younger American generation, raised in the ethos of multiculturalism, does indeed appear to be far more tolerant of others, especially compared to past generations. Nonetheless, as indicated by the growing number of hate groups in the United States (described earlier), racism, prejudice, and discrimination persist. Americans are not alone in questioning the validity of the "salad bowl" theory. In a February 2011 speech to the Munich Security Conference, British prime minister David Cameron blasted multiculturalism as a complete failure. He spoke of the importance for all immigrants of learning the language of their new home and becoming educated in the elements of a common culture and curriculum. To that end, Cameron said, "Frankly, we need a lot less of the passive tolerance of recent years and much more active, muscular liberalism" (BBC News 2011). Cameron claims that multiculturalism has failed in other societies as well.

Amalgamation

Interestingly, we may be witnessing people accomplishing, via voluntary amalgamation, what social-policy makers have failed to achieve. **Amalgamation** involves the "genetic blending" of two or more previously distinct racial or ethnic groups. It occurs when two people from different races have children either through intermarriage or interdating. Marriages between people of different races are often referred to as "mixed marriages," although the term "interracial marriage" is more acceptable. In the past, interracial marriages were outlawed in various parts of the United States because of public sentiment (and government policy). "In 1958, only 4 percent of whites approved of white-black marriages, according to a national Gallup Poll survey. Blacks were not included in the 1958 survey. By 1997, the approval rate among whites had increased to 61 percent. Later Gallup polls found that black approval rates rose from 56 percent in 1968 to 77 percent in 1997" (Pugh 2001, p. A5). So-called antimiscegenation laws were declared unconstitutional by a landmark Supreme Court decision in 1967.

Although interracial marriages accounted for just 5 percent of all U.S. marriages in 2001, the total number of interracial marriages represents a tenfold increase over 1960 (Pugh 2001). In 2001, there were 1.5 million black-white marriages. Adding Hispanics and Asians who marry outside their racial or ethnic groups increases the total number of mixed marriages to 3 million (Pugh 2001). "Four states with large minority populations—California, Texas, New York, and Florida—are home to nearly half of U.S. mixed marriages. Nearly one of every four such couples lives in California" (Pugh 2001, p. A5). The steady growth in interracial marriages reveals an increasing acceptance of such diversity in marriage, especially in geographic areas that have a high rate of racial and ethnic diversity.

As the number of relationships between members of racially (and ethnically) diverse groups continues to increase, the total number of children of "mixed" race increases more dramatically. The number of people not of one specific race has increased so much over the past decade that the U.S. census, as well as other government and official forms, now allows people to indicate "Other" when asked to identify their race. As La Ferla (2004) indicates, "Nearly 7 million Americans identified themselves as members of more than one race in the 2000 Census, the first time respondents were able to check" such a category (p. D1).

Have you ever met someone whose race you could not determine by looking at and talking with him or her? The term "racial passing" is applicable here. *Racial passing* once referred to people who tried to "pass" for members of another race (such as light-skinned African Americans who attempted to pass as white in order to avoid discrimination); today, the term is more applicable to people who are not obviously biracial. In other words, such people can pass for any number of racial or ethnic categories. A number of actors (e.g., Jessica Alba), athletes (e.g., Tiger Woods), and entertainers (e.g., Christina Aguilera) have this ethnically ambiguous quality as they are neither black nor white nor even obviously biracial (La Ferla 2004) (see "Connecting Sociology and Popular Culture" Box 8.6 for a discussion of famous multiracial persons).

As the amalgamation trend continues, it will become increasingly difficult to tell the difference between racial and ethnic groups in the United States. In addition, as diverse groups around the world continue to move from nation to nation, the amalgamation trend occurring in the United States will likely become dominant elsewhere as well. Perhaps as people become less dissimilar, they will learn to concentrate on the similarities among them rather than the differences. Ideally, this will lead to a more racially and ethnically tolerant world—one where ethnic stratification is replaced by ethnic ambiguity.

Many Americans, such as Jessica Alba shown here, have a combination of multiple races and/or ethnicities.

What Do You Think?

Are racism, prejudice, discrimination, and intolerance permanent fixtures of society? What do you think?

SUMMARY

The terms "race" and "ethnicity" are socially constructed means of categorizing people based on specific criteria. "Race" refers to a group of people who are socially recognized based on some sort of physical characteristic, generally skin color. "Ethnicity" refers to a group of people who are recognized as a distinct group based on social or cultural factors. Historically, people belonging to minority groups (those lacking in socioeconomic and political power) have faced such inequalities as racism, prejudice, and discrimination. Generally, like-minded groups, including racial and ethnic groups, identify with one another and come to use the expression "we" in a natural forum. Out-groups come to be viewed as "they" groups. Concentrating on the differences between groups of people leads to ethnic stratification. Ethnic stratification is a system of ranking ethnic groups in society with the dominant group on top and the less powerful groups taking positions lower in the hierarchy. Utilizing this system of ethnic stratification, sociologists are able to distinguish majority-minority and dominant-subordinate social systems.

Connecting Sociology and Popular Culture

Box 8.6 Famous Multiracial Persons

Numerous famous multiracial persons have become pop-culture icons while starring in their specific fields. Among today's most admired actresses is Jessica Alba, the Dark Angel herself. Known for her exotic looks, Alba received her first break in the television series *Dark Angel*. Since, she has gone on to star in numerous feature films and can be seen in a variety of advertisements. Born in Pomona, California, on April 28, 1981, Alba has an ethnic background consisting of Danish, French, and Mexican heritages.

One of the most popular singer-songwriters of her generation, Christina Aguilera was born on December 18, 1980, in Staten Island, New York. Aguilera is a bilingual singer of Irish (mother's side) and Ecuadorian (father's side) ancestry. Her self-titled debut album went platinum ten times over. She has received many honors, including Grammy nominations, MTV awards, a Teen Choice Award, and so on. She also has many commercial endorsements. Aguilera was a child actor on the New Mickey Mouse Club from 1993 to 1994. She continued to draw attention for her singing ability throughout her childhood, and she remains a top performer in her twenties.

Considered one of the world's most popular athletes (at least until his infidelity scandal in 2009), Tiger Woods dominates his sport (golf) like no other. Woods has been in the limelight since he first putted a golf ball as a two-year-old for Bob Hope on *The Mike Douglas Show*. Born in Cypress, California, on December 30, 1975, Woods has pursued Jack Nicklaus's record for majors victories (eighteen) ever since he turned professional. He is perhaps one of the most famous multiracial people of all. His father, Earl, was of mixed African American (50 percent), Chinese (25 percent), and Native American (25 percent) ancestry; Woods's mother, Kultida, originally from Thailand, is of mixed Thai (50 percent), Chinese (25 percent), and Dutch (25 percent) ancestry. This makes Tiger one-quarter Chinese, one-quarter Thai, one-quarter African American, one-eighth Native American, and one-eighth Dutch. He refers to his ethnic makeup as "Cablinasian"—a term he coined to combine syllables from Caucasian, black (American), Indian, and Asian. (Woods used this term to describe himself during an appearance on *The Oprah Winfrey Show*.)

Barack Obama, perhaps the most powerful man in the world, is a descendent of biological parents of different races. Obama was born on August 4, 1961, in Honolulu, Hawaii. His father, Barack Obama Sr., was of Luo ancestry and came from the Nyanza Province of Kenya. His mother, Stanley Ann Dunham, was raised in Wichita, Kansas, and was of primarily English ancestry. Obama's parents met at the University of Hawaii's Manoa campus. A number of Dunham's ancestors had been antislavery activists in the mid- and late-1800s. Seemingly appearing out of nowhere in his relatively modest position as the freshman U.S. senator from Illinois, in 2008 Obama was elected the forty-fourth president of the United States; his victory was attributed in large part to his popularity among younger and minority voters. Because he is the son of parents of two different races, Obama is sometimes referred to as the nation's first multiracial president. Others, however, refer to him as the first black U.S. president. Perhaps ending this debate, when he filled out his 2010 census form, Obama responded to Question 9 by checking "Black, African American, or Negro" as his race. As described earlier in this chapter, he could have chosen "white" (because of his mother) or checked the last category on the form, "Some other race."

What Do You Think?

What other famous multiracial people can you think of? Do multiracial people hold a certain appeal that single-race people do not? What do you think?

Most societies are stratified based on race or ethnicity. In the United States, whites make up the majority group. However, the number of minority groups is growing rapidly, especially the number of Hispanics or Latinos, who now represent the largest minority group, followed by African Americans, Asian Americans, Native Americans, and Pacific Islanders. The term "minority," from a sociological standpoint, has less to do with statistical realities and more to do with identifying people who are disadvantaged in terms of socioeconomic and political power. In many cases, the dominant group attempts to hold onto its power via institutional racism—widespread, large-scale, structured discrimination on the basis of race or ethnicity.

Although tolerance and acceptance of ethnic diversity have been growing, prejudice and discrimination still exist throughout society. There are a number of possible explanations as to why intolerance toward others exists in society; this chapter has discussed psychological, normative, and power-conflict theoretical explanations. One extreme form of prejudice comes in the form of hate crimes. A hate crime, also known as a bias crime, is a criminal offense committed against a person, property, or society that is motivated, in whole or in part, by the offender's bias against a race, religion, disability, sexual orientation, ethnicity, or national origin.

Patterns of interracial and interethnic contact have also resulted in many negative consequences, including expulsion or population transfers, annihilation or genocide, segregation, and slavery. Possible solutions to the negative effects of intergroup contact include assimilation, pluralism or multiculturalism, and amalgamation.

Glossary

Amalgamation—The physical blending of two or more previously distinct racial or ethnic categories of people.

Assimilation—The cultural blending of two or more previously distinct categories of people.

Discrimination—Behavior that treats people unequally on the basis of an ascribed status, such as race or gender.

Enslavement—The literal ownership of a population of people, whereby owners have complete control over slaves.

Ethnic stratification—A system of ranking ethnic groups in society with the dominant group on top and the less powerful groups taking positions lower in the hierarchy.

Ethnicity—A category of people who are recognized as distinct based on social or cultural factors (e.g., nationality, religion, language, geographic residence, and values).

Ethnocentrism—The tendency of people from one cultural group to judge other cultures by the standards of their own.

Expulsion or population transfer—The forced uprooting and ejection of a minority group from the society of the dominant majority.

Genocide—The intentional attempt by a dominant population to exterminate a race of people.

Hate crime—A criminal offense committed against a person, property, or society that is motivated, in whole or in part, by the offender's bias against a race, religion, disability, sexual orientation, ethnicity, or national origin; also known as a bias crime.

Individual racism—Unequal treatment and behavior directed by a member or group of one race against a person or group of another race.

Institutional racism—Widespread, large-scale, structured discrimination on the basis of race or ethnicity.

Minority group—A disadvantaged group of citizens; specifically, the underprivileged at the lower end of the stratification hierarchy.

Pluralism—The idea that all groups have something positive to add to the greater society and that each racial and ethnic group ("we" group) should maintain its cultural heritage.

Prejudice—Negative beliefs and overgeneralizations concerning a group of people.

Race—A category of people who share socially recognized physical characteristics (such as skin color or hereditary traits) that distinguish them from other categories of people.

Racism—Any attitude, belief, behavior, or social arrangement that has the intent, or the ultimate effect, of favoring one category of people (or individual) over another category of people (or individual).

Segregation—The separation of races; the formal restriction of contact between racial or ethnic groups, with denial of equal access to superior facilities and opportunities to subordinate groups.

Discussion Questions

1. How do you and your friends view race in the United States? Are there growing signs of tolerance, or do prejudice and discrimination prevail?
2. What can you do to stop prejudice and discrimination in your community? What have you already done?
3. Do you think it is necessary to have hate-crime legislation? Are stiffer penalties justified when a bias is involved? Why or why not?
4. Do you have membership in "we" groups? If so, what parameters distinguish "we" from "them"?

5. Is society becoming ethnically ambiguous? Or do people still see black and white (and other distinctive categories of people)?

Web Links

To learn more about the Southern Poverty Law Center, visit www.splcenter.org.
To learn more about promoting tolerance, visit www.tolerance.org.
To learn more about hate crimes, visit the U.S. Congress' website www.fbi.gov/hq/cid/civilrights/hate.htm.
To learn more about the "Beer Summit" and to see a video clip, visit www.politico.com/news/stories/0709/25637.html.
For an up-to-date look at U.S. and World Population figures, visit www.census.gov/main/www/popclock.html.

9 GENDER INEQUALITY

Maria Pepe, who attempted to be the first girl to play Little League Baseball in 1972, is shown here throwing out the opening pitch at a 2004 Little League World Series game.

Chapter Nine

- Introductory Story
- The Social Construction of Gender
- Learning Gender Roles and Gender Appropriateness
- Understanding Gender Stratification
- Feminism
- Lesbian, Gay, Bisexual, and Transgendered Persons
- Summary, Glossary, Discussion Questions, and Web Links

INTRODUCTORY STORY

In the "Bart Star" (1997a) episode of *The Simpsons,* which first aired on November 9, 1997, eight-year-old Lisa Simpson appears at a youth football tryout prepared for one of her trademark confrontations by asking head coach Ned Flanders, "What position have you got for me?" Lisa continues, "That's right. A girl wants to play football. How about that?" Lisa is dumbfounded when Flanders replies, "Well, that's super-duper, Lisa. We've already got four girls on the team." As it turns out, Lisa is about twenty-five years too late in her quest to become a trailblazer for women's rights in sports. Had she made such a proclamation in the early 1970s, she might have been the first girl to play organized youth football.

Unlike Lisa Simpson, Maria Pepe of Hoboken, New Jersey, was a true trailblazer in the women's rights movement as it pertains to sports. For, despite the popularity in the early 1950s of a Broadway comedy featuring a girl with a passionate desire to play football (*Time Out for Ginger* by Ronald Alexander), in real life it was accepted without question that "contact" sports were for boys only.

This attitude began to change with the feminist movement of the 1960s and the growing gender-equity movement of the 1970s. In the summer of 1972, twelve-year-old Maria Pepe struck the blow that Lisa Simpson had hoped to when she shattered the gender barrier in Little League Baseball. Pepe, who had a deep passion for and desire to play baseball, coupled with a mean fastball, tried out for the local Little League Baseball team. She made it and played in three games. The governing Little League then ruled her ineligible—because girls were not allowed to play—and threatened to strip the Hoboken Young Democrats team of its status as a member of the Little League Association. After her coach informed Pepe of the news, with a heavy heart she turned in her uniform.

But her plight gained national attention. The National Organization for Women (NOW) worked with Pepe's family in an attempt to get her reinstated. Two years later, the New Jersey Superior Court ruled that girls must be allowed to play Little League Baseball. For Pepe, it was too late as she no longer met the age requirement. However, since then, more than 5 million girls have played Little League (Read 2005). Today, no one would even consider forbidding a girl from trying out. Pepe's brief participation in Little League was enough to make ESPN's (2007) top ten "Greatest U.S. Women's Sports Moments" list, coming in at number five.

As this chapter shows, gender roles and expectations have undergone quite a transition during the past couple of generations. Nonetheless, gender stratification still exists in North American society today.

THE SOCIAL CONSTRUCTION OF GENDER

In Chapter 8, we learned that the concepts of race and ethnicity are socially constructed. **Social construction** itself refers to the idea that all concepts exist because humans created, or built, them. In this regard, concepts are not defined by laws of nature. Socially constructed terms are dependent on human social experiences, needs, values, and interests. Thus, social construction is contingent not only on ideas about things but also on beliefs that have been shaped by social forces. Socially constructed reality is also viewed as an ongoing, dynamic process rather than a static perspective on social reality. This is certainly true with regard to the concepts of sex, gender, and gender roles.

We begin with a distinction between the terms "sex" and "gender." **Sex** refers to an individual's biological classification (male or female). Males and females differ biologically with regard to their internal and external reproductive organs, types and levels of hormones, and chromosomal structure (females have an XX and males an XY design) (Leonard 1988). However, to be born a male or female in any given society entails much more than a biological distinction. Culture predicates the transformation of biological classifications into gender ones.

Before we discuss gender, it should be pointed out that, on occasion, a person is born with both male and female genitalia. In such cases, the term "intersex person" is applied. An *intersex person* is born with or develops mixed sexual physiology (e.g., an abnormally small penis and a large clitoris). Some individuals do not discover they are intersex until they reach puberty (see "Connecting Sociology and Popular Culture" Box 9.1 for a further discussion of intersexuality).

The term "hermaphrodite" was once used to describe persons with mixed sexual physiology, but it has fallen out of favor in describing humans. A hermaphrodite is an organism having both male and female reproductive organs. In many species, hermaphroditism is a common part of the life cycle, enabling a form of sexual reproduction in which mating partners are not separated into distinct male and female categories. Hermaphroditism most commonly occurs in invertebrates, although it is also found in some fish and to a lesser degree in other vertebrates. The 1990 book and 1993 film *Jurassic Park* featured dinosaurs that exhibited a sequential hermaphrodite transformation, and the aliens in the film *District 9* were described as reproducing like earthworms (simultaneous hermaphroditism).

Gender refers to socially determined expectations placed on individuals because of their sexual category. In most societies, the prevailing culture expects males to display certain "masculine" behaviors and females to display certain "feminine" behaviors. Each society, then, determines what constitutes expected and proper behavior for males and females based on cultural and gender appropriateness; these expectations are expressed in the form of gender roles. Gender roles extend to all realms of social life: attitudes and emotional-response patterns; mannerisms, tone of voice, and body language; style of dress and ornamentation; and "appropriate" activities, including sports. **Gender roles** can be defined as sets of cultural expectations associated with being a male (masculinity) or female (femininity). Sociologists point out that as gender roles are learned and culturally defined, they vary from one culture to the next.

LEARNING GENDER ROLES AND GENDER APPROPRIATENESS

Regardless of individual personalities, in every society people face an incalculable number of behavioral expectations based solely on their gender. These behavioral expectations lead to a number of societal ideals of gender "appropriateness" that are applied more or less universally to all members of a specific gender. For example, throughout most of Western history until the twentieth century, it was the norm

Connecting Sociology and Popular Culture

Box 9.1 Judging on One's Sex: The Case of Caster Semenya, Track Star

In most cases, it seems rather simple to determine one's sex; after all, people are either males or females, correct? Well, not quite. As our discussion of intersex persons reveals, some people possess a mixed sexual physiology. People with intersex conditions may choose to live exclusively as either male or female by wearing gender-specific clothing and utilizing key social cues of gender behavior; they may also undergo hormone replacement therapy or genital surgery. Other intersex persons may choose to live their lives with the physiology of a male and a female. Some men have a condition called Klinefelter's syndrome (also known as the XXY maleness), caused by having an extra X chromosome in most of their cells. The syndrome can affect different stages of physical, linguistic, and social development. Because they do not produce as much of the male hormone testosterone as other boys, teenagers with Klinefelter's syndrome may have less facial and body hair and be less muscular than other boys (Medicine Plus 2009b).

Another variation of an intersex person is the result of androgen insensitivity syndrome (AIS). A person with AIS is genetically male (has one X and Y chromosome) and is resistant to male hormones called androgens. As a result, the person has some or all the physical characteristics of a woman, despite having the genetic makeup of a man (Medicine Plus 2009a). A person with complete AIS appears to be female but has no uterus and has very little armpit and pubic hair. In addition, persons with AIS may have both male and female physical characteristics; many will have partial closing of the outer vaginal lips, an enlarged clitoris, and a short vagina (Medicine Plus 2009a).

Seldom does the topic of intersex persons reach the domain of the mass media and popular culture; after all, how many people have to "prove" their sexuality? The world of athletics provides us with such a case with the South African runner and Pretoria University student Caster Semenya, a sprinter who was eighteen years old when she won the women's eight hundred meters at the World Championships on August 19, 2009. She beat her opponents so convincingly (by two full seconds), and performed so much better (by eight seconds) than her own eight-hundred-meter time of just a year earlier, that people began to question her sexuality (Litke 2009). The International Association of Athletics Federations (IAAF) said "it was obliged to investigate" as her stunning performance in this and the 1,500-meter race amounted to "the sort of dramatic breakthroughs that usually arouse suspicion of drug use." The organization also required her to take a gender test, which "takes weeks

for women and girls in American society to wear skirts or dresses. Only men and boys wore pants. And while women wore "dungarees" for sports and blue-collar labor as early as the World War I years, not until the 1960s did public schools begin allowing girls to attend class in pants, and a number of formal restaurants continued to require skirts and dresses "for ladies" until the 1980s. In fact, during Hillary Clinton's run for the presidential nomination in 2008, many commentators felt compelled to remark on her wardrobe, as she consistently wore pantsuits rather than skirts or dresses. Interestingly, although today it is acceptable for women to wear either skirts or pants, this liberal form of thinking did not extend to males as it is still, generally speaking, not considered appropriate for men to wear skirts.

to complete, requires a physical medical evaluation, and includes reports from a gynaecologist, endocrinologist, psychologist, an internal medicine specialist and an expert on gender" (D. Smith 2009). News of this unusual testing circulated into the mainstream media, and Semenya's sexuality became the target of late-night talk show host's jokes. What should have been a crowning moment in the life of a young track star was overshadowed by doubt. The early days that followed her victory left Semenya feeling humiliated, which in turn led to her attempt to escape media scrutiny.

Who is Caster Semenya? Sports columnist Jim Litke (2009) explains, "Semenya's tale begins with a tomboy who always wore pants to school, didn't mind playing rough, and endured plenty of taunts from the boys she regularly competed against in a poor village 300 miles north of Johannesburg. The head of her secondary school thought Semenya was a boy until Grade 11" (p. B3). Her parents raised her as a girl and insist that she is female. As Semenya is very muscular and has a deep voice, a number of her competitors openly questioned her sexuality at the 2009 World Championships. Early preliminary medical tests revealed that Semenya had three times the normal female level of testosterone in her body (Hart 2009). Over the next few weeks, additional test results leaked to the media revealed that she has both male and female sexual organs. Semenya has no ovaries but rather internal male testes that produce large amounts of testosterone (Fanhouse 2009).

In November 2009, South Africa's sports ministry announced that Semenya would keep the gold medal and prize money she had won at the World Championships in August 2009. After completing a number of gender tests, the IAAF in July 2010 cleared Semenya to compete as a woman in all future international track and field events. It is unclear whether she had any medical procedures or treatments prior to the IAAF's final decision, as the federation said medical details of her case would remain confidential (*Los Angeles Times*, 7/7/10).

In essence, a sports governing body decided the gender of Caster Semenya. As the Semenya case clearly demonstrates, biology alone cannot determine a person's gender. Instead, gender is a matter of social construction, and biology is one aspect of this determination.

What Do You Think?

What criteria should be used to determine one's sex? Why should a gender expert and psychologist be involved in a sexuality test? Does Semenya have an unfair advantage over her opponents considering that she produces significantly higher amounts of testosterone than "normal" women as a result of her internal testes? What do you think?

In 2006, Michael Coviello, a senior at Hasbrouck Heights High School in New Jersey, made the national news when he won the right to wear a skirt to school. You may ask, What was his motivation to wear a skirt to school? Was he trying to make a political statement? Coviello's fight to wear a skirt began when he was barred from wearing shorts because of a school policy prohibiting them from October 1 to April 15. Coviello felt that since girls could wear skirts and expose their legs, boys should be afforded the same privilege (Givhan 2006).

When discussing gender, sociologists generally focus their attention on women and their fight for equality. As Lorne Tepperman and Jenny Blain explain, "It used to be that if sociologists spoke of gender, people thought they meant

What Do You Think?

Why did Coviello have to fight for the right to wear a skirt? Should men feel comfortable wearing a skirt or dress to class or work? What do you think?

something that affected women. Now we see men and masculinities as constructed by society and culture—as equally 'gendered'" (2006, p. 163). In other words, there were sociologists who taught gender and forgot about one-half of the equation: men. This is a mistake, as the concept of masculinity is as much the result of social construction as the notion of femininity (Gilbert 2005). So, what about men? If gender expectations change for women, do they not also change for men? (See "Connecting Sociology and Popular Culture" Box 9.2 for a closer look at what it means to be a "manly" man.)

Although most men do not want to wear skirts, they are unsure about a growing number of social norms associated with gender appropriateness. Consider the male hug. The embrace has long been reserved for women, American men celebrating sports victories, and men from other countries (Brown 2005). While female friends comfortably greet each other with a hug and perhaps a kiss on the cheek, American males have generally relied on a handshake as an appropriate greeting. However, this norm is disappearing, and a greater number of males have found it appropriate to hug each other—albeit with certain restrictions. Douglas Brown (2005) describes three different categories of hugging between men: "the hip-hop" (men greet each other with handshakes of various styles, pull themselves in toward each other, then bump their inside shoulders); "the half-and-half" (guys greet each other with standard handshakes, then reach around each other's shoulders with their left arms and pat each other's backs); and "the bear" (guys dispense with handshakes altogether and drape one arm over their partner's right shoulder and the other arm around his waist; one hand usually pats the partner's back as well). The male hug represents a transition in gender appropriateness as evidenced by the realization that most male hugs do not last much longer than one second. Male hugs that last two or more seconds are generally interpreted as romantic rather than friendly. Furthermore, because the level of acceptability in society is still mixed, many males are asking themselves when they greet a male friend, Should I shake, or should I hug? Making the wrong choice is potentially embarrassing socially.

Jet Black, shown here, has made a career of dressing as a woman.

Connecting Sociology and Popular Culture

Box 9.2 The "Man Laws": Don't Fruit the Beer

In the later years of the first decade of the 2000s, the Miller Lite beer brand introduced a "Man Laws" advertising campaign. In these TV commercials, the manly men of the "Square Table" (a takeoff on King Arthur's round table) analyze a number of social situations and provide words of masculine authority known as "man laws." Male viewers are expected to abide by these rules because, well, they are men. The Square Table is chaired by Burt Reynolds and members include actors, athletes, an astronaut, and a regular "Joe." In the first "Man Laws" commercial, the men discuss whether it is okay to date a woman who has dumped your friend. Most men have encountered this situation at one time or another, and that is the point of these rules: to establish guidelines, or rules, for expected behavior in typical life situations. Astronaut Brian Binnie suggests, "You've got to wait at least a month." Moderator Burt Reynolds disagrees, "No, not a month." Comedian Eddie Griffin offers an alternative view: "I was always taught you've got to wait two Saturdays or a new hairdo, whichever comes first." Again, Reynolds strongly disagrees. He reminds the group of the informal male expectation that, due to honor among male friends, it is ethically wrong to date a woman who has wronged a pal. Nearing a group decision, comedian Jackie Flynn, asks, "But what if she's drop-dead gorgeous?" At this prospect, even Reynolds realizes a compromise must be reached. Eventually the group agrees that a six-month waiting period must be enforced. The ruling becomes a "man law" and is recorded as such by an elderly scribe.

In another "Man Laws" commercial, the group contemplates whether it is okay to put fruit in their beer. One member suggests that it helps to prevent scurvy, to which the elderly scribe replies, "I had scurvy once." Reynolds is dead set against putting fruit in beer. He suggests that they might as well put a little umbrella in it and call it a "beera colada." The Man Law solution: "Don't fruit the beer." The implication of this rule is that putting fruit in one's beer is unmasculine. It is interesting to note that this commercial was a direct attack against Corona beer, whose commercials show people enjoying beer with a slice of lime. Today, other companies fruit their beers. Blue Moon, for example, is served with an orange slice. What would Reynolds have to say about such a trend?

FHM, a popular magazine for "manly men" that regularly includes photos of gorgeous women, has also embraced the "man laws" mantra by running a series of ads and sponsoring a website that features additional rules for men. One *FHM*-sponsored "man law" states, "No man shall own a dog smaller than a football." Readers are encouraged to take photos of violators and to upload them to the website—a type of public shaming. A 2007 *FHM* calendar features a "man law" for each month.

The "man laws" mantra reflects one set of ideals for male gender appropriateness. However, there is undoubtedly a growing social current in contemporary society for men to break the traditional laws of masculinity by, for instance, gelling their hair, wearing fragrant cologne (for means other than disguising body odor), shaving their chest hair, body waxing, getting their nails done, and using exfoliating creams. Many men have opted for cosmetic surgery, and male television announcers would not dream of going on the air without makeup. In short, there exists an ambiguity in contemporary society regarding what constitutes gender appropriateness for males.

What Do You Think?

Should men act "manly," or should they be willing to show their feminine side? What characteristics best describe the contemporary male? What characteristics best describe the "ideal" man? What do you think?

> **What Do You Think?**
>
> Do you observe that women seem to be more comfortable hugging and kissing while greeting one another than men? If you are, or if you were, a male, would you find it comfortable to hug and kiss a friend when you greeted one another in a college hallway? Why or why not? What do you think?

Gender Roles and the Socialization Process

How is it that we come to view certain acts and behaviors as appropriate for men and others as suitable for women? The answer lies in cultural expectations that are taught through the socialization process via the agents of socialization. As we learned in Chapter 5, the socialization process begins with the family, especially one's parents. Each of us was taught about certain aspects of gender appropriateness by our parents (or primary caregivers). As Susan Greendorfer (1993) explains, "It is through the process of gender role socialization that we learn, from infancy, about the relationship between biological sex and behavior, mannerisms, dress, and activities. This learning is shaped by ideological beliefs pertaining to gender—namely, those that clearly distinguish what males are, do, and should be from what females are, do, and should be.... Gender role socialization has two outcomes, produced by emphasis on differences between the sexes rather than on similarities: (a) Parents treat sons and daughters differently, and (b) we learn at a very early age to distinguish between male and female" (p. 4). While it is true that some parents treat their sons and daughters differently based on their gender, sociological analysis reveals that not all children are raised by parents in a gender-appropriate manner. There are parents who treat their sons and daughters equally (without sex-type expectations), allowing them to express themselves without regard to societal gender expectations. In 2011, a Toronto couple (Kathy Witterick and David Stocker) went to the "extreme" of trying to raise a "genderless" baby by withholding the child's sexual category (Gillies 2011). The couple share the sex of their baby, named Storm, with sons Jazz and Kio, a close family friend, and two midwives who helped deliver the baby. Witterick and Stocker hope that Storm will remain untouched by the connotations of pink versus blue and male versus female, so that the child can develop its own sexual identity without conforming to social stereotypes and predetermined expectations associated with gender (Gillies 2011).

Regardless of how they raise their children, parents serve as role models. They provide both direct and indirect socialization regarding gender appropriateness. Boys are especially influenced by their fathers (Raley and Bianchi 2006; Badalament 2010). Fathers serve as the first role model for boys and contribute to infant development (Pruett 1998; Young et al. 1995). Thus, if we revisit the "male hug" topic, boys who were raised in an environment where fathers openly displayed signs of emotional expressiveness (hugging and kissing) toward their sons are more likely to utilize the male hug because they learned that it is okay to express themselves in an intimate manner. This is just one of countless examples of how parents may influence their children with regard to gender role expectations. Each of us can examine the messages we received from our parents and consider the extent to which they were sex typed. For example, students with opposite-sex siblings can recall whether they received different messages on gender appropriateness in such areas as the age at which they were first allowed to walk to the store alone or to go on a date, their curfew as teenagers, and so on. Students without opposite-sex siblings can compare the gender appropriateness of messages they received from their parents with those received by their classmates.

Much attention has been given to the role of the media and its portrayal of gender appropriateness. Often, girls and women in the media (e.g., television, film, and advertising) are shown in stereotypical fashion as young, thin, sexy, smiling, acquiescent, provocative, and available homemakers and caregivers. Men, on the other hand, are usually portrayed as independent, powerful, successful, tough, natural leaders, and breadwinners (Godwyll and Annin 2007). We are not passive receptors of media presentations, however. We engage with the information given to us and construct our own ways of behaving, sometimes imitating, sometimes resisting models offered to us (Tepperman and Blain 2006). Consider, for example, the fact that many of the feminists of the 1960s and 1970s watched 1950s sitcoms wherein women were shown as homemakers and men as breadwinners. These television shows did not stop feminists from seeking gender equity. Still, today, young girls (ages eight to twelve) are bombarded with unrealistic media images of beauty, and they grow up thinking that if they do not look like the supermodels adorning the covers of nearly every magazine on newsstands, there is something wrong with them. Young girls are often concerned with issues that confront women, such as body fat, perfume, eyeliner, lipstick, rouge, and whether they should have a nose job. Teenage girls are having breast-augmentation surgery—in high school, a period when most girls are still developing.

Teens, especially girls, receive numerous messages from the media, such as the teen magazines shown here, that discuss how they should look, act, and dress.

The workplace represents a social institution in transition as it relates to gender roles. The days when mothers were expected to stay at home have disappeared. The idea that women should be allowed to work—in any profession—is nearly universally accepted in the United States. What has not disappeared, however, is the glass ceiling. The term "glass ceiling" is a metaphor describing how many women find their

What Do You Think?

How much influence do the media have on how boys and girls believe they are supposed to look and act? Are some boys and girls more susceptible than others to the media's influence? What do you think?

attempts to reach the very top of the occupational hierarchy hampered by a rigid barrier (the ceiling concept). Women will be promoted through many ranks and may find themselves so close to the top that they can see it (the glass concept), and yet, they never quite attain the top positions. Consider, for example, that in 2010, of the Fortune 500 companies, only fifteen had female CEOs (CNNMoney.com 2010). At Xerox, Ursla Burns became the first woman CEO to replace a woman, Anne Mulcahy, as a Fortune 500 chief (CNNMoney.com 2010). With this description in mind, we can define the **glass ceiling** as a barrier that interferes with the promotion of a qualified person within an organizational hierarchy because of sex discrimination. Victims of glass ceiling practices and policies may suffer from emotional pain and distress, degradation, shame, humiliation, and loss of dignity.

Gender roles and the workplace provide another very important area of study for sociologists: the concept of equal pay for equal work. When men were expected to be the primary breadwinners for their families, employers felt it necessary, in general, to pay them a higher salary than women. The reasoning was that men needed to take care of their families. As women entered the workplace in large numbers (over the past few decades), they increasingly demanded "equal pay for equal work." Today, in most cases, opposite-sex coworkers are probably being paid fairly equally for similar job descriptions when they have similar qualifications and experience. Still, many people point to overall differences in earnings between men and women as an indicator of gender inequality in the workplace. For example, in 2007, women earned about eighty cents for every dollar men earned (U.S. Bureau of Labor Statistics 2008a). This statistic can be interpreted, on face value, as evidence of gender inequity in pay. Sociologists dig deeper, however, and analyze why such a difference occurs. We find that all women do not make 20 percent less than their male counterparts at their specific workplaces; rather, many women hold lower-paying service jobs—more women than men are child-care workers, waitresses, and nurse's aides, for example. These lower-paying service jobs are referred to as **pink-collar jobs**. Women also tend to pursue the lowest-paying professional careers, most notably in teaching and occupational therapy (U.S. Bureau of Labor Statistics 2011). Because a disproportionate number of women work in lower-paying jobs than men, when the salaries of all men and all women are combined, the difference in average salary between them equals about 20 percent. In some cases, women may prefer these types of jobs because the more flexible hours help them accommodate family obliga-

Relatively low-paying service jobs that are traditionally held by women are referred to as "pink collar" jobs.

tions. In other cases, women are relegated to such positions because they are not given equal opportunities in the higher-paying occupations.

> **What Do You Think?**
>
> In the jobs you have held, did your opposite-sex coworker(s) make more, less, or the same amount of money as you? Were opportunities for promotion the same for male and female workers? Was this fair? What do you think?

Another social influence on norms of gender appropriateness is the institution of religion. Within Christianity, different denominations have been struggling with questions of male and female roles and how literally (or not) to interpret biblical teachings on such questions. Roman Catholicism continues to ordain only men as priests, for example. The Southern Baptist denomination's rather specific view of the roles of men and women was reaffirmed during its 1998 convention. Among the resolutions to be adhered to were that "'a wife is to submit graciously to the servant leadership of her husband even as the church willingly submits to the headship of Christ.' . . . Husbands and wives are of 'equal worth before God' and both bear 'God's image,' but in differing ways, the statement said. A wife 'has the God-given responsibility to respect her husband and to serve as his helper in managing her household and nurturing the next generation'" (Stammer 1998, p. A1). Most Southern Baptist congregations adhere to a literal interpretation of the Bible, which includes citing various New Testament references that distinguish the roles of women from those of men. For example, the New International Version Bible states, "A woman should learn in quietness and full submission. I do not permit a woman to teach or to have authority over a man; she must be silent" (1 Timothy 2:11–14).

Female rabbis also face discrimination because of gender role expectations. The largest Jewish congregations do not have female senior rabbis, and annual salary discrepancies between rabbis of the same level vary by as much as $28,000 (Zelizer 2004). This practice has engendered the phrase "stained-glass ceiling" to refer to women who are denied promotion or relegated to "lesser" roles (e.g., specialized ministries like music, youth, or Bible studies) within the institution of religion (Van Biema 2004).

As this brief review of the impact of the agents of socialization on gender appropriateness and gender roles reveals, men and women are not treated equally in society. As a result, society is stratified by gender, just as it is by economics and race and ethnicity.

UNDERSTANDING GENDER STRATIFICATION

Why is society stratified by gender? A number of theoretical explanations are provided later in this chapter, but for now, let us examine the role of patriarchy. **Patriarchy** refers to male-dominated societies wherein socioeconomic and political power is controlled primarily by males. In contrast, a **matriarchy** refers to female-dominated societies. Historically, most nations have been patriarchal in design. That few societies are egalitarian (i.e., socioeconomic and political power is shared equally) all but guarantees a system of gender stratification that has left many women in a subservient position.

Karl Marx and Friedrich Engels traced the origins of gender stratification to the prehistoric form of the family, where women, because they were biologically capable of bearing and nursing children, took on the role of primary caregiver, while men, more or less by default, took on the role of primary provider (e.g., hunting for food). Women, because they were responsible for taking care of the children, became dependent on men to provide food, clothing, and shelter. This dependence came to be viewed as both a necessity and a sign of weakness (Tucker 1978). The average male has always been physically stronger and faster than the average female, so this perceived "weakness" became further reinforced in patriarchal societies.

Differential placement in society's social structure as a result of gender stratification has led to an unequal opportunity and reward system that often disadvantages women in many social institutions. Furthermore, gender stratification leads to sexism and sexual harassment.

Sexism and Sexual Harassment

Sexism is defined as behavior, conditions, or attitudes that foster stereotypical social roles based on sex and lead to discrimination against members of one sex due to preferential treatment of members of the other sex. Historically, women have been victims of sexism far more often than men, but both men and women may be victimized. There are two primary forms of sexism, ideological and institutional. **Ideological sexism** is the belief that one sex is inferior to another and stresses gender appropriateness based on gender roles. **Institutional sexism**, on the other hand, refers to systematic practices and patterns within social institutions (e.g., the glass ceiling) that lead to inequality between men and women.

Sexual harassment is a byproduct of sexist attitudes. That is, a sexist attitude is similar to prejudice in that it refers to a belief, and sexual harassment is like discrimination because it refers to behavior (see Chapter 8 for a discussion of the differences between prejudice and discrimination). A violation of U.S. law, sexual harassment involves making deliberate or repeated, unwanted, and offensive verbal comments, gestures, or sexual advances that tend to create a hostile or offensive environment. The most commonly recognized form of sexual harassment occurs in the workplace. Victims of sexual harassment in the workplace may sue under Title VII of the Civil Rights Act of 1964. The two primary forms of workplace sexual harassment involve quid pro quo bargaining and hostile work environments. Quid pro quo is a Latin term meaning, "something for something"; it refers to the performance of some act in return for something else. Thus, a harasser might tell a victim, "I will give you a promotion if you provide me with sexual favors." A hostile work environment exists when an employee experiences workplace harassment and fears going to work because of the offensive, intimidating, or oppressive atmosphere. Because workplace supervisors are more often than not males, females are more likely to be victims of workplace sexual harassment.

If we revisit the introductory story for this chapter, we will recall that in 1972, girls were not allowed to play Little League baseball. Girls and women were discriminated against in sports as well as most other social institutions. The passage of Title IX led to the removal of institutional sexism in sport within educational settings (see "A Closer Look" Box 9.3 to learn more about Title IX and its impact on fighting institutional sexism).

Theories of Gender Stratification

The functionalist approach mirrors Marx's belief that the division of labor can be traced to the role of men and women in the family because of women's role in reproduction. Whereas Marx was more concerned about the power relationships that developed because of the division of labor, functionalists put forth the practical aspect of such an arrangement. That is, some people need to raise and nurture the next generation, and others need to provide subsistence. Thus, men as providers and women as nurturers serve vital, or functional, roles within the family structure in particular and within society in general. In short, functionalists argue that a gendered division of labor helps to secure the survival of the human species. The functionalist perspective was very popular in the first half of the twentieth century.

In the 1960s—which, as we know, were characterized by significant changes in many major social institutions, including the role of women in the family and the workplace—functionalism was eclipsed by the conflict perspective. Conflict theorists argued that traditional gender role expectations were exploitative of women and caused a great imbalance in social power between the sexes. Because men held the power, maintaining it was in their best interest. The conflict perspective argues that men use various devices (e.g., the glass ceiling) to keep their privileged position. Gender stratification exists because those in power (men) value controlling the means of production. Conflict theorists and feminists (feminism is discussed later in this chapter) attempt to reveal that gender roles are man-made

A Closer Look

Box 9.3 The Impact of Title IX

The most significant single event to occur for women in sports was the passage of Title IX of the Education Amendments of 1972 (20 USC 1681). Title IX was the first comprehensive federal legislation created to prohibit sex discrimination in education programs that receive federal financial assistance. This includes public elementary, secondary, and postsecondary schools and public and private universities. Since nearly every educational institution receives some type of federal funding, nearly all are required to comply with Title IX. Title IX is enforced by the Office for Civil Rights (OCR) of the U.S. Department of Education. This legislation requires educational institutions to maintain policies, practices, and programs that do not discriminate against anyone based on sex. Under this law, males and females are to receive equal funding and treatment in all areas of education including athletics. The OCR has the authority to develop policies regarding the regulations it enforces.

Before Title IX, athletic budgets were overwhelmingly slanted toward male sports. As an example, a friend who attended a public high school in the 1960s remembers being one of many girls who baked cookies for bake sales to help raise money for the school to buy a "weight machine" (similar to today's Nautilus training apparatus). When the machine was successfully purchased, it was proudly displayed at a school dance—and no girls were allowed to touch it. It was for the exclusive use of the boys in the school. Title IX was designed to eliminate such widespread examples of discrimination in educational settings. Three basic aspects of Title IX apply to athletics: participation and accommodation (offering sports programs), athletic financial assistance (scholarships), and "other" athletic program areas. The implementation of Title IX meant that male students would have to share the better facilities (gymnasium, weight rooms, swimming pool, etc.), the better practice times (previously, women were usually given late-night or early-morning practice times), and, most importantly, financial resources. "The impact of Title IX has been clear and dramatic. In 1972 only one girl in twenty-seven played a sport sponsored by her high school, and colleges spent a total of $100,000 on athletic scholarships for women. By 1996, one girl in three played a sport sponsored by her high school, and colleges spent a total of $180 million on athletic scholarships for women. The participation of women in college sports increased fourfold between 1970 and 1999, from 31,000 to 110,000" (Porto 2003, pp. 13–14).

Title IX does not require that men's programs be cut to accommodate women's programs. It is each school's choice whether to cut men's programs in an effort to comply with Title IX or to add women's programs. Due to the decreasing amount of money available to an increasing number of schools, cutting men's sports programs is often viewed as the best fiscal decision. Numerous men's gymnastics, wrestling, swimming, track and field, water polo, and baseball teams have been cut over the past three decades, and Title IX compliance is usually cited as the reason (Delaney and Madigan 2009a). Because Title IX is supposed to fight discrimination based on sex, men have attempted, generally unsuccessfully, to use the law to stop cuts to their sports programs. In 2005, for example, the Supreme Court rejected the National Wrestling Coaches Association's claim that Title IX was a form of discrimination against male athletes because of the large number of cuts in wrestling programs across the United States.

What Do You Think?

There have been many reactions to Title IX. A large number of male athletes feel threatened by this legislation because they worry that their sports programs will be weakened or even eliminated. Conversely, female athletes feel that its implementation is critical for female sports participation to continue. What do you think?

and therefore amenable to change. Change that leads to equality between men and women is the goal of the conflict perspective.

A third approach to explaining gender stratification is symbolic interactionism, which focuses on the meanings and symbolism involved in the social construction of gender role stratification. Especially important in the creation and maintenance of gender stratification are the messages we receive and the manner in which we interpret them. Let us revisit Charles Horton Cooley's looking glass self theory—which states that our self-image is a product of messages we receive from others—and apply it to gender stratification. This theory suggests that if boys and girls (and men and women) receive different messages for the same behavior, they will see themselves as different.

For example, say a young boy falls from a tree branch, lands awkwardly, and scrapes his knee, causing it to bleed. He then goes inside the house, crying to his mother for help. If his mother tells him, while she is bandaging his knee, "Big boys don't cry. Now go back outside and play," he has been told, in essence, to suppress his emotions and go face his obstacles. These are masculine traits. Now, say this boy has a twin sister, who falls from the same tree branch, lands awkwardly, and scrapes her knee, causing it to bleed. She goes running inside the house, crying to her mother. And the mother tells her, while she is bandaging her knee and hugging her daughter, "There, there, let it all out. Mommy will take care of you. Why don't you go play with your doll on the couch and watch some television?" The daughter has received a completely different message than her brother. She has been encouraged to express her emotions and engage in a passive activity (watching TV) while being overly nurtured. She has been feminized. Thus, if the same situation (falling from a tree branch) elicits entirely different reactions from a significant caregiver based on sex, the recipients learn to see differences between the genders; different roles are assigned to people based on their gender. When a significant number of people in society buy into specific expectations of individuals based on sex, gender stratification results.

Gender Stratification in Other Cultures

The United States, of course, is not the only nation where gender stratification will be found. Some societies are less stratified, while others are more so. According to the World Economic Forum's (WEF) "Global Gender Gap Report 2010," the Nordic nations of Iceland, Norway, Finland, and Sweden have the greatest equality between men and women (see Table 9.1). The report measures equity in politics,

What Do You Think?

Three sociological theories have been presented in an attempt to explain why gender stratification exists in society. Which theory seems the most plausible? What do you think?

TABLE 9.1 Global Gender Gap Index

2010 RANK	COUNTRY	2009 RANK
1	Iceland	1
2	Norway	2
3	Finland	3
4	Sweden	4
5	New Zealand	5
6	Ireland	8
7	Denmark	7
8	Lesotho	10
9	Philippines	9
10	Switzerland	13

Source: World Economic Forum 2010.

education, employment, and health (WEF 2010). The United States' rank rose from thirty-first in 2009 to nineteenth in 2010, primarily because of a higher number of women in President Barack Obama's administration and a reduction in the country's gender pay gap.

Among the nations in which gender is much more stratified are Afghanistan, Saudi Arabia, and Kenya. In Afghanistan, life is slightly better today for women than under the rule of the Taliban, but according to Human Rights Watch (2007), soldiers, police, and terrorists frequently attack women. Many women do not leave their homes because they fear being kidnapped, raped, or robbed.

In Saudi Arabia, where breast cancer is considered a taboo, women often ignore growing tumors in their breasts until it is too late for treatment. Documented cases reveal that women fear seeing a male doctor, and men divorce women diagnosed with the disease; in one incident, an angry crowd dragged a woman from a mammogram machine because the technicians were men (Abu-Nasr 2007). In 2004, Saudi women were not allowed to vote or run for office in Saudi Arabia's first nationwide election. Saudi women suffer a number of indignities because of the influence of the religious establishment: they must have written permission from a male guardian to travel, get an education, or work. Even with "permission" they are not allowed to drive, mingle with men in public, or leave the home without covering themselves with an abaya. An abaya is a loose, usually black, cloak or robe worn by Muslim women, especially in Arabic-speaking regions, covering the body from head to toe and often worn with a headscarf and veil.

In parts of Kenya, a girl's value is equivalent to the dowry price she can fetch for her father (usually a few goats and blankets). Girls are also subjected to genital mutilation—the cutting away or removal of all or some of the external genital organs, especially the clitoris. The United Nations has opposed female genital mutilation since the early 1950s, but the practice is still widespread throughout Africa (Dixon 2004). Traditionally, girls faced the procedure around age seventeen, but village elders have been targeting girls as young as eight, when they are less likely to resist, because an increasing number of girls (with and without their mothers' blessing) are fleeing their villages to avoid mutilation. The girls are running away because the procedure is both humiliating and painful. The first cut, made during an annual public ceremony, is small and symbolic. "The girls are then taken to a seclusion [*sic*] hut where the major operation takes place using a knife or blade and no anesthetic to remove the external sexual organs, including all or part of the clitoris and labia" (Dixon 2004, p. A12). Girls who scream out in pain bring shame to their families. Furthermore, because such operations are typically performed under nonsterile conditions, they can cause infections and septicemia; the long-term effects of such mutilation include the formation of scar tissue that can cause recurrent urinary tract infections and interfere with intercourse or childbirth (United Nations Population Fund 2009).

Girls in Kenya forced to endure the painful ritual of genital mutilation, women lacking the right to vote and dress as they please in Saudi Arabia, and women in Afghanistan who fear for their lives in venturing outside their homes represent the tip of the iceberg of gender stratification found around the world. Although gender stratification is not as severe in the United States, it is a land that professes "equality for all."

In March 2008, Secretary of State Condoleezza Rice hosted the first-ever U.S.-led summit to combat violence against women (representatives from seventeen countries attended). Rice believes that ending violence against women should be a global priority. She is especially devoted to ending human trafficking, which she calls "the slave trade of the modern world" (Winik 2008, p. 10). In more than one hundred nations around the world, women and children are the victims of human trafficking. Human trafficking is the modern version of slavery wherein the victims are forced into involuntary servitude and prostitution; some are forced to become child soldiers (generally boys). "The State Department estimates that 800,000 people are moved across international borders each year by traffickers and millions more are forcibly transported within their own countries" (Winik 2008, p. 10).

Perhaps the leading force in the fight for equality among the genders is feminism. Our attention thus turns to feminism, which represents both an ideological platform to fight for the rights of women everywhere and a social movement designed to bring about an end to gender stratification.

FEMINISM

Feminism may be defined as a social movement and an ideology in support of the idea that a larger share of scarce resources (e.g., wealth, power, income, and status) should go to women. Feminists hope to show that gender stratification is the result of historic, man-made conditions, not natural, biological differences.

Feminism is a women-centered approach to the study of human behavior. It advocates for oppressed women. Through analysis of gender roles and gender appropriateness, feminist theory demonstrates how women have historically been subjected to a double standard in both their treatment and the evaluation of their worth.

Although a number of activists from diverse backgrounds have worked to improve women's position in society for the past few centuries, two clearly identifiable waves of feminism in the United States made significant inroads toward this goal. The first significant wave of feminism began in the 1830s as part of the abolitionist movement. These early feminists strove to gain equal rights for women in all social institutions, but especially within the family, education, and the sociopolitical realm. In 1848, a group of women led by Lucretia Mott, a Quaker preacher, and Elizabeth Cady Stanton, wife of an abolitionist lawyer, organized the first Women's Rights Convention in Seneca Falls, New York. The convention brought to light many of the social institutions designed to discriminate against women (institutional sexism). For example, "Once a woman married, she forfeited her legal existence. She couldn't sign a contract, make a will, or sue in a court of law. If she received property from her father or some other source, her husband could sell it and keep the money for himself" (Gurko 1974, p. 8).

More than three hundred people attended this conference on women's rights. Besides shining a light on the inequality women faced in society, it also established the "Declaration of Sentiments." Modeled after the Declaration of Independence, this document addressed concrete issues that concerned early feminists. The Women's Rights Convention also marked the beginning of a seventy-two-year battle to gain women the right to vote in the United States. As a result of this convention, Seneca Falls has gained the distinction of being the birthplace of American feminism. This first wave of feminism continued for more than seventy years, culminating in 1920 with the passage of the Nineteenth Amendment to the U.S. Constitution, which guarantees women the right to vote.

The birthplace of feminism and the women's rights movement in the United States is located in Seneca Falls, NY. Shown here is the site of the first Women's Rights Convention held in 1848.

The second, and contemporary, wave of feminism began in the 1960s and was influential in the passage of a number of pieces of landmark legislation, including the Equal Pay Act of 1963, the Civil Rights Act of 1964, and Title IX in 1972 (discussed earlier in this chapter). Although a constitutional amendment stating that equal rights under the law shall not be denied on the basis of sex passed both houses of Congress in 1972, it failed to gain the required ratification by two-thirds of the fifty states within the ten-year time limit. In 2009, one of President Barack Obama's first acts as president was to sign the Lilly Ledbetter Fair Pay Act into law. The contemporary wave of feminism has focused on gaining women equal rights through legal reform and legislating antidiscriminatory policies.

Modern-day feminists are concerned about civil rights, gay and lesbian issues, homelessness, AIDS activism, environmental concerns, and human rights in general. The growth of women's studies programs on college campuses has further assisted the feminist agenda.

Variations of Feminist Thought

A variety of feminist approaches emerged as a result of this second wave of feminism. They include liberal (sometimes called egalitarian) feminism, Marxist feminism, radical feminism, socialist feminism, and postmodern feminism.

- *Liberal feminism* is the most mainstream variation. It is based on the idea that all people are created equal and should be treated equally. Liberal feminists believe that the greatest obstacle to gender equity is sexism. Sexism leads to prejudice and discrimination against women and therefore serves as a barrier against equality.
- *Marxist feminism* is inspired by the ideas of Karl Marx and conflict theory. Like Marx and Engels, Marxist feminists trace the origins of gender stratification to the gender role expectations found in the family. "Marxist feminists stress that only a revolutionary restructuring of property relations can change a social system where women are more likely to be exploited than men" (Delaney 2005, p. 206).
- *Radical feminism* views the patriarchal system as a sexual system of power wherein men possess political and economic power and control the resources necessary to maintain their power position. They too view sexism as an ultimate tool of power. Radical feminists also believe that men use violence in the form of rape, incest, sexual harassment, and battery as a weapon of sexual power in an attempt to subjugate women. Radical feminists are against all existing social structures because they are believed to have been created by men.
- *Socialist feminism* points to the role of women in the family and the capitalist system as the major cause of gender inequality in society. Capitalism creates a class-based system. Inherent in any class-based socioeconomic system is the realization that there will always be people on the bottom social rungs. Socialist feminists argue that unpaid housework is a prime example of devaluing the role of women in society. In short, "socialist feminists argue that change in women's social status will occur only through a transformation of the economic system, along with a change in the way household work is evaluated" (Delaney 2005, p. 208).
- *Postmodern feminism* criticizes the dominant social order, especially its patriarchal aspects, from a postmodern theoretical perspective. Postmodernists argue that the concepts and outlooks used to examine the world in the

> past no longer apply to the analysis of the world today. Thus, basic forms of knowledge come into question, including the roles of men and women in society. Postmodern feminism encourages a careful consideration of the taken-for-granted gender-stratified world and stresses equality between men and women.

I routinely ask my college students if they consider themselves to be feminists, and most respond no. This does not mean, however, that college students are not in favor of equality between the sexes; they are. Here is the big question: is feminism dead? The National Organization for Women would say that feminism is alive and well. According to its website, NOW is the largest organization of feminist activists in the United States. Located in all fifty states and the District of Columbia, NOW has 550 total chapters and over half a million members (NOW 2009). Since its inception in 1966, NOW has striven to take action to bring about equality for women; eliminate discrimination and harassment in the workplace, schools, the justice system, and all other spheres of society; secure abortion, birth-control, and reproductive rights for all women; end all forms of violence against women; eradicate racism, sexism, and homophobia; and promote equality and justice in American society (NOW 2009).

The efforts of NOW are evidence of the vitality of the feminist movement. Certainly, the advantages women of today enjoy compared to women of the past result, in great part, from the feminist movement. Nonetheless, many social commentators and educators question whether younger women today embrace the feminist ideal. For a view of feminism from a younger perspective, see "A Closer Look" Box 9.4.

LESBIAN, GAY, BISEXUAL, AND TRANSGENDERED PERSONS

Stephen Maddison (2000) explains that the rhetoric and ideology of the women's movement during the 1960s and 1970s assisted the gay liberation movement that followed. The attention that feminists brought to gay and lesbian issues led to a specialized subfield of sociology concerned with lesbian, gay, bisexual, and transgendered (LGBT) persons. There has been so much academic discourse about these individuals that the acronym LGBT has automatic meaning to sociologists. However, as Brian de Vries (2007) states, "*LGBT* has become a ubiquitous acronym. Its reference to lesbian, gay, bisexual, and transgender people suggests an inclusive community united by sexual identity or sexual orientation" (p. 18). As de Vries indicates, lesbian, gay, bisexual, and transgendered persons do not all share similar life experiences. Furthermore, additional letters have been added to the LGBT acronym—most notably, *Q* for "queer."

A Closer Look

Box 9.4 Younger Women's View of Feminism

Sandy Banks, a columnist for the *Los Angeles Times,* wrote a column on April 10, 2009, titled, "A Younger View of Feminism." Banks describes a panel she sat on a month earlier at a West Hollywood Women's Leadership Conference titled "The F Word: Reflections of Feminism of Women in the Media." She was struck by the fact that today's twenty-something women are beneficiaries of feminism, and yet the movement does not resonate with them. The twenty-something women whom Banks and other panelists describe enjoy getting "dolled up" and looking sexy—not that there is anything wrong with that. "What's wrong is that the 'consumer culture' has become such a defining force in young women's search for identity. It's what you're wearing, what your weight is, rather than what you believe in, how you think" (Banks 2009, p. A2). One panelist at the conference stated, "A poll of seniors at her daughter's private school found that only one of 125 girls considered herself a feminist" (Banks 2009, p. A2). Banks (2009) further states, "Our panelists were talking about politics and ideology. Our daughters are talking more about social equality.... Our history is not their history. They cannot remember a time when abortion was illegal; when a star female soccer player couldn't expect a college scholarship.... Now, as panelist Katie Buckland noted, you've got 'feminist strippers' who consider sexuality a route to female empowerment, rather than a reflection of male domination" (p. A2).

Syndicated columnist Suzanne Fields discussed the glass ceiling concept from a contemporary feminist perspective in a June 22, 2009, column titled "Goal: Break Glass Ceiling or Get Glass Slipper?" Fields (2009) states, "No one any longer regards it as worth remarking when a woman becomes a doctor, lawyer, editor, astronaut, or CEO. Women have shattered a lot of glass ceilings, and when nobody notices the broken glass, that's a sign of progress. If women haven't gained equality (or superiority) in numbers sufficient to please feminist advocates, few argue that women can't compete with men on level playing fields.... All they have to do is show up.... Women have higher high school and college graduation rates, and they're healthier and live longer than men" (p. A12). Fields explains that feminists are upset that men have not completely bought into the ideals of feminism but warns that there may be a bigger problem: the revolution of young women. This "revolution" is tied to some of the same things described by Sandy Banks. Fields makes note of the current little-girl fashion craze for "princess dresses" (see "Connecting Sociology and Popular Culture Box 5.1 for a discussion of princess socialization). Fields (2009) states, "Little girls yearn to be a pink sleeping beauty, a lavender Rapunzel or a pale-blue Cinderella, wouldn't dream of suiting up in pants like their mothers. They're dreaming of a glass slipper, not the glass ceiling" (p. A12).

What Do You Think?

I have asked my students for years if they consider themselves feminists, and very few say yes. Despite this, nearly all women indicate that they want equality. Is it possible to seek gender equity without being a feminist? Are Banks and Fields correct in their assessment of twenty-something women and their perspective on feminism? What do you think?

Being "Queer"

The *Q* of LGBTQ is of particular interest because, in the past, calling a gay person "queer" was considered an offensive insult. Alyssa Howe (2004) explains that the term "queer" became popularized in the early 1990s because it includes gay men, lesbians, bisexuals, transgendered persons, and other "sexual radicals (those who practice sadomasochism, bondage and discipline, etc.)" (p. 251). The title of "queer" serves to rally gay people under one umbrella "identity" (Howe 2004). Sociologist Maayan-Rahel Simon (2005), for example, claims that she has chosen "to identify as queer because where *lesbian* suggests only that my orientation is sexually related, *queer* associates me with a movement to reclaim myself and come out from under my oppression.... To embrace the term *queer* within 'gay and lesbian culture' is to finally put an accurate name to all the feelings of awkwardness and insecurity in being comfortable with our desires and affections as nonheterosexual individuals in a heterosexist society" (p. 14). Thus, as Simon explains, the term "queer" is embraced by many gay people because it represents a social movement as much as an identity. This movement is quite popular, as nearly every major regional and national sociology conference has numerous sessions on "queer-related" topics (e.g., queer studies). The queer movement embraced a slogan so popular—"I'm here, I'm queer, get used to it"—that its usage has passed into popular culture.

That gay people may embrace the term "queer" indicates the growing acceptance of and openness in discussing the gay identity. Throughout most of history, gay people have generally hidden their sexual orientation. Around the 1970s and 1980s, gay people started "coming out of the closet" and openly displayed their sexual identities. Contemporary television shows such as *The Simpsons* discuss the gay identity in a fairly open manner. *The Simpsons* addresses the "queer" issue in the episode appropriately named "Homer's Phobia" (1997b). In this episode, Homer discovers that his new friend John is gay and reveals his homophobia. John asks Homer what he has against gays. Homer replies, "They turned the navy into a floating joke. They ruined all of our best names. Like Bruce, Lance, and Julian. Those were the toughest names we had. Now, they're just, ah—" John interrupts Homer and says, "Queer?" Homer nods in agreement and adds, "And that's another thing. I resent that you people use that word. That's our word for making fun of you. We need it." This conversation mirrors the changes in the meaning and application of the word "queer" in recent years.

It should be noted, however, that it is primarily the younger generation of gays who have adopted the "queer" term. Older gay people are not as comfortable using it as their younger counterparts. Furthermore, as Howe (2004) explains, using the term "queer" comes with problems as differences of race, class, and gender within the gay community are minimized or ignored. Further complicating our understanding of the *Q* word is the realization that the letter *Q* also applies those who are questioning their sexual identities (de Vries 2007).

Transgendered Persons

Transgendered people have a unique status that does not seem to fit the LGBT collective category. "They include people who present themselves as male or female, or both, in varying situations. They include people who may be postoperative, preoperative (e.g., transitioning), or nonoperative male-to-female (MTF) or female-to-male (FTM) in status" (de Vries 2007, p. 20). A **transgendered person** is not necessarily gay. Transgendered people believe that they were born into the opposite-sex body to the gender with which they identify. Typically, a transgendered person struggles internally with his or her sexual identity. Such individuals may experience emotional distress that most others cannot possibly understand. Often, when a transgendered person begins to experiment with behaviors generally expected of an opposite-sex person, family members and friends react negatively.

A transgendered person may eventually reach a point in his or her life when a sex change operation is deemed necessary to stop "living a lie." (Note: The 2005 film *Transamerica* provides a glimpse into the world of a person going through the sex-change procedure.) Once the decision is made to have a sex change, hormone therapy and psychological counseling, sometimes spanning several years, begin (Young 2000). This eventually leads to sex-reassignment surgery (the existing genitals are removed and replaced with those of the new sex). Next, the transgendered person faces the need to change his or her forms of identification (e.g., driver's license, passport, Social Security card, etc.), which accompanies a name change. For example, I know of a person born as a male and named "Daniel," who, after a sex-change operation, changed her name to "Danielle."

Changing sexual identities does not necessarily bring the satisfaction that transgendered persons hope for, as family members and close friends may shun them—this has been the case for the person I knew formerly as Daniel. Danielle informs me that she has received one form of inner peace but still suffers from others' inability to accept her in the same way she sees herself.

As with queers, it may be argued that placing transgendered persons under a collective umbrella such as LGBTQ has its problems because it deemphasizes the different life experiences and other socioeconomic variables that help to identify individuals. However, a justification for using this collective term rests with the realization that many persons under the LGBTQ umbrella face harassment, name-calling, and physical assault.

LGBTQ Victimization

All LGBTQ persons face prejudice and discrimination. They risk being misunderstood and mislabeled by members of the predominant heterosexual society. LGBTQ persons are especially vulnerable to prejudice and discrimination during the teenage years; this is particularly true at school. As Sarah Holmes and Sean Cahill (2005) explain, "Gay, lesbian, bisexual, and transgender (GLBT) youth are coming out younger, on average at the age of sixteen. Many become dangerously isolated—rejected by family and friends, harassed and attacked by their peers in school, and demeaned by society. Because of their youth, many lack independent resources and may have a hard time accessing support" (p. 63).

According to the Southern Poverty Law Center (SPLC) (2007), "LGBTQ students, as well as students perceived by peers to be gay, are the most common targets of harassment at school. That harassment can reach its most fevered pitch in middle school. . . . In 2005, 64 percent of middle school students reported anti-gay bullying and name-calling as major problems in their schools—18 percentage points higher than what was reported by high school students" (p. 32). As a result of this bullying and the increasing number of straight students who find bullying unacceptable in their schools, a number of gay-straight alliances (GSA) have formed. These student-run clubs create safe spaces for gay youth and their allies. GSA clubs also organize campus-wide events designed to increase acceptance of marginalized groups and reduce prejudice, discrimination, and bullying.

One of the most popular events organized by GSAs is the "Day of Silence" celebrated by students across the nation. On this day, held in April each year (e.g., April 25 in 2008), students go through an entire day without speaking, often wearing rainbow ribbons or black armbands, in recognition of the daily harassment faced by LGBTQ students (SPLC 2007).

A gay rights parade in Manchester, England, in 2011 with participants carrying placards that state, "Some People Are Gay."

It is against U.S. law to discriminate against anyone. However, as we learned in Chapter 8, when a crime is perpetrated against a person, property, or society that is motivated, in whole or part, by the offender's bias against a person's sexual orientation (or race, religion, disability, ethnicity, or national origin), a hate crime has been committed. Bias crimes against transgendered persons are now recognized as hate crimes. In May 2009, a jury in Colorado convicted Allen Andrade of beating eighteen-year-old Angie Zapata to death with a fire extinguisher after discovering she was biologically male (*The Citizen,* 8/19/09). In August 2009, a Syracuse, New York, laborer became the second person in the nation to be convicted of a hate crime in a transgender slaying that drew a twenty-five-year sentence. Dwight DeLee received the harshest penalty allowed for manslaughter as a hate crime in the November 2008 slaying of Moses Lateisha Green. Green was born a male but began living as a woman at age sixteen and dressed frequently in women's clothing (*The Citizen,* 8/19/09).

What Do You Think?

Have you ever participated in a "Day of Silence"? Does your campus participate in this event? What else do you believe can be done to end harassment, name-calling, and physical assault against LGBTQ persons? What do you think?

Despite legislation designed to protect LGBTQ persons, many still face prejudice, discrimination, bullying, teasing, and physical assaults. LGBTQ persons are sometimes discriminated against on television, too (see "Connecting Sociology and Popular Culture Box" 9.5 to learn more about being gay on TV).

LGBTQ persons are protected from discriminatory practices in the United States and most Western societies. This was not always the case in the United States as antisodomy laws were in existence, in some cases directed against homosexuals and in others against homosexuals and heterosexuals. On June 26, 2003, the U.S. Supreme Court ruled 6–3 that sodomy laws are unconstitutional. However, gay sex is still illegal in eighty countries, and at least seven impose the death penalty for homosexual acts—usually under Islamic law (Jubera, Paterik, and Lewis 2010). Homosexual acts are punishable by death in Iran, Saudi Arabia, the United Arab Emirates, Yemen, Mauritania, and parts of Nigeria and Sudan (Jubera, Paterik, and Lewis 2010). In the African nation of Malawi, in May 2010, a judge sentenced a male couple to the maximum fourteen years in prison with hard labor under Malawi's antigay legislation. Crowds outside the courthouse cheered magistrate Nyakwawa Usiwa-Usiwa's decision, and many said they believed the sentence was too lenient (*Post-Standard,* 5/23/10). Twenty-year-old Tiwonge Chimbalanga, a hotel janitor, and Steven Monjeza, unemployed, were arrested on December 27, 2009, the day after they celebrated their engagement with a party at the hotel where Chimbalanga worked—an apparent first in Malawi. The magistrate ruled that the couple had committed unnatural acts (sodomy) and gross indecency. (Note: Gay marriage is discussed further in Chapter 10.)

Amidst nearly global condemnation of the sentence levied against Monjeza and Chimbalanga, Bingu wa Mutharika, president of Malawi, announced on May 29, 2010, that he would release the two gay men. Mutharika was quoted in newswire reports as having said, "These boys committed a crime against our culture, our religion and our laws; however, as the head of state I hereby pardon them and therefore ask for their immediate release with no conditions.... I have done this

Connecting Sociology and Popular Culture

Box 9.5 Being Gay on TV

A number of organizations such as the SPLC track incidents of prejudice and discrimination against LGBTQ persons. Some watchdog groups keep an eye on specific private sectors. In the world of entertainment, for example, the Gay & Lesbian Alliance Against Defamation (GLAAD) monitors depictions of gays and lesbians in the media. To this end, GLAAD presents awards to the television networks that best portray positive images of gay persons, thereby fostering an inclusive society.

In its fourth annual Network Responsibility Index, GLAAD found that MTV scored the highest among fifteen networks for its representation of gay characters during the 2009–2010 television season. Of MTV's 207.5 hours of original prime-time programming, 42 percent included content reflecting the lives of gay, bisexual, and transgendered people. As a result, MTV earned the first ever "excellent" rating from GLAAD. GLAAD president Jarrett Barrios praised MTV's programs *The Real World* and *America's Best Dance Crew* for offering richly diverse portrayals of gay and transgendered people that help Americans better understand the LGBT community (F. Moore 2010). Among the broadcast networks, 35 percent of the CW's content reflected the lives of lesbian, gay, bisexual, and transgendered persons; the Fox network, 30 percent; and ABC, 26 percent. As a result, these three networks received a "good" rating from GLAAD. NBC was rated "adequate" (13 percent), and CBS earned a "failing" grade (7 percent). Among the cable networks, ABC Family (37 percent), TNT (34 percent), Showtime (32 percent), Lifetime (31 percent), and HBO (26 percent) all received a "good" rating. GLAAD assigned a "failing" grade to USA (4 percent), A&E (3 percent), and TBS (2 percent) (F. Moore 2010).

For its report, GLAAD reviewed all prime-time programming—totaling 4,787.5 hours—on the major networks between June 1, 2009, and May 31, 2010, and all original prime-time programming—1,227.5 hours—on ten prominent cable networks. Programming includes dramas, comedies, unscripted fare, and newsmagazines. GLAAD also acknowledged positive parenting portrayals both in the depiction of gay couple Mitchell and Cameron, who are raising an adopted daughter on ABC's *Modern Family,* and in the story line on Fox's *Glee* in which high school student Kurt comes out as gay to his father.

What Do You Think?

Do the networks provide enough positive coverage of gay characters and issues on prime-time TV? Which shows portray gay characters and issues in a negative light? What are some differences between the portrayal of LGBT characters on TV and the actual lives of LGBT persons? What do you think?

on humanitarian grounds, but this does not mean that I support this" (*Post-Standard,* 6/2/10, p. A10). UN Secretary-General Ban Ki-moon, who visited Malawi at the end of May and met with Mutharika, is pressing the president to change the nation's law banning homosexuality. Because homosexuality goes against the culture and religion of Malawi, such a change will difficult. Gay-rights activists around the world are likely to continue pressing Malawi to change its antihomosexuality laws. Will the United States be the nation to lead the way in equality between persons whether they are gay or not?

SUMMARY

Like race and ethnicity, the concepts of sex, gender, and gender roles are socially constructed. Whereas sex refers to one's biological classification, gender refers to the socially determined expectations for behavior. These expectations become routinized as gender roles. Gender roles and notions of gender appropriateness are determined by each society's cultural norms and values. Sociologists argue that gender roles are inculcated by the agents of socialization and the socialization process.

Because they are patriarchal in design, gender stratification is a predominant characteristic of most societies. Due to gender stratification, many women occupy a subservient position in society. Gender stratification manifests itself in a variety of ways, primarily as a result of sexism and sexual harassment. In some cases, gender stratification is so widespread that institutional sexism exists.

The fight for gender equity is an ongoing battle that started in earnest with the feminist movement of the 1960s. Although there exists a number of variations of feminism, feminists generally support the idea that females and males should share equally in society's benefits and resources. Modern-day feminists have also led the fight to gain equality and fair treatment for lesbian, gay, bisexual, transgendered, and "queer" persons. LGBTQ persons are often subject to prejudice and discrimination themselves. A number of gay-straight alliances have organized on school campuses across the nation in an effort to stop bullying, harassment, physical assaults, and the general misunderstanding of LGBTQ persons.

Glossary

Feminism—A social movement and ideology in support of the idea that a larger share of scarce resources (e.g., wealth, power, income, and status) should go to women.

Gender—The set of socially determined expectations placed on individuals because of their sexual category.

Gender roles—Sets of cultural expectations that are associated with being a male (masculinity) or female (femininity).

Glass ceiling—The barrier that exists in workplaces that interferes with the promotion of qualified persons within the hierarchy of an organization because of sexual discrimination.

Ideological sexism—The belief that one sex is inferior to another and stresses gender appropriateness based on gender roles.

Institutional sexism—Systematic practices and patterns within social institutions (e.g., the glass ceiling) that lead to inequality between men and women.
LGBT—An acronym used to describe lesbians, gays, bisexuals, and transgendered persons. In some instances the letter *Q* is added to refer to "queers."
Matriarchy—Female-dominated societies in which socioeconomic and political power is controlled primarily by females.
Patriarchy—Male-dominated societies in which socioeconomic and political power is controlled primarily by males.
Pink-collar jobs—Lower-paying service jobs generally held by women.
Sex—A biological classification of male or female.
Sexism—Behavior, conditions, or attitudes that foster stereotypical social roles based on sex and that lead to discrimination against members of one sex due to preferential treatment for members of the other sex.
Social construction—The idea that all concepts exist because humans created, or built, them.
Transgendered person—A person whose gender identity or expression is different from his or her physical sex, or the sex to which the person was born.

Discussion Questions

1. Discuss how the terms "sex" and "gender" are socially constructed.
2. What does gender appropriateness mean? Have you ever been told that you were not behaving properly for your gender? Explain.
3. Are you a feminist? Why or why not? Do you believe feminism is dead or alive and kicking?
4. Have you ever noticed bullying, harassment, or physical assault against a fellow student? If yes, what did you do about it?
5. Do you believe we, as a society, are closer to eliminating racism or sexism? Explain.

Web Links

To learn more about the National Organization for Women (NOW), visit its website at www.now.org.
To learn more about the U.S. Bureau of Labor Statistics, visit its website at www.bls.gov.
To learn more about threats against human rights worldwide, visit the Human Rights Watch website at www.hrw.org.
To learn more about hate crimes against transgendered persons, visit www.civilrights.org/publications/hatecrimes/lgbt.html.
To learn more about LGBTQ-related news stories, visit the GLAAD website at www.glaad.org.

MARRIAGE AND FAMILY 10

FBI TEN MOST
WANTED FUGITIVE
UNLAWFUL FLIGHT TO AVOID PROSECUTION - SEXUAL CONDUCT WITH A
NOR, CONSPIRACY TO COMMIT SEXUAL CONDUCT WITH A MINOR; RAPE AS
AN ACCOMPLICE
WARREN STEED JEFFS

Warren Jeffs, polygamist sect leader of the Fundamentalist Church of Jesus Christ of Latter Day Saints, is known to his followers as the "Prophet."

Chapter 10

- Introductory Story
- Romantic Love, Marriage, and Divorce
- The Family
- Dimensions and Functions of the Family
- The Changing Family
- Family Abuse and Violence
- Summary, Glossary, Discussion Questions, and Web Links

INTRODUCTORY STORY

Generally, students find the subject of marriage and family quite relevant to their lives. After all, nearly everyone comes from some sort of a family, and most people are likely to get married some day (if they are not already married). In many cases, people marry more than once during their lifetimes—this is known as serial monogamy. In rare cases, someone may have multiple spouses at the same time. This type of marriage is known as polygamy. In the United States, polygamy is illegal. However, in other parts of the world, including certain areas of Africa and some Islamic countries, polygamy is legal and condoned by religious teachings.

The precise meanings of such terms as monogamy and polygamy are explained later in this chapter; for now, let us examine your perception of polygamy. When you hear the word "polygamy," what images come to mind? Do you think of HBO's popular television drama *Big Love,* a series revolving around the fictional character Bill Henrickson, his three wives, and their combined family of seven children, who live together in three neighboring houses in Sandy, Utah, a suburb of Salt Lake

City? Or do you think of such real-life polygamist leaders as Warren Jeffs—known to his followers as "The Prophet"—and his community, the Fundamentalist Church of Jesus Christ of Latter-Day Saints (FLDS)? It should be noted that the Church of Jesus Christ of Latter-Day Saints officially banned polygamy over one hundred years ago as a condition of Utah's becoming a part of the United States. The Mormon Church also excommunicates members who engage in polygamy.

The romanticized polygamist depictions of *Big Love,* which premiered on March 12, 2006, are quite different from the realities of separatist polygamist communities, such as those led by real-life polygamists like Jeffs. Polygamist communities, such as the one at Jeffs's West Texas compound, are characterized by women who are treated as chattel, young boys who are kicked out of the community so that older adult males can marry underage female relatives, and environments where incest is common. **Incest** is defined as sexual relations between persons so closely related that their marriage is illegal or forbidden by custom. In the United States, for example, sexual relations between siblings and between parents (or grandparents) and their biological children are considered incestuous. In twenty-five U.S. states, marriage between first cousins is illegal and falls under the incestuous umbrella. In nineteen states first-cousin marriage is legal, and in six states marriage is allowed under certain circumstances (National Conference of State Legislatures 2010).

When the secrets of his community were revealed, Jeffs was confronted with the laws of the land. He faced numerous charges and, as of late 2009, was serving two consecutive terms of five years to life in Utah for rape as an accomplice in the arranged marriage of a fourteen-year-old girl and her nineteen-year-old cousin (Jeffs performed the marriage). Fifth District Court judge James L. Shumate noted in his ruling that the polygamous sect leader knew marrying a fourteen-year-old girl to her cousin was illegal. In Utah, marriage between first cousins is allowed if both are sixty-five or older or if both are fifty-five or older and one is unable to reproduce (National Conference of State Legislatures 2010). The two counts of rape as an accomplice were based on Jeffs's failure to intervene when the girl objected to having sex with her cousin (husband). Appeals are pending.

This chapter discusses monogamy, serial monogamy, polygamy, and many other marriage-related topics. The ever-changing family structure is also a focus. Chances are students will see a connection between much of this material and their own lives.

ROMANTIC LOVE, MARRIAGE, AND DIVORCE

Have you ever heard the children's nursery rhyme "First comes love, then comes marriage, then comes a baby in a baby carriage"? At one time, this rhythm reflected the traditional American view of the proper order of things. This romanticized view of love, marriage, and family has changed quite a bit in contemporary society. As Max Weber might say, Let's use this ideal type and compare it to reality.

Romantic Love

Certainly some people first fall in love, then date, marry, and eventually start a family together. But what is love—and more specifically, romantic love? **Romantic love** involves a deep physical and emotional attraction. Many have pondered, How do people fall in love? Social psychologists Alfred Lindersmith, Anselm Strauss, and Norman Denzin (1991) describe the process of falling in love as similar to getting hooked on drugs. It begins as a weekend habit, and as the involvement continues and becomes more serious—often without the realization of the participants—the two become progressively more psychologically dependent on each other. As they learn more about each other and the relationship becomes more intimate, a mutual trust and dependency develops. The lovers discover that nobody else can provide them with the same high that they experience with each other. The two begin to crave each other's company and often find themselves daydreaming about each other when apart. Romantic lovers may even experience withdrawal distress when separated. At this point, they are hooked on each other.

Romantic lovers only see the positive attributes of their partners. They ignore each other's faults because they are in love. However, when lovers are asked why they love each other, the answers are often varied and unilluminating. "Like heroin users who praise the drug in exaggerated terms, lovers often extol the virtues of their partners in extremely unrealistic terms. Both love and drug addiction have their honeymoon periods when habits are new, before reality intrudes itself and brings the individual back to earth" (Lindersmith, Strauss, and Denzin 1991, p. 310).

Over time, romantic lovers may fall out of love. This involves a breaking-away process that is generally very emotional and agonizing. Withdrawal from a romantic love may be as difficult as withdrawal from a heroin addiction. The pain can stay with people for a lifetime. On the other hand, romantic love may be transformed into a more realistic and committed love that allows couples to acknowledge the flaws that each partner possesses. This is important, as deep romantic love generally only lasts a few years. In order for the relationship to survive the test of time, the couple must learn to grow beyond the limits of romantic love; they must build a relationship on shared goals, commitment, loyalty, and compromise. This type of relationship serves as a solid foundation on which to build a marriage. And that is why romantic love is idealized in American culture—because many still view it as a prerequisite to marriage.

Variations of Marriage

An interracial couple on their wedding day.

The idea that romantic love serves as a precursor to marriage is not universal. In many societies, love has little or nothing to do with getting married. Instead, families help their sons and daughters find a lifelong partner through an "arranged marriage." Cultures that embrace this custom believe that love will follow the marriage, which is viewed not in a romantic and idealistic framework but rather in terms of more pressing social concerns, such as property, power, social class, and so on. According to the 2001 *Guinness Book of World Records,* the youngest marriage recorded involved an eleven-month-old baby boy and a three-month-old girl in Bangladesh. The marriage took place in order to end a twenty-year feud between the children's families.

Sociologists examine a number of characteristics of marriage. First, we should define marriage. **Marriage** is a relatively enduring, socially approved sexual and socioeconomic relationship between at least two persons for the purpose of creating and maintaining a family. (Note: Variations and family types are discussed later in this chapter.) Being married has a number of advantages over being single. For example, married men and women—especially men—are likely to live longer than those who are not married (Waite 2002). Research conducted by the National Center for Health Statistics (2008) also reveals that married people tend to be healthier than unmarried people. Married people are sick less often and are more active. They smoke and drink less and, in general, feel better than the single, divorced, never married, or cohabitating. These advantages are explained, at least in part, by the realization that married couples may enjoy more economic resources, provide social and psychological support for one another, and support and encourage healthier lifestyles.

Despite the many advantages of being married, the number of married couples has been declining for decades. In 2005, the U.S. census estimated that just 49.7 percent (or 55.2 of the nation's 111.1 million total households) of U.S. households consisted of married couples (S. Roberts 2002). This was the first time that less than half of U.S. households comprised married couples. People are also waiting longer to get married and are increasingly likely to be unwed and better educated than they were two decades ago. The Pew Research Center's 2010 Executive Summary summarizes many of these findings:

> **Age**—Mothers of newborns are older now than their counterparts were two decades ago. In 1990, teens had a higher share of all births (13 percent) than did

women ages 35 and older (9 percent). In 2008, the reverse was true—10 percent of births were to teens, compared with 14 percent to women ages 35 and older. Each race and ethic group had a higher share of mothers of newborns in 2008 who are ages 35 and older, and a lower share who are teens, than in 1990.

Marital Status—A record 41 percent of births were to unmarried women in 2008; in 1990, 28 percent of births were to unmarried women. The unmarried-mother share of births has increased most sharply for whites and Hispanics, although the highest share is for black women.

Education—Most mothers of newborns (54 percent) had at least some college education in 2006, an increase from 41 percent in 1990. According to David Popenoe, codirector of the National Project at Rutgers University, later marriage is very strongly associated with higher levels of education and that is why people in the Northeast have such a late age of marriage (the Northeast has the highest average level of education by region) (Ohlemacher 2005).

Perhaps one of the most important variables involved with marriage is finding a mate—not necessarily finding the "right" mate but having the opportunity to find a partner. In China, for example, the large male-to-female ratio has left many men wondering whether they will be able to find a mate at all (see "A Closer Look" Box 10.1 for details).

A number of marriage patterns are based on cultural norms, or societal laws. For example, some norms promote endogamy. **Endogamy** limits marriage to people of the same race, religion, social class, or ethnic group. For example, miscegenation laws in the United States once prohibited marriages between races. The U.S. Supreme Court ruled such laws unconstitutional in 1967. In contrast to endogamy is the exogamy marriage pattern. **Exogamy** involves marriage between people from different racial, religious, or ethnic groups—for example, when a member of a royal family marries a commoner or someone from a wealthy socioeconomic class marries someone from a poorer one.

Perhaps the most important distinction among marriage patterns is that between monogamy and polygamy. **Monogamy** permits an individual to be married to only one other person at a given time. (In some instances, monogamy may mean that one person is married to only one other person in a lifetime.) This is the legal system of marriage in the United States and most Western societies. According to the *Guinness Book of World Records* (2005), the world's longest monogamous marriage lasted eighty years between Percy and Florence Arrowsmith of Hereford, England. A variation of monogamy is serial monogamy. **Serial monogamy** is the practice of having more than one spouse during the course of a lifetime, but only one at a time. According to the *Guinness Book of World Records* (1997), Glynn "Scotty" Wolfe holds the record for the most marriages, with twenty-nine.

A Closer Look

Box 10.1 The Shortage of Female Mates in China

The men of China are confronted with a unique barrier in their attempts to marry. The Chinese proclivity to abort female fetuses has led to a noticeable gender imbalance among newborns. It is estimated that more than 24 million Chinese men of marrying age could find themselves without a woman to wed by 2020 because of this imbalance (Neilan 2010). The shortage of women is attributed to the Chinese government's one-child policy, which was introduced in 1979. In the early 1970s, the fertility rate averaged almost 6 births per woman; this dropped to about 1.6 after 2000 (Davidson, Bunnell, and Yan 2008). The Chinese culture's tendency to value males has led to a change in China's sex ratio of males to females at birth from 106 male births per 100 female births in 1975 to 120 male births per 100 female births (Davidson, Bunnell, and Yan 2008). A leading cause of the increased male-to-female sex ratio is technology, especially in the form of ultrasound scans, introduced in the late 1980s. This technology has enabled Chinese parents to opt for sex-specific abortions. That Chinese males face difficulty in finding a female mate is a social problem in its own right, but a number of other social problems are related to the shortage of women. China's National Population and Family Planning Commission reports that abductions and trafficking of women are "rampant" in areas with excessive numbers of men and that illegal marriages and forced prostitution are also problems in those areas (Neilan 2010).

What Do You Think?

China's large population was a contributing factor in the government's decision to try to limit family size. As explained in this box, the one-child policy, coupled with the Chinese cultural preference for males, has resulted in many unforeseen consequences. What steps could the Chinese government pursue to try to correct the shortage of marriage-aged women in China? What do you think?

His twenty-ninth wife, Linda Essex-Wolfe, had been married twenty-two previous times. Guinness stopped tracking this category for fear that people would marry just to break the record.

In contrast to monogamy is polygamy. **Polygamy**, as this chapter's introductory story reveals, involves the marriage of one person to more than one other person at any given time. Polygamy has two subcategories: polyandry and polygyny. *Polyandry* (literally meaning "many wives") refers to the practice of a female having two or more male marriage partners; *polygyny* refers to a male having two or more wives. Polygamy is illegal in the United States; however, a number of groups still practice this form of marriage. Polygamy often involves child abuse, incest, arranged marriages involving children as young as ten years of age, and intermarriage between related persons. Polygamous clans generally adhere to a code of silence. Only when the code is broken does the outside world intervene. Such was the case with Warren Jeffs. According to a 2004 Gallup poll, 91 percent of Americans consider polygamy morally wrong (*USA Today,* 9/13/04). Nonetheless, it appears that the number of people in polygamist communities in the United States has increased over the years. "Polygamist marriages have been growing steadily since the 1800s, says Mary Batchelor, acting director of *Principle Voices,* a nonprofit group that advocates for Utah decriminalizing polygamy. She says most polygamists are living within the general population" (M. Scott 2008, p. D1).

The U.S. census does not track polygamy; still *Principle Voices* estimates that 37,000 people, including children, live in polygamy in the western United States and British Columbia. That is up from 30,000 in 2000, according to the group's informal survey of independent fundamentalists. "The largest known polygamist community in the United States is the Fundamentalist Church of Jesus Christ of the Latter Day Saints, headed by Jeffs. That group, with about 8,000 members, broke from the Mormon church after the latter disavowed polygamy more than a century ago" (M. Scott 2008, p. D1). Because polygamy itself is illegal—although enforcement of such laws varies from state to state—polygamists generally try to abide by as many federal laws as possible—for example, limiting marriage to women who are at least eighteen. Marriages between older men and girls under eighteen do occur, however, because of the coercive nature of polygamist communities. Children do not know any better than to follow their elders' rules. To further their own cause, the adults keep children undereducated. The girls take care of younger siblings, and boys typically work fourteen hours a day (M. Scott 2008). Because older males view younger males as a threat, boys are often kicked out of the community. They become known as "lost boys" (see "Connecting Sociology and Popular Culture" Box 10.2 about lost boy Brent Jeffs).

Gay Marriage

The issue of gay marriage has taken on a great deal of prominence in the United States, as well as other nations, in the twenty-first century (Green 2006). Societal attitudes toward same-sex marriage, once a taboo, have changed dramatically over the past decade. Gay people believe that they have the same right to marry as heterosexual people. They want to be allowed to marry for the same socioeconomic reasons as opposite-sex couples. Most of these reasons deal with the basic social rights and benefits granted opposite-sex couples, including full consideration in child-custody cases, hospital visitation rights, the power to make medical decisions with regard to a partner, and access to health insurance coverage offered by employers to workers' spouses.

An increasing number of U.S. states allow gay couples to marry. Shown here are Ellen DeGeneres and Portia de Rossi on their wedding day.

The legal landscape in the United States is in constant flux when it comes to states that do or do not allow gay marriage. In early 2008, only Massachusetts allowed an actual gay marriage. A number of states at that time allowed civil unions. A **civil union** grants the same legal rights as marriage but not the label of being married. In June 2008, California allowed gay marriage for the first time. Among the gay couples rushing to the altar on that first day (June 16, 2008) were George Takei, who played Sulu on the original *Star Trek,* and his partner of twenty-one years, Brad Altman. Their gender-neutral marriage license read, "Party A" and "Party B" instead of "bride" and "groom." Months later, the legality of their marriage, along with that of every other gay marriage in California (about 18,000), was thrown into doubt as California voters passed a constitutional amendment against gay marriage—a heartbreaking defeat for the gay-rights movement that elated religious conservatives. California gay-rights lawyer Evan Wolfson, who heads a group called Freedom to Marry, proclaimed, "There's something deeply wrong with putting the rights of a minority up to a majority vote" (*Post-Standard,* 11/6/08, p. A6).

With the passage of the state constitutional ban on gay marriage in California behind them, gay-rights activists turned their attention to the left-leaning Northeast. Consider these recent developments in the gay-marriage debate.

Connecting Sociology and Popular Culture

Box 10.2 Excerpts from "Lost Boy" Brent Jeffs

The polygamist clan headed by Warren Jeffs is described in this chapter's introductory story and in the discussion of polygamy. Young women have great value to polygamist clans as they are expected to marry the adult males, bear many children, and help take care of their extended families. Young males, conversely, are not valued; they are seen as competition by the older, dominant men of the clan. Consequently, boys are often sent away from polygamist communities. With no real place to go, these castaways become known as "lost boys." One such castoff of the FLDS community was Brent Jeffs, nephew to clan leader Warren Jeffs. He chronicles his ordeal in the aptly named popular-culture book *Lost Boy*.

Brent Jeffs was the first FLDS member to file a sexual-abuse lawsuit against his uncle. In *Lost Boy* Jeffs describes how girls are valued property and boys are expendable. He describes how every child believes he or she is special—or at least likes to think of him- or herself as such. Excerpts from Jeffs's book reveal how he once thought of himself as special but later came to believe this was not so true. He describes how his family had what his church called "royal blood" because they were direct descendants of their prophet (Joseph Smith). "When I was little, my family was favored, in the church's elite. I was assured that there was a place for me in the highest realms of heaven and at least three wives for me right here on earth once I attained Melchizedek priesthood. I was in a chosen family in a chosen people, visiting sacred land near end times. I would one day become a god, ruling over my own spinning world" (ABC News 2009).

This excerpt from *Lost Boy* reveals how Jeffs came to realize he was not really that special:

> When you are number ten of twenty, with three 'sister-mothers'—two of whom are full-blooded sisters—and a grandfather whom thousands of people believe speaks directly to God, it can be hard to figure out what 'special' really means. All told, I have roughly sixty aunts and uncles on my dad's side and

What Do You Think?

In a democratic society, should the will of the majority supersede the will of the minority? If a majority vote were to decide every civil rights issue, would the rights of the minority be compromised? What do you think?

- In July 2008, the Massachusetts Senate voted to repeal a 1912 law used to bar out-of-state same-sex couples from marrying in the state—a law that critics say was originally aimed at interracial marriages.
- In November 2008, same-sex partners were allowed to marry in Connecticut. The Connecticut Supreme Court ruled 4–3 on October 10, 2008, that same-sex couples have the right to wed rather than accept a 2005 civil union law designed to give them the same rights as married couples.
- In April 2009, Vermont and Iowa joined Connecticut and Massachusetts as states that allow gay marriage.
- By early June 2009, New Hampshire had passed legislation to legalize same-sex marriages.
- As of July 2010, five states—California, Nevada, New Jersey, Oregon, and Washington—grant essentially all the rights of marriage to same-sex couples without the authorization of marriage itself.

> twenty-two on my mom's—with probably thousands of cousins. In families as large as mine, even keeping track of your own siblings—let alone cousins and aunts and uncles—is difficult.... It simply isn't possible for all of the women and children to get their needs met. Just making sure the children are fed, clothed, and physically accounted for is an ongoing challenge. Simply keeping dozens of children physically safe is close to impossible. (ABC News 2009)

Jeffs elaborates on the meaning of the term "lost boy" by pointing out that many FLDS families had lost a young child, frequently due to accidents that better supervision could have prevented. In addition, many children are "lost" because of the genetic disorder that runs through the FLDS church. (Note: Genetic disorders are common in families and clans characterized by in-breeding.) Jeffs points out that FLDS members refuse to acknowledge the scientific knowledge linking genetic disorders to marriages among closely related families. Still, the primary reason the term "lost boys" is applied to young males in polygamist communities stems from basic math: half of all children born are boys. In order for some men to have many wives, other males must either leave, recruit new females, or go unmarried. As a result, being born a boy in the FLDS does not entail the privilege it may seem to. To reach the privileged rank, boys must kowtow to leaders and attempt to maintain perfect obedience to constantly changing demands and hierarchies.

In 2011, a Texas jury convicted polygamist sect leader Warren Jeffs of child sexual assault for taking two young followers as brides in what his church calls "spiritual marriages." Jeffs, who acted as his own lawyer, claimed his religious rights were being trampled by civil law and vowed that God would seek revenge against those who prosecuted him (*Post-Standard,* 8/5/11, p. A11).

What Do You Think?

Brent Jeffs's description of polygamy presents a counterperspective to the idea that all men benefit from this patriarchal power structure. Are the boys as victimized by this socioreligious system as the girls? What do you think?

- In November 2009, voters in Maine voted down gay marriage; as a result of that setback, legislatures in New York and New Jersey failed to schedule long-expected votes on bills to recognize such unions.
- In March 2010, same-sex marriage was legalized in Washington, D.C.
- In July 2010, Hawaii governor Linda Lingle vetoed a law that would have permitted same-sex civil unions.
- Chief U.S. District Judge Vaughn Walker overturned California's gay-marriage ban in August 2010. Because an appeal was expected, one that could reach the U.S. Supreme Court (to decide whether gays have a constitutional right to marry), gay marriage was not allowed to resume immediately.
- In February 2011, President Barack Obama directed the Justice Department to stop defending the Defense of Marriage Act (1996), which bars federal recognition of same-sex marriages, against lawsuits challenging the act as unconstitutional.
- In May 2011, Delaware governor Jack Markell signed a bill that gives same-sex couples additional legal protections and recognition beginning in 2012.

- In June 2011, Illinois began granting licenses for civil unions.
- In July 2011, New York State became the sixth and most populous state to legalize same-sex marriage.

Despite the seemingly growing support for gay marriage, a number of states adamantly oppose legalizing such relationships. As of April 2009, the following states had constitutional bans on gay marriage: Alabama, Alaska, Arizona, Arkansas, California, Colorado, Florida, Georgia, Hawaii, Idaho, Kansas, Kentucky, Louisiana, Michigan, Mississippi, Missouri, Montana, Nebraska, Nevada, North Dakota, Ohio, Oklahoma, Oregon, South Carolina, South Dakota, Tennessee, Texas, Utah, Virginia, and Wisconsin. A number of these states passed constitutional bans on gay marriage in reaction to the 2004 Massachusetts law that legalized same-sex marriages.

It would be safe to suspect that the gay-marriage debate will continue for years to come as many people feel very strongly about this issue. In an odd form of mild protest concerning the debate over who should and should not be allowed to marry, Benton County, Oregon, commissioner Linda Modrell banned all marriages—gay and heterosexual. Benton County includes Corvallis, home to Oregon State University, viewed by many as a bastion of liberalism (CNN.com 2004).

Outside the United States, a number of nations allow gay marriage. The Netherlands legalized gay marriage in 2001. Belgium, Spain, and Canada followed the Dutch initiative. Spain's legalizing gay marriage is especially significant in light of the powerful presence of the Catholic Church in that country. The church opposes gay marriage and urged Spaniards to oppose the law. Pope Benedict XVI has condemned gay marriage as an expression of anarchic freedom (Ross-Thomas 2005). In December 2009, legislatures in Mexico City also turned aside opposition from the Roman Catholic Church by approving a far-reaching gay-rights bill that allows people of the same sex to marry and adopt children, inherit, obtain joint housing loans, and share insurance policies (*Post-Standard,* 12/22/09). In Africa, most nations do not allow gay marriage; in fact, they are intensely and officially against homosexual behavior. Police officers broke up a gay wedding in Kikambala, Kenya, in February 2010, for example, arresting several guests. The police said that they arrested the guests for their own protection against an angry mob that had assembled to stone the wedding party to death. Homosexuality is outlawed in Kenya, and violations are punishable by up to fourteen years in prison (Gettleman 2010). When asked to explain the intense feelings about homosexuality in Kenya, a Kenyan police spokesperson, Eric Kiraithe, stated, "It's culture, just culture. It's what you are taught when you are young and what you hear in church. Homosexuality is unnatural. It's wrong" (Gettleman 2010, p. 1). This police spokesperson's comments sum up the debate about gay marriage and nearly every other social topic: culture and how one was raised will impact one's feelings toward same-sex marriage and other social issues.

What Do You Think?

Gay marriage is a hotly debated topic. Some people feel that gay people have a right to marry one another. Other people feel strongly against gay marriage. Should gay people be allowed to marry? What do you think?

Divorce

Married people are supposed to be happier than single people. They have confessed their love for one another and promised to remain loyal until death do them part. Such an agreement is not made lightly, and a marriage is a legal (and often religious) ceremony. Entering into marriage is, perhaps, the single most important decision a person can make. As we just learned, gay people are fighting for the right to participate in this social institution. Clearly, then, marriage must be a wonderful thing that lasts a lifetime. Unfortunately, this is not the case, as nearly half of all first marriages end in divorce. A **divorce** is a legal termination of a marriage by a court in a legal proceeding, requiring a petition or complaint for divorce (or dissolution in some states) by one party. There are two types of divorce—fault (e.g., marital misconduct) and no-fault (e.g., irreconcilable differences between the married persons). According to the National Center for Health Statistics, for example, 43 percent of marriages break up within fifteen years (Meckler 2002). U.S. Census Bureau statistics indicate that second marriages have a much higher failure rate (estimates range from 60 to 67 percent) and third marriages an even higher divorce rate (around 75 percent) (AboutDivorce.org 2011).

Why do people divorce? Presumably, they were once in love, or the arranged partnership was planned according to custom and tradition. A number of factors contribute to divorce. Martin Daly and Margo Wilson (2000) state, "The strength of the alliance depends on each partner's perception of the benefits and costs of continuing or terminating it, and these perceptions are grounded in a peculiar calculus that is affected by shared interests in the welfare of children, sexual fidelity, pressures from collateral kin, and the opportunity costs of marital decisions" (p. 91).

Divorce has a great impact on family life. David Popenoe and Barbara Whitehead (2002) argue that nothing has affected family life (and therefore happiness and personal well-being) more negatively than divorce. They believe children are especially hurt by it. Furthermore, Popenoe and Whitehead (2002) claim that the widespread prevalence of divorce is a major contributor to the significantly decreasing percentage of households with children. Jennifer Morse (2006) argues that the legal innovation of unilateral divorce has reduced marriage to nothing more than a temporary association of individuals. Morse adds that if marriage is merely a free association of individuals, then there is no justifiable reason to

What Do You Think?

In an attempt to be "green conscious," should divorce be discouraged for the sake of the planet? What do you think?

exclude same-sex couples, or even larger groupings of sexual partners, from the right to marry.

Interestingly, divorce is also eco-unfriendly. That is right—divorce can be bad for the environment. When people divorce, the result is two new households. Households with fewer people are not as efficient as those with more. After all, a house requires the same amount of heating or air conditioning whether one or four people live there. "Per person, divorced households spent more per person per month for electricity compared with a married household, as multiple people can be watching the same television, listening to the same radio, cooking on the same stove or eating under the same lights" (Schmid 2007, p. A1).

As the following pages show, marriage and divorce are among the many forces that have contributed to dramatic changes in the family structure.

THE FAMILY

The family is a social group, and like all other social groups, it has norms and rules with corresponding sanctions (punishments) for violation. For example, most of us had a curfew when we were young, and if we violated the curfew, we were confronted with some sort of punishment (e.g., grounding). As we learned in Chapter 5, the family is much more than a social group; it is a primary group that exerts great impact on the development of its members. The family is so important that many claim it "is the bedrock of society" (Gubrium and Holstein 1990, p. 13). In this manner, the family is often looked upon as a social institution vital to the general well-being of society.

Defining the Family

One's family is determined by kinship. **Kinship** refers to a network of relatives. Undoubtedly, we have all heard the statement "The name of the victim has not been released pending notification of the next of kin." This statement reflects the importance of family over other concerns such as the media's ability to provide the public with information about an auto accident. After all, imagine a parent's first learning about a tragedy involving a child's death on the news.

Sociologist Rosemary Hopcroft (2009) argues that kinship creates a type of altruism within a family that helps to establish familial stability: "Children create shared genetic interests in the family, as both father and mother have an equal genetic stake in their children. This encourages cooperation between parents and joint investment in children" (p. 393). Citing the research of others (Amato and

Cheadle 2005; Carlson, McLanahan, and England 2004), Hopcroft (2009) also believes that other types of family structures, such as those established via second marriages, disrupt the joint investment in children and tend to have negative effects on children: "Remarriage generally does not ameliorate problems. Children brought up in other arrangements receive less education and have lower occupational achievement than children brought up by their biological parents or even their mother alone" (p. 393). Hopcroft (2009) goes so far as to suggest that "through both giving and receiving altruism within the family, married people live longer, healthier lives, and are less likely to suffer mental illness" (p. 393). Although Hopcroft's beliefs may seem a little radical to some, the basic point of her research is to highlight the value of kinship.

Definitions of the family have changed over the past few decades. Traditionally, the family was defined as a household with two or more people related by blood, marriage, or adoption. Lauer and Lauer (1997) add an emotional component to this traditional description and define the family as "a group united by marriage, blood, and/or adoption in order to satisfy intimacy needs and/or bear and socialize children" (p. 26). The limitations of this definition do not reflect the realities of the modern era, as a wide variety of social units may be recognized as "families" including childless unions. Thus, changes had to be made to the traditional definition of a family. The contemporary definition views the **family** as a social group of two or more people related by blood, marriage, or adoption or who live together and cooperate economically. This definition allows for a number of alternative lifestyles to the traditional interpretation of the family and does not require marriage. Redefining the family in light of social changes reflects the notion that definitions of the family are a matter of social construction in the same manner as race, ethnicity, and gender.

It is also important to note that the term "family" represents a particular discourse for describing human relations in or out of the household that involve other terms such as "parent," "son," "daughter," "brother," and "sister," among other titles (Gubrium and Holstein 1990). This admission reveals another feature of the family common to all social groups—namely, that the family structure involves a hierarchy wherein certain members, usually the parent(s), oversee norms and expectations.

What Do You Think?

Based on the contemporary definition of a family, college roommates could be considered a family. What do you think?

The Parental Role

Perhaps the most important role within the family is that of the parent. People become parents in one of three ways: through pregnancy, adoption, or stepparenting. The timing of becoming a parent also varies. John Santrock (2007) explains that, for some couples, the parental role is well planned and coordinated; however, for others, the discovery that they are about to become parents comes as a big surprise. In either scenario, the lives of expectant parents change dramatically. These individuals will have to find a way to balance their own needs with their commitment to their partners and to raising their children. As the primary caregivers, parents are responsible for nurturing, protecting, and teaching their children. The importance of the parental role is commonly expressed by outside societal members when a young person gets in trouble, resulting in a question such as, Where are his or her parents? The implication is that the primary role of parenting involves knowing what children are doing at all times and taking responsibility for their actions. In addition, the parental role involves taking on a number of responsibilities, developing interpersonal skills, meeting emotional demands, and nurturing and guiding children.

As we see later in this chapter, the family structure has changed over the years. In regard to the parental role, the most significant change involves the realization that many families are headed by a single parent. Most single-parent families are headed by women; consequently, the role of mother has changed quite dramatically in many families. "The cultural image of the American mother has changed from the cheery, doting homemaker to the frenzied, sleepless working mom. The conventional wisdom accompanying this change is that as today's mothers juggle the dual roles of worker and family caregiver, they must spend less time with their children, and receive little help from fathers" (Bianchi, Robinson, and Milkie 2006, p. 1). Single parents are often emotionally distressed, socially isolated, financially disadvantaged, overworked, and able to spend too little time at home with their children (Ambert 2001).

The Grandparent Role

Another interesting development in regard to parenting involves the role of grandparents. There are many types of grandparents, from those who are relatively young, perhaps in their early forties, and enjoy actively participating in their grandchildren's lives to those who are quite elderly and choose to take on the role of bestowing wisdom. Some grandparents enjoy spending time with their grandchildren, and others live far away and as a result spend little time with them. Most grandparents view their role as distinct from the parental role. They spend quality time with grandchildren and occasionally babysit them.

In some cases, grandparents may desire to spend more time with their grandchildren than the parents allow. There might be any number of reasons for this, including a parent's belief that the grandparent is unfit to spend time with his or her grandchildren. Parents who divorce or are fighting over custody of children may attempt to punish spouses by forbidding their parents (the grandparents) from seeing the grandchildren. This type of punishment may harm both the grandchildren and the grandparents emotionally. As a result, many grandparents have banded together in an attempt to secure legal rights to visit their grandchildren. For example, in 1984, the Grandparents Rights Organization, a national volunteer nonprofit organization, was formed to advocate for the rights of grandparents.

> **What Do You Think?**
>
> Some grandparents believe that they should have the right to visit their grandchildren whenever they want. What do you think?

Another interesting development in the role of grandparents involves the realization that an increasing number of grandparents have taken on the role of surrogate parent. A surrogate parent assumes the responsibilities of child care due to a number of reasons, including parents' illness, incarceration, substance abuse, death, or general inability to raise their children. An increasing number of grandparents have assumed the custodial care of their grandchildren; as a result, their role has changed dramatically (see "A Closer Look" Box 10.3).

DIMENSIONS AND FUNCTIONS OF THE FAMILY

There exist a number of specific dimensions, or types, of family structures, and various functions performed within these family structures are dictated by cultural norms and values.

Dimensions of Family Types

The most common family type in the United States, especially among the middle class, is the nuclear (basic, central, or cardinal) family. The **nuclear family** is an individual's immediate family; it generally consists of parents and their children. The **extended family**, in contrast, consists of multiple generations (grandparents, parents, and children, as well as other relatives such as aunts, uncles, and cousins) all living together in a single dwelling or in close proximity. As Steinmetz, Clavan, and Stein (1990) explain, there are variations of the extended family: "An extended family can be made up of adult siblings and their offspring sharing a household; it may be a *stem family* in which the eldest son, his wife, and their offspring reside with his parents; or it may be the *joint family* in which all adult male children, with their wives and offspring, live with their parents" (p. 18). The extended family is the most common type of family worldwide. In the United States, it is more common among families of upper and lower socioeconomic

A Closer Look

Box 10.3 Grandparents as Parents

According to U.S. census figures, at least 6.7 million children in the United States were being raised by grandparents or other relatives in 2006 (Meyersohn and McFadden 2007). "That equates to roughly one in 12 children, about 10 times the number of children in the U.S. foster care system" (Meyersohn and McFadden 2007, p. 1). The Ohio State University Extension (2008) estimates that 5 percent of American families are grandparent-grandchild families, 10 percent of all grandparents are raising grandchildren, and 4 million children live in a household headed by a grandparent.

For many grandparents, raising grandchildren is a financial burden. The census estimates that one in four grandparents raising grandchildren lives below the poverty level (Traster 2000). As a result, many caregiver grandparents are in need of child-welfare benefits. Some states have enacted kinship-care systems designed to increase the stipend paid to nonparents raising children of their kin (Traster 2000). "Kinship care" is the term used to describe situations that involve grandparents, other relatives, or other persons with a close emotional connection to a child who become his or her foster parent(s). Kinship-care programs serve many functions, including enabling children to live with people they know and trust, reducing the trauma of living with persons who initially are unknown, helping to keep siblings together, encouraging families to rely on their own family members and resources, and reducing the stigma that children may experience from being labeled "foster children."

Kinship-care legislation is also designed to assist grandparents (and other relatives) raising grandchildren who also face emotional, medical, and legal complications due to their new role as parent. Grandparents have complained about their lack of legal rights in a number of situations, including enrolling children in school, accessing and authorizing medical treatment, maintaining public housing leases, obtaining affordable legal services, and accessing a variety of federal benefits and services (Child Welfare League of America 2007).

What Do You Think?

Grandparents as parents serve as stabilizing figures for children whose parents can no longer care for them, but many of these caregivers face legal and financial challenges. What do you think can be done to help them? Would you support kinship-care legislation? Explain.

status. Due primarily to recent dire societal economic conditions, the number of U.S. multigenerational households has increased 30 percent since 2000. Still, the number of extended family households is relatively small (6.6 million) compared to nuclear family households (Schnurnberger 2010). According to the U.S. Bureau of Labor Statistics (2010b) there are roughly 110 million households in the United States with an average size of 2.59 persons.

Sociologists also distinguish between the family of orientation and the family of procreation. The *family of orientation* refers to the family that one is born into as a son or daughter. The *family of procreation* is the family one creates on marrying and having children. In this regard, the roles of wife-mother and husband-father are established.

Functions of the Family

The family possesses a number of key characteristics or functions. And yet, despite the wide variety of family types found around the world, ethnographic research has generated six "bedrock features" that characterize "the family" (Berger 2002). A brief review of these key functions is summarized below:

1. *Replacement of members of society:* The family of procreation ensures the survival of the human species. As Berger (2002) explains, there is a "taken-for-granted acceptance that the core function of [the family] revolves around the procreation and protection of children" (p. 4).
2. *Regulation of sexual activity:* Within every society certain sexual taboos lead to distinctions between appropriate and inappropriate behavior. Berger (2002) describes this as "the organization of human sexuality by means of some form of marriage that serves to socially legitimize the sexual union, regardless of whether manifested in the form of monogamy or polygamy and its subcategories" (p. 3). For example, in the United States, as in most Western societies, age restrictions are placed on those who may have sexual intercourse (e.g., an adult cannot have sex with a minor), and the incest taboo forbids sex between immediate family members. Interestingly, in a number of U.S. states, marriage between first cousins is not outlawed. Among these states are New York, California, Texas, and Florida. Furthermore, despite the stigma attached to marriage between first cousins, researchers at Stanford University and the National Society of Genetic Counselors report that the number of genetic birth defects in the offspring of first cousins (due to recessive genes that both parents pass on to their children) is not that much higher than for the general population (Willing 2002).
3. *Acknowledgment of rights and duties between family members:* As the primary agents of socialization, family members play a critical role in individual development. Parents are responsible for creating a nurturing environment that includes love and support, affection, and protection. Children are responsible for abiding by the rules established by their parents as well as by the greater society.
4. *Establishment of a household:* Some sort of clear residential arrangement is designated for parents and children, typically referred to as a household.
5. *Establishment of a set of reciprocal social and economic obligations between parents and children:* The parents are responsible for providing

What Do You Think?

In many U.S. states, marriage between first cousins is legal. Marriage between first cousins still carries a stigma, however. What do you think?

economically for themselves and their children, and children are expected to help their parents within the household environment.

6. *Provision of a source of identity:* The family provides a socially legitimate system for reckoning descent. Parents provide children with an identity in terms of race or ethnicity and ancestry, as well as initial socioeconomic status and religion.

THE CHANGING FAMILY

In many families, it is the father who has the primary responsibility for taking care of the children.

The once traditional family (the breadwinner father, stay-at-home mother, and dependent children all residing under one roof) has changed dramatically over the past few decades (see "Connecting Sociology and Popular Culture" Box 10.4 for a description of a fictional TV traditional family). "Many argue that changes away from the more 'traditional' two-parent families have created much of the social malaise that Americans experience" (Tepperman and Blain 2006, p. 174). Whether the demise of the traditional family is responsible for the "social malaise" found in American society is up for debate. It is clear, however, that such factors as geographic relocation, an increasing number of women in the workplace, the high divorce rate, and changing cultural norms have led to a wide variety of family types. The following pages take a quick look at the changing family.

Commuter Marriages

In a commuter marriage, spouses live apart from one another for long stretches because they have jobs or careers in different geographic locations. This is similar to a long-distance relationship, except the couple is married. Although these marriages are unconventional, to say the least, the number of commuter marriages jumped 30 percent between 2000 and 2005 to 3.6 million couples, according to an analysis of census figures (Cullen 2007). The primary reasons for commuter marriages are job relocation or military deployment of one spouse. Cullen (2007) explains, "While military deployments, migratory jobs and economic need have long forced couples around the world to live apart, in America today, it is more likely the woman's career that drives the separation." Businesses often gain great benefits from hiring commuting couples because they get the best of both worlds: the desired stability associated with married persons as well as an employee who can dedicate more time to work without the interference of the day-to-day obligations of marriage and raising a family.

Connecting Sociology and Popular Culture

Box 10.4 The Simpsons as an Idealized Traditional Family

One of the most recognizable American families worldwide is the Simpson family from the highly popular and long-running television show *The Simpsons.* (Note: On May 20, 1997, *Time* magazine named *The Simpsons* the twentieth century's best television show.) The Simpson family includes Homer Simpson, his wife Marge, and their three children, Bart, Lisa, and Maggie. So popular is *The Simpsons* that 22 percent of Americans can name all five Simpson family members, compared to just 1 in 1,000 (0.1 percent) who can name all five First Amendment freedoms (Delaney 2008b). Right now, you are wondering what the five basic freedoms are, right? For those among the 99.99 percent who do not know, the five basic rights are freedom of speech, press, religion, petition for redress of grievances, and peaceful assembly.

From the start, *Simpsons* creator Matt Groening made it clear that the Simpson family was to be anything but normal, let alone traditional. Despite Groening's claim, the Simpson family is far more normal than many care to admit. In the series's fourth episode ("There's No Disgrace Like Home" 1990), Homer, a working-class husband and father, is driving with his family to the home of his billionaire boss, Mr. Burns, for an employee party. Homer needs to make a good impression on Mr. Burns, and he informs his family, "Now remember, as far as anyone knows, we're a nice normal family." When *The Simpsons* first aired, a number of politicians and family organizations believed that the Simpson family was too atypical. Former president George H. W. Bush famously stated during a January 1992 National Religious Broadcasters convention that he preferred to see the United States as "a lot more like the Waltons and a lot less like the Simpsons" (Ortved 2007, p. 94). *The Waltons* (1972–1981) was a TV show about a 1930s-era family. Cleverly, and quickly, *The Simpsons* responded to Bush's criticism by having the Simpson family seated in front of the television listening to Bush's comments, with Bart responding, "Hey! We're just like the Waltons. We're praying for an end to the Depression, too."

Despite criticisms from Bush and others, the Simpson family is now the rare example of the traditional ("normal") nuclear family consisting of a breadwinner husband-father, a stay-at-home wife-mother, and dependent children all living under the same roof. Most estimates indicate that only 5 percent of all American families now fit this once ideal type. One might argue that watching *The Simpsons* affords viewers the same nostalgic look at America's past that *The Waltons* once did.

What Do You Think?

How does your family compare to the Simpson family? Are the Simpsons the ideal type of the once-dominant family form? What do you think?

Voluntary Childlessness

As the term implies, voluntary childlessness refers to the choice not to have children. Voluntarily childless married couples represent a small percentage of families. In many cases, such couples face pressure from other family members and close friends and questions as to why they do not want children. This is because, as mentioned earlier, a primary function of family is procreation to guarantee the survival of the species. Nonetheless, having children is not the ideal for all married couples. Married couples without children have more time for each other, themselves, and their careers.

What Do You Think?

If you were an only child who married and decided not to have children, would you likely face pressure from your parents to give them grandchildren. How do you think you would respond? What do you think?

Cohabitation

As recently as 2007, unmarried couples who lived together in North Dakota were considered criminals. Legislation was narrowly passed to get rid of a law that listed cohabitation by an unmarried man and woman as a sex crime, on a par with rape, incest, and adultery (Rivoli 2007). As of 2004, seven U.S. states still had anticohabitation laws on the books. Is it any wonder that the number of unmarried couples living together only began to rise in the 1970s, a relatively liberal period that followed the radical 1960s? During this era cohabitation was openly discussed; still, it was not accepted by conservative members of society. Further, people who lived together in a sexual relationship without being married were described as "living in sin." This attitude was evident when all three major television networks passed on the 1977 mid-season replacement show *Three's Company* because the concept of unmarried men and women living together was taboo. (Note: In this show, an unmarried man lives with two unmarried women, but they do not have sex with each other.) ABC eventually agreed to air the show. Sponsors were boycotted, but *Three's Company* became a huge success. By today's standards, it is a rather tame show.

As described above, **cohabitation** involves a couple living together in an intimate, sexual relationship without being legally married (Lauer and Lauer 1997). Some people think of cohabitation as a "trial marriage," while others just prefer this lifestyle choice. Research has shown that couples who cohabit tend to have more egalitarian relationships, as well as less stable relationships, than married couples (Hohmann-Marriott 2006). In 1991, there were 3 million unmarried opposite-sex persons cohabitating. In 2006, there were 5.2 million (U.S. Census Bureau 2006a). The U.S. Census Bureau (2006a) also estimates that 413,000 households contained unmarried male couples, and 363,000 contained unmarried female couples. Clearly, cohabitation is becoming a normative life experience—especially compared to past perceptions and realities (Raley 2000).

Delayed Marriage

It was once common for men and women to marry shortly after high school. Now, an increasing number of people are delaying marriage for many reasons. For one, the increasing number of people who cohabitate and view such a lifestyle as a trial run for marriage implies that if and when they marry, they will be older. Other people delay marriage because of "the availability of sexual relations among singles, the emphasis on personal growth and freedom, the unwillingness to 'settle down' before one has many experiences, and fears about commitment and the high divorce rates" (Lauer and Lauer 1997). People may also delay marriage until they are economically stable, especially if they want children.

Dual-Earner Families

As articulated earlier in this chapter, the old family ideal of the breadwinner father and stay-at-home mother has all but disappeared. Today, 80 percent of families with both parents living in the same household are characterized by dual-income couples (Cullen 2007). As the term implies, in dual-earner families both parents work. In many cases, both parents work out of economic necessity. In other situations it is the result of women's progress in the workforce and their desire to gain an identity, in the same manner as men, through what they do outside the home (Hertz and Marshall 2001).

Single-Parent Families

The fastest-growing family form in the United States is the single-parent family. Such families may be the result of a woman giving birth "out of wedlock," divorce, or the death of a spouse. Most typically, single-parent families are the result of single women having children. Since the 1960s, the number and proportion of all births that occur out of wedlock have increased tremendously (Lauer and Lauer 1997). According to a report from the National Center for Health Statistics (2009), the proportion of births to unmarried mothers in the United States has risen steeply over the past few decades, consistent with the proportions in other countries (see Table 10.1 for international percentage rates of births to unmarried mothers). Between 1980 and 2007, the proportion of births to unmarried women in the United States more than doubled from 18 percent to 40 percent.

> **What Do You Think?**
>
> A characteristic of the twenty-first-century family is that both parents earn an income. Are there advantages, disadvantages, or both to this reality? What do you think?

While a great deal of attention is often paid to births to unmarried teens, six out of ten births to women between the ages of twenty and twenty-four were among unmarried women in 2007 (see "Connecting Sociology and Popular Culture" Box 10.5 for a discussion of an adult single parent who generated a great deal

TABLE 10.1 2007 Births to Unmarried Mothers: An International Comparison

COUNTRY	PERCENTAGE
Iceland	66
Sweden	55
Norway	54
France	50
Denmark	46
United Kingdom	44
United States	40
The Netherlands	40
Ireland	33
Germany	30
Canada	30
Spain	28
Italy	21
Japan	2

Source: National Center for Health Statistics 2009.

Note: Data for Iceland, France, the United Kingdom, Ireland, Spain, and Canada are for 2006.

of media coverage when she gave birth to octuplets). Birthrates among unmarried U.S. mothers are highest for Hispanic women (106 births per 1,000 unmarried Hispanic women), followed by non-Hispanic black women (72 per 1,000) and non-Hispanic white women (32 per 1,000) (Centers for Disease Control and Prevention 2009a).

Many single parents face a number of disadvantages financially as well as in terms of social capital (Ambert 2001). Because many single parents must be employed for long hours, they are often less involved in their children's lives. Moreover, because many single-parent families reside in neighborhoods with a high concentration of similarly economically poor families, the probability of children becoming delinquent or turning to gangs increases (Ambert 2001). It should be pointed out, however, that single-parent families do not cause delinquency, though they are a risk factor (Trojanowicz, Morash, and Schram 2001).

Remarriage

Remarriage refers to marrying again after the end of a first marriage. Generally, this occurs when a divorced person marries for a second time. As high as divorce rates are for first marriages, second marriages have a higher probability of failure. Second marriages create stepfamilies and blended families. "Cultural beliefs and values wield strong influences on the ways in which stepfamily members think about their relationships, interact together, and feel about each other" (Ganong and Coleman 2004, p. 25). In other words, the social and psychological environments of stepfamilies are influenced by the attitudes, values, and norms of the members involved and the culture in which they reside. In American society, remarriage is fairly common and socially accepted.

Remaining Single

Most people will eventually marry. Because of this cultural norm, people who remain single often feel socially isolated. They cannot share in stories about spouses and raising children. Research repeatedly indicates that married people are happier than single people; companies generally prefer to hire married people,

Connecting Sociology and Popular Culture

Box 10.5 The Octomom

With single mothers as commonplace as they are today, it takes a rare instance for one particular mom to become a dominant topic of conversation in popular culture. Such is the case with Nadya Suleman (full name, Nadya Denise Doud-Suleman Guitierrez), better known as the "Octomom." Suleman, who was already a single mother of six, gave birth to octuplets on January 26, 2009. Only the second full set of octuplets born alive in the United States, the Suleman octuplets are the only set to surpass one week in age. Such a feat was bound to draw enormous attention from the mass media. Suleman was on the cover of numerous magazines and discussed on news programs and by nearly all those connected to the mass media. After all, people were curious about this mystery woman. "Curiosity about Suleman turned to outrage after it became clear that the single, unemployed mother had been using student loans and Social Security disability payments to help pay for her children's care" (*The Citizen,* 8/11/09, p. A2). Furthermore, because she had gone to a fertility clinic, the indignation intensified. The Medical Board of California also investigated the fertility clinic for possible irregularities. (Note: All Suleman's children were conceived via in vitro fertilization. In each of her five previous pregnancies, Suleman was implanted with six embryos resulting in four single births and one fraternal-twin birth, with four boys and two girls born between 2001 and 2006.) Suleman has kept secret the identity of the man who she says fathered the octuplets as well as the six children she already had.

In April 2009, Suleman appeared on *Good Morning America* and happily gave the audience a tour of the babies' nursery in her La Habra, California, home. In a June interview, however, she expressed deep regret over her historic birth of octuplets saying, "I screwed my life up, I screwed up my kids' life. What the heck am I going to do? I have to put on this strong face, and I have to pretend like I don't regret it" (Ferran 2009, p. 1). But what can Suleman do? She must persevere for the children. With a mostly angry public against her, any attempts to capitalize on media opportunities to raise money to support her children and herself became slim and met with accusations of opportunism. On August 10, 2009, the Fox network announced that it would air a two-hour special on the life of the "Octomom" based on footage bought from an online company that paid for access to her life. *Octomom: The Incredible Unseen Footage* broadcast on August 19, 2009. Fox executive Mike Darnell said that the network had set up a six-figure account for the children; none of the money went directly to Suleman.

What Do You Think?

Many people believe that it was immoral or unethical for Suleman to go to a fertility clinic to increase her chances of becoming pregnant, especially in light of the fact that she was an unemployed single mom who already had six children. Is the fertility clinic that assisted Suleman guilty of unethical or immoral behavior? What do you think?

married people receive a discount on insurance rates, and so forth. Despite all this, there is growing cultural acceptance of those who never marry and remain single.

According to the U.S. Census Bureau, 96 million people in the United States had no spouse in 2009. That means 43 percent of all Americans over the age of eighteen were single. In the bureau's 2009 "America's Families and Living Arrangements" survey, single adults included those who have never been married, are divorced, or are widowed (CNN.com 2010a). In terms of changing family structures, the present discussion concerns those single people who never married. The U.S. census states, "Of the singletons, 61 percent [of the 96 million] have never said 'I do'" (CNN.com 2010a). A vast majority of never-married single people live alone (others may live with aging parents or share a residence with someone). Some people never marry for any number of reasons; in some cases it is by choice, and in others it may not be. Among other things, single people enjoy the privacy that such a lifestyle affords; they enjoy the freedom to come and go as they please, and they can be as tidy or as messy as they want within their own living quarters.

Generation Yo-Yo

Traditionally, the dreams of most young adult Americans included graduating from high school and either attending college, finding a job, or joining the military. This certainly implied moving out of the parental home to enjoy their freedom and establish lives outside direct parental influence. After all, living at home is never a good sign of having attained adulthood and fiscal responsibility for one's self. This cultural norm was illustrated in the *Seinfeld* episode titled "The Puffy Shirt" (1993). In this episode, George Costanza moves back in with his parents for financial reasons—he mentions that he only has $714 in his bank account. Jerry points out that it is never a good sign when an adult has to move back in with his parents, because it is like probation or rehabilitation.

Such thinking, apparently, has changed. Generations X and Y have been transformed into Generation Yo-Yo because of the increasing number of adults in their twenties and thirties who live with their parents (many of whom moved back home after moving out). More than 18 million Americans age eighteen to thirty-four live in their parents' homes. According to the 2005 College Graduation Survey, more than 60 percent of 2005 college graduates moved back into the homes of their parents after graduation (Aproberts 2006). So much for planning for the future. In 2007, Bill Cosby commented, "Human beings are the only creatures on Earth that allow their children to come back home."

As the discussion of the changing family reveals, the traditional nuclear family that consisted of a breadwinner father, a stay-at-home mother, and their children all living together has changed dramatically and in a variety of ways over the past couple of generations. So long as family members feel loved and nurtured, the type of family they are a part of is not so important. Unfortunately, a large number of families are not peaceful and loving. Many involve violence and abuse.

FAMILY ABUSE AND VIOLENCE

Determining the true incidence of family abuse and violence is difficult due to dramatic underreporting. However, evidence indicates that abuse and violence are serious problems in many families. The limited space allocated for family abuse and violence in this chapter barely does justice to this grim social problem; nonetheless, the topic must at least be introduced.

As for the idea that family violence is dramatically underreported, students should ask themselves whether they have ever had any violent confrontations with their siblings and, if they did, whether these acts of violence were reported to police. Chances are that students with siblings got into fights with them while growing up, no? In most cases, fights between siblings do not qualify as examples of abuse. In other cases, however, they may. Regardless, sibling physical confrontations represent the mere tip of the abuse and violence iceberg that plagues many families. As Lauer and Lauer (1997) state, "Next to death, separation, and divorce, family violence is the most difficult experience people have to cope with.... It is easy to understand the severity of the trauma. After all, we expect our families to be a source of comfort and support, a refuge from an often difficult world" (p. 369).

Stress

One of the leading causes of abuse and violence in the home is stress. Stress involves pressures or hardships confronting a person. Many people experience stress. Students may feel stress when impending exams and term-paper deadlines converge. In addition to the demands of academic work, students may experience stress with a dating partner, in family life, or in their living conditions. Family stress can stem from such factors as the birth of child, the death of a family member, severe illness, family problems (e.g., alcoholism, drug or gambling addiction, criminal arrest), loss of income, bankruptcy, divorce, and remarriage. Research has shown that marital distress is associated with emotional distress in children, causing them to act out inappropriately (VanderValk et al. 2007). Children's misbehavior may result in further stress for parents. Parents who fail to cope with stress may take out their frustration on each other, their children, or their aging parents.

Abuse and Violence

Abuse and violence in the family take many forms, including sibling violence; marital rape; spousal, child, and parent abuse; and abuse of the elderly. Abuse may be

Ideally, the home is the safest environment for children; unfortunately, this is not always the reality.

emotional or physical. With physical abuse—which is the result of violence—the scars are visible; emotional abuse, however, scars the victim on the inside (e.g., the human psyche).

Family violence can be defined as an act carried out with the intention of, or perceived as having the intention of, physically hurting one's partner (in marriage, dating, or cohabitation), child, parent, or sibling (Steinmetz, Clavan, and Stein 1990). Examples of family violence and abuse are nearly infinite. One needs only to read a daily newspaper to find current instances. Consider these recent headlines:

- Woman says father held her in cellar for twenty-four years and raped and impregnated her.
- Father sentenced in sex crime.
- Man locked son in room for three years.
- Woman sentenced for making stepchildren gorge.
- Parents who caged children found guilty.
- Increased potential for child abuse as more children live with nonparents.
- Daughter charged in mother's starving death.
- Public heaps scorn on male victims of abusive women.

> **What Do You Think?**
>
> How does your family of orientation compare to those described in this chapter? How will your family of procreation look?

As we have learned in this chapter, there is a wide variety of marriages and families. Some marriages last a lifetime and are filled with more love than sorrow; conversely, some marriages last less than a few months. Families, too, are quite diverse. A number of families consist of two parents and their children; other families do not involve children, marriage, opposite-sex partners, or two parents.

SUMMARY

Marriage takes many forms. Although it always involves at least two persons (monogamy), in some cases it involves more (polygamy). In the United States, the cultural ideal is for romantic love to precede marriage. In other societies, marriages are arranged, and romantic love has little or nothing to do with such unions. The issue of gay marriage has come to the forefront of discussion in the United States and other nations. While there appears to be a growing acceptance of homosexuality in the United States, many people are so opposed to gay marriage that a number of states have reinforced their constitutions to stipulate that a marriage can only involve a man and a woman. Whether gay or straight, a large number of marriages and civil unions end in divorce. The increasing frequency and social acceptance of divorce have contributed to a number of social problems for the families involved and changes in the family structure as a whole.

The family is a social group, and like all other social groups, it has norms and rules with corresponding sanctions (punishments) for their violation. The family is also a primary group that exerts great influence on the development of its members. A vital social institution and cornerstone of human society, the family has nonetheless undergone quite a few changes over the past couple of generations. Today, the family may involve grandparents serving as parents, commuter marriages, voluntary childlessness, cohabitation, delayed marriage, dual-income couples, single parents, remarriage, and adult children moving back in with their parents; an increasing number of people are also remaining single rather than marrying. Regardless of its structure, the family is ideally a social environment in which all members feel safe and secure. Due to family violence and abuse, however, this is not always the case.

Glossary

Civil union—A legal status granting the rights of marriage but not the marriage label.

Cohabitation—The state of living together in an intimate, sexual relationship without being legally married.

Divorce—A legal termination of a marriage by a court in a legal proceeding, requiring a petition or complaint for divorce (or dissolution in some states) by one party.

Endogamy—Marriage between people of the same race, religion, social class, or ethnic group.

Exogamy—Marriage between people from different racial, religious, or ethnic groups.

Extended family—A family that consists of multiple generations living together in a single dwelling or in close proximity.

Family—A social group comprising two or more people who are related by blood, marriage, or adoption or who live together and cooperate economically.

Family violence—Acts carried out with the intention of, or perceived as having the intention of, physically hurting one's partner (in marriage, dating, or cohabitation), child, parent, sibling, or another member of an extended family living in the home, such as a grandparent or cousin.

Incest—Sexual relations between persons who are so closely related that their marriage is illegal or forbidden by custom.

Kinship—A network of relatives.

Marriage—A relatively enduring, socially approved, sexual and socioeconomic relationship between at least two persons for the purpose of creating and maintaining a family.

Monogamy—A marriage pattern that permits one individual to be married to one other person at a given time.

Nuclear family—An immediate family that generally consists of parents and their children.

Polygamy—A marriage pattern that permits an individual to be married to more than one person at any given time.

Romantic love—A deep physical and emotional attraction.

Serial monogamy—The practice of having more than one spouse during the course of a lifetime, but only one at a time.

Discussion Questions

1. Do you think people like Warren Jeffs should be allowed to have a polygamous family? Explain.
2. Do you believe romantic love should precede marriage? Or are arranged marriages a better idea?
3. Some people argue that it is too easy to get divorced and that is why the divorce rate is so high. Do you agree?
4. Perhaps rather than divorce it is marriage that is too easy to attain. What do you think?
5. Will you be a part of Generation Yo-Yo? Or will you be prepared to live on your own after graduation?

Web Links

To learn more about polygamy, visit http://principlevoices.org/archives/category/polygamy.

To learn more about the rights of grandparents and the Grandparents Rights Organization, visit www.grandparentsrights.org.

To learn more about the relationship between marriage and health, visit the National Center for Health Statistics at www.cdc.gov/nchs.

To learn more about divorce in the United States, visit the CDC's National Center for Health Statistics website at www.cdc.gov/nchs/fastats/divorce.htm.

11

EDUCATION AND RELIGION

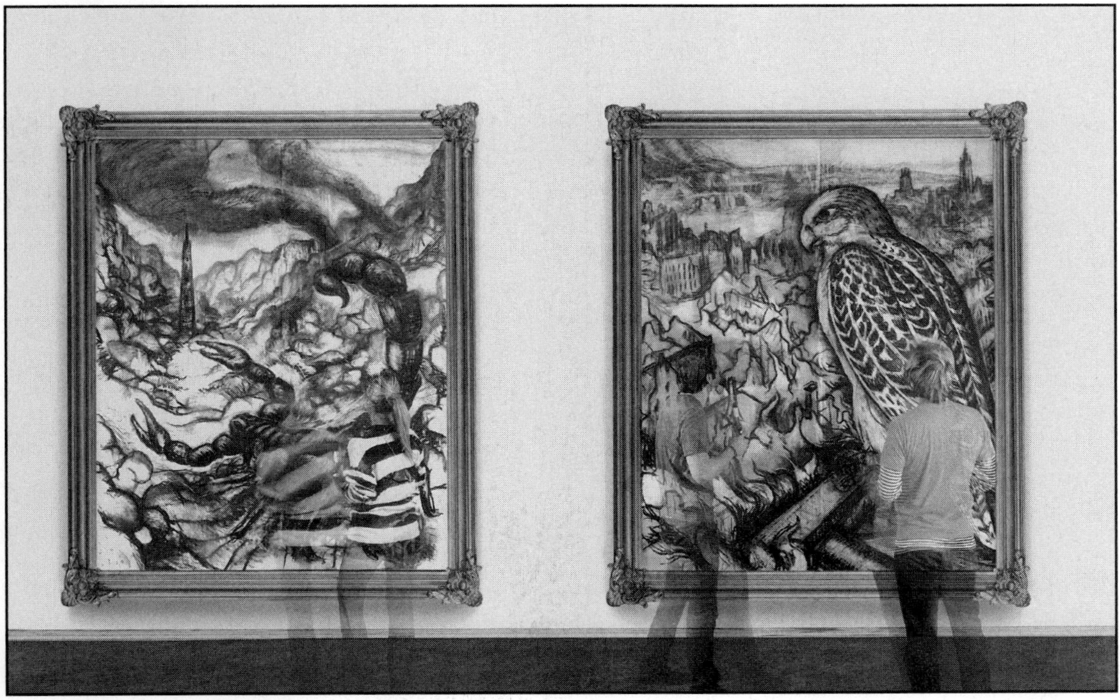

College life is much more than attending class, studying, taking exams, and writing term papers. There are plenty of opportunities to attend sporting events and art exhibits. In this photo, students are shown moving through an art gallery.

Chapter 11

INTRODUCTORY STORY

Choosing which college to attend can be difficult. After all, there are numerous variables to consider when choosing the right college. Economic costs, for example, have become an increasing concern for many students (and their parents). Scholarship offers that lower the overall financial costs of attending college must be factored into the economic decision. The reputation of the college and, more importantly, of the specific program of study is also a critical factor in the decision-making process. Some students may decide that a two-year degree is sufficient for their career aspirations. Other students will realize that a four-year degree is a minimum requirement for the jobs they aspire to attain. Attending a two-year school first and then transferring to a four-year school is an option that many students seeking a bachelor's degree will choose. Some students want to be close to home; others want to move away. Whether a college is wireless accessible has become increasingly important for incoming students. And there are still other factors to weigh, such as the social life on campus, the quality of the dorms and cafeteria food, the aesthetics and safety of the campus, and the reputation of the professors. Some students may want to attend the same college as their parents to fulfill some sort of romantic legacy. Yes, choosing the right college to attend involves many variables, and making the proper decision seems quite important.

Chances are, however, that most students have not factored in nearly as many variables when choosing their religion. This is because most people are indoctrinated into the religion of their parents and hold onto it for the rest of their lives. This is quite interesting when you think about it. Attending a certain college may or may not affect one's future, and it is unlikely that the college one graduates from encompasses all aspects of the personal lifespan. Religion, on the other hand, represents a way of life that is supposed to guide one's entire life. Why is it, then, that people do not explore all the religions of the world, then weigh in which, if any, will work best for them? Religion is, after all, very important to most people. Should they not spend as much time in researching which religion to practice as they do in evaluating which college to attend?

This chapter focuses on important issues related to education and religion. Although the review of each of these two major social institutions and agents of socialization is brief, the sociological relevance of both is properly covered.

EDUCATION: A RIGHT FOR ALL?

As a college professor, I often ask students, "Why are you in college?" The first response for most students is a pragmatic one: "To get a job." Idealistically, I wish that students would respond, "To increase my level of knowledge so that I can speak intelligently on a number of diverse topics." Realistically, however, I do realize that most students are attending college to find a job—although I remind them that if all they wanted was a job, they should be working instead of attending college! Students really mean, of course, that they want a good job, and in most cases, that means a job in a professional career that pays well. In light of current economic conditions, students are correct in their basic belief that attending college will help them to land a higher-paying job, thus earning them more money over the course of their lifetimes than will be possible for those with less education.

This belief echoes the idea that higher education is tied to social mobility via significant economic and noneconomic benefits (Karen and Dougherty 2005). Furthermore, as Joel Spring (2000) explains, "Since the 1970s, income and wealth are increasingly related to years of education as wages increase for jobs requiring technological skills and wages decline for low-skilled jobs" (1). Thus, while jobs are available, the lower-skilled jobs are lower paying than those that require technological and specialized skills taught at colleges and universities. As a means of illustration, data provided by the U.S. Bureau of Labor Statistics (2010a) reveal that the 2009 median weekly earnings for college graduates (bachelor's degree) were $1,025; yet it was just $454 for those with less than a high school diploma. The average median weekly salary for all U.S. workers in 2009 was $774 (see Table 11.1 for a complete listing of 2009 median weekly earnings by level of education).

TABLE 11.1 2009 Median Weekly Earnings by Level of Education

LEVEL OF EDUCATION	MEDIAN WEEKLY EARNINGS ($)
Doctoral degree	1,532
Professional degree	1,529
Master's degree	1,257
Bachelor's degree	1,025
Associate's degree	761
Some college, no degree	699
High school graduate	626
Less than a high school diploma	454

Source: U.S. Bureau of Labor Statistics 2010a.

As the information in Table 11.1 clearly demonstrates, the higher one's level of education, the higher one's salary will be (on average). The U.S. Bureau of Labor Statistics does not clarify what is meant by a professional degree or how it differs from a doctoral degree. Generally, however, PhD's are considered research doctorates, whereas professional degrees are not. A professional degree prepares a person for a specific profession, such as engineering. A PhD qualifies the holder for a wider range of occupations.

Formal Education

Formal education involves training and developing people in knowledge, skills, intellect, and character, in structured and certified programs. Thus, **formal education** can be viewed as a process of teaching and learning in which some people (e.g., teachers and professors) cultivate knowledge, skills, intellect, and character, while others (students) take on the role of learner. The value of a formal education lies not simply in the knowledge one gains but the provision of **credentials** (e.g., diplomas, certificates, security clearances, and powers of attorney) that are needed in a technologically advanced society. A credential is issued by a third party with the relevant authority or assumed competence to do so. It indicates that

Connecting Sociology and Popular Culture

Box 11.1 Celebrities and Formal Education

As already noted in this chapter, a positive correlation exists between one's education level and income, on average. Of course, there are always exceptions to the rule. For example, as we learned in Chapter 7, one of the richest people in the world, Bill Gates, did not graduate from college. He would fall into the "some college, no degree" category. (Many people claim some college when asked about their level of education; this has the same meaning as having attended college, even if just one class or for one semester.) Famous celebrities, by implication, are almost always quite wealthy, but not all of them have benefited from formal education. Child actors, especially those on successful television series, are often tutored in studios. Other celebrities have some college but no degree. And still others have college degrees. Let us take a look at a select sampling of celebrities and the education they have attained.

Many celebrities, including Natalie Portman shown here, have college degrees and encourage others to pursue higher education.

Paris Hilton is a high school dropout who later earned her General Educational Development (GED) certificate; Angelina Jolie graduated from Beverly Hills High School; Brad Pitt attended the Missouri School of Journalism at the University of Missouri, Columbia; Sean Penn attended Santa Monica College; Madonna attended the University of Michigan; Denzel Washington attended the University of Oklahoma, dropped out, and later earned his bachelor's in drama and journalism from Fordham University (1977); Sylvester Stallone came within a few credit hours of graduating from the University of Miami but later received his degree from that institution (1999) after receiving credit for his acting and life experiences; Samuel L. Jackson graduated from Morehouse College in Atlanta (1972); and Lucy Liu is a graduate of the University of Michigan (Varner 2008).

A number of celebrities have graduated from prestigious Ivy League schools, including Natalie Portman, with a psychology degree from Harvard; John Krasinski, with a playwriting degree from Brown; Brooke Shields, with a French literature degree from Princeton; Julia Stiles, with an English degree from Columbia; Conan O'Brien, with an American history degree (magna cum laude) from Harvard; and David Duchovny, with a master's degree in English literature from Yale. (Parade.com 2009). Jennifer Connelly earned a degree in English from the equally prestigious Stanford University (Parade.com 2009).

What Do You Think?

Considering the platform provided to celebrities by the media to offer us their opinions on a variety of topics, including politics, is it important that they have a college education? What do you think?

the possessor is competent to perform or qualified for a specific job or position. There are some jobs, such as acting, wherein advanced formal education is not needed to be successful (see "Connecting Sociology and Popular Culture" Box 11.1 for a select look at celebrities and their corresponding levels of education).

Formal education is a relatively new phenomenon. Historically, different groups of people, such as the early hunters and gatherers, transmitted the skills necessary for survival from one generation to the next. In agrarian societies, agricultural skills were also passed down from generation to generation. People were too busy fighting for survival to worry about intellectual pursuits. Eventually, with the development of written language, a privileged few were taught to read and write. The peasants, for the most part, were left to toil while select members of society began to learn the laws of mathematics and science. Books were handwritten and, understandably, few in number. By the 1500s, Europeans had been introduced to the Bible, but because few could read, it was up to the clergy to inform peasants about its contents and their interpretation.

Martin Luther (1497–1550), the person responsible for starting the Protestant Reformation and for whom Lutheranism is named, believed that everyone should have the right to learn to read and write. Specifically, Luther wanted all to be able read the Bible for themselves so that they could make their own personal meaning from the holy book. The Catholic Church, the dominant social institution of Western Europe at the time, was against the idea of mass education because it wanted to maintain control of and influence over the masses. The right to universal public education never emerged during Luther's lifetime. In fact, it would not materialize until centuries later. Instead, education was limited to high-status groups.

Mass education began with industrialization as society needed literate people to operate machinery and develop further technology. In the United States, mandatory education laws were finally instituted in the early 1900s. With the formation of community colleges and state universities during the twentieth century, far more opportunities became available for all American citizens to attain a college education. Meanwhile, in many parts of the world, mass education was far less of a reality. As a result, in 1948, the UN General Assembly adopted and proclaimed the Universal Declaration of Human Rights, which called for all member countries to publicize the text of the declaration. Of particular note is Article 26, which states that "everyone has the right to education" and that "education shall be free, at least in the elementary and fundamental stages," adding that

What Do You Think?

The government-funded formal education system in the United States provides educational opportunities through high school for all citizens. Should the government provide a college education for all citizens who qualify for admissions into public universities? Where would the funding come from to support such a system? What do you think?

"elementary education shall be compulsory" (Universal Declaration of Human Rights 1998). The need for a universal right to education ties directly into the economic correlation between education level and income pointed out earlier in this chapter.

SOCIOLOGICAL PERSPECTIVES ON EDUCATION

Sociologists are among the vast majority of academics who view education as one of society's most important social institutions. It is deemed so essential that it is often promoted as the solution to nearly every social problem that exists. For example, when people display racist and sexist attitudes, the teaching of tolerance is emphasized. Political candidates attempt to educate the populace about why they should be voted into office. Government programs such as DARE are introduced to elementary school students in an attempt to educate them about the potential dangers of illegal drug use. In short, education is promoted by a wide variety of social policy makers as a means of battling nearly all social problems. And yet, despite the near-universal acceptance of the idea that education is the solution to most problems, there exist differing opinions, or perspectives, regarding how educational programs should be introduced to students. The functionalist, conflict, and interactionist perspectives offer their own views on the role of education in society.

The Functionalist Perspective

The functionalist perspective analyzes the manifest (intended or stated) and latent (unintended or hidden) functions of society. According to functionalists, the manifest functions of education include the following:

- *Transmission of culture:* School-age children are educated in the norms, values, and beliefs of the greater society. Functionalists argue that it is important for children and immigrants to learn the ways of the dominant culture, including its history and language, in order to better fit into and function properly within the society in which they reside.
- *Promotion of social integration:* The mainstreaming of children and immigrants assists with the integration process and helps to form a unified society in which all members share a sense of community or belonging. Creating a community ideal is so important that most colleges and universities require freshmen (and, in some cases, sophomores) to live on campus.
- *Screening and selecting:* Education serves as a screening-and-placement system to prepare people for society's occupational structure through the acquisition of proper credentials. Possessing key credentials provides

opportunities for upward mobility. Thus, education helps to stimulate people to perform well in school so that they can be successful in the socioeconomic system.

- *Research and development:* Higher education institutions, especially universities and technological schools, have a commitment to developing new knowledge to benefit present and future generations. In this regard, education serves as an agent of social change.
- *Creation of well-rounded persons:* The expression "educating the whole person" comes into play here. College students often wonder why they have to take "general education" courses. The answer is quite simple: college graduates should be educated in a wide variety of topics so that they can think and speak intelligently on a wide variety of topics, including the arts, natural sciences, social sciences, history, and popular culture. At some colleges, students receive a break on their tuition for attending sporting and cultural events.

Religious-based colleges and universities, such as Notre Dame University, use sports as a means of reaffirming a sense of community and solidarity through religious symbolism, such as the image of Jesus Christ raising his arms (as if to indicate a touchdown) in mural form on the campus's library building. This image of Jesus is affectionately known as "Touchdown Jesus" among Notre Dame supporters.

The functionalist perspective also recognizes a number of latent functions of education:

- *Matchmaking:* Although you will seldom, if ever, find in your college handbook the promotion of this idea, many students will find their future spouses in college. This is not an important feature of higher education, but it is a nice bonus.
- *Development of social networks:* Creating networks of friendships and social connections is important as these people may help you find a job in the future.
- *Social life:* As suggested in the introductory section of this chapter, some students will choose a school based on its social life. These students may be attracted to the idea of attending a college with big-time sports programs or those known as party schools. Clearly, administrators do not embrace the "party school" label.

What Do You Think?

Some people, including employers, feel that the value of a degree is negatively compromised if it comes from a party school. What is your school's reputation, and will this reputation help or hinder your job search? What do you think?

The Conflict Perspective

Whereas the functionalist perspective concentrates on the (mostly positive) functions of a social institution, the conflict perspective generally focuses on the social inequalities found within a given institution. Conflict theorists, for example, believe that the norms, values, and beliefs taught by educators are dictated by those with power, or the social elites. Listed below are some of conflict theorists' primary concerns with the education system:

- *The hidden curriculum:* Conflict theorists believe that schools are essentially "control devices" that indoctrinate the younger generation, including immigrants, in the nonacademic knowledge, values, attitudes, norms, and beliefs of the dominate group in society. This perspective also argues that the rules enforced by administrators (puppets of the powerful) are designed to quell creativity and the expression of individual thought. These administrators, many of whom are not directly involved with education, mandate that teachers meet certain standards, such as assessment testing, in the classroom. Because students and parents primarily interact with teachers, the teachers must deal with the discontent associated with the **hidden curriculum**. This dissatisfaction is not a new phenomenon and was perhaps best articulated in popular culture more than thirty years ago in Pink Floyd's popular refrain from "Another Brick in the Wall": "We don't need no education. We don't need no thought control. No dark sarcasm in the classroom. Teachers, leave them kids alone." The irony of this refrain is cleverly demonstrated with a protest against education via the use of poor grammar.
- *Education as a capital commodity:* While functionalists view the research-and-development function of education in a positive light, conflict theorists view such innovative developments as necessary to maintaining the capitalist order. For example, technological advancements that increase production and reduce costs have value because they increase profits for capitalists. Capitalists, then, encourage people to become educated so that they can directly or indirectly increase production as a result of this newly developed knowledge. Thus, from this Marxist-conflict perspective, education serves to support the system of production run by those who control the means of production.
- *Credentialism:* Once again, the conflict perspective differs from the functionalist in its view of a similar topic. For conflict theorists, credentialism (an emphasis on certificate or degree attainment to show that people have certain skills required for specific jobs) reinforces social inequality because people with limited financial resources do not have the same resources necessary to pursue the credentials that come with higher education.
- *Tracking:* **Tracking**, sometimes called ability grouping or streaming, involves placing students in specific curricular groups based on academic ability (based on test scores). Although proponents of tracking point out its strengths (e.g., it allows teachers to better tailor lessons for a specific ability group, properly challenges high-ability students, and encourages students of low academic ability to achieve in specialized vocations), conflict theorists

point out the negative aspects of such a policy. These include reinforcement of the idea that society has given up on economically disadvantaged youths, as well as the tendency for less-experienced teachers to teach low-track classes, for lessons taught in low-track classes to lack the comprehensiveness of high-track lessons, and for high-track students to look down on those placed in low-track classes.

The Interactionist Perspective

In regard to the educational setting, symbolic interactionists are primarily concerned with two related issues: the self-fulfilling prophecy and the teacher-expectancy effect. The term "**self-fulfilling prophecy**," coined by sociologist Robert Merton ([1949] 1968), refers to a prediction that comes true, either directly or indirectly, through one's own actions. For example, worrying that she is going to have a bad game might alter an athlete's actions so that this prediction is fulfilled by her own behavior. In school, the **teacher-expectancy effect**—the impact of a teacher's expectations on a student's ability to perform—often generates a self-fulfilling prophecy. Thus, a teacher's telling a student from a lower socioeconomic class that he is "no good" and will "never amount to anything because he is stupid" may exert a strong negative influence over that student. The student may opt not to study for an exam because of the teacher's expectations and consequently fail, leading to a self-fulfilling prophecy. On the other hand, a teacher who constantly praises a student may influence him or her to study more so as not to disappoint the teacher.

What Do You Think?

Which of the three sociological perspectives on education best summarizes your academic experiences? What do you think?

PROBLEMS IN EDUCATION

Although education is often promoted as the solution to nearly all society's social problems, this institution is far from perfect. Problems in education begin with the fact that most schools—including statewide school systems—struggle to define their primary goals.

Goals

There is a lack of consensus as to what the goals of education should be. That is, should general knowledge or vocational training be emphasized? Should there be open enrollment or strict admissions requirements? How much homework is appropriate? At all levels of education, there is a lack of agreement as to what constitutes a basic education. Ideally, at least at the secondary level, basic skills such as reading, writing, math, science, physical health, and civic responsibility should be included as the primary goals of education. Most people directly or indirectly affiliated with education agree that some sort of standards should be put into place, but when specific questions are asked, educators are divided about how to answer them. The current buzzword of educational standards is "assessment." Assessment measurements are often vague and originate with bureaucrats far removed from the daily realities of teaching and learning. University professors generally argue that a student's grade represents an assessment; consequently, politically motivated assessments are unnecessary and highly subjective.

Bureaucratization of Schools

As mentioned earlier in the discussion of the hidden curriculum, administrators have introduced a number of "control devices" into education that have the ultimate effect of bureaucratizing schools. The bureaucratization of the classroom limits students' creativity and instructors' teaching approaches. Standardized testing and assessments and evaluations are ploys on the part of politicians and education administrators who care more about standardization in accountability than the furthering of creative knowledge. Teachers argue that assessments of students' learning are accomplished via subject examinations. Bureaucrats disagree and have increasingly insisted on some sort of standardized testing. For example, "accountability" is an important aspect of the No Child Left Behind Act of 2001. Each state must establish strong standards for what every child should know and learn in reading and math in grades three through eight. Student progress and achievement are measured for every child, every year. The basic intention of the No Child Left Behind legislation is good, as each child will theoretically have equal access to a quality education. Critics claim, among other things, that teachers are forced to "teach to a test." That is, teachers emphasize materials found on the assessment tests at the expense of other general areas of study. At colleges and universities, the bureaucratization of schools results in an increasingly bloated administrative body that emphasizes an increasing number of written rules and regulations, an increasing number of required general education classes, and the hiring of fewer teachers, which means fewer elective courses offered to students.

In 2007, the Pew Research Center for the People and the Press conducted research on Americans' feelings regarding the effectiveness of the No Child Left Behind legislation. A great deal of the research centered on questions about standardized testing. Among Pew's findings were the following:

- Just 30 percent of public school parents said that the No Child Left Behind Act made their children's schools better.

- Of African American parents, 37 percent reported that the act made schools better, compared to 33 percent of white parents; 22 percent of African American parents reported that the act made schools worse, compared with 27 percent of white parents.
- Forty-five percent of the public and 43 percent of parents with children in public schools said that the law overemphasizes standardized testing.
- Democrats (49 percent) and Independents (47 percent) were more likely to say that the law overemphasizes testing than Republicans (38 percent).
- Level of education presented a notable difference in views about standardized testing. Of college graduates, 64 percent reported that the act places too much emphasis on standardized testing, compared with 44 percent of those with some college, and 32 percent of those with a high school education or less.
- In addition, nearly half of college grads (48 percent) said there is too much federal influence over schools under the No Child Left Behind Act, compared with 37 percent of those with some college, and 39 percent of those with a high school diploma or less.

Unequal Funding

Despite the idealism of the No Child Left Behind legislation, schools are not funded equally. This is true when comparing private schools to public schools and when comparing public schools in some districts to those in others. As a result, some schools do not have enough books for their students and lack other necessary equipment, while other schools can afford their students access to computers and other superior facilities. Funding also influences classroom size. Schools with enough money to hire additional teachers are able to reduce the teacher-student ratio, and educational experts believe that the smaller the ratio, the better the educational experience of the student. Unequal funding is tied directly to local taxes, especially property taxes. A way to alleviate this unequal funding from district to district is to pool all the money collected in all districts and divide it equally. Naturally, people from wealthier districts oppose this idea, and many politicians are afraid to establish such a system for fear of not being reelected.

What Do You Think?

When you look back at your elementary and high school education, do you believe there was too much, too little, or just the right amount of standardized testing? Now that you are in college, do you believe there is too much, too little, or just the right amount of standardized testing? What about the role of the state and/or federal government at your school? Is it too big, too little, or just right? What do you think?

Needs of the Majority Versus the Needs of the Minority

This educational problem centers on the need of teachers to keep a certain "pace" in the classroom. Teachers and professors have a teaching plan centered on how much material they hope to cover in a given class period, as well as across the entire semester. In order to accomplish their goals, teachers must move along at a certain pace. This results in some students not quite comprehending the material, thus lagging behind. If a teacher slows the pace so that the slower learners can catch up, the advanced students in the classroom will not be properly stimulated. At most schools and colleges, remedial courses are available to help students with special needs. However, an increasing number of colleges and universities is eliminating remedial courses, arguing that college is a place not to catch up but rather to accelerate. Conversely, far fewer secondary schools and colleges offer programs for "gifted" students as a means to stimulate elite learners. An honors program, for example, is designed to challenge the brightest students.

School Violence

Perhaps the most disturbing problem in education is school violence, which occurs at all levels of education (elementary, middle, and high school, as well as college). According to the Centers for Disease Control and Prevention (CDC 2008b), an estimated 55 million students are enrolled in prekindergarten through twelfth grade. Another 15 million students attend college and universities across the country. Most U.S. schools are relatively safe, but parents, teachers, administrators, and students themselves would agree that any amount of violence is unacceptable. Acts of violence disrupt the learning process and have a negative effect on students, the school itself, and the greater community (CDC 2008b). The CDC's 2008 fact sheet on violence in schools lists the following findings:

- Approximately 38 percent of public schools reported at least one incidence of violence to police during the 2005–2006 school year.
- In 2005, 24 percent of students reported the presence of gangs at their schools. Students in urban schools were more likely to report gang activity than suburban and rural students.
- From 2003 to 2004, 10 percent of teachers in city schools reported that they were threatened with injury by students, compared with 6 percent of teachers in suburban schools and 5 percent in rural schools.
- In 2005, students ages twelve to eighteen were victim to about 628,200 violent crimes at school, including rape, both sexual and aggravated assault, and robbery.
- About 30 percent of students reported moderate ("sometimes") or frequent ("once a week or more") bullying. This included 13 percent reporting as a bully, 10.6 percent as a victim, and 6.3 percent as both.
- Young people who bully are more likely to smoke, drink alcohol, get into fights, vandalize property, skip school, and drop out of school.

Bullying is an all-too-common occurrence at many schools across the nation.

- Of boys who were bullies in middle school, 60 percent had at least one criminal conviction by age twenty-four.
- Violent deaths at schools accounted for less than 1 percent of the homicides and suicides among children ages five to eighteen.

The most horrific school shooting case on a college campus occurred at Virginia Tech on April 16, 2007. On that violent day, Virginia Tech student Seung-Hui Cho killed thirty-two people and wounded many others before taking his own life. The shooting took place at two separate locations: a dorm (West Ambler Johnston Hall) and a classroom (Norris Hall). Not only the deadliest school shooting, this was also the deadliest shooting rampage by a single gunman in U.S. history (ABC News 2007).

Dropouts

It has already been established that a positive correlation exists between educational attainment and income. High school dropouts earn significantly less income than college graduates. The obvious conclusion is that students need to stay in school if they want to improve their chances of succeeding in life. Students who drop out of high school harm more than themselves, however; they also harm the immediate community and the greater society.

How many students drop out of high school? The answer is alarming. "Collectively, America's more than 20,000 high schools graduate just 71% of their students. This means 1.2 million young people a year—about 7000 every school day—are dropping out without the necessary skills to get and keep a good job" (Tyre 2009, p. 10). Dropout rates vary from school district to school district, but students from inner-city public schools face the greatest likelihood of failure.

How do dropouts negatively affect the community and society? To begin with, low graduation rates affect America's ability to compete in the global workplace. "A 2008 report from the nonprofit organization Education Trust found that the United States is the only industrialized country where teens are less likely than their parents to earn a high school diploma" (Tyre 2009, p. 10).

Economists estimate that the students who drop out each year result in \$320 billion in lost wages, taxes, and productivity. Adults who are high school dropouts are more likely to draw on government resources like welfare and Medicaid. Dropouts are also more likely to get into trouble and end up in jail (Tyre 2009). In short, it is in the best interests of all to find ways to decrease the dropout rate in our schools.

Lowering Academic Standards

As education becomes increasingly important, lowering academic standards is one of the last things administrators should consider. And yet, there is an alarming trend toward dumbing down the curriculum (at all levels of education) in many school districts across the United States. Examples include social promotion (e.g., advancing a student to the next grade level simply because of his or her age); lowering qualifying exam scores, passing-grade standards, and minimum scores (e.g., a school determines that the lowest grade a teacher may give a student is fifty out of one hundred); and rewarding students simply because they tried to do well. Trying is not doing. Students must do the work. They must learn the assigned materials. School administrators and teachers must raise, not lower, academic standards if they want students to achieve and to excel in society. (And bearing in mind the previous discussion of dropouts, it is also important for the greater community and society to maintain high standards in schools.)

A number of education-reform critics argue that establishing national standards of education is the key to improving the overall educational system. Education reform, they argue, should include "common standards" whereby good teachers receive merit pay, and students who perform well move on to the next grade. It will be difficult to establish national standards as the role of public education is pretty much left to the states, and the states usually pass authority off to local school districts, of which there are now more than 13,000 in the United States (Isaacson 2009). "The Federal Government provides less than 9% of the funding for K–12 schools. That is why it has proved impossible thus far to create common curriculum standards nationwide" (Isaacson 2009, p. 32). Those who promote common standards hope to achieve "universal proficiency" levels in such basic courses as reading and math.

Whether or not one agrees with the idea of common standards or some other sort of education reform, it is clear—in light of the United States' worldwide rankings in math and reading scores—that something must be done. Compared to other nations, the United States ranks a dismal twenty-fifth in math and fifteenth in reading proficiency (see Table 11.2).

TABLE 11.2 Nations Ranked by Reading and Math Proficiency Among Fifteen-Year-Olds

READING (2003)	MATH (2006)
1. Finland	1. Finland
2. South Korea	2. South Korea
3. Canada	3. The Netherlands
4. Australia	4. Switzerland
5. New Zealand	5. Canada
6. Ireland	6. Japan
7. Sweden	7. New Zealand
8. The Netherlands	8. Belgium
9. Belgium	9. Australia
10. Norway	10. Denmark
11. Switzerland	11. Czech Republic
12. Japan	12. Iceland
13. Poland	13. Austria
14. France	14. Germany
15. United States	15. Sweden
16. Denmark	16. Ireland
17. Iceland	17. France
18. Germany	18. United Kingdom
19. Austria	19. Poland
20. Czech Republic	20. Slovak Republic
21. Hungary	21. Hungary
22. Spain	22. Luxembourg
23. Luxembourg	23. Norway
24. Portugal	24. Spain
25. Italy	25. United States
26. Greece	26. Portugal
27. Slovak Republic	27. Italy
28. Turkey	28. Greece
29. Mexico	29. Turkey
	30. Mexico

Source: Time 2009. There is a difference in the number of countries listed in the "Reading" and "Math" columns because the results were tallied in different years.

OTHER ISSUES IN EDUCATION

> **What Do You Think?**
>
> Many problems are associated with the U.S. education system. What problems do you consider most important? What can be done to correct the many problems confronting education in the United States? What do you think?

A number of other issues in education are worth mentioning, including compensatory education, alternatives to traditional public schools, community colleges, and whether religion should be taught in school. **Compensatory education** programs are U.S.-government-funded programs designed to help preschool children from lower socioeconomic classes. Perhaps the best known such program is Head Start. According to information provided on the Head Start website, the mission of this national program is to promote "school readiness by enhancing the social and cognitive development of children through the provision of educational, health, nutritional, social and other services to enrolled children and families" (U.S. Department of Health and Human Services 2008). In general, children who go through the Head Start program score higher on intelligence and achievement tests and are less likely to be placed in special education. These children also develop a higher self-image and self-concept.

For a number of reasons (e.g., the previously discussed problems in education), parents have opted to send their children to private, magnet, or charter schools instead of the traditional public school. In other cases, parents have decided to homeschool their children. **Private schools** may be religiously based or privately funded by wealthy persons or endowments. Private schools are not open to the public and generally entail the payment of tuition or other, related fees. **Public schools**, in contrast, are paid for by the taxpayers. According to the U.S. Department of Education's National Center for Education Statistics, private school enrollment was 6.2 million in 2007, or 11 percent of enrolled students for that year. Based on an analysis of U.S. census data, the state of Delaware and Washington, D.C., have the highest rates of private school enrollment (19 percent) in the United States (Essoyan 2008). Hawaii follows at 18 percent. At 4 percent, Utah and Montana have the lowest rates of private school enrollment. Nevada is the next lowest at 5 percent (Essoyan 2008).

Magnet schools differ from private schools in that they are a part of the public school system. They differ from public schools in that they offer a specialized focus, for instance, emphasizing computer applications, performing arts, math and science, honors programs, or the basics. **Charter schools**, while receiving taxpayer money, have a different organizational model from magnet schools (e.g., they have their own school administration, which does not follow the public school system's bureaucracy). Big Picture Learning schools represent another alternative to traditional teaching by employing such unique (some might say radical) techniques as not assigning homework, filling out report cards, or giving class tests; encouraging internships; and having students design their own learning plans (Doran 2008). According to its website, Big Picture Learning's mission "is to lead vital changes in education, both in the United States and internationally, by generating and sustaining innovative, personalized schools that work in tandem with the real world of the greater community" (Big Picture Learning 2009). This nonprofit organization claims that its students score, on average, much higher in English and math and have high college acceptance rates (Doran 2008).

Some parents and guardians believe that the education of their children is better conducted in the home rather than a formal setting. This type of education is known as *homeschooling* or home learning. As the name implies, homeschooling involves the education of children at home, usually by parents but sometimes by tutors. Before mandatory education laws, most schooling was conducted at home. Now, considered an alternative form of education, this schooling method has gained renewed interest and increased in frequency in both the United States and Canada over the past decade (Tepperman and Blain 2006). Although total numbers are still low, the U.S. Department of Education (2003) estimates that more than 1 million (roughly 2.2 percent) American students are homeschooled. Proponents of homeschooling like the idea that students are not exposed to peer pressure, receive one-on-one instruction, do not face violence, and are free of the other problems often associated with public schooling. Critics of homeschooling argue that homeschooled children are socially awkward because they have fewer social interactions with peers. According to the U.S. Department of Education (2003), homeschoolers score, on average, sixty-seven points higher than the national average on the Scholastic Aptitude Test, or SAT.

After graduating from high school or attaining the equivalent level of education, for instance, by getting a GED, students may opt to attend a community college or a vocational or occupational college. Community colleges were originally established to benefit low-income students as a stepping-stone to better jobs and higher income (Santibanez et al. 2007). Because community colleges are so important for the economically poor, some states (e.g., California) have an open admissions policy. There is a debate as to whether an open-door policy should be offered at the collegiate level. An open admissions policy creates a classroom with students who possess differing degrees of preparedness for college-level work. Furthermore, due in part to the ever-increasing expenses associated with attending a four-year college, many students attend a community college first and then transfer to a four-year school. The nearly 1,200 community colleges in the United States are responsible for educating about half the nation's undergraduates (Santibanez et al. 2007). Occupational and vocational colleges are designed to teach adults "professional service skills" in order to qualify them for specific jobs (Deil-Amen 2006). Occupational and vocational training offers hands-on instruction by individuals with professional experience in specialized fields (e.g., plumbing, electrical, or computer repair). Beyond training, vocational and occupational colleges offer relevant certifications and accelerated training, qualifying graduates for immediate employment without the overwhelming debt that most college students accumulate.

Another important issue in education involves whether religion should be taught in schools. The primary controversy stems from the U.S. Constitution's First Amendment, which calls for a separation of church and state. The term "state" refers to governments (federal, state, and local), while the term "church" refers to religious denominations (R. Thomas 2007) (see "A Closer Look" Box 11.2 for the main arguments of this hotly debated issue).

A Closer Look

Box 11.2 Religion in Public Schools

The U.S. Constitution's First Amendment, the first section of the Bill of Rights, guarantees citizens five basic rights. Most Americans are quick to demand their rights; yet, very few can actually name them. Do you know what they are? (See "Connecting Sociology and Popular Culture Box 10.2 for the answer.) The roots of the First Amendment can be traced to a bill written by Thomas Jefferson, who wanted to ensure that all citizens were free of and from a state-mandated religion. In brief, Jefferson opposed having a state religion to which all citizens were compelled to belong.

Despite the First Amendment, people from many communities across the United States feel strongly that religion should be a part of the school curriculum. Christianity, in particular, has a long history of influence in American government. As a result, many in the Christian majority feel that religion should have a strong presence in schools, including the recitation of religious prayers at the start of the school day. The trend in court decisions, however, has been toward curtailing prayer in school settings. "But prayer is permitted in the form of students praying individually on their own initiative or small groups using their free time to pray together" (R. Thomas 2007, p. 130). Proponents of religion in schools worry that not permitting religion is akin to endorsing secular humanism. (Note: Secular humanism is discussed later in this chapter.) And although secular humanism is important to some people, the total number of its adherents pales in comparison to the number supporting religious-based teachings.

Opponents to teaching, or endorsing, religion in school cite the First Amendment but also point out how many different religions exist in the United States and Canada at present. Endorsing one religion at the expense of others promotes religious intolerance, critics claim. Sociologists point out that the idea of schools endorsing one dominant religion (e.g., Christianity) is hegemonic in thinking. **Hegemony** refers to the dominance of one group over another. Perhaps the strongest argument against teaching religion in school is this counterargument: should the church teach science, math, and other subjects? Religion, after all, is a belief system, whereas science, math, and the other subjects are fact based.

What Do You Think?

Should religion be taught in school? Why or why not? Should science and mathematics be taught in church? Why or why not? What do you think?

THE INSTITUTION OF RELIGION

Religion is one of the oldest social institutions of human society. It arose out of the human need to explain and understand life's mysteries. Primitive humans, who were smart enough to outwit animals, were not intelligent enough to explain such simple things as lunar and solar eclipses. Lacking intellect, primitive people blamed such cosmic occurrences on angry gods rather than simple planetary alignments. With the rise of science, many of life's mysteries were explained quite rationally. However, many other questions remained unanswered, so people continued to rely on religion and their faith that the unknown was the bailiwick of a supreme being or beings. In short, religion continues as a major social institution because it brings comfort to people, carries out important social functions, and encompasses a great variety of organizations.

Defining Religion

As stated above, religion developed as a explanation for life's uncertainties. Religious explanations are not based on scientific research and empirical data; instead, they are based on beliefs. For most people, religion is a predominant influence on their lives, and when science provides evidence that counters their beliefs, a discord is created. Should one maintain faith in a belief system or accept the intellectual explanation of things? As Plato explained long ago, there is a difference between knowledge and science and opinion and religious belief (Lindsay 1943). Science and religion are often at odds because of their fundamental structural differences. Science is grounded by a commitment to empirical testing of theoretical postulates. Religion, on the other hand, is consumed by spirituality and a structure centered around belief. As Davies states, "The world's major religions, founded on received wisdom and dogma, are rooted in the past and do not cope easily with changing times" (1983, p. 2). Religious adherents are told to rely on faith and their spiritual beliefs. Beliefs are ideas that people presume to be true, when they may or may not be. Every religion is based on a system of beliefs. Religious beliefs are

Diverse students find a common bond through prayer.

ideals to which members of a particular religion adhere. Adherents are expected to abide by such beliefs and accept their validity even without empirical verification.

Some religious adherents abide by beliefs blindly, even when they contradict the norms and laws of the prevailing society. For example, in the United States, as with other Western societies, parents are expected to provide the best health care possible to their children. When parents choose to ignore the law in favor of a religious belief, they run the risk of civil punishment. Such was the case for Dale Neumann, a central Wisconsin man found guilty of killing his eleven-year-old daughter Madeline because he and other family members prayed for the ill girl instead of seeking medical care for her. Prosecutors contended that Neumann should have rushed his daughter to a hospital when she could not walk, talk, eat, or drink. "Instead, Madeline died on the floor of the family's rural Weston home as people surrounded her and prayed.... Neumann, who once studied to be a Pentecostal minister, testified that he believed God would heal his daughter and he never expected her to die. God promises in the Bible to heal, he said" (*Post-Standard,* 8/2/09, p. A4). Neumann testified that if he went to a doctor, he would be putting the doctor before God, and he believed that was the wrong thing to do, based on his religious beliefs.

Neumann's expression of religious faith, although extreme, reflects the general idea of religion and its connection to an unearthly higher power. George Sage (1989) states, "Religion is the belief that supernatural forces influence human lives" (p. 271). Intelligent design theories argue against natural selection and evolution theories, insisting that the complexities of human existence are beyond random chance and must, therefore, involve the existence of either God or some supernatural designer. Among the many problems with intelligent design theories is the fact that their premises remain untestable and therefore unscientific. Most people believe in a god or creator of some sort. Science needs empirical validity. Although there is a wide variety of religions around the world, religion is universally found in nearly all human societies. "As a social institution, religion is a system that functions to maintain and transmit beliefs about forces considered to be supernatural and sacred. It provides codified guides for moral conduct and prescribes symbolic practices deemed to be in harmony with beliefs about the supernatural" (Sage 1989, p. 271).

With these ideas in mind, **religion** can be defined as a system of beliefs and rituals that binds people together in a social group while attempting to answer the dilemmas and questions of human existence by making the world more meaningful to adherents. And by many accounts, religion is very meaningful in the lives of most Americans (See "Connecting Sociology and Popular Culture" Box 11.3).

Connecting Sociology and Popular Culture

Box 11.3 Religion in Contemporary American Society

How religious are Americans? And how much meaning does religion hold for them? To answer these questions, let us look at data that measure a variety of religious views and practices in the contemporary United States. According to data provided by the Pew Forum on Religion & Public Life (2009),

- about three-quarters of U.S. adults (in 2008) described themselves as Catholic (24 percent) or as belonging to one of the various Protestant denominations (51 percent);
- 39 percent of Americans pray at least once a week, another 33 percent pray once or twice a month or a few times a year, and 27 percent seldom or never pray;
- Jehovah's Witnesses (82 percent) and Mormons (75 percent) are the most likely to pray, while atheists (4 percent) are the least likely to pray;
- 63 percent of those with children pray or read holy texts with their children, with Mormons (91 percent) the most likely to do so;
- 42 percent of Americans agree with the statement "I often feel that my values are threatened by Hollywood and the entertainment industry," with Mormons (67 percent) most likely to agree and Jews (25 percent) the least likely;
- 50 percent of Americans accept homosexuality as a way of life, with Jews (79 percent) the most accepting and Mormons (24 percent) the least accepting (*Los Angeles Times*, 6/28/08).

The Pew Forum on Religion & Public Life (2009) provides us with other survey results on Americans' religious attitudes and practices, including the following:

- Men (20 percent) are more likely than women (13 percent) to claim no religious affiliation.
- Among people who are married, 37 percent are married to a spouse with a different religious affiliation (this figure includes Protestants married to another Protestant from a different denomination).
- Hindus (78 percent) and Muslims (71 percent) are the most likely to be married and to be married to someone of the same religion (90 and 83 percent, respectively).
- Mormons (20 percent) and Muslims (15 percent) are the religious categories with the largest families, as defined by having three or more children living at home.
- Of all the major racial and ethnic groups in the United States, black Americans (75 percent) are the most likely to report a formal religious affiliation.
- Those reporting no religious affiliation are likely to be younger than those claiming an affiliation.

What Do You Think?

What do you think of the data provided here? Are Americans more or less religious than you previously thought? How do you compare with the rest of Americans in terms of religious views and practices? What do you think?

Sociology and Religion

Karl Marx, who influenced the creation of conflict theory, argued that religion was the "opiate of the masses" because it existed chiefly to pacify the poor by turning their attention away from the misery of their lives in this world toward a happier afterlife (Glock and Stark 1965; McLellan 1987). Marx argued that religion existed to help the ruling elite keep the masses docile, controllable, and exploitable. He referred to it as an explicitly evil form of slavery that hampered men's attempts to reach their full human potential (Carlebach 1978). For Marx, the existence of a higher entity than man was not even conceivable (Aptheker 1968). He believed that man made the world, it was up to him to change it for the better, and no amount of churchgoing or prayer could save the world. Consequently, for Marx, religion was not necessary; it was universal only because exploitation is universal.

Sociologist Max Weber used religion to help explain the growth of capitalism. In *The Protestant Ethic and the Spirit of Capitalism,* Weber ([1904–1905] 1958) traced the impact of Protestantism—primarily Calvinism—on the rise of the spirit of capitalism. He found that other religions were "irrational" in foundation and therefore not conducive to the growth of a rational economic system (capitalism).

Whereas Marx and Weber examined religion primarily from sociopolitical and economic points of view, Emile Durkheim described religion as a system of beliefs and practices relative to sacred things that unites like-minded people in a kind of moral community (Durkheim 1915). **Sacred** items are those that we set apart and revere; the sacred is felt to be holy. The opposite of the sacred is the profane. The **profane** consists of society's ordinary, mundane, and secular items. Durkheim argued that religion was, at each moment of history, the totality of beliefs and sentiments of a group of people. His own abandonment of religion drove him to higher levels of patriotism and led him to accept and promote French secularism. Secularism comes about as society becomes increasingly dominated by science and the "worship" of mundane items. **Secularization**, then, is the process by which the influence of religion in a society declines. It involves a reliance on science to provide answers to life's dilemmas and uncertainties. As a proponent of secularism, Durkheim encouraged the worship of society—rather than of God or religion.

SOCIOLOGICAL PERSPECTIVES ON RELIGION

Marx, Weber, and Durkheim were among the early theorists to present ideas on religion. Sociologists continue to examine the institution of religion from a variety of sociological perspectives. Just as we examined education from the point of view of the three major sociological perspectives earlier in this chapter, we now look at religion from the same three perspectives.

The Functionalist Perspective

Functionalists acknowledge that religion provides both functional and dysfunctional aspects. Religion helps to give order to the lives of adherents, it serves to explain and justify one's place in the world, and it tells its believers that humans are not a mere accident of history but a creation of God. Religion offers a version of reality that provides meaning and makes sense of a vast, ever-changing, confusing, and seemingly meaningless world. Thus, according to functionalists, religion meets many basic human needs, which explains its near universality. The specific functions of religion include the following:

- *Social solidarity:* The word "religion" derives from the Latin *religare,* meaning "to bind together." Religion, then, is a vehicle for getting a large number of like-minded people to accept and conform to common beliefs and values, where shared perspectives shape a "we" feeling among members.
- *Social control:* The social bonding of religious adherents extends beyond civil concerns to issues of morality that are articulated in such holy scriptures as the Ten Commandments, the Golden Rule, and the Koranic rules. Through sacred rules, religion attempts to control the behaviors of its followers by telling them what they need to do in order to gain salvation. Violating the rules can lead to strong negative sanctions. Religious people often turn to holy teachings when choosing courses of actions deemed to be right and proper. In some societies, religion is the dominating force behind social-control efforts.
- *Ceremonies of status:* Religion serves to confer legitimacy on a society's norms and values via ceremonies of status that represent passage from one level to the next. Baptisms, bar mitzvahs, confirmations, and other religious ceremonies mark the passage of children through the developmental stages of life. Members of the religious community celebrate these passages in such a manner that adherents feel blessed to be a part of the community.
- *Self-esteem and identity:* Participation in religious ceremonies, prayers, and activities gives adherents a sense of identity and generally increases self-esteem. To have a member of one's family serve as a clergy person, for example, is almost always a guaranteed form of positive identity and esteem.
- *Psychological support:* A primary function of religion is providing emotional and spiritual support to followers. Psychological support is especially important when a family member is sick or has recently died. The religious community unites and provides much-needed support for the grieving family. Psychological support is also critical during times when people question

their faith and purpose in life. Many find much-needed comfort in the religious guidance of their leaders.

As Robert Merton ([1949] 1968) explained, one should not assume that just because a social institution exists, all aspects of that institution are functional. Any item of a social system may have negative consequences, which lessens its overall effectiveness and contribution to the social system. For example, religion often promotes solidarity, but it can only serve this function on the societal level if there is a consensus among all the members of society. Religion is one of the leading causes of war and conflict throughout human history. It continues to be a source of intolerance today. History has also shown that many people have been victimized by religious persecution throughout time. A general dislike for people of different religious persuasions has been used as a justification for oppression and any number of violent acts; consider, for instance, the Inquisition, the burning of witches at the stake, and the offering of virgin sacrifices. Furthermore, in its attempt to provide explanations for the meaning of life and human existence, religion has often offered irrational, unscientific, and empirically unverified answers, insisting that adherents take them on faith.

The Conflict Perspective

As we have learned already, the conflict perspective was inspired by the ideas of Karl Marx. As a humanist, Marx wanted everyone to reach his or her full human potential while on earth. He promoted such an idea because he was not convinced that there was an afterlife. Marx reasoned that if there is no guarantee of an afterlife, should people not live their lives here on earth to the fullest? He argued that people in power use religion as a form of social control. When people are convinced that a certain way of life leads to rewards in the hereafter, they have no reason to fight for equality in the present. Students should ask themselves, If it were a fact that there isn't an afterlife, would I lead my life differently? Marx attempted to stimulate people to ask such a question. He believed that once they realized this could be their only chance for happiness, people would abandon religion and pursue full lives here on earth. Marx attributed the willingness of people to blindly accept the teachings of their religious leaders as an example of false consciousness—the inability to see what is in one's own best interest.

Conflict theorists, like their functionalist counterparts who acknowledge the dysfunctional aspects of religion, argue that religion is a leading cause of social disruption, violence, and war. Since like-minded people find it natural to use the expression "we" as a form of identification with others of the same religion, the obvious consequence is the formation of a "they" group. (Note: The "we-they" concept is discussed in Chapter 8.) And this "they" group consists of all people who adhere to a different religion. As anyone with even a superficial knowledge of the world realizes, the world is currently filled with examples of intolerance based on religious beliefs. The negative aspects of the "we-they" concept also serve to legitimize the many forms of social inequality that exist in societies around the world.

The Symbolic-Interactionist Perspective

Although the macro approaches of functionalism and conflict theory seem best suited to explaining the role of religion from a sociological point of view, the micro-oriented symbolic-interactionist perspective is also relevant. Recall from Chapter 2 that symbolic interactionism is a theory based on the idea that social reality is constructed in each human interaction through the use of symbols. In short, we interact with one another through the use of symbols.

Religion is filled with symbolic behavior; in fact, it is nearly dependent upon the use of symbols and rituals. Religious adherents combine ritualistic behaviors with the use of symbols during ceremonies of passage, while saying prayers, and when wearing certain types of clothing at specific events. Adherents abide by certain symbolic protocols without consciously thinking about their behavior—for example, when kneeling, standing, and sitting during church services. The ritualistic behavior of repeating the same acts over and over leads to near involuntarily actions. But symbolic interactionists remind us that such behavior is learned; it is not innate. Ritualistic religious behaviors may seem natural to adherents, but they are the result of conditioning. Symbolic interactionists also point out that the effectiveness of any religion and its leaders is also the result of the conditioned behavior.

Consider, for example, that a Catholic who walks into a Catholic church will place his or her hand in holy water, make the sign of the cross, and kneel in the aisle directly in front of the altar. Catholics do this routinely. And they are certainly not alone in their rituals. All adherents of major religions have ritualistic behaviors that they engage in. Profane items, such as two pieces of wood crossed to form a small *t* come to symbolize a sacred, holy cross for those who believe in the cross's symbolism and meaning. Once again, all major religions give symbolic meaning to otherwise profane items.

What Do You Think?

Attend a service of a religion about which you have little or no previous knowledge. Observe the behaviors of the adherents and look for examples of ritualistic behavior. See if you can spot the symbols of the greatest importance. Compare these with your own religion. If you are not religious, visit a second religion's services. Do you see any common behaviors from a symbolic-interactionist perspective? What do you think?

ORGANIZING RELIGION

With the introduction of the terms "sacred," "profane," and "secularization," it becomes necessary to point out other important concepts of relevance to the sociological study of religion. Specifically, we are concerned here with various forms of religious organization, including the church, denominations, sects, and cults. Analysis begins with the term "church."

Church

The term "**church**" is often used generically by sociologists (and laypersons) to refer to all varieties of religious organization. A church is a religious organization that is viewed as legitimate within mainstream society. The goal of any church is to reinforce its beliefs among believers and to convert or persecute nonbelievers. When a church is the official religion of a state, it will endorse the existing political and socioeconomic institutions of that society. The United States is one of the few nations that has never had an official state religion. Even so, Christianity is the prevailing faith in the United States.

Denomination

Smaller subdivisions of churches are known as "denominations." A **denomination** is a large group of religious congregations united under a common faith and name and organized under an administrative and legal hierarchy. A denomination accepts the larger society and the legitimacy of other religions. Examples of denominations in the United States include Methodism, Lutheranism, Roman Catholicism, and Reform and Conservative Judaism.

Sect

A **sect** is a type of religious organization that claims legitimacy but stands independently from the greater society. Sects are smaller in size than denominations. Like churches, sects claim to have found the path to salvation for their adherents. Unlike a church, a sect does not attempt to convert or persecute nonbelievers. Instead, members attempt to live their lives peacefully within a society, yet removed from its prevailing sentiments, values, and norms. Examples include the Amish, Jehovah's Witnesses, and Hasidic Jews.

Cult

Generally speaking, a **cult** can be defined as a religious movement that has little or nothing in common with other types of religious organizations found in the same society. Although cults can be formal or informal organizations, they are likely to be regarded as unconventional or unusual from the standpoint of prevailing churches, denominations, and sects. A cult usually originates with a leader who has a revelation or message from God. The leader's personal charisma sustains the life of the cult. The cult leader becomes a source of fresh religious ideas for those who are seeking solutions to various life issues.

THE MAJOR WORLD RELIGIONS AND ESTIMATED MEMBERSHIP

The major religions of the world are generally theistic. "Theism" refers to a belief in God. The term "monotheism" means a belief in one God, while the term "polytheism" refers to a belief two or more gods. Most of the major religions began as polytheistic and evolved into monotheistic faiths. Our review of the major world religions is chronological, beginning with the oldest major religion, Hinduism. Global and U.S. membership estimates are also provided.

Hinduism (Origins Dating to 4000–2500 BCE)

The origins of Hinduism can be traced to the Indus Valley (India and Pakistan) civilization dating back to between 4000 and 2500 BCE. Although generally described as a polytheistic religion, Hinduism is founded on a belief in the unity of everything. This totality is called Brahma, the greatest deity. For Hindus, the goal in life is to reach enlightenment. One's path, or progress, toward enlightenment is measured by his or her karma. *Karma* is the idea that a person's behavior in the present life will determine his or her position in the next life. Good deeds are rewarded and lead the individual to a higher level of enlightenment. Bad deeds are punished and lead the individual to a lower level of social standing in the next life. The idea that individuals have multiple lives is reflected by the Hindu belief in reincarnation. A fundamental Hindu concept, *reincarnation* is the belief that the human soul does not die but is reborn. Worldwide, there are nearly 1 billion Hindus (Adherents.com 2007). According to the Pew Research Center (2008), approximately 0.4 percent of Americans (a little more than 1 million people) are Hindu.

Of note, the popular TV show *My Name Is Earl* is based on the idea of karma. The lead character, Earl, and his brother Randy have harmed many people during their lives. Earl learns about karma and decides to make amends. He creates a list of all the people he has harmed and crosses their names off the list once he has made up for what he did to them. In so doing, Earl becomes more enlightened. Earl also learns, however, that the path to enlightenment is filled with challenges.

Judaism (Origins Dating to 2000–1600 BCE)

Judaism began as polytheistic and evolved into a monotheistic religion. The name itself originates from that of Jacob's fourth son, Judah. Jews believe in a God that watches over people to monitor their activities, with good being rewarded and evil punished. Because the human soul is immortal, if good deeds are not rewarded in this life, they will be rewarded in the afterlife. Salvation, then, is attained through action (a way of life) and belief. Among the most important figures of the Jewish faith are Abraham and Moses. (Note: Muslims also trace their lineage to Abraham.) Moses is recognized as the greatest Jewish leader because the Jews believe that God revealed to him the Torah (the first five books of the Bible). The core belief of Judaism is "love of God." Jews believe themselves to be the "chosen" people and await Judgment Day when the Messiah will resurrect the dead and restore the Jerusalem Temple destroyed in 70 CE. There are roughly 14 million Jews worldwide (Adherents.com 2007), with approximately 6 million living in the United States.

Buddhism (Origins Dating to 560–490 BCE)

Buddhism is another religion that originated in India. Some forms of Buddhism are polytheistic, others monotheistic. This religion developed from the teachings of Siddhartha Guatama, who reached enlightenment around 535 BCE and assumed the title of "Buddha." Buddhism arose as a rejection of Hinduism, but it retains a belief in reincarnation. Individuals go through a number of life cycles wherein they attempt to detach themselves from all desires in order to reach salvation. Salvation can be attained through knowing and living by "noble truths." Ultimately, Buddhists seek nirvana. **Nirvana** is a state of perfect bliss in which the self is freed from suffering and desire. It represents the final freeing of the soul. A type of supreme happiness, nirvana is possible when the soul relinquishes passion, hatred, and delusion. Worldwide, there are approximately 376 million Buddhists (Adherents.com 2007). In the United States, 0.7 percent (less than 3 million) of Americans are Buddhist (Pew Research Center 2008).

What Do You Think?

Do you believe people can reach nirvana? What does "nirvana" mean to you? Has Kurt Cobain, deceased former lead singer of Nirvana, reached nirvana? What do you think?

Confucianism (Origin Dated to 500 BCE)

Confucianism is based on the principles of Confucius (K'ung Fu Tzu) who lived from 551 to 479 BCE in the Chinese state of Lu. Confucius traveled across China giving advice to rulers and offering teachings about ethical and philosophical rules for proper conduct. Confucianism emphasizes the importance of many virtues (wisdom, loyalty, self-control, and self-development). It is unique among major world religions in that it values proper conduct for its own sake, not to attain some sort of salvation or reward in an afterlife. Thus, people are supposed to be good for goodness' sake, not because they will be rewarded for it. Proponents of Confucianism value self-control, rationality over emotion, and the virtues of being dignified and polite. There are approximately 394 million adherents of Confucianism worldwide (Adherents.com 2007). In the United States, the number is so small that Confucianism does not register on the list of major U.S. religious traditions (Pew Research Center 2008).

Christianity (Origin Dated to 33 CE)

Christianity began as a sect of Judaism nearly 2,000 years ago. The feature that distinguishes Christianity from Judaism is the Christian belief in Jesus Christ as the son of God. Thus, all who believe in Jesus Christ as the son of God are known as Christians. Jesus, who was born a Jew, is regarded as a divine being who came into this world to achieve salvation for all people. Jews do not recognize Jesus as their savior. During his lifetime, Jesus is credited with having performed many miracles; as a result, he acquired a number of followers, or disciples. Jesus's disciples would form the foundation of Christianity. Having proclaimed himself the "son of God" sent to earth to save humanity, Jesus would be crucified on a cross for his teachings. Christians believe that he rose from the dead, appeared to his disciples, and told them to go forth and spread his words of wisdom and salvation. Among the leading disciples to spread the word of Jesus was St. Paul. Like Jesus, Paul preached against many of the Jewish customs. As a result, the Jewish rejection of Christianity relates primarily to the teachings of Paul.

The Bible is the holy book for Christians. With more than 2.1 billion Christians worldwide, Christianity has more adherents than any other single religion. Nearly half of all Christians are Catholic. Christianity is by far the most popular religion in the United States, with just under 80 percent of Americans claiming a Christian denomination. Specifically, 51 percent of Americans are Protestant, and 24 percent are Catholic.

Religion speaks to people in different ways. Most religious leaders are happy if adherents embrace their faith's teachings regardless of the means by which the message was delivered. Christian rock, for example, has become an effective method for reaching the younger generation (see "Connecting Sociology and Popular Culture" Box 11.4 for a description of Christian rock).

Connecting Sociology and Popular Culture

Box 11.4 Christian Rock: Salvation Through Music

A group of college students leave their dorm dressed appropriately for a rock concert. When the students arrive at the stadium, they are joined by tens of thousands of other young adults in frenzied anticipation of listening to their favorite rock bands. But the rock bands they are here to see are not stadium favorites like Pearl Jam, the Rolling Stones, or any other top-grossing band. Instead, these revelers are ready to sing along—drug and alcohol free—with their favorite Christian rock bands.

Christian rock band Switchfoot performs at DTE Energy Music Theatre, Clarkston, Michigan, July 18, 2010.

The Christian rock culture has inspired a type of religious revival among a generation of Christian young people. Fans of Christian rock attend the performances of such bands as 12 Stones, Disciple, Run Kid Run, and Neon Cross. Older generations of Christians, however, may view such performances as blasphemous because the lyrics seem to take the Lord's name in vain. Ah . . . once again, rock music is at the center of a generation gap.

With Christian rock, we see a transformation of the mundane into the sacred. For one thing, this rock music is laced with lyrics that encourage spirituality and teach the word of God, rather than encouraging deviant behavior. Second, music halls and arenas that host Christian rock festivals are often decked out to resemble church-like settings. In this regard, attending a Christian rock performance becomes a religious experience.

The formation of Christian rock should not surprise regular churchgoing folks as music has long been a standard feature of many religions. In Christian religions, for example, organ music generally accompanies the choir. The introduction of mundane rock music into the world of the sacred began innocently enough a few decades ago when traditional churches began to incorporate acoustic guitar music into Sunday services. Many traditional churches viewed this laid-back music playing as a way to bring young people to religious services. Over time, additional musical instruments became accepted during church worship.

Just like rock itself, there are variations of Christian rock. For example, there exist Christian alternative rock, Christian metal, Christian punk, and contemporary Christian music. Although Christian rock is mostly an American phenomenon, this genre is becoming increasingly popular in other Western societies.

What Do You Think?

If you are a Christian, would you consider Christian rock a blessing or blasphemous? If you are not a Christian, is there a musical incorporation of beliefs in your faith? If you are nonreligious, is there any category of music that reflects your beliefs? What do you think?

Although Christian rock is the most common religion-based genre of popular-culture music in the United States, there are many other variations of religiously centered forms of music, including Christian rap and R&B; gospel music and Reggae gospel; Jewish songs, hymns, and prayers from the Old Testament, as well as other Jewish music; Islamic spirituality—the list goes on and on. To find music or a genre that reflects your religious beliefs, simply conduct a Google search.

Islam (622 CE)

The most recent of the major world religions, Islam was founded in Arabia in 622 CE by Muhammad (570–632 CE), whom Muslims regard as a prophet. Islam is linked to Judaism and Christianity, but Muhammad believed that adherents of those faiths misinterpreted the teachings of Abraham, Moses, and Jesus. Muslims believe that the words of Allah, the one true God, were given to Muhammad in the sacred text the Koran. They believe in a creator who is just and rewards those who adhere to the teachings. They also believe that sinners are condemned to hell. Among the their core tenets, Muslims believe that "God is great," meaning that God is more important than civil society and the rules dictated by the world-wide community, and that on Judgment Day, evil will be punished and good will be rewarded. Worldwide, there are more than 1.5 billion Muslims, making Islam the second-largest religion by membership (Adherents.com 2007). In the United States, there are approximately 4 million Muslims (Pew Research Center 2008).

The Unaffiliated and the Obscure

Although most people belong to one major religion, many are unaffiliated with any particular faith. According to the Pew Research Center (2008), 16.1 percent (roughly 50 million) of Americans are unaffiliated with any religion. Among the unaffiliated are atheists (those who do not believe in a God) (1.6 percent of Americans), agnostics (2.4 percent), the secular unaffiliated (6.3 percent), and the religious unaffiliated (5.8 percent) (Pew Research Center 2008).

Research conducted by the American Religious Identification Survey (ARIS) suggests that the unaffiliated—or "nones" as ARIS calls those who answer "none" to the question "What is your religious identity?"—represent just 15 percent of the American population (Grossman 2009). Nonetheless, ARIS reports that this figure is nearly double the percentage of Americans who claimed no religion at all

What Do You Think?

Many college campuses have religiously based groups that receive public funding in one form or another, such as access to public buildings to hold meetings. Some students have complained that they are excluded from such groups because they are not believers. Should campus religious groups be allowed to exclude nonbelievers? What do you think?

in 1990 (8 percent) (Grossman 2009). In the past, those who claimed no religious affiliation were more likely to be young, politically independent males living in the West (ARIS 2008). Today, however, the unaffiliated more closely resemble the general population as their ranks increase.

The category of "none," or no affiliation, outnumbers every other major U.S. religious group except Catholics and Baptists. The ARIS report concluded that the challenge to Christianity's dominance in the United States does not come from other religions but from a rejection of organized religion itself (Grossman 2009).

Millions of people identify with small, nonmajor religious groups. According to the 2008 ARIS report, the survey does not define nearly 2.8 million people who identify with dozens of religious movements, calling themselves Wiccan, pagan, or Spiritualist (Grossman 2009). Like the unaffiliated, these people find spirituality outside organized religion. Wicca, a contemporary form of paganism, involves goddess worship and reverence for nature. The Wiccan religion has become accepted enough in contemporary society that, as of 2007, the Pentagon allows Wiccan soldiers to be buried in Arlington National Cemetery with a five-pointed-star symbol on gravestones. On April 22, 2007, a Wiccan spokesperson stated, "We are pleased to announce that VA agreed today to add the Wiccan emblem of belief to its approved list" (Davis 2007).

What Do You Think?

Have you or has someone you know recently switched religions or dropped religion? Or are you more committed to your religious identity than ever before? What are the implications for society if people continue to drop their religious identities? What do you think?

There also exist a number of very small religions in the United States. According to the 2001 ARIS, these religious groups are Ethical Culture (4,000 members); Rastafarianism (11,000); Santeria (22,000); Eckankar (26,000); Druidism (33,000); Taoism (40,000); Deity (49,000); Scientology (55,000); Sikhism (57,000); New Ageism (68,000); Baha'i (84,000); Native American (103,000); Spiritualism (116,000); Wicca (134,000); and Paganism (140,000) (Kosmin, Mayer, and Keysar 2001). Asylum.com (2010) has identified a number of other small religious groups including Heavy Metal, Jediism, the Church of Google, the Church of the Flying Spaghetti Monster, and the Iglesia Maradoniana

Arlington National Cemetery permits a variety of religious markings on gravestones, including the Wiccan pentagram and the Christian cross shown here.

(Maradona Church). The Church of Heavy Metal is based on a faith that involves worshipping heavy metal music. Rock magazine *Metal Hammer* claims 10,000 followers of this new religion. Jediism, also known as the Temple of the Jedi Order, is based on the philosophic teachings of the *Star Wars* Jedi. Proponents claim that Jediism is a blend of Taoism and Buddhism. The Church of Google, also known as Googlism, is based on a belief that Google is omniscient and omnipresent and is the closest thing humans will come to know as a god. The Church of the Flying Spaghetti Monster, also known as Pastafarianism, was created as a satirical protest against the decision by the Kansas State Board of Education to require the teaching of intelligent design as an alternative to evolution in public schools. The Maradona Church, also known as The Hand of God Church, was created in honor of Argentinian soccer star Diego Maradona, who once claimed that he had scored a World Cup soccer goal via the hand of God. He has since admitted that he cheated and used his own hand to guide the ball into the goal box (Delaney and Madigan 2009b). The religion lives on even though its basic tenet has been disproved.

Fans of the hit TV show *Seinfeld* celebrate Festivus, a secular holiday introduced on the show as an alternative to the overly commercialized holidays of the major religions. Promoted as a "festival for the rest of us," Festivus is celebrated each year on December 23. Adherents of Festivus engage in "feats of strength" and "air their grievances" with friends and family members. And yes, there is a Church of Festivus, which promotes the secular notion of Festivus, a holiday to be celebrated by all people regardless of their religious affiliation or lack thereof. The Church of Festivus also promotes "freedom of religion" and doing "that which is right."

Changing and Losing One's Religion

Despite the many choices of religion available to people, the vast majority will maintain the religious affiliation they were raised in throughout their lifetime. However, more than one in four American adults (28 percent) has left the faith in which he or she was raised in favor of another religion—or no religion at all (Pew Forum on Religion & Public Life 2009). Changing religion may cause friction within a person's immediate family, but Western societies in general seldom frown on such a freedom of choice. "In the West it is generally taken for granted that people have a perfect, indeed sacred, right to follow their own religious path, and indeed to invite—though never compel—other people to join them. The liberal understanding of religion lays great emphasis on the right to change belief" (*The Economist,* 7/26/08, p. 29). The United States, a nation founded by Europe's Christian dissidents, has long supported the right of individuals to follow and propagate any form of religion, without impediment or help, from the state (*The Economist,* 7/26/08).

In other nations, especially Muslim states, changing religions is not a viable option. "In Malaysia, people who try to desert Islam can face compulsory 're-education.' Under the far harsher regime of Afghanistan, death for apostasy is still on the statute book" (*The Economist,* 7/26/08, p. 30). In 2007, Egypt's grand mufti, Ali Gomaa, claimed that a Muslim can choose a religion other than Islam in light of three verses in the Koran: (1) "Unto you your religion, and unto me my religion"; (2) "Whosoever will, let him believe, and whosoever will, let them disbelieve"; and (3) "There is no compulsion in religion." Nonetheless, Gomaa states that "anyone who deserts Islam is committing a sin and will pay a price in the hereafter, and also that in some historical circumstances (presumably war between Muslims and non-Muslims) an individual's sin may also amount to 'sedition against one's society'" (*The Economist,* 7/26/08, p. 30).

Some people may choose to abandon religion altogether because they have, reminiscent of REM's song "Losing My Religion," lost faith in their religion. (Note: REM's song goes, in part, "That's me in the corner. That's me in the spotlight losing my religion, trying to keep up with you. And I don't know if I can do it.") Survey results presented by the Pew Forum on Religion & Public Life (2009) indicate that "the number of people who say they are unaffiliated with any particular faith today (16.1 percent) is more than double the number who say they were not affiliated with any particular religion as children. Among Americans ages 18–29, one-in-four say they are not currently affiliated with any particular religion."

What Do You Think?

In general, do Americans place too much, too little, or just the right amount of emphasis on religion? Do people in other nations around the world place too much, too little, or just the right amount of emphasis on religion? What do you think?

SUMMARY

This chapter discussed two very important social institutions: education and religion. Education, once reserved for the ruling or privileged classes, is now viewed as a universal right for all. Mandatory education laws require that all people be educated into their high school years. It is not, however, mandatory that everyone graduate from high school. Fundamentally, advanced education results in an increased level of general knowledge. However, from a practical standpoint comes the realization that income and wealth are positively correlated to one's level of education. Despite the idea that education is the solution to nearly all social problems, the field of education is beset with a number of its own problems, including a lack of consensus on goals, the bureaucratization of schools, unequal funding, teachers' need to maintain a pace (thereby leaving some students to fall behind), school violence, and the lowering of academic standards.

Religion, as one of the oldest social institutions in human history, remains a powerful influence on the vast majority of people around the world. Religion arose as an attempt to provide answers to life's many complicated mysteries. This is still true today even though the secular world of science is capable of providing rational and logical insights into once unexplainable phenomena. Religion remains a powerful social institution because it brings comfort to people and because it serves many roles in society. Because religion is faith based, firm believers view their religion as "right" and competing religions as "wrong." Inevitably, this reality has, at times, lead to religiously based intolerances that, in turn, have led to conflicts and wars.

Glossary

Charter schools—Schools that receive taxpayer money but are different from traditional public schools because they have their own administration.

Church—A religious organization that is viewed as legitimate within mainstream society.

Compensatory education—Federally funded programs designed to help preschool children from lower socioeconomic classes.

Credentials—Evidence of authority, such as diplomas, certificates, security clearances, and powers of attorney, issued by a third party and indicating that the possessor is competent to perform, or qualified for, a specific job or position.

Cult—A religious movement that has little or nothing in common with other types of religious organizations found in the same society.

Denomination—A large group of religious congregations united under a common faith and name and organized under an administrative and legal hierarchy.

Formal education—The process of teaching and learning in which some people (e.g., teachers and professors) cultivate knowledge, skills, intellect, and character, while others (students) take on the role of learner.

Hegemony—The dominance of one group over another.

Hidden curriculum—The educational control practices that involve the indoctrination of the next generation in the nonacademic knowledge, values, attitudes, norms, and beliefs of the dominate group in society.

Magnet schools—Schools that are part of the public school system but offer a specialized teaching focus.

Nirvana—A state of perfect bliss in which the self is freed from suffering and desire.

Private schools—Schools that may be religiously based or privately funded by wealthy persons or endowments, or by parents who pay tuition or other related fees, in order for their children to attend.

Profane—That which is ordinary, mundane, and secular.
Public schools—Schools that are funded by taxpayers.
Religion—A system of beliefs and rituals that binds people together in a social group while attempting to answer the questions and resolve the dilemmas of human existence by making the world more meaningful to adherents.
Sacred—That which is set apart and revered.
Sect—A type of religious organization that claims legitimacy but stands independently from the greater society.
Secularization—The process by which the influence of religion in a society declines.
Self-fulfilling prophecy—A prediction that comes true, either directly or indirectly, through one's own actions.
Teacher-expectancy effect—The impact of a teacher's expectations on a student's ability to perform. This effect often generates a self-fulfilling prophecy.
Tracking—The placing of students in specific curricular groups based on academic ability (based on test scores); sometimes called ability grouping or streaming.

Discussion Questions

1. How will earning a college degree affect your wealth and income over your lifetime?
2. How much time did you take to choose your college? How much time did you take in deciding your religious affiliation?
3. Based on your experiences, what are the greatest problems facing education?
4. What, if any, beliefs are shared among the world's major religions? What are the core differences between them?
5. Can someone be moral and ethical without being religious? Explain.
6. Of the three major sociological perspectives, which best explains the role of education in society? Which perspective best describes the role of religion in society?

Web Links

To learn more about Head Start, visit the program's website at www.acf.hhs.gov/programs/hsb/about/index.html.
To learn more about and listen to Christian rock, visit www.christianrock.net.
To learn more about religion being taught in public schools, visit www.religioustolerance.org/ps_pray.htm.

To learn more about statistics on religion in the United States, visit http://religions.pewforum.org/reports.

To learn more about secular alternatives to organized forms of religion, visit www.churchoffestivus.com.

12

ECONOMICS AND POLITICS

The U.S. Debt Clock as displayed on a building in midtown Manhattan, New York, on August 2, 2011.

Chapter 12

- Introductory Story
- Economics: Development, Sectors, and Modern Systems
- Consumerism
- Globalization and Multinationals
- Sociological Perspectives on Economics
- Politics: Systems and Parties
- The Possession of Political Power, Authority, and Influence
- Sociological Perspectives on Politics
- Summary, Glossary, Discussion Questions, and Web Links

INTRODUCTORY STORY

In every society, economics and politics are intertwined. That is to say, a nation's political system influences the economic system and vice versa. The **political system** is the governmental framework in which certain individuals and groups hold power to make decisions over others. The economic system refers to the coordinated processes by which goods and services are produced and distributed. In democratic societies, political leaders attempt to balance the needs of individuals with those of the greater society. In capitalistic societies, individuals, businesses, and corporations attempt to maximize profits, often at the expense of others (the competition).

The United States, of course, is a democratic-capitalistic society. Thus, the economic system guarantees that some people will flourish while others will struggle. However, everyone, theoretically, has a chance to prosper because the democratic political system proclaims that all people are equal. Realistically, some people have more resources at their disposal than others in their attempts to reach economic security; as a result, they are more likely to thrive.

So, how do we gauge whether our political leaders are doing a good job balancing the needs of individuals with those of the greater society? A number of measurements exist to estimate the effectiveness of our leaders. One of the most interesting indicators is the state of the economy. If you enjoy a quick and frank glance at the state of economic affairs in the United States, take a look at the "U.S. National Debt Clock" (www.brillig.com/debt_clock), which provides a running tally of the outstanding public debt. The debt is updated every day. As of March 14, 2011, the national debt had exceeded $14 trillion ($14,179,106,645,970.00). Two years earlier, the national debt was $9.3 trillion. The estimated U.S. population is also provided so that each citizen's share of the debt can be calculated. On this same March 2011 date, the U.S. population was 310,199,915; thus each member owed $45,709.58. A number of individuals will have a hard time paying off "their share" of the debt. The national debt has continued to increase by an average of $4.09 billion per day since September 28, 2007. Pages of news links relevant to the national debt are also provided on the debt clock website. So, the question can be asked once again: how good of a job are our political leaders doing in the economic realm of society?

ECONOMICS: DEVELOPMENT, SECTORS, AND MODERN SYSTEMS

In Chapter 7, we learned about social stratification on the basis of power, prestige, and economics (see Chapter 7 for a review of key economic terms such as wealth, income, socioeconomic status, and a description of the distinct social-stratification systems). Although most people want a certain amount of power and prestige, many believe that money will provide both. And certainly, we all want, at the very least, enough money to sustain a pleasant lifestyle. Consequently, personal finances are important to all of us. After all, money can buy happiness, right? Perhaps you have heard that the opposite is true, that money cannot buy happiness. Although the debate over whether money can buy happiness seems philosophical, sociologists would point out that many things we would like to do, purchase, or consume come with a monetary cost—one that money can overcome. So, it is true that money can help people attain objects from the domain of the material culture, but it cannot help with the nonmaterial aspects of culture. (Note: Material and nonmaterial culture were discussed in Chapter 4.) Economists Daniel Kahneman and Angus Deaton (2010) argue that money can buy life satisfaction when people earn about $75,000 annually. Research conducted by Kahneman and Deaton centers on the premise that emotional well-being is tied to an individual's life experiences of joy, stress, sadness, anger, and affection, which make one's life pleasant or unpleasant. Having a high annual income ($75,000), the economists conclude, buys life satisfaction (but not necessarily happiness) because money gives people the opportunity to purchase the basic necessities of life (e.g., food, clothing, shelter, and health care). Kahneman and Deaton also indicate that annual income much higher than $75,000 does not correspondingly increase life satisfaction, and they warn that low income is associated both with low life evaluation and low emotional well-being.

When we speak of the economy and of economic systems and sectors, however, we are not discussing personal financial well-being; instead, we are taking a macro look at a very complex web of interrelated social systems, theories, policies, and people. Because this is an introductory sociology book, the analysis of the economy in this chapter is basic and reflects a sociological perspective.

Economic Development

The word "economy" derives from the Greek *oikonomos,* meaning "one who manages a household" (*American Heritage Dictionary* 2006). As described above and in the chapter's introductory story, today, the term "**economy**" refers to the social system that coordinates a society's production, distribution, and consumption of goods and services. With such responsibilities as overseeing production and distribution of goods (e.g., necessities and luxury items) and services (e.g., police, fire, and health care), the economy clearly also represents a major social institution.

Early humanity employed an economic system much different from today's, as early societies were made up of hunters and gatherers who lived off the land. Hunter-gatherer societies represent the most basic level of economic development, at which there was no cultivation or manufacturing. People hunted animals for food and/or ate wild berries and other natural food sources. Hunter-gatherers were nomadic people, meaning they moved from place to place based on the availability of food supplies. In short, they lived on what they could attain directly from the natural environment. Hunter-gatherer societies were predominant until roughly 10,000 BCE. Very few such societies exist today (in Arctic regions and remote areas).

The evolution of economic systems began with the transition from hunter-gatherer to agricultural economies. It should be noted that horticultural societies emerged as forerunners to agricultural societies. Horticultural societies worked a small area of land until the soil could no longer provide subsistence. The people would then move on to another area and start all over again. People in agricultural societies had learned growing techniques that eliminated the need to move from place to place. Agricultural systems stimulated advancements that led to surplus food production—the first step in economic inequality. Surplus food also meant that some people were free to perform tasks beyond food production. Inevitably, these other tasks led to invention and discovery—two critical elements in the introduction of industry.

Industrial economies emerged with early industrialization in Western Europe during the late eighteenth century (see Chapter 1 for a discussion of the Industrial Revolution). Industrial economies are characterized by economic production based on manufacturing. The use of machines led to the mass production of a vast array of products (goods). Inventions and the expansion of technology led to previously unthinkable developments in production and consumption.

The end of World War II marked the beginning of a new economic system known as the postindustrial economy. Postindustrial economies are characterized by a shift in production emphasis from goods (manufacturing) to services (e.g., education, computer programming, health care). The United States is an example of a postindustrial economy. That does not mean manufacturing jobs are nonexistent; rather, they are decreasing in total numbers (see "Connecting Sociology and Popular Culture" Box 12.1 for an overview of products made in the United States). Manufacturing jobs have been replaced by service-related jobs. According to Daniel Cohen (2006), "In wealthy countries industrial and agricultural employment account for less than 20 percent of total employment, while the service sector accounts for nearly 80 percent" (p. 52). Service jobs require specialized skills and advanced education. Chances are that most students are in college to find a service-related professional job rather than a job in a factory.

The Shifting Labor Market

As indicated in "Connecting Sociology and Popular Culture" Box 12.1 and Table 12.1, the United States remains as a major producer of consumer products in the world economic system. Nonetheless, the economic system of the United States has altered its focus from manufacturing to service, and the resultant shift in the labor market has had a profound effect on millions of Americans.

Connecting Sociology and Popular Culture

Box 12.1 Products Made in the USA

We often hear the expression "buy American." The idea behind this sentiment is to encourage consumers to purchase products made in the United States so that the American economic system remains viable and Americans stay employed. Although the concept of buying American is admirable, many of our consumer products turn out to have been made abroad as industry attempts to maximize profits via cheap foreign labor. Furthermore, some products are made in the United States, but the materials come from abroad; or the materials may come from the United States, but the products are made overseas. Thus, before we take a look at what products are still made in the United States, it is important to clarify what is meant by "Made in the USA."

The Federal Trade Commission (FTC) determines what is "American made." A government agency charged with preventing deception and unfairness in the marketplace, the FTC also has the power and authority to bring law enforcement actions in response to false or misleading claims that a product is of U.S. origin. "Traditionally, the Commission has required that a product advertised as Made in USA be 'all or virtually all' made in the U.S. After a comprehensive review of Made in the USA and other U.S. origin claims in product advertising and labeling, the Commission announced in December 1997 that it would retain the 'all or virtually all' standard" (FTC 2009). Not all products made in the United States are necessarily labeled as such. However, federal law requires that U.S. content must be disclosed on automobiles and textile, wool, and fur products. Any product sold in the United States that claims to be "Made in the USA" must meet the "all or virtually all" standard. Specifically, the "all or virtually all" standard means that "all significant parts and processing that go into the product must be of U.S. origin. That is, the product should contain no—or negligible—foreign content" (FTC 2009). The FTC website provides a number of scenarios in which a product meets the "Made in the USA" standard as well as examples of products that do not meet the standard. (Note: The FTC website is provided at the end of this chapter.)

How does the United States rank compared to other nations in products produced domestically? The answer may surprise you. "America still produces more goods than any other country—$1.6 trillion worth, according to the federal Bureau of Economic Analysis. While some analysts predict that China will soon overtake the U.S. as the world's leading producer, America currently accounts for about 20% of all manufacturing output" (*Parade,* 4/19/09, p. 10). The United States is losing ground in its world market share of consumer-goods production, but it continues to have a relatively strong hold on higher-end products like machinery, capital equipment, tractors, and aircraft, as well as chemicals and food (see Table 12.1 for a listing of the top U.S.-made products and the number of Americans employed per category).

An Internet search for "Made in the USA" products will quickly yield a wide-range of options for those who wish to purchase American-made items. The Americans Working website, for example, provides an *A–Z* listing of "Made in the USA" products. (The site is provided at the end of this chapter.) Some retailers offer only U.S.-made products in their stores. For example, the Made in America Store in suburban Buffalo, New York, offers products like maple syrup tapped from U.S. trees and bottled in U.S.-made containers. Toys are shrink-wrapped in American-made plastic; clothing and American flags are stitched with home-grown thread. Furthermore, everything is displayed on American-made hangers, and the shelving comes from a closed Ford dealership (CBS News 2010).

What Do You Think?

Many people feel that it is very important to purchase "Made in the USA" products as a means to keep the American economy strong. What do you think?

TABLE 12.1 Top U.S.-Made Products

PRODUCT	DOLLAR VALUE IN 2007 (BILLIONS)	AMERICANS EMPLOYED (MILLIONS)
Chemical products (e.g., pharmaceuticals, cosmetics, soaps, paints, fertilizers)	$250	0.83
Transportation equipment (e.g., motor vehicles and parts, aerospace products, trains, ships)	$195	1.4
Processed food, beverage, and tobacco products (e.g., cookies, coffee, cigarettes, prepared meals)	$175	1.7
Computers and electronics (e.g., computer peripherals, communications equipment)	$146	1.2

Source: Parade, 4/19/09.

According to research data provided by the Institute for Supply Management (ISM), the service-sector index rose to 53.2 percent in September 2010 (*New York Times,* 10/5/10). The ISM reports that nearly 83 percent of workers in the private sector are employed in the service industries. A March 2011 ISM report states that the thirteen nonmanufacturing industries reporting growth in February 2011, in order, were real estate; rentals and leasing; accommodation and food services; mining; utilities; professional, scientific, and technical services; educational services; transportation and warehousing; finance and insurance; other services; public administration; wholesale trade; management of companies and support services; and retail trade (ISM 2011). A January 2011 report in *Time* (written by Bill Saporito) also indicates that the primary economic growth areas are service related. Business editor Bill Saporito described specific corporations with a need for mechanical engineers, rocket scientists (to work on refrigeration technologies, not rockets!), and tax specialists. Saporito (2011) also reiterated that low-end manufacturing jobs are increasingly disappearing.

The economic shift to a service-based economy has left many people unemployed and homeless and has contributed to the development of an underclass. Although unemployment, homelessness, and poverty have been discussed previously (see Chapter 7), these topics, understandably, come to light once again in a discussion of the economy. After all, economic stability helps to provide many of the most important things in life. Yes, love, happiness, friends, and family are also important, but financial security (e.g., having a good job) provides people with the means to live life more comfortably and safely. In short, we have many needs in life, and these needs come at a cost. Psychologist Abraham Maslow (1954) explained that all humans try to fulfill a hierarchy of five basic needs:

1. *Physiological/biological:* Everyone has basic survival needs, such as for food and shelter.
2. *Safety and security:* This refers to stability, protection, and freedom from fear.
3. *Love and belongingness:* Everyone wants to feel as though he or she belongs to a group or family and especially to have someone special with whom to share a loving relationship.
4. *Self-esteem:* This entails feeling good about oneself—having self-respect, confidence, and a positive reputation.
5. *Self-actualization:* In this stage, a person has found peace within him- or herself. There is a sense of having reached one's full human potential. One accepts oneself and is relatively independent.

The sociological implications of Maslow's hierarchy of needs are very evident. As Maslow himself argued, for children, the first three needs are met by the family (the primary agent of socialization); if a child is raised in an environment where these first three needs are met, there is a good chance of his or her attaining the next two levels. Adults must fend for themselves when seeking to fulfill the hierarchy of needs. It should be evident that the primary needs for food, clothing, shelter, safety, and security are tied to the realm of economics. Steady employment and a decent living wage are critical elements of satisfying basic needs for any individual or family. A person who constantly struggles for economic survival, according to Maslow's description of the hierarchy of needs, has little chance of self-actualization.

The shifting labor market did not occur overnight; the signs have been in existence for a long period. Many people took heed of the changing economic reality and prepared themselves for the service, or postindustrial, society. Other people, however, for a variety of reasons, are not as well prepared. Survival in the service economy generally implies the possession of higher education credentials. And as most students can attest, the costs of higher education can themselves be overwhelming. People at the lower end of the socioeconomic ladder may become especially isolated from the higher-paying service jobs because of the costs associated with attending college.

What Do You Think?

With the number of factory jobs quickly diminishing, what are the employment options for people without a college education? Are there enough jobs for the people willing and able to work? Should our economic system be changed or modified? If so, how? What do you think?

The Underclass

The changing nature of America's economic system has dramatically changed many urban areas. The loss of significant numbers of manufacturing jobs has left many inner-city persons without gainful employment opportunities. When people are unemployed, their financial stability is greatly compromised. Anyone who remains unemployed for an extended period generally ends up poor. Many of the nation's poor live in the core of America's cities. The term "underclass" (popularized by William Wilson in his 1987 book *The Truly Disadvantaged*) generally refers to the extremely poor who live in neighborhoods, or census tracts, where the poverty rate exceeds 40 percent. Underclass members are generally poorly educated, unskilled in terms of the economic market, likely to have been in the poverty category for generations, and dependant on the welfare system; they appear to have little chance to break out of the cycle of poverty (Wilson 1987, 1996). The term "underclass" is not meant to refer to a racial or ethnic group, but because the vast majority of the underclass are racial minorities, some oppose the use of the term. Among the critics are Randall Shelden, Sharon Tracy, and William Brown (2001): "This term is used to, in effect, stigmatize those who fall within the general category of the 'underclass'—the homeless, those who live in 'the projects,' addicts, young poor women with babies, and of course gang members. Needless to say, the term is often used interchangeably with racial minorities" (p. 193).

During the 1970s, the shift in the labor market began to have its most negative effect on American blacks. Blacks were heavily represented in manufacturing, and the decline in production in such sectors as automobiles, rubber, and steel hurt urban African Americans profoundly. Blacks were also adversely affected by the mechanization of southern agriculture and the large number of baby boomers and white women who entered the labor market in the 1970s. These socioeconomic factors contributed greatly to the large number of blacks in the underclass. Thus, Wilson argued that public policies, such as race-based programs and policies, were doomed to fail because they ignored the core economic explanation of poverty, delinquency, and gang membership: the elimination of industry-based jobs. Wilson's use of the term "underclass" was not racist; instead, it was a condemnation of government policies that disadvantaged blacks more than any other group of people. African Americans are overrepresented in the underclass, generally because of social and economic forces that they cannot control. Criticism of the term "underclass" might be a little more appropriate if it were aimed at the person who first coined the term in 1982: Ken Auletta, a writer for *The New Yorker*. Auletta used the word broadly to include individuals with "behavioral and income deficiencies" (Papadimitriou 1998).

The inner cities have suffered the most from the shifting labor market. When industries move (capital flight), they take with them job opportunities and the tax revenue necessary to maintain the areas they have abandoned. When economic opportunities disappear, those who can afford to move will also abandon the deprived area (termed "white flight," referring to the exodus of middle- and upper-class persons, generally white people). These developments lead to lower tax revenues and eventually impoverished neighborhoods lacking in basic civil services and the political power and representation needed to help the community. The lack of political power is exemplified in a number of ways, including the inability of poorer communities to stop civic projects that rip them apart. The location and building of freeways is a clear example of whether a community has political power. In *Going Down to the Barrio,* Joan Moore (1991) explains how freeways ripped apart Mexican American neighborhoods. Robert Powell, in *We Own This Game* (2003), describes how expressways bisected Overtown, a poor section of Miami that had been a vibrant neighborhood once considered the Harlem of the South.

It is interesting to note that the United States is not the only country to apply the term "underclass" to a group of statistically poor people. In Australia, social researchers have used the term "rural underclass" to describe rural Victoria. Bureau of Statistics data revealed that not a single full-time job had been created in rural Victoria in thirteen years (between 1990 and 2003), leaving it a land of part-time work despite a decade of solid economic growth in Australia. The lack of full-time jobs has led to the formation of a rural underclass with countless people in country towns stuck in low-income jobs or unemployed altogether, caught in a poverty trap: they cannot afford to move, and they cannot afford to stay. The problem is not unique to rural Victoria, as throughout Australia almost two-thirds of all jobs created since 1990 have been part-time (*The Age,* 4/26/03). Industrial leaders argue that it is not viable to set up businesses in country towns. It is up to the government to provide legitimate economic opportunities for these citizens to meet their survival needs.

What Do You Think?

Some people find the term "underclass" offensive. Others argue that using it is okay because it is meant as a criticism of failed political policies. What do you think?

Economic Sectors

The different stages of economic development are reflected in a society's dominant economic sector. Economies may contain up to three basic sectors: primary, secondary, and tertiary. The **primary sector** consists of the direct extraction of natural resources from the environment. Examples include drilling for oil, mining, fishing, ranching, and farming. Certain aspects of the primary sector were the dominant economy of hunter-gatherer and agricultural economies. The **secondary sector** (manufacturing) involves transforming raw materials into physical products (goods). Examples include refining petroleum into gasoline, turning metals into automobiles, and mass-producing a wide variety of consumer products. The secondary sector is the central feature of industrial societies. The **tertiary sector** (service) consists of producing and processing information and providing services. Examples include research, engineering, finance, technological support, entertainment, sports, and teaching. The tertiary sector dominates postindustrial economies.

Modern Economic Systems

Modern economic systems vary tremendously based on the ownership of the means of production. That is, a society's economic system can range from free enterprise (productive capacity is privately owned) to a planned economy (production is state controlled).

The economic system most familiar to the majority of American college students is capitalism. **Capitalism** is an economic system that encourages free enterprise (private ownership). Capitalism emerged as a result of rapid improvement in technological skills. By design, it involves the mass production of goods, competition and consumer choice, and the pursuit of profit. Although the term "capitalism" seems simple enough, there exist four different categories of capitalistic economies:

1. *State-guided capitalism:* The government tries to guide the market, most generally by supporting particular industries that it expects to become successful.
2. *Oligarchic capitalism:* The bulk of power and wealth is held by a small group of individuals and families.
3. *Big firm capitalism:* The most significant economic activities are carried out by giant enterprises (corporations).
4. *Entrepreneurial capitalism:* A significant role is played by small, innovative firms (Baumol, Litan, and Schramm 2007).

What Do You Think?

The United States is one of the most highly capitalistic nations in the world. Which category of capitalism, or combination of categories, best describes the U.S. economic system? What do you think?

In contrast to the capitalist ideal of free enterprise is the socialist doctrine of state-owned production. **Socialism** is a theory of socioeconomic organization based on government ownership, management, and control of the means of production, distribution, and exchange of goods and services. At one time, socialism was quite popular. Jeffry Frieden (2006) states, "Within five years of the end of

World War Two, socialism stretched from the center of Europe to the Pacific" (p. 322). The People's Republic of China, Cuba, Venezuela, and some of the former Soviet Bloc nations employ a socialistic economic model.

The word "socialism" is sometimes used interchangeably with the term "communism." **Communism** is based on the economic concept of common ownership of the means of production and distribution based on need. As articulated by Karl Marx and Friedrich Engels in *The Communist Manifesto,* communism was intended as an economic system controlled by the people without government interference. A number of societies labeled as communistic employ a one-party system to oversee the production and distribution of goods and services.

The basic premise of communism and socialism is shared wealth, or communal ownership of all state assets, including money. Have you ever wondered whether you would be better off than you are now if all the money in the world was divided equally among all the people of the world? As explained by Marilyn vos Savant (a columnist for *Parade* and record holder for the highest recorded IQ in the world), "The global money supply is about $60 trillion. (Economists call this figure the M3 value; it includes much more than currency.) Say that we take it all—which means that you and Bill Gates would have nothing in the bank—and then distribute it equally among every individual, about 6.8 billion people. Each man, woman, and child would receive about $9000. So, if your household now has less than $9000 per person you would gain. If you have more, you would lose" (vos Savant 2009, p. 18).

What Do You Think?

Now, would you like to share all the world's money communally? Would it change the lives of people dramatically? What do you think?

Many of today's modern societies employ some combination of capitalism, socialism, and communism in their economic systems. These societies are said to have a **mixed economic system**. With mixed economies, some means of production are privately owned, and some are publicly owned. Thus, a nation with a mixed economy may encourage the private production of a number of goods but offer a socialized health care system (service) to benefit all members of society.

What Do You Think?

Which of the modern economic systems described above do you believe best benefits your life chances? Which system best benefits the greater society? What do you think?

CONSUMERISM

Capital accumulation is a fundamental driving force of capitalistic economies (Glyn 2006). In order for the capitalistic system to be successful, it must mass-produce items (goods) designed for consumption. Robert J. Samuelson (2008) explains, "For the past quarter-century, Americans have been on an unprecedented consumption binge—for cars, TVs, longer vacations.... It was the ever-expanding stream of consumer spending that pulled the U.S. economy and, to a lesser extent, the global economy forward.... In 1980, Americans spent 63 percent of national income (gross domestic product) on consumer goods and services. For the past five years, consumer spending equaled 70 percent of GDP" (p. A21). The consumer-driven U.S. capitalist economic system not only depends upon the mass production of goods but fuels the existence and expansion of warehouse stores such as Costco and Sam's Club. Although buying in bulk sometimes helps consumers save money, bulk purchasing also leads to waste when consumers purchase more items than necessary (Bick 2007).

When corporations or individuals develop products that consumers desire or demand, great profits can be realized. Conveniently, a free enterprise system such as capitalism provides plenty of opportunities for people to become wealthy. On the other hand, capitalism hinders any chance of the collectivity sharing the total economic wealth of a society. Thus, capitalism has become a system in which the needy are without income and the well-heeled are without needs, and this radical inequality is simply assumed (Barber 2007). This inequality, however, also leaves capitalistic nations with a dilemma, for if the poor cannot be enriched enough to become consumers, then the production-consumption-centered economic system becomes compromised (Barber 2007).

Consequently, capitalistic nations must find a way to ensure that the vast majority of citizens have enough disposable income to consume products, or they must find foreign markets to purchase their goods. Much of the world is eager to consume, and people consume a wide variety of goods and services, including elements of popular culture (see "Connecting Sociology and Popular Culture" Box 12.2).

Historians love to dispute the origins of consumerism. Traces of consumer interest and behavior extend throughout much of human history. Ultimately, consumerism became significant in late-eighteenth-century Western Europe (Stearns 2001). That industrialization emerged at the same time is no coincidence. Historians trace the beginnings of the consumer revolution to the introduction of shopkeepers. "The most easily measured aspect of eighteenth-century consumerism consisted of an explosion of shops and new marketing methods.... Older types of exchange, with peddlers and fairs, continued as well, and in some cases expanded in bringing hints of consumer goods to remote areas. But it was the shopkeeper and his methods that anchored the first iteration of a consumer society" (Stearns 2001, p. 16).

With the rise of the leisure class by the end of the nineteenth century, consumerism had become so common that Thorstein Veblen (1857–1929) wrote

Connecting Sociology and Popular Culture

Box 12.2 Global Consumption of U.S. Popular Culture

The entities responsible for creating mass-produced products are aggressive pushers of consumerism. They attempt to flood global markets via marketing and advertising. They encourage shopping simply for shopping's sake. "Shop and buy!" is the battle cry of societies that rely on mass consumer consumption of products. American culture is especially dependent upon consumerism, and most citizens have bought into the idea that consumption is a good and necessary aspect of life. For example, most of us, especially students, consume music and entertainment via such devices as iPods, iPads, cell phones, and laptop computers. Students might want to compare the many ways they consume products with how past generations did.

Although many advanced industrial and postindustrial societies attempt (often successfully) to sell their goods and services around the world, few, if any, come near the United States in their exportation of popular culture. One area of U.S. popular culture in particular is now globally consumed. This area is the media, especially television programming, feature films, and sound recordings. Yes, indeed, any American who travels around the world is likely to find a media-related reminder of home. So, how is it that the United States became the world leader in media-related popular-culture consumption? Lane Crothers (2007) explains that media development itself is "a Western phenomenon in which various competing groups and interests developed, adapted, and sometimes stole technologies and markets to serve capitalist profit-centered ends. The U.S. experience, however, was quite different from Europe's. This difference, and recording, developed—ultimately favoring the competitive position of American media" (p. 35). Crothers (2007) further explains,

> Much, if not most, of the music, films, and television programming generated by the major popular culture corporations carries an American label regardless of the nation of origin of the company that owns it; moreover, much, if not most, of this programming—especially the programming that has sufficient backing to be marketed and distributed around the world—derives its life and context from the economic, social, and technological forces that led U.S. companies to take a global lead in the production of popular culture. Accordingly, American popular culture is a global phenomenon that is as embedded in the context of globalization as is any other facet of our contemporary era. (p. 63)

The spread of American popular culture via television, film, and music tends to emerge from core

of conspicuous leisure and conspicuous consumption, both of which are tied to human behavior. According to Veblen (1899), **conspicuous leisure** refers to nonproductive use of time, and **conspicuous consumption** refers to purchasing items not necessary for basic survival. Nixon and Frey (1996) add to this account by describing conspicuous consumption as "a public display of material goods, lifestyles, and behavior in a way that ostentatiously conveys privileged status to others for the purpose of gaining their approval or envy" (p. 211). Although persons from all socioeconomic groups may participate in conspicuous consumption, wealthy persons are in the best position to flaunt their advantageous economic status. For example, Katie Holmes reportedly spent \$7,500 for a Birkin handbag—a

American values (Crothers 2007). In this regard, the global spread of popular culture is akin to the global spread of American culture in general. This might be a frightening thought to some, especially when one considers that a television show like *The Simpsons* possesses a global following. In many parts of the world, *The Simpsons* characters are as identifiable as such American logos as the Nike swoosh and McDonalds's golden arches. "Large numbers of *The Simpsons* brand of products (e.g., figurines, board games, apparel, snacks, holiday decorations, and so on) are prominently displayed in a variety of fashions by millions of people around the world.... *The Simpsons,* for better or worse, has become a symbolic American icon throughout the global community that eagerly consumes US popular culture" (Delaney 2008b, p. 31).

Another example of an American-based popular-culture global phenomenon is Oprah. She is so popular that her mere endorsement of a product all but guarantees its success; this includes books, merchandise that she displays or wears, and even herself as an entity. As Gwendolyn Audrey Foster (2005) explains, Oprah may call her audience "my people" or "my readers," but she should simply call them her consumers (p. 23).

The 2008 release of *Indiana Jones and the Kingdom of the Crystal Skull,* starring Harrison Ford as an archaeologist competing in 1957 with an evil KGB agent, played by Cate Blanchett, to find a skull endowed with mystic powers, upset members of Russia's present-day Communist Party. The party members claimed that the Soviet Union did not send terrorists to the United States but did launch a satellite "which evoked the admiration of the whole world" (*Post-Standard,* 5/25/08, p. A2). The different interpretations of past events reflect the sociopolitical perspectives of an American director (and his values) and a once-dominant governmental ideology.

Despite the attempts of some governments around the world to limit the impact of American popular culture on their societies, the United States' "established position and the increasing spread of satellites, VCRs, DVD players, and streaming Internet content, American movies, music, and television programming can be expected to retain their position as the most watched, most used, and most traded types of popular culture around the world" (Crothers 2007, p. 150).

What Do You Think?

For many people around the world, the primary view of the United States is based on what they see and hear in American television, film, and music. Does such an image accurately portray Americans? What do you think?

handbag! Numerous stars, such as Paris Hilton, Sandra Bullock, and Billy Joel, shop at the Beverly Hills Mutt Club, where dog beds cost as much as $1,000 and jewel-encrusted dog collars fetch $300 (Scott 2008).

Today, the principle of conspicuous consumption further fuels consumerism as people are enticed to overspend on unnecessary and luxury items. Many people are willing to purchase items they cannot afford and wind up in debt. Some will go into further debt by purchasing on credit or taking out loans. But is it any wonder that a large number of people are in debt when one considers the huge operating budget deficit the federal government works on? It seems that people really do follow the behaviors of political leaders.

GLOBALIZATION AND MULTINATIONALS

The discussion of global consumerism, in essence, introduced us to the concept of globalization. A term that has been in vogue for the past few decades, "globalization" generically refers to discussions of world affairs. In around the mid-1980s, it appeared in such forms as "global governance," "global markets," and "global ecology," replacing the word "international" (as in "international studies" and "international markets") (Scholte 2000b). Thus, usage of the term "globalization" represents a more contemporary look at the international world. Still, discussions of globalization center on socioeconomic concerns. Tavis (2000) explains, "The process that has come to be called globalization is the integration of economic activity across the world. It involves an unparalleled movement not only of capital but also of goods and services, technologies, and even people" (p. 13). With these ideas in mind, **globalization** may be defined as a socioeconomic process in which the constraints of geography on social and economic arrangements recede and people become increasingly aware that they live in an interconnected world. Globalization represents the evolution of heterogeneous cultures into a homogeneous culture that transcends geographic boundaries. Economists, politicians, sociologists, and governments of the world debate whether this evolutionary growth has a negative or positive influence on individual societies.

The ever-growing, single-integrated economic system seems to work for multinational corporations (MNCs, discussed below), as they enjoy greater profits for themselves and their stockholders; such a system, however, has left less developed nations in a state of uneasiness and even hostile resentment. Douglas Kellner (2002) argues that accelerating globalization strengthens the dominance of a world capitalist economic system and erodes local cultures and traditions through the imposition of a global culture. Kought and Walker (2001) believe that "the globalization of financial markets and the concomitant restructuring decisions of firms challenge the historical legacy of national systems of governance" (p. 317). Frieden (2006), however, argues that globalization is a choice requiring supportive governments, and supportive governments need domestic political support: "International economic affairs depend on political backing from powerful countries and from powerful groups in those countries" (p. xvii).

Most sociologists agree that globalization has caused a number of problems. Domestically, an ever-growing number of American workers are losing their jobs due to competition from cheaper wage earners outside the United States. The terms "downsizing" and "outsourcing" are used to explain this economic reality. **Downsizing** refers to reductions in a company's workforce as a result of negative economic conditions, and **outsourcing** occurs when a company seeks an outside provider or manufacturer in order to cut costs. Increasingly, outsourcing markets are found in "developing" nations.

Images of global economic expansion, social injustice, and Western cultural dominance upset opponents of continued globalization (Holton 2005). Production and distribution systems under globalization have contributed to the continuing disparity between the rich and the poor. As Raphael Kaplinsky (2005) explains, "Most of the individuals making decisions about the allocation of resources which drive globalization and economic growth fail to recognize the importance of poverty and distribution. Their focal point is the accumulation of personal and aggregate social wealth" (p. 27). Because of this focus, many third world nations have become welfare states dependent upon financial aid from wealthier nations. Furthermore, Vandana Shiva (2000) argues that globalization has contributed to the deregulation of environmental policies designed to protect ecological life forms (e.g., plants and vegetation).

Multinational Corporations

Globalization is fueled by the wealth and influence of multinational corporations. As the name implies, a **multinational corporation** is a business with operations, holdings, and subsidiaries in more than one country. The individual companies may be linked to the parent via merger, operating as subsidiaries, or maintain relative autonomy. An MNC relies on the resources of each company under its umbrella. In some cases, the finished product of an MNC, such as a major auto company (Ford, Chevrolet, or Toyota), combines resources taken from multiple subsidiaries.

A factory worker is shown packing chocolates at multinational corporation Nestlé.

MNCs are not a new phenomenon, as commerce among nations dates back at least to the time of the Phoenicians, whose trading ships sailed from what is now Lebanon to foreign lands more than 3,000 years ago. From that point on, trading routes via shipping have crisscrossed the globe, seeking and trading silk, gold, spices, tools, and, today, oil. The American colonies were heavily impacted by the presences of such MNCs as the Hudson's Bay Company and the Dutch

East India Company. In his *The Theory of Business Enterprise* (1904), Veblen described shipping as an evolutionary accomplishment of business management that fed the primary motive of business: pecuniary gain. Nations that dominated shipping were able to take necessary natural resources from other, less developed nations. Clearly, companies tied to shipping were advantageously positioned to enjoy huge profits. At one time, what is now the United States was a victim of European multinationals. Today, the United States is in a position of power, and its MNCs are taking advantage of European companies. Thus, the United States exemplifies how a nation once dominated by foreign MNCs can become the dominator if it is rich in natural resources and develops advanced technology through scientific and cultural achievements (Delaney 2005). Furthermore, not all MNCs are headquartered in wealthy nations. Brazil, Taiwan, Kuwait, and Venezuela are classified as part of the developing world; yet, these nations are home to several MNCs.

Presently, MNCs are often viewed as utilitarian enterprises that possess too much political and economic power in the business world and have little or no regard for the cultural or economic well-being of the nations in which they operate. In reality, this perception is only partially true. MNCs do often exert influence on public policy in their parent nations by threatening to move jobs overseas (e.g., outsourcing), and they are primarily concerned with profit over other concerns such as the environment. However, MNCs that operate outside the parent nation must still abide by the laws of the land in which they operate. Paying low wages to workers is certainly an advantage for MNCs, but such workers are seldom effective in high-tech jobs. Also, some developing nations are characterized by instability, and MNCs generally prefer to operate in politically stable countries with a functioning infrastructure (Nizamuddin 2007). Other important variables for MNCs to consider when looking to expand to other nations include market size, cultural openness, corruption, geographic distance, corporate tax rates, and tariffs (Bognanno, Keane, and Yang 2005). If foreign nations are as generous to corporations as the United States, they will not pay much in tax. According to a 2004 study by the U.S. Government Accountability Office, 61 percent of American corporations, including 39 percent of the large companies, paid no corporate income taxes between 1996 and 2000 (Weiss 2008). In 2007, corporations paid just 14.4 percent of the total U.S. tax burden, compared to 50 percent in 1940 (Weiss 2008). When corporations do not pay U.S. taxes, doing so is up to the American taxpayers.

What Do You Think?

Many people feel that corporations should pay more taxes, especially when compared to the average taxpayer. What do you think?

SOCIOLOGICAL PERSPECTIVES ON ECONOMICS

Sociological analyses of the economic system are as varied as the theoretical perspectives found in sociology. Our sociological analysis of social institutions has centered on the functionalist, conflict, and symbolic-interactionist perspectives. As is consistent with their core focus, functionalists and conflict theorists concentrate on the macro aspects of economics, while symbolic interactionists employ a micro approach.

The Functionalist Perspective

Because functionalists tend to concentrate on the positive aspects of social institutions, they view the economic system as a vital social institution that assists with society's overall functionality. Among the functions of the economic system are the provision of jobs, the manufacture of consumer and industrial products, the distribution of these products, and the presentation of many methods of consumption to consumers.

This chapter's opening discussion described the United States as a democratic-capitalistic society with an economic system that guarantees that some people will flourish while others will struggle. As we shall discover shortly, conflict theorists see this reality in a negative light. Functionalists, however, would argue that an economic system designed to reward those who reach top positions with an accompanying high salary serves as a motivation to the rest of the workers to work hard in an attempt to achieve such lofty positions. Furthermore, functionalists believe that those who rise to the top should be paid more money because they have reached culturally desired goals. Thus, from the functionalist perspective, a medical doctor deserves more money than a hospital custodian because the doctor worked harder to reach such a distinguished position.

The functionalist perspective is often criticized for its analysis of the economic system. First, many of the jobs available to workers are low paying with little or no opportunity for advancement. Second, many corporations, seeking the desired goal of maximizing profits, do so at the expense of American workers by closing domestic plants in favor of foreign locations that provide a cheaper labor force. In turn, these corporations exploit the workers of the foreign markets by paying lower salaries. Third, the functionalist perspective seems to ignore that some people have an easier path toward economic success because of such social advantages as being born into a wealthy family, having a chance to attend good schools, and so on.

The Conflict Perspective

Conflict theorists, especially those in the Marxist tradition, view the economic system as the root of all evil because the imbalance of power among people is rooted in this social institution. You may recall from Chapter 2 that power is the most critical variable for conflict theorists. From an economic standpoint, those with power control the means of production. The workers are employed by and subordinate to those who control the means of production. Those with power will use their economic advantage to control the workers. Tension and alienation are inevitable between those who control the means of production and those who do not. Thus, conflict theorists would argue that the economic system should reward workers more evenly; otherwise, the class struggle between the haves and the have-nots will never cease.

The conflict perspective views globalization in a negative light because it is feared that the ever-growing, single-integrated economic system works to the advantage of multinational corporations (those who control the means of production) at the expense of the have-nots in the developing nations. As described earlier in this chapter, the production and distribution systems under globalization have contributed to the continuing disparity between the rich (the powerful) and the poor (the workers).

Critics of the conflict perspective will point out that under a globalized economic system, the overall levels of production have increased. Many workers enjoy a better lifestyle than they would have in the past because the salaries they earn afford them an opportunity to meet their basic needs and purchase consumer goods. A large number of people have affordable health care because of their corporate employment. (Note: We discuss health care in Chapter 13.)

The Symbolic-Interactionist Perspective

The symbolic-interactionist approach pays close attention to the impact of the economic system on individuals, families, and small groups. Symbolic interactionists, among other things, are especially interested in the work experiences of people, the day-to-day interactions of workers, the meaning workers place on their jobs, and the effects of economic position on self-esteem.

The work experience is connected to the day-to-day interactions of workers in a number of ways. Consider that all workers must learn the rules, both formal and informal, of their workplace. For example, the workday may end formally at 5:00 p.m., but management might expect its professional workers to stay later to assure that projects are completed on time. A worker who leaves every day at 5:00 p.m. while others stay behind is subject to a poor job-performance review by a supervisor. This worker will also be evaluated by coworkers as well. The day-to-day interactions of these coworkers will certainly be impacted by this behavior. Furthermore, because most of us work in a diverse workplace, individuals need to find a way to get along with a wide variety of personalities.

The economic institution has a great impact on an individual's sense of self as well. For example, it is generally understood that people have a higher sense of self while they are employed than when they are not. Upon graduation, college students will feel much better about themselves when they find a job because this will help to validate the decision to go to college in the first place. Having gainful employment affords one the chance to pay bills and contribute positively to society. However, being employed might not be enough for people with high expectations. College students, for example, certainly hope to find a "good" job upon graduation—that is, a job in their field, a high-paying job, or both. A person's self-esteem will certainly take a hit if he or she cannot find a job that has meaning.

The micro approach to the study of economics is beneficial because it can provide an in-depth analysis of how individuals feel about their place in the economic system, but the micro focus comes at the expense of macro considerations. The economic system is larger than any one individual's needs and desires. Many people do not find great meaning in their jobs but perform regardless because they need to feed a family. While a college graduate may feel angst that it is taking too long to find a good job, it is imperative to understand that during times of recession, one might be happy to find any type of employment.

What Do You Think?

Each of these theoretical perspectives offers sociological insights about the economic system. Analyze each of these perspectives in terms of your employment outlook after graduation and ask yourself which one you believe to be most relevant. What do you think?

POLITICS: SYSTEMS AND PARTIES

As mentioned in the opening paragraph of this chapter, economics and politics are intertwined. Now that we have learned about the economic system, it is time to focus on the political system.

Politics is generally viewed as the guiding influence of governmental policy. The political system operates on behalf of the government. The **government** is the political unit that exercises authority via laws and customs. Collective actions, such as voting, marches, and rallies, are also considered to be political if the state is the target of such mass activity (Armstrong and Bernstein 2008).

Global Political Systems

Present-day global political systems can be categorized in a number of ways, but the most critical distinction is based on power distribution. Political systems that

High-level politicians, such as then-Governor Sarah Palin shown here at a local event in Auburn, New York, generally rely on a number of predictable backdrops, including visible American flags, well-dresssed local politicians standing in support in the background, and various corresponding ceremonies such as ribbon-cutting events.

limit power to a few, or one absolute leader, are referred to as authoritarian governments, whereas systems that give power to the people are known as democratic governments.

Authoritarian governments expect unquestioned obedience to authority. With authoritarian governments, great power is given to political leaders, and people have little or no say in who their leaders will be. An authoritarian government is unconcerned about the needs of the people and places the needs of leaders above all else. Authoritarian leaders generally rule for life. Monarchies are the oldest form of authoritarian government and are typically associated with agrarian societies. In a monarchy, leadership is hereditary, vested, for instance, in a royal family. Monarchs usually have a royal title such as king, queen, or emperor. Often, the monarch is also the leader of a national religion, which further reinforces the ruler's position of authority. Beyond monarchies, other examples of authoritarian governments include totalitarian regimes, dictatorships, military juntas, and oligarchies. The rise of industrialization helped to transform many authoritarian governments into democracies. Nonetheless, a number of authoritarian governments exist today.

In a democracy, the political system is designed to empower the people, and leaders are chosen periodically, in contested elections, to represent the needs of the people. In fact, democracy literally means "rule by the people." In a democracy, power rests with the position and not with the elected person. Thus, Bill Clinton once had a great deal of power, but this power stemmed from the position he held and did not reside in himself. Although most Americans think of the United States as a democracy, it is really a "representative democracy,"—meaning that the people elect others to make decisions for them. The people are allowed to vote for propositions. However, even when people pass a proposition, it risks being overturned by judges and political leaders. Thus, the rule of the majority—an assumed characteristic of democracy—is not always the case.

What Do You Think?

If the people of a particular state overwhelming pass a proposition, should a judge or political leader be allowed to overturn this decision? What do you think?

Political Parties

As described above, the United States has a representative democracy. While Americans do vote for candidates (although they do not vote directly for the president as the presidency is determined by the electoral college), they seldom vote directly on issues. In this manner, citizens are placed at a distance from truly ruling themselves. This distance is lengthened by the introduction of political parties, a characteristic of democratic systems. George Washington, the first president of the United States, warned of the danger of political parties in his farewell address: "Let me warn you in the most solemn manner against the baneful effects of the spirit of party." Washington considered political parties the "worst enemy" of popular government (Hershey 2007, p. 5).

Why was Washington so worried about political parties so long ago? And why are so many Americans upset with the two-party system that dominates the U.S. democratic system today? In order to answer these questions, we must understand what a political party is. A **political party** is an organization designed to gain power for itself via its candidates. Political parties are formed based on a prevailing ideology. For example, in the United States, conservatives tend to belong to the Republican Party, and liberals tend to belong to the Democratic Party. Some people vote strictly along party lines rather than learning for themselves the traits that characterize a particular candidate. Not only did Washington worry about political parties, but he believed in rule by an educated elite as he feared power in the hands of the masses. Many people today are dissatisfied with the two-party system primarily because they recognize that parties "try to teach or propagandize citizens" (Hershey 2007, p. 10).

There have been occasional attempts to form a third party. During the 1992 presidential election, for example, Ross Perot formed the Reform Party and ran for president. Ralph Nader has also run for president as the Green Party candidate in 1996 and 2000 and as an independent candidate in 2004 and 2008. Perot and Nader shared the same fate; it is nearly impossible to win a major election without the backing of one of the two major parties. In 2009, the populist Tea Party movement emerged. Although generally characterized as a political party whose members oppose "big government" taxation and spending, this most recent of the third-party movements in the United States is so diverse and decentralized that, as of July 2010, sixty-nine Tea Parties exist in Missouri and twenty-four in Kansas. The Tea Party movement has attracted people fed up with concerns beyond taxation and spending, including antiminority racists, according to the National Association for the Advancement of Colored People (NAACP). At the 2010

NAACP convention in Kansas City, a resolution was passed calling on all people—including Tea Party leaders—to condemn racism within the Tea Party movement. "The resolution asserts that tea party supporters have engaged in 'explicitly racist behavior, displayed signs and posters intended to degrade people of color generally and President Barack Obama specifically'" (Thomas and Campbell 2010, p. 1). The resolution led to sharp criticisms from Tea Party organizers and claims that most people who participate in the Tea Party movement are not racist. David Webb, spokesperson for the National Tea Party Federation, which represents sixty-one Tea Party groups around the United States, acknowledges that "fringe elements" do exist in the movement but claims they represent the exception rather than the rule (Drake 2010). These fringe elements include radio talk show host Mark Williams, who responded to the NAACP resolution by promptly confirming it and then producing a racist parody that included nearly every racist stereotype since the Jim Crow era. The National Tea Party Federation expelled Williams and his organization, the Tea Party Express, over the racist blog post (Gerson 2010). Attempting to defuse the claims of racism directed toward the Tea Party movement and its members (known as Tea Baggers), President Obama and Vice President Joseph Biden stated that they do not believe the Tea Party is a "racist organization" but acknowledge that "elements" of the movement clearly harbor such views (Drake 2010).

Racist accusations levied against the Tea Party aside, most Tea Baggers (many students are likely aware of the Urban Dictionary's definition of "tea bagger" and that its original meaning has nothing to do with politics) are citizens upset with the current political-economic situation in the United States. Citizens across the globe share this concern, whether they belong to a Tea Party or not. This discussion of the Tea Party movement is meant to highlight the fact that economics and politics are indeed intertwined as the movement was started by people unhappy with both their present economic status and their belief that their political leaders are too inept to solve current economic problems.

A growing number of Americans are disappointed with the two-party political system and the perceived growing influence of the government on people's lives. Shown here, Tea Party members carry signs and demonstrate in front of the California State Capitol Building in April 2010.

A large number of people disagree with George Washington and contemporary critics of the political parties. Instead, proponents of political parties see value in this system. Keefe and Hetherington (2003) claim that "the parties have made important contributions to the development and maintenance of a democratic political culture and to democratic institutions and practices. In essence, the parties form the principal institution for popular control of government, and this achievement is remarkable given the limitations under which they function" (p. 29). From this standpoint, the political parties are viewed as positive entities because they are set up to involve people in the political system via grassroots campaigns and "get-out-the-vote" promotions.

What Do You Think?

Will the Tea Party flourish where other third parties have failed? What do you think?

Great athletes are popular in most societies. Many become cultural icons and fixtures in the lives of citizens. Thus, their sociological relevance is rather obvious. However, athletes who become politicians eventually move away from the identities they once possessed and enter the domain of political figures capable of influencing their representatives, as well as people outside their constituencies. Let us take a closer look at Republican senator Jim Bunning of Kentucky (mentioned in "A Closer Look" Box 12.3). In late February 2010, Bunning utilized a political ploy known as a filibuster to single-handedly kill a bill designed to extend unemployment benefits. A *filibuster* is an obstructive tactic designed to prevent the adoption of a measure generally favored by the majority of lawmakers in a particular legislative body. A filibuster is accomplished by means of a very long speech that may last for a day or days.

What Do You Think?

Are political parties a threat to or the protector of democracy? What do you think?

The package bill targeted by Bunning's filibuster would extend not only unemployment insurance but also COBRA (medical health insurance) benefits and employment for thousands of federal highway workers. The bill was expected to receive unanimous support in the Senate. So why would Bunning oppose the bill? Bunning explained, "If we cannot pay for a bill that all 100 senators support, how can we tell the American people with a straight face that we will ever pay for anything? (Lopez 2010, p. A4). In a clear example of how economics and politics are intertwined, Bunning used his political right to exercise a filibuster against a bill that would result in continued deficit spending. The fact that all senators were perceived to favor the bill and yet still could not find the funding to support it alarmed Bunning. On the other hand, millions of people across the nation were (temporarily) affected by the actions of one politician. Ultimately, only nineteen senators objected to the deficit spending bill, but the filibuster had triumphed nonetheless.

A Closer Look

Box 12.3 Athletes in Politics

A wide variety of people are attracted to politics. For some, politics is a career or a calling to public service. Some enter the domain of politics (especially at the local level) to fight or promote a specific cause. Many candidates have studied law; thus, many lawyers become politicians. Celebrities may attempt to capitalize on their status as public figures and decide to run for office. And athletes, many of whom have celebrity status, may also throw their hats into the ring and run for office after their sports careers have ended. In *The Sociology of Sports,* Delaney and Madigan (2009a) discuss many former athletes in politics.

For example, a number of U.S. presidents were involved in sports, or were sportsmen, before their political careers began. Abraham Lincoln was an equestrian, swimmer, wrestler, runner, and jumper; Theodore Roosevelt played baseball, lacrosse, polo, tennis, and football, as well as participated in horseback riding, boxing, and rowing; Woodrow Wilson played and coached football; Franklin D. Roosevelt swam, rode horseback, and sailed; Harry Truman was an avid walker and umpired baseball games; Dwight D. Eisenhower played baseball and football in his youth and in later life enjoyed golfing and fishing; John F. Kennedy swam, sailed, golfed, and played tennis and touch football; Lyndon B. Johnson was a swimmer, equestrian, hunter, and fisherman; Richard M. Nixon played football at Whittier College; Gerald Ford played football at Michigan (earning the most valuable player award in 1934 and participating in two All-Star games) and later coached at Yale while pursuing his law studies (he also turned down professional offers from the Green Bay Packers and Detroit Lions); Jimmy Carter played basketball in high school; Ronald Reagan played football at Eureka College); and George H. W. Bush was the captain of his baseball team. As these examples demonstrate, political leaders at the highest level participated in sports before they turned to politics. The following discussion of other athletes who have successfully run for political office is not, of course, exhaustive but provides ample evidence that the worlds of athletics and politics often intersect (Delaney and Madigan 2009a).

Among the more popular, or well-known, former U.S. athletes who have gone on to political careers are Jack Kemp, Bill Bradley, Steve Largent, and Jesse "The Body" Ventura. Jack Kemp was a star quarterback for thirteen years with the American Football League's (AFL) Buffalo Bills and San Diego Chargers. He led the Bills to back-to-back AFL championships in 1964 and 1965. Kemp cofounded the AFL Players Association and was elected president for five terms. His sports exploits and name recognition helped his initial election bid. A Republican, Kemp served in the U.S. House of Representatives (representing the Buffalo area and Western New York) from 1971 to 1989. He failed in a 1988 bid to win the Republican Party presidential nomination but served as secretary of housing and urban development for four years in George H. W. Bush's administration. Kemp was selected as Bob Dole's 1996 presidential running mate against Bill Clinton (and Al Gore). Clinton and Gore won in a landslide victory (Delaney and Madigan 2009a).

Bill Bradley, a Rhodes scholar after a starring career with Princeton's basketball team—he was a three-time All-American, averaging 30.2 points per game throughout his three-year varsity career—played with the National Basketball Association (NBA) for ten years and won two NBA championships with the New York Knicks (1970 and 1973). Bradley's excellence in professional basketball was honored by the Knicks when they retired his number twenty-four jersey. Bradley also served as captain of the 1964 gold-medal-winning U.S. Olympic men's basketball team. Bradley turned his popularity in basketball into immediate success in the political arena. After retiring from the sport in 1977, he ran for the U.S. Senate in New Jersey in 1978. He won and served seventeen years in that body. Bradley ran unsuccessfully for the 2000 Democratic presidential nomination, losing out to Al Gore (Delaney and Madigan 2009a).

Steve Largent, never the fastest or most gifted wide receiver, worked hard throughout his fourteen-year NFL career with the Seattle Seahawks and earned his induction into the Hall of Fame. The Oklahoma native was elected to the U.S. House of Representatives as a Republican in 1994. He was reelected three times, always with a margin of over 60 percent of the vote. He identified himself with the religious Right and led a revolt against House Speaker Newt Gingrich, whom he blamed for congressional losses in 1998. Largent relinquished his House seat to run for state governor in 2002. He lost his bid in a close election, being defeated by state senator Brad Henry by less than 7,000 votes. He is currently the CEO of a cellular phone lobbying organization (Delaney and Madigan 2009a).

Other notable American athletes have also gone into politics. For example, Benjamin Nighthorse Campbell (son of a Portuguese immigrant mother and Northern Cheyenne Indian father), is a former Republican senator from Colorado (he did not seek reelection in 2004). Elected to the U.S. Senate in 1992, Campbell was the first Native American to serve in that body in more than sixty years. He also served in the U.S. House of Representatives from 1987 to 1992. Campbell is a former three-time U.S. national judo champion (1961 to 1963) and represented the United States at the 1964 Olympic Games in Tokyo. While serving in the Senate, Campbell was a member of the Committee on Indian Affairs. He remains an outspoken critic of the use of Indian nicknames, mascots, and logos in sports. Major League Baseball Hall of Fame pitcher Jim Bunning, who had 1,000 strikeouts and one hundred wins in both leagues, is a senator from Kentucky. Jim Ryun (R-KS), a three-time Olympic track star and former mile and 1,500-meter world-record holder, is a congressman. J. C. Watts, a two-time Orange Bowl most valuable player with the University of Oklahoma, played in the Canadian Football League (CFL). Upon the completion of his CFL career, Watts was elected to the U.S. House of Representatives in 1994. Watts served four terms in Congress before leaving politics in 2003. He was one of the highest-profile African Americans in the Republican Party (Delaney and Madigan 2009a).

What Do You Think?

Are athletes qualified to serve as politicians? Would you vote for your favorite athlete as governor or senator for your state? What sort of qualification would your favorite athlete need to possess, other than athletic skill, for you to vote for him or her? What do you think?

The United States is not the only country with political leaders who were previously sports stars. Throughout the world, former athletes have entered the realm of sports. Just as in the United States, some of these athletes have risen to the ranks of president. Russia's former president and current prime minister, Vladimir Putin, a one-time KGB agent, is a martial arts expert who still enjoys putting on displays. Sebastian Coe, a British middle-distance runner who dominated the 800- and 1500-meter races during the early 1980s, is the only man to win the Olympic gold medal in the 1500 twice (Moscow 1980 and Los Angeles 1984). He is one of the most decorated athletes in British history. Coe, a Conservative, served in Parliament from 1992 to 1997 but lost his reelection bid. In 2000, Coe was elected to the House of Lords. He led London's successful bid to host the 2012 Summer Olympic Games and now serves as president of the organizing committee for those games. Coe had to convince members of the International Olympic Committee that London's transport system could be overhauled and that there was public support for the games (Delaney and Madigan 2009a).

A number of former Canadian National Hockey League (NHL) players have enjoyed success in the political arena after their playing careers were over. Howie Meeker's sporting and political professions overlapped as he won the federal by-election in the Ontario riding of Waterloo South in 1951 while he was still playing hockey for the Toronto Maple Leafs. The Conservative MP did not seek reelection in 1953. After retiring from hockey, Meeker became a Canadian hockey broadcasting icon who entertained viewers for thirty years with his trademark folksy phrases. Frank Mahovlich, who played professional hockey for twenty-two years (NHL and the World Hockey Association), never ran for political office but was appointed to the Senate in 1998. He belongs to the Fisheries and Oceans and National Finance Senate committees. Ken Dryden, a former goaltender for the Montreal Canadians, successfully ran for Parliament and was named to the cabinet as minister of social development. There are rumors that Dryden ultimately plans on running for prime minister. It is reasonable to assume that if Wayne Gretzky stepped into Canada's political arena, he could successfully run for nearly any political office, including prime minister (Delaney and Madigan 2009a).

What Do You Think?

It is the right of a politician to utilize the filibuster approach to protest a perceived political injustice. On the other hand, many people, especially those directly affected by Bunning's filibuster, felt they were victims of political-economic injustice. Where do you stand on this issue? What do you think?

THE POSSESSION OF POLITICAL POWER, AUTHORITY, AND INFLUENCE

A number of sociologists, economists, and political scientists have attempted to explain the concepts of power and authority, their roles, and how they operate in society. Power and authority are exercised in nearly all social relationships, by both small groups and large organizations and societies.

Distinguishing Between Power and Authority

Conflict theorists emphasize the role of power as a force that reveals social inequality throughout society. They claim that the dominant power group forces its values upon the rest of society, the subordinate groups. Lewis Coser, for example, argued that the level of power held by any group depends on its relation to other groups. Those who control the means of production, or valued rewards, are in a position of power. Thus, Coser (1956) defined power as "the chance to influence the behavior of others in accord with one's own wishes" (p. 134). C. Wright Mills examined the role of power in society and concluded that an elite power group consisting of political, military, and economic institutions—the so-called triangle of power—dictated the course of behavior in American society. Mills (1956) described three types of power:

1. *Authority:* power that is justified by the beliefs of the voluntarily obedient
2. *Manipulation:* power that is wielded unbeknownst to the powerless
3. *Coercion:* the final form of power, whereby the powerless are forced to obey the powerful

Major decisions throughout history, according to Mills, have always been made by the triangle of power and not by average citizens. Mills, then, argued that democracy is an illusion.

Sociologist Max Weber viewed **power** as the ability to exercise one's will over others, despite their resistance. In this regard, anyone who can control others' behavior has power. Weber defined **authority** as power attached to a social position (e.g., athletic director or head coach). Authority is a legitimate relation of domination and subjection; thus, authority is described as legitimate power. Weber identified three types of authority:

1. *Rational-legal:* authority based on rational grounds, anchored in rules, and legally enacted or contractually established. Authority resides in the office or social position, not the individual. This type of authority is the most common in contemporary sports.
2. *Traditional:* authority based on tradition. Dominant in premodern societies, this type of authority is rare in sports today.
3. *Charismatic:* authority that rests on the appeal of leaders who claim allegiance because of their extraordinary virtuosity, whether ethical, heroic, or religious. In this authority type, the power resides with the individual, not the social position or role. In sports, a person may gain a position of power, but, ultimately, if the position is to be maintained, it will become rationalized.

Today, most nations, especially in the West, have governments based on rational-legal principles. Political leaders have authority to act on behalf of their constituencies or in the interests of national security and stability. Governments seek equilibrium in society because social systems and organizations are very complex and depend on relative efficiency in order to maintain smooth operations. People with power have the ability to mobilize resources to attain the system's goals (Parsons 1960).

Political Influence

Political leaders are not the only people with power. In reality, many people and organizations have the ability to exert political influence—another form of power—over others. The media and special-interest groups are entities with such a capability.

The media's role in politics is so strong that the media themselves collectively carry such tags as "the fourth branch of government," "a political institution," "an integral part of the American political system," and "a tool for governing" (Graber 2000, p. xi). As these tags indicate, the media can have a significant impact on the political system. Depending on one's perspective, this impact may be both positive and negative. In authoritarian societies the media generally serve as a vehicle for the propaganda of the government and political leader(s). Media outlets that attempt to criticize government operations within an authoritarian society are heavily scrutinized and eventually silenced. In democratic societies, the media are granted far greater freedom to pass judgment on the government. In the United States, the freedom of the press is deemed so important that it is one of the five basic freedoms guaranteed by the U.S. Constitution. Michael Gurevitch and Jay Blumler (2000) suggest that the media perform a number of functions and services for the political system, including surveilling the sociopolitical environment, identifying the key issues of the day, providing platforms for politicians and interest groups, presenting a diverse range of views, creating mechanisms for holding officials accountable for their behavior, encouraging citizens to participate in politics, and advocating for a continued "freedom of the press" mentality.

Critics of the role of the media in politics point out that most news outlets are controlled by a few giant media corporations (Gurevitch and Blumler 2000). Control of the news by a few conglomerates undermines the democratic system. As a result, many people learn about news events from alternative news sources, including the Internet, which provides a wide sampling of political views. For example, liberals find the website MoveOn.org to their liking. Conservatives will prefer TheConservativeVoice.com. The Internet is not the only alternative source for news. Recent technology has created another option in news coverage: Twitter (see "Connecting Sociology and Popular Culture" Box 12.4 to learn about Twitter and its political influence).

Most forms of the media, including Twitter, the Internet, and alternative and traditional news sources, are often guilty of media coverage bias. That is, a news outlet general supports one political approach over another and allows such a bias to distract subtly (or not so subtly) from the truth. Other criticisms of the political media include that it perpetuates "sound bite democracy" (by presenting politics in a simplified and slanted manner); presents incomplete coverage (ignoring some candidates or issues); and imposes "coverage charges" (it costs a lot of money to advertise on television, and only the richest candidates can afford to use this medium) (Tepperman and Blain 2006).

Above, this chapter briefly reviewed political parties. Although each party attempts to dominate the sociopolitical landscape with its prevailing ideology, each has a relatively diverse set of political agendas. In other words, claiming an allegiance to one political party over another does not guarantee that special attention will be granted to all the areas of concern among party members. To that end, special-interest groups were created. And there exists "a profusion of interest groups of nearly every conceivable variety and size" (R. Smith 2008, p. 157).

Special-interest groups have become increasingly powerful and prevalent in American politics since the inception of the U.S. Constitution. Such groups are much more active today than in the past, but they are indeed as old as the nation itself. Consider, in 1757, that local merchants donated liquor to bribe voters during George Washington's run for election to the Virginia House of Burgesses (Sabato 1984; Rozell and Wilcox 1999). So, what is a special-interest group? An **interest group** may be defined as an organized collection of people working together on behalf of or strongly supporting a specific interest or cause in an attempt to influence politicians, government, and legislation (see "A Closer Look" Box 12.5 to learn more about special-interest groups).

SOCIOLOGICAL PERSPECTIVES ON POLITICS

We employ the same three sociological perspectives used to analyze economics earlier in the chapter to analyze politics here. Once again, the functionalist and conflict perspectives utilize a macro approach, while symbolic interactionism focuses on micro issues. The underlying variable of greatest importance in our discussion of politics is power, who possesses it, and how it is exercised.

The Functionalist Perspective

Chapter 2 explained that functionalism has two basic assumptions: the idea that all society's institutions are interconnected and share a general consensus on values. Functionalists would posit that within a democratic political system, the needs of the majority are met by politicians because people put politicians into office. In addition, because eligible citizens elect politicians, they also possess power. Giving citizens the power to vote for elected officials is functional because it should contribute to a general consensus of values in society. The functionalists would also submit that the "checks and balances" political system contributes to the smooth functioning of society because no single branch of the government (executive, legislative, or judicial) can gain a monopoly on power.

Barack Obama evoked the "general consensus on values" component of functionalism with his 2008 presidential campaign slogan "Yes We Can." Obama attempted to unite the diverse American population with his speeches promoting a "coming together" attitude. For example, during his speech in South Carolina, after he won the Democratic presidential primary, Obama used such phrases as "You can see it in the faces here tonight. There are young and old, rich and poor. They are black and white, Latino and Asian and Native American"; "Make no mistake about what we're up against. We're up against the belief that it's alright for lobbyists to dominate our government, that they are just part of the system in Washington"; and "Don't tell me we can't change. Yes, we can. Yes, we can

Connecting Sociology and Popular Culture

Box 12.4 Twitter and Politics

According to information from its website, Twitter is a privately funded startup with offices in San Francisco, California. Founded by Jack Dorsey, Biz Stone, and Evan Williams, Twitter started as a side project in March 2006 (launched publicly in July 2006) and has now grown into a real-time short messaging service that works over multiple networks and devices. In countries around the world, people follow the sources most relevant to them and access information via Twitter as it happens—from breaking world news to updates from friends (Twitter 2009). Twitter and simplicity go hand in hand. Twitter asks one question: "What are you doing?" Answers must be under 140 characters in length and can be sent via mobile texting, instant messaging, or the Web (Twitter 2009). The messages sent and read, known as "tweets," are text-based posts that resemble microblogging. A Twitter subscriber creates a profile page and becomes an "author" of tweets. The people who receive the tweets are known as "followers." Authors may restrict delivery of tweets to those within their circle of followers or allow access to all who subscribe to Twitter (the default setting). As of April 2011, there was an average of 155 million tweets per day, triple the number of a year earlier (Kirkpatrick 2011).

A number of celebrities use Twitter as a means of communicating with fans, friends, and family. Celebrities enjoy this social-networking site because they control the flow of information. Many followers of famous celebrity Twitter authors wait impatiently for updates about their daily activities; many tweets include such mundane information as lunch menus, shopping updates, and so on. Fans of such celebrities as Charlie Sheen, Ashton Kutcher, Britney Spears, Ellen DeGeneres, Oprah Winfrey, Anderson Cooper, Shaq, and Terrell Owens number in the millions. As Twitter continues to grow, it faces some of the troubling issues experienced by other Internet sites—most specifically, spam. *Businessweek* writer Sarah Lacy (2009) blames this on Ashton Kutcher (regular users of Twitter know that Kutcher was the first author to have 1 million followers): "He was one of the earliest and most visible celebrities to seize on Twitter as a way to lure fans and drive traffic. And in social media, where mainstream celebs go, D-listers and sex peddlers follow" (p. 1). In 2010, Kutcher posted the first thirteen minutes of his new film *Killers* on his Twitter home page as a means of promoting his film and entertaining his more than 5 million followers. Based on the posted number of followers on their Twitter home pages (in March 2011), 310 people or organizations had more than 1 million followers. As of September 2011, Lady Gaga led the way with more than 13.2 million followers, with Justin Bieber (12.4 million), Barack Obama (9.9 million), Katy Perry (9.6 million), Kim Kardashian (9.5 million), Britney Spears (9.3 million), Shakira (8.2 million), Taylor Swift (7.8 million), Ashton Kutcher (7.5 million), Ellen DeGeneres (7.4 million), Rihanna (7.3 million), Oprah Winfrey (7.2

change. Yes, we can" (CNN Politics 2008). Obama's constant use of "we" not only reflects the functionalist perspective but reminds us of Charles Horton Cooley's idea of primary groups and the shared sense of "we-ness." The constant use of "we" by Obama was a deliberate attempt to connect himself to the people, as if "we" are all one family (a primary group) and "we" are together in this fight to keep American strong.

Functionalists would also argue that because of the complexity of the social system, it is functional to break the political system into parts designed to take

million), and Selena Gomez (7.1 million) rounding out the top thirteen (Twitter 2011).

But Twitter has its proponents beyond celebrity stargazers and people who want to keep up with friends and family. In other words, it goes beyond social networking; it serves political purposes and has been used in emergencies and criminal proceedings. In politics, Twitter became a rage during the 2008 U.S. presidential campaign primarily because of Obama's use of it. Journalists have used Twitter to provide real-time coverage of news events as they occur around the world. The June 2009 presidential election in Iran propelled the credibility of Twitter in the world of politics. Protestors took to the streets of Tehran after accusations that hard-line president Mahmoud Ahmadinejad had stolen his reelection. The Iranian government was able to control traditional news outlets, but it was no match for people who sent tweets of the events in Iran. Twitter was considered such an important source of news during the Iranian postelection demonstrations that a State Department official e-mailed Twitter co-founder Jack Dorsey to delay scheduled maintenance of its global network while Iranians were using it to swap information and inform the outside world about the mushrooming protests around Tehran. Twitter complied with the request (*Post-Standard,* 6/21/09). It should be pointed out, however, that tweets are unconfirmed sources of information and are often ripe with biased opinions about events, especially political events.

Nonetheless, Twitter has been found to be helpful during emergencies because people in the middle of such events can provide immediate and firsthand information about them as they take place. This can be especially important during emergencies caused by earthquakes, hurricanes, tornados, and snowstorms; authors may post information about road closings and direct emergency personnel to hot spots and people most in need of help. When US Airways Flight 1549 experienced multiple bird strikes and was forced to attempt a water landing in the Hudson River, an onboard passenger was the first to send photos to the public before any other media arrived at the scene. Law enforcement officials also have access to Twitter. They have interrupted planned violent attacks by reading tweets posted online. In Mexico, for example, two people face thirty-year sentences for terrorism and sabotage in what may be the most serious charges ever brought against anyone using a Twitter account. Mexican prosecutors say the defendants helped to cause a chaos of car crashes and panic due to tweets posted on their Twitter accounts (*Post-Standard,* 9/5/11, p. A9). Authorities in England had to temporarily shut down cellular service when rioters used Twitter to organize riots in London and other English cities in August 2011.

What Do You Think?

Many people highlight the virtues of Twitter, while others emphasize the negative aspects. What is your conclusion about the role Twitter plays in politics and other real-life social events? What do you think?

care of specific needs. These parts include, but are not limited to, oversight committees that serve as watchdogs of society; agencies responsible for distributing funds for such programs as unemployment insurance, Medicaid, and Medicare; legislative bodies that create laws; law enforcement personnel who enforce the laws and norms of society; and judicial courts that determine whether justice has been served.

The primary criticism of the functionalist perspective of the political system resides with its unrealistic portrayal of equality among citizens. All people are not

A Closer Look

Box 12.5 Political Interest Groups

Interest groups hold a unique position in American and other democratic societies as their primary mission is "to give voice to the voiceless" (Strolovitch 2007, p. 17). Giving voice to the people is a fundamental aspect of democracy. Consequently, it should come as no surprise that numerous groups and organizations have special-interest groups working for them. For example, gun advocates have the National Rifle Association, college professors have the American Association of University Professors, laborers have the American Federation of Labor–Congress of International Organizations, pro-environment advocates have the Sierra Club and Friends of the Earth, most ethnic groups have political interest groups acting on their behalf, and so on. Interest groups are very prevalent and operate at the local, state, and national levels (R. Smith 2008).

All special-interest groups attempt to influence public opinion via advertisements, ground-level petitions, letter-writing campaigns, and so on. They also attempt to influence sympathetic candidates by supporting their campaigns. Special-interest groups also hire lobbyists who deal directly with government officials and attempt to influence them on behalf of the groups (Delaney 2008b). On the surface, there is nothing wrong with special-interest groups; after all, they do represent the needs and concerns of people. They also provide information to candidates and politicians on topics they might otherwise be ignorant of. When special-interest groups cross over to corrupting (or attempting to corrupt) politicians and government officials, however, the political system becomes compromised (Delaney 2008b). Corruption is possible because special-interest groups donate money to politicians' campaign operations, and because most politicians rely on political donations, special-interest groups are in a position to influence the success or failure of a campaign.

Interest groups have a high degree of political involvement in the United States as a result, at least in part, of the distinctive characteristics of the American government. Mark Rozell and Clyde Wilcox (1999) describe these distinctive characteristics as follows: governmental decision making offers multiple incentives and opportunities for influencing policy; the major political parties welcome outside interest groups to join their ranks; American elections are much more frequent than those of other Western democracies; and the fact that only a small percentage of eligible Americans vote makes those who do vote likely to vote based on individual interests. Despite the impact and power of political special-interest groups, in the United States they rarely have any sort of official status within the government (R. Smith 2008).

What Do You Think?

Many people vote based on personal interests rather than the interests of the greater society. Is voting based on personal interests a good thing? What do you think?

equal in society, and much of this has to do with the connection between economics and politics. That is, people with money can afford to contribute to election campaigns and influence government officials to act in their best interests. The wealthy can also afford to finance special-interest groups, which negatively affects the idea of a general consensus on values and norms.

The Conflict Perspective

The functionalist perspective of rallying people behind the idea of a consensus on values is illustrated with then-Senator Barack Obama's 2008 presidential campaign slogan of "Yes we can."

The primary criticism of the functionalist approach is directly related to the basic premise of conflict theory—namely, that a great disparity in power exists among citizens in any given society. The underlying principle of the conflict perspective rests with the idea that society's predominant values and norms are those of the dominant power group, which are imposed on the masses by power elites. The power elites control the means of production. Controlling the means of production implies dominance in the economic realm of society, but this dominance is exercised and legitimized via the political system.

Because the power elite are small in number and yet control the economic and political systems, conflict theorists argue that the state serves the needs of the few at the expense of the masses. The power that regular citizens feel they possess is an example of false consciousness from the conflict perspective. Conflict theorists argue that the masses generally accept the existing social system even though it is used to exploit them. From time to time, however, the people revolt. Sometimes they are successful in their rebellion, but in many cases they fail. Karl Marx's era saw a great number of people's revolts. Marx tried to unite the workers of all lands in a mass proletariat rebellion. He would have been pleased by the people's attempt to fight the power elite during the 2011 "Winter of Discontent" (see "Closer Look" Box 12.6).

Functionalists criticize the conflict perspective by downplaying the existence of the power elite. Functionalists argue that the conflict perspective overestimates the degree to which any democratic society is run by a few powerful people and entities (e.g., the oil industry and gun manufacturers), and they do not accept the

A Closer Look

Box 12.6 Social Change and the 2011 "Winter of Discontent"

From time to time, the people revolt against their political leaders. During the Northern Hemisphere's winter months of 2011, a great number of "people's revolts" occurred, especially in northern Africa. The people were unhappy with their political leaders and sought social change.

The spark of social change in the 2011 Winter of Discontent began modestly in Tunisia with the act of an otherwise unassuming young man named Mohammed Bouazizi. For seven years, Bouazizi sold vegetables from a cart on the dusty streets of Sidi Bouzid, an impoverished town about 190 miles south of the capital, Tunis. On December 17, 2010, Bouazizi's livelihood was threatened when a policewoman confiscated his unlicensed vegetable cart and its goods. This had happened before, but it would not happen again. Bouazizi went to the provincial headquarters to complain to local municipal officials, but they refused to see him. Fed up with the way he was being treated and seeing no end to his misery as a have-not, Bouazizi covered himself in fuel and set himself on fire. He did not die right away but lived until January 4, 2011 (Time.com 2011a). Outrage over his ordeal led President Zine el Abidine Ben Ali, the Tunisian dictator, to visit Bouazizi on December 28, 2010, in the hospital to try to comfort him. Ben Ali was also trying to ease the anger of the masses in Tunisia, but to no avail. Just ten days after his visit to Bouazizi, Ben Ali's twenty-three-year rule of Tunisia was over (Time.com 2011a).

Bouazizi did not set out to be a martyr. But he became the spark that lit the flame of Tunisia's people's revolution. The success in Tunisia crept into the minds of young Egyptians who sought to break free of their country's thirty-year dictatorship. On January 25, 2011, the people of Egypt took to the streets of Cairo chanting, "Mubarak must go!" Using modern technology, including mobile phones, Facebook, and Twitter, young Egyptians communicated with one another to organize protests and rallies. The first, planned for January 25, 2011, was coordinated almost entirely online, when 85,000 people pledged on Facebook to attend a nationwide antigovernment protest. The Facebook page, called "Revolution Day," presented a list of demands for President Hosni Mubarak, ranging from raising the minimum wage to limiting presidential terms (Time.com 2011b). Within weeks, the people's revolution in Egypt was a success, and Mubarak was out of office (*The Telegraph,* 2/12/11). Only time will tell if the people are happy with the new regime.

With people's revolts successful in Tunisia and Egypt, revolutions sprung up in other North African nations. In Libya, the people attempted to overthrow the dictatorship of Col. Muammar Gadhafi. Revolutionists seized early victories by overthrowing government authorities in a number of cities throughout the country. They vowed to march to Tripoli and oust Gadhafi. In late February 2011, it looked as though the protestors would win control of Libya. Ever-defiant, Gadhafi vowed to die "a martyr" rather than surrender his political power (Butt and Landay 2011). Keeping his vow not to "go down without fighting," Gadhafi retaliated against the rebels using his massive weaponry, authorizing his military to strike by land and sea despite the likelihood that innocent citizens would die as a result of the firepower. Because Gadhafi was willing to use his military against his own people, the tide of revolution had shifted by mid-March. The rebels turned to the outside world for help. But just as the rest of the world remained neutral in Tunisia and Egypt, it also avoided getting involved in Libya—that is, until March 17, 2011, when the United Nations approved a "no-fly zone" over the nation. Gadhafi responded to the UN resolution by stating he would not recognize the mandate. On the last winter's day of 2011, his warplanes took to the air to repel the rebels. One was immediately shot down by French fighter jets. Hours later, the United States and other nations joined in to enforce the no-fly zone established over Libya. The people's revolution in Libya appeared as if it had failed, but by the end of the 2011 summer, the rebels had taken Tripoli. Once again, only time will tell what lies ahead in Libya.

Inspired by the events in Tunisia and Egypt,

people's revolutions were launched in Bahrain, Jordan, Saudi Arabia, Iraq, Yemen, and Algeria. In each case, the people attempted to oust existing political regimes and restore power to the people. In Bahrain, the apartheid regime led by the Sunni monarchy (the Sunni are a minority in Bahrain), used the same technique as Gadhafi—tanks, guns, and tear gas (provided by the United States)—to control the Shiite majority (Kristof 2011). In Iraq, thousands of Shiites rallied in support of their brethren in Bahrain, requesting that their government send troops to Bahrain. The Persian Gulf's Sunni nations readied to send troops to Bahrain if Iraq pulled such a move. Security forces in Yemen struck against protestors across the nation to halt the push calling for the ouster of longtime president Ali Abdullah Saleh, a key U.S. ally in the fight against Al-Qaeda. As the Winter of Discontent ended, none of the other North African nations' revolutionists had reached their goals. What does the future hold?

Meanwhile, the Winter of Discontent was evident in the United States as well. Once again, the have-nots were battling the haves. As in North Africa, angry crowds flooded the streets, occupied capitol buildings (e.g., the Wisconsin State Capitol), and vowed to fight to the end. The protestors in Wisconsin and other states were trying to exercise their political power in the name of the people. The power elites—namely, a number of state governors and especially Wisconsin governor Scott Walker—stood their ground and vowed to push on with their agendas. And their primary agenda was to bury labor unions by crippling their right to bargain collectively.

Governor Walker claimed that he was trying to cut the state's budget deficit. Instead of going after big business and the banks (e.g., eliminating government bailouts and tax breaks and shelters for the rich) or insisting on an end to the wars in the Middle East, which have cost taxpayers more than the combined deficits of all U.S. states, Walker argued that public-sphere union workers make too much money and that their unwillingness to compromise on collective bargaining rights was somehow responsible for Wisconsin's deficit. (Note: According to the nonpartisan Center on Budget and Policy Priorities [2010], virtually the entire U.S. deficit is the result of the economic downturn, the Bush tax cuts for the rich, and the wars in Afghanistan and Iraq.) The unions countered that they had made, and were willing to make more, concessions on salary, medical benefits, and retirement contributions. Union representatives also claimed that public-sphere workers do not make more money than private-sphere workers. The governor's attack on public employees was a scapegoating technique wherein he blamed the unions for the state's deficit (*On Campus* 2011). Such scapegoating defies logic and reason; consequently, there has to be another reason to attack unions other than state budget shortages.

Governor Walker's proposals to eliminate the collective bargaining rights of union workers were supported by the state's Republican majority. As a general rule, the Republicans support the status quo and power elites because of their commitment to big business (e.g., tax cuts for the rich and powerful organizations). In essence, Walker admitted to working for the best interests of the power elites when he spoke to a prank caller claiming to be billionaire conservative businessman David Koch. Fully believing that he was talking with Koch, Walker explained his antiunion stand and his attempts to bust them. The phone call was recorded and released via the Buffalo Beast, a left-leaning website in New York. The audio quickly spread across the Web. Democrats, who typically support unions and working-class people, used the audio tape to indicate that Walker represented the needs of the rich and powerful (Dwyer and Khan 2011). Koch responded by donating $300,000 in television advertising to support Walker (Dwyer and Khan 2011).

Governor Walker, a political leader who represents the needs of the power elite, succeeded in drastically reducing the collective power of union workers. Union workers vowed to fight him in an attempt to restore their power. (Note: In May 2011, a Wisconsin State supreme court judge voided the collective bargaining law passed by the Republicans and Governor Walker.) One of the most fascinating aspects of this ordeal, from a conflict perspective, is Governor Walker's portrayal of union workers as the haves, or the wealthy. In an attempt to rally a number of Wisconsin citizens, Walker tried to paint a picture of union members as elites. In reality, of course, union workers have always been, and remain, representatives of the people, the working class. There is a saying that when union workers are strong, all workers are strong. This is so because when union workers receive their fair share of profits, all workers can point to the salaries and benefits of union workers when making demands for themselves in the private sector. That a number of nonunion workers see unions in a negative light is a clear example of what Karl Marx called false consciousness—the inability to clearly see where one's best interest lies. The workers should stick together and point to a common threat, or enemy: the owners of the means of production and the administrators who work for them. In education, the real power elites, or haves, are the administrators—people who earn three to five times as much as teachers and professors. For example, school superintendents in Syracuse, New York, receive annual salaries ranging from $176,163 to $199,000 (Moses 2011). Teachers and professors typically make one-third to one-fourth that amount. So, who are the haves and the have-nots?

As the Winter of Discontent came to an end in 2011, the struggle of the people continued.

What Do You Think?

Do unions represent power elites or the working class? Should the money being used to wage war be applied instead to the U.S. deficit? Should tax cuts be extended to the wealthy? What do you think?

premise of the conflict perspective that the politically powerful dictate key values and norms to the masses.

The Symbolic-Interactionist Perspective

The political system may appear to be beyond its scope, but the symbolic-interactionist perspective's focus on individuals and small groups is especially relevant to an examination of the characteristics of politicians that may sway voters. Symbolic interactionists would also examine the manner in which events influence voters' perceptions of candidates and politicians as well as people's interactions with one another.

Local political and organizational elections are of particular interest to symbolic interactionists as well. In many instances, local and organizational elections may hold greater meaning for voters because the connection between the candidate or official and the voter is closer than that between a voter and U.S. senator. Herbert Blumer (1969), who coined the term "symbolic interactionism," insisted that the perspective's fundamental premise is that humans act toward things on the basis of meanings. When an election has particular meaning to folks, their involvement is stronger and involves an emotional component.

The symbolic-interactionist approach to politics is beneficial because it can provide an in-depth analysis of candidates' and politicians' leadership styles and personality traits, as well as their perception by voters. However, critics of this micro focus say that it ignores the greater complexity of the political system. An analysis of power is enlightening when it comes to small-group relationships, but critics say it lacks substance when applied to the greater political system.

What Do You Think?

Which of these theoretical perspectives on the political system best applies to Jim Bunning's filibuster, described earlier in this chapter? What do you think?

SUMMARY

In every society, economics and politics influence one another. The economic system refers to the coordinated processes by which goods and services are produced and distributed. With such responsibilities as overseeing the production and distribution of goods (e.g., necessities and luxury items) and services (e.g., police, fire, and health care), the economy clearly also represents a major social institution. When we speak of the economy and economic systems and sectors, we are taking a macro look at a very complex web of interrelated social systems, theories, policies, and people.

The political system is the governmental framework in which certain individuals and groups hold power to make decisions over others. Politics are generally viewed as the guiding influence of governmental policy. The political system operates on behalf of the government. The government is the political unit that exercises authority via laws and customs. The study of politics centers on the concepts of authority, power, and political influence. Political and governmental leaders possess power and authority, but they are not the only ones. In reality, many people and organizations have the ability to exert political influence—another form of power—over others. The media and special-interest groups are among those entities with such a capacity.

Glossary

Authority—Power that is justified by the beliefs of the voluntarily obedient.

Capitalism—An economic system that encourages free enterprise (private ownership).

Communism—The economic concept of common ownership of the means of production and distribution based on need.

Conspicuous consumption—The purchase of items not necessary for basic survival.

Conspicuous leisure—Nonproductive use of time.

Downsizing—Reductions in a company's workforce as a result of negative economic conditions.

Economy—The social system that coordinates a society's production, distribution, and consumption of goods and services.

Globalization—A socioeconomic process in which the constraints of geography on social and economic arrangements recede and people become increasingly aware that they live in an interconnected world.

Government—The political unit that exercises authority via laws and customs.

Interest group—An organized collection of people working together on behalf or in strong support of a specific interest or cause in an attempt to influence politicians, government, and legislation.

Mixed economic system—An economic system in which some of the means of production are privately owned and some are publicly owned.

Multinational corporation—A business with operations, holdings, and subsidiaries in more than one country.

Outsourcing—The use by a company of outside providers or manufacturers in order to cut costs.

Political party—An organization designed to gain power for itself via its candidates.

Political system—The governmental framework in which certain individuals and groups hold power to make decisions over others.

Power—The ability to exercise one's will over others despite their resistance.

Primary sector—The part of the economy that consists of the direct extraction of natural resources from the environment.

Secondary sector—The part of the economy that involves transforming raw materials into manufactured physical products (goods).

Socialism—A theory of socioeconomic organization based on government ownership, management, and control of the means of production, distribution, and exchange of goods and services.

Tertiary sector—The part of the economy that consists of producing and processing information and providing services.

Discussion Questions

1. Would the United States be better off with more elements of socialism (e.g., universal health care) incorporated into its sociopolitical system? Or should it remain as democratic as possible?
2. Could you see yourself working for a political interest group? If so, which one(s)? If not, why not?
3. Is your future profession threatened or enhanced by globalization? Explain.

4. Do you think the media have too much influence on politics? Are special-interest groups necessary or a hindrance to democracy? Explain.

5. Do you vote? Why or why not? What types of personality characteristics do you think are important for political leaders to possess?

Web Links

To learn more about the national debt, visit www.brillig.com/debt_clock.

To learn more about the Federal Trade Commission and "Made in the USA" product standards, visit www.ftc.gov/bcp/edu/pubs/business/adv/bus03.shtm.

The Americans Working website provides an *A–Z* listing of American-made products at www.americansworking.com.

To learn more about the United States' socioeconomic position in comparison to other nations, see the "Measure of America" findings at www.globalresearch.ca/index.php?context=va&aid=9621.

To learn more about the Made in America Store, visit www.saveourcountryfirst.com.

To learn more about special-interest groups, visit www.moveon.org and www.theconservativevoice.com.

To learn more about American political parties, visit www.politics1.com/parties.htm.

13 HEALTH CARE AND THE ENVIRONMENT

Many people have strong opinions about how health care should be managed, and they often resort to protesting to express their views. Shown here is an anti–health care reform rally in Portsmouth, New Hampshire, in 2009.

Chapter 13

- Introductory Story
- The Sociological Perspective on Health and Medicine
- Health Care in the United States
- Mental Health
- The Environment
- Threats to the Environment
- Saving the Ecosystem
- Sociological Perspectives on the Environment
- Summary, Glossary, Discussion Questions, and Web Links

INTRODUCTORY STORY

Test day: a day of stressful anxiety for some students and a day to shine for others. On test day, professors often receive phone calls or e-mails from students complaining that they are too sick to take the exam. To enhance claims of illness, a phone message is accompanied by a terrible-sounding cough, grunt, or other disturbing noise. (This cannot be accomplished via an e-mail for it would look silly to type, "I am too sick—cough, cough—to take the exam today.") Some professors will give the student the benefit of the doubt. Others may wonder whether such claims of being sick are legitimate.

When someone claims to be sick, he or she is taking on the sick role, which carries with it a specific set of expectations, including efforts toward regaining good health. In fighting a cold or the flu, for example, getting plenty of bed rest is commonly cited as a leading method toward restoring health. As a graduate student–instructor at the University of Nevada, Las Vegas, during the early 1990s, I can remember a student calling claiming to be too sick to take the scheduled introductory sociology exam that Friday. She spoke quietly, coughed quite a few times, apologized for being sick, and asked about taking a makeup exam the following week. I took her at her word, wished her well, and informed her that I would create a makeup exam for her. Later that evening, at a nightclub with some friends, I spotted this gravely ill student dancing up a storm on the dance floor. She was drinking an alcoholic beverage and laughing loudly. The minute she spotted me observing her, she realized she was busted. She was not living up to the expectations that coincide with the sick role. She also realized that any hope for a makeup exam had disappeared along with her false claim of being sick.

The sick role is just one of many aspects related to the topic of health discussed in this chapter. Along with health, the highly important subject of the environment is also discussed in this chapter.

THE SOCIOLOGICAL PERSPECTIVE ON HEALTH AND MEDICINE

Anyone who is legitimately sick, of course, hopes to get healthy as quickly as possible. Just as obvious is the desire of healthy people to remain healthy. Not only is it the goal of everyone to be healthy, but from a functionalist perspective, healthy people are better able to contribute to society. Consequently, functionalists view ill health as a dysfunction, for it detracts from the goals attained through good health. Modern societies, especially capitalistic ones, require healthy people so that they can perform their work function of producing goods and providing services. For this reason, most employers offer health insurance to their employees. But how does this functional imperative on behalf of employers help the unemployed or those employed people who do not have health insurance coverage? Conflict theorists will reply that the U.S. health care system has a harmful effect on the unemployed and underemployed as they will most likely go without health insurance.

Naturally, all people desire good health as good health contributes to our quality of life. Good health and adequate health care are important issues in contemporary society. As a result, it is important to understand what we mean by the term "health." Health involves the general condition of the body or mind, as in the phrases "good health" or "poor health." Sociologists are also concerned about individuals' social health. Thus, from a sociological perspective, **health** is defined as a state of physical, mental, and social well-being wherein the individual is free from disease or ailment. Being physically ill is an example of poor health. As described in the chapter's introductory story, when sick, people are assigned a sick role. From a symbolic-interactionist perspective, the **sick role** is a social role performed by sick persons that is recognized by others and exempts them from normal obligations. In this manner, a person who misses work all week and stays in bed is not labeled a "slacker" but instead as "sick." With less severe forms of sickness and ailments, individuals are expected to recover in a normal time frame and abandon the sick role in favor of their normal social roles. An individual who appears to cling to the sick role for an extended period or who claims a sickness without medical verification may be stigmatized as a "malingerer" (someone pretending to be sick) or a "hypochondriac" (a person who constantly believes he or she is ill or is about to become ill). Hypochondria is a mental disorder in which a person suffers torment resulting from an excessive preoccupation with his or her own health, usually focusing on some particular symptom. (Note: Mental health is discussed later in this chapter.)

In regard to physical health, a distinction is made between acute and chronic disorders. *Acute disorders* are illnesses (e.g., appendicitis and influenza) that come on suddenly and are of limited duration and from which the afflicted person either recovers or dies relatively quickly. *Chronic disorders* are long-term or permanent illnesses that are rarely cured completely. Examples of chronic disorders include cancer, heart disease, diabetes, arthritis, and some sexually transmitted diseases. As individuals age, they become more likely to suffer from chronic illnesses. "Nearly half of Americans have a chronic condition, and 75% of the $2.6 trillion spent annually on health care goes to treat patients with long-term health problems, says Kenneth Thorpe, a professor at Atlanta's Emory University and head of the Partnership to Fight Chronic Disease" (Szabo 2009, p. 2D). The seriousness of chronic disorders is illustrated by the fact that in the United States, chronic disorders account for approximately 70 percent of all deaths and a similar proportion of all health care costs.

When sick, people generally seek treatment in the form of medicine. **Medicine** refers to the scientific system developed to treat illness or to preserve good health by such means as diagnosis, drug treatment, or manipulation. The United States has perhaps the best medical system in the world—for those who can afford it. Unfortunately, nearly 17 percent of the U.S. population is without health insurance. According to the U.S. census, 50.7 million (16.7 percent) Americans were uninsured in 2009, up from 46.3 million in 2008 (Wolf 2010). The primary reason cited by the U.S. census for the dramatic one-year increase was the recession—companies dropping employee health insurance benefits and families going without coverage to cut costs (so that they could secure the necessities of food, clothing, and shelter).

HEALTH CARE IN THE UNITED STATES

Although everyone wants good health, and nearly all of us understand that sooner or later we will need health care, there is a great debate among politicians and citizens alike as to who is economically responsible for providing health care and how it should be paid for. The interconnectedness of economic and political responsibility, discussed in Chapter 12, becomes quite relevant in this chapter's discussion of health care. In 2009, President Barack Obama promoted the idea that drastic changes in the health care system were needed. He attempted to persuade politicians and the public to accept his many economic proposals because of his belief that health care should be available to all Americans. Toward this desired end, Obama suggested that public—government-controlled—health care was the direction to take. His many detractors countered that promoting such government-controlled health care was socialist and ill-advised, primarily because the government was viewed as incapable of handling such an important and massive program.

Complaints about universal health care as a socialist ideal are mostly pointless as socialist principles are already fully entrenched in American society in such programs as Medicare, Medicaid, Social Security, and the Veterans Administration. In brief, the government already pays for nearly half of American health care costs while private insurance pays for about one-third; the remaining health care expenses are paid for out of pocket.

Detractors of Obama's health care plan were also concerned about how such a program would be funded. This is a legitimate concern, especially in light of the data presented in Chapter 12 revealing that the national debt is greater than $14 trillion. However, worries over government funding should be countered with the realization that people without health insurance often have their costs covered by taxpayer dollars anyway. Consider, for example, the number of uninsured people who go to the emergency room (ER) because they do not have health insurance. Who covers these costs? Ultimately, it is the taxpayer.

But uninsured patients are not the only ones using the ER for nonurgent care. "With too few primary-care doctors to go around, many patients turn to the ER when they can't get an appointment with their regular physician, says Sandra Schneider, vice president of the American College of Emergency Physicians" (Szabo 2009, p. 2D). How many people go to the ER? According to a *USA Today* Gallup poll, 41 percent of Americans reported that they had gone to a hospital emergency room in the past twelve months (Gonzalez 2009). Of those respondents who went to the ER, only 34 percent did so because of a possibly life-threatening condition (the primary purpose of ERs); 29 percent went because their doctor's office was closed; 26 percent went for a non-life-threatening condition that could not be treated by the patient's primary doctor; and 9 percent went to the ER because it was their main source of medical care (Gonzalez 2009).

Going to the ER may be convenient (beyond the wait time), but it does come at a hefty cost. Based on 2009 research conducted by the University of Virginia, the average cost for an emergency room visit is $558 compared to $161 for primary care (Szabo 2009). The same study found that the most common causes of ER visits are back pain ($303 average ER cost); upper respiratory problems, such as the flu ($198); chest pain ($718); headache ($511); and dental disease ($142) (Szabo 2009).

Finding a financial solution to the health care problem is challenging, to say the least. Some proponents of Obama's plan argued that the costs of health care could be covered if the billions of dollars spent daily to wage war were directed toward health for Americans instead. Such a sentiment represents the opposite political perspective to that opposing universal health care.

Idealistically, members of a civil society should be in favor of all citizens receiving affordable health care with reasonable premiums and quality doctors, nurses, and other health care professionals. After all, even people with health insurance are confronted with sky-high costs for prescriptions (especially nongenerics), copayments that keep going up, the need for referrals to see specialists, caps on total coverage, and so on. Thus, many people with health insurance already face a less-than-ideal situation. There is another scenario to consider. Say a person has a job with health insurance but finds a better job. In many instances this person could be denied health care insurance at the new job because of a preexisting condition.

In March 2010, Obama's comprehensive health care reform bill, after being passed by the Senate (56–43), was passed by the House of Representatives (220–211) and signed into law by the president (Herszenhorn and Pear 2010). Highlighting the political nature of health care reform, all Republican congressional representatives (and thirty-four Democrats) voted against it. The nearly 3,000-page bill was filled with a number of "political riders" (add-ons that have little or nothing to do with health care reform); consequently, the bill's extent is beyond

What Do You Think?

Should a person who wishes to leave one job for another be penalized for a preexisting medical condition? What do you think?

the scope of an introductory sociology text. However, in short, the ten-year, $938 billion bill extended coverage to 32 million uninsured Americans and banned insurance companies from denying coverage to people with preexisting medical conditions (Werner 2010). Other highlights of the bill include barring insurance companies from putting lifetime dollar limits on coverage and from canceling policies except in cases of fraud; providing funding for community health centers (in 2011); and standardizing insurance company paperwork to reduce administrative costs (2013). As of early 2011, detractors of Obama Care (as it is popularly known) were still trying to get rid of the universal health care legislation.

What Do You Think?

Do you have adequate health care? How would you or your family members pay for major medical expenses without health care coverage? Do you think universal health care is a good idea? What do you think?

Health Care Fraud

One of the few things people of all political ideologies can agree on when it comes to health care is the need to end fraud; after all, health care fraud inevitably increases the cost of health care for everyone. The National Health Care Anti-Fraud Association (NHCAA) (2009) defines **health care fraud** as "an intentional deception or misrepresentation that the individual or entity makes knowing that the misrepresentation could result in some unauthorized benefit to the individual or the entity or to some other party." There are many types of health care fraud. "The most common kind of fraud involves a false statement, misrepresentation or deliberate omission that is critical to the determination of benefits payable. Fraudulent activities are almost invariably criminal, although the specific nature or degree of the criminal acts may vary from state to state" (NHCAA 2009). The NHCAA conservatively estimates that more than $60 billion is lost each year due to fraud; this figure represents 3 percent of the more than $2 trillion the United States spent on health care in 2008. "This loss directly impacts patients, taxpayers and government through higher health care costs, insurance premiums and taxes. Additionally, health care fraud often hurts patients who may be subjected to unnecessary or unsafe procedures or who may be the victims of identity theft" (NHCAA 2009).

Discovering health care fraud can be problematic. People with inside knowledge (whistle-blowers) initiate around 90 percent of health care fraud suits. "Whistle-blowers helped authorities recover at least $9.3 billion from health care providers accused of defrauding states and the federal government, according to an analysis of Justice Department records" (Freking 2008b, p. D7). The $9.3 billion was recovered between 1996 and 2005. It should be noted that many additional cases begun during this same period were still pending. For example, not included was the eventual $920 million recovery from Tenet Healthcare Corp, one of the nation's largest hospital chains, in 2006 (Freking 2008b). At the time of the Tenet case, this was the largest health care settlement to date. In September 2009, American pharmaceutical giant Pfizer Inc. and its subsidiary Pharmacia & Upjohn Company Inc. agreed to pay $2.3 billion to the U.S. Justice Department in the largest health care fraud settlement in Justice Department history. Pfizer agreed to the record payment to resolve criminal and civil liability arising from the illegal promotion of certain pharmaceutical products (U.S. Department of Health and Human Services 2009b).

Health Care Expenditures

As previously noted, the United States spent over $2 trillion for health care in 2008. The total cost of health care soars every year. The National Coalition on Health Care (NCHC) (2009) estimates that the national health care spending will reach $2.5 trillion in 2009, accounting for 17.6 percent of gross domestic product (GDP). The United States spends a greater percentage of its GDP on health care than any other country in the world (Wallechinsky 2007). In 2006, the United States also spent more money per person ($7,026) on health care than any other nation (Freking 2008a). Based on current estimates, in 2017 health spending will total $4.3 trillion in the United States, an average expenditure of $13,101 per person (Freking 2008a). By 2012, the Medicare and Medicaid programs will account for 50 percent of all national health care spending (NCHC 2009).

Reflecting rising national health care spending is a corresponding increase in health care costs for employers and employees. Consider the following bits of research data provided by the NCHC (2009):

- Over the last decade, employer-sponsored health insurance premiums have increased by 119 percent.
- Employees have seen their share of job-based coverage increase at nearly the same rate during this period, jumping from $1,543 to $3,354.
- The cumulative raises in employer-sponsored health insurance premiums have increased at four times the rate of inflation and wages increases during the last decade. This increase has made it much more difficult for businesses to continue to provide coverage to their employees and for those workers to afford coverage themselves.
- The average employer-sponsored premium for a family of four is close to $13,000 a year, and the employee foots about 30 percent of this cost. Health insurance costs overtook profits in 2008, and the gap grows steadily.
- About 1.5 million families lose their homes to foreclosure every year due to unaffordable medical costs.

The United States spends a great deal of money on health care, more than any other nation; yet, it does not lead the world in quality health care. On the positive side, the United States is tied for first (with at least twenty other nations) in terms of its citizens having access to clean water and sanitation facilities (Wallechinsky 2007). However, there is a down side, beyond the high employer and employee costs and the large number of people without any or without adequate health insurance. For example, in 2008 the "Mothers' Index" (compiled by Save the Children, a U.S.-based, global humanitarian organization) ranked the United States twenty-seventh among the best nations in which to be a mother and a child. The index is calculated based on such criteria as mothers' and children's health (e.g., infant and maternal mortality rates), access to quality health care facilities, and educational and economic status. New Zealand and a number of Nordic countries (Sweden, Norway, Iceland, and Denmark) dominate as the best places to be a mother and child, while sub-Saharan African nations (Niger, Chad, Yemen, Sierra Leone, Angola) are largely the worst places to be a mother (Save the Children 2008).

The United States lags behind many other nations in a number of other significant areas of health care as well. Consider these alarming statistics:

- Forty-three nations have more doctors per capita.
- Forty-nine nations have more hospital beds per capita.
- Thirty-three nations have a lower infant-mortality rate.
- Twenty-eight countries have a lower maternal-mortality rate.
- Twenty-nine nations have a higher life expectancy for women, and twenty-seven have a higher life expectancy for men. (Note: The average life expectancy is 79.5 years for an American woman and 74.1 years for an American man.)
- In all the above health care categories, the United States' position has steadily declined over the last twenty years (Wallechinsky 2007).

As the sampling of health care statistics listed above indicates, the U.S. health care system is far from the best in the world. This leads health care reformists to believe that the system needs to be modified. The U.S. health care system is riddled with inefficiencies, excessive administrative expenses, inflated prices, poor management and inappropriate care, waste, and fraud (NCHC 2009). Amending the health care system is a daunting task. Among the biggest needs to be addressed within the health care system is the creation of many new jobs. Although jobs in health care have already increased by 45 percent in the last fifteen years, in order to meet the needs of Americans, the United States will need more than 500,000 new nurses by 2016 (Brenner 2008). The United States will also need many more family doctors and pediatricians, as many present-day medical students are pursuing higher-paying fields like dermatology (average salary: $390,274) and plastic surgery (average salary: $412,000) instead of urgent care (Brenner 2008). According to Dr. Ted Epperly, president of the Kansas-based American Academy of Family Physicians, the country will need to add another 40,000 to the existing 100,000 doctors over the next decade to the meet the growing need (Leblanc 2009). "The need for more primary care doctors comes as the country's shortage of all doctors is expected to worsen, according to a study by the Association of American Medical Colleges, which found the rate of first-year enrollees in U.S. medical schools has declined steadily since 1980. If current patterns persist, the study shows the country will have about 159,000 fewer doctors than it needs by 2025" (Leblanc 2009, p. A9).

The need for all these new doctors and nurses is compounded by the aging population. Although the United States ranks behind nearly thirty other nations in average life expectancy, the life expectancy for the average American is 77.7 years (Centers for Disease Control and Prevention 2009a). (Note: Life expectancy refers to the length of time a child born in a specific year is expected to live, assuming mortality trends stay constant.) The U.S. life expectancy has grown by 1.4 years over the past decade, and this increase is attributed mainly to declining mortality due to almost all leading causes of death, federal health officials said (*Post-Standard,* 6/12/08). The increase in life expectancy has contributed to the growing number of centenarians. Data provided by the U.S. Census Bureau reveal that there were 66,000 Americans older than one hundred in 2011 (Civic Ventures 2011). There are more centenarians in the United States than any other nation (Civic Ventures 2011). As people continue to age, further demands are placed on the health care system. Elderly folks who live in nursing homes, for example, need health care service. Nearly 1.4 million seniors already live in nursing homes in the United States (National Consumer Voice 2011).

Japan has long boasted that it has among the highest life expectancies for both men and women. According to Japan's Ministry of Health, Labor, and Welfare, the average life expectancy is 85.59 for women and 78.64 for men (in 2004) (Red Orbit 2005). The World Bank estimates that the average life expectancy for all Japanese citizens in 2010 was 83 years (Fackler 2010). Japanese officials claim that Japanese citizens' long life is a testament to a society with a superior diet and a commitment to its elderly that is unrivaled in the West. However, this claim to longevity is now being questioned after police found the body of a man thought to be one of Japan's oldest at 111 years, mummified in his bed, dead for more than three decades. His daughter, eighty-one at the time of the discovery in 2010, hid his death to continue collecting his monthly pension payments, the police said (Fackler 2010). The discovery of this insurance fraud led to further investigations.

Within a short period, Japanese authorities failed to find more than 281 Japanese listed in records as one hundred years old or older (Fackler 2010).

Social Epidemiology

It is worth repeating that the wealthiest Americans enjoy access to great health care service in the United States, whereas the poor generally do not. It is also true that some of us are healthier than others. How do we explain such discrepancies? The field of social epidemiology attempts to answer these types of questions. **Social epidemiology** is the study of the causes, frequency, distribution, and social determinants of health, disease, and impairment throughout a population. Social epidemiologists commonly use two concepts: incidence and prevalence. *Incidence* refers to the number of new cases of a specific disorder or disease (e.g., type 2 diabetes) occurring in a given period, usually a calendar year. *Prevalence* refers to the total number of cases of a particular disorder or disease.

A bulimic girl hovers over a dirty toilet as part of her unhealthy lifestyle.

In brief, social epidemiologists have learned that differences in individual genes (biology), socioeconomic variations, and lifestyle choices contribute to differences in an individual's health and ability to afford quality health care. Biology affects health in a number of ways, including differences in how the cells of the immune system work together to combat infection (such as one caused by a flu virus); differences in metabolism (as a method to combat obesity); differences in individuals' movable joints, making range of motion possible (this can affect a person's exercise routine); and differences in digestive systems (which dictate what types of food—healthy or unhealthy—an individual can consume).

Socioeconomic variations in health include age, sex, race or ethnicity, and social class. The very young and the elderly are the most vulnerable to illness and death as the mortality rate drops significantly shortly after birth but begins to rise significantly during middle age. By the time an individual reaches age sixty-five, he or she is likely to suffer from at least one chronic disorder (e.g., arthritis, impaired vision or hearing), and the probability of mortality increases rapidly. As a result, the elderly are more likely to require health care on a regular basis than are younger people (ages fifteen to forty-four). As for gender and health, women do live longer, but they generally suffer from more chronic diseases than do men. Women are also more likely to visit a doctor. Macho men (those who think it is a sign of weakness to seek help for health ailments) put off seeing a doctor until it is absolutely necessary, whereas many women visit doctors on a regular basis. Thus, women are more likely to use health care than men.

As we learned in Chapter 7, race and ethnicity are often connected to social class. Recall that African Americans and Hispanics/Latinos are far more likely to live in poverty than are whites. It stands to reason, then, that blacks and Hispanics are less likely to be able to afford quality health care and that whites and Asians are more likely not only to be able to afford health care but to engage in preventive health care as well. Occupations of the poor are generally more labor intensive (e.g., mining, oil drilling, and work in textile mills) and therefore carry with them a greater risk of injury and premature death. In short, "poor people suffer from higher rates of illness and have a lower life expectancy than rich people" (Tepperman and Blain 2006, p. 267).

Another important variable that affects an individual's health involves lifestyle choices. Generally speaking, either people can choose to live a healthy lifestyle that involves regular exercise and a proper diet, or they can opt to engage in a number of activities likely to compromise their health. Among the unhealthy lifestyle choices that many people engage in are illegal drug use; unprotected sex (which may lead to acquiring a sexually transmitted disease); the consumption of unhealthy foods (e.g., those that are high in saturated fats and processed foods high in sodium); eating disorders (e.g., anorexia nervosa and bulimia); the failure to exercise regularly (a minimum of thirty minutes of cardiovascular activity five days a week is recommended); excessive consumption of alcohol; and smoking tobacco. Ironically, the most deadly causes of preventable premature death—tobacco and alcohol consumption and the consumption of unhealthy foods combined with poor exercise—are legal.

The question has been asked countless times, Why is tobacco legal when it is responsible for so many premature deaths? Part of the answer has always resided in the simple fact that tobacco has been a cash crop since the formation of the colonies in what is now the United States. The undeniable power of the tobacco industry (a special-interest group) is revealed in both the economic and political arenas. The billions of dollars generated by the tobacco industry secure its economic stability. In turn, the industry spends vast amounts of money to buy political favors among legislators via lobbying efforts. Historically, the tobacco industry has been powerful culturally as well. For decades, especially in the 1950s and 1960s, tobacco was portrayed positively in television and feature films. It seemed like all the coolest characters smoked. The present-day popular TV show *Mad Men* (about a fictional 1960s advertisement firm) reflects the popularity of smoking in office buildings and the idea that smoking was cool. The tobacco conglomerates enjoyed free reign to bombard citizens with advertisements about the coolness of smoking. As a result, generation after generation of folks were raised in an environment where tobacco was viewed as a harmless and cool consumer product just waiting for purchase.

Smoking is no longer viewed as cool; in fact, it now has the opposite reputation. This is because we know all about the harmful effects of smoking tobacco. Citizens are now bombarded with messages about the dangers of smoking. The candy cigarettes once sold in candy stores and advertisements that appeared in all types of magazines have disappeared. The television and movie industries rarely portray smoking in a positive manner. As a result, the number of smokers has decreased. Today, just one in five adults smokes tobacco. In 2009, the Centers for Disease Control and Prevention (CDC) reported that 46 million adults (20.6 percent) were current cigarette smokers in 2008 (CDC 2009b). Many of these 46 million Americans are addicted to the nicotine in tobacco and cannot quit the habit, even though they are trying. Others, however, find enjoyment in smoking and do not care to have their tobacco use demonized.

What Do You Think?

Are tobacco smokers being demonized in society? What do you think?

Tobacco consumption causes the deaths of more than 443,000 Americans every year, costing the nation $96 billion in health care costs annually (CDC 2009b). To put this statistic in another form, if your introductory sociology course met for one hour today, more than fifty Americans died because of tobacco use while you were in class. Cardiovascular diseases (heart disease, hypertension, and stroke) cause the largest number of smoking-related deaths, followed by various cancers (e.g., lung and throat), respiratory diseases (e.g., chronic airway obstruction, pneumonia, bronchitis, and emphysema), and other causes, such as burn deaths. Secondhand smoke is even more dangerous to those exposed to its deadly effects. This is especially important as nearly half of all nonsmoking Americans are regularly exposed to secondhand smoke (U.S. Department of Health and Human Services 2006). The CDC (2009b) reports that those with low education levels and those who work in the hospitality and service industries face the greatest risks posed by secondhand smoke.

Typically, nonsmokers will live twelve years longer than smokers; even so, many smokers will reach an elderly age.

Secondhand smoke is especially harmful to babies and youth as its harmful effects can have adverse affects on their development. According to the World Health Organization (WHO), "Around 40 percent of children and one in three adults around the world are regularly exposed to secondhand smoke, a substance that kills more than 600,000 people every year" (CTV News

2010). The research provided by WHO (which appeared in *The Lancet* medical journal) also indicates that 5.1 million deaths per year are caused by smoking (CTV News 2010). Along with death, secondhand smoke can trigger allergies, asthma attacks, other breathing problems, and ear infections. Is it any wonder smoking is banned in an increasing number of public areas, including outdoor parks? In addition, discarded cigarette butts are not just an ugly form of litter; nearly all cigarette butts consist of plastic-like cellulose acetate fibers that can take decades to decompose.

In short, the health of smokers and nonsmokers is compromised (e.g., smokers live, on average, twelve fewer years than nonsmokers), and the rising costs of health care caused by smokers are passed on to nonsmokers in the form of higher health care costs (e.g., insurance premiums).

The deadly effects of tobacco are certainly not limited to the United States. According to WHO (2009), "Tobacco is the second major cause of death in the world. It is currently responsible for the death of one in ten adults worldwide (a little more than 5 million deaths each year). If current smoking patterns continue, it will cause some 10 million deaths each year by 2020. Half the people that smoke today—that is about 650 million people—will eventually be killed by tobacco" (p. 1). The negative effects of tobacco on health and health care costs extend beyond the death of smokers and secondhand smoke victims. As explained by WHO (2009), "Tobacco is the fourth most common risk factor for disease worldwide. The economic costs of tobacco use are equally devastating. In addition to the high public health costs of treating tobacco-caused diseases, tobacco kills people at the height of their productivity, depriving families of breadwinners and nations of a healthy workforce. Tobacco users are also less productive while they are alive due to increased sickness."

What Do You Think?

In an attempt to save American lives, the U.S. government is currently waging a war against terrorism. Perhaps the government should wage a war against tobacco companies to save American lives. What do you think?

Tobacco smokers are well aware of the high cost of a pack of cigarettes. A two-pack-a-day smoker spends nearly $100 week for cigarettes. For people who are unemployed or earning a relatively low salary, these costs come at the expense of other household needs. WHO recognizes this concern as well:

> Tobacco and poverty are inextricably linked. Many studies have shown that in the poorest households in some low-income countries as much as 10% of total household expenditures are on tobacco. This means that these families have less money to spend on basic items such as food, education and health care. In addition to its direct health effects, tobacco leads to malnutrition, increased health care costs and premature death. It also contributes to a higher illiteracy rate, since money that could have

been used for education is spent on tobacco instead. Tobacco's role in exacerbating poverty has been largely ignored by researchers in both fields. (WHO 2009)

The potentially hazardous effects of tobacco use are certainly not limited to the economically poor. Anyone who uses tobacco products is risking compromised health or death. See "Connecting Sociology and Popular Culture" Box 13.1 for a brief review of the tragic, premature death of Amy Winehouse, a talented singer whose lifestyle choices helped to contribute to her early demise.

In some instances, one's health may be compromised by a combination of factors (biology, socioeconomic variables, and lifestyle choices). Let us consider the expanding problem of obesity in the United States (and around the world), for example. Americans consume more calories per capita than the citizens of any other nation. Not surprisingly, the United States leads the world in the predominance of obesity (see "A Closer Look" Box 13.2 for a discussion of obesity). Mex-

Connecting Sociology and Popular Culture

Box 13.1 Amy Winehouse, Lifestyle Choices, and Emphysema

By most accounts, Amy Winehouse was a talented singer and entertainer. Many media stories describe her as a major partier who enjoyed drinking, smoking, and consuming illegal drugs. According to at least a few reports, Winehouse suffered from a number of health problems, including signs of emphysema. All these stories about Winehouse were linked together by lifestyle choices.

Amy Winehouse was an English singer and songwriter who possessed strong, soulful vocals and mixed a variety of musical genres, including R&B, soul, jazz, rock, and ska. Her debut album *Frank* was an instant commercial and critical success in Britain. After that, Winehouse won numerous awards, such as the Brit Award (Best British Female Artist) and the Ivor Novello Award (three times); in 2008, at the Fiftieth Annual Grammy Awards, Winehouse won awards for Best Pop Vocal Album, Best Female Pop Vocal Performance, Best New Artist, Song of the Year ("Rehab"), and Record of the Year (*Rehab*). She became the first British woman to win five Grammy's in one year.

With as much attention as Winehouse garnered for her singing ability, she maintained her presence in the world of popular culture even more for her behavior offstage. *Los Angeles Times* writer Jeannine Stein (2008) explains, "English singer Amy Winehouse is no stranger to tabloid headlines—routinely grabbing attention for her alleged drug use, brushes with the law, bizarre onstage behavior and curious fashion choices" (p. F3). Anyone with even modest knowledge of the world of popular culture is certainly aware of Winehouse's battles with substance abuse and her self-disclosed interview statements admitting to problems with self-harm, depression, and eating disorders. She often went through periods of heavy drinking and drug use, violent mood swings, and bouts of exhaustion and ill health that caused her to cancel numerous shows (especially in August 2007 in the United Kingdom and Europe). Winehouse also admitted to taking (and overdosing on) heroin, ecstasy, cocaine, ketamine, and alcohol. She was also arrested for assault. Winehouse chose

Amy Winehouse represents a perfect case study of a person whose unhealthy lifestyle choices contributed to premature death. Winehouse is shown here in concert in London, in 2007.

ico, by the way, ranks as the second-fattest population in the world due to the rising popularity of soft drinks and fast-food restaurants, with more than 71 percent of Mexican women and 66 percent of Mexican men overweight (*Post-Standard,* 3/22/08).

As this brief review of social epidemiology reveals, a number of variables are likely to influence a person's physical health and

to partake in all these destructive behaviors, at least initially. Drug addictions, once established, are very difficult to break. Rehabilitation did not always work for Winehouse, as she routinely slipped back into her old, self-destructive behaviors. It is somewhat ironic that her most popular song, "Rehab," has the refrain, "They tried to make me go to rehab but I said, 'no, no, no,'" when she herself had been in rehab many times.

One behavior was constant with Winehouse: smoking. She was a chain smoker who added to her health issues by often smoking crack cocaine as well. In 2008, it was revealed (by her U.S. publicist, Tracey Miller) that Winehouse was showing signs of emphysema (Stein 2008). Although Winehouse's chain-smoking and other drug addictions were more extreme than those of most people, this twenty-seven-year-old's bout with emphysema was not that uncommon for someone so young. "Health experts say that young adult smokers are no strangers to mild emphysema, a shortness of breath caused by damage to the lung's small air sacs. Smoking can permanently deteriorate the lungs, irreversibly diminishing lung capacity—and the damage starts young, even in teens who smoke five cigarettes a day. . . . But many smokers don't show symptoms for years, leading them to believe no damage is being done when, in fact, it is accruing all the time" (Stein 2008, p. F3). Emphysema is caused by some of the 4,000 to 5,000 toxic chemicals in cigarette smoke. None of these chemicals is known to be a source of emphysema, but collectively they create chaos in the lungs. During the early stage of emphysema, the lungs are said to be operating at less than 80 percent of their total capacity. This is because the dangerous chemicals are already breaking down the lung's tiny air sacs, called alveoli (Stein 2008).

Amy Winehouse's lifestyle choices were all intertwined. She had a great singing voice but threatened it by choosing to smoke and ingest other damaging chemicals and drugs. Her health became compromised, and in July 2011 she died prematurely as a result of her risky lifestyle choices, which included abusing drugs (both legal and illegal ones), alcohol, and tobacco.

What Do You Think?

Many talented people, such as Amy Winehouse, risk their health and lives by participating in dangerous lifestyle behaviors. What compels people to do this? What do you think?

A Closer Look

Box 13.2 The Obesity "Epidemic"

More than 60 percent of Americans aged twenty years and older are overweight. According to the CDC, the prevalence of obese persons (both adults and children) has increased from 15 percent in the late 1970s to nearly 33 percent in 2004 (CDC 2007). The American Heart Association claims that the obesity rate among American men nearly tripled to 28 percent between 1960 and 2002, and it more than doubled to 34 percent for women (McCutcheon 2006). You may be wondering how obesity (and overweight) is measured. One of the most commonly used measurements to determine whether someone is overweight or obese is the body mass index (BMI). The BMI is an index of weight adjusted for the height of an individual. The BMI formula is calculated by dividing a person's weight by his or her height squared and multiplying by 703. (Note: A link is provided at the end of the chapter so that you can ascertain your own BMI.) Adults with a BMI of twenty-five or higher are considered overweight, and those with a BMI score of thirty or more are considered obese. In short, an obese person is someone with an excessive amount of fat.

Obesity is such a problem that it represents the second-leading cause (behind tobacco) of preventable deaths in the United States. The highest obesity rates are in the South, with Mississippi leading the way, followed by Alabama, and West Virginia (Freking 2006). Only four states have an obesity rate below 20 percent (Jackson 2006). If the current trend in obesity continues, the United States may actually see a drop in life expectancy over the next generation (Jackson 2006). Obesity and inactivity strongly increase the risk of type 2 diabetes, the sixth-leading cause of death in the United States. Furthermore, like tobacco, obesity and inactivity increase the risks for heart disease, cancer, and cerebrovascular ailments, including strokes (Delaney 2008a).

Just like tobacco, obesity is causing a major strain on health care resources. Unlike tobacco-related health problems, medical personnel face unique problems when dealing with obese persons. For example, the rise in obesity among Americans is taking a toll on rescue workers, who must load patients onto stretchers and get them into and out of ambulances. In a survey conducted by the National Association for Emergency Medical Technicians, 47 percent of respondents reported suffering back injuries while performing their duties. The rising number of calls involving obese patients is a major factor in the high injury rate (McCutcheon 2006). Worldwide, sales of stretchers specially designed for obese patients and special lift systems are increasing at a rapid rate.

Although some people may have a genetic predisposition toward being overweight (e.g., those with thyroid problems or low metabolism), this does not explain the tremendous increase in overweight and obese persons in one generation. The most plausible explanation of obesity involves lifestyle choices of poor diet and lack of physical exercise. In other words, the convenience of fast food (which is generally high in sodium), combined with increases in computer-driven work and sedentary computer and

well-being. (Note: The effects of the physical environment on health are discussed later in this chapter.)

MENTAL HEALTH

Just as they influence physical health, social factors also influence mental health. Furthermore, physical health is an important component of mental health.

television entertainment, is contributing to the growing waistlines of Americans, as well as many other people around the world (Jackson 2006). The expansion of fast-food restaurants such as McDonald's around the globe is not the only reason for poor food options. Many people have chosen to consume high-fat, high-energy products instead of basic fruits and vegetables. Sugar- and fat-based products abound in the United States and other Western societies.

But how did this all come about? Families in the 1950s and 1960s regularly enjoyed home-cooked meals, but today many parents—primarily due to economic demands—are too busy working to prepare healthy home-cooked meals and opt to stop at the fast-food drive-thru on the way home from work instead. Schools that provide cafeteria meals are competing with vending machines that offer soda and candy. Schools and organizations (e.g., the Girl Scouts) regularly have fund-raisers, but they almost always sell unhealthy foods to raise money. We want to support the organization, but now we "have" to eat junk food. Schools that sell cookies and other sweet treats are sending ill-advised messages to students about proper nutrition. Food companies that sell candy and other unhealthy foods spend billions advertising their products in an attempt to influence consumer purchasing decisions. And let's face it, many of the tastiest foods are filled with empty calories; yet, we love our snacks. Finding healthy foods is easier for some people than the rest. Many neighborhoods do not have grocery stores that stock fresh vegetables and fruits. Instead, a number of neighborhoods are overwhelmed with liquor and convenience stores and fast-food restaurants. In an effort to help combat the growing epidemic of obesity, an increasing number of restaurants have been mandated by law to post calorie and fat counts alongside prices on menus. This has inspired fast-food restaurants to provide healthy options, like salads.

Because child obesity is as big a concern as adult obesity, it is important that parents provide their children with healthy snacks, such as fresh fruit, raisins, water, grain cereals, or trail mix, instead of fast food and junk food. A proper diet is one of the keys in fighting obesity. It is also especially important that young people exercise regularly so that they do not grow up to be overweight or obese. Perhaps one of the best illustrations of the problem of obesity among young people resides with military recruiting. Obesity is the number one reason why applicants are denied entry to the military. "About 75 percent of the country's 17- to 24-year-olds are ineligible for military service, largely because they are poorly educated, overweight, and have physical ailments that make then unfit for the armed forces" (Davenport and Brown 2009, p. 1). Military leaders are concerned that the growing obesity problem in the United States threatens the country's ability to defend itself, especially in a time when the all-volunteer military is already strained fighting two wars (Davenport and Brown 2009).

What Do You Think?

Is obesity the result of biology, lifestyle choices, socioeconomic status, or a combination of any three of these variables? How can the obesity epidemic be reversed? What do you think?

Other features of mental health include the absence of mental illness, how we feel about ourselves, how we feel about others, and how we are able to meet the demands of life. Thus, **mental health** may be defined as a state of emotional and psychological well-being that allows an individual to function, both cognitively and emotionally, in society; to meet the regular demands of everyday life, including relationships with other people; and to adapt to change and cope with adversity.

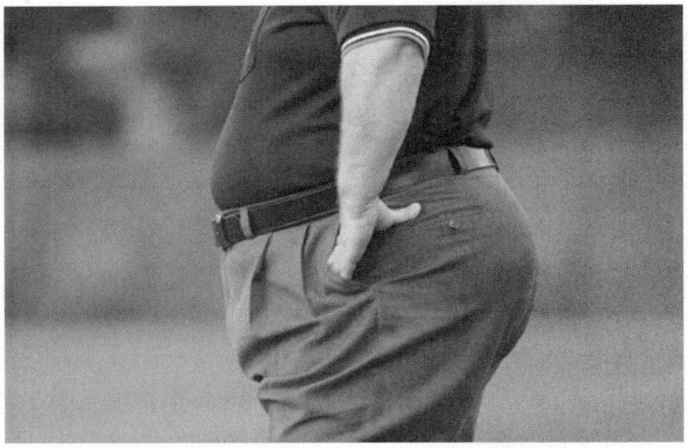

Obesity has become so commonplace in the United States, and is associated with so many negative health risks, that some health care officials argue that it has become epidemic.

The mental-health profession, a branch of medicine that deals with the achievement and maintenance of psychological well-being, has made many advances in the past few decades. Mental-health professionals examine the brain's functionality through the study of neuroscience, have researched and developed effective medications and therapies, and have standardized diagnostic codes for mental illness. The mental-health profession also recognizes social factors such as stress and self-esteem and their effect on one's mental health.

Mental health is very important as one cannot be truly healthy without being mentally healthy. In addition, mental health affects our physical and social health. Research in health psychology indicates that mental disorders, such as depression, affect outcomes of pregnancy, gastrointestinal disorders, and heart disease (Tsai 2008). A **mental disorder** is a condition that alters thinking, mood, or behavior (or some combination thereof) and makes it difficult or impossible for a person to cope with everyday life.

Mental Illness

Mental illness represents the opposite end of the mental-health spectrum. Thus, **mental illness** refers to all mental disorders. Due in large part to the advances in the medical health profession, millions of people around the world are identified as suffering from some sort of mental illness. WHO (2007b) claims that 450 million people worldwide are affected by mental, neurological, or behavioral problems at any given time. In extreme cases, people who suffer from a mental illness may opt to commit suicide. WHO estimates that 873,000 people die by suicide every year (worldwide).

There are too many categories of mental illness to discuss them all here, but a few examples deserve mention because of their social nature. The first example of a mental illness is depression. According to WHO (2007a), depression is a mental disorder characterized by a depressed mood, loss of interest or pleasure, feelings of guilt or low self-esteem, disturbed sleep or appetite, low energy, and poor concentration. Depression affects roughly 121 million people worldwide. In 2009, Tasnime Akbaraly et al. published their research findings linking depression to diet in the *British Journal of Psychiatry*. The scientists found that people who regularly consume fish, fruit, and vegetables reduce their chances of suffering from depression. Conversely, people whose diet consisted of processed meats, sweetened desserts, fried foods, refined cereals, and high-fat dairy products were more likely to suffer from depression. The researchers indicated that a bad diet does not cause depression but is a contributing factor.

Another fairly common type of mental illness is popularly referred to as a nervous breakdown. "Nervous breakdown" (or "mental breakdown") is not a clinical term; instead, a number of disorders fall under this umbrella, including generalized anxiety, panic disorder, panic attacks, trauma disorders, psychotic disorders (e.g., schizophrenia), and mood disorders (e.g., bipolar disorder). The word "breakdown" is the key to understanding this disorder, as the afflicted person has difficulty performing daily functions due to such circumstances as career burnout, academic stress, the death or loss of a loved one, a romantic breakup, unemployment, and postwar trauma.

Stress is sometimes thought of as a type of mental illness, but there are different kinds of stress. According to the CDC (2008a), there are three types: positive stress, tolerable stress, and toxic stress. *Positive stress* includes stress that most people deal with on a temporary basis. For example, this chapter's introductory story described "test day," a potential source of anxiety for some students. Meeting new people, going on job interviews, and confronting mild inconveniences may be viewed as examples of positive stress. This type of stress causes minor physiological changes, including an increase in heart rate and changes in hormone levels. The CDC (2010b) describes this type of stress as beneficial in helping people develop the skills they need to cope with and adapt to new and potentially threatening situations throughout life.

The CDC (2008a) defines *tolerable stress* as stemming from "adverse experiences that are more intense but still relatively short-lived. Examples include the death of a loved one, a natural disaster, a frightening accident, and family disruptions such as a separation or divorce" (p. 3). *Toxic stress* results from intense adverse experiences that may be sustained over a long period. In childhood such stress can lead to permanent changes in the development of the brain (CDC 2008a). Toxic stress may require long-term medication and assistance from mental-health personnel. Toxic stress is linked to impaired judgment, delusions and paranoia, and suicide; it is therefore included in the domain of mental illness.

Undoubtedly, most students have heard of posttraumatic stress disorder (PTSD). PTSD is an extreme form of long-term stress caused by a high level of trauma. Soldiers who have seen combat often report PTSD when they return home. Victims of brutal attacks may also experience PTSD. A person with PTSD will suffer anxiety attacks, depression, reoccurring nightmares, night sweats, flashbacks, and extreme emotional and physical reactions to reminders of the traumatic incident (CDC 2010a).

How prevalent is anxiety and mental illness among college students? A new study conducted by Jean Twenge et al. indicates that five times as many high school and college students are dealing with anxiety and other mental-illness issues as youths of the same age studied in the Great Depression era (Irvine 2010). Twenge et al. analyzed data collected from over 77,000 high school or college students who, from 1938 through 2007, took the Minnesota Multiphasic Personality Inventory. Six times as many students from 2007 scored high in "hypomania," a measure of anxiety and unrealistic optimism (from 5 percent of students in 1938 to 31 percent in 2007), and six times as many students in 2007 rated high in depression (from 1 to 6 percent) (Irvine 2010). Twenge and her researchers speculate that popular culture plays a major role in the increased rates of mental-health issues among young people today. The researchers cite pop culture's focus on individuals' external features—wealth, looks, and status—as the major contributing cause of increased anxiety among the younger generation. The high expectations of people who are overly optimistic (an aspect of hypomania) are often crushed by the disappointment associated with personal shortcomings (e.g., an unexpected low grade on a test, the inability to find a high-paying job).

What Do You Think?

Twenge et al. argue that popular culture and the expectations of the younger generation have increased anxiety and stress among high school and college students. What do you think?

Despite the large number of people who suffer from mental illness, the mentally ill are often targets of discrimination and stigma. Stigmatization of and discrimination against the mentally ill are attributed to a number of factors, including the traditional lack of understanding of mental illness, the historical mistreatment of the mentally ill, ineffective and barbaric forms of ancient treatment (e.g., exorcisms, bleeding, drilling holes in the skulls of the afflicted in order to release demons), and the television and film industries' portrayal of the mentally ill as violent characters.

The negative effects of mental illnesses on an afflicted person worsen over time. The key to helping the mentally ill is treatment. But treatment can be costly, and there is a debate among politicians and health officials, as well as the general public, about who should foot the bill to treat the mentally ill. The government used to take responsibility for their care. This changed with the deinstitutionalization movement that began in the 1960s and reached its height during the Reagan era. **Deinstitutionalization** refers to the practice of discharging patients from mental hospitals into the community. Deinstitutionalization is a cost-saving mechanism that eliminates custodial homes and programs designed to help the severely mentally ill. Many facilities were closed, and patients were released without supervision. Many of these people had no place to go except the streets, where they lived among other homeless persons. Without medication and proper supervision, some of the mentally ill caused harm to themselves as well as to others.

> **What Do You Think?**
>
> Should the mentally ill be treated at government expense? What if a mentally ill person who is living on his own commits a crime because he has not received treatment; is he accountable for his actions? What do you think?

THE ENVIRONMENT

Our discussion of the environment is combined with that of health care because of the great impact the environment has on people's physical and mental health. The relationship between the environment and health is evident in a variety of ways, many of which are described in the remainder of this chapter. It should also be noted that a branch of public health—environmental health—exists in order to study (and protect) humans (and other organisms) from the effects of environmental hazards that can adversely affect health or the ecological balances essential to human health and environmental quality (U.S. Department of Health and Human Services 1998).

So, what does the term "environment" actually mean? In simplest terms, the environment refers to one's surroundings—as in, "I need peace and quiet in my work environment." The ecological environment refers to the natural world of land, sea, air, plants, and animals—as in, "nuclear waste is harmful to the environment." The sociological analysis of the environment involves the study of natural and social forces. Thus, sociologists look at the **environment** as the totality of social and physical conditions that affect nature (land, water, air, plants, and animals) and humanity and their influence on the growth, development, and survival of organisms.

Of all the Earth's organisms, humans place the highest demands on the environment. And yet, humans also represent the greatest threat to it. It is important to note that Earth has a limited carrying capacity to support life. **Carrying capacity** refers to the maximum feasible load, just short of the level that would end the environment's ability to support life (Catton 1980). In other words, carrying capacity is tied to the number of organisms that can be supported in a given area, based on the natural resources available, without compromising present and future generations. The carrying capacity for any specific area is not necessarily fixed, as food-production capacity, for example, can be improved through technology. However, once the environment is sullied, the carrying capacity shrinks, negatively altering its ability to sustain life.

Over the generations, but especially recently, the Earth's carrying capacity has stretched to its limit due to a number of threats to the environment. Let us examine some of these threats.

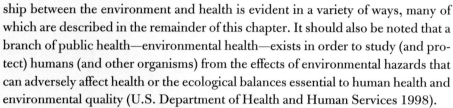

THREATS TO THE ENVIRONMENT

There are numerous threats to the environment, including the spread of deserts, the destruction of forests by acid rain, deforestation, the stripping of large tracts of land for fuel, radioactive fallout, and overpopulation that exceeds the carrying capacity of local agriculture in many areas. Human dependency on the conversion of fossil fuels (e.g., into gasoline, diesel, and heating oil) to meet energy needs has led to a number of serious problems (e.g., global warming and the greenhouse effect) that are being felt around the world.

Overpopulation: Are There Too Many People in the World?

For centuries, social thinkers have pondered whether the Earth's carrying capacity has been compromised by human overpopulation. For example, Thomas Malthus, in *An Essay on the Principle of Population* (1798), claimed that the world's population was growing too quickly in proportion to the amount of food available. Although his theory was rather simple and harshly criticized by later scholars, such as Karl Marx and Friedrich Engels (who called his conception "false and childish"), has Malthus's concern about the number of people and the available food supply been proven accurate today? First, let us take a brief look at Malthus's theory from Marx and Engels's point of view. Malthus "stupidly" reduces two complicated issues—natural reproduction of the species and natural reproduction of edible plants (or means of subsistence)—to two natural theorems, one (population) geometric and the other (food supply) arithmetic (Marx and Engels 1978, p. 276). Marx and Engels are correct in that human population does not grow geometrically; nor has our ability to grow food grown arithmetically. In fact, our ability to produce food has grown dramatically since the time of Malthus through such means as advanced machinery to replace human and animal labor and large corporate farms that produce far more food than traditional family farms. However, Marx and Engels (1978) were concerned about overpopulation, stating, "There are *too many* people. Even the existence of men is a pure luxury; and if the worker is 'ethical,' he will be *sparing* in procreation" (p. 97). Their concern for population control was directed at those who could not afford (based on such criteria as the worker's ability to provide adequate food and shelter for his children) to bring children into the world, suggesting that it is unethical for people to have children if they cannot provide for them.

Despite any criticism of Malthus's theory of population growth and the environment's capacity to provide enough food to feed the masses, millions of people around the world are without adequate food, and many die of starvation. CARE (2008) estimates that more than 840 million people around the world are malnourished—799 million of whom live in the developing world. Malnutrition can severely affect a child's intellectual development and physical growth. In addition, 6 million children under the age of five die every year as a result of hunger. The rising cost of food (especially such staples as rice and grains) will jeopardize an increasing number of people worldwide. In short, close to 1 billion people face hunger, and this hunger could trigger global social unrest.

What Do You Think?

Are there too many people in the world? Should people be able to afford children, as suggested by Marx and Engels, if they choose to procreate? What do you think?

The Five Horrorists: The Destroyers of Life

Although environmentalists worry about the future of our planet, maybe our focus should remain on people and other organisms. Most likely, the planet will survive any tragedy, human-made or natural, bestowed upon it. The key question is whether humans and other organisms will be able to live in an environment that is greatly modified due to some disaster (e.g., global warming, a nuclear holocaust).

If we revisit Malthus and his concern with overpopulation, we learn that he believed nature would fight to protect itself, even from the threat of humanity. That is, nature would provide "forces" of relief from the strain created by human abuse in the form of the "Four Horsemen." These Four Horsemen (war, famine, pestilence, and disease), which have biblical roots, would provide the function of population control. According to Malthus, the Four Horsemen were the destroyers of human life. From this standpoint, nature would find a way to maintain its carrying capacity by drastically reducing humanity. Herbert Spencer, who argued that the fight for scarce resources would lead to the survival of the fittest (see Chapter 2), correctly pointed out that the Four Horsemen are not merely the product of nature but rather a combination of natural and social forces.

An artist's depiction of the "Five Horrorists," an updated interpretation of the "Four Horsemen" that threaten the very existence of humanity.

In an attempt to update Malthus's and Spencer's ideas, in 2005 I coined the term "**five horrorists**" to represent an advanced evolutionary interpretation and development of the Four Horsemen concept. "Breaking completely from the religious roots and de-emphasizing the natural component of the four horsemen, the Five Horrorists emphasize the social forces that will lead to the destruction of humanity, if left unchecked by global powers." It was necessary to infuse the social element of the destroyers of life because famine, pestilence (e.g., plagues caused by locusts and other swarms of insects), and disease are as much the result of human conditions as they are natural ones. War, of course, is completely human-made and not caused by nature. The fifth horrorist refers to another concept I coined in 2005: the "enviromare." An **enviromare** is an environmentally produced nightmare that causes great harm to humanity. This fifth destroyer of humanity represents a recent human creation that threatens the ecosystem, biosphere, and so on.

Enviromares are all associated with some type of pollution that causes a problem for the environment. Among the enviromares are water pollution and shortages of drinkable water (due, among other things, to toxins dumped into bodies of potable water); land pollution (especially as the result of overgrazing by domesticated animals, deforestation, agricultural mismanagement, the increased use of chemical fertilizers and pesticides, erosion, urban sprawl, and strip mining); solid waste pollution (Americans produce more than 4.5 pounds of garbage per person, per day); noise pollution (mostly an urban problem resulting from high-density living); celestial pollution (yes, space is already littered with trash); air pollution (caused by both nature and humanity); and chemical and nuclear pollution (dangerous chemicals, radiation, and radioactive fallout). It is important to point out that nature also plays a part in compromising clean air as volcanic eruptions spill a variety of toxins into the air, and lightning emits nitrogen dioxide and ignites wildfires (see Delaney's *Contemporary Social Theory* [2005] for a complete description of the five horrorists). It stands to reason that all these types of pollution can compromise the health of humans and other organisms.

What Do You Think?

Enviromares represent a threat to the ecosystem and humanity. Is it possible to eliminate the enviromares of the world? What do you think?

Threats to the environment come in many forms. Oil spills, such as the 2010 BP oil spill in the Gulf of Mexico, cause a great deal of damage to a variety of species specifically and the environment in general.

Human Dependency on Fossil Fuels

For more than a century, humans have become increasingly dependent on fossil fuels, such as crude oil and coal, especially for transportation and heating. The burning of fossil fuels has compromised the quality of the air we breathe as well as the ozone layer. The ozone layer is the Earth's upper atmosphere, which screens out a great deal of the sun's harmful ultraviolet rays. Acid rain, the greenhouse effect, and global warming are among the other concerns raised by our reliance on fossil fuels.

Global warming and the greenhouse effect are especially dangerous threats to the environment as rising global temperatures lead to melting glaciers, rising sea levels, lower crop yields, shortages of drinking water, increased health problems (especially for poorer nations), and strained power grids. Although most scientists and world leaders recognize global warming as a reality, a few people still deny its existence (see "Connecting Sociology and Popular Culture" Box 13.3 for a closer examination of global warming). But let us examine the facts: scientists have detailed that the Arctic perennial sea ice has been decreasing at a rate of 9 percent per decade since a first satellite sensor image began its tracking in 1970; Greenland's glaciers are also thawing (huge chunks of ice have been breaking off the Sermeq Kujalleq glacier for years); melting glaciers threaten low-lying areas; the Siberian permafrost is melting; and rainforests in Brazil are being depleted (rainforests are needed to cleanse the atmosphere of carbon dioxide and to produce oxygen).

Africa, a region among the least responsible for climate change and the least able to afford the costs of adaptation, is suffering from global warming due to the pollution caused by other nations. "The United Nations environment agency unveiled a new atlas [June 2008] showing while Africa produces only 4 percent of the world's total carbon dioxide emissions, its inhabitants could suffer the most from its consequences. Signs include the 50 percent shrinkage of glaciers on Mount Kilimanjaro in Tanzania and the Rwenzori mountains in Uganda, the drying up of Lake Chad and falling water levels in Lake Victoria" (*Post-Standard,* 6/13/08, p. A16). Africa is also losing 10 million acres of forest each year—twice the world's average deforestation rate. Some areas of Africa are losing over 55.12 tons of soil per 2.5 acres each year (*Post-Standard,* 6/13/08, p. A16). The rapid deforestation around the world is diminishing the planet's supply of oxygen, the most critical element of survival for life forms on Earth.

In 2009, Switzerland expanded its border at Italy's expense because of melting glaciers in the high Alps. "The Swiss government Wednesday approved shifting the border up to 164 yards into Italian territory because the Swiss Federal Office of Topography ruled the watershed that determined the border in 1942 had moved because of melting glaciers and snow fields. The shift moves the final stop of the Furggsattel Sesselbahn ski station, near the famed Matterhorn peak, onto Swiss territory" (*Post-Standard,* 8/20/09, p. A13). The changing borders of Switzerland and Italy represent the tip of the iceberg (pun intended) when it comes to dramatic changes that will occur in the physical environment if current glacier thaw continues.

As pointed out earlier, nature does play a role in compromising the ecosystem. Unfortunately, we cannot control nature; we can only attempt to modify human

Connecting Sociology and Popular Culture

Box 13.3 Global Warming: An Inconvenient Truth or a Bunch of Hot Air?

Scientists believe that global warming is an indisputable reality. This "reality" insinuated itself into popular culture in a number of ways, including slang and fictional and nonfictional films. Among the more common slang terms used in relation to global warming are "fossil fools" and "greenhouse asses." *Fossil fools* (a play on the term "fossil fuels") are people who fail to recognize the negative impact of driving fuel-inefficient vehicles such as Humvees and sport utility vehicles. The fossil fools concept has become so popular that throughout North America people celebrate "Fossil Fools Day" on April 1 as a way to connect the eco-unfriendly behavior of driving gas-guzzlers to other forms of foolish behavior. "Fossil Fools Day" has become increasingly popular on college campuses and in communities throughout the United States (especially in the Northwest) as well as Canada. Proponents of "Fossil Fools Day" encourage people to kick the oil habit and avoid acting like a fossil fool by walking, cycling, taking public transportation, or car-pooling whenever possible; buying fuel-efficient vehicles (e.g., hybrids); living as close to work as possible; shopping at local stores; and buying regionally and seasonally produced food whenever possible. *Greenhouse asses* are people who insist that the environment is in fine shape and believe that preserving it is unnecessary. Perhaps only time will tell who the real fools and asses are, but if environmentalists and world scientists are correct, we need to take drastic steps now to save our planet. One thing is clear: with the dramatic increase in the price of gas during the later years of the first decade of the 2000s, would it not be foolish to drive a fuel-inefficient vehicle?

Global warming and the greenhouse effect have infiltrated the public's consciousness via a variety of media sources, including print and televised news, talk radio programs, television shows, musician and actor activism, and films. Fictional movies such as *The Day After Tomorrow* (2004) and *The Simpsons Movie* (2007) are two examples of the gloom and doom predicted by climatologists and environmentalists. In *The Day After Tomorrow,* the underlying theme is that global warming is triggering an abrupt and catastrophic shift in the planet's climate. The central theme of *The Simpsons Movie,* a film about the animated Simpson's family, centers on saving Lake Springfield from the ravages of pollution. In this film, the rock band Green Day is killed when the pollution in the lake erodes their barge. President Arnold Schwarzenegger decides to save the rest of the country from Springfield's environmental mess by enclosing the city in a giant glass dome. Al Gore's nonfiction account of the environment in his documentary film *An Inconvenient Truth* (2006) has had the largest impact on popular culture and debate between people who find it necessary to save the planet and those who feel it is fine just as it is. The film (which won an Academy Award) points out a number of environmental problems confronting humanity.

What Do You Think?

Has the concern over global warming been blown out of proportion, or are people not taking this environmental threat seriously enough? What do you think?

behavior. However, people in the developed nations of the world like their luxury items, and they like their products to be as cheap as possible. But how much longer can we live as we do before permanently destroying the ecosystem or depleting limited natural resources? Ironically, attempts to kick our dependency on oil through such means as ethanol plants have triggered further food shortages. In other words, trying to solve one problem may create bigger problems. What can conscientious people do?

SAVING THE ECOSYSTEM

Conscientious people who want to do their part to save the ecosystem can heed the warnings of scientists, including climatologists, about the many threats to our planet—the only one (that we are aware of) that can sustain human life. The **ecosystem** refers to the interaction of a community of organisms within their physical environment. Although it is relatively comforting to know that science is trying to save the ecosystem, thus humanity, it will take action on the part of people, big business, and governments around the world if we hope to prevail. As individuals, we can only do the little things, such as recycling, driving fuel-efficient automobiles, reducing waste, supporting "green-friendly" organizations, and so on. Perhaps our biggest contribution to saving the ecosystem comes in the form of demanding that our political leaders take drastic steps to protect the environment. After all, the little things that people can do to save the environment pale in comparison to what we need businesses and governments to do.

Going Green

It has almost become a cliché to say, "We are going green." "Going green" is a general expression that incorporates a wide variety of behaviors that people can adopt in an attempt to become eco-friendly. Going green is so popular that it qualifies as a social movement. A **social movement** is a persistent and organized effort on the part of a relatively large number of people who share a common ideology and try to bring about or resist change. Nearly everyone (e.g., businesses, schools, individuals) claims to be going green in one form or another. But what does it mean to go green? There are many answers to this question.

Developing New Technology

Developing new technology to lessen our dependency on fossil fuels is an example of going green. This can include pursuing alternative energy sources such as solar, wind, and nuclear power to replace our reliance on oil and oil-related products. We can reduce our addiction to gasoline by driving fuel-efficient automobiles, carpooling, taking mass transit, and working more from home whenever possible. Some people are installing various gas-saving devices in their existing cars, especially devices that make use of hydrogen. For example, the Hydrogen Hurricane, a gas-saving gizmo available via the Internet, can increase gas mileage by nearly 40 percent. The main component of this device is a steel cylinder filled with distilled water. With the electricity supplied from the car's battery, the unit makes bubbles of hydrogen and oxygen through a process called electrolysis. A hose carries the hydrogen and oxygen to the engine's air intake (Knauss 2008). A Chevrolet Prizm that gets thirty-five miles per gallon (on the highway) can get fifty miles per gallon after the installation of the Hydrogen Hurricane (Knauss 2008). Jay Leno, host of NBC's *The Tonight Show,* boasts about owning and driving hydrogen-powered automobiles that use no gasoline and emit zero emissions into the air. Why are we not all driving such cars? We need to demand that the auto industry mass-produce such vehicles. For that matter, we need political and business leaders to do this on their own.

Protecting and Saving Natural Resources

Natural resources are finite. Consequently, it is important to use nature's resources as sparingly as possible and to recycle resources whenever possible. Recycling is an easy way for humans to contribute to maintaining the ecosystem's carrying capacity. Before the recycling of soda and beer bottles and cans became law, these items appeared as litter on city streets and rural roads. Today, empty plastic water bottles and energy drink cans pollute roadsides, parks, and other private and public areas. Pending legislation will require that these products also be charged a deposit fee in order to encourage recycling. Remember, if you place just one soda can or beer bottle in the trash, you have wasted more energy than the 1 billion people suffering from malnourishment or hunger (because they do not even have access to a soda can or beer bottle). On the other hand, individuals are at times nearly powerless in their attempts to recycle. Consider, for example, that about one-third of what the average American throws away is packaging! As consumers, we do not ask to be overwhelmed with so much packaging, especially such harmful products as Styrofoam "peanuts." What can consumers do about this? Well, we can demand that manufacturers be more eco-friendly in their packaging practices.

Reducing solid waste is another important goal of the green movement. Solid waste is a term for garbage. And Americans produce a great deal of it: four pounds of solid waste per day, per person, for a staggering 1 trillion pounds of garbage each year (Paul 1986; Levine 1988). Americans also waste 1.3 pounds of food every day, and food waste can decompose into methane in a landfill (Miller 2004). People around the world litter and thus create garbage. In a 2008 report released by the Ocean Conservancy, nearly 7.2 million items (trash) were collected by volunteers on a single day in September 2007 on shorelines in seventy-six countries (including forty-five

U.S. states) (Herbert 2008). The most common trash items collected were cigarettes and cigarette filters (1.97 million items), food wrappers and containers (0.69 million), caps and lids (0.65 million), and bags (0.58 million). The 378,000 worldwide volunteers on average collected 182 pounds of trash for every mile of shoreline (Herbert 2008). It does not take an environmentalist to plead, "Keep our oceans and waterways clean!"

While some people still question the validity of global warming, what is not debated are the harmful effects of destroying the rainforest.

Globally, one of the top priorities for saving the ecosystem centers on protecting the rainforest. As mentioned earlier, the rainforest helps to balance the Earth's ecosystem by turning carbon dioxide into oxygen. In effect, the rainforest cleans the atmosphere to help us breathe. The Amazon rainforest is such a critical producer of oxygen that it has been described as the "lungs of our planet." As such, the Amazon rainforest produces about 20 percent of the Earth's oxygen. Unfortunately, more than half of the Earth's rainforests have been destroyed in the past half century. About 20 percent of the Amazon rainforest has been forever lost. In short, worldwide, over 150 acres of rainforest are destroyed per minute (Lakshmanan 2006).

One other important strategy for saving the ecosystem involves the controversial topic of population control. If Malthus, Spencer, and Marx were concerned about overpopulation in their time, imagine how they would react today! There are nearly 7 billion people worldwide, and every one of them places demands on the limited natural resources. How will we provide for them all?

What Do You Think?

In how many ways do you help to save the ecosystem? Other than what has already been mentioned in the text, what other ways are there to save the planet? What do you think?

SOCIOLOGICAL PERSPECTIVES ON THE ENVIRONMENT

Democrats and Republicans, liberals and conservatives, socialists and communists, and moderates alike should all be able to agree on the importance of protecting the environment; after all, we all share the same one. And although people can agree that breathing fresh air is better than breathing smoggy air, and drinking clean, clear water is better than drinking contaminated, dirty water, and clean beaches are better than polluted ones, somehow socioeconomic-political agendas interfere with the methods that best guarantee a sustainable environment for future generations. Sociologists certainly want to contribute positively to the maintenance of a viable environment, but they too look at the environment from different theoretical perspectives.

The Functionalist Perspective

Functionalists examine how all the social institutions are intertwined together to form a larger social system. They also recognize that humans and social institutions reside within the natural environment. Consequently, the natural environment serves a function. Because the natural environment is functional, it is in our best interest to maintain and preserve it. Preservation of the environment is the only logical conclusion from a functionalist standpoint. Despite the necessity to protect the environment, functionalists acknowledge that humans are also the biggest culprits in harming it. From this standpoint, humans are dysfunctional in their dealings with the environment. On the other hand, functionalists point out that it is often more profitable for business to treat the environment as if it were a self-sustaining system capable of withstanding anything humans can throw at it. This reality explains, in part, why some people do not believe in global warming or climate change. It is in the best interest of people who benefit from harming the environment to deny that humans can do so (e.g., via burning fossil fuels). Denial, in this regard, is functional for those who profit economically from disregarding environmental concerns.

The Conflict Perspective

Like functionalists, conflict theorists recognize the value of sustaining the environment. But, true to their basic tenet, they explore the role of power when it involves environmental concerns and social discourse. Conflict theorists point to social injustices that the poor are subjected to when decisions are made about environmental issues such as highway construction, toxic-waste storage facilities, and landfill locations that have a direct impact on local residents. No neighborhood, for example, wants to be the site of a toxic dump facility or garbage trucked in from municipalities hundreds of miles away. The common protest involves the proclamation, "Not in my backyard!" Neighborhoods that are politically or economically powerful will manage to pressure officials into favorable decisions. But if a landfill of some sort is needed, eventually it will find a home. And, as the conflict perspective points out, it will end up in a neighborhood where the residents are not as politically and economically powerful. We see the same scenario when roads and interstates need to be built or expanded. Inevitably, they are built in poorer areas, destroying the very fabric of the neighborhood.

Conflict theorists argue that those who control the means of production violate the environment in a number of harmful ways that include strip mining, logging, hydrofracking, corporate agriculture, and oil drilling. When the industrialists secure all the natural resources from a region, they move on, often leaving a devastated environment behind. The powerful industries repeat this behavior around the world. They exploit developing nations by taking their natural resources. It is the imbalance of power that allows this to occur.

What Do You Think?

Both the functionalist and conflict perspectives offer a sociological look at the environment. Which one do you believe to be the most realistic? What do you think?

SUMMARY

Everyone strives for good physical and mental health. There are many social components of health, including the healthy role, which is the expectation that all of us strive toward, and the "sick role," which encompasses efforts to get healthy through such means as taking medicine. Medicine is much more than treatment (e.g., taking a prescribed drug); it is a scientific system implemented to restore health by treating illness or to preserve good health through such means as diagnosis, drug treatment, and manipulation. There are many social inequalities involved with health care. Generally, the wealthy enjoy access to outstanding health care (both physical and mental), including top doctors, whereas millions of economically poor people go without any health care whatsoever. In addition, millions of employed Americans go without adequate health care coverage.

The environment refers to our surroundings, both social and physical. All living organisms, including humans, are dependent on a healthy environment. And yet, all the Earth's creatures, including humans, place high demands on the limited natural resources available from the environment. Earth, however, has limitations, or a "carrying capacity" for supporting life. Such extreme demands have been placed on the Earth that the entire ecosystem is in danger. Among the most significant threats to the environment are the destruction of the rainforest, human dependency on fossil fuels, human overpopulation, and global warming. Going green, developing new technologies, and protecting and saving natural resources are among the possible solutions to saving the ecosystem.

Glossary

Carrying capacity—The maximum feasible load just short of the level that would end the environment's ability to support life.

Deinstitutionalization—The practice of discharging patients from mental hospitals into the community.

Ecosystem—The interaction of a community of organisms within their physical environment.

Enviromare—An environmentally produced nightmare that causes great harm to humanity.

Environment—The totality of social and physical conditions that affect nature (land, water, air, plants, and animals) and humanity and influence the growth, development, and survival of organisms.

Five horrorists—An advanced evolutionary interpretation and development of the Four Horsemen concept.

Health—A state of physical, mental, and social well-being wherein the individual is free from disease or ailment.

Health care fraud—Intentional deception or misrepresentation by an individual or entity in the knowledge that the misrepresentation could result in some unauthorized benefit to the individual, entity, or some other party.

Medicine—The system designed to restore health by treating illness or to preserve good health by such means as diagnosis, drug treatment, and manipulation.

Mental disorder—A condition that alters thinking, mood, or behavior (or some combination thereof), making it difficult or impossible for a person to cope with everyday life.

Mental health—A state of emotional and psychological well-being that allows an individual to function, both cognitively and emotionally, in society; to meet the regular demands of everyday life, including relationships with other people; and to adapt to change and cope with adversity.

Mental illness—A term that refers to all mental disorders.

Sick role—A social role performed by sick persons that is recognized by others and exempts them from normal obligations.

Social epidemiology—The study of the causes, frequency, distribution, and social determinants of health, disease, and impairment throughout a population.

Social movement—A persistent and organized effort on the part of a relatively large number of people who share a common ideology and try to bring about or resist change.

Discussion Questions

1. If you were the president of the United States, what would you do about the health care system? Specifically, would you shift the responsibility from employers to the government?
2. Describe how socioeconomic factors affect health care in the United States.

3. Considering how many people die prematurely each year because of tobacco smoking, should tobacco be outlawed?

4. What shape will the Earth's ecosystem be in ten years from now? In one hundred years? In two hundred years?

5. In what specific ways does your college or university claim to be "green"? What other things should your school do in its efforts to be green?

Web Links

To learn more about "fossil fools" and "Fossil Fools Day," visit the Global Exchange website at www.globalexchange.org/war_peace_democracy/oil/fossilfoolsday.html.

To determine your body mass index, use the BMI calculator available at www.whathealth.com/bmi/calculator.html.

To learn more about "going green," visit www.treehugger.com/gogreen.php.

Watch the number of people being added to the world's total population by the second at www.ibiblio.org/lunarbin/worldpop.

To learn more about the 2010 health care bill, visit www.cbsnews.com/8301-503544_162-20000846-503544.html.

14 SOCIOLOGY'S PLACE IN SOCIETY

Completing the Connection

In the film Precious, *the lead character, Precious (shown here), and her friends were surprised to learn that there are male nurses because they associate the nursing profession with women. This reaction should remind students of the discussion in Chapter 9 on "pink-collar" jobs.*

Chapter 14

- Introductory Story
- The Importance of Introductory Sociology Courses
- The Value of Sociology
- Careers and the Liberal Arts Degree
- Careers and the Undergraduate Sociology Degree
- Careers and the Graduate Sociology Degree
- The Future of Sociology: Not a Conclusion, but a Continuation . . .

INTRODUCTORY STORY

As discussed in Chapter 11, most students attend college to find a job, rather than simply to increase their base of cumulative knowledge. Thus, students are naturally curious about what types of jobs they will qualify for with their major degree. The answers are a little clearer with some majors than they are with others. For example, students with a degree in business assume that they are qualified to find a job in business. Education majors will most likely teach. Prelaw students expect to go on to graduate school and eventually find a profession in the area of law, perhaps as a lawyer. There are some majors, however, where future job opportunities are a little less clear. For example, what will a student do with a degree in philosophy or history? More relevant to our discussion, what type of career can someone expect to find with a degree in sociology? That is certainly a fair question, and one that will be answered by the end of this chapter.

Before we turn our attention to a discussion of career opportunities in sociology, let us examine the importance of introductory sociology courses specifically and the role of sociology in society in general. After all, it is important for sociology majors and sociologists that sociology has a secure place in society.

THE IMPORTANCE OF INTRODUCTORY SOCIOLOGY COURSES

As with history, philosophy, and a number of other disciplines, one of the biggest obstacles confronting sociology is attracting students. During the height of American student political activism in the 1960s and to a lesser extent the 1970s, the discipline of sociology enjoyed far greater enrollment than it does today. Why are more students not interested in sociology as a major in college? First of all, proportionately few high school students are exposed to sociology (as compared to subjects like math, science, English, psychology, and business). Second, because students are preoccupied (and rightfully so) with future financial considerations, many will choose a major based on how much money they believe they can earn after graduation. Luckily for sociology, introductory sociology fulfills a "general education" requirement at most colleges and universities. Ideally, if taught by energetic and knowledgeable introductory sociology professors who demonstrate the relevancy of sociology to everyday life, more students will choose sociology as a major.

Introductory Sociology

It is vital to the profession that sociologists attempt to attract students to the discipline. Because introductory sociology is generally the first course a student takes in the discipline, introductory professors are the key to the discipline's success. It is vital that introductory instructors point out the validity of the field. I constantly remind students that we live sociology on a daily basis. Hopefully, by now, you have come to realize that the subject areas discussed in your introductory sociology course are reflected in your daily activities. (Note: This becomes increasingly important for students looking for a career based on a sociology degree.) Hopefully, the preceding thirteen chapters have demonstrated the relevancy of sociology to the everyday life of students and established sociology's place in society.

Equally important is the fact that, regardless of one's major, sociology serves as an excellent complement to all disciplines. In that regard, sociology as a minor should be a serious consideration for any student. For example, if you are a business major, you will need to be able to relate to a diversity of people. In the ever-expanding global-economic market, it is more important than ever before to understand the values, norms, and customs of people different from ourselves. Ask your introductory sociology professor to explain how sociology complements your major, and you will be happy to learn of the positive relationship between sociology and any other discipline.

What Do You Think?

How is sociology relevant to your everyday life? What do you think?

THE VALUE OF SOCIOLOGY

Now that you have been exposed to the discipline, perhaps you are considering sociology as a major, a dual major, or a minor. If this is the case, you are most likely wondering about sociology's value and its place in society. As Alfred McClung Lee (1978) once asked, for whom do we do sociology? Is it for ourselves or for others; if it is for others, which others? The answers to these questions are that we do sociology for ourselves, for our students, and for society. Sociologists are the experts in the study of human social behavior, and as a result we need to show our value to ourselves, our students, and our society. Demonstrating the value of sociology to society helps to ensure our majors can find jobs upon graduation.

Students may also wonder about the marketability of a sociology degree and the reputation of sociology among potential employers. Further, what are current sociologists doing to maintain and improve the positive image of sociology in the marketplace? That is, how are sociologists promoting their field in society? After all, if sociologists primarily study human behavior in the context of cultural norms and values at the societal, organizational, and group levels, what are they doing to show their relevancy to society? These are valid concerns and questions for those eventually seeking a career armed with a bachelor's degree in sociology. The answers to these questions are addressed in our discussion of promoting and popularizing sociology via the "four *R*'s."

The Four *R*'s

Many sociology professors do much more than meet their primary responsibilities of teaching, conducting scholarship, and providing service to the college and community. They are active participants in promoting the field of sociology in hopes of elevating the prestige of the discipline. Undoubtedly, your sociology professor has encouraged you all term to become an active participant in making society a better place to live. Armed with sociological knowledge, you can potentially make a quite significant contribution to society. If you have embraced the ideal of making society better and helping others, you are ready to do sociology as a career. Helping others as a reformist is a critical aspect of sociology and the first of the four *R*'s.

1. Reformists

As we learned in Chapter 1, the sociological tradition has its roots in social reform. This reformist attitude addresses the concern over sociology's *mission*. From the time of early industrialization, sociologists have focused on issues related to social problems and social change. Courses in social problems and social change are both common and relatively popular with college students. Sociologists, including sociology majors, must continue this persistent study of the social conditions and processes that help to create social problems—such as racism, sexism, domestic abuse, poverty, homelessness, environmental degradation, gang violence—and offer solutions for the successful eradication of these problems. It is not necessary for every sociologist to focus on social change and social problems, but reformist ideals should be emphasized by all. Sociologists should make a loud claim to being experts in the study of social change and social problems—it is what we do! Furthermore, sociology students should also embrace this mantra as it will serve them well in future endeavors.

2. Relevancy

The value of sociology to society and the marketplace is clearly demonstrated by its relevancy. The relevancy of sociology is the *focus* of our discipline. Every topic discussed in this text is relevant to student lives and/or society. Sociology examines social institutions, organizations, cultures, entire societies, and human behaviors. It is hard to imagine a student's future life that will not involve these elements. Sociology students should never underestimate the value of education and the relevancy of their degree.

3. Research and Theory

Along with its commitment to moral reform, sociology is firmly entrenched in empirical science. Sociology *is* science. It is research guided by *theory*. Sociologists do not merely speculate on observable behavior; we attempt to document and explain it. Sociological theory courses are designed to stimulate critical and abstract thinking, tools that come in handy in one's professional life. Research methodology courses will prepare students for a number of professions, some directly involved with data collection and analysis and others that value the ability to analyze and apply qualitative and quantitative research.

4. Public Relations

It often seems as though sociology suffers from an identity crisis, as the public generally has little idea what a sociologist does. Sociology clearly needs more public exposure, especially positive coverage in the media. It is important to get the sociological word out in the public domain. In this manner, promoting and popularizing sociology with the public serves a self-preservation function. In short, sociology needs a Dr. Joyce Brothers or even a Dr. Phil who becomes synonymous with the discipline via mass and popular appeal as these individuals have done with the field of psychology.

As with every discipline, a number of sociologists attempt to promote the field by serving as media experts who offer sociological insights on a wide variety of topics to various news outlets (newspapers, radio, and television). Nearly every college and university has a public relations department that sends a questionnaire to faculty members asking them what topic areas, if any, they are comfortable serving as a media expert for. Faculty members choose from a PR-generated list and usually claim their teaching area(s) as the category(s) for which they are willing to respond to media requests. (Ask your professor if he or she serves as a media expert and, if he or she does, in what areas.) In this manner, once a news outlet sends out a general request (via the Internet) or contacts a specific school to find out if anyone on staff is qualified to be interviewed on a specific news event, the PR department will put the outlet in touch with the appropriate faculty member. Students who wish to be in the public eye will enjoy working for public relations firms. Gaining knowledge from sociologists who serve as media experts will assist you in this career pursuit.

Beyond serving as media experts, a number of sociologists write books with a popular appeal. This is another effective means of getting the sociological word out. Sociologists who write on topics of general interest are likely to enjoy an elevated status in the media and thus serve as the torchbearers shining the light on the discipline. Dr. Pepper Schwartz (University of Washington) is a prime example of a sociologist who is attempting to popularize the field. And it is no wonder she is popular in the media as her primary area of study is sex! Schwartz has received many academic awards over the course of her professional career. She is the author of several books, many of them quite popular, including *The Great Sex Weekend, The Lifetime Love and Sex Quiz Book, Everything You Know About Love and Sex Is Wrong,* and *Ten Talks Parents Must Have with Their Children About Sex and Character.*

Because of the popularity of her books and her willingness to promote the discipline (along with herself), Pepper Schwartz has contributed to many magazines, journals, and newspapers. She appears on local news programs (in Seattle) and national news shows. Schwartz has also been on some of the most popular TV shows, including a number of appearances on *The Oprah Winfrey Show*. Oh yeah, she still manages to teach courses at the University of Washington. As a sociologist who attempts to promote the field via popular means, Schwartz is admired by many. On the other hand, she is scorned by some traditional sociologists for the same reason. But Schwartz is not alone her attempt to popularize sociology. Many sociologists, including Jacque Lynn Foltyn, are also attempting to popularize the field (See "Connecting Sociology and Popular Culture" Box 14.1 for an interview with Foltyn).

Sociologists who are willing to provide their expertise in a public forum are contributing to the field in an invaluable fashion. These sociologists not only provide great free exposure to the field but help elevate the overall positive image of the field in the greater society. A recent article in the American Sociological Association's (ASA) *Footnotes* concurs with this sentiment of promoting sociology's value to the labor market: "Approximately 30,000 newly minted sociology majors will graduate this spring [2009]. In addition to enduring the usual post-graduation jitters, this year's graduates will also have to contend with a rapidly deteriorating job market, soaring debt, and unparalleled economic uncertainty. As a result, stressing the value of a sociology degree in the labor market is particularly pressing" (2009, p. 4).

As revealed in this discussion of the four *R*'s, many sociologists are actively trying to promote their field. Promoting sociology in the popular media helps the discipline, the universities and colleges that employ these sociologists, the professors themselves, and, of course, sociology majors. After all, the more popular sociology becomes and the more widespread the positive recognition of sociology, the better it is for sociology majors who seek employment with a sociology degree.

CAREERS AND THE LIBERAL ARTS DEGREE

The vast majority of introductory sociology students are not sociology majors. Ideally, however, after completing the introductory sociology course, students will have a better understanding of and appreciation for the field. With this newfound understanding and appreciation, perhaps you are now considering majoring in sociology and contemplating what type of career or profession to pursue. Deciding on a major, and by extension a future profession, is often tough for students. There are so many things to consider, including job availability, salary, and benefits packages. Most likely, as a student, you have already been advised to pick a career that you can honestly see yourself in for the rest of your life. After all, why would you want a career in a field that you do not particularly care about?

When choosing a major and future profession, it might also be important to consider your own sociopolitical ideology. At least, that is the conclusion of two sociologists who recently conducted research in the area of jobs and politics. Neil Gross (University of British Columbia) and Ethan Fosse (Harvard University, doctoral student) believe that sociopolitical "typecasting" has a great influence on the profession one chooses. For example, liberals are more likely to seek the occupation of college professor, author, journalist, creative artist, social worker, and bartender, while conservatives are more likely to seek occupations such as religious worker, building manager, physician, dentist, and law enforcement officer (P. Cohen 2010) (see "A Closer Look" Box 14.2 for more information about careers and sociopolitical ideology).

Robin Williams (shown here) is a comedian and an actor, and he is among the many famous celebrities with a sociology degree.

Gross and Fosse (2010) also point out that job typecasting is not just a matter of political ideology. The researchers suggest that certain jobs are gender typecast. For example, less than 6 percent of nurses today are males, and although discrimination against men is a possible explanation for their low numbers in nursing, according to Gross and Fosse, most people consider nursing to be a woman's career. Students should recall Chapter 9's discussion of gender and careers and the introduction of the term "pink-collar." Pink-collar jobs are, at least in part, the result of typecasting. In the Oscar-nominated film *Precious,* the lead character and her friends were asked if they had ever seen a male nurse before, and they all giddily answered no (P. Cohen 2010).

The Liberal Arts Degree and Overcoming Roadblocks in Employment

Before we examine specific career opportunities for students who graduate with a sociology degree, let us first look at career opportunities from a more general perspective: the liberal arts degree. Kate S. Brooks, director of liberal arts career services at the University of Texas, Austin, and author of *You Majored in What? Mapping Your Path from Chaos to Career* (2009), offers a number of tips to students seeking employment with a liberal arts degree. Brooks (2010) also indicates that there are three major hurdles to clear in achieving gainful employment.

Many students realize that the job search begins long before graduation. Those who wait until graduation, however, will face the first roadblock in finding a job: the lack of knowledge about the workplace, typical entry-level

Connecting Sociology and Popular Culture

Box 14.1 Popularizing Sociology

In November 2009, I interviewed Jacque Lynn Foltyn, associate professor of sociology and chair of the Department of Social Sciences at National University, La Jolla, California. Her studies focus on human beauty, fashions in beauty, fashion photography, the cult of dead celebrities, and representations of death in art and popular culture. Her cultural critiques have appeared in a variety of forums, including fashion and lifestyle magazines, such as *Allure, More,* and *Sunday Life* (AU), and newspapers, such as the *New York Times,* the *Chicago Tribune,* the *Times* (UK), and the *Guardian* (UK). As a scholarly expert, she helped shape and appeared on a July 7, 2009, *CBS National News/48 Hours Mystery* special on the death of Michael Jackson. Dr. Foltyn has also made many guest appearances on a variety of TV shows.

Q. Are you trying to popularize sociology? If so, how?

A. I popularize sociology with examples from popular culture in my classes, no matter what course I am teaching.... I have helped popularize sociology by serving as a sociological expert for mainstream fashion, beauty, and lifestyle magazines, major newspapers, and radio and television program specials. Another way I have popularized sociology is by serving as a consultant for catalogues for museum exhibits (e.g., Science Museum of Minnesota regarding body image) and for a project headed by journalist Nancy Friday for Revlon Corporation. I have been interviewed by television producers for my expertise, contributing to a story about ugliness on *Oprah,* about human height on *NBC Dateline,* and about the evolution of beauty on *60 Minutes Australia.*

Q. What are the possible benefits of popularizing sociology?

A. Popularizing the sociology major at universities, elevating the overall prestige of the academic discipline, and keeping it relevant.

Q. What are the possible drawbacks of trying to popularize sociology?

A. I cannot think of any, other than concerns voiced by some academics that think attention in the mass media trivializes the research. I regard such thinking as creating a false and asymmetrical binary position about academic and public forums of information.

Q. Should sociology have a public relations firm working for it in an attempt to popularize the field?

A. Many universities already promote the work of their academics, whatever the disciplines. I think

positions, and how to find them. Brooks (2010) recommends that students (1) talk to an alumnus in the field and use their liberal arts research skills (e.g., search the Internet) to learn about potential opportunities, typical entry-level positions, the "lingo" of the field, and where job opportunities are posted; (2) get direct experience (e.g., do an internship, volunteer, or get a part-time job in the field—and do not worry about the job title); and (3) work with the college career center (e.g., attend workshops, create a resume, secure letters of recommendation, etc.).

it would be a good idea for the ASA [American Sociological Association] and perhaps the PSA [Pacific Sociological Association] to do more with press releases, etc.

Q. What popular shows have you appeared on? Do you like promoting your work and sociology in pop culture?

A. Answered above. I do like working with the media in pop culture and serious news venues. It is rewarding to help shape the discourse about, for example, beauty standards, plastic surgery, and the fascination with dead celebrities and forensics. I have received letters of appreciation from members of the public and also been a subject of high level blogs, including by the scientist Richard Dawkins at Oxford University, and the cultural critic Bryan Appleyard.

Q. How do celebrities, such as Oprah, view sociology?

A. I can only answer that by speculating. Because media personalities interview sociological experts, they must be searching for an additional layer of meaning that sociological research and analysis can supply. The doctorate matters.

Q. In your opinion, what is the perception of sociology in the general society?

A. Mixed. There are those who would view it as not utilitarian enough at the BA degree level ("What do you do with that degree?"). There are those who do not trust any social scientists or academics. There are those who value the insights of the "sociological imagination." The fact that President Reagan and First Lady Michele Obama majored in sociology gives sociology a higher profile. Joy Behar, a member of *The View,* who also hosts her own *CNN HLN* TV show, talks frequently about having majored in sociology, and when I listen to her, I notice her quips and analysis often reflect her sociological education.

What Do You Think?

Sociologists disagree about whether the field should be popularized as a method of informing the public about sociology's place in society. What do you think about Jacque Lynn Foltyn and her attempt to popularize sociology? Has her vast experience stimulated ideas for ways in which you can apply your sociology degree? What do you think?

Students need to recognize the applicability of their degree, or they risk confronting the second roadblock in seeking a career: not fully understanding and adequately selling their education to potential employers. Brooks (2010) recommends that graduating students have full confidence in their degree and knowledge of its application in the marketplace in order to convince employers to hire them. In essence, you have to learn how to be your own salesperson, that is, to sell yourself as the best candidate for the job because of, not despite, your degree. (Note: This reflects the importance and relevance of sociologists promoting and

A Closer Look

Box 14.2 Careers and Political Ideology

In their research article "Why Are Professors Liberal?" Gross and Fosse (2010) ascertained that instead of asking, "Why are most professors liberal?" one should ask, "Why do liberals want to be professors?" As previously stated, Gross and Fosse argue that many professions are typecast based on sociopolitical ideology. That is, the profession of college professor is perceived as liberal; therefore, liberal-thinking college students are more likely to consider teaching at a university as a possible career than conservative-thinking students. Gross and Fosse state, "The theory we advance—which, we contend, ranks highly in terms of comprehensiveness, realism, and parsimony—holds that the liberalism of professors is a function not primarily of class relations, but rather of the systematic sorting of young adults who are already liberally- or conservatively-inclined into and out of the academic profession, respectively" (Charbonneau 2010, p. 1). The statistics support Gross and Fosse's claim (and the general public's perception) that most professors are left-wing. Columnist Leo Charbonneau (2010) cites *The Chronicle's* "2009 Almanac of Higher Education," stating that 55.8 percent of academics reported that they considered themselves either "far left" or "liberal," while just 15.9 percent claimed to be either "far right" or "conservative." The remaining 28.4 percent self-identified as "middle of the road" (or moderate).

In research conducted by Neil Gross and the *New York Times,* 43 percent of college professors identified themselves as liberal, 48 percent as moderate, and just 9 percent as conservative (P. Cohen 2010). See Table 14.1 for data on other professions and political ideology.

What Do You Think?

Should you consider your sociopolitical ideology when considering a major? Do you believe your ideal future profession reflects your sociopolitical ideology? What do you think?

popularizing sociology as discussed earlier in the chapter. If employers are convinced of the validity of an academic field, the value of the degree increases, and the odds of finding a job are increased.)

Upon graduation, some students may put off the job search because they feel that the challenge is too daunting. Brooks claims this fear leads to the third roadblock: failure to develop personal commitment and a desire to tackle the job search. Brooks recommends that students (1) develop focus (e.g., create a plan of attack and set attainable goals); (2) take action (e.g., be an active job hunter, pursue all leads, and work with alumni); and (3) notice what does and does not work and keep adjusting their plans accordingly (e.g., if your resume is not getting noticed, consider revising it; do mock interviews with friends and professionals you know; visit a career counselor).

Armed with these job-seeking tips, the sociology major is now ready to find a job!

These data illustrate an interesting variable when students consider what their major should be in college. For example, sociology is generally considered a liberal discipline in that it supports empiricism and social reform; as a result, liberal- and moderate-thinking students tend to find sociology appealing while ultraconservative-thinking students are less likely to do so. Consequently, when choosing a major for the primary purpose of future employment, students may want to take their sociopolitical ideology into account.

TABLE 14.1 Occupation and Ideology

OCCUPATION	LIBERAL (%)	MODERATE (%)	CONSERVATIVE (%)
Professors	43	48	9
Authors and journalists	37	52	11
Creative artists	33	54	13
Social workers	28	58	14
Bartenders	27	68	5
Law enforcement officers	11	60	29
Physicians and dentists	17	52	31
Building managers	10	58	32
Religious workers	15	39	46

Source: P. Cohen 2010.

CAREERS AND THE UNDERGRADUATE SOCIOLOGY DEGREE

A degree in sociology serves as a qualification for a number of jobs. Do not expect, however, to find a category listed alphabetically under *S* for "sociologist" in the newspaper want ads or on an online job finder. Instead, students who graduate with a bachelor's degree in sociology are likely to find employment in the helping professions, business, and various public-sector positions. According to the ASA's 2008 "Majoring in Sociology: A Guide for Students" pamphlet, "Employment opportunities for those with Bachelor's degrees in sociology include entry-level positions in the following areas: administration, advertising, banking, counseling (family planning, career, substance abuse, and so forth), community planning, health services, journalism, group and recreational work, marketing and market research, sales, teaching (if certified), human resources/personnel work, social services, and social research."

In other words, a sociology degree, like most undergraduate degrees, is an applied degree. "Contrary to what many believe, there is no 'one-to-one' relationship between academic majors and careers. One does not necessarily need a degree in business administration or marketing to land a successful career in the corporate world. On the contrary, a degree in sociology provides an excellent springboard for entering the world of business, industry, and organization" (*ASA Footnotes* 2009b, p. 4). In short, one has to apply the sociology degree to specific desired jobs.

Students who realize a sociology degree is as valuable as any other undergraduate degree when seeking a career after graduation become attracted to the discipline for a number of reasons beyond employment. The ASA reports (from *Pathways to Job Satisfaction: What Happened to the Class of 2005?*) that the most cited reason graduating seniors gave for majoring in sociology was the discipline's "interesting concepts" (*ASA Footnotes* 2009b). One-third of respondents reported that sociology helped them to understand their lives better. Just one-fourth of graduating sociology majors cited that they majored in the field because they thought it would prepare them for a job they wanted or for graduate or professional schools. "The lure of the sociology major may not be the promise of a particular career, but what students graduate with is a distinctive and transferable skill-set. . . . Sociology majors, equipped with the sociological imagination, are in a position to be more aware of their social context, as well as able to effectively navigate within it. This social competency, which is merely the application of sociological knowledge to an individual situation, is extremely useful" (*ASA Footnotes* 2009b, p. 4).

For students concerned about specifics, a number of career opportunities are open to those who major in sociology. This includes work in research, policy making, urban planning, government and nongovernment agencies, business, and public relations.

A Sampling of Specific Career Opportunities

There are many reasons why research methodology courses represent a fundamental requirement for sociology majors everywhere, both nationally and internationally. The most relevant reason with regard to career opportunities resides with the fact that many sociology majors find employment in the field of research. "Research is a major activity of many social scientists, who use a variety of methods to assemble facts and construct theories. Applied research usually is designed to produce information that will enable people to make better decisions or manage their affairs more effectively" (U.S. Bureau of Labor Statistics 2008b). Sociology majors are especially qualified to conduct research in a variety of employment settings, including at a university; a public agency at the local, state, or federal level; a business, industrial, or corporate firm; a research institute; or a nonprofit or advocacy organization. Some sociologists are self-employed as researchers and sell their data to a variety of firms; other sociologists have created their own research companies and consulting firms. Sociologists are especially suited for positions as research consultants because of their knowledge of research design and methodology, focus group studies, and data analysis. As a bit of career advice, be sure to emphasize your research skills on your resume (just as you list your computer skills). Ongoing research conducted by the ASA reveals that "sociology graduates who communicate to employers the skills learned as undergraduates enhance the likelihood that they will actually use these skills on the job and will have greater job satisfaction than those who do not communicate that they have these skills" (Spalter-Roth and Van Vooren 2008).

Knowledge of research, combined with the general training that sociology majors receive, contributes to potential opportunities for securing policy-making positions. As Rebecca Maynard and Thomas Corbett explain, "Policymakers have increased their demands for research to sharpen their understanding of social problems and goals, identify the menu of policy and program options to address particular needs, assess the relative strengths and limitations of options, and shape the development of detailed policy implementation guidelines. Program directors have developed an appreciation for and are increasingly relying on research to guide them in the translation of policy program support into client intervention and service strategies" (2003, p. 303). Knowledge in social and demographic analysis will further assist the sociology major seeking a job in policy making.

Policy planning is an applied profession that becomes marketable in a number of ways, such as in urban planning. Beth Perry and Alan Harding (2002) claim that "the future of urban sociology is bright, due to the continued importance of distinctly sociological interpretations of contemporary debates on the urban, cities, and globalization and due to the opportunities offered by interdisciplinarity to combine urban sociological concerns with those of other disciplines" (p. 851). Urban sociologists are trained to analyze social and demographic data and trends, and they have been taught to understand and appreciate cultural diversity.

Many sociology majors find work at all levels of the government. Sociologists may conduct research-and-evaluation projects, manage programs, engage in policy analysis, work in human resources, serve as counselors and advisors, and hold management positions. Most government jobs held by sociologists are with various federal agencies, such as the Department of Health and Human Services, the National Institute of Aging, the Bureau of the Census, Housing and Urban

Development, and so on. A number of private nongovernment agencies also hire sociologists, including the World Bank, the Children's Defense Fund, and the Peace Corps.

Sociology majors may also find employment in the private sector—in business. Opportunities include, but are not limited to, sales, human resources, management, consulting, marketing, advertising, telecommunications, insurance, and public relations. (Perhaps the ASA will hire a future sociology graduate to help promote the field, as suggested earlier in this chapter.) Sociology departments that teach public relations skills will qualify graduates for a number of job opportunities, as most colleges, agencies, businesses, sports organizations, media outlets, and so on, employ public relations personnel. As a reminder, it is critical that sociology majors (like most other students) are familiar with the latest computer programs and data-analysis techniques, as most businesses try to keep up with the latest innovations in their field. The employee who remains on the cutting edge of technological advancements will always be marketable in a number of private business and government agencies.

A General List of Occupational Opportunities for Sociology Majors

The description above represents a sampling of specific job opportunities for sociology majors. Below is a general sampling of occupational opportunities for sociology majors. For a complete listing of job opportunities with a sociology degree, as well as a listing of current job openings, visit the ASA's website at www.asanet.org.

Administrative assistant
Adoption agent
Affirmative action worker
Banker
Business manager
Case aide worker
Child-welfare officer
Civil engineer
College-placement specialist
Community organizer
Consultant
Consumer-survey advisor
Correctional case worker
Customer relations

Admissions counselor
Advertising agent
Alcohol- and drug-abuse case worker
Budget analyst
Career-services counselor
Census worker
City planner
Clergy
Community-relations director
Compensation/benefits worker
Consumer advocate
Convention organizer
Criminologist
Data analyst/processor

Day-care worker
Demographic analyst
Editor
Family planner
Financial-aid director
Gerontologist
Government worker
Health-care worker
Housing coordinator
Industrial sociologist
Job analyst
Life-quality researcher
Market analyst/researcher
Mass-communication analyst
Motivational speaker
Nutritionist
Park forest ranger
Peace Corps/VISTA worker
Personnel interviewer
Policy analyst
Probation officer
Program director
Public health educator
Public-opinion surveyor
Real estate agent/manager
Resident planner
Research analyst
Sales-campaign planning
School counselor
Social-movements organizer
Social-survey director
Statistician
Substance-abuse counselor
Teacher
Urban planner
Volunteer-program coordinator
Writer/author

Delinquency counselor
Dietitian
Environmental organizer
Family guidance/services counselor
Foster-care worker
Group-home worker/director
Group therapist
Hospital administrator
Human resources manager
Insurance agent
Labor-relations analyst
Manufacturing representative
Marriage and family therapist
Medical social worker
News correspondent
Occupational career counselor
Parole officer
Penologist
Personnel specialist
Population analyst/specialist
Professor
Public administrator
Public health supervisor
Public relations specialist
Recreation director/therapist
Reporter
Research director
Sales representative
Secret service agent
Social scientist/analyst
Social welfare examiner
Survey-research specialist
Telemarketer
Therapy aide worker
Veterans Affairs specialist
Welfare counselor
Youth-outreach worker/manager

It is worth noting that a number of former sociology majors have gone on to become quite famous in such areas as politics, sports, and the arts (including entertainment) (see "Connecting Sociology and Popular Culture" Box 14.3 for a sampling).

Connecting Sociology and Popular Culture

Box 14.3 Famous Sociology Majors

This chapter has discussed a wide variety of specific and general job opportunities for sociology majors. And yet, you might find it interesting to realize that a number of famous people graduated from college with a degree in sociology. The ASA (2009) provides a number of examples.

In politics: Rev. Martin Luther King Jr.; Ronald Reagan, former U.S. president; Michele Obama, First Lady; Rev. Jesse Jackson; Wellington Webb, former Denver mayor; Brett Schundler, mayor of Jersey City; Annette Strauss, former mayor of Dallas; Roy Wilkins, former head of the NAACP; Rev. Ralph Abernathy; Shirley Chisholm, former congresswoman from New York; Maxine Waters, congresswoman from Los Angeles; Barbara Mikulski, U.S. senator from Maryland; Cardinal Theodore McCarrick, archbishop of Washington, D.C.; Saul Alinsky, father of community organizing; Emily Balch, 1946 Nobel Peace Prize winner; Francis Perkins, social reformer and secretary of labor; and Richard Barajas, chief justice, Texas Supreme Court.

In the arts and entertainment: Dr. Ruth Westheimer, the "sex doctor"; Regis Philbin, TV host and personality; Saul Bellow, novelist; Dan Aykroyd, actor/musician; Robin Williams, actor/comedian; Dinah Shore, singer; Joy Behar, TV personality; and Paul Shaffer, bandleader on *The Late Show with David Letterman* (and before that on *Saturday Night Live*).

From the world of sports: Joe Theisman, NFL quarterback/TV sports analyst; Alonso Mourning, NBA; Bryant Stith, NBA; Brian Jordan, MLB; Eric Bjornson, NFL; Bobby Taylor, NFL; and Ahmad Rashad, TV sportscaster.

What Do You Think?

Of these famous sociology majors, which person do you consider the most impressive representation of the field? What can you do to make this list? What do you think?

CAREERS AND THE GRADUATE SOCIOLOGY DEGREE

According to the ASA, 224 academic departments awarded at least one master's degree in sociology in the 2006–2007 academic year. More than half (122) of these departments completed the online survey of the ASA's Research Department and Task Force on the Master's Degree in Sociology about their programs. Of the 122 responding departments, 85 percent reported a freestanding master's program, while 15 percent reported not offering a separate master's program but instead awarding the master's en route to a PhD. Enrollment in the freestanding programs varied a great deal, from three to seventy-two students, with a median of twenty students currently enrolled. Almost two-thirds of master's programs (64 percent) were found in freestanding sociology departments, while 18 percent were found in combined sociology and anthropology departments, followed by 8 percent in combined sociology and criminal justice programs, 5 percent in programs combining sociology with more than one discipline, and 4 percent in a broader social science division (ASA 2009).

The ASA's task force found that most departments offering a master's degree in sociology only track the careers of their PhD graduates. The ASA has a strong commitment to tracking the careers of sociology graduate students and states: "When the first wave of the student survey is complete we will know more about the characteristics of the students in these different types of programs, including labor force status, their finances, their racial and ethic background, their future goals, and whether the programs they attend are meeting their needs" (ASA 2009, p. 5). We do know that advanced degrees qualify sociology majors in the field of education as teachers and professors. A master's or doctorate in sociology will qualify persons for the same types of jobs as a bachelor's degree, but (usually) at a higher level within an agency, business, or organization (including the government).

Furthermore, sociology cracked the top ten in a 2009 best careers list. According to marketing research conducted by CareerCast.com, sociologist ranked as the eighth most appealing job in the new website's analysis of two hundred occupations. The ranking, which appeared in CareerCast's "2009 Jobs Rated Report," is based on various job characteristics, including perceived work environment, income, employment outlook, physical demands, security, and stress (Needleman 2009). According to the study, mathematicians fare the best, in part because they typically work in favorable conditions—indoors and in places free of toxic fumes or noise—unlike those toward the bottom of the list, like sewage-plant operators, painters, and bricklayers. This top-ten recognition for sociology came on the heels of an online *Forbes* feature listing sociologist as one of the nation's highest-paying rare jobs (ASA 2009).

THE FUTURE OF SOCIOLOGY: NOT A CONCLUSION BUT A CONTINUATION ...

What does the future hold in store for sociology? Does it have a place in society? The simple answer is, Yes, sociology does have a secure place in society. It is secure for a number of reasons, but primarily because of the relevancy of the field. Every human behavior has a social component. This is true whether we are talking about individuals, groups, organizations, communities, or entire societies. Furthermore, as the world continues to shrink into an ever-interlocking global community, the importance of sociology expands.

The significance of sociology in the global community is relevant because it examines all aspects of social life (as demonstrated throughout this volume). As a science, sociology offers empirical observations about social life. As with the other sciences, especially the social sciences, sociology develops theories and attempts to support them with research. In this regard, sociology fulfills two of the most commonly cited tasks of science: discovery and explanation. However, sociology partakes in a third, equally important element of science: prediction. After all, discovering and explaining a social phenomenon is one thing, but the ability to predict future events is the real goal of science. Sociologists are embracing the importance of the mantra that the goal of science is to predict behavior so that we can better assist people in improving their quality of life.

Concern over people's quality of life reveals that sociology also has a sensitive side. And this is reflected in its commitment to fight injustice. Remember, sociology is at least as much about demonstrating a reformist attitude as it is a social science. As Joe Feagin and Hernan Vera (2001) state, "Sociology can help liberate when humanistic concern, critical reflectivity, and empathetic reason are applied to the everyday problems that create misery for human beings" (p. 263).

The future of humanity seems to be in peril. People around the world face an assortment of major social problems: hunger, homelessness, lack of proper sanitation, war, the threat of terrorism, economic inequality, lack of health care, shortages of energy and drinkable water, and so on. Many politicians and world leaders have failed to provide their people with an adequate quality of life. They need help! Sociologists are among the people qualified to help solve the social problems of the world. It is, after all, what we do.

Thankfully, a number of talented people are already in the profession. But there is always room for more. So, the call to arms is extended to all students who share a sociological commitment to making the world a better place for all humans and all living organisms. However, whether you become a sociologist or not, it is the hope of introductory sociology professors everywhere that you will now be capable of looking at the world from a sociological perspective. Armed with this knowledge, we also hope that your place in society involves making the world a better place to live for all people.

SUMMARY

In an ideal world, people would attend college to advance their level of knowledge, both general and specific. However, as we do not live in an ideal world, most people attend college in order to gain a degree that will enable them to embark on a career. Thus, it becomes inevitable that students will want to know what types of career opportunities are open to them with their respective degrees. Sociology majors, naturally, wonder the same thing.

Although most people do not like to hear the truth about four-year degrees, the fact remains that most undergraduate degrees are relatively equal in value. The possession of an undergraduate degree informs potential employers that an individual is trainable, educable, and capable of overcoming a number of difficult challenges. As described in this chapter, a sociology degree is as valuable to students as most other degrees. However, even with a college degree (in any discipline), it is still up to the graduate to apply his or her diploma to the job market. Sociology majors are as well equipped to survive in the real world as graduates in any other major—perhaps more so because of the nature of sociological subject matter.

Apply your degree and your sociological imagination, and you will do well!

Discussion Questions

1. Should the American Sociological Association hire a public relations firm to help promote the field?

2. The sociology degree is as valuable as nearly any other undergraduate degree. Is this the perception of the sociology degree at your college or university? What is the perception of the value of the sociology degree at your school?

3. What are the primary assets of sociology for employers?

4. What are the primary assets of a student who graduates with a sociology degree?

Web Links

To learn more about the work of the ASA Task Force on the Master's Degree in Sociology, visit www.asanet.org/about/taskforces/masters.cfm.

To learn more about the nation's best and worse jobs, visit www.careercast.com/jobs/content/JobsRated_10BestJobs.

REFERENCES

ABC News. 2007. "Police Cite Person of Interest in Va. Tech Dorm Killing; Dead Gunman Yet to Be ID'd." April 16. Available at http://abcnews.go.com/print?id=3045574.

———. 2009. "Inside Warren Jeffs's Polygamous Group" (excerpts from his *Lost Boy*). Available at http://abcnews.go.com/GMA/Books/Story?id=7633887&page=1.

AboutDivorce.org. 2011. "Divorce Rate—USA." Available at www.aboutdivorce.org/us_divorce_rates.html.

Abu-Nasr, Riyadh. 2007. "Muslim Women Fight Breast Cancer Taboo." *Post-Standard,* October 25, p. A4.

Acredola, Linda, and Susan Goodwyn. 2006. *A Parent's Guide to the Baby Signs Program.* Vacaville, CA: Baby Signs, Inc.

Adams, Bert, and R. A. Sydie. 2001. *Sociological Theory.* Thousand Oaks, CA: Pine Forge Press.

Adherents.com. 2007. "Major Religions Ranked by Size." Available at www.adherents.com/religions_by_adherents.html.

Adorno, Thomas W., Else Frenkel-Brunswik, Daniel J. Levinson, and R. Nevitt Sanford. 1950. *The Authoritarian Personality.* New York: Harper.

Age, The. 2003. "Part-Time Work Spawns Rural Underclass." April 26. Available at www.theage.com.au/articles/2003/04/25/1050777401309.html.

Akbaraly, Tasnime N., Eric J. Brunner, Jane E. Ferrie, Michael G. Marmot, Mike Kivimaki, and Archana Singh-Manoux. 2009. "Dietary Pattern and Depressive Symptoms in Middle Ages." *British Journal of Psychiatry* 195: 408–413.

Alderson, Priscilla. 2004. "Ethics." Pp. 97–112 in *Doing Research with Children and Young People,* edited by Sandy Fraser, Vicky Lewis, Sharon Ding, Mary Kellett, and Chris Robinson. Thousand Oaks, CA: Sage.

Amato, P. R., and J. Cheadle. 2005. "The Long Reach of Divorce: Divorce and Child Well-Being Across Three Generations." *Journal of Marriage and Family* 67: 191–206.

Ambert, Anne-Marie. 2001. *The Effects of Children on Parents.* 2nd ed. New York: Haworth.

American Civil Liberties Union (ACLU). 2005. "Racial Profiling: Definition." Available at www.aclu.org/racialjustice/racialprofiling/21741res20051123.html.

American Heritage Dictionary. 2006. 4th ed. Houghton Mifflin. Available at http://dictionary.reference.com/help/adh4.html.

American Religious Identification Survey. 2008. "American Religious Identification Survey (ARIS) 2008." Available at www.americanreligionsurvey-aris.org/reports/ARIS_Report_2008.pdf.

American Sociological Association. 2005. "Famous Sociology Majors." Available at www2.asanet.org/student/famoussocs.html.

———. 2006. "Code of Ethics." Available at www.asanet.org/about/ethics.cfm.

———. 2008. "Majoring in Sociology: A Guide for Students." Washington, DC: American Sociological Association.

———. 2009. "What Can I Do with a Master's in Sociology? The Department as Context." Washington, DC: American Sociological Association. Available at www.asanet.org/research/masters.cfm.

Anders, George. 2009. "How Our Salaries Are Changing." *Parade,* April 12, pp. 6–8.

Aproberts, Alison. 2006. "Generation Yo-Yo." *Post-Standard* (originally appeared in *Sacramento Bee*), March 27, p. D1.

Aptheker, Herbert. 1968. *Marxism and Christianity.* New York: Humanities Press.

Argetsinger, Amy, and Roxanne Roberts. 2009. "Tareq and Michaele Salahi Crash Obamas' State Dinner for India." *Washington Post,* November 26. Available at www.washingtonpost.com/wp-dyn/content/article/2009/11/25/AR2009112504113.html.

Armstrong, Elizabeth A., and Mary Bernstein. 2008. "Culture, Power, and Institutions: A Multi-Institutional Politics Approach to Social Movements." *Sociological Theory* 26(1): 74–99.

ASA Footnotes. 2009a. "Sociology Makes Top-Ten Careers List." February. Washington, DC: American Sociological Association.

———. 2009b. "The Undergraduate Sociology Degree's Real-World Application." May–June. Washington, DC: American Sociological Association.

Asylum.com. 2010. "Is Heavy Metal the World's Weirdest Religion?" Available at www.asylum.com/2010/01/27/heavy-metal-religion-2011-census-jediism-weird-religions/?icid=m.

Aviv, Rachel. 2007. "Black Tie (and Pants) Optional." *Post-Standard,* January 8, p. D2.

Babbie, Earl. 1988. *The Sociological Spirit.* Belmont, CA: Wadsworth.

———. 1989. *The Practice of Social Research.* 5th ed. Belmont, CA: Wadsworth.

Badalament, John. 2010. "How to Be a Good Dad" (an excerpt from *The Modern Dad's Dilemma*). *The Good Men Project Magazine,* June 1. Available at http://goodmenproject.com/2010/06/01/how-to-be-a-good-dad.

Baillargeon, R. 2004. "Infants' Physical World." *Current Directions in Psychological Science* 13: 89–94.

Banks, Sandy. 2009. "A Younger View of Feminism." *Los Angeles Times,* April 10, p. A2.

Banned Books and Authors. 2011. "Mississippi School District Bans Book on Censorship: *Fahrenheit 451* by Ray Bradbury." Available at www.banned-books.com/bbarticle-miss.html.

Barber, Benjamin R. 2007. *Consumed: How Markets Corrupt Children, Infantilize Adults, and Swallow Citizens Whole.* New York: Norton.

Barker, Olivia. 2001. "Couples Do Variations on Marriage Themes." *USA Today,* June 26. Available at www.usatoday.com/life/2001-06-26-theme-weddings.htm.

Bartol, Curt R. 1995. *Criminal Behavior: A Psychosocial Approach.* 4th ed. Englewood Cliffs, NJ: Prentice Hall.

Bartol, Curt A., and Anne M. Bartol. 2005. *Criminal Behavior: A Psychological Approach.* 7th ed. Upper Saddle River, NJ: Prentice Hall.

Baumol, William J., Robert E. Litan, and Carl J. Schramm. 2007. *Good Capitalism, Bad Capitalism and the Economics of Growth and Prosperity.* New Haven, CT: Yale University Press.

Baumrind, Diana. 1966. "Effects of Authoritative Parental Control on Child Behavior." *Child Development* 37(4): 887–907.

———. 1967. "Child Care Practices Anteceding Three Patterns of Preschool Behavior." *Genetic Psychology Monographs* 75(1): 43–88.

BBC News. 2007. "Shetty Questioned over Gere Kiss." September 16. Available at http://news.bbc.co.uk/go/pr/fr/-/2/hi/entertainment/7016745.stm.

———. 2011. "State Multiculturalism Has Failed, Says David Cameron." February 5. Available at www.bbc.co.uk/news/uk-politics-12371994.

Beaubien, Jason. 2006. "African Farmers Face Critical Loss of Fertile Land." National Public Radio, April 27. Available at www.npr.org/templates/story/story.php?storyId=5360696&ps=rs.

Becker, Howard. 1963. *The Outsiders.* New York: The Free Press.

Belczyk, Jaclyn. 2010. "Obama Administration Announces $3.4 Billion Indian Trust Settlement." Jurist Legal News and Research. Available at http://jurist.law.pitt.edu/paperchase/2009/12/obama-administration-announces-34php.

Belk, Russell. 1988. "Possessions and the Extended Self." *Journal of Consumer Research* 15 (September): 130–168.

Beller, Emily, and Michael Hout. 2006. "Intergenerational Social Mobility: The United States in Comparative Perspective." *The Future of Children* 16(2): 19–36.

Benzaquen, Adriana S. 2006. *Encounters with Wild Children: Temptation and Disappointment in the Study of Human Nature.* Montreal: McGill–Queens University Press.

Berger, Brigitte. 2002. *The Family in the Modern Age.* New Brunswick, NJ: Transaction.

Bertaux, Daniel, and Paul Thompson. 2005. "Introduction." Pp. 1–12 in *Between Generations: Family Models, Myths, and Memories,* edited by Daniel Bertaux and Paul Thompson. New Brunswick, NJ: Transaction.

Best, Jacqueline. 2006. "Co-Opting Cosmopolitanism? The International Monetary Fund's New Global Ethics." *Global Society* 20(3): 307–327.

Best, Joel. 2001. *Damned Lies and Statistics: Untangling Numbers from the Media, Politicians, and Activists.* Berkeley, CA: University of California Press.

Best, Joel, and David F. Luckenbill. 1994. *Organizing Deviance.* 2nd ed. Englewood Cliffs, NJ: Prentice Hall.

Bianchi, Suzanne M., John P. Robinson, and Melissa A. Milkie. 2006. *Changing Rhythms of American Family Life.* New York: Sage.

Bick, Julie. 2007. "24 Rolls of Toilet Paper, a Tub of Salsa, and a Plasma TV." *New York Times,* January 28, p. 3.

Big Picture Learning. 2009. "About Us." Available at www.bigpicture.org/about-us.

Bilefsky, Dan. 2010. "Changing Face in Poland: Skinhead Puts on Skullcap." *New York Times,* February 27. Available at www.nytimes.com/2010/02/28/world/europe/28poland.html.

Birnbaum, Michael H. 2000. "Decision Making in the Lab and on the Web." Pp. 3–34 in *Psychological Experiments on the Internet,* edited by Michael H. Birnbaum. New York: Academic Press.

Black, Donald. 1995. "The Epistemology of Pure Sociology." *Law and Social Inequality* 20 (summer): 829–870.

Blumer, Herbert. 1937. "Social Psychology." Pp. 44–98 in *Man and Society,* edited by Emerson P. Schmidt. New York: Prentice Hall.

———. 1969. *Symbolic Interactionism.* Englewood Cliffs, NJ: Prentice Hall.

Bogart, Leo. 2005. *Over the Edge.* Chicago: Ivan R. Dee.

Bognanno, Mario F., Michael P. Keane, and Donghoon Yang. 2005. "The Influence of Wages and Industrial Relations Environments on the Production Location Decisions of U.S. Multinational Corporations." *Industrial and Labor Relations Review* 58(2): 171–200.

Brenner, Lynn. 2004. "How Did You Do?" *Parade,* March 14, pp. 4–12.

———. 2008. "How Does Your Salary Stack Up?" *Parade,* April 13, pp. 6–12, 15–17.

Brewer, John, and Albert Hunter. 1989. *Multimethod Research: A Synthesis of Styles.* Newbury Park, CA: Sage.

Brooks, Kate S. 2009. *You Majored in What? Mapping Your Path from Chaos to Career.* New York: Viking.

———. 2010. "Making the Most of Your Liberal Arts Degree." Pp. 18–19 in *Job Choices 2010,* edited by the National Association of Colleges and Employers (NACE). Bethlehem, PA: NACE.

Brown, Douglas. 2005. "Embracing the Male Hug." *Post-Standard* (originally appeared in the *Denver Post*), June 12, p. H1.

Bryant, J. Alison, and Jennings Bryant. 2003. "Effects of Entertainment Televisual Media on Children." Pp. 195–218 in *The Faces of Televised Media: Teaching, Violence, Selling to Children,* edited by Edward L. Palmer and Brian M. Young. 2nd ed. Mahwah, NJ: Lawrence Erlbaum.

Buffalo News. 1999. "Tennessee Man's Dream to Marry Car Thwarted." March 6, p. A5.

Buford, Bill. 1991. *Among the Thugs.* New York: Vintage.

Butler, Kristin. 2009. "In Muslim Culture, Honor Killings Not Out of Date." Available at www.crosswalk.com/root/news/religiontoday/11603889.

Butt, Ameera, and Jonathan S. Landay. 2011. "Gadhafi Losing Grip over Libya." *Post-Standard,* February 26, p. A1.

Calhoun, Thomas C., Rhonda Fisher, and Julie Ann Harms Cannon. 1998. "The Case of Amateur Stripping: Sex Codes and Egalitarianism in a Heterosocial Setting." Pp. 47–61 in *Youth Culture: Identity in a Postmodern World,* edited by Jonathon S. Epstein. Westport, CT: Greenwood Press.

Campbell, Anne. 1984. *The Girls in the Gang.* New York: Basic Blackwell.

Campbell, Bradley. 2009. "Genocide as Social Control." *Sociological Theory* 27(9): 150–172.

CARE. 2008. "Facts About Hunger." Available at www.care.org/campaigns/world-hunger/facts.asp.

Carlebach, Julius. 1978. *Karl Marx and the Radical Critique of Judaism.* Boston: Routledge and Kegan Paul.

Carlson, M. S., S. McLanahan, and P. England. 2004. "Union Formation in Fragile Families." *Demography* 2: 237–261.

Cartwright, Dorwin, and Alvin Zander, eds. 1968. *Group Dynamics.* 3rd ed. Evanston, IL: Peterson.

Carvajal, Doreen. 2010. "France Vows to Continue Deporting Roma." *New York Times,* August 25. Available at www.nytimes.com/2010/08/26/world/europe/26iht-roma.html.

Catholic Church Religion News Blog. 2002. "Mother Teresa's Diary Reveals Her Crisis in Faith." Available at www.religionnewsblog.com/00001315.

Catton, W. R. 1980. *Overshoot: The Ecological Basis of Revolutionary Change.* Urbana: University of Illinois Press.

CBS News. 2010. "NY Shop Sells Item Made in USA, Packaging and All." May 30. Available at http://wcbstv.com/local/made.in.usa.2.1724024.html.

———. 2011. "New Facebook Status Options Applauded by Gay Users." February 18. Available at www.cbsnews.com/stories/2011/02/18/ap/national/main20033739.shtml.

Center on Budget and Policy Priorities. 2010. "Critics Still Wrong on What's Driving Deficits in Coming Years: Economic Downturn, Financial Rescues, and Bush-Era Policies Drive the Numbers." June 28. Available at www.cbpp.org/cms/index.cfm?fa=view&id=3036.

Centers for Disease Control and Prevention (CDC). 1988. "Current Trends Operational Criteria for Determining Suicide." December 23. Available at www.cdc.gov/mmwr/preview/mmwrhtml/00001318.htm.

———. 2007. "Obesity and Overweight: Introduction." Available at www.cdc.gov.

———. 2008a. "The Effects of Childhood Stress on Health Across the Lifespan." Available at www.cdc.gov/Ncipc/pub-res/pdf/Childhood_Stress.pdf.

———. 2008b. "Understanding School Violence: Fact Sheet." Available at www.cdc.gov/violenceprevention/pdf/SchoolViolence_FactSheet-a.pdf.

———. 2009a. "Life Expectancy." Available at www.cdc.gov/nchs/fastats/lifexpec.htm.

———. 2009b. "Press Release." November 12. Available at www.cdc.gov/media/pressrel/2009/r091112.htm.

———. 2009c. "The Tuskegee Timeline." Available at www.cdc.gov/tuskegee/timeline.htm.

———. 2010a. "Coping with a Traumatic Event." Available at www.cdc.gov/masstrauma/factsheets/public/coping.pdf.

———. 2010b. "Coping with Stress." Available at www.cdc.gov/features/HandlingStress.

———. 2010c. "Suicide: Facts at a Glance." Summer 2010. Available at www.cdc.gov/violenceprevention/pdf/Suicide_DataSheet-a.pdf.

Chambliss, William. 1988. *On the Take.* 2nd ed. Bloomington: Indiana Press.

Champion, Dean John. 2004. *The Juvenile Justice System.* 4th ed. Upper Saddle River, NJ: Prentice Hall.

Charbonneau, Leo. 2010. "The Latest on Lefty Profs." University Affairs, January 25. Available at www.universityaffairs.ca/margin-notes/tag/neil-gross-and-ethan-fosse.

Child Welfare League of America. 2007. "Summary of the Kinship Caregiver Support Act (s.985)." Available at www.cwla.org/advocacy/summarykinshipact.htm.

Chu, Don. 2006. *The Department Chair Primer: Leading and Managing Academic Departments.* Bolton, MA: Anker.

Citizen, The. 2007. "Study Finds That Veterans Are a Quarter of the Homeless." November 8, p. D8.

———. 2009. "Even Riskier: Texting While Driving Trumps Driving Drunk, Studies Show." August 13, p. A16.

———. 2009. "Fox Network to Air Two-Hour 'Octomom' Special." August 11, p. A2.

———. 2009. "Jury Awards $675K in Music Downloading Case." August 1, p. A5.

———. 2009. "Syracuse Man Gets 25 Years for Transgender Hate Killing." August 19, p. A3.

———. 2009. "Teen 'Sexters' Getting Charged with Child Porn." February 5, p. B6.

———. 2010. "Student's Stunning Suicide Illustrates Dangers of Internet." October 1, p. B6.

———. 2010. "Turning to Twitter to Fix Restaurant Complaints." September 26, p. C4.

Civic Ventures. 2011. "Fact Sheet on Older Americans." Available at www.civicventures.org/publications/articles/fact_sheet_on_older_americans.cfm.

Cloward, Richard, and Lloyd Ohlin. 1960. *Delinquency and Opportunity.* New York: Free Press.

CNN Politics. 2008. "Obama Speech: 'Yes, We Can Change.'" January 26. Available at http://articles.cnn.com/2008-01-26/politics/obama.transcript_1_change-time-iowa?_s=PM:POLITICS.

CNN.com. 2004. "Oregon County Bars All Marriage." March 23. Available at http://us.cnn.com/2004/US/West/03/23/marriage.ban.reut/index.html.

———. 2010a. "Single? You're Not Alone." August 19. Available at http://articles.cnn.com/2010-08-19/living/single.in.america_1_single-fathers-single-mothers-single-parents?_s=PM:LIVING.

———. 2010b. "Twitter Now Getting More Traffic Than MySpace." September 22. Available at http://current.com/technology/92694096_twitter-now-getting-more-traffic-than-myspace.htm.

———. 2011. "OMG! Oxford English Dictionary Adds New Words." Available at http://articles.cnn.com/2011-03-25/living/oxford.new.words_1_new-words-oxford-english-dictionary-usage?_s=PM:LIVING.

CNNMoney.com. 2010. "Women CEOs." May 3. Available at http://money.cnn.com/magazines/fortune/fortune500/2010/womenceos.

CNSNews.com. 2009. "Madonna Booed in Bucharest for Defending Gypsies." August 27. Available at www.cnsnews.com/news/article/53160.

Cockerham, William. 1995. *The Global Society*. New York: McGraw-Hill.

Cohen, Bernard P. 1989. *Developing Sociological Knowledge*. Chicago: Nelson-Hall.

Cohen, Daniel. 2006. *Globalization and Its Enemies,* translated by Jessica B. Baker. Cambridge, MA: MIT Press.

Cohen, Patricia. 2010. "Professions? Study Explores Why Professors and Bartenders Lean Left and Cops and Doctors Lean Right." *New York Times* (as it appeared in the *Post-Standard*), January 24, p. E1.

Columbia Presbyterian Medical Center. 2010. "The Nuts and Bolts of Bone Marrow Transplants." Available at http://cumc.columbia.edu/dept/medicine/bonemarrow/bmtinfo.html.

comScore. 2009. "Press Release: Americans View 34 Percent More Online Videos in November 2008 Compared to Year Ago." Available at www.marketingcharts.com/television/middle-agers-help-hulu-grow-490-9125/nielsen-top-three-sites-video-viewing-ages-35-49-april-2009jpg.

Cooley, Charles. 1902. *Human Nature and the Social Order*. New York: Scribner.

———. 1909. *Social Organization*. New York: Scribner.

Cooper, Derrick. 1991. "On the Concept of Alienation." *International Journal of Contemporary Sociology* 28: 7–26.

Coser, Lewis. 1956. *The Functions of Social Conflict*. New York: Free Press.

———. 1977. *Masters of Sociological Thought*. 2nd ed. New York: Harcourt Brace Jovanovich.

Cressey, Donald. 1969. *Theft of the Nation*. New York: Harper & Row.

Creswell, John W. 1994. *Research Design: Qualitative and Quantitative Approaches*. Thousand Oaks, CA: Sage.

Crothers, Lane. 2007. *Globalization and American Popular Culture*. Lanham, MD: Rowan & Littlefield.

CTV News. 2010. "Second-Hand Smoke Kills 600,000 Every Year: WHO." November 26. Available at www.ctv.ca/CTVNews/Health/20101126/secondhand-smoke-lancet-101126.

Cullen, Lisa Takeuchi. 2007. "Till Work Do Us Part." *Time,* September 27. Available at www.time.com/time/priority/o,8816,1666269,00.html.

Curran, Daniel J., and Claire M. Renzetti. 1994. *Theories of Crime*. Boston: Allyn and Bacon.

Curtiss, Susan. 1977. *Genie: A Psycholinguistic Study of a Modern-Day "Wild Child."* Boston: Academic Press.

Cuzzort, R. P., and Edith W. King. 1995. *Twentieth-Century Social Thought*. 5th ed. Fort Worth, TX: Harcourt Brace.

Daly, Martin, and Margo I. Wilson. 2000. "The Evolutionary Psychology of Marriage and Divorce." Pp. 91–110 in *The Ties That Bind: Perspectives on Marriage and Cohabitation,* edited by Linda J. Waite. New York: Aldine de Gruyter.

Davenport, Christian, and Emma Brown. 2009. "Girding for an Uphill Battle for Recruits." *Washington Post,* November 5. Available at www.washingtonpost.com/wp-dyn/content/article/2009/11/04/AR2009110402899.html.

Davidson, Shannon, Jennifer Bunnell, and Fei Yan. 2008. "Gender Imbalance in China." Stanford University: Asia Health Policy Program. Available at http://asiahealthpolicy.stanford.edu/news/gender_imbalance_in_china_20081027.

Davis, Pete Pathfinder. 2007. "Wiccan VA Headstone Pentacle Settlement." April 22. Available at www.witchvox.com/va/dt_va.html?a=uswa&c=military&id=11738.

Davis-Delano, Laurel R. 2009. "The Problems with Native American Mascots." Pp. 118–125 in *Sport in Contemporary Society,* edited by D. Stanley Eitzen. Boulder, CO: Paradigm.

Davis-Kimball, Jeannine. 2002. *Warrior Women.* New York: Warner Books.

de Vries, Brian. 2007. "LGBT Couples in Later Life: A Study in Diversity." *Generations* (fall): 18–23.

Deil-Amen, Regina. 2006. "To Teach or Not to Teach 'Social' Skills: Comparing Community Colleges and Private Occupational Colleges." *Teachers College Record* 108(3): 397–421.

Delaney, Tim. 2001. *Community, Sport, and Leisure.* 2nd ed. Auburn, NY: Legend Books.

———. 2002. "Ethical Issues in Social Research." Pp. 281–314 in *Values, Society, and Evolution,* edited by H. James Birx and Tim Delaney. Auburn, NY: Legend Books.

———. 2004. *Classical Social Theory: Investigation and Application.* Upper Saddle River, NJ: Pearson/Prentice Hall.

———. 2005. *Contemporary Social Theory: Investigation and Application.* Upper Saddle River, NJ: Pearson/Prentice Hall.

———. 2006a. *American Street Gangs.* Upper Saddle River, NJ: Pearson.

———. 2006b. *Seinology: The Sociology of Seinfeld.* Amherst, NY: Prometheus Books.

———. 2007. "Popular Culture: An Overview." *Philosophy Now* (November–December): 6–7.

———. 2008a. *Shameful Behaviors.* Lanham, MD: University Press of America.

———. 2008b. *Simpsonology: There's a Little Bit of Springfield in All of Us!* Amherst, NY: Prometheus.

Delaney, Tim, and Tim Madigan. 2009a. *The Sociology of Sports: An Introduction.* Jefferson, NC: McFarland.

———. 2009b. *Sports: Why People Love Them!* Lanham, MD: University Press of America.

Delaney, Tim, and Allene Wilcox. 2002. "Sports and the Role of the Media." Pp. 199–215 in *Values, Society, and Evolution,* edited by Harry Birx and Tim Delaney. Auburn, NY: Legend Books.

DeNavas-Walt, Carmen, Bernadette D. Proctor, and Cheryl Hill Lee. 2006. *Income, Poverty, and Health Insurance Coverage in the United States in 2005.* Washington, DC: U.S. Department of Commerce.

Department of Human Services. 2010. "Death with Dignity Act: FAQs About the Death with Dignity Act." Available at www.oregon.gov/DHS/ph/pas/faqs.shtml#insurance.

Deutscher, Guy. 2010. "Does Your Language Shape How You Think?" *New York Times,* August 29. Available at www.nytimes.com/2010/08/29/magazine/29language-t.html?scp=1&sq=%93Does%20Your%20Language%20Shape%20How%20You%20Think?%94&st=cse.

Diener, Edward, and Martin E. P. Seligman. 2002. "Very Happy People." *Psychological Science* 13: 81–84.

District Six Museum. 2003. "Recalling District Six." Available at www.southafrica.info/about/history/districtsix.htm.

Dixon, Robyn. 2004. "Rejecting a Ritual of Pain." *Los Angeles Times,* July 3, pp. A1, A12, A13.

Dobbin, Frank, Alexandra Kalev, and Erin Kelly. 2007. "Diversity Management in Corporate America." *Contexts* 6(4): 21–27.

Doctors Without Borders. 2010. "Homepage: About Us." Available at www.doctorswithoutborders.org/aboutus.

Dodds, Paisley. 2011. "By Jove! I Think She's Got It." *Post-Standard,* April 3, p. A13.

Dollard, John, Neal E. Miller, Leonard W. Doob, O. H. Mowrer, and Robert R. Sears. 1939. *Frustration and Aggression.* New Haven, CT: Yale University Press.

Domhoff, G. William. 2010. "Power in America: Wealth, Income and Power." Department of Sociology, University of California, Santa Cruz. Available at http://sociology.ucsc.edu/whorulesamerica/power/wealth.html.

Doob, Christopher Bates. 1999. *Racism: An American Cauldron.* New York: Longman.

Doran, Elizabeth. 2008. "LaFayette Unveils a New Kind of School." *Post-Standard,* August 13, pp. A1, A6.

Dorell, Oren. 2006. "Lottery Winners' Good Luck Can Go Bad Fast." *USA Today,* February 26. Available at www.usatoday.com/news/nation/2006-02-26-lotteryluck_x.htm.

Dorfman, Joseph. [1934] 1961. *Thorstein Veblen and His America.* New York: Viking.

Doyle, Charles. 2002. "CRS Report for Congress: The USA PATRIOT Act, a Sketch." Order Code RS21201. Federation of American Scientists, April 18. Available at www.fas.org/irp/crs/RS21203.pdf.

Drake, Bruce. 2010. "Tea Party Not a 'Racist Organization,' Biden Says." Politics Daily, July 18. Available at www.politicsdaily.com/2010/07/18/tea-party-not-a-racist-organization-biden-says.

Du Bois, W. E. B. 1903. *The Souls of Black Folk.* Chicago: A. C. McClurg & Co.

———. [1903] 2007. "The Souls of Black Folk." Pp. 54–58 in *Classical Readings in Society,* edited by Eve L. Howard. Belmont, CA: Wadsworth.

Dugger, Celia W. 2007. "World Bank Neglects African Farming, Study Says." *New York Times,* October 15. Available at www.nytimes.com/2007/10/15/world/africa/15worldbank.html.

Durkheim, Emile. [1895] 1951. *Suicide.* New York: Free Press.

———. [1914] 1973. "The Dualism of Human Nature and Its Social Condition." Pp. 149–163 in *Emile Durkheim: On Morality and Society,* edited by K. Bellah. Chicago: University of Chicago Press.

———. 1915. *The Elementary Forms of the Religious Life.* London: Allen & Unwin.

Dwyer, Devin, and Huma Khan. 2011. "'I Don't Hide': Wisconsin Gov. Defends Comments on Prank Phone Call." ABC News, February 23. Available at http://abcnews.go.com/Politics/gov-scott-walker-pranked-reporter-posing-david-koch/story?id=12980381.

Eckholm, Erik. 2009. "Last Year's Poverty Rate Was Highest in 12 Years." *New York Times,* September 11. Available at www.nytimes.com/2009/09/11/us/11poverty.html.

Economist, The. 2008. "Briefing Religious Conversions: The Moment of Truth." July 26, pp. 29–31.

Eitzen, D. Stanley. 1999. *Fair and Foul: Beyond the Myths and Paradoxes of Sport.* New York: Rowan & Littlefield.

Eitzen, D. Stanley, and George H. Sage. 1989. *Sociology of North American Sport.* 4th ed. Dubuque, IA: William C. Brown.

Elkind, David. 2001. *The Hurried Child: Growing Up Too Fast Too Soon.* 3rd ed. Cambridge, MA: Perseus.

Elkins, Edward. 2010. "Legally Blonde—Law School in Pink." *Orlando Law School Examiner,* August 23. Available at www.examiner.com/law-school-in-orlando/legally-blonde-law-school-pink.

Emeigh, John Grant. 2010. "Suicide: Montana Crying for Help." *Montana Standard,* February 1. Available at www.mtstandard.com/news/local/article_d8c9808b-5159-5717-a685-c443601192f5.html.

Encyclopedia.com. 2011. "Military-Industrial Complex." Available at www.encyclopedia.com/topic/Military-Industrial_Complex.aspx.

Engerman, Stanley L., and Kenneth L. Sokoloff. 2006. "The Persistence of Poverty in the Americas: The Role of Institutions." Pp. 43–78 in *Poverty Traps,* edited by Samuel Bowles, Steven N. Durlauf, and Karla Hoff. Princeton, NJ: Princeton University Press.

Ernst, Moritz Manasse. 1947. "Max Weber on Race." *Social Research* 14: 191–221.

ESPN. 2007. "Greatest U.S. Women's Sports Moments." ESPN. Available at http://espn.go.com/page2/s/list/movements/uswomen.html.

Essoyan, Susan. 2008. "The Private." *Honolulu Star-Bulletin,* January 13, p. A4.

Facebook. 2010. "Press Release: Statistics." Available at www.facebook.com/press/info.php?statistics.

Fackler, Martin. 2008. "Internet Addicts Get Help." *Honolulu Star-Bulletin,* January 13, p. A9.

———. 2010. "Japan, Checking on Its Oldest, Finds Many Gone." *New York Times,* August 14. Available at www.nytimes.com/2010/08/15/world/asia/15japan.html?_r=1.\

Family Guy. 2002. "Road to Europe." First aired February 7.

———. 2007. "Peter's Daughter." First aired November 25.

Fanhouse. 2009. "Semenya's Gender Tests Results Are In." Available at www.fanhouse.com/news/main/caster-semenya-gender-test-results/666103?icid=main|main|dl1|link4|http%3A%2F%2Fwww.fanhouse.com%2Fnews%2Fmain%2Fcaster-semenya-gender-test-results%2F666103.

Fantasy Sports Ventures. 2009. "Homepage." Available at www.fantasysportsventures.com.

Farran, D. C., and R. Haskins. 1980. "Reciprocal Influence in the Social Interactions of Mothers and Three-Year-Old Children from Different Socioeconomic Backgrounds." *Child Development* 51: 780–791.

Feagin, Joe R., and Clairece Booher Feagin. 2004. "Theoretical Perspectives in Race and Ethnic Relations." Pp. 18–34 in *Rethinking the Color Line,* edited by Charles A. Gallagher. 2nd ed. Boston: McGraw-Hill.

Feagin, Joe, and Hernan Vera. 2001. *Liberation Sociology.* Cambridge, MA: Westview.

Federal Bureau of Investigation. 2004. "Hate Crimes." Available at www.fbi.gov/ucr/cius_04/offenses-reported/hate_crime/index.html.

———. 2006. "Financial Crimes Report to the Public Fiscal Year 2006." Available at www.fbi.gov/publications/financial/fcs_report2006/financial_crime_2006.htm.

———. 2007. "Hate Crime Statistics." Available at www.fbi.gov/ucr/hc2007.htm.

———. 2008a. "Incidents and Offenses: Hate Crime Statistics, 2007." Available at www.fbi.gov/ucr/hc2007.

———. 2008b. "Wanted: By the FBI." Available at www.fbi.gov/wanted/fugitives/vc/murders/said_y.htm.

———. 2009. "Preliminary Annual Uniform Crime Report, 2009." Available at www.fbi.gov/ucr/2009prelimsem/index.html.

Federal Trade Commission. 2009. "Complying with the Made in the USA Standard." Available at www.ftc.gov/bcp/edu/pubs/business/adv/bus03.shtm.

Ferran, Lee. 2009. "Octomom: 'I Screwed My Life Up.'" ABC News, June 5. Available at http://abcnews.go.com/GMA/story?id=7762688&page=1.

Feuer, Alan. 2008. "Judge Says Use of MySpace May Violate a Court Order." *New York Times,* February 14. Available at www.news.com.

Fields, Suzanne. 2009. "Goal: Break Glass Ceiling or Get Glass Slipper?" (as it appeared in the *Post-Standard*), June 22, p. A12.

Finckenauer, James. 2002. "Crime and Criminals." Pp. 1426–1429 in *Encyclopedia of Crime and Punishment,* edited by David Levinson. Vol. 3. Thousand Oaks, CA: Sage.

Flavel, John, Patricia H. Miller, and Scott A. Miller. 2002. *Cognitive Development.* 4th ed. Upper Saddle River, NJ: Prentice Hall.

Flick, Uwe, Ernst von Kardorff, and Ines Steinke. 2004. *A Companion to Qualitative Research.* Thousand Oaks, CA: Sage.

Forbes.com. 2009. "The World's Billionaires: #1 William Gates III." Available at www.forbes.com/lists/2009/10/billionaires-2009-richest-people_William-Gates-III_BH69.html.

Foster, Brooke Lea, J. Scott Orr, and Laura Laing. 2009. "The Mentally Ill in Prison." *Parade,* June 28, p. 6.

Foster, Gwendolyn Audrey. 2005. *Class-Passing: Social Mobility in Film and Popular Culture.* Carbondale, IL: Southern Illinois University Press.

Frankel, Martin. 1983. "Sampling Theory." Pp. 21–67 in *Handbook of Survey Research,* edited by Peter H. Rossi, James D. Wright, and Andy B. Anderson. New York: Harcourt Brace Jovanovich.

Frankenberg, Erica, Chungmei Lee, and Gary Orfield. 2003. "A Multiracial Society with Segregated Schools: Are We Losing the Dream?" Civil Rights Project, University of California, Los Angeles. Available at http://civilrightsproject.ucla.edu/research/k-12-education/integration-and-diversity/a-multiracial-society-with-segregated-schools-are-we-losing-the-dream.

Freking, Kevin. 2006. "31 States Show a Rise in Obesity Among Adults." *Post-Standard,* August 30, p. A4.

———. 2008a. "Health Care Costs to Hit $4.3 Trillion by 2017." *Post-Standard,* February 26, p. A3.

———. 2008b. "Whistle-Blowers Lead to US Recouping $9.3B." *Post-Standard,* September 2, p. D7.

Frey, James H. 1989. *Survey Research by Telephone.* 2nd ed. Newbury Park, CA: Sage.

Frieden, Jeffry A. 2006. *Global Capitalism: Its Fall and Rise in the Twentieth Century.* New York: Norton.

Friedman, Milton. 1962. *Capitalism and Freedom.* Chicago: University of Chicago Press.

Frost, Greg. 2006. "Extra Credit." *Boston College Chronicle* 14(14) (March 30). Available at www.bc.edu/bc_org/rvp/pubaf/chronicle/v14/mr30/extracredit.html.

Fulwood, Sam, III. 1998. "Nationwide Ordered to Pay $100 Million in Federal Suit over Racial Redlining." *Buffalo News,* October 28, p. A8.

Gallagher, Charles A. 2009. "Color-Blind Privilege: The Social and Political Functions of Erasing the Color Line in Post Race America." Pp. 90–94 in *Race and Ethnicity in Society,* edited by Elizabeth Higginbotham and Margaret L. Andersen. 2nd ed. Belmont, CA: Wadsworth/Cengage.

Gandossy, Taylor. 2009. "TV Viewing at 'All-Time High,' Nielsen Says." CNN Entertainment, February 24. Available at http://articles.cnn.com/2009-02-24/entertainment/us.video.nielsen_1_nielsen-company-nielsen-spokesman-gary-holmes-watching?_s=PM:SHOWBIZ.

Ganong, Lawrence, and Marilyn Coleman. 2004. *Stepfamily Relationships: Development, Dynamics and Interventions.* New York: Kluwer Academic/Plenum.

Garber, Jeffrey. 2010. "Make Experience Count When Searching for Work." *Post-Standard,* February 1, p. 3.

Garner, Roberta, ed. 2000. *Social Theory.* Orchard Park, NY: Broadview.

Gaynor, Tim. 2010. "U.S. Puts Brakes on 'Virtual' Border Fence." Reuters (Phoenix), March 16. Available at www.reuters.com/article/idUSTRE62F61T20100316.

Gerson, Michael. 2010. "Some Small Signs of Sanity." *Post-Standard,* July 22, p. A14.

Gerstenfeld, Phyllis B. 2004. *Hate Crimes: Causes, Controls, and Controversies.* Thousand Oaks, CA: Sage.

Gettleman, Jeffrey. 2010. "Kenyan Police Disperse Gay Wedding." *New York Times,* February 13. Available at www.nytimes.com/2010/02/13/world/africa/13kenya.html.

Gilbert, James. 2005. *Men in the Middle: Searching for Masculinity in the 1950s.* Chicago: University of Chicago Press.

Gillies, Rob. 2011. "A Genderless Baby." *Post-Standard,* May 28, p. A9.

Ginsberg, Thomas. 2003. "Latinos Surge Past Blacks." *Buffalo News,* January 22, p. A1.

Givhan, Robin. 2006. "Skirting: The Issue." *Post-Standard* (originally appeared in the *Washington Post*), February 3, p. E2.

Glock, Charles, and Rodney Stark. 1965. *Religion and Society in Tension.* Chicago: Rand McNally.

Glyn, Andrew. 2006. *Capitalism Unleashed: Finance Globalization and Welfare.* New York: Oxford University Press.

Godbout, Todd M. 1993. "Employment Change and Sectoral Distribution in 10 Countries, 1970–90." *Monthly Labor Review* (October): 3–20.

Godwyll, Francis Ebenezer, and Collins Annin. 2007. "Perpetuation of Racism and Sexism in the US: Subtle Reinforcement by Popular Culture." *International Journal of Diversity* 6(4): 41–49. [see http://ijd.cgpublisher.com/product/pub.29/prod.381]

Goffman, Erving. 1959. *Presentation of Self and Everyday Life.* Garden City, NY: Anchor.

———. 1963. *Stigma: Notes on Management of Spoiled Identity.* Englewood Cliffs, NJ: Prentice Hall.

Goffman, Ken. 2004. *Counterculture Through the Ages.* New York: Villard.

Gongloff, Mark. 2002. "Bush Seeks New Business Ethic." CNNMoney.com. Available at http://money.cnn.com/2002/07/09/news/bush/index.htm.

Gonzalez, Alejandro. 2009. "USA Today Gallup Poll: Heading to the ER: A Familiar Trip for Many." *USA Today,* September 9, p. 2D.

Good Morning America. 2009. "The Dangers of Winning the Lottery." September 2. Available at www.suite101.com/content/the-dangers-of-winning-the-lottery-a144771.

Goode, Erich. 2001. *Deviant Behavior.* 6th ed. Upper Saddle River, NJ: Prentice Hall.

Goodnough, Abby. 2009a. "911 Tape Raises Questions in Gates Case." *New York Times,* July 28. Available at www.nytimes.com/2009/07/28/us/28gates.html?scp=6&sq=Henry+Louis+Gates&st=nyt.

———. 2009b. "Harvard Professor Jailed; Officer Is Accused of Bias." *New York Times,* July 21. Available at www.nytimes.com/2009/07/21/us/21gates.html?ref=henry_louis_jr_gates.

Gottfredson, Michael R., and Travis Hirschi. 2003. "Crime and Low Self-Control." Pp. 57–64 in *Current Controversies in Criminology,* edited by Ronald Weitzer. Upper Saddle River, NJ: Prentice Hall.

Graber, Doris A., ed. 2000. *Media Power in Politics.* 4th ed. Washington, DC: CQ Press.

Graham, Jefferson. 2008. "YouTube Expands Its Horizons, and Its Time Limits for Videos." *USA Today,* October 24, p. 12B.

Green, Adam Isaiah. 2006. "Until Death Do Us Part? The Impact of Differential Access to Marriage on a Sample of Urban Men." *Sociological Perspectives* 49(2): 163–189.

Greenberg, Elizabeth, Eric Dunleavy, and Mark Kutner. 2008. "Literacy Behind Bars: Results from the 2003 National Assessment of Adult Literacy Prison Survey Chapter 1: Introduction." *Journal for Vocational Special Needs Education* 30(2) (winter): 20–26.

Greendorfer, Susan L. 1993. "Gender Role Stereotypes and Early Childhood Socialization." Pp. 3–14 in *Women in Sport: Issues and Controversies,* edited by Greta L. Cohen. Newbury Park, CA: Sage.

Gross, Neil, and Ethan Fosse. 2010. "Why Are Professors Liberal?" (an as-of-yet-unpublished paper that was highly publicized in multiple media outlets). Available at www.soci.ubc.ca/fileadmin/template/main/images/departments/soci/faculty/gross/why_are_professors_liberal.pdf.

Grossman, Cathy Lynn. 2009. "Most Religious Groups in USA Have Lost Ground, Survey Finds." *USA Today,* March 9. Available at www.usatoday.com/news/religion/2009-03-09-american-religion-ARIS_N.htm.

Gubrium, Jaber F., and James A. Holstein. 1990. *What Is Family?* Toronto: Mayfield.

Guinness Book of World Records. 1997. Available at www.guinnessbookofworldrecords.

———. 2001. Available at www.guinnessbookofworldrecords.

———. 2005. Available at www.guinnessbooksofworldrecords.

Gunter, Barrie, Caroline Oates, and Mark Blades. 2005. *Advertising to Children on TV: Content, Impact, and Regulation.* Mahwah, NJ: Lawrence Erlbaum.

Gurevitch, Michael, and Jay G. Blumler. 2000. "Political Communication Systems and Democratic Values." Pp. 24–35 in *Media Power in Politics.* 4th ed. Washington, DC: CQ Press.

Gurko, Miriam. 1974. *The Ladies of Seneca Falls.* New York: Schocken Books.

Gurza, Agustin. 2000. "Spanking: An Idea Whose Time Has Gone." *Los Angeles Times,* March 21, p. B1.

Habitat for Humanity. 2010. "Homepage: About Habitat for Humanity." Available at www.habitat.org/cd/giving/lander/default.aspx?media=GooglePd&source_code=DHQOQ1107W1GGL&keyword=brand&tgs=OS83LzIwMTEgMTozMDo1OSBQTQ%3d%3d.

Hadden, Richard W. 1997. *Sociological Theory: An Introduction to the Classical Tradition.* Orchard Park, NY: Broadview.

Hale, Phil. 2008. "The Black KKK." *Playboy,* June, pp. 63–64, 122–128.

Hammersley, M., and R. Gomm. 1997. "Bias in Social Research." *Sociological Research Online* 2(1). Available at www.socreonline.org.uk/2/1/2.html.

Harlan, Lane, and Richard Pillard. 1976. *The Wild Boy of Aveyron.* Cambridge, MA: Harvard University Press.

Harms, William. 2007. "America's Individualist Culture Influences the Ability to View Others' Perspectives." *University of Chicago Chronicle* 26(9). Available at http://chronicle.uchicago.edu/070712/perspectives.shtml.

Harold, Christine. 2007. *Our Space.* Minneapolis: University of Minnesota Press.

Harris, Marvin. 2004. "How Our Skins Got Their Color." Pp. 7–9 in *Rethinking the Color Line: Readings in Race and Ethnicity,* edited by Charles A. Gallagher. 2nd ed. Boston: McGraw-Hill.

Harris, Scott Duke. 2010. "Study: Americans Spending More Time on Social Websites." *San Jose Mercury News* (as it appeared in the *Post-Standard*), August 3, p. A2.

Hart, Simon. 2009. "World Athletics: Caster Semenya Tests Show High Testosterone Levels." *Telegraph,* August 24. Available at www.telegraph.co.uk/sport/othersports/athletics/6078171/World-Athletics-Caster-Semenya-tests-show-high-testosterone-levels.html.

Henderson, Harry. 2001. *Terrorism.* New York: Facts on File.

Henriques, Diana B., and Jack Healy. 2009. "Madoff Goes to Jail After Guilty Pleas." *New York Times,* March 13. Available at www.nytimes.com/2009/03/13/business/13madoff.html?_r=1&ref=bernard_l_madoff.

Herbert, H. Josef. 2008. "1 Day at World's Beaches Nets 6m Pounds of Trash." *Post-Standard,* April 16, p. A4.

Hershey, Marjorie Randon. 2007. *Party Politics in America,* 12th ed. New York: Pearson/Longman.

Herszenhorn, David M., and Robert Pear. 2010. "Final Votes in Congress Cap Battle on Health Bill." *New York Times,* March 25. Available at www.nytimes.com/2010/03/26/health/policy/26health.html.

Hertz, Rosanna, and Nancy L. Marshall. 2001. *Working Families.* Berkeley, CA: University of California Press.

Higginbotham, Elizabeth, and Margaret L. Andersen, eds. 2009. *Race and Ethnicity.* 2nd ed. Belmont, CA: Wadsworth/Cengage.

Hirschi, Travis. 1969. *Causes of Delinquency.* Berkeley: University of California Press.

Hitwise US. 2008. "Top 20 Websites—January, 2008." Available at www.hitwise.com/datacenter/rankings.php.

Hofstede, Geert. 2001. *Culture's Consequences.* 2nd ed. Thousand Oaks, CA: Sage.

Hohmann-Marriott, Bryndl. 2006. "Shared Beliefs and the Union Stability of Married and Cohabitating Couples." *Journal of Marriage and Family* 68 (November): 1015–1028.

Holmes, Sarah E., and Sean Cahill. 2005. "School Experiences of Gay, Lesbian, Bisexual, and Transgendered Youth." Pp. 63–76 in *Gay, Lesbian, and Transgendered Issues in Education: Programs, Policies, and Practices,* edited by James T. Sears. New York: Harrington Park Press.

Holton, Robert J. 2005. *Making Globalization.* New York: Palgrave Macmillan.

Holy Bible: Authorized King James Version. 1989. Grand Rapids, MI: World Bible Publishers.

Homans, George. 1961. *Social Behavior: Its Elementary Forms.* New York: Harcourt, Brace & World.

Hoover, Kenneth R. 1976. *The Elements of Social Scientific Thinking.* New York: St. Martin's Press.

Hopcroft, Rosemary L. 2009. "The Evolved Actor in Sociology." *Sociological Theory* 27(4): 390–406.

Howe, Alyssa Cymene. 2004. "Queer Pilgrimage: The San Francisco Homeland and Identity Tourism." Pp. 248–264 in *Life in America,* edited by Lee D. Baker. Malden, MA: Blackwell.

Hsu, Spencer S. 2010. "Work to Cease on 'Virtual Fence' Along the U.S.-Mexico Border." *Washington Post,* March 16. Available at www.washingtonpost.com/wp-dyn/content/article/2010/03/16/AR2010031603573.html.

Hu, Winnie. 2010. "Legal Debate Swirls over Charges in a Student's Suicide." *New York Times,* October 1. Available at www.nytimes.com/2010/10/02/nyregion/02suicide.html?ref=newjersey.

Human Rights Watch. 2007. "Civilian Accounts: Attacks Targeting Civilians." Available at www.hrw.org/reports/2007/afghanistan0407/3.htm.

Hunter-Gault, Charlayne. 2006. "In Tanzania, Women See a Path Out of Poverty." National Public Radio, August 10. Available at www.npr.org/templates/story/story.php?story?Id=5632059.

ILO News. 1999. "Americans Work Longest Hours Among Industrialized Countries." World History Archives, September 6. Available at www.hartford-hwp.com/archives/26/077.html.

Institute for Research on Poverty. 2009. "How Many Children Are Poor?" Available at www.irp.wisc.edu/faqs/faq6.htm.

Institute for Supply Management (ISM). 2011. "February 2011 Non-Manufacturing ISM *Report on Business,*" March. Available at www.ism.ws/ISMReport/NonMfgROB.cfm.

Intelligence Report. 2008 (spring). Issue 129. Montgomery, AL: Southern Poverty Law Center.

International Labour Organization. 2010. "Forced Labour." Available at www.ilo.org/global/Themes/Forced_Labour/lang—en/index.htm.

International Monetary Fund (IMF). 2008a. "About the IMF." Available at www.imf.org/external/about.html.

———. 2008b. "What the IMF Does." Available at www.imf.org/external/work.html.

Irvine, Martha. 2009. "The Princess Syndrome." *Post-Standard,* July 23, p. C2.

———. 2010. "Stressed-Out Students." *Post-Standard,* January 14, p. C2.

Isaacson, Walter. 2009. "How to Raise the Standard in America's Schools." *Time,* April 27, pp. 32, 34–36.

Jackson, Derrick Z. 2006. "Diabetes, Obesity Greatest Foes." *Post-Standard,* October 4, p. A10.

James, Susan Donaldson. 2008. "Wild Child Speechless After Tortured Life." ABC News, May 7. Available at http://abcnews.go.com/Health/story?id=4804490&page=1.

Janis, Irving L. 1972. *Victims of Groupthink.* Boston: Houghton Mifflin.

———. 1982. *Groupthink: Psychological Studies of Policy Decisions and Fiascoes.* Boston: Houghton Mifflin.

Jewell, Mark. 2005. "Don't Ignore Genetics, Say Drug Researchers." *Post-Standard,* July 15, p. A3.

Joan Shorenstein Center on the Press, Politics, and Public Policy. 2007. "Young People and the News." Scribd, July. Available at www.scribd.com/doc/11033695/Young-People-and-News-2007.

John, D. R. 1999. "Consumer Socialization of Children: A Retrospective Look at Twenty-Five Years of Research." *Journal of Consumer Research* 26(3): 183–213.

Johns Hopkins Medicine. 2011. "Conventional Wisdom Unwise: Study Shows Young Black Patients on Kidney Dialysis Do Much Worse—Not Better—Than White Counterparts." Press release, August 9. Available at www.hopkinsmedicine.org/news/media/releases/conventional_wisdom_unwise_study_shows_young_black_patients_on_kidney_dialysis_do_much_worse___not_better___than_white_counterparts.

Johnson, Scott. 2009. "Alien Nation." Newsweek.com. Available at www.newsweek.com/id/213805.

Jones, James H. 1993. *Bad Blood: The Tuskegee Syphilis Experiment.* New York: Free Press.

Jubera, Drew, Stephanie Paterik, and Katherine Lewis. 2010. "Developed World Leads on Gay Rights." *Parade,* April 25, p. 12.

Juette, Melvin, and Ronald J. Berger. 2008. *Wheelchair Warrior: Gangs, Disability, and Basketball.* Philadelphia: Temple University Press.

Kahneman, Daniel, and Angus Deaton. 2010. "High Income Improves Evaluation of Life but Not Emotional Well-Being." *Proceedings of the National Academy of Sciences.* Available at www.pnas.org/content/early/2010/08/27/1011492107.full.pdf+html.

Kaiser Commission on Medicaid and the Uninsured. 2007. "Learning from History: Deinstitutionalization of People with Mental Illness as Precursor to Long-Term Care Reform." Kaiser Family Foundation, August. Available at www.kff.org/medicaid/upload/7684.pdf.

Kang, Cecilia. 2010. "Cellphone Cancer Study Inconclusive; Researcher Urges More Study." *Washington Post,* May 16. Available at http://voices.washingtonpost.com/posttech/2010/05/cell_phone_cancer_study_produc.html.

Kaplinsky, Raphael. 2005. *Globalization, Poverty, and Inequality: Between a Rock and a Hard Place.* Malden, MA: Polity Press.

Karen, David, and Kevin J. Dougherty. 2005. "Necessary but Not Sufficient: Higher Education as a Strategy of Social Mobility." Pp. 33–57 in *Higher Education and the Color Line: College Access, Racial Equity, and Social Change,* edited by Gary Orfield, Patricia Marin, and Catherine L. Horn. Cambridge, MA: Harvard University Press.

Karp, Harvey. 2004. *The Happiest Toddler on the Block.* New York: Bantam.

Katz, Elihu, and Paul Felix Lazarsfeld. 1955. *Personal Influence: The Part Played by People in the Flow of Mass Communications.* Glencoe, IL: Free Press.

Keefe, William J., and Marc J. Hetherington. 2003. *Parties, Politics, and Public Policy in America.* 9th ed. Washington, DC: CQ Press.

Kellner, Douglas. 2002. "Theorizing Globalization." *Sociological Theory* 20(3): 285–305.

Kelton Research and Support. 2008. "News & Information." Available at http://sev.prnewswire.com/computer-electronics.

Kerr, Alistair W., Howard K. Hall, and Stephen K. Kozub. 2002. *Doing Statistics with SPSS.* Thousand Oaks, CA: Sage.

Kerr, Jennifer C. 2005. "Growing Number Join Ranks of Poor." *Post-Standard,* August 31, p. A8.

Keveney, Bill. 2007. "'LOST' Philosophy: Something to Think About." *USA Today,* March 28, p. 7D.

Keyes, Cheryl. 2002. *Rap Music and Street Consciousness.* Urbana: University of Illinois Press.

Keys, Laurinda. 2001. "Mother Teresa's Writings Reveal Fear of Losing God." *Buffalo News,* September 15, p. A2.

King, C. Richard, and Charles Fruehling Springwood. 2001. *Team Spirits: The Native American Mascots Controversy.* Lincoln: University of Nebraska Press.

Kirkpatrick, Marshall. 2011. "There Are Now 155m Tweets Posted per Day, Triple the Number a Year Ago." ReadWriteWeb, April 6. Available at www.readwriteweb.com/archives/there_are_now_155m_tweets_posted_per_day_triple_th.php.

Kirschstein, Ruth. 2000. "Objectivity in Research." U.S. Department of Health and Human Services. Available at www.hhs.gov/ohrp/coi/kershstein.htm.

Knauss, Tim. 2008. "Drive to Innovation." *Post-Standard,* June 5, p. A1.

Koggel, Christine M. 2007. "Empowerment and the Role of Advocacy in a Globalized World." *Ethics and Social Welfare* 1(1): 8–21.

Kosmin, Barry A., Egon Mayer, and Ariela Keysar. 2001. *American Religious Identification Survey.* Graduate Center of the City University of New York. Available at www.gc.cuny.edu/facultyresearch_studies/aris.

Kought, Bruce, and Gordon Walker. 2001. "The Small World of Germany and the Durability of National Networks." *American Sociological Review* 66 (June): 317–335.

Kraft, Dina. 2000. "DNA Study Genetically Links Jews and Arabs: Research Backs Biblical Account of Abraham as Common Ancestor." *Buffalo News,* May 5, p. A10.

Kratcoski, Peter C., and Lucille Dunn Kratcoski. 1996. *Juvenile Delinquency.* 4th ed. Upper Saddle River, NJ: Prentice Hall.

Kristof, Nicholas D. 2011. "Bahrain Pulls a Qaddafi." *New York Times,* March 16. Available at http://search.aol.com/aol/search?enabled_terms=&s_it=comsearch50&q=Nicholas+D.+Kristof%2C+NY+Times%2C+Bahrain%27s+apartheid.

Kroll, Luisa. 2008. "World's Billionaires." Forbes.com, March 5. Available at www.forbes.com/2008/03/05/richest-people-billionaires-billionaires08-cx_lk_0305billie_land.html.

Krug, Gary. 2005. *Communication, Technology, and Cultural Change.* Thousand Oaks, CA: Sage.

La Ferla, Ruth. 2004. "Generation E. A.: Ethnically Ambiguous." *Post-Standard,* January 5, p. D1.

Lacy, Sarah. 2009. "Is Twitter Pimping Porn to Family Users?" *Businessweek,* September 1. Available at www.businessweek.com/technology/content/sep2009/tc2009091_567323.htm?chan=technology_technology+index+page_top+stories.

Lakshmanan, Indira A. R. 2006. "A Living Tree Emits Oxygen. A Dead One Emits Carbon Dioxide." *Boston Globe,* December 6, p. A9.

Landouceur, Robert, Jean-Marie Boisvert, Michel Pepin, Michael Lorranger, and Caroline Sylvain. 1994. "Social Cost of Pathological Gambling." *Journal of Gambling Studies* 10(4): 399–409.

LaPiere, Richard T. 1994. "Attitude vs. Actions and the Pitfalls of Quantitative, 'Survey' Research." Pp. 49–56 in *Empirical Approaches to Sociology,* edited by Gregg Lee Carter. New York: Macmillan.

Lastowka, Greg. 2010. *Virtual Justice: The New Laws of Online Worlds.* New Haven, CT: Yale University Press.

Lauer, Robert H., and Jeannette C. Lauer. 1997. *Marriage and Family: The Quest for Intimacy.* 3rd ed. Boston: McGraw-Hill.

Lavoie, Denise. 2008. "Obama Related to Pitt, Clinton to Jolie." AOL News. Available at http://news.aol.com/elections/story/_a/obama-related-to-pitt-clinton-to-jolie/20080325.html.

Leblanc, Steve. 2009. "Is a Doctor In?" *Post-Standard,* September 14, p. A9.

Lee, Alfred McClung. 1978. *Sociology for Whom?* New York: Oxford.

Leiss, William, Stephen Kline, and Sut Jhally. 1986. *Social Communication in Advertising.* New York: Methuen.

LeMay, Michael C. 2005. *The Perennial Struggle: Race, Ethnicity and Minority Group Relations in the United States.* Upper Saddle River, NJ: Pearson/Prentice Hall.

Lemert, Edwin M. 1951. *Social Pathology.* New York: McGraw-Hill.

Lengermann, Patricia Madoo, and Jill Niebrugge-Brantley. 1998. *The Women Founders.* Boston: McGraw-Hill.

———. 2000. "Early Women Sociologists and Classical Sociological Theory: 1830–1930." Pp. 289–321 in *Classical Sociological Theory,* by George Ritzer. Boston: McGraw-Hill.

Leonard, Wilbert M., II. 1988. *A Sociological Perspective of Sport.* New York: Macmillan.

Lesieur, Henry. 1998. "Costs and Treatment of Pathological Gambling." Pp. 153–171 in *The Annals,* edited by James H. Frey. Thousand Oaks, CA: Sage.

Levine, Michael. 1988. "The Trash Mess Won't Be Easily Disposed of." *Wall Street Journal,* December 15, p. 14.

Levi-Strauss, Claude. 1962. *The Savage Mind.* Chicago: University of Chicago Press.

Liegeois, Jean-Pierre, and Nicolae Gheorghe. 1995. *Roma/Gypsies: A European Minority.* MRG International Report 95/4. London: Minority Rights Group International. Available at www.unhcr.org/refworld/pdfid/469cbfd70.pdf.

Lindersmith, Alfred R., Anselm L. Strauss, and Norman K. Denzin. 1991. *Social Psychology.* 7th ed. Englewood Cliffs, NJ: Prentice Hall.

Lindsay, Alexander. 1943. *Religion, Science, and Society in the Modern World.* New Haven, CT: Yale University Press.

Lipschutz, Ronnie. 2005. "Networks of Knowledge and Practice: Global Civil Society and Global Communications." Pp. 17–33 in *Global Activism, Global Media,* edited by Wilma de Jong, Martin Shaw, and Neil Stammers. Ann Arbor, MI: Pluto Press.

Litke, Jim. 2009. "Another Story That Sounds Too Good to Be True?" *The Citizen,* August 21, p. B3.

Livingstone, Sonia. 2002. *Young People and New Media: Childhood and the Changing Media Environment.* Thousand Oaks, CA: Sage.

Locke, John. [1689] 1991. *Letter Concerning Toleration.* London: Routledge.
Longman, Jere. 2009. "South African Runner's Sex-Verification Result Won't Be Public." *New York Times,* November 20. Available at www.nytimes.com/2009/11/20/sports/20runner.html.
Lopez, Kathryn Jean. 2010. "Hey, Critics, Bunning Did the Right Thing." *The Citizen,* March 11, p. A1.
Los Angeles Times. 2008. "Beliefs: Religious Views and Practices in America." June 28, p. B2.
———. 2010. "Semenya Cleared to Compete as a Woman." July 7, p. C6.
LOST. 2004. "Tabula Rasa." First aired October 6.
Loy, John, and Alan Ingham. 1981. "Play, Games, and Sport in the Psychological Development of Children and Youth." Pp. 189–216 in *Sport, Culture and Society,* edited by John Loy, Gerald Kenyon, and Barry McPherson. Philadelphia: Lea & Febiger.
Luo, Y., and R. Baillargeon. 2005. "When the Ordinary Seems Unexpected: Evidence for Incremental Physical Knowledge in Young Infants." *Cognition* 95: 297–328.
MacDonald, Laura M. 2007. "America's Toe-Tapping Menace." *New York Times,* September 2. Available at www.nytimes.com/2007/09/02.
MacDowall, Luke. 2010. "The Washington Redskins, the Laches Doctrine and Secondary Meaning: Why Time Doesn't Heal All Wounds." *Wake Forest Intellectual Property Law Journal,* March 16. Available at http://ipjournal.law.wfu.edu/2010/03/16/the-washington-redskins-the-laches-doctrine-and-secondary-meaning-why-time-doesn%E2%80%99t-heal-all-wounds.
Macionis, John J. 2010. *Social Problems.* 4th ed. Boston: Prentice Hall/Pearson.
Maddison, Stephen. 2000. *Fags, Hags, and Queer Sisters: Gender Dissent and Heterosocial Bonds in Gay Culture.* New York: St. Martin's Press.
Malthus, Thomas. 1798. *An Essay on the Principle of Population.* London: J. Johnson.
Manson, Neil A. 2003. "Introduction." Pp. 1–23 in *God and Design,* edited by Neil A. Manson. New York: Routledge.
Maps of World. 2008. "Top Ten Poorest Countries." Available at www.mapsofworld.com/world-top-ten/world-top-ten-poorest-countries-map.html.
Marger, Martin N. 2006. *Race and Ethnic Relations: American and Global Perspectives.* 7th ed. Belmont, CA: Thomson/Wadsworth.
Marks, James S. 2002. "Chronic Illness." Healthline. Available at www.healthline.com/galecontent/chronic-illness.
Marsico, Katie. 2010. *The Trail of Tears: The Tragedy of the American Indians.* Tarrytown, NY: Marshall Cavendish Benchmark.
Martineau, Harriet. 1836–1837. *Society in America,* 2 vols. London: Charles Knight and Company.
Marx, Karl, and Friedrich Engels. [1845–1846] 1970. *The German Ideology,* Part I, edited by C. J. Arthur. New York: International Publishers.
———. 1978. *The Marx-Engels Reader,* edited by Robert C. Tucker. 2nd ed. New York: W. W. Norton.
Maslow, Abraham. 1954. *Motivation and Personality.* New York: Harper & Row.
Masnick, Mike. 2010. "Court Reduces Award in Jammie Thomas-Rasset Case from $80,000 per Song to $2,250." Available at www.techdirt.com/articles/20100122/1010047873.shtml.
Masten, Ann S., and Abigail H. Gewirtz. 2006. "Resilience in Development: The Importance of Early Childhood." Encyclopedia on Early Childhood Development, March 15. Available at www.child-encyclopedia.com/documents/Masten-Gewirtz ANGxp.pdf.
Maynard, Rebecca A., and Thomas Corbett. 2003. "Where We Go from Here." Pp.

303–320 in *Policy into Action,* edited by Mary Claire Lennon and Thomas Corbett. Washington, DC: Urban Institute Press.

McCool, Grant, and Martha Graybow. 2009. "Madoff Gets 150 Years for Massive Investment Fraud." Reuters, June 29. Available at www.reuters.com/article/2009/06/29/us-madoff-idUSTRE55P6O520090629.

McCracken, Grant. 1990. *Culture and Consumption.* Bloomington: Indiana University Press.

McCutcheon, Chuck. 2006. "Feeling the Strain." *Post-Standard,* September 18, p. D2.

McFarland, Melanie. 2004. "Young People Turning Comedy Shows into Serious News Source." *Seattle Post-Intelligencer,* January 22. Available at www.seattlepi.com/tv/157538_tv22.html.

McLellan, David. 1987. *Marxism and Religion.* New York: Harper & Row.

McPherson, Miller, Lynn Smith-Lovin, and Matthew E. Brashears. 2006. "Social Isolation America: Changes in Core Discussion Networks over Two Decades." *American Sociological Review* 71(3) (June): 353–376.

Mead, George Herbert. 1934. *Mind, Self, and Society,* edited and with introduction by Charles W. Morris. Chicago: University of Chicago Press.

Meckler, Laura. 2002. "Marriage Study Reveals Divorce-Related Factors." *Post-Standard,* July 25, p. A1.

Medicine Plus. 2009a. "Androgen Insensitivity Syndrome." Available at https://www.google.com/health/ref/Androgen+insensitivity+syndrome.

———. 2009b. "Klinefelter's Syndrome." Available at www.nlm.nih.gov/medlineplus/klinefelterssyndrome.html.

Meekand, James Gordon, and Jose Martinez. 2009. "Photo Shows Tareq and Michaele Salahi Getting Face Time with President Obama." *Daily News,* November 27. Available at www.nydailynews.com/news/politics/2009/11/27/2009-11-27.

Menzel, Peter. 1995. *Material World: A Global Family Portrait.* San Francisco: Sierra Club Books.

Merton, Robert. 1938. "Social Structure and Anomie." *American Sociological Review* 3: 672–682.

———. [1949] 1968. *Social Theory and Social Structure.* New York: Free Press.

Meyer, John M., ed. 2002. *American Indians and U.S. Politics: A Companion Reader.* Westport, CT: Praeger.

Meyersohn, Jon, and Cynthia McFadden. 2007. "Grandparents Being Parents." ABC News, February 27. Available at http://abcnews.go.com/Primetime/story?id=2904559&page=1.

Michelmore, Bill. 2000. "Cataracts Big Suicide Lure." *Buffalo News,* May 1, p. A1.

Miller, Chaz. 2004. "Food Waste." *Waste Age,* March 1. Available at http://wasteage.com/mag/waste_food_waste_2.

Mills, C. Wright. 1956. *The Power Elite.* New York: Oxford University Press.

———. 1959. *The Sociological Imagination.* New York: Oxford University Press.

Missoulian (Missoula, Montana). 2010. "Race Complicates Reservation Crime Fight." September 6. Available at http://missoulian.com/news/state-and-regional/article_93264637-753a-58e5-a83d-d8cd25ee0160.html.

Mohr, Fred A. 2003a. "Indian Costume Caper Nets Charge." *Post-Standard,* November 20, p. B1.

———. 2003b. "Intruder Targets College Teacher." *Post-Standard,* November 9, p. B1.

Moore, Frazier. 2010. "Study: MTV Leads in Showing Gay Characters." *Post-Standard,* July 24, p. C4.

Moore, Joan. 1991. *Going Down to the Barrio.* Philadelphia: Temple University Press.

Moore, Joan, and John Hagedorn. 2001. "Female Gangs: A Focus on Research." *OJJDP Juvenile Justice Bulletin.* Washington, DC: U.S. Department of Justice.

Moos, Bob. 2008. "Wii Bowling Rolls a Strike with Seniors." *The Post-Standard,* January 4, p. A2.

Morse, Jennifer Roback. 2006. "Why Unilateral Divorce Has No Place in a Free Society." Pp. 74–99 in *The Meaning of Marriage,* edited by Robert P. George and Jean Bethke Elshtain. Dallas: Spence.

Moses, Sarah. 2010. "Donor Dilemma: She's Multiracial." *Post-Standard,* January 6, p. A5.

———. 2011. "Superintendents Resist Pay Cap." *Post-Standard,* March 15, pp. A1, A6.

MSNBC. 2004. "'Virgin Mary Grilled Cheese' Sells for $28,000." November 23. Available at www.msnbc.msn.com/id/6511148/#.

———. 2010. "Reports on College Literacy Levels Sobering." January 20. Available at www.msnbc.msn.com/id/10928755.

Museum of Learning. 2010. "Page Act of 1875." Museum Stuff. Available at www.museumstuff.com/learn/topics/Page_Act_of_1875.

Nardi, Peter M. 2003. *Doing Survey Research: A Guide to Quantitative Methods.* Boston: Allyn & Bacon.

National Alliance to End Homelessness. 2008. "Veterans." Available at www.endhomeless.org/section/policy/focusareas/veterans.

National Assessment of Adult Literacy (NAAL). 2009. "Three Types of Literacy: Publications and Products." National Center for Education Statistics. Available at http://nces.ed.gov/naal/literacytypes.asp.

National Association for the Advancement of Black People. 2011. "Homepage." Available at www.orgsites.com/ct/blackpeople.

National Center for Health Statistics. 2008. "NCHS ... Monitoring the Nation's Health." Centers for Disease Control and Prevention. Available at www.cdc.gov/nchs.

———. 2009. "Press Release: Increase in Unmarried Childbearing Also Seen in Other Countries." Available at www.cdc.gov/media/pressrel/2009/r090513.htm.

National Coalition for the Homeless. 2007. "How Many People Experience Homelessness? NCH Fact Sheet #2." Available at www.nationalhomeless.org/publications/facts/why.

National Coalition on Health Care (NCHC). 2009. "Health Insurance Costs." Available at www.nchc.org/facts/cost.shtml.

National Conference of State Legislatures. 2010. "State Laws Regarding Marriages Between First Cousins." Available at www.ncsl.org/default.aspx?tabid=4266.

National Consumer Voice. 2011. "Nursing Home Transparency." Available at www.theconsumervoice.org/advocate/issueindex/nursinghometransparency.

National Health Care Anti-Fraud Association (NHCAA). 2009. "What Is Health Care Fraud?" Available at www.nhcaa.org/eweb/DynamicPage.aspx?webcode=anti_fraud_resource_centr&wpscode=ConsumerAndActionInfo.

National Organization for Women. 2009. "Homepage." Available at www.now.org/organization/info.html.

National Poverty Center. 2009. "Poverty in the United States." Available at www.npc.umich.edu/poverty.

Needleman, Sarah. 2009. "Doing the Math to Find the Good Jobs." *Wall Street Journal,* January 6. Available at http://online.wsj.com/article/SB123119236117055127.html.

Neilan, Terence. 2010. "World Dearth of Women to Leave 24M Chinese Men Unwed Coming Soon: New Commenting Experience." Outbrain. Available at www.sphere.com/world/article/shortage-of-women-in-china-poses-marriage-challenge/19311767?.

Nelson, Jessica. 2009. "Who Are the Working Poor?" Oregon Labor Market Information System. Available at www.qualityinfo.org/lomisj.

New American Bible. 1971. Nashville, TN: Thomas Nelson Publishers.

New York Times. 2010. "U.S. Service Sector Expanded in September." October 5. Available at www.nytimes.com/2010/10/06/business/economy/06econ.html?_r=1.

———. 2010. "Senator: Pull Up Your Pants." April 1 (as it appeared in the *Post-Standard,* April 4, p. A13).

New York Tribune. 1910. "Whites and Blacks Riot." Library of Congress, July 5. Available at http://chroniclingamerica.loc.gov/lccn/sn83030214/1910-07-05/ed-1/seq-2/;words=Riots+RIOT+riot+riots+rioting+RIOTS+.-Rioting#.

Newton, Michael. 2002. *Savage Girls and Wild Boys: A History of Feral Children.* London: Faber and Faber.

NGO.org. 2010. "Alphabetical List of NGOs Affiliated with the United Nations." Available at www.ngo.org/links/list.htm.

Nielson Online. 2009. "Middle-Agers Help Hulu Grow 490%." Marketing Charts. Available at www.marketingcharts.com/television/middle-agers-help-hulu-grow-490-9125/nielsen-top-three-sites-video-viewing-ages-35-49-april-2009jpg.

Nixon, Howard, II, and James H. Frey. 1996. *A Sociology of Sport.* Belmont, CA: Wadsworth.

Nizamuddin, Ali M. 2007. "Multinational Corporations and Economic Development: The Lessons of Singapore." *International Social Science Review* 82, nos. 3–4): 149–162.

O'Brien, Terrence. 2008. "'Sexting' from Your Cell Phone Is Hot New Flirting Trend, Study Finds." *USA Today,* December 10. Available at www.switched.com/2008/12/10/sexting-from-your-cell-phone-is-hot-new-flirting-trend.

O'Shea, Michael. 2005. "Better Fitness." *Parade,* November 27, p. 8.

Office of Juvenile Justice and Delinquency Prevention. 2000. "1998 National Youth Gang Survey." Available at www.ncjrs.gov/pdffiles1/ojjdp/183109.pdf.

Ohio State University Extension. 2008. "Grandparents as Parents Again." Available at http://ohioline.osu.edu/ss-fact/o157.html.

Ohlemacher, Stephen. 2005. "Northeasterners Wait Longer to Get Married." *Post-Standard,* October 17, p. D2.

———. 2006a. "9.5 Hours a Day Spent with Media." *Post-Standard,* December 15, p. A4.

———. 2006b. "Diversity Growing in Nearly Every State." *Post-Standard,* August 15, p. A5.

———. 2006c. "Do Violent Video Games Make Kids Aggressive?" *Post-Standard,* October 26, p. C1.

———. 2007. "Poverty Rate in U.S. Shows Decline for 2006." *Post-Standard,* August 29, p. A7.

Omi, Michael, and Howard Winant. 2004. "Racial Formations." Pp. 9–17 in *Rethinking the Color Line: Readings in Race and Ethnicity,* edited by Charles A. Gallagher. 2nd ed. Boston: McGraw-Hill.

On Campus. 2011. "Defending Public Services." 30(4) (March–April): 8–10.

Organization for Economic Co-Operation and Development (OECD). 2009. "Average Annual Hours Actually Worked per Worker." OECD Stat Extracts. Available at http://stats.oecd.org/Index.aspx?DataSetCode=ANHRS.

Orshansky, Mollie. 1963. "Children of the Poor." *Social Security Bulletin* 26 (July): 3–13.

———. 1965. "Children of the Poor." *Social Security Bulletin* 28 (January): 3–29.

Ortved, John. 2007. "Simpson Family Values." *Vanity Fair,* August, pp. 94, 96, 98, 100, 102–104.

Pampel, Fred. 2000. *Sociological Lines and Ideas.* New York: Worth Publishers.

Papadimitriou, Dimitri. 1998. "Employment Policy, Community Development, and the Underclass." Ideas RePEc, February 10. Available at www.ideas.repec.org/p/wpa/wuwpma/9802016.html.

Parade. 2008. "Intelligence Report: Where Your Money Goes." March 16, p. 14.

———. 2009. "Intelligence Report: What's Made in the USA." April 19, p. 10.

———. 2009. "What People Earn: Our Annual Report." April 12, pp. 1, 6–8, 10–12.

Parade.com. 2009. "Hollywood's Star Students." Available at www.parade.com/export/sites/default/celebrity/slideshows/editors-pick/hollywood-star-students.html.

Park, Robert E. 1950. *Race and Culture.* Glencoe, IL: Free Press.

Parsons, Talcott. [1937] 1949. *The Structure of Social Action.* Glencoe, IL: Dorsey Press.

———. 1954. *Essays in Sociological Theory.* Glencoe, IL: Free Press.

———. 1960. *Structure and Process in Modern Societies.* New York: Free Press.

Patrick, James. 1973. *A Glasgow Gang Observed.* London: Methuen.

Paul, Bill. 1986. "Congregation Is Rapidly Coming of Age." *Wall Street Journal,* March 2, p. 6.

Peace Corps. 2008. "Mission." September 26. Available at www.peacecorps.gov/index.cfm?shell=about.mission.

Pearson, Jake. 2010. "Sen. Eric Adams Fights 'Crack' Epidemic by Launching Ads Urging Youth to Pull Up Saggy Pants." *Daily News,* March 28. Available at www.nydailynews.com/ny_local/2010/03/28/2010-03-28_fight_the_crack_epidemic_pol_puts_up_ads_urging_youths_to_pull_up_their_pants.html.

Peel, J. D. Y. 1971. *Herbert Spencer: The Evolution of a Sociologist.* New York: Basic.

Peffer, George Anthony. 1986. "Forbidden Families: Emigration Experiences of Chinese Women under the Page Law, 1875–1882." *Journal of American Ethnic History* 6(1) (fall): 28–46.

Perry, Beth, and Alan Harding. 2002. "The Future of Urban Sociology: Report of Joint Sessions of the British and American Sociological Associations." *International Journal of Urban and Regional Research* 26(4) (December): 844–853.

Peters, Ruth. 2003. *Laying Down the Law: The 25 Laws of Parenting to Keep Your Kids on Track, out of Trouble, and (Pretty Much) under Control.* New York: St. Martin's Press.

Pew Center on the States. 2008. "One in 100: Behind Bars in America 2008." February 28. Available at www.pewcenteronthestates.org/report_detail.aspx?id=35904.

———. 2009. "1 in 31 U.S. Adults Are Behind Bars, on Parole, or Probation." March 2. Available at www.pewcenteronthestates.org/news_room_detail.aspx?id=49398.

Pew Forum on Religion & Public Life. 2009. "U.S. Religious Landscape Survey: Summary of Key Findings." Available at http://religions.pewforum.org/reports.

Pew Research Center. 2008. "The U.S. Religious Landscape Survey Reveals Diverse Pattern of Faith." February 25. Available at http://pewresearch.org/pubs/743/united-states-religion.

———. 2011. "The New Demography of American Motherhood." Available at http://pewresearch.org/pubs/1586/changing-demographic-characteristics-american-mothers.

Pew Research Center for the People and the Press. 2007. "'No Child Left Behind' Gets Mixed Grades." June 13. Available at http://people-press.org/report/337/no-child-left-behind-gets-mixed-grades.

Pham, Alex. 2010. "5 Years Old and 2 Billion Videos a Day." *Los Angeles Times* (as appeared in the *Post-Standard*), May 19, p. A2.

Piaget, Jean. [1936]1952. *The Origins of Intelligence in Children.* New York: International Universities Press (original work published in French).

———. 1954. *The Construction of Reality in the Child.* New York: Basic Books.

Popenoe, David, and Barbara Dafoe Whitehead. 2002. "The Personal and Social Costs of Divorce." Pp. 33–46 in *Marriage, Health, and the Professions,* edited by John Wall, Don Browning, William J. Doherty, and Stephen Post. Grand Rapids, MI: William B. Eerdmans.

Porto, Brian. 2003. *A New Season: Using Title IX to Reform College Sports.* Westport, CT: Praeger.

Post-Standard. 1996. "Bride Weds Man of Her Dreams—Except He's Dead." September 1, p. A6.

———. 2003. "German Says Victim Wanted to Be Eaten." December 4, p. A3.

———. 2004. "Cracker Barrel Pays to Settle Racism Suit." September 10, p. A3.

———. 2004. "Hunters' Killings Baffle Authorities, Residents." November 23, p. A6.

———. 2005. "Snack Food May Look Familiar, but Fails to Reach Miraculous Price." December 7, p. A2.

———. 2005. "Some Make It Big, Others Barely Making It." September 5, p. A8.

———. 2007. "Did You See?" December 15, p. A2.

———. 2008. "'Jones' Leaves Commies Cold." May 25, p. A2.

———. 2008. "Africa and Global Warming." June 13, p. A16.

———. 2008. "Calif. Votes to Stop Permitting Gay Marriage." November 6, p. A6.

———. 2008. "Millionaire Tally Tops 10,000,000." June 25, p. A1.

———. 2008. "Survey: Mexico Ranks as Second-Fattest Country." March 22, p. A3.

———. 2008. "U.S. Life Expectancy Tops 78 as Top Diseases Decline." June 12, p. B7.

———. 2009. "Despite the Recession, Crime Rates Keep Falling." December 22, p. A13.

———. 2009. "Father Found Guilty in Girl's Diabetic Death." August 2, p. A4.

———. 2009. "Glacier Shrinks, and Country Grows." August 20, p. A13.

———. 2009. "Heart Failure Strikes Blacks More Often." March 19, p. A1.

———. 2009. "Jury Rules Against Woman in Music Downloading Case." June 19, p. A15.

———. 2009. "Mexico City Legalizes Same-Sex Marriage." December 22, p. A2.

———. 2009. "Pitbull Gets Key to City." August 21, p. A2.

———. 2009. "Report: 12% of Indian Deaths Due to Alcohol." August 22, p. A12.

———. 2009. "State Department to Twitter: Please Don't Go Down During an International Crisis." June 21, p. A2.

———. 2010. "First Things First." June 2, p. A10.

———. 2010. "Malawian Gay Couple Sentenced to 14 Years." May 23, p. A17.

———. 2010. "Study Says Cell Phone, Cancer Link Inconclusive." May 17, p. A10.

———. 2011. "Polygamist Sect Leader Convicted of Sex Crime." August 5, p. A11.

———. 2011. "Twitter Users Face Terror Charges." September 5, p. A9.

Powell, Robert Andrew. 2003. *We Own This Game.* New York: Atlantic Monthly Press.

Pruett, Kyle D. 1998. "Role of the Father." *Pediatrics* 102(5): 1253–1261.

Pugh, Tony. 2001. "Mixed Marriages Soar in U.S., Indicate Crumbling of Racial Walls." *Buffalo News,* March 25, p. A5.

Pyle, Richard. 2000. "Batch of New Words for Dictionary," CBS News, June 27. Available at www.cbsnews.com/stories/2000/06/27/tech/main210016.shtml%20or%20www.merriam-webster.com/info/newwords09.htm.

Quicker, John. 1983. *Homegirls: Characterizing Chicana Gangs.* San Diego, CA: International Universities Press.

Quinney, Richard A. 1977. *Class, State, and Crime: On the Theory and Practice of Criminal Justice.* New York: David McKay.

Raley, R. Kelly. 2000. "Recent Trends and Differentials in Marriage and Cohabitation: The United States." Pp. 19–39 in *The Ties That Bind,* edited by Linda J. Waite. New York: Aldine de Gruyter.

Raley, Sara, and Suzanne Bianchi. 2006. "Sons, Daughters, and Family Processes: Does Gender of Children Matter?" *Annual Review of Sociology* 32: 401–421.

Rauh, Sherry. 2009. "10 Ways to Raise a Spoiled Child: Plus Tips to Reverse the Damage by Fine-Tuning Your Approach to Child Discipline." WebMD. Available at www.webmd.com/parenting/features/10-ways-to-raise-spoiled-child.

Read, Philip. 2005. "They Took Her Uniform." *Post-Standard,* May 8, p. D2.

Real, Michael R. 1996. *Exploring Media Culture: A Guide.* Thousand Oaks, CA: Sage.

Red Orbit. 2005. "Japan's Life Expectancy Renews Record in 2004." July 22. Available at www.redorbit.com/news/health/183539/japans_life_expectancy_renews_record_in_2004.

Regoli, Robert M., and Jon D. Hewitt. 2003. *Delinquency in Society.* 5th ed. Boston: McGraw-Hill.

ReligiousTolerance.org. 1997. "Heaven's Gate: Christian/UFO Believers." March 25. Available at www.religioustolerance.org/dc_highe.htm.

———. 2006. "The Da Vinci Code." May 18. Available at www.religioustolerance.org/davinci11.htm.

Resnick, Michael D., P. S. Bearman, R. W. Blum, K. E. Bauman, K. M. Harris, J. Jones, J. Tabor, T. Beuhring, R. E. Sieving, M. Shew, M. Ireland, L. H. Bearinger, and J. R. Udry. 1997. "Protecting Adolescents from Harm: Findings from the National Longitudinal Study on Adolescent Health." *Journal of Medical Association* (September 10): 823–832.

Reuter, Peter. 1983. *Disorganized Crime: The Economics of the Visible Hand.* Cambridge, MA: MIT Press.

———. 1985. *The Organization of Illegal Markets.* Washington, DC: Diane Publishing.

Reynolds, Larry. 1993. *Interactionism: Exposition and Critique.* 3rd ed. Dix Hills, NY: General Hall.

Ringer, Benjamin B., and Elinor R. Lawless. 1989. *Race—Ethnicity and Society.* New York: Routledge.

Rios, Delia M. 2004. "Listen Up, You Guys." *Post-Standard,* May 13, p. E3.

Ritzer, George. 2000a. *The McDonaldization of Society.* Thousand Oaks, CA: Pine Forge Press.

———. 2000b. *Sociological Theory.* 5th ed. Boston: McGraw-Hill.

Rivoli, Jonathan. 2007. "North Dakota Legislature Repeals Cohabitation Law." *Bismarck Tribune,* March 1. Available at www.bismarktribune.com/articles/2007/03/01/news/update.

Roberts, J. M. 1996. *A History of Europe.* New York: Allen Lane, Penguin Press.

Roberts, Sam. 2002. "The Married Minority: They Slip to 48.7 Percent of Households." *Post-Standard,* October 15, p. A23.

Rose, Peter. 1981. *They and We: Racial and Ethnic Relations in the United States.* 3rd ed. New York: Random House.

Rosen, Bernard, and H. J. Crockett Jr. 1969. *Achievement in American Society.* Cambridge, MA: Schenman.

Rosenberg, Morris. 1965. *Society and the Adolescent Self-Image.* Princeton, NJ: Princeton University Press.

Rossi, Peter H., James D. Wright, and Andy B. Anderson. 1983. "Sample Surveys: History, Current Practice, and Future Prospects." Pp. 1–20 in *Handbook of Survey Research,* edited by Peter H. Rossi, James D. Wright, and Andy B. Anderson. New York: Harcourt Brace Jovanovich.

Ross-Thomas, Emma. 2005. "Spain Legalizes Same-Sex Marriage; Catholic Church Appalled." *Post-Standard,* July 1, p. A6.

Rozell, Mark J., and Clyde Wilcox. 1999. *Interest Groups in American Campaigns: The New Face of Electioneering.* Washington, DC: CQ Press.

Ryan, John, and William M. Wentworth. 1999. *Media and Society.* Boston: Allyn and Bacon.

Rymer, Russ. 1994. *Genie: A Scientific Tragedy.* New York: Harper Perennial.

Sabato, Larry J. 1984. *PAC Power.* New York: Norton.

Sage, George H. 1989. "Religion, Sport, and Society." Pp. 271–282 in *Sport in Contemporary Society,* edited by D. Stanley Eitzen. 3rd ed. New York: St. Martin's Press.

———. 1993. "Introduction." Pp. 1–17 in *Racism in College Athletics: The African-American Athletics Experience,* edited by Ronald C. Althouse and Dana D. Brooks. Morgantown, WV: Fitness Information Technology.

Samantha Who. 2009. "With this Ring." First aired July 23.

Samuelson, Robert J. 2008. *Washington Post,* April 23, p. A21.

Sanders, William B. 1994. *Gangbangers and Drive-by's: Grounded Culture and Juvenile Gang Violence.* Hawthorne, NY: Aldine DeGryter.

Santibanez, Lucrecia, Gabriella Gonzalez, Peter A. Morrison, and Stephen J. Carroll. 2007. "Methods for Gauging the Target Populations That Community Colleges Serve." *Population Research & Policy Review* 26: 51–67.

Santrock, John W. 2007. *Children.* 10th ed. New York: McGraw-Hill.

Saporito, Bill. 2011. "Where the Jobs Are." *Time,* January 17, pp. 12, 14–19.

Sapsford, Roger, and Victor Jupp, eds. 2006. *Data Collection and Analysis.* London: Sage.

Saunders, Peter. 2005. *The Poverty Wars: Reconnecting Research with Reality.* Sydney: University of New South Wales Press.

Save the Children. 2008. "Mother's Day Report Card: The Best and Worst Countries to Be a Mother." Available at www.savethechildren.org/newsroom/2008/best-worst-countries-motherhtml.

Schaffer, H. R. 1984. *The Child's Entry into a Social World.* New York: Harcourt Brace Jovanovich.

Schmalleger, Frank. 2004. *Criminology Today.* 3rd ed. Upper Saddle River, NJ: Prentice Hall.

Schmid, Randolph. 2007. "Divorce Is Also Hard on the Planet." *Post-Standard,* December 4, p. A1.

Schmidt, Susan. 2005. "Casino Bid Prompted High-Stakes Lobbying." *Washington Post,* March 13. Available at www.washingtonpost.com/wp-dyn/content/article/2005/03/25/AR2005032508287.html.

Schneider, Stephen. 2002. "Organized Crime—Global." Pp. 1112–1118 in *Encyclopedia of Crime and Punishment,* edited by David Levinson. Vol. 3. Thousand Oaks, CA: Sage.

Schnurnberger, Lynn. 2010. "Happiness Is a Full House." *Parade,* May 2, p. 6.

Scholte, Jan Aart. 2000a. "Civil Society and a Democratisation of the International Monetary Fund." Pp. 91–116 in *Poverty in World Politics: Whose Global Era?* edited by Sarah Owen Vandersluis and Paris Yeros. New York: St. Martin's Press.

———. 2000b. *Globalization: A Critical Introduction.* New York: St. Martin's Press.

Schwartz, John. 2010. "Bullying, Suicide, Punishment." *New York Times,* October 2. Available at www/nytimes.com/2010/10/03/weekinreview/03schwartz.html?scp=Bullying,%20Suicide,%20Punishment&st=cse.

Scott, Megan K. 2008. "Polygamy Gets More Attention: But That Doesn't Seem to Slow Its Growth." *Post-Standard,* April 10, p. D1–D2.

Scott, Walter. 2008. "Personality Parade." *Parade,* May 25, p. 2.

Seely, Hart. 2007. "The Upshot of Downloading." *Post-Standard,* December 23, p. A1.
Seinfeld. 1993. "The Puffy Shirt." First aired September 23.
———. 1998. "The Bookstore." First aired April 9.
Shaer, Matthew. 2009. "English Gets Millionth Word, Site Says." *Christian Science Monitor,* June 10. Available at http://news.aol.com/article/one-millionth-word-web-20/522727?cid+main.
Shahzad, Syed Saleem. 2003. "Brothels and Bombs in Saudi Arabia." Asia Times Online, December 3. Available at www.atimes.com/atimes/Middle_East/EL09Ak01.html.
Shelden, Randall G., Sharon K. Tracy, and William B. Brown. 2001. *Youth Gangs in American Society.* 2nd ed. Belmont CA: Wadsworth.
Shibutani, Tamotsu. 1955. "Reference Groups as Perspectives." *American Journal of Sociology* 6: 562–569.
Shibutani, Tamotsu, and K. M. Kwan. 1965. *Ethnic Stratification: A Comparative Approach.* New York: Macmillan.
Shiva, Vandana. 2000. "The World on the Edge." Pp. 112–129 in *Global Capitalism,* edited by Will Hutton and Anthony Giddens. New York: The New Press.
Shoemaker, Donald. 2000. *Theories of Delinquency.* New York: Oxford University Press.
Siegel, Larry J., Brandon C. Welsh, and Joseph J. Senna. 2003. *Juvenile Delinquency.* 8th ed. Belmont, CA: Wadsworth.
Siegel, Robert. 2004. "Lyndon Johnson's War on Poverty." National Public Radio, January 8. Available at www.npr.org/templates/story/story.php?storyId=1589660.
Silverman, David. 2001. *Interpreting Qualitative Data: Methods for Analysis Talk, Text and Interaction.* Thousand Oaks, CA: Sage.
Simmel, Georg. [1908] 1971. "The Poor." Pp. 150–178 in *Georg Simmel,* edited by D. Levine. Chicago: Chicago Press.
Simon, Maayan-Rahel. 2005 "On Being Queer." Pp. 13–15 in *Gay, Lesbian, and Transgendered: Issues in Education,* edited by James T. Sears. New York: Harrington Park Press.
Simpsons, The. 1990. "There's No Disgrace Like Home." First aired January 28.
———. 1997a. "Bart Star." First aired November 9.
———. 1997b. "Homer's Phobia." First aired February 15.
Smith, Cooper. 2011. "'Sexting,' 'Retweet,' 'Cyberbullying' Added to *Concise Oxford English Dictionary.*" Huffington Post, August 27. Available at www.huffingtonpost.com/2011/08/18/sexting-retweet-cyberbullying-concise-oxford-english-dictionary_n_930347.html.
Smith, David. 2009. "Caster Semenya Row: 'Who Are White People to Question the Makeup of an African Girl?' It Is Racism." *The Observer,* August 23. Available at www.guardian.co.uk/sport/2009/aug/23/caster-semenya-athletics-gender.
Smith, Raymond A. 2008. *The American Anomaly: US Politics and Government in Comparative Perspective.* New York: Routledge.
Smith, Stacy L., and Charles Atkin. 2003. "Television Advertising and Children: Examining the Intended and Unintended Effects." Pp. 301–326 in *The Faces of Televised Media: Teaching, Violence, Selling to Children,* edited by Edward L. Palmer and Brian M. Young. 2nd ed. Mahwah, NJ: Lawrence Erlbaum.
Sniffen, Michael. 2005. "Study: Blacks, Hispanics Fare Worse in Traffic Stop." *Post-Standard,* August 25, p. A7.
Snow, David. 1999. "1998 PSA Presidential Address: The Value of Sociology." *Sociological Perspectives* 42(1): 1–22.
So, Alvin. 1990. "Class Theory or Class Analysis? A Re-examination of Marx's Unfinished Chapter on Class." *Critical Sociology* 17: 35–55.

Southern Poverty Law Center (SPLC). 2000a. "101 Tools for Tolerance." Montgomery, AL: Southern Poverty Law Center.

———. 2000b. *Ten Ways to Fight Hate: A Community Response Guide.* 2nd ed. Montgomery, AL: SPLC.

———. 2007. "Harassment. Name-Calling. Physical Assault." *Teaching Tolerance* (spring): 32–36.

———. 2009. "Fighting Hate: Hate Group Numbers Surge." *SPLC Report* 39(1) (spring): 1.

———. 2010. "Who We Are." Available at http://splcenter.org/who-we-are.

———. 2011. "The Year in Hate & Extremism." *Intelligence Report* 141 (spring): 41–67.

Spalter-Roth, Roberta, and Nicole Van Vooren. 2008. "What Skills Do Sociology Majors Learn and What Is the Pathway to Using Them on the Job?" *Footnotes* 37(2) (May–June): 1, 8.

Spencer, Herbert. 1864. *The Principles of Biology.* New York: Appleton.

———. 1898. *Principles of Sociology.* New York: Appleton.

Spencer, William. 1987. "Self-Work in Social Interaction: Negotiating Role-Identities." *Social Psychology Quarterly* 50(2): 131–142.

Spring, Joel. 2000. *The Universal Right to Education.* Mahwah, NJ: Lawrence Erlbaum Associates.

Stammer, Larry B. 1998. "A Wife's Role Is 'to Submit,' Baptists Declare." *Los Angeles Times,* June 10, pp. A1, A27.

Stangor, Charles. 2004. *Research Methods for the Behavioral Sciences.* 2nd ed. New York: Houghton Mifflin.

Stashenko, Joel. 2004. "Reform of Drug Laws Took Time." *Post-Standard,* December 10, p. A14.

Stearns, Peter N. 2001. *Consumerism in World History: The Global Transformation of Desire.* New York: Routledge.

Stein, Jeannine. 2008. "Smoking's Early Risks." *Los Angeles Times,* June 30, p. F3.

Steinmetz, Suzanne, Sylvia Clavan, and Karen F. Stein. 1990. *Marriage and Family Realities: Historical and Contemporary Perspectives.* New York: Harper & Row.

Stiglitz, Joseph E. 2002. *Globalization and Its Discontents.* New York: Norton.

Stillwell, Cinnamon. 2008. "Honor Killings: When the Ancient and the Modern Collide." *San Francisco Chronicle,* January 23. Available at http://articles.sfgate.com/2008-01-23/opinion/17119909_1_honor-killings-so-called-honor-muslim.

Stith, John. 2010. "Poverty in US Suburbs Rising, but CNY Steady, Report Says." *Post-Standard,* January 21, p. A6.

Streshinsky, Maria. 2009. "Triumph and Tragedy in Indian Country." *The Atlantic.* Available at www.theatlantic.com/doc/200912u/cobell-indian-trust-settlement.

Strolovitch, Dara Z. 2007. *Affirmative Advocacy: Race, Class, and Gender in Interest Group Politics.* Chicago: University of Chicago Press.

Sun Sentinel. 2010. "Justin Bieber Music Video Becomes Most-Watched YouTube Clip Ever." July 16. Available at http://southflorida.sun-sentinel.com/entertainment/sfl-ent-justin-bieber-video-071610,0,6186982.story.

Sutherland, Edwin. [1949] 1983. *White Collar Crime.* New Haven, CT: Yale University Press.

Sutherland, Edwin, and Donald R. Cressey. 1978. *Criminology.* 10th ed. Philadelphia: Lippincott.

Swarns, Rachel L., and Jodi Kantor. 2009. "In First Lady's Roots, a Complex Path from Slavery." *New York Times,* October 8. Available at www.nytimes.com/2009/10/08/us/politics/08genealogy.html.

Swartz, Jon. 2004. "Behind Fun Façade, Professional Wrestling Sees 65 Deaths in 7 Years." *USA Today,* March 12, p. 1A.

Sykes, Gresham M., and David Matza. 1957. "Techniques of Neutralization: A Theory of Delinquency." *American Sociological Review* 22: 664–670.

Szabo, Liz. 2009. "Chronic Conditions Crank Up Health Costs." *USA Today,* September 9, p. D1–D2.

Tapper, Jake. 2006. "Cracker Barrel May Face Another Lawsuit." ABC News, October 17. Available at http://abcnews.go.com/US/LegalCenter/story?id=2577627.

Tavis, Lee A. 2000. "The Globalization Phenomenon and Multinational Corporate Developmental Responsibility." Pp. 13–36 in *Global Codes of Conduct,* edited by Oliver F. Williams. Notre Dame, IN: University of Notre Dame Press.

Telegraph. 2011. "Egypt Protests: The Resignation of Mubarak as It Happened." February 12. Available at www.telegraph.co.uk/news/worldnews/africaandindianocean/egypt/8320161/Egypt-protests-the-resignation-of-Mubarak-as-it-happened-day-18.html.

Tepperman, Lorne, and Jenny Blain. 2006. *Think Twice! Sociology Looks at Current Social Issues.* 2nd ed. Upper Saddle River, NJ: Pearson/Prentice Hall.

Thevenin, Tine. 1987. *The Family Bed.* Wayne, NJ: Avery.

Thomas, Devon. 2010. "Lady Gaga Beats President Obama to 10 Million Facebook Fans." *CBS News,* July 6. Available at www/cbsnews.com/8301-31749_162-20009733-10391698.html.

Thomas, Judy L., and Matt Campbell. 2010. "NAACP Resolution Addresses Tea Parties." *Kansas City Star,* July 13. Available at www.kansascity.com/2010/07/13/2081369/naacp-resolution-denounces-racism.html.

Thomas, R. Murray. 2007. *God in the Classroom: Religion and America's Public Schools.* Westport, CT: Praeger.

Thomas, Stephen B., and Sandra Crouse Quinn. 1991. "The Tuskegee Syphilis Study, 1932–1972: Implications for HIV Education and AIDS Risk Programs in the Black Community." *American Journal of Public Health* 81: 1503.

Thompson, Kenneth. 1975. *Auguste Comte: The Foundation of Sociology.* New York: Wiley & Sons.

Thompson, Paul. 2005. "Family Myth, Models, and Desires in the Shaping of Individual Life Paths." Pp. 13–38 in *Between Generations: Family Models, Myths, and Memories,* edited by Daniel Bertaux and Paul Thompson. New Brunswick, NJ: Transaction.

Time. 2009. "Us Against the World: Nations Ranked by Performance of Their 15-Year-Olds." April 27, p. 35 (original data source: National Governor's Association).

Time.com. 2011a. "Bouaziz: The Man Who Set Himself and Tunisia on Fire." January 21. Available at www.time.com/time/world/article/0,8599,2043557,00.html.

———. 2011b. "Is Egypt About to Have a Facebook Revolution?" January 24. Available at www.time.com/time/world/article/0,8599,2044142,00.html.

Translogic. 2010. "New Car Apps Will Save You Money, Time While Driving." July 15. Available at http://translogic.aolautos.com/2010/07/15/new-car-apps-will-save-you-money-time-while-driving.

Traster, Tina. 2000. "When Grandparents Are 'Parents' Again." *Parade,* March 26, p. 5.

Trojanowicz, Robert C., Merry Morash, and Pamela J. Schram. 2001. *Juvenile Delinquency.* 6th ed. Upper Saddle River, NJ: Prentice Hall.

True, June Audrey. 1989. *Finding Out: Conducting and Evaluating Social Research.* 2nd ed. Belmont, CA: Wadsworth.

Tsai, Grace. 2008. "What Is Mental Health?" *Discovery Health.* Available at http://health.discovery.com/centers/mental/whatis_print.html.

Tucker, Robert C., ed. 1978. *The Marx-Engels Reader.* 2nd ed. New York: Norton.

Turner, Jonathan H. 2003. *The Structure of Sociological Theory.* 7th ed. Belmont, CA: Wadsworth.

———. 2006. *Sociology.* Upper Saddle River, NJ: Pearson/Prentice Hall.

Twenge, Jean. 2006. *Generation Me.* New York: Free Press.

Twenge, Jean, and W. Keith Campbell. 2009. *The Narcissism Epidemic: Living in the Age of Entitlement.* New York: Simon & Schuster.

Twitter. 2009. "About Twitter." Available at http://twitter.com/about.

———. 2010. "The 1000 Most Popular Twitter Users." Available at http://twittercounter.com/pages/100.

———. 2011. "Twitter Counter: Top 100 Most Followed on Twitter." Available at http://twittercounter.com/pages/100:.

Tyre, Peg. 2009. "Coaching Students to Stay in School." *Parade,* June 7, p. 10.

U.S. Attorney Southern District of New York. 2009. "Press Release: Bernard L. Madoff Pleads Guilty to Eleven-Count Criminal Information and Is Remanded into Custody." March 12. Available at www.justice.gov/usao/nys/pressreleases/March09/madoffbernardpleapr.pdf.

U.S. Bureau of Labor Statistics. 2008a. "Overview of BLS Statistics on Wages, Earnings, and Benefits." Available at www.bls.gov/bls/wages.htm.

———. 2008b. "Social Scientists, Other." In *Occupational Outlook Handbook, 2008–09.* Available at www.bls.gov/oco/printucos954.htm.

———. 2009a. "Employment by Major Industry Sector." Available at www.bls.gov/emp/ep_table_201.htm.

———. 2009b. "Economic News Release: Regional and State Employment and Unemployment Summary." Available at http://data.bls.gov/cgi-bin/print.pl/news.release/laus.nr0.htm.

———. 2009c. "Education Pays." Available at www.bls.gov/emp/ep_chart_001.htm.

———. 2010a. "Education Pays." Available at www.bls.gov/emp/ep_chart_001.htm.

———. 2010b. "Fact Sheet." Available at http://factfinder.census.gov/servlet/SAFFFacts.

———. 2011. "Occupational Employment Statistics." Available at www.bls.gov/oes.

U.S. Census Bureau. 2000. "Fifteen Largest Ancestries: 2000." Available at www.census.gov/prod/2004pubs/c2kbr-35.pdf.

———. 2005. "Census Data." Available at www.census.gov/data.

———. 2006a. "Opposite Sex Unmarried Partner Households." Available at www.census.gov/population/socdem/hh-famcps.

———. 2006b. "Poverty Overview." Available at www.census.gov/poverty.

———. 2007. "Poverty Overview." Available at www.census.gov/poverty.

———. 2008a. "Household Income Rises, Poverty Rate Unchanged, Number of Uninsured Down." Available at www.census.gov/Press-elease/www/releases/archives/income_wealth/012528.html.

———. 2008b. "United States: Fact Sheet." Available at http://factfinder.census.gov/servlet/ACSSAFFFacts.

———. 2009. "Poverty: Definitions." Available at www.census.gov/hhes/www/poverty/definitions.html.

———. 2010a. "Guide to U.S. Census Bureau Data Stewardship/Privacy Impact Assessments (DS/PIAs)." Available at www.census.gov/po/pia/pia_guide.html.

———. 2010b. "Income, Poverty and Health Insurance Coverage in the United States: 2009." Available at www.census.gov/newsroom/releases/archives/income_wealth/cb10-144.html.

U.S. Customs and Border Protection. 2006. "Fact Sheet: SBInet: Securing U.S. Bor-

ders." Department of Homeland Security. Available at www.dhs.gov/xlibrary/assets/sbinetfactsheet.pdf.
U.S. Department of Education. 2003. "National Center for Education Statistics: Homeschooling in the United States: 2003." National Center for Education Statistics. Available at http://nces.ed.gov/pubs2006/homeschool.
———. 2008. "National Center for Education Statistics: Fast Facts." National Center for Education Statistics. Available at http://nces.ed.gov/fastfacts/display/asap?id=65.
U.S. Department of Health and Human Services. 1998. "An Ensemble of Definitions of Environmental Health." Available at www.health.gov/enviornment/definitionsofenvhealth/ehdef/2.htm.
———. 2005. *National Vital Statistics Reports* 54(20). Available at www.cdc.gov/nchs/data/nvsr/nvsr54/nvsr54_20.
———. 2006. "New Surgeon General's Report Focuses on the Effects of Secondhand Smoke." Available at www.hhs.gov/news/press/2006pres/20060627.html.
———. 2008. "About the Office of Head Start." Available at www.acf.hhs.gov/programs/hsb/about/index.html.
———. 2009a. "The 2009 HHS Poverty Guidelines." Available at http://aspe.hhs.gov/poverty/09poverty.shtml.
———. 2009b. "Justice Department Announces Largest Health Care Fraud Settlement in Its History: Pfizer to Pay $2.3 Billion for Fraudulent Marketing." Available at www.hhs.gov/news/press/2009pres/09/20090902a.html.
U.S. Department of Justice. 2002. "Acquaintance Rape of College Students." Community Oriented Policing Services. Available at www.cops.usdoj.gov/pdf/e03021472.pdf.
U.S. Department of Labor. 2008. "A Profile of the Working Poor, 2006." Bureau of Labor Statistics, August. Available at www.bls.gov/cps/cpswp2006.pdf.
U.S. Department of State. 2010. "Trafficking in Persons Report 2010." June 14. Available at www.state.gov/g/tip/rls/tiprpt/2010.
U.S. Marshals Service. 2010. "History—Incident at Wounded Knee." Available at www.usmarshals.gov/history/wounded-knee/index.html.
U.S. National Archives and Records Administration. 2010. "Chinese Exclusion Laws." Available at www.archives.gov/pacific/education/curriculum/4th-grade/chinese-exclusion.html.
Uniform Crime Report. 2008. "Crime in the United States: Table 1." Federal Bureau of Investigation. Available at www2.fbi.gov/ucr/cius2008/data/table_01.html.
United Nations Population Fund. 2009. "Gender Equality: Calling for an End to Female Genital Mutilation/Cutting." Available at www.unfpa.org/gender/practices1.htm.
Universal Declaration of Human Rights. 1998. "Fiftieth Anniversary of the Universal Declaration of Human Rights 1948–1998." United Nations. Available at http://www.un.org/overview/rights.html.
UPI.com. 2009. "Rapper C-Murder Gets Life for 2002 Killing." August 14. Available at www.upi.com/Top_News/2009/08/14/Rapper-C-Murder-gets-life-for-2002-killing/UPI-66731250279665.
Urdan, Timothy G. 2001. *Statistics in Plain English.* Mahwah, NJ: Lawrence Erlbaum Associates.
USA Today. 2003. "Barbie Deemed Threat to Saudi Morality." September 10. Available at www.usatoday.com/news/offbeat/2003-09-10-barbie_x.htm.
———. 2004. "Snapshots." September 13, p. D1.
———. 2009. "USA Today Snapshots: Most Visited Art Museums." April 14, p. A1.
Van Biema, David. 2004. "Rising Above the Stained-Glass Ceiling." Time.com, June 21. Available at www.time.com/time/magazine/article/0,9171,655431-1,00.html.

Vandenburgh, Henry. 2004. *Deviance: The Essentials.* Upper Saddle River, NJ: Prentice Hall.

VanderValk, Inge, Martijn de Goede, Ed Spruijt, and Wim Meeus. 2007. "A Longitudinal Study on Transactional Relations Between Parental Marital Distress and Adolescent Emotional Adjustment." *Family Therapy* 34(3): 169–190.

Varner, Marcus. 2008. "Education of the Stars." Classes and Careers.com Available at www.classesandcareers.com/education/2008/01/02/education-of-the-stars-2.

Veblen, Thorstein. 1899. *The Theory of the Leisure Class.* New York: Macmillan.

———. 1904. *The Theory of Business Enterprise.* New York: Scribner.

———. 1964. *The Writings of Thorstein Veblen,* edited by Leon Ardzrooni. New York: Viking.

Virginia Tech News. 2006. "Transportation Institute Releases Findings on Driver Behavior and Crash Factors." Available at www.vtnews.vt.edu/articles/2006/04/2006-237.html.

Virginia Tech Transportation Institute (VTTI). 2009. "New Data from VTTI Provides Insights into Cell Phone Use and Driving Distraction." Available at www.vtti.vt.edu/PDF/7-22-09-VTTI-Press_Release_Cell_phones_and_Driver_Distraction.pdf.

Volberg, Rachel. 1994. "The Prevalence and Demographics of Pathological Gamblers: Implications for Public Health." *American Journal of Public Health* 84: 237–241.

———. 1996. "Prevalence Studies of Problem Gambling in the United States." *Journal of Gambling Studies* 12: 111–128.

vos Savant, Marilyn. 2005. "Ask Marilyn." *Parade,* September 14, p. 20.

———. 2009. "Ask Marilyn." *Parade,* August 23, p. 18.

Waite, Linda J. 2002. "The Health Benefits of Marriage." Pp. 13–32 in *Marriage, Health and the Professions,* edited by John Wall, Don Brownie, William J. Doherty, and Stephen Post. Grand Rapids, MI: William B. Eerdmans.

Walker, Sam. 2006. *Fantasyland: A Season on Baseball's Lunatic Fringe.* New York: Viking.

Wallechinsky, David. 2007. "Is America Still No. 1?" *Parade,* January 14, pp. 4–6.

Walston, John. 2006. *The Buzzword Dictionary: 1,000 Phrases Translated from the Pompous to English.* Oak Park, IL: Marion Street Press.

Warhol, Andy. 1968. *Andy Warhol* (catalog for his photo exhibition in Stockholm, February–March).

Watts, Duncan J., and Peter Sheridan Dodds. 2007. "Influentials, Networks, and Public Opinion Formation." *Journal of Consumer Research* 34 (December): 441–458.

WBZTV.com. 2009. "Gates Arresting Officer: Obama 'Way Off Base.'" Available at http://wbztv.com/local/obama.comment.cambridge.2.1097782.html.

Webb, Jim. 2009. "Why We Must Fix Our Prisons." *Parade,* March 29, pp. 4–5.

Weber, Max. [1904–1905] 1958. *The Protestant Ethic and the Spirit of Capitalism.* New York: Scribner.

———. [1926] 1975. *Max Weber: A Biography,* translated and edited by Harry Zohn. New York: Wiley & Sons.

———. 1978. *Economy and Society,* edited by Guenter Roth and Claus Wittich. Berkley: University of California Press.

Weinberg, Daniel H. 2006. "Measuring Poverty in the United States: History and Current Issues." Center for Economic Studies, U.S. Census Bureau. Available at www.ces.census.gov/index.php/cespapers.

Weir, Tom. 2004. "Online Sports Betting Spins Out of Control." *USA Today,* August 22, p. A1.

Weisman, Steven R. 2006. "IMF Votes to Enhance Power of China and Others." *New*

York Times, September 19. Available at www.nytimes.com/2006/09/19/business/worldbusiness/19fund.html.
———. 2007a. "IMF Faces a Question of Identity." *New York Times,* September 28. Available at www.nytimes.com/2007/09/28/business/worldbusiness/28imf.html.
———. 2007b. "The World Bank, the Little-Noticed Big Money Manager." *New York Times,* October 17. Available at www.nytimes.com/2007/10/17/business/worldbuisness/17Worldbank.html.
Weiss, Gary. 2008. "Are You Paying for Corporate Fat Cats?" *Parade,* April 13, p. 18.
Werner, Erica. 2010. "Obama to Sign Today and Take It on Road." *Post-Standard,* March 23, p. A11.
White, Josh. 2005. "Suicide Tries Linked to Increasing Despair." *Post-Standard,* November 2, p. A5.
White, Kevin. 2010. "Personal Interview." November 2.
Whitehouse, Tom. 1998. "From the Wild: Feral Boy Prefers Living with Dogs." *Daily Breeze,* July 7, p. A7.
Whittaker, David, ed. 2001. *The Terrorism Reader.* New York: Routledge.
Whoriskey, Peter, and William Branigin. 2006. "Abramoff Is Sentenced for Casino Boat Fraud." *Washington Post,* March 30. Available at www.washingtonpost.com/wp-dyn/content/article/2006/10/13/AR2006101300740.html.
Williams, Frank P., and Marilyn D. McShane. 1994. *Criminological Theory.* Englewood Cliffs, NJ: Prentice Hall.
Willing, Richard. 2002. "Research Downplays Risk of Cousin Marriages." *USA Today,* April 4, p. 2A.
Wilson, William. 1987. *The Truly Disadvantaged.* Chicago: University of Chicago Press.
———. 1996. *When Work Disappears: The World of the New Urban Poor.* New York: Vintage Books.
Winik, Lyric Wallwork. 1999. "There's a New Generation with a Different Attitude." *Parade,* July 18, p. 7.
———. 2002. "Intelligence Report: How to Prevent Suicide." *Parade,* September 29, p. 7.
———. 2008. "Intelligence Report: Ending Violence Against Women." *Parade,* April 6, p. 10.
Winn, Marie. 2002. *The Plug-In Drug: Television, Computers, and Family Life.* New York: Penguin.
Wolf, Richard. 2010. "Number of Uninsured Americans Rises to 50.7 Million." *USA Today,* September 17. Available at www.usatoday.com/news/nation/2010-09-17-uninsured17_ST_N.htm.
Wolff, Edward N. 2010. "Recent Trends in Households Wealth in the United States: Rising Debt and the Middle-Class Squeeze—an Update to 2007." Levy Economics Institute. Working Paper No. 589, March. Available at www.levyinstitute.org/pubs/wp_589.pdf.
Woodward, Curt. 2006. "Same-Sex Marriage Faces New Setback." *Post-Standard,* July 27, p. A9.
World Economic Forum (WEF). 2010. "The Global Gender Gap Report 2010." Available at www.weforum.org/en/Communities/Women%20Leaders%20and%20Gender%20Parity/GenderGapNetwork/index.htm.
World Health Organization (WHO). 2007a. "Depression." Available at www.who.int/mental_health/management/depression/definition/en.
———. 2007b. "Mental Health" Available at www/who.int/mental_health/en.
———. 2009. "Tobacco Free Initiative: Why Is Tobacco a Public Health Priority?" Available at www.who.int/tobacco/health_priority/en/index.html.

Wortham, Jenna. 2010. "As Facebook Users Die, Ghosts Reach Out." *New York Times,* July 17. Available at www.nytimes.com/2010/7/18/technology/18death.html?_r=1&emc=etal.

Young, Antonia. 2000. *Women Who Become Men.* New York: Oxford.

Young, Margaret H., Brent C. Miller, Maria C. Norton, and E. Jeffrey Hill. 1995. "The Effect of Parental Supportive Behaviors on Life Satisfaction of Adolescent Offspring." *Journal of Marriage and the Family* 57(3) (August): 813–822.

Zambito, Thomas, and Greg B. Smith. 2008. "Feds Say Bernard Madoff's $50 Billion Ponzi Scheme Was Worst Ever." *Daily News,* December 13. Available at www.nydailynews.com/news/ny_crime/2008/12/13/2008-12-13.

Zelizer, Gerald L. 2004. "Time to Break the 'Stained Glass' Ceiling." *USA Today,* September 16, p. 11A.

INDEX